CITY OF NORFOLK VIRGINIA

COURT ORDER BOOK 2
1770–1782

An unexplored source of potential vital records!

COMPILED AND TRANSCRIBED BY
Kristina Deluise

Heritage Books
2024

HERITAGE BOOKS

AN IMPRINT OF HERITAGE BOOKS, INC.

Books, CDs, and more—Worldwide

For our listing of thousands of titles see our website
at
www.HeritageBooks.com

Published 2024 by
HERITAGE BOOKS, INC.
Publishing Division
5810 Ruatan Street
Berwyn Heights, MD 20740

Heritage Books by the author:
City of Norfolk, Virginia Court Order Book 1, 1761–1769
City of Norfolk, Virginia Court Order Book 2: 1770-1782
City of Norfolk, Virginia Marriage Records, 1850–1859
City of Norfolk, Virginia Marriage Records, 1860–1869
City of Norfolk, Virginia Marriage Records, 1870–1879
City of Norfolk, Virginia Marriage Records, 1880–1889
City of Norfolk, Virginia Marriage Records, 1890–1899
City of Norfolk, Virginia Will Book 1, 1784–1800
City of Norfolk, Virginia Will Book 2, 1800–1810
City of Norfolk, Virginia Will Book 3, 1810–1820
City of Norfolk, Virginia Will Book 4, 1820–1828
City of Norfolk, Virginia Will Book 5, 1828–1835
City of Norfolk, Virginia Will Book 6, 1835–1841
City of Norfolk, Virginia Will Book 7, 1841–1846
City of Norfolk, Virginia Will Book 8, 1846–1868
City of Norfolk, Virginia Will Book 9, 1869–1885
City of Norfolk, Virginia Will Book 10, 1886–1894

International Standard Book Number
Paperbound: 978-0-7884-4300-8

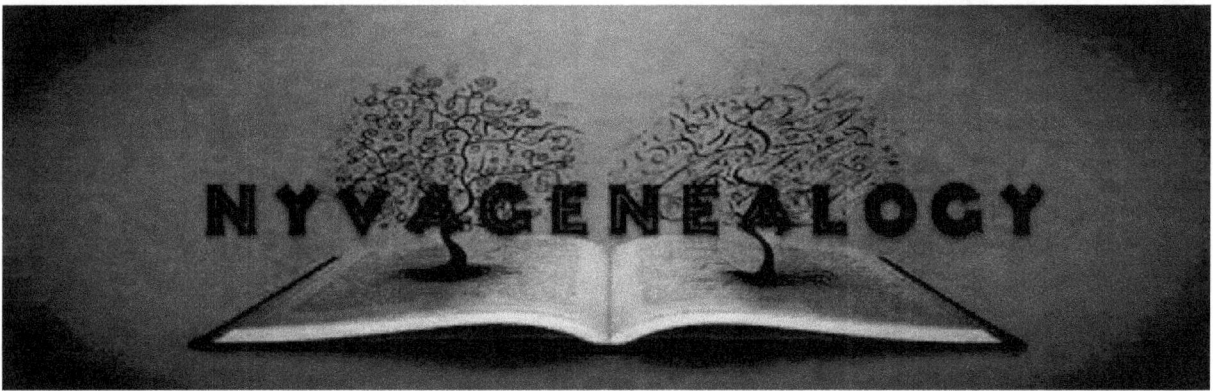

My name is Kristina Deluise and I am the owner of a website called New York Virginia Genealogy.
www.nyvagenealogy.homestead.com **Which also focuses on the City/County/Borough of Norfolk**
http://nyvagenealogy.homestead.com/NORFOLKCOUNTY.html
And on Princess Anne County http://nyvagenealogy.homestead.com/Princess-Anne-County.html

The Court Order Books has been a learning experience. I have learned a lot about life in Norfolk during the 1760s and forward. I have also learned new or should I say OLD legal terms. One item to mention first is that books 1-3 are only numbered on the left side of the page, So I marked the left side of the page as PAGE 1 and the right side of the page as PAGE 1B.

Also, a note for book 2, page 225 is completely blank. And page number 228 is used twice with different information. So you will see PAGE 228 and PAGE 228B, then PAGE 228-2, and PAGE 228-B2.

Oh, and it wasn't my idea to say T.A.B. it was the Clerk's abbreviation for Trespass Assault & Battery

I liked the first Clerk in the first book because he wrote everything out. And he included "and Jane his wife" in most of the statements. The Clerk in the second book was even better because he had much better handwriting, and he too wrote everything out. In the 3rd book, the Clerk said, " And his wife". The first Clerk said JOHN SMITH and JOSEPH SMITH executors of THOMAS SMITH. The 2nd Clerk did a little of that, but by the 3rd book, it was Thomas Smith's executors, which was highly annoying.

Some Examples:
The first clerk was wonderful, and he wrote out Everything. The clerks that followed not so much The first clerk would say: JOHN SMITH and JANE his wife.
The rest: JOHN SMITH and his wife.
The first clerk would say JANE SMITH executrix of JOHN SMITH.
The rest would say: JOHN SMITH'S Executrix.
The first clerk would say NEIL JAMIESON, JAMES TAYLOR, MATHEW PHRIPP, and BASSETT MOSELEY Executors of JACOB ELLEGOOD. The rest would say Jacob Ellegood's Executor's.
The First Clerk would write:
JOHN SMITH VS JOHN SMITH. IN CASE. Continued. (Giving you that "In Case" information)
JOHN SMITH VS. JOHN SMITH. IN DEBT. Continued. (Giving you that "In Debt information) The new clerks write:
JOHN SMITH VS JOHN SMITH. Continued JOHN
SMITH VS JOHN SMITH. Continued.
So, to save space and my fingers in the later books you will see

JOHN SMITH VS JOHN SMITH. Continued (2X)

I know some of you might have an issue with some of the alterations that were made to this book, but to be honest some of them were done by me and some of them were done by Microsoft word.

Some of my alterations: ATTORNIES was changed to ATTORNEY'S, and Microsoft word kept telling me "ies" was wrong, so I changed it. Another alteration was the fact that until ten o'clock tomorrow was always spelled out and I changed it to 10 o'clock. And Gentlemen was never spelled out in the original book and I always spelled it out.

ALL HATH, was changed to "have" or "has" depending on the wording in the sentence. After an internal debate and checking several OLD dictionaries. ENQUIRY was changed to INQUIRY. Microsoft Word did not like TILL so all was changed to UNTIL. Another change made by me that appears often is CLAIMOUR was changed to claims. These books use DEFENCE and I changed it to DEFENSE. One last change of note was with the occupation of TAILOR, they wrote TAYLOR.

Some of the Clerk's wrote March 3, 1777 and some of them wrote the whole thing out. And as you know if you have purchased any of my previous books, I always change one thousand seven hundred and seventy-seven to the actual number 1777.

You will also note "*" symbol next to a name, that's for me, to let me know that's exactly how the name was spelled and not to go verifying it a million times. Or changing it to fit other places in the book.

There are several "surname" issues that drove me crazy, because I know for a fact that the name will be spelled one way in future books, having done will & marriage books in the past. And knowing even in future newspaper articles, a name could be spelled 3 different ways in the same article. So, because the Clerk's handwriting was neat and you could clearly see a name spelled one way on one page and a different way on the next page. And "all" versions of the name are the SAME person, because in most of the instances they involve "all" the same person or persons: SIMON VERSION & VASHON. And GHISLEN is spelled in the beginning GEEZLIN, and other ways before ending with GHISLEN. Oh, and PRYOR later becomes PRIOR. A name spelling change that was all me, was VALLENTINE, it's spelled with 2 "L" throughout most of books 1-3, I changed it for my own sanity to 1 "L" didn't want to go through the rest of my life spelling Valentine's Day wrong. Thanks for understanding.

Another name issue is DAVID W. ok sometimes just DAVID and sometimes DAVID W. However, his last name is spelled DIFFERENTLY every time I have seen it. DAVID MECHKIN/MCMEEKIN/ MCMECAN. In book 3 1783-1785 in the book on page 175 it's MCMICKIN OR MCMECKEN and in the index it's MCMECAN.

Another name that drove this compiler crazy was GOLDSBURY/BERRY HACKET. The name appears 70 plus times in the book and for the first 117 pages it's clearly written GOLDSBURY and for the rest of the book it's clearly written GOLDSBERRY.

Also, there are many instances were partners are involved in the law suit and most of them are labeled as PHRIPP & BOWDOIN OR BALFOUR & BARRAUD or ARCHIBALD WHITE & COMPANY. So, if the name is listed only once on the page and I was completely unsure of the first name, it will appear in the index as MR. PHRIPP and MR. BOWDOIN. However, it the names appear again on the same page in full then they will be listed in the index as MATTHEW PHRIPP and PREESON BOWDOIN. Also keep in mind that sometimes the comma or the & isn't there. I am trying to catch them as I proofread, so keep in mind PHRIPP BOWDOIN is not a person, it's PHRIPP & BOWDOIN as previously mentioned. And PREESON BOWDOIN will remain the "surviving" partner of PHRIPP & BOWDOIN for over 40 years until his death in 1804. And MARSDEN MAXWELL is not a person but MARSDEN & MAXWELL or JAMES MARSDEN and JAMES MAXWELL.

In order book 2, towards the end, there are several entries, GREIVE LOUDON & ROB. And as much as I looked, I couldn't decide if it was GREIVE, COMMA, LOUDON & ROB, or GREIVE LOUDON & ROB. So, I left it as written and put in the index as 3 individuals, MR. GREIVE, MR. LOUDON and MR. ROB.

Just wanted to mention that the ONLY hint or implied acknowledgment of the American Revolutionary War comes in Court Order Book 1 on page 104:

Liberty Liberty sweet Liberty Remember the first of November 1765

Author's Note: This is the day the Stamp Act went into effect.

A Few final notes of interest. When an Aldermen was involved in a Court Case, they would always write:

ABSENT: PAUL LOYALL GENTLEMEN

And then there would be a Court case involving the individual Alderman

And then they would say PRESENT: PAUL LOYALL GENTLEMEN.

A small note of interest When Anthony Lawson Esquire was Deputy Recorder, he was listed as a separate line item when listing Gentlemen Aldermen in attendance for that day, his name was the only name I have seen thus far listed this way.

I spent hours looking up or to put it bluntly, "trying to find" some of these legal terms SOMEWHERE! I don't know about you, but search engines don't work very well for me. It's all knowing the "where" to look. So, to save you some time, I have included a "mini" dictionary with this introduction. You will notice throughout the book there are words in addition to the names that are capitalized. That is because Microsoft word always said they were spelled wrong.

Regards,

Kristina Deluise

DEFINITIONS:

Because I ended up looking up a lot of these terms for 2 reasons, 1 to learn how to spell them and 2 to learn what they mean. I decided to include them in this book.

ABSCOND: To go in a clandestine manner out of the jurisdiction of the courts or to lie concealed in order to avoid their process.

ALIAS: At another time. An alias writ is a second writ issued in the same cause, where a former writ of the same kind had issued without effect. In such case, the language of the second writ is, we command you as we have before commanded you.

ARCTA ET SALVA CUSTODIA: In strict and safe custody or keeping. When a Defendant is arrested on a capias ad satisfaciendum, he is to be kept Arcta et Salva custodia.

ASSUMPSIT: A promise or engagement by which one person assumes or undertakes to do some act or pay something to another.

BREACH OF PROMISE: Failure to perform a contracted for or agreed upon act, or to comply with a legal duty owed to another person. Most times usually referred to as marriage.

CAPIAS AD RESPONDENDUM: By which actions at law were frequently commenced and which commands the sheriff to take the defendant and him safely keep so that he may have his body before the Court on a certain day to answer the Plaintiff actions.

CAPIAS AD SATISFACIENDUM- Also known as: CA. SA.
In practice. A write of execution (usually termed for brevity, ca.sa.) which a party may issue after having recovered judgement against another in certain actions at law. It commands the sheriff to take the party named and keep him safely, so that he may have his body before the court on a certain day to satisfy the party the party by whom it is issued, the damages or debt and damages recovered by the judgment. It is effect is to deprive the party taken of his liberty until he makes the satisfaction awarded.

CAPIAS EXTENDI FACIAS: A writ of execution issuable in England against a debtor to the crown, which commands the Sheriff to take or arrest the body and cause to be extended the lands and goods of the debtor.

CERTIORARI: The name of a writ issued by a Superior Court directing an inferior court to send up to the former some pending proceeding, or all the record and proceedings in a cause before verdict with it's certificate to the correctness and completeness of the record for review or trial

COMITIA: An assembly

COMITATUS: Dignity and office of a Person holding rank or position of importance. And or a companion or fellow traveler, a troop or company of robbers.

COMMITTITUR: Order or minute setting forth that the person named in it is committed to the custody of the Sheriff.

COMMON BAIL: The form of entering merely fictitious bail, in cases where special bail is not required. A species of bail intended only to express the appearance of a Defendant.

CONDEMNATION: A sentence or judgement which condemns someone to do, to give or to pay something or which declares that his claims or pretensions are unfounded. And in regards to money, the damages which the party failing in an action is adjudged or condemned to pay, *sometimes simply called the condemnation.* As used in an appeal bond, this phrase means the damages which should be awarded against the appellant by the judgement of the court. It does not embrace damages not included in the judgement.

COPARTNERY: The contract of co-partnership. A contract by which the several partners agree concerning the communication of loss or gain arising from the subject of the contract.

DE BENE ESSE: The Courts will allow evidence to be taken out of the regular course, in order to prevent the evidence being lost by the death or absence of the witness. This is called taking the evidence "De Bene Esse" and is looked upon as a temporary and conditional examination to be used only in case the witness cannot afterwards be examined in the suit in the regular way.

DECEIT: A fraudulent and cheating misrepresentation, artifice or device, used by one or more persons to deceive and trick another who is ignorant of the true facts, to the prejudice and damage of the party imposed upon.

DEDIMUS ET CONCESSIMUS: We have given power or we have given and granted.

DEDIMUS POTESTATEM: A writ issued by royal authority empowering an Attorney to appear for a Defendant. Prior to the statute of Westminster. 2. A party could not appear in Court by Attorney without this writ.

DEMANDANT: The plaintiff or party suing in a real action.

DEMURRER: A formal allegation that facts as stated in the pleadings even if true are not legally sufficient for the case to proceed.

DENTINUE: A form of action which lies for the recovery of personal chattels from one who acquired possession of them lawfully, but retains it without right, together with damages for this detention.

DETINUIT: In pleading. An action of replevin is said to be in the DETINUIT when the plaintiff acquires possession of the property claimed by means of the writ. The right to retain is of course subject to such as to the judgement of the court upon his title to the property claimed.

EJECTMENT: At common law, this was the name of a mix action which law for the recovery of the possession of land and for damages for the unlawful detention of it's possession. The action was highly fictitious being in theory only for the recovery of a term for years and brought by a purely fictitious person, as lessee in a supposed lease from the real party in interest.

ENFEOFF: To invest with an estate by feoffment. To make a gift of any corporeal hereditaments to another.

ENFEOFFMENT: The act of investing with any dignity or possession. Or Instrument or deed by which a person is invested with possessions.

ESCHEATED OR ESCHEATORS: The land demanded by an ejectment, being agreed to be part or parcel of the said territory or track of land. The lessor of the Plaintiff in ejectment was and always had been a citizen of Virginia and in his pursuance of his said patent entered into the land in quest and was thereof possessed prior to the institution of the said action of ejectment.

ESTOP: To stop, bar, impede or prevent.

EX PARTE- when it is taken or granted at the instance and for the benefit of one party only, and without notice to or contestation by any person adversely interested. Or It is made by a person who is not a party to the proceeding, but who has a interest in the matter which entitles him to make his application.

FELONIOUSLY- (Felon), (Taken away, stolen)

FIERI FACIAS: A writ of execution commanding the sheriff to levy and make the amount of a judgment from the goods and chattels of the judgement debtor.

FIERI FECI- I have caused to be made. The name given to the return made by a sheriff or other officer to a Writ of Fieri facias where he has collected the whole or part of the sum directed to be levied.

HABERE FACIAS SEISINAM: That you cause to have seisin. The writ of execution in real actions, directing the sheriff to cause the demandant to have seisin of the lands recovered. It was the proper process for giving seisin of a freehold as distinguished from a chattel interest in lands.

INFAMIS: A persons whose right of reputation was diminished, involving the loss of some of the rights of citizenship, either on account of his infamous avocation or because of conviction for a crime.

IMPARL: To have license to settle a litigation amicably, to obtain delay for adjustment.

IMPARLANCE: In early practice, imparlance meant time given to either of the parties to an action to answer the pleading of the other. It thus amounted to a continuance of the action to a further day. Literally the term signified leave given to the parties to talk together with a view to settling their differences amicably but it is modern practice denotes a time given to the defendant to plead.

JOINDER IN DEMURRER: When a defendant in an action tenders an issue of call called a demurrer, the plaintiff if he means to maintain his action, must accept it, and this acceptance of the defendant's tender is signified by the plaintiff in a set form of words.

JUSTIFICATION: Maintaining or showing a sufficient reason in court why the defendant did what he is called upon to answer, particularly in an action of libel.

MESSUAGE: dwelling house

NEXT FRIEND: A Competent person, who although not an appointed guardian, but usually a relative, acts on behalf of the infant, married woman or other person of some disability but not sui juris. A Next Friend is not considered a party to the suit but is regarded as an agent or Officer of the Court to protect the rights of the disabled person.

NIHIL DICIT: He says nothing. When a person aka defendant fails to make a pea or answer the plaintiff's declarations.

NIL DEBET: He owes nothing. The form of the general issue in all actions of debt on simple contract.

NON-ASSUMPSIT- The general issue in the action of assumpsit: being a plea by which the defendant avers that he did not undertake or promise as alleged.

NON DENTINUE: He's not detaining the item in question mentioned in **DENTINUE:**

NON DETINET: He does not detain. The name of the general issue in the action of detinue. The general issue in the action of replevin where the action is for the wrongful detention only.

NON EST FACTUM: A plea by way of traverse, which occurs in debt on bond or other specialty. It denies that the deed mentioned in the declaration is the Defendants Deed. Under this the defendant may contend at the trial that the deed was never executed in point of fact but can't deny its validity.

NON PERFORMANCE: Neglect or failure or refusal to do or perform the act that was stipulated to be done. Failure to keep the terms of the contract or covenant, in respect to acts or doings agreed upon.

ONEROUS CAUSE: In Scotch law. A good and legal consideration.

OYER: Hearing of a deed read, which a party sued on a bond, etc. might pray or demand and it was then read to him by the other party: the entry on the recording, and it is to read to him in these words.

OYER AND TERMINER: A half French phrase applied in England to the assizes which are so called from the commission of OYER and TERMINER directed to the judges, empowering them to inquire, hear and determine all treasons, felonies and misdemeanors. This Commission is now issued regularly, but was formerly used only on particular occasions as upon sudden outrage or insurrections. In any place. In the United States the higher criminal Courts are called Courts of OYER & TERMINER.

POTENTATE: A person who possesses great power or sway, a prince, sovereign or monarch.

REPLEVY: The act of replevin, to recover a possession of personal property unlawfully withheld from the plaintiff and damages for its detention.

SCIRE FACIAS- A judicial writ. Founded upon some record and requiring the person against whom it is brought to show cause why the party bring it should not have advantage of such record or in the case of a SCIRE FACIAS to repeal letters patent why the record should not be annulled and vacated.

The most common application of this writ is as a process to revive a judgment after the lapse of a certain time or on a change of parties or otherwise to have execution of the judgment in which cases it is merely a continuation of the original action. It is used more rarely as a mode of proceeding against special bail on their recognizance and as a means of repealing letters patent in which cases it is an original proceeding.

SCIRE FECI- The name given to the sheriff's return to a writ of SCIRE FACIAS that he has caused notice to be given to the party or parties against whom the writ was issued.

SEISIN IN FACT: The possession with intention the part of him who holds it to claim a freehold interest. Or in law: a right of immediate possession to the nature of the estate.

SEQUESTRATION: In equity practice. A writ authorizing the taking into custody of the law of the real and personal estate (or rents, issues, and profits) of a defendant who is in contempt and holding the same until he shall comply.

SEQUESTRATOR: One who is appointed or chosen to perform a sequestration or execute a writ.

SPECIE: Coin of precious metals or of a certain weight.

SWEARING THE PEACE: Showing to a magistrate that one has just cause to be afraid of another in consequence of his menaces, in order to have him bound over to keep the peace.

T.A.B. (clerk's idea not mine.) Trespass, Assault & Battery

TROVER: For the recovery of damages against a person who had found another's goods and wrongfully converted them to his own use.

UMPIRE: when matters in dispute are submitted to two or more arbitrators and they do not agree in their decisions. It is usually for another person to be called in as a umpire to whose sole judgment it is then referred.

Writ of Dower: or a Writ of right of dower, where by a widow seeks to recover the remainder of the dower to which she is entitled.

Writ of Inquiry: In Common law practice. A writ which issues after the plaintiff in an action has obtained a judgement by default, on an unliquidated claim, directing the sheriff with the aid of a jury, to inquire into the amount of the plaintiff's demand and assess his damages.

PAGE 1
NORFOLK BOROUGH
At a Hustings Court Held this 22ⁿᵈ day of January 1770
PRESENT: MAXIMILIAN CALVERT ESQUIRE MAYOR
GENTLEMAN ALDERMEN: GEORGE ABYVON, LEWIS HANSFORD, PAUL LOYALL, JAMES TAYLOR, CHARLES THOMAS, CORNELIUS CALVERT

Ordinary License is granted JOHN DUNN, STEPHEN TANKARD, Ferry Keepers DUGAL GILCHRIST and JAMES ATKINSON on their complying with the law.

DUGAL GILCHRIST against OBEDIAH DOEGOOD dismissed.

MISTERS CAPEL* and OSGOOD HANBURY against EDWARD HACK MOSELEY, THOMAS TABB Dismissed.

HALCOT PRIDE against CHARLES COWPER. Order against the Defendant and JOSEPH CALVERT Sergeant.

WILLIAM M. COX against JOHN HARDIE Dismissed.

ROBERT SHEDDEN and COMPANY against ROBERT BRYCE. The Plaintiff by their Attorney moves for Special Bail which is granted. Where upon SAMUEL BACON came into Court and entered himself Special Bail for the Defendant and thereon the Defendant by his Attorney prayed an Imparlance.

JOHN LEE against FRANCES FRASIER administratrix of RICHARD FRASIER Imparlance.

ANDREW MORANO against JOHN DAVEREUX. The Plaintiff by his Attorney moves for Special Bail which is granted. Where upon THOMAS BURKE Gentleman came into Court and entered himself Special Bail for the Defendant and thereon the Defendant by his Attorney prayed an Imparlance.

On the Petition of PAUL WATLINGTON against ROBERT GILMOUR administrator of JAMES GRAY for 3 pounds, 13 shillings and 10 pence said to be due by account. This day came the parties by their Attorneys and the Plaintiff proving his demand to be just by his own oath. Therefore, it is considered by the Court that the Plaintiff recover the same against the said Defendant together with his costs by him in this behalf expended to be levied of the Goods and Chattels of the said intestate if so, much the said ROBERT GILMOUR has in his hands to be administered and if he has it not then the costs are to be levied of his proper goods and chattels and the said Defendant in mercy.

JONATHAN DISON and SARAH, his wife against JOHN ASHLEY an Imparlance.

PAGE 2
JOHN CHAPMAN Plaintiff
Against: *Ejectment for one Messuage, one Tenement and a piece or parcel of land with appurtenances lying and being the Borough of Norfolk situate on the South Side of Main Street.*
HENRY HOLDFAST
This day came as well the Plaintiff by WILLIAM ROSCOW WILSON CURLE Gentleman his Attorney as PETER DALE who being admitted Defendant in this suit in the room of the said HENRY HOLDFAST by his Attorney pleaded the General issue, Not Guilty and confessed the lease Entry and Ouster in the Declaration supposed and agreed to insist on the Title only at the day of Trial.

WALTER MC CLURG assignee of JAMES MCCAA against HUMPHREY MASSENBURG Dismissed.

WALTER MC CLURG against CHARLES COOPER. The Plaintiff by his Attorney moved for Special Bail which is granted. Where upon WRIGHT WESTCOTT came into Court and entered himself Special Bail for the Defendant and thereon the Defendant by his Attorney prayed an Imparlance.

MARY ROSS against JOHN SMITH. The Plaintiff by her Attorney moved for Special Bail which is granted. Where upon STEPHEN TANKARD came into Court and entered himself Special Bail for the Defendant and thereon the Defendant by his Attorney prayed an Imparlance

WILLIAM SIMPSON against GEORGE BLINN Dismissed.
WILLIAM SIMPSON against EDWARD VOSS and ELDRED FISHER Dismissed.

FRANCES WALDROND Plaintiff
Against Re: On a Writ of Scire Facias
MATHEW PHRIPP Defendant
This day came the Plaintiff by WILLIAM ROSCOW WILSON CURLE Gentleman his Attorney and the Defendant being duly warned and not appearing. It is ordered that the Judgement be entered for the Plaintiff against the said Defendant for 5 pounds 17 shillings and 3 pence, also 236-pound net tobacco and 15 shillings or 150 pounds of tobacco and one shilling and 3 pence. That he have execution for the same and also for the costs of suing forth and prosecuting this suit.

THOMAS NEWTON SR. and JOHN TAYLOR Executors of ROBERT TUCKER deceased against PAUL LOYALL an Imparlance.

PAGE 2B

ROBERT TUCKER against ARCHIBALD AVEN Dismissed.

GEORGE VEAL JR. and NATHANIEL BURGESS executors of HARDRESS LAMOUNT deceased against EDWARD VOSS. The Plaintiffs by their Attorney moved for Special Bail which is granted. Where upon ELDRED FISHER came into Court and entered himself Special Bail for the defendant and thereon the Defendant by his Attorney prayed an Imparlance.

MARGARET BANNERMAN Plaintiff
Against Re: In Chancery
BENJAMIN BANNERMAN Defendant

This day came the Plaintiff by WILLIAM ROSCOW WILSON CURLE Gentleman her Attorney and the Commissioners appointed to Sequester the Estate of the defendant, this day made their report in these words to wit: "In Obedience to an Order of the Norfolk Borough Court of the 23rd Instant to us directed. We have entered on and taken into possession all the land and tenements within our knowledge as also taken an account of the rents, thereof as under mentioned. Sept 1, 1768. JAMES ARNOT'S lease for 3 years commenced 18 pounds per annum has already paid in part to B. BANNERMAN 9 pounds 6 shillings and 5 half penny. Balance due September 1, 1769, 8 pounds 13 shillings and 6 half penny. August 1, 1769. JOHN BELL entered upon rent in the house he lives 15 pounds per annum. On December 11, 1768, MAXIMILLIAN GRIMES entered upon rent in the house he lives at 8 pounds per annum he is allowed 3 pounds 5 shillings for repairs out of his rent. August 8, 1768, CHRISTOPHER THOMPSON entered upon rent in the house he lives at 29 pounds per annum has granted his bond with security for one year's rent to BANNERMAN. July 1769 BATHSHEBA BOYD entered upon rent in the house she lives at 8 pounds per annum. Note: two small tenements vacant frequently let at 7 or 8 pounds per annum. Witness our hands this 24th day of August 1769. THOMAS VEALE, HUMPHREY ROBERTS, AMOS ETHERIDGE, ROBERT SHEDDEN, PORTSMOUTH September 12, 1769. On information we whose names are here unto subscribed went to the dwelling house of MRS. BANNERMANS and there secured agreeable to an order in Court, one feather bed, one Bolster, two pillows, one sheet, one pair blanket, one rug, one counterpane belonging to the Estate of MR. B. BANNERMAN, AMOS ETHERIDGE, JAMES MARSDEN. On consideration there of it is ordered and decreed that the tenants of the Defendant in the report mentioned attorn to the said Commissioners and that the said Commissioners or any three of them sell the goods that they may have taken in their hands at public sale for read money and apply the same with the rents that they shall receive from time to time in support of the Plaintiff agreeable to a former decree in this suit made and that they return an account of their proceedings here in to the next Court.

PAGE 3

RALPH SAUNDERS was this day brought before the Court by Warrant under the hands and seal of PAUL LOYALL Gentleman and PHILIP CARBERY having sworn the peace against him. It is ordered that the Sergeant take him and keep him in Custody until he gives bond and security himself in 50 pounds and 2 securities in 25 pounds each for the said RALPH SAUNDERS keeping the peace for 6 months and that he pays the costs of this prosecution.

WILLIAM KEETON was this day brought before the Court by warrant under the hand of CHARLES THOMAS Gentleman and HARMON HILL having sworn the peace against him. It is ordered that the Sergeant take him and keep him in Custody until he gives bond and security himself in 50 pounds and 2 securities in 25 pounds each for the said WILLIAM KEETON keeping the peace for 6 months and that he pays the costs of this prosecution.

WILLIAM PLUME Plaintiff
Against Re: In Case for Slander
JOHN HARDIE Defendant

This day came the parties by their Attorney's and the Jury that was sworn in this Court at the last Court not returning any verdict are discharged and ordered that the Sergeant Summon a new jury to appear at the next Court and also that he summon WILLIAM GRAY, JOHN DISON and WILLIAM BICKERDICK who were jurymen in the said cause to appear at the next Court to show cause why they did not appear at the last Court to be held for this Borough.

JOHN MCLAIN was this day brought before the Court by warrant under the hand of CHARLES THOMAS Gentleman and RICHARD BICKERDICK having sworn the peace against him. It is ordered that the Sergeant take him and keep him in Custody until he gives bond and security in 50 pounds and two securities in 25 pounds each for the said JOHN MCCLAIN keeping the peace for 6 months and that he pays the costs of this prosecution.

JOHN CRAMMOND Plaintiff
Against Re: In Case
JAMES WEBB and APHIA his wife Executors of WILLIS LANGLEY deceased Defendants

This day came the Defendants by their Attorney and the Plaintiff though solemnly called came not but made default nor his suit further prosecuted. Therefore, on the prayer of the Defendants. It is considered that they recover against the Plaintiff 5 shillings current money and their costs by them about their defense in this

PAGE 3B

Behalf expended, according to the form of the Act of Assembly and the Plaintiff for his false claims be in mercy. (Error) Vide Folio 5

This Court is adjourned until tomorrow 10 o'clock, MAXIMILLIAN CALVERT MAYOR, TESTE: JOHN BOUSH D.C.

NORFOLK BOROUGH

At a Hustings Court Held this 23rd day of January 1770
PRESENT: MAXIMILIAN CALVERT ESQUIRE MAYOR
GENTLEMAN ALDERMEN: GEORGE ABYVON, JAMES TAYLOR, CHARLES THOMAS, CORNELIUS CALVERT, LEWIS HANSFORD

Ordinary License is granted JAMES DIXON, JOSEPH GREAR and MATTHEW KELLY on their complying with the law.

THOMAS NEWTON SR. and JOHN TAYLOR executors of ROBERT TUCKER deceased against GEORGE BLINN. On motion of the Defendant by his Attorney a DEDIMUS is granted him to take the deposition of ZACHERIAH BEAN, JOHN WALKE and JOHN HUNT giving the Plaintiff reasonable notice.

THOMAS ARCHER assignee of JOHN NEWTON COOKE Plaintiff
Against Re: In Debt
GEORGE COOKE Defendant
This day came the parties by their Attorneys and there upon came also a Jury to wit: BASSETT MOSELEY, RALPH SAUNDERS, JOHN BOWNESS, THOMAS FARRER, PETER MCNABB, RICHARD BASSET, RICHARD BICKERDICK, JOHN RICHARDSON, JAMES WEBB, JOHN SMITH, JOHN SELDEN, and JOHN MACLEAN who being elected tried and sworn the truth to speak upon the issue joined upon their oath do say that the Defendant has not paid the debt in the declaration mentioned. Therefore, it is considered that the Plaintiff recover against the said Defendant his debt aforesaid amounting to 38 pounds 16 shillings and 4 pence and his costs by him about his suit in this behalf expended and the said Defendant in mercy. But this judgement is to be discharged by the payment of 19 pounds, 8 shillings and 2 pence with interest for the same at the rate of 5% per annum to be computed from June 3, 1768, to the time of payment and costs.

PAGE 4
FEREBEE HODGES Executor of WILLIAM HODGES Plaintiff
Against Re: In Debt
AARON BARBER and ZACHERIAS MARSINGALE Defendants
This day came the parties by their Attorney's and there upon came also a Jury to wit:
BASSET MOSELEY, RALPH SAUNDERS, JOHN BOWNESS, THOMAS FARRER, PETER MCNABB, RICHARD BASSETT, RICHARD BICKERDICK, JOHN RICHARDSON, JAMES WEBB, JOHN SMITH, JOHN SELDEN, and JOHN MACLEAN who being elected tried and sworn the truth to speak up on the issue joined upon their oath do say. That the Defendants have not paid the debt in the declaration mentioned. Therefore, it is considered that the Plaintiff recover against the said Defendants his debt aforesaid amounting to 25 pounds 13 shillings and his costs by him about his suit in this behalf expended and the said defendants in mercy. But this judgement is to be discharged by the payment of 12 pounds 16 shillings and 6 pence with interest for the same at the rate of 5% per annum to be computed from January 23, 1767, to the time of payment and the costs.

JOHN CRAMOND Plaintiff
Against Re: In Case
EDWARD VOSS Defendant
This day came the parties by their Attorney's and there upon came also a Jury to wit:
BASSET MOSELEY, RALPH SAUNDERS, JOHN BOWNESS, THOMAS FARRER, PETER MCNABB, RICHARD BASSETT, RICHARD BICKERDICK, JOHN RICHARDSON, JAMES WEBB, JOHN SMITH, JOHN SELDEN, and JOHN MACLEAN who being elected tried and sworn the truth to speak up on the issue joined upon their oath do say. That the Defendant did assume in manner and form as the Plaintiff against him has declared and assess the Plaintiffs damages by occasion of the nonperformance of that assumption to 35 pounds 12 shillings and 6 pence besides his costs. Therefore, it is considered that the Plaintiff recover against the said Defendant his damages aforesaid in form aforesaid and his costs by him about his suit in this behalf expended. And the Defendant in mercy.

CORNELIUS CALVERT an Infant under the age of 21 year by CORNELIUS CALVERT his next friend Plaintiff
Against Re: In Trespass, Assault and Battery
JOSEPH CALVERT Defendant
This day came the parties by their Attorney's and there upon came also a Jury to wit: JOHN LAWRENCE, JOHN EILBECK, WILLIAM SKINKER, JOHN STANHOPE, JOHN EVE, ALEXANDER MOSELEY, GEORGE BLINN, PETER TAYLOR, HARDRESS WALLER, GEORGE OLDNER, EDWARD HANSFORD and CHAPMAN MANSON who being elected tried and sworn the truth to speak upon
PAGE 4B
The issue joined upon their oath do say that the Defendant is guilty of the Trespass, Assault and Battery in the declaration mentioned in manner and form as the Plaintiff against him has declared and do assess the Plaintiff damages by occasion thereof to 1 pound. Therefore, it is considered that the Plaintiff recover against the said Defendant his damages aforesaid in form aforesaid assessed and the said Defendant may be taken.

JOHN WILLOUGHBY Plaintiff
Against Re: In Case
CONSTANTINE RIDDICK Defendant
This day came as well the Plaintiff by JAMES HOLT Gentleman his Attorney as the Defendant in Custody of the Sergeant of this Borough and says that he cannot gainsay the Plaintiffs action nor but that he did assume in manner and form as the Plaintiff against him has declared. Therefore, it is considered that the Plaintiff recover against the said Defendant 7 pounds, 19 shillings and his costs by him about his suit in this behalf expended. And the said Defendant in Mercy. And the said Defendant being ruled to give Special Bail and failing so to do. On the Motion of the Plaintiff by his Attorney aforesaid the Defendant is continued in Custody of the said Sergeant until he shall have satisfied this judgement and the costs.

RICHARD POOK Plaintiff
Against Re: In Trespass, Assault and Battery
PHILIP CARBERY Defendant
This day came the parties by their Attorney's and there upon came also a Jury to wit: RICHARD BROWN, WILLIAM WALKER, RICHARD BICKERDICK, JAMES WEBB, BASSETT MOSELEY, JOHN RICHARDSON, JOHN SMITH, NATHANIEL BOUSH, JOHN CALVERT, SAMUEL CALVERT, MATHEW KELLY and ROBERT STEAL who being elected tried and sworn the truth to speak upon the issue joined upon their oath do say that the Defendant is guilty of the Trespass, Assault and Battery in the declaration mentioned in manner and form as the Plaintiff against him has declared and do assess the Plaintiff damages by occasion thereof to 2 pounds. Therefore, it is considered that the Plaintiff recover against he said Defendant his damages aforesaid in form aforesaid assessed and his costs by him about his suit in this behalf expended and the said Defendant may be taken.

JAMES DUNLOP against PRINCE GORHAM. The Defendant pleaded that he did not assume issue joined and referred.
WILLIAM COAKLEY against ANTHONY MOSELEY. The Defendant pleaded that he did not assume issue joined and referred.

PAGE 5
FRANCISCO PACHICO against JOHN HUTCHINGS administrator of CHARLES SMALLWOOD. The Defendant pleaded that he did not assume issue joined and referred.

LEWIS DE LA COUDRE against MATHEW KELLY. The Defendant pleaded that he did not assume issue joined and referred.
PHILIP CARBERY against GEORGE KELLY and RICHARD POOK. The defendant pleaded not guilty separately. Issue joined and referred.
JOHN TUCKER against THOMAS SMITH Dismissed.
JOHN WILSON against CHARLES GODFREY and JOHN GODFREY. The Defendant pleaded payment. Issue joined and referred.
JAMES DAWSON against CHARLES COOPER. The Defendant pleaded not guilty. Issue joined and referred.
ROBERT WATERS against STEPHEN TANKARD. The Defendant pleaded that he did not assume issue joined and referred.
WILLIAM FREEMAN against JOHN BALLENTINE. The Defendant pleaded payment. Issue joined and referred.
CHARLES COOPER against JAMES DAWSON. The Defendant pleaded that he did not assume issue joined and referred.
THOMAS NEWTON SR. and JOHN TAYLOR executors of ROBERT TUCKER deceased against ALEXANDER BELL. The Defendant pleaded that he did not assume issue joined and referred.

THOMAS NEWTON SR. and JOHN TAYLOR executors of ROBERT TUCKER deceased against JOHN WILSON. The Defendant pleaded that he did not assume issue joined and referred.

Order is granted GEORGE KELLY against RICHARD POOK for 50 pounds tobacco for 2 days attendance in his suit against PHILIP CARBERY.

Order is granted BARTHOLOMEW THOMPSON against RICHARD POOK for 50 pounds tobacco for 2 days attendance in his suit against PHILIP CARBERY.

This Court is adjourned to Court in Course. GEORGE ABYVON SR. ALDERMAN

JOHN CRAMOND Plaintiff
Against Re: In Case
JAMES WEBB and APHIA his wife executors of WILLIS LANGLEY deceased Defendants
This day came the Parties by their Attorney's whereupon came also a Jury to wit:
PAGE 5B
GEORGE SPARLING, PETER MCNABB, JOSEPH GREAR, ALEXANDER MOSELEY, NATHANIEL BOUSH, WILLIAM WALKER, RICHARD BICKERDICK, ANTHONY MOSELEY, CHARLES BOUSHNELL, EDWARD HANSFORD, RALPH SAUNDERS and JOHN BANKS who being elected tried and sworn the truth to speak upon the issue joined upon their oath do say that the Defendants testator did assume in manner and form as the Plaintiff did assume in manner and form as the Plaintiff against them has declared and do assess the Plaintiff damages by occasion of the non-performance of that assumption to 1 pound 7 shillings and 56 pence. Therefore, on the prayer of the Defendant it is considered that they recover against the Plaintiff 5 shillings current money and their costs by them in this behalf expended according to the form of the act of assembly and the Plaintiff for his false claims be in mercy.

This Court is adjourned to Court in Course. GEORGE ABYVON SR. ALDERMAN. TESTE: JOHN BOUSH D.C.

NORFOLK BOROUGH
At a Hustings Court Held this 19th day of February 1770
PRESENT: MAXIMILIAN CALVERT ESQUIRE MAYOR
ANTHONY LAWSON ESQUIRE DEPUTY RECORDER
GENTLEMAN ALDERMEN: GEORGE ABYVON, LEWIS HANSFORD, ARCHIBALD CAMPBELL, JAMES TAYLOR, PAUL LOYALL, CORNELIUS CALVERT, CHARLES THOMAS,

JOHN MARCOM HERBERT against JAMES YARD. Order against the Defendant and WILLIAM AITCHESON his bail.

MATHEWS MCVIE and JANE, his wife against DAVID DUGAN Dismissed.

WILLIAM and THOMAS FARRER against ALLEN WOOD Dismissed.

ANDREW ESTAVE against JOHN BALLENTINE by Petition and summons. Judgement is granted the Plaintiff for 4 pounds 1 shilling and 4 pence. It is ordered that the Defendant pay the same unto the Plaintiff with costs and fee.

FRANCIS WILLIS JR. assignee of RICHARD DUNBAR against ROBERT TUCKER. The Plaintiff by his Attorney moved for Special Bail which is granted. Where upon WILLIAM SKINKER came into Court and entered himself Special Bail for the defendant and thereon the Defendant by his Attorney prayed an Imparlance.

PAGE 6
WILLIAM FREEMAN against JOHN BALLENTINE in debt. JOHN MCLACHLAN who was his Special Bail this day surrendered him up and on motion of the Plaintiff by his Attorney, the said Defendant is remanded into Custody of the Sergeant.

HARDRESS WALLER against JOHN CRAMOND Dismissed.

EDWARD HACK MOSELEY against ARCHIBALD INGRAM and JAMES INGRAM and COMPANY. The Plaintiff by his Attorney moved for Special Bail, which is granted where upon NEIL JAMIESON came into Court and Entered himself Special Bail for the Defendant and there on the Defendant by their Attorney prayed a Special Imparlance.

JOSHUA WRIGHT against JOHN HARDY an Imparlance.
HOWARD POOLE against THOMAS THOMPSON a Special Imparlance.

NEIL JAMIESON, JAMES TAYLOR, MATHEW PHRIPP and BASSETT MOSELEY Executors of JACOB ELLEGOOD deceased against STEPHEN TANKARD. The Defendant pleaded that he did not owe issue joined and referred.

SEYMOUR POWELL against JOHN COLEMAN. The Plaintiff by his Attorney moved for Special Bail which is granted whereupon JOSEPH CALVERT came into Court and entered himself bail and the Defendant being called and not appearing a conditional order against him.

ROBERT BANKS who as well against JOHN HUNT an Imparlance. And on Motion of the Plaintiff by his Attorney a DEDIMUS has granted him to take the deposition of ROBERT SHEPHERD giving the Defendant notice.

ROBERT BANKS who as well against OWEIN * CRUMLESS and CATHERINE his wife a Special Imparlance. On motion of the Plaintiff by his Attorney a DEDIMUS has granted him to take the deposition of ROBERT SHEPHERD giving the defendant reasonable notice.

BARNABAS LORAIN against NICHOLAS ANDREW Discontinued.

JAMES KEMPE and CHARLES WILLIAMSON against JAMES MURDAUGH and JOHN MACLEAN. The Plaintiff by their Attorney file their Bill of Injunction and time is allowed the Defendant to consider it and ordered that the Plaintiff give bond and security in the Clerk's Office.

JOHN WILSON against CHARLES GODFREY and JOHN GODFREY dismissed.

PAGE 6B
On the motion of ARCHIBALD CAMPBELL to withdraw his bond against GEORGE ABYVON administration of NICHOLAS WINTERON out of the Office is allowed.

HARDRESS WALLER joiner, WILLIAM and JONATHAN SIMPSON Butchers and partners BASSET and ALEXANDER MOSELEY Merchants and Partners PAUL LOYALL Gentleman CHARLES GODFREY Mariner FRANCIS and GRIFFIN PEART Merchants and Partners NICHOLAS WONYCOTT Merchant, EDWARD ARCHER Merchant, LEWIS HANSFORD and Company Merchants JAMES BALFOUR and DANIEL BARRAUD Merchants and Partners against SARAH WINTERTON an infant daughter and heiress of NICHOLAS WINTERTON deceased. ANN WINTERTON Widow and GEORGE ABYVON administrator of the said NICHOLAS WINTERTON deceased Chancery. This day came as well the Plaintiff by JAMES HOLT Gentleman their Attorney as the Defendants by their Attorney and leave is given to amend the bill and make JONATHAN DISON Carpenter, JOSEPH CALVERT, JOHN WILSON Merchants, JOHN RAMSAY and JAMES TAYLOR Practitioners of Physician and Partners JOHN TAYLOR and THOMAS NEWTON Executors ROBERT TUCKER deceased. SAMUEL BOUSH Gentleman, GEORGE GORDON, DAVID CHEVIS, DAVID CROSS Merchants WILLIAM RASCOW WILSON CURLE Gentleman, WILLIAM CHISHOLM and JOHN BOWNESS Merchants and Partners, WILLIAM BOLDEN and JOHN LAWRENCE and Company Merchants and Partners ARCHIBALD WHITE and Company Merchants DUNCAN CAMPBELL Mariner, JOHN CORRIS Merchant NEIL MCCOUL Merchant, WILLIAM JACOB, Planter, JOHN GAWITH Mariner, ARCHIBALD CAMPBELL Gentleman, THOMAS BRESSIE Merchant complainants to this bill and time is allowed them to consider it.

BAULTIS ECHORD was this day brought before the Court by Warrant under the hand and seal of GEORGE ABYVON Gentleman for being a person of lewd life and conservation and common disturber of the peace and CORNELIUS CALVERT Gentleman having sworn the peace against the said ECHORD. It is ordered that the Sergeant take him and keep him in Custody until he gives bond and security in 50 pounds and 2 securities and 25 pounds each for his keeping the peace for 6 months and that he pay the costs of this prosecution

PAGE 7
FRANCISCO PACHICO Plaintiff
Against Re: In Case
JOHN HUTCHINGS administrator of CHARLES SMALLWOOD deceased Defendant

This day came the parties by their Attorney's and thereupon came also a Jury to wit: WRIGHT WESTCOTT, GEORGE BLINN, WILLIAM BICKERDICK, NATHANIEL YOUNG, JAMES DAWSON, RALPH SAUNDERS, RICHARD KELSICK, HARDRESS WALLER, STEPHEN TANKARD, CHARLES COOPER, JOHN HARDIE and JOHN STANHOPE who being elected tried and sworn the truth to speak upon the issue joined upon their oath do say. That the Defendants intestate did assume in manner and form as the Plaintiff against him has declared and do assess the Plaintiff damages by occasions of the non-performance of that assumption to 107 pounds, 5 shillings and 3 farthings besides his costs. Therefore, it is considered that the Plaintiff recover against the said Defendant his damages aforesaid in form aforesaid assessed and his costs by him about his suit in this behalf expended to be levied of the goods and chattels of the said intestate if so much the said JOHN HUTCHINGS has in his hands to be administered and if he has it not then the costs are to be levied of his proper goods and chattels and the said Defendant in mercy.

LEWIS DE LA COUDRE Plaintiff
Against Re: In Case
MATTHEW KELLY Defendant
This day came the parties by their Attorney's and thereupon came also a Jury to wit: PHILIP CARBERY, WILLIAM PLUME, JOHN NEWTON COOKE, WILLIAM GRAY, GEORGE FARRER, RICHARD BICKERDICK, SAMUEL DENBY, PETER TAYLOR, ALEXANDER BELL, SAMUEL WHITE, BARTHOLOMEW THOMPSON and ROBERT BANKS who being elected tried and sworn the truth to speak upon the issue joined upon their oath do say that the Defendant did assume in manner and form as the Plaintiff against him has declared and do assess the Plaintiff damages by occasion of the non-performance of that assumption to 4 pounds besides his costs. Therefore, it is considered that the Plaintiff recover against the said Defendant his damages aforesaid in forma foresaid assessed and his costs by him in this behalf expended. And the said Defendant in mercy.

PAGE 7B
SAMUEL DENBY Plaintiff
Against Re: In Case
JAMES WEBB & APHIA his wife executors of WILLIS LANGLEY deceased Defendants
This day came the parties by their Attorney's and thereupon came also a Jury to wit: WRIGHT WESTCOTT, GEORGE BLINN, WILLIAM BICKERDICK, NATHANIEL YOUNG, JAMES DAWSON, RALPH SAUNDERS, RICHARD KELSICK, HARDRESS WALLER, STEPHEN TANKARD, CHARLES COOPER, JOHN HARDIE and JOHN STANHOPE who being elected tried and sworn the truth to speak upon the issue joined upon their oath do say. That the Defendants testator did assume in manner and form as the Plaintiff against him has declared and do assess the Plaintiff damages by occasions of the non-performance of that assumption to 11 pounds, 4 shillings, 8 pence 3 farthings besides his costs. Therefore, it is considered that the Plaintiff recover against the said Defendant his damages aforesaid in form aforesaid assessed and his costs by him about his suit in this behalf expended to be levied of the goods and chattels of the said intestate if so, much the said JAMES WEBB & APHIA his wife have in their hands to be administered and if they have it not then the costs are to be levied of his proper goods and chattels and the said Defendant in mercy.

Order is granted NICHOLAS GAUTIER, JANE MUNROE, PETER BISER and ROBERT MOORIE against LEWIS DE LA COUDRE for 25 pounds tobacco for one day's attendance each in his suit against MATHEW KELLY.

Order is granted ALEXANDER BELL against SAMUEL DENBY for 25 pounds of tobacco for 1 day's attendance in his suit against JAMES WEBB and APHIA his wife executors of WILLIS LANGLEY deceased

This Court is adjourned until tomorrow 10 o'clock. MAXIMILIAN CALVERT MAYOR, TESTE: JOHN BOUSH D.C.

PAGE 8
NORFOLK BOROUGH
At a Hustings Court Held this 20th day of February 1770
PRESENT: MAXIMILIAN CALVERT ESQUIRE MAYOR
ANTHONY LAWSON ESQUIRE DEPUTY RECORDER
GLENTLEMAN ALDERMEN: GEORGE ABYVON, LEWIS HANSFORD, ARCHIBALD CAMPBELL, JAMES TAYLOR, CHARLES THOMAS, CORNELIUS CALVERT,

ANN WALLACE and NICHOLAS POOLE against SAMUEL MIDDLETON. Answers filed and time to consider it.

JOHN WILCOCKS assignee of CHARLES BIRKBICK* Plaintiff
Against Re: In Case
THOMAS THOMPSON Defendant
This day came the parties by their Attorney's and there upon came also a Jury to wit: WRIGHT WESTCOTT, RICHARD BICKERDICK, JOHN WILLS, SETH POINTER, JOHN CALVERT, ALEXANDER MOSELEY, JOHN WOODSIDE, MARK TALBOTT, ELDRED FISHER, STEPHEN TANKARD, WILLIAM GRAY and ROBERT BANKS who being elected tried and sworn the truth to speak upon the issue joined upon their oath do say that the Defendant did assume in manner and form as the Plaintiff against him has declared and do assess the Plaintiff damages by occasion of the non-performance of that assumption to 28 pounds, 12 shillings and 10 pence half penny besides his costs. Therefore, it is considered that the Plaintiff recover against he said Defendant his damages aforesaid in form aforesaid and costs by him about his suit in this behalf expended and the said defendant in mercy.

THOMAS NEWTON SR. and JOHN TAYLOR Executors of ROBERT TUCKER against JOHN WILSON Dismissed. The Defendant to pay Clerk and Sergeant fees and tax.

6

MASON MILLER against EDWARD VOSS and JOHN WOODSIDE Dismissed.

WILLIAM PLUME Plaintiff
Against Re: In Case for Slander
JOHN HARDIE Defendant
This day came the parties by their Attorney's and there upon came also a Jury to wit: JAMES DUNN, JONATHAN MEREDITH, JOHN NEWTON COOKE, CHARLES COOPER,
PAGE 8B
NATHANIEL BOUSH, JAMES DAWSON, THOMAS OAKS, JAMES WEBB, BARTHOLOMEW THOMPSON, JAMES ROGERS, RICHARD BASSETT and JOSIAH DEANS who being elected tried and sworn the truth to speak upon the issue joined upon their oath do say that the Defendant is guilty of speaking the slanderous words in manner and form as in the declaration against him is alleged and do assess the Plaintiff damages by occasions of the Speaking the slanderous words in the declaration mentioned to 2 pounds and 6 pence besides his costs. Therefore, it is considered that the Plaintiff recover against the said Defendant his damages aforesaid in form aforesaid assessed and his costs by him in this behalf expended and the said defendant in mercy.

WALTER BRUCE and SUSANNAH BAILY, a Free Negro were this day brought before the Court by a warrant under the hand and seal of GEORGE ABYVON Gentleman for being persons of lewd life and conservation and common disturber of the peace by keeping a disorderly house and entertaining gentleman slaves and the same being proved. It is ordered that the Sergeant take them and keep them in Custody until they respectively give bond and security in 50 pounds each and 2 securities each in 25 pounds each for their being of good behavior for 6 months and pay the costs of this prosecution.

WILLIAM COAKLEY Plaintiff
Against Re: In Case
ANTHONY MOSELEY Defendant
This day came as well the Plaintiff by JAMES HOLT Gentleman their Attorney as the Defendant in his proper person and by consent the continuance in this Cause yesterday is set aside, and the said Defendant relinquishing his former plea says that he cannot gainsay the Plaintiff action nor but that he did assume in manner and form as the Plaintiff against him has declared. Therefore, it is considered that the Plaintiff recover against the said Defendant 6 pounds 5 shillings and his costs by him about his suit in this behalf expended and the said Defendant in mercy.

WILLIAM FREEMAN against JOHN BALLENTINE Dismissed at the Defendants costs.

PAGE 9
ROBERT WATERS Plaintiff
Against Re: In Case
STEPHEN TANKARD Defendant
This day came the parties by their Attorney and the Defendant by his Attorney relinquishing their former plea says that he cannot gainsay the Plaintiffs action nor but that he did assume in manner and form as the Plaintiff against him has declared. Therefore, it is considered that the Plaintiff recover against the said Defendant 22 pounds 7 shillings and 6 pence and his costs by him about his suit in this behalf expended and the said defendant in mercy.

JOHN HORNIBLOW Plaintiff
Against Re: On a Writ of SCIRE FACIAS
JOSEPH CALVERT & WILLIAM IVY who were Special Bond for WILLIAM VERLING Defendants.
This day came the Plaintiff by WILLIAM RASCOW WILSON CURLE GENTLEMAN his Attorney and the defendants being duly warned and not appearing. Ordered that Judgement be entered for the Plaintiff against JOSEPH CALVERT one of the defendants for 9 pounds 6 shillings and 2 pence, also for 236 pounds of neat tobacco and 15 shillings or 150 pounds of tobacco and 1 shilling and 3 pence. That he have execution for the same and also for the costs of suing forth and prosecuting this suit and discontinued against WILLIAM IVY the other defendants.

Order is granted CATHERINE MARSHALL ANN SCOTT and ALEXANDER CARR against WILLIAM PLUME for 150 pounds tobacco for 6 days attendance each in his suit against JOHN HARDY.

Order is granted TUBIPHILL* HUGHES against WILLIAM PLUME for 25 pounds of tobacco for 1 day's attendance in his suit against JOHN HARDY.

RALPH CARR Plaintiff
Against Re: In Case
ZACHERIAS MARSINGALE Defendant
This day came the parties by their Attorney's and thereupon came also a Jury to wit:
WRIGHT WESTCOTT, STEPHEN TANKARD, WILLIAM GRAY, ALEXANDER MOSELEY, JOHN CALVERT, JOHN WOODSIDE, ELDRED FISHER, BARTHOLOMEW THOMPSON, HARDRESS WALLER, JOHN DISON, PAGE 9B
ROBERT BANKS and JOHN STANHOPE who being elected tried and sworn the truth to speak upon the issue joined upon their oath do say that the Defendant did assume in manner and form as the Plaintiff against him has and do assess the Plaintiff damages by occasion of the non-performance of that assumption to 14 pounds 8 shillings and 9 pence half penny besides his costs. Therefore, it is considered that the Plaintiff recovered against the said Defendant his damages aforesaid in form aforesaid assessed and his costs by him in this behalf expended and the said Defendant in mercy.

MARGARET BANNERMAN Plaintiff
Against Re: In Chancery
BENJAMIN BANNERMAN Defendant
This day came the Plaintiff by WILLIAM RASCOW WILSON CURLE Gentleman her Attorney and the Commissioners appointed to sequester the estate of the Defendant this day made their report in these words to wit: We the subscribers being appointed by Norfolk Borough Court to take into possession all the Estate of BENJAMIN BANNERMAN both real and personal. In obedience to the same we have further taken into Custody and Committed to the goal 3 Negroes men named EDINBURGH ABERDEEN and FRANK GIVEN and our hands this 20th February 1770. JAMES MARSDEN, HUMPHREY ROBERTS, AMOS ETHERIDGE, ROBERTS SHEDDEN. On consideration where of it is ordered and decreed that the said commissioner make sale of the two slaves named EDINBURGH and ABERDEEN in the said report mentioned on Thursday the 22nd of March Next, giving notice thereof in the PUBLIK GARETTE unless any person or persons having any right or title to the said 2 slaves named EDINBURGH and ABERDEEN do appear at the next Court to be held for the said Borough on Monday the 19th of March Next and claim the same and it is further ordered and decreed that the said Commissioners make sale of the said Negro FRANK in the said report also mentioned on Saturday the 24th instant giving notice thereof at the Court house door and that they return the money arising thereby together with the produce of the said 2 slaves EDINBURGH and ABERDEEN if sold into the Clerk's office for the use of the Plaintiff agreeable to a former decree in this suit made and that use of the Plaintiff agreeable to a former decree in this suit made and that they report their proceedings there in to the Court and it is said to the Sergeant of the said Borough

PAGE 10
That he keep the said slaves in his custody until the day of sale or otherwise discharged by the Court.

Order is granted THOMAS BRESSIE and EDWARD STRANG against RALPH CARR for 175 pounds of tobacco each for 7 days attendance in his suit against ZACHERIAS MARSINGALE.

Order is granted JOSIAH NICHOLS against RALPH CARR for 75 pounds tobacco for 3 days attendance in his suit against ZACHERIAS MARSINGALE.

PHILIP CARBERY Plaintiff
Against Re: In Trespass
GEORGE KELLY and RICHARD POOK Defendants
This day came the parties by their Attorney's and thereupon came also a Jury to wit: WRIGHT WESTCOTT, ALEXANDER MOSELELY, JOHN CALVERT,STEPHEN TANKARD, WILLIAM GRAY, JOHN WOODSIDE, ELDRED FISHER, HARDRESS WALLER, JONATHAN DISON, ROBERT BANKS, JOHN STANHOPE and SAMUEL DENBY who being elected tried and sworn the truth to speak upon the issue joined upon their oath do say that the Defendant GEORGE KELLY is not guilty of the Trespass as the Plaintiff against him has declared and that the said RICHARD POOK is guilty of the Trespass in the declaration mentioned in manner and form as the Plaintiff against him has declared and do asses the Plaintiff damages by occasion thereof to 2 shillings and 9 pence. Therefore, it is considered that the Plaintiff take nothing by his bill against KELLY but for his false claims be in mercy. And the said Defendant go hence without day and recover against the Plaintiff his costs by him about his defense in this behalf expended. And it is further considered that the Plaintiff recover against the Defendant POOK 2 shillings and 9 pence damages by the jurors aforesaid in this verdict assessed and his costs by him in this behalf expended. The Court being of opinion that the Trespass as to POOK was willful and the said Defendant in mercy.

JAMES DAWSON against CHARLES COOPER. Dismissed at the Plaintiff Costs.
SETH POINTER against GEORGE ABYVON. The Defendant pleaded not guilty. Issue joined & referred.
THOMAS FARRER against NICHOLAS GAUTIER issue (not Guilty) and referred.

PAGE 10B
WILLIAM MOORE against HENRY BROWN Discontinued.

LEWIS HANSFORD Plaintiff
Against Re: In Chancery
EDWARD HACK MOSELEY Defendant
This day came as well the Plaintiff in his proper person as the Defendant by WALTER LYON Gentleman his Attorney and the said Plaintiff not further prosecuting his suit the same is discontinued at his costs. Therefore, it is considered that the Defendant recover against the Plaintiff his costs by him about his defense in this behalf expended.

EDWARD HANSFORD against JOHN SMITH Continued and ordered that the parties be prepared for trail in April Next.

JONATHAN MEREDITH against WILLIAM SMITH. The Defendant pleaded that he did not assume issue joined and referred.
MATHEW CRAWFORD against TALBOT THOMPSON. The Defendant pleaded not guilty. Issue joined and referred.

JOHN CHALMERS and Company against JOHN WILSON surviving partners of WILSON & IRWINE. The Defendants pleaded that they did not assume issue joined and referred.

JOHN HARDIE against JOHN WILSON. The Defendant plead OYER of the bond which is granted him.
JOHN GREENHOW against JAMES ATKINSON and MARY his wife. The Defendant pleaded that they did not assume with leave. Issue joined and referred.

MISTERS GEORGE STORR and ELLIS against JOHN BRICKELL discontinued.
JAMES DUNLOP against ELDRED FISHER. The Defendant pleaded that he did not assume. Issue joined and referred.

THOMAS BUTT against JOSEPH MITCHELL. The Defendant pleaded that he did not assume issue joined and referred.

PAGE 11
GEORGE ABYVON Plaintiff
Against Re: In Debt
EDWARD VOSS Defendant
This day came the Plaintiff by JAMES HOLT Gentleman his Attorney and the Defendant being solemnly called and not appearing. Ordered that the former order of this Court against the said Defendant and WILLIAM MCCAA his bail be confirmed. Therefore, it is considered that the Plaintiff recover against the said Defendant and WILLIAM MCCAA his bail aforesaid his debt amounting to 71 pounds, 13 shillings and 4 pence and his costs by him in this behalf expended and the said Defendant in mercy. But this Judgement is to be discharged by the payment of 35 pounds 16 shillings and 8 pence with interest for the same at the rate of 5% per annum to be computed from October 15th, 1768, to the time of payment and the costs.

JOHN TUCKER against LEWIS HANSFORD. The former order of this Court against him the said Defendant and ROBERT TAYLOR his bail be confirmed, and a Writ of Inquiry is awarded him for his damages.

This Court is adjourned to Court in Course. MAXIMILIAN CALVERT MAYOR. TESTE: JOHN BOUSH D.C.

PAGE 11B
NORFOLK BOROUGH
At a Hustings Court Held this 19th day of March 1770
PRESENT: MAXIMILIAN CALVERT ESQUIRE MAYOR
GENTLEMAN ALDERMEN: GEORGE ABYVON, CHARLES THOMAS, ARCHIBALD CAMPBELL, LEWIS HANSFORD, PAUL LOYALL, CORNELIUS CALVERT,
It is ordered that the rates and liquor, diet and lodging for man and corn oats for horses be at the following price and that no Ordinary Keeper in this Borough take greater prices for the same under the penalty of the law.

RUM PUNCH made with double refined sugar per quart	0.1.4
Rum Punch made with Marovado Sugar per quart	0.0.8
Rum Quart	0.2.6
Arrack by the gallon	2.0.0
Virginia Brandy by the Quart	0.2.6
French Brandy by the Quart	0.5.0
Madeira Wine by the Quart	0.3.0
Tenerife Wine by the Quart	0.2.0
Claret by the bottle	0.4.0
Port Wine by the Bottle	0.3.0
Bristol Beer in London Stout by the Bottle or Quart	0.1.3
English Cider by the Bottle	0.1.4
Virginia and Hughs crab by the bottle or quart	0.0.7
Virginia Common Cider by the bottle or quart	0.0.4
A meal of hot victuals	0.1.3
A meal of cold victuals	0.1.0
Lodging for the night	0.0.6
Pasturage and fodder for a horse for the night	0.0.6
Corn and oats by the gallon	0.0.4

EDWARD PARK against WILLIAM BROWN. The Plaintiff by his Attorney moved for Special Bail which is granted. Where upon ALEXANDER BELL came into Court and entered himself Special Bail for the defendant and thereon the Defendant by his Attorney prayed an Imparlance.

PAGE 12
MARGARET BANNERMAN Plaintiff
Against Re: In Chancery
BENJAMIN BANNERMAN Defendant
This day came the Plaintiff by WILLIAM ROSCOW WILSON CURLE Gentleman her Attorney and GEORGE DONALD having produced a bill of sale for the two Negroes Named EDINBURGH and ABERDEEN in a former decree in this suit mentioned. On consideration where of it is ordered and decreed that the Commissioners by consent of the said GEORGE DONALD make sale of the said Negroes agreeable to the said

9

former decree mentioned and keep the money in their hands until the said GEORGE ascertains his demand at the Next Court to be held for this Borough.

JOHN GOODRICH Plaintiff
Against Re: In Debt
ROBERT SHEDDEN Admin of BENJAMIN REED Defendant
This day came the Plaintiff by WILLIAM ROSCOW WILSON CURLE Gentleman his Attorney as the Defendant in his proper person and the said Defendant acknowledges the Plaintiffs action for 332 pounds 10 shillings and 10 pence. Therefore, it is considered that the Plaintiff recover against the said Defendant his debt aforesaid and his costs by him in this behalf expended when assets to be levied of the goods and chattels of the said intestate is so much the said ROBERT SHEDDEN has in his hands to be administered and if he has it not then the costs are to be levied of his proper goods and chattels and the said ROBERT in mercy. But this Judgement is to be discharged by the payment of 165 pounds 3 shillings and 6 half penny with interest for the same at the rate of 5% per annum to be computed from August 23, 1768, to the time of payment and the costs.

JOHN WILSON Plaintiff
Against Re: On a SCIRE FACIAS
WILLIAM BROAK COTTON and JOHN GODFREY Defendants
This day came the Plaintiff by WILLIAM ROSCOW CURLE Gentleman his Attorney, and the Defendants being duly warned and not appearing. Ordered that the judgement be entered for the Plaintiff against the said Defendants for 16 pounds, also 140 pounds of neat tobacco and 15 shillings or 150 pounds of tobacco and 1 shilling and 3 pence that he have execution for the same and

PAGE 12B
Also, for the costs of suing forth and prosecuting this Suit. But this Judgement is to be discharged by the payment of 4 pounds 8 shillings, also 140 pounds of neat tobacco and 15 shillings or 150 pounds of tobacco and one shilling and 3 pence with interest on the said sum of 4 pounds 8 shillings at the rate of 5% per annum to be computed from April 10th, 1768, to the time of payment and the costs.

JACOB OADS against THOMAS SLACK Dismissed.
WILLIAM SMITH against EDWARD NEIL Dismissed.
JOHN CRAMOND against ELDRED FISHER "Oyer of the Record" is granted the Defendant.

ROBERT BURCHALL against JOHN CALVILL by Petition and Summons. Judgement is granted the Plaintiff for 3 pounds 6 shillings and 4 pence half penny. It is ordered that the Defendant pay the same unto the Plaintiff with costs and fees.

SAMUEL SAMWAYS against JOHN ASHLEY continued and MATHEW GODFREY undertakes for the Plaintiff that he will pay to the Defendant all such damages costs and charges as shall be awarded against him by the Court.

WALTER MCCLURG against HENRY BATTS. Order against the Defendant and CHARLES COOPER his bail.
JOHN IVY admin of WILLIAM IVY against PETER DALE Dismissed.

MATHEW KELLY who as well against JOHN MCNEIL an Imparlance. On the motion of the Plaintiff by his Attorney a DEDIMUS is granted him to take the deposition of JONATHAN MEREDITH giving the Defendant reasonable notice.

JAMES LEITCH against JOHN DISON by Petition and Summons. Judgement is granted the Plaintiff for 1 pound 11 shillings and one penny half penny. It is ordered that the Defendant pay the same unto the Plaintiff with costs and fees.

HENRY RITTER against JONAS MISSAR a Special Imparlance
MARY ANN THELABALL against JOHN CALVILL an Imparlance.
MISTERS CAPLE and OSGOOD HANBURYS against EDWARD H. MOSELEY an Imparlance. (LISTED 2X)

PAGE 13
MISTERS CAPLE and OSGOOD HANBURYS against EDWARD H. MOSELEY An Imparlance

CHARLES COOPER Plaintiff
Against Re: In Case
JAMES DAWSON Defendant
This day came the parties by their Attorney's and there upon came also a Jury to wit: NICHOLAS POOLE, SAMUEL WHITE, WILLIAM MCCAA, WILLIAM GRAY, CHARLES BUSHNELL, SAMUEL TUMBLINSON, STEPHEN TANKARD, EDWARD MITCHELL, JOHN RICHARDSON, JOHN EVE, GEORGE JACKSON and HUGH WARDEN who being elected tried and sworn the truth to speak upon the issue joined upon their oath do say that the Defendant did assume in manner and form as the Plaintiff against him has declared and do assess the Plaintiff damages by occasion of the non-performance of that assumption to 25 pounds, 15 shillings besides his costs. Therefore, it is considered that the Plaintiff recover against he said Defendant his damages aforesaid in form aforesaid and costs by him about his suit in this behalf expended and the said Defendant in mercy.

EDWARD HACK MOSELEY against LEWIS HANSFORD replication and commission.

JOHN CHALMERS and COMPANY Plaintiff
Against Re: In Case
JOHN WILSON Surviving Partner of WILSON and IRVIN Defendants

This day came the parties by their Attorney's and the Defendant by his Attorney relinquishing his former plea, says that he cannot gainsay the Plaintiff's action nor but that he did assume in manner and form as the Plaintiff against him have declared. Therefore, it is considered that the Plaintiff recover against the said Defendant 85 pounds, 5 shillings and 6 pence and their costs by them in this behalf expended and the said Defendant in mercy.

JONATHAN MEREDITH against WILLIAM SMITH Dismissed at the Defendants Cost.
THOMAS BUTT against JOSEPH MITCHELL Dismissed.

Ordinary License is granted JAMES ROGERS and JOHN MCNEIL on their complying with the law.

Order is granted JOHN NEWTON COOKE against JAMES DAWSON for 75 pounds tobacco for 3 days attendance in the Suit of CHARLES COOPER against him.

PAGE 13B
Order is granted HARDRESS WALLER against CHARLES COOPER for 75 pounds tobacco for 3 days attendance in his suit against JAMES DAWSON.

JOHN TUCKER Plaintiff
Against Re: In Case
LEWIS HANSFORD Defendant
This day came the Plaintiff by JAMES HOLT Gentleman his Attorney and there upon came also a Jury to wit: JOHN GILCHRIST, JOHN INGRAM, JOHN STANHOPE, HARDRES WALLER, CHARLES COOPER, EDMOND KEETON, THOMAS FARRER, JAMES GILCHRIST, ROBERT SHEDDEN, BARTHOLOMEW THOMPSON, JOHN NEWTON COOKE and JOHN WILSON who being sworn well and truly to enquire of damages in this suit upon their oath do say that the Plaintiff has sustained damages in the declaration mentioned to 98 pounds, 14 shillings and 11 pence besides his costs. Therefore, it is considered by the Court that the Plaintiff recover against the Defendant and ROBERT TAYLOR his bail his damages aforesaid in form aforesaid assessed and his costs by him in this behalf expended and the said Defendant in mercy.

JAMES FLETCHER was this day brought before the Court by 2 warrants from under the hands and seal of MAXIMILIAN CALVERT and GEORGE ABYVON for being a person of lewd life and conversation and a Common Disturber of the peace and the same being proved by his own confession it is ordered that the Sergeant take him and keep him in Custody until he gives bond and security himself in 100 pounds and 2 securities in 50 pounds each for the said JAMES FLETCHERS keeping the peach for 12 months and that he pay the costs of this prosecution.

This Court is adjourned to Court in Course: MAXIMILIAN CALVERT MAYOR, TESTE: JOHN BOUSH D.C.

PAGE 14
NORFOLK BOROUGH
At a Hustings Court Held this 21 day of May 1770
PRESENT: MAXIMILIAN CALVERT ESQUIRE MAYOR
ANTHONY LAWSON ESQUIRE DEPUTY RECORDER
GENTLEMAN ALDERMEN: GEORGE ABYVON, LEWIS HANSFORD, PAUL LOYALL, JAMES TAYLOR, CHARLES THOMAS, CORNELIUS CALVERT,

GEORGE CARLTON against WILLIAM GRAY agreed dismissed each parting paying their own costs.
JOHN GREENWOOD against ALEXANDER BELL discontinued at the defendants' costs.
WALTER MCCLURG against HENRY BATTS dismissed at the defendants' costs.
BENJAMIN BANNERMANS Petition is rejected.
JAMES JOLLIF SR. against JOHN BRICKELL a Special Imparlance

Ordinary License is granted MARY ROSS and PAUL HERITTER on their complying with the law.

ROBERT BOWERS against JOHN WILLS by Petition and Summons. Judgement is granted the Plaintiff for 3 pounds, 8 shillings and 3 pence. It is ordered that the Defendant pay the same unto the Plaintiff with costs and fees.
STEPHEN TANKARD against JOSEPH HUDSON dismissed.

RICHARD JOHNSON JR. against MASON MILLER. The Plaintiff by his Attorney moved for Special Bail which is granted. Where upon JAMES MURPHREE came into Court and entered himself Special Bail for the defendant and thereon the Defendant by his Attorney prayed an Imparlance and Oyer.

ROBERT TUCKER against RICHARD DUNBAR dismissed.

ROBERT TUCKER against ALEXANDER BELL by Petition and Summons. Judgement is granted the Plaintiff for 2 pounds, 13 shillings and 7 pence half penny. It is ordered that the defendant pay the same unto the Plaintiff with costs and fees.

GEORGE JOSEPH FENWICK against WILLIAM KEETON a Special Imparlance.

PAGE 14B
JOHN MCLACHLAN against ARCHIBALD AVEN by Petition and Summons. Judgement is granted the Plaintiff for 2 pounds. It is ordered that the Defendant pay the same unto the Plaintiff with costs and fees.

THOMAS WILLIS Plaintiff
Against Re: In Case
JOHN GUY Defendant
This day came as well the Plaintiff by WALTER LYON Gentleman his Attorney as the Defendant in his proper person and the said defendant says that he cannot gainsay the Plaintiffs action nor but that he did assume in manner and form as the Plaintiff against him has declared. Therefore, it is considered that the Plaintiff recover against the said Defendant 6 pounds, 2 shillings and his costs by him in this behalf expended and the said Defendant in mercy.

SAMUEL SAMWAYS against JOHN ASHLEY An Imparlance.

JAMES FLETCHER was this day brought before the Court by a Warrant under the hand and seal of CHARLES THOMAS Gentleman for Breach of the Peace and the same being proved it is ordered that the Sergeant take the said JAMES FLETCHER and keep him in Custody until he gives bond and security himself in 20 pounds and 2 securities in 10 pounds each for the said JAMES FLETCHER keeping the peace 6 months and pay the costs of this prosecution.

CATHERINE CRUMLESS was this day brought before the Court and it appearing to the said Court that she is a person of lewd life and conversation and a common disturber of the peace. It is Therefore, ordered that the Sergeant take her and keep her in Custody until she gives bond and security herself in 20 pounds and 2 securities in 10 pounds each for the said CATHERINE CRUMLESS being of good behavior 6 months and pay the costs of this prosecution.

The King by JACOB WILLIAMS against BARNABAS LORAIN dismissed at the Plaintiffs costs.
JOHN MACNEIL was this day brought before the Court by Warrant under the hand and seal of MAXIMILIAN CALVERT and GEORGE ABYVON Gentleman for being a person of lewd life and conversation and keeping a disorderly house and dealing with Gentleman slaves and the same being proved.

PAGE 15
It is ordered that that the Sergeant take him and keep him in Custody until he gives bond and security himself in 50 pounds and 2 securities in 25 pounds each for the said JOHN MACNEIL being of good behavior and for 12 months and pay the costs of this prosecution. And it is further ordered that the said MACNEILS license be suppressed.

JOHN SMITH was this day appointed CONSTABLE in the room of GEORGE WILSON and he having taken the oaths to the Government and subscribed the test, also the oath of constable enters on the execution of his office.

BARNABAS LORAIN is discharged from his office of Constable.

THOMAS BROWN and THOMAS BIRCH Plaintiff
Against Re: In Case
DAVID CROSS Defendant
This day came the parties by their Attorney's and there upon came also a Jury to wit:
WILLIAM MARSH, BARTHOLOMEW THOMPSON, JAMES MILLER, CHARLES GODFREY, JOHN RICHARDSON, RICHARD BROWN, ELDRED FISHER, NATHANIEL YOUNG, THOMAS FARRER, JAMES MURPHREE, JOHN BROWN, and JOHN WILLS who being elected tried and sworn the truth to speak upon the issue joined withdrew and not returning any verdict the Course is continued.

THOMAS NEWTON SR. and JOHN TAYLOR executor of ROBERT TUCKER deceased against ALEXANDER BELL Dismissed.

GEORGE OLDNER Plaintiff
Against Re: In Case
JOHN GODREY Defendant
This day came the parties by their Attorney's and there upon came also a Jury to wit: GEORGE SPARLING, HUGH WARDEN, JOHN GREENWOOD, THOMAS MORRIS, NICHOLAS POOLE, JOHN SMITH, JOHN CALVERT, BASSET MOSELEY, JOHN KELSO, SAMUEL TUMBLINSON, JOHN GILCHRIST and STEPHEN TANKARD who being elected tried and sworn the truth to speak upon the issue joined upon their oath do say that the Defendant did assume in manner and form as the Plaintiff against him has declared and do assess the Plaintiff damages by occasion of the non-performance of that assumption to 10 pounds, 5 pence besides his costs.

PAGE 15B
Therefore, it is considered that the Plaintiff recover against he said Defendant his damages aforesaid in form aforesaid and costs by him about his suit in this behalf expended and the said defendant in mercy.

MARGARET BANNERMAN Plaintiff
Against Re: In Chancery
BENJAMIN BANNERMAN Defendant
This day came as well the Plaintiff by WILLIAM ROSCOW WILSON CURLE Gentleman Attorney her Attorney as GEORGE DONALD Gentleman in his proper person who pursuant of a former decretal order of this Court this day produced his demand of 196 pounds, 8 shillings and 10 pence against the said Defendant BENJAMIN BANNERMAN with several exhibits thereto annexed to ascertain the same. On consideration where of it is the opinion of this Court that the same is justly due him from the said Defendant. And it is hereby ordered and decreed that his said demand be allowed him and that the bond taken by the Sequestrator for the 2 Negroes in the said former decretal order mentioned be delivered up to the said GEORGE DONALD and that the receipt in these words to wit: 1769 June 27th then received of CAPTAIN BENJAMIN BANNERMAN one HHO run quantity 114 gallons payable in October in good Merchantable wheat at the market price to be delivered at

RICHMOND LANDING. ZACH ROWLAND to his Court produced by the said GEORGE DONALD Lodged in the Clerk's office be delivered up by the Clerk of this Court to the Plaintiff MARGARET BANNERMAN and it is further ordered and decreed that the said GEORGE DONALD pay the costs.

JOHN STODDART Plaintiff
Against Re: In Case
ALEXANDER LIVINGSTON Defendant
This day came the Defendant by WILLIAM ROSCOW WILSON CURLE Gentleman his Attorney and the Plaintiff though solemnly called came not but made default nor is his suit further prosecuted. Therefore, on the prayer of the Defendant it is considered that he recover against the Plaintiff 5 pounds current money and his costs by him about his defense in this behalf expended according to the form of the Act of Assembly and the Plaintiff for his claims in mercy.

The Court is adjourned until tomorrow 10 O'clock MAXMILIAN CALVERT MAYOR
PAGE 16
NORFOLK BOROUGH
At a Hustings Court Held this 22nd day of May 1770
PRESENT: MAXIMILIAN CALVERT ESQUIRE MAYOR
ANTHONY LAWSON ESQUIRE DEPUTY RECORDER
GENTLEMAN ALDERMEN: GEORGE ABYVON, LEWIS HANSFORD, ARCHIBALD CAMPBELL, JAMES TAYLOR, PAUL LOYALL, CORNELIUS CALVERT, CHARLES THOMAS

THOMAS NEWTON SR. & JOHN TAYLOR Executors of ROBERT TUCKER deceased against MATHEW ROTHERY Dismissed.

JAMES DUNLOP Plaintiff
Against Re: In Case
PRINCE GORHAM Defendant
This day came the parties by their Attorney's and there upon came also a Jury to wit: WILLIAM MARSH, JAMES MILLER, NATHANIEL YOUNG, JOHN RICHARDSON, RICHARD HOGG, CHARLES GODFREY, JAMES MURPHREE, BARTHOLOMEW THOMPSON, THOMAS FARRER, RICHARD BROWN, ELDRED FISHER and JOHN WILLS who being elected tried and sworn the truth to speak upon the issue joined upon their oath do say that the Defendant did not assume as in the pleading he has alleged. Therefore, it is considered that the Plaintiff take nothing by his bill for his false claims be in mercy. And the defendant go hence without day and recover against the Plaintiff his costs by him about his defense in this behalf expended.

Ordinary License is granted RICHARD BASSET on his complying with the law.

SETH POINTER Plaintiff
Against Re: In Case
GEORGE ABYVON Defendant
This day came the parties by their Attorney's and thereupon came also a Jury to wit: WILLIAM MCCAA, RICHARD BASSET, BASSET MOSELEY, JOHN WILSON, SAMUEL BACON, JONATHAN EILBECK, JOHN BOWNESS, JOHN ARDISS, JOHN MADDOX, JONATHAN DISON, NICHOLAS WONYCOTT and JOHN MACLEAN who being elected tried and sworn the truth to speak upon the issue joined upon their oath
PAGE 16B
do say that the Defendant did not assume as in the pleading he has alleged. Therefore, it is considered that the Plaintiff take nothing by his bill for his false claims be in mercy.
And the defendant go hence without day and recover against the Plaintiff his costs by him about his defense in this behalf expended.

Order is granted ELIZABETH DAVIS, ELIZABETH GODFREY, ALEXANDER BELL, and CHARLES GODFREY against GEORGE ABYVON for 100 pounds tobacco each for 4 days attendance each in the suit of SETH POINTER against them.
Order is granted CHARLES COOPER against SETH POINTER for 50 pounds tobacco for 2 days attendance in his suit against GEORGE ABYVON.

RICHARD BROWN was this day appointed constable he having first taken the oaths to the government and subscribed the test also the oath of a constable enters on the execution of his office.

THOMAS FARRER Plaintiff
Against Re: In Case for Slander
NICHOLAS GAUTIER Defendant
This day came the parties by their Attorney's and thereupon came also a jury to wit: JOHN CALVERT, JAMES GODFREY, JONATHAN DISON, JOHN ARDISS, JOHN MADDOX, JONATHAN EILBECK, SAMUEL BACON, JOHN BOWNESS, NICHOLAS WONYCOTT, BASSET MOSELEY, JOHN WILSON and RICHARD BASSET who being elected tried and sworn the truth to speak upon the issue joined upon their oath do say that the defendant is guilty of speaking the slanderous words in manner and form as in the declaration against him is alleged and do assess the Plaintiff damages by occasion of the speaking the slanderous words in the declaration mentioned to 8 pounds besides his costs. Therefore, it is considered that the Plaintiff recover against the said defendant his damages aforesaid in form aforesaid assessed and his costs by him in this behalf expended and the said defendant in mercy.

MATHEW CRAWFORD Plaintiff

Against Re: in Case

TALBUT THOMPSON Defendant

This day came the parties by their Attorney's and thereupon came also a jury to wit: WILLIAM MARSH, ALEXANDER MOSELEY, CHARLES GODFREY, RICHARD HOGG,

PAGE 17

ELDRED FISHER, JOHN WILLS, BARTHOLOMEW THOMPSON, NATHANIEL YOUNG, THOMAS FARRER, RICHARD BROWN, WILLIAM FARRER, and STEPHEN TANKARD who being elected tried and sworn the truth to speak upon the issue joined upon their oath do say that the defendant is not guilty as in pleading he has alleged. Therefore, it is considered that the Plaintiff take nothing by his bill but for his false claims be in mercy and the defendant go hence without day and recover against the Plaintiff his costs by him about defense in this behalf expended.

JOHN GREENHOW Plaintiff

Against Re: In Case

JAMES ATKINSON and MARY, his wife Defendant

This day came the Defendants by JAMES HOLT Gentleman Attorney and the Plaintiff though solemnly called came not but made default no is his suit further prosecuted. Therefore, on the prayer of the Defendant it is considered that he recover against the Plaintiff 5 shillings current money and the costs by them about this defense in this behalf expended according to the form of the Act of Assembly and the Plaintiff for his claims be in Mercy.

Order is granted WILLIAM WALKER against THOMAS FARRER for 150 pounds for 6 days attendance in his suit against NICHOLAS GAUTIER.

Order is granted BARNABAS LORAIN against NICHOLAS GAUTIER for 150 pounds tobacco for 6 days attendance in the suit of THOMAS FARRER against him.

JOSEPH MITCHELL Plaintiff

Against Re: In Debt

JONATHAN DISON Defendant

This day came the parties by their Attorney's and the Defendant by his Attorney relinquishing his former plea acknowledges the Plaintiffs action for 47 pounds 2 shillings. Therefore, it is considered that the Plaintiff recover against the said Defendant his debt aforesaid and his costs by him in this behalf expended and the said Defendant in Mercy. But this judgement is to be discharged the payment of 14 pounds 4 shillings and 11 pence half penny with interest for the same at the rate of

5% per annum to be computed

PAGE 17B

From July 14th, 1768, to the time of payment and the costs.

JAMES DUNLOP Plaintiff

Against Re: In Case

ELDRED FISHER Defendant

This day came the parties by their Attorney's and there upon came also a Jury to wit: WILLIAM SKINKER, WILLIAM MARSH, THOMAS FARRER, RICHARD BROWN, ALEXANDER MOSELEY, CHARLES GODFREY, JONATHAN EILBECK, BARTHOLOMEW THOMPSON, JOHN WILLS, RICHARD HOGG, NATHANIEL YOUNG and STEPHEN TANKARD who being elected tried and sworn the truth to speak upon the issue joined upon their oath do say that the Defendant did assume in manner and form as the Plaintiff against him has declared and do assess the Plaintiff damages by occasion of the non-performance of that assumption to 20 pounds, 1 shilling, 4 pence half penny besides his costs. Therefore, it is considered that the Plaintiff recover against he said Defendant his damages aforesaid in form aforesaid and costs by him about his suit in this behalf expended and the said Defendant in mercy.

THOMAS BROWN and THOMAS BIRCH Plaintiff

Against Re: In Case

DAVID CROSS Defendant

This day came the parties by their Attorney's and there upon came also a Jury to wit: WILLIAM MARSH, BARTHOLOMEW THOMPSON, JAMES MILLER, CHARLES GODFREY, JOHN RICHARDSON, RICHARD BROWN, ELDRED FISHER, NATHANIEL YOUNG, THOMAS FARRAR, JAMES MURPHREE, JOHN BROWN and JOHN WILLIS who being elected tried and sworn the truth to speak upon the issue joined upon their oath do say that the Defendant did assume in manner and form as the Plaintiff against him has declared and do assess the Plaintiffs damages by occasion of the non-performance of that assumption to 75 pounds, 9 shillings, 3 pence half penny besides his costs. Therefore, it is considered that the Plaintiff recover against he said Defendant his damages aforesaid in form aforesaid and costs by him about his suit in this behalf expended and the said defendant in mercy. And the Court says the said Sterling Money may be discharged in Current Money at 15% differences of exchanged.

PAGE 18

EDWARD HANSFORD against JOHN SMITH publication of the deposition and set for hearing.

MATHEW ROTHERY against SAMUEL GRIFFIN. The Defendant pleaded not Guilty issue joined and referred.

THOMAS BRESSIE against MALACHI MAUND. Covenant performed with leave issue joined and referred.

JOHN SMITH against WILLIAM CHISHOLM, billed filed and time to consider it.

JOHN HARDIE against JOHN WILSON performance and time issue joined and referred.

14

MALACHI MOUND against WILLIAM WALLACE discontinued at the Plaintiff's Costs.

WILLIAM WALLACE against MALACHI MOUND covenant not broken issue joined and referred.

JOHN MADDOX against ALEXANDER MORRISON. The Defendant pleaded that he did not assume issue joined and referred.

THOMAS ARCHER against JAMES MAXWELL. The Defendant pleaded that he did not detain issue joined and referred.

JOSIAH BUTT against SAMUEL SIMMONS. The Defendant pleaded that he did not assume issue joined and referred.

THOMAS DAVIS against JOSEPH LOCKHART abates by the Plaintiff deaths.

This Court his day rated flour at 12 shillings and 6 pence.

The Court is adjourned to Court in Course. MAXIMILIAN CALVERT MAYOR.TESTE: JOHN BOUSH D.C.

PAGE 18B
NORFOLK BOROUGH
At a Hustings Court Held this 25th day of June 1770
PRESENT: CHARLES THOMAS ESQUIRE MAYOR
GENTLEMAN ALDERMEN: GEORGE ABYVON, LEWIS HANSFORD, MAXIMILIAN CALVERT, JAMES TAYLOR

ROBERT BALLARD against WALTER LYON abates by the Plaintiffs death.

GEORGE ABYVON executor of HENRY ROTHERY against MATHEW ROTHERY an Imparlance.

ROBERT COUDEN against THOMAS ROBERTS Dismissed.

THOMAS ROBERTS against JOHN ASHLEY an Imparlance.

LEMUEL ROBERTS against JOHN GUY order against the Defendant and THOMAS TALBOT his bail.

WILLIAM and JOHN DURELL against JOHN MACNEIL by petition dismissed.

WILLIAM and JOHN DURELL against JOHN MACNEIL in case dismissed.

WILLIAM MARSH & COMPANY against WILLIAM and JOHN BROWN Dismissed.

JOHN CRAMOND against ROBERT STEELE and SARAH his wife executrix of JOHN CANN deceased an Imparlance.

WILLIAM SIMPSON against JOHN BALLENTINE by Petition and summons judgement is granted the Plaintiff for 2 pounds 15 shillings and 9 pence. It is ordered that the Defendant pay the same unto the Plaintiff with costs and fees.

WILLIAM SIMPSON against ARCHIBALD AVEN. The Plaintiff by his Attorney moved for Special Bail which is granted. Where upon THOMAS BURKE Gentleman came into Court and entered himself Special Bail for the Defendant and thereon the Defendant by his Attorney prayed an Imparlance.

PAGE 19
WILLIAM SIMPSON against CHARLES COOPER order against the Defendant and JAMES DUNN his bail.

WILLIAM SIMPSON against JOHN SMITH in debt. The Plaintiff by their Attorney moves for Special Bail which is granted. Where upon STEPHEN TANKARD came into Court and entered himself Special Bail for the Defendant and thereon the Defendant by his Attorney prayed an Imparlance,

WILLIAM SIMPSON against JOHN SMITH In Case: The Plaintiff by their Attorney moves for Special Bail which is granted. Where upon STEPHEN TANKARD came into Court and entered himself Special Bail for the Defendant and thereon the Defendant by his Attorney prayed an Imparlance.

MARY ROSS against JOHN COLVILLE. The Plaintiff by their Attorney moves for Special Bail which is granted. Where upon NATHANIEL BOUSH came into Court and entered himself Special Bail for the Defendant and thereon the Defendant by his Attorney prayed an Imparlance.

MALACHI MAUND against CHARLES JENKINS Executor of JOSEPH LOCKHART. Order against the Defendant and THOMAS CREECH his bail.

JOSEPH GREAR against JOHN GRANFIELD Dismissed.

JOHN HARDIE against WILLIAM SIMPSON and HARMON HILL Dismissed.

TERESA BOYD against NATHANIEL STROUDS abates by the Plaintiffs marriage.

ROBERT BANKS who as well against JOHN HUNT dismissed.

HENRY RITTER against JONAS MERCER dismissed.

JOHN HARDIE against JOHN WILSON replication and issue.

CORNELIUS CALVERT against WILLIAM CALVERT. The Defendant pleaded payment. Issue joined and referred.

ANN WALLACE against SAMUEL MIDDLETON set for hearing on the bill & answer.

PAGE 19B
EDWARD PARKE Plaintiff
Against Re: In Case
WILLIAM BROWN Defendant
This day came the Plaintiff by WILLIAM ROSCOW WILSON CURLE Gentleman this Attorney and there upon came also a Jury to wit: JOHN MCLEAN, STEPHEN TANKARD, GEORGE SPARLING, CHARLES GODFREY, ALEXANDER MOSELEY, DANIEL HUTCHINGS, ROBERT HATTON,

EDMOND KEETON, JAMES LEITCH, ROBERT STEEL, JOHN CRAMOND and WILLIAM BELL who being sworn well and truly to enquire of damages in this suit upon their oath do say that the Plaintiff has sustained damages in the declaration mentioned to 9 pounds, 10 shillings besides his costs. Therefore, it is considered by the Court that the Plaintiff recover against the Defendant and ROBERT TAYLOR his bail his damages aforesaid in form aforesaid assessed and his costs by him in this behalf expended and the said Defendant in mercy.

THOMAS ARCHER Plaintiff
Against Re: In Detinue for 2 Negroes Slaves
JAMES MAXWELL Defendant
This day came the parties by their Attorney's and there upon came also a Jury to wit:
JOHN MCLEAN, STEPHEN TANKARD, GEORGE SPARLING, CHARLES GODFREY, ALEXANDER MOSELEY, DANIEL HUTCHINGS, ROBERT HATTON, EDMOND KEETON, JAMES LEITCH, ROBERT STEEL, JOHN CRAMOND and WILLIAM BELL who being elected tried and sworn the truth to speak upon the issue joined upon their oath do say that the Defendant did detain the 2 Negroes in the declaration mentioned in manner and form as the Plaintiff against him has declared and that the said slaves are of the value of to wit: KATE 30 pounds and HENRIETTA 8 pounds 11 shillings and 6 pence besides his costs. Therefore, it is considered by the Court that the Plaintiff recover against the Defendant the sales aforesaid if they may be had or the value of them if they not to be had together with his damages

PAGE 20

aforesaid in form aforesaid assessed and his costs by him in this behalf expended and the said Defendant in mercy.

JOHN G. FRASIER against WRIGHT WESTCOTT. The Defendant pleaded that he did not assume issue joined and referred.
JOHN HUNTER against JOHN G. FRAZIER. The Defendant pleaded that he did not assume issue joined and referred.

THOMAS NEWTON SR. and JOHN TAYLOR Executors of ROBERT TUCKER deceased Plaintiffs
Against Re: In Debt.
JOHN TATEM and THOMAS THOMPSON Defendants
This day came the Plaintiffs by JAMES HOLT Gentleman their Attorney and the defendant JOHN TATEM being solemnly called and not appearing ordered that the former order of this Court against him the said Defendant JOHN and JOSEPH CALVERT Sergeant his bail be confirmed. Therefore, it is considered that the Plaintiff recover against the said defendant and JOSEPH CALVERT his bail aforesaid his debt amounting to 63 pounds, 6 shillings and their costs by them in this behalf expended and the said defendant JOHN in mercy. But this judgement is to be discharged by the payment of 31 pounds 13 shillings with interest for the same at the rate of 5% per annum to be computed from April 25, 1768, to the time of payment and costs. And the other Defendant THOMAS THOMPSON pleaded payment issue joined and referred.

THOMAS NEWTON SR. and JOHN TAYLOR Executor of ROBERT TUCKER against JOHN WILSON and ELDRED FISHER. The Defendants pleaded payment issue joined and referred.

EDMOND KEETON against JAMES MARSHALL. The Defendant pleaded not guilty. Issue joined and referred.
JAMES LEITCH against PAUL WATLINGTON and RICHARD BICKERDICK. The Defendants pleaded payment. Issue joined and referred.

PAGE 20B
King by BARNABAS LORAIN against JAMES ANDERSON Dismissed.

EDWARD HANSFORD Complainant
Against Re: In Chancery
JOHN SMITH Defendant
This cause was this day heard on the bill, answer and replication and depositions and the arguments of the Council on both sides. On Consideration whereof it is ordered and decreed that the defendant convey unto the Plaintiff his heirs by a good and sufficient deed an indefeasible estate in fee simple of and in the parcel of land with the appurtenances in the bill mentioned and it is further ordered and decreed that the Defendant pay rents unto the Plaintiff his costs by him about his suit in this behalf expended from which decree the Plaintiff by his Attorney prayed an appeal to the 3rd day of the next General Court which on his giving security of prosecution at or before the next Court to be held for this Borough is allowed.

The Court this day rated Flour 12 pounds 6 shillings
This Court is adjourned to Court in Course: CHARLES THOMAS MAYOR, TESTE: JOHN BOUSH D.C.

PAGE 21
NORFOLK BOROUGH
At a Hustings Court Held this 23rd day of July 1770
PRESENT: ANTHONY LAWSON ESQUIRE DEPUTY RECORDER
GENTLEMAN ALDERMEN: GEORGE ABYVON, JAMES TAYLOR, ARCHIBALD CAMPBELL, CORNELIUS CALVERT, LEWIS HANSFORD

HENRY NEWTON against JOHN GRIFFIN Dismissed at the Defendants Costs.
WILLOUGHBY MORGAN and UNICE his wife against JAMES MARSHALL dismissed at the Defendants Costs.
WILLOUGHBY MORGAN and UNICE his wife against JAMES MARSHALL dismissed at the Defendants Costs.

RICHARD POINDEXTER against JOHN BIRCH Dismissed.
ARCHIBALD WHITE and Company against JAMES ROGERS Dismissed.
MATTHEW KELLY who as well against OWEN CRUMLESS and CATHERINE his wife an Imparlance.

JOHN BAKER and ELIZABETH his wife Plaintiff

Against Re: In Case for Slander

ELIZABETH CROFT Defendant

This day came the Defendant by JAMES HOLT Gentleman her Attorney and the Plaintiffs though solemnly called came not but made default nor is their suit further prosecuted. Therefore, on the prayer of the Defendant it is considered that she recover against the Plaintiffs 5 shillings current money and costs by her about her defense expended according to the form of Act of Assembly and the Plaintiff for their false claims be in mercy.

PAGE 21B

ARCHIBALD WHITE & COMPANY Plaintiffs

Against Re: In Debt.

JOHN DISON Defendant

This day came the parties by their Attorney's and the defendant by his Attorney acknowledges the Plaintiffs action for 23 pounds, 2 shillings and 6 pence. Therefore, it is considered that the Plaintiff recover against the said Defendant their debt aforesaid and their costs by them in this behalf expended. And the said Defendant in mercy. But this Judgement is to be discharged by the payment of 10 pounds with interest for the same at the rate of 5% per annum to be computed from May 8, 1767, to the time of payment and the costs.

ARCHIBALD WHITE & Company against MARY NICHOLAS. The Plaintiff by their Attorney moved for Special Bail which is granted. Where upon ARCHIBALD CAMPBELL and WALTER LYON Gentleman entered themselves Special Bail for the Defendant and thereon the Defendant by her Attorney prayed a Special Imparlance.

JOHN HURT against SAMUEL SMITH THURMER by Petition and Summons. Judgement is granted the Plaintiff for 2 pounds 8 shillings and 2 pence. It is ordered that the defendant pay the same unto the Plaintiff with costs.

LOGAN GILMOUR and Company against JOHN TATEM. The Plaintiff by their Attorney moved for Special Bail which is granted. Where upon SAMUEL PORTLOCK came into Court and entered himself Special Bail for the defendant and thereon the Defendant by her Attorney prayed an Imparlance.

JOHN WOODSIDE against CHARLES JENKINS executor of JOSEPH LOCKHART. Imparlance.

PHILOMON RUSSELL against ALEXANDER BELL. An Imparlance.

PAGE 22

ALEXANDER BELL against JOSIAH BUTT. An Imparlance.

SAMUEL SWANN against ALEXANDER MORRISON. The Plaintiff by his Attorney moved for Special Bail which is granted. Where upon JOHN WILSON came into Court and entered himself Special Bail for the defendant and thereon the Defendant by his Attorney prayed an Imparlance

SAMUEL CALVERT and PEGGY, his wife and JOHN ROSS, ALEXANDER ROSS and ROBERT ROSS, infants by the said SAMUEL their guardian against ANDREW SPROWLE and WILLIAM ORANGE executors of JOHN ROSS time to consider.

WILLIAM CHISHOLM and LATIMORE HALSTEAD against JAMES MARSHALL by Petition and Summons. Judgement is granted the Plaintiffs for 1 pound 10 shillings and 3 pence. It is ordered that the Defendant pay the same unto the Plaintiff with costs and fees.

JAMES MARSHALL was this day brought before the Court by warrant under the hand of CHARLES THOMAS ESQUIRE for Breach of the Peace and the same being proved. It is ordered that the Sergeant take him and keep him in Custody until he gives bond and security himself in 20 pounds and 2 securities in 10 pends each for the security of JAMES MARSHALL keeping the peace 6 months and pay costs.

Order is granted SAMUEL DENBY against WILLOUGHBY MORGAN and UNICE his wife for 25 pounds tobacco for 1 day's attendance in the complaint of his wife against JAMES MARSHALL.

Order is granted ELIZABETH HARDY against JAMES MARSHALL for 25 pounds tobacco for 1 day's attendance in the Complaint of UNICE MORGAN against him.

PAGE 22B

ANN KELLY was this day brought before the Court by Warrant under the hand of CHARLES THOMAS ESQUIRE for Breach of the Peace and the same being proved. It is ordered that the Sergeant take the said ANN KELLY and keep her in custody until MATTHEW KELLY her husband gives bond and security on behalf of his wife in 40 pounds and 2 securities in 20 pounds each for the said ANN KELLY'S keeping the peace for 12 months and pay costs of this prosecution.

Order is granted MARGARET SHURLEY against CATHERINE CRUMLESS for 25 pounds tobacco for one day's attendance in her Complaint against ANN KELLY.

THOMAS BRESSIE

Against Re: In Covenant

MALACHI MAUND and RICHARD TEMPLEMAN Defendant

This day came the parties by their Attorney's and the defendants by their Attorney relinquishing their former plea, say that they cannot gainsay the Plaintiff's action nor but that they have broken their Covenants with the Plaintiff in manner and form as the Plaintiff against them have declared. Therefore, it is considered that the Plaintiff recover against the said Defendant 36 pounds 4 shillings and 5 pence and his costs by them in this behalf expended. And the said defendant in mercy. And the Plaintiff agrees to stay the execution of this judgement 6 months.

ROBERT TUCKERS executors against JOSEPH CALVERT. On motion of the Plaintiffs by their Attorney a DEDIMUS is granted to take JOHN GREENHOW'S deposition.

Order is granted SOLOMON HANBURY against THOMAS BRESSIE for 50 pounds of tobacco for 2 days attendance in his suit against MALACHI MAUND & RICHARD TEMPLEMAN.

JOHN MACNEIL and MARGARET, his wife against WILLIAM KEETON dismissed at Plaintiffs costs.

PAGE 23
WILLIAM WALLACE Plaintiff
Against Re: In Covenant
MALACHI MAUND Defendant
This day came the parties by their Attorney's and there upon came also a Jury to wit:
JAMES MURPHREE, JOHN ASHLEY, JOHN MADDOX, EDMOND KEETON, DANIEL HUTCHINGS, WILLIAM CALVERT, WILLIAM CHISHOLM, JOHN ARDIS, JOHN WILSON, WILLIAM FREEMAN, PHILIP CARBERY and JOHN WALKER who being elected tried and sworn the truth to speak upon the issue joined upon their oath do say that the Defendant has broken his covenant with the Plaintiff as the said Plaintiff against the said Defendant has declared and that the Plaintiff has sustained damages by occasion thereof to 25 pounds besides his costs. Therefore, it is considered that the Plaintiff recover against the said Defendant his damages aforesaid in form aforesaid assessed and his costs by him in this behalf expended and the said Defendant in mercy.

Order is granted JOHN SOUTHERLAND SR., JOHN SOUTHERLAND JR. and TAYLOR SEVILLS against WILLIAM WALLACE for 50 pounds of tobacco for 2 days attendance and JESSE WILLIAMS for 25 pounds tobacco for 2 days attendance in his suit against MALACHI MAUND.

MATTHEW ROTHERY Plaintiff
Against Re: In Case
SAMUEL GRIFFIN Defendant
This day came the parties by their Attorney's and there upon came also a Jury to wit: JOHN WALKER, JOHN ARDIS, JOHN CRAMOND, JOHN ASHLEY, JOHN MADDOX, PHILIP CARBERY, WILLIAM CHISHOLM, WILLIAM CALVERT, JAMES MURPHREE, EDMOND KEETON, DANIEL HUTCHINGS, and WILLIAM FREEMAN
PAGE 23B
Who being elected tried and sworn the truth to speak upon the issue joined withdrew and not returning any verdict the cause is continued.

The Court is adjourned until tomorrow 10'Clock: ANTHONY LAWSON DEPUTY RECORDER, TESTE: JOHN BOUSH D.C.

NORFOLK BOROUGH
At a Hustings Court Held this 24th day of July 1770
PRESENT: ANTHONY LAWSON ESQUIRE DEPUTY RECORDER
GENTLEMAN ALDERMEN: GEORGE ABYVON, JAMES TAYLOR, LEWIS HANSFORD, CORNELIUS CALVERT

JOSEPH MITCHELL against GEORGE ABYVON Executor of HENRY ROTHERY Dismissed.
MATHIAS GALE against GEORGE ABYVON Executor of HENRY ROTHERY discontinued at the Plaintiffs cost.

JOHN SHERLOCK against JOSHUA EDWARDS. The Defendant pleaded that he did not assume issue joined and referred.
GEORGE PAGAN & Company against JOHN WILSON. The Defendant pleaded that he did not assume issue joined and referred.

WILLIAM MURPHREE against JOHN MACNEIL and MARGARET his wife. The former order of this Court against them the said Defendants and GEORGE WILSON and PETER BISER, their bail be confirmed, and a Writ of Inquiry is awarded him for his damages.

ELIAS ELLERY against NATHANIEL YOUNG and JOHN SMITH. The Defendants pleaded that they did not assume issue joined and referred.

PAGE 24
THOMAS TAYLOR against JOHN YOUNG. The Defendant pleaded that he did not assume issue joined and referred.
JOHN COX against GEORGE ABYVON Executor of HENRY ROTHERY discontinued.
JANE MUNROE against JOSEPH GREAR and ELSE his wife. The Defendants pleaded that the Plaintiff made first assault issue joined and referred.
SAMUEL WARNER against JOHN CANNON continued and on motion of the Plaintiff by his Attorney a DEDIMUS is granted him to take depositions giving legal notice.
ROBERT TUCKER against WILLIAM MCCAA. The defendant pleaded that he did not assume issue joined and referred.
ANN BOUCHER administrator of DANIEL ROTHERY deceased against MATTHEW ROTHERY. The Defendant pleaded he did not assume issue joined and referred.
EDMOND BRUCE against MATTHEW KELLY and ANN his wife. The Defendant pleaded not guilty issue joined and referred.
MATTHEW KELLY and ANN, his wife against JUDITH ALLEN. The Defendant pleaded not guilty issue joined and referred.
THOMAS BYCROFT against JOHN MARNIX. The Defendant pleaded that he was not guilty issue joined and referred.
CHARLES COOPER and CHAPMAN MANSON against GEORGE FARRER. The Defendant pleaded not guilty issue joined and referred.
JOHN FIFE against JAMES ARCHDEACON removed by Certiorari.

DUNCAN SHARP against JOHN MCKERROLL. The Defendant pleaded that he did not assume issue joined and referred.

JOHN MCFARLAN against JOHN MACKERROL. The Defendant pleaded that he did not assume issue joined and referred.

THOMAS ROBERTS against ROBERT STEAD. The Defendant pleaded that he did not assume issue joined and referred.

WILLIAM SMITH against THOMAS GRANT plea and time.

GEORGE OLDNER against JOHN CHESHIRE. The Defendant pleaded that he did not assume issue joined and referred.

JOHN EILBECK and WILLIAM CHALMERS against JONATHAN MEREDITH and ELIZABETH his wife. The Defendants pleaded that they did not assume issue joined and referred.

MOORY MALICOTE against CHARLES COOPER. The Defendant pleaded that he did not assume issue joined and referred.

HALCOTT PRIDE against CHARLES COOPER. The former order of this Court against him the said Defendant against him the said Defendant and JOSEPH CALVERT Sergeant his bail be confirmed, and a Writ of Inquiry is awarded him for damages.

ROBERT SHEDDEN and Company against ROBERT BRYCE. The Defendant pleaded that he did not assume issue joined and referred.

JOHN LEE against FRANCES FRASIER administrative of RICHARD FRASIER. The Defendant pleaded that she did not assume issue joined and referred.

JOHN MADDOX Plaintiff
Against Re: In Case
ALEXANDER MORRISON Defendant
This day came the parties by their Attorneys and there upon came also a Jury to wit:

WILLOUGHBY MORGAN, BARTHOLOMEW THOMPSON, ELDRED FISHER, JAMES LEITCH, ROGER PIERCE, WILLIAM STEVENSON, CHRISTOPHER RATSEY, WILLIAM IVY, GEORGE SPARLING, FRANCES HATTON, JOEL MOHUN and MASON MILLER who being elected tried and sworn the truth to speak upon the issue joined upon their oath do say that the Defendant did not assume as in pleading he has alleged. Therefore, it is considered that the Plaintiff take nothing by his bill but for his false claims be in mercy and the Defendant go hence without day and recover against the Plaintiff his costs by him about his defense in this behalf expended.

MATTHEW ROTHERY Plaintiff
Against Re: In Case
SAMUEL GRIFFIN Defendant
This day came the parties by their Attorney's and there upon came also Jury to wit: JOHN WALKER, JOHN ARDIS, JOHN CRAMOND, JOHN ASHLEY, JOHN MADDOX, PHILIP CARBERY, WILLIAM CHISHOLM, WILLIAM CALVERT, JAMES MURPHREE, EDMOND KEETON, DANIEL HUTCHINGS, and WILLIAM FREEMAN who were yesterday elected tried and sworn the truth to speak upon the issue joined upon their oath do now say that the Defendant did assume in manner and form as the Plaintiff against him has declared and do assess the Plaintiffs damages by occasion of the non-performance of that assumption to 35 pounds besides costs. Therefore, it is considered that the Plaintiff recover against the said Defendant his damages aforesaid in form aforesaid assessed and his costs by him in this behalf expended and the said Defendant in mercy.

Order is granted GILES RANDOLPH and FRANCIS HATTON against MATTHEW ROTHERY for 75 pounds of tobacco for 3 days attendance and JOSEPH MITCHELL for 50 pounds tobacco for 2 days attendance in his suit against SAMUEL GRIFFIN.

Order is granted JOHN GRANT against SAMUEL GRIFFIN for 50 pounds tobacco for 2 days attendance in the suit of MATTHEW ROTHERY against him.

JOSIAH BUTT Plaintiff
Against Re: In Case
SAMUEL SIMMONS Defendant
This day came the parties by their Attorney's and thereupon came also a Jury to wit: JOHN CRAMOND, NICHOLAS WONYCOTT, PHILIP CARBERY, WILLIAM FREEMAN, WILLIAM CHISHOLM, JOHN ARDIS, JOHN ASHLEY, WILLIAM CALVERT, DANIEL HUTCHINGS, EDMOND KEETON, JOHN MADDOX and JAMES MURPHREE who being elected tried and sworn the truth to speak upon the issue joined upon their oath do say that the Defendant did assume in manner and form as the Plaintiff against him has declared and do assess the Plaintiff damages by occasion of the non-performance of that assumption to 6 pounds 10 shillings besides his costs. Therefore, it is considered that the Plaintiff recover against the said Defendant his damages aforesaid in form aforesaid assessed and his costs by him in this behalf expended and the said Defendant in mercy.

It is ordered that the Clerk deliver HUGH WARDENS Indenture to JOHN CRAMOND which were filed in the said warden's suit against JOHN CRAMOND.

JOHN HARDIE Plaintiff
Against Re: In Debt
JOHN WILSON Defendant
This day came the Parties by their Attorney's and there upon came also a Jury to wit: BARTHOLOMEW THOMPSON, WILLOUGHBY MORGAN, JAMES LEITCH, ROGER PIERCE, WILLIAM STEVENSON, CHRISTOPHER RATSEY, WILLIAM IVY, ELDRED FISHER, GEORGE SPARLING, FRANCIS HATTON, JOEL MOHUN and MASON MILLER. Who being elected tried and sworn the truth to speak upon the issue joined upon their oath do say that the Defendant has not performed the bond item

PAGE 26

Of the writing obligatory in the declaration mentioned but the same has broken as the Plaintiff in his replication has alleged and do assess the damages of the Plaintiff by occasion thereof besides his costs to 40 pounds. Therefore, it is considered that the Plaintiff recover against the said Defendant his debt amounting to 50 pounds and his damages aforesaid in form aforesaid assessed together with this costs by him in this behalf expended and the said Defendant in mercy. But this judgement is to be discharged by the payment of the said damages and costs.

CORNELIUS CALVERT Plaintiff
Against Re: In Debt
WILLIAM CALVERT Defendant
This day came the parties by their Attorney's and the Defendant by his Attorney relinquishing his former plea acknowledges the Plaintiffs actions for 74 pounds, 17 shillings and 6 pence. Therefore, it is considered that the Plaintiff recover against the Defendant his costs aforesaid and his costs by him in this behalf expended. And the said Defendant in mercy. But this judgement is to be discharged by the payment of 37 pounds 8 shillings and 9 pence with interest for the same at the rate of 5% per annum to be computed from August 24, 1765, to the time of payment and the costs.

JOHN GIRRAGE FRASIER Plaintiff
Against Re: In Case
WRIGHT WESTCOTT Defendant
This day came the parties by their Attorney's and thereupon came also a Jury to Wit: JOHN ARDIS, PHILIP CARBERY, JOHN CRAMOND, WILLIAM CHISHOLM, WILLIAM CALVERT, JAMES MURPHREE, EDMOND KEETON, JOHN ASHLEY, JOHN MADDOX,

PAGE 26B

DANIEL HUTCHINGS, WILLIAM FREEMAN and NICHOLAS WONYCOTT who being elected tried and sworn the truth to speak upon the issue joined upon their oath do say that the Defendant did assume in manner and form as the Plaintiff against him has declared and do assess the Plaintiff damages by occasion of the non-performance of that assumption to 29 pounds, 6 shilling besides his costs. Therefore, it is considered that the Plaintiff recover against the said Defendant his damages aforesaid in form aforesaid assessed and his costs by him in this behalf expended. And the said Defendant in mercy.

JOHN HUNTER Plaintiff
Against Re: In Case
JOHN GIRRAGE FRASIER Defendant
This day came the parties by their Attorney's and the Defendant by his Attorney relinquishing his former plea says that he cannot gainsay the Plaintiffs action nor but that he did assume in manner and form as the Plaintiff against him has declared. Therefore, it is considered that Plaintiff recover against the said Defendant 25 pounds 8 shillings and his costs by him in this behalf expended and the said Defendant in mercy.

THOMAS NEWTON SR. & JOHN TAYLOR Executors of ROBERT TUCKER Deceased Plaintiffs
Against Re: In Debt
THOMAS THOMPSON Defendant
This day came the parties by their Attorney's and the Defendant by his Attorney relinquishing his former plea acknowledges the Plaintiffs action for 63 pounds, 6 shillings. Therefore, it is considered that the Plaintiff recover against the said Defendant their debt aforesaid and their costs by them in this behalf

PAGE 27

Expended and the said Defendant in mercy. But this Judgement is to be discharged by the payment of 31 pounds, 13 shillings with interest for the same at the rate of 5% per annum to be computed from April 25, 1768, to the time of payment and the costs.

THOMAS NEWTON SR. & JOHN TAYLOR Executor of ROBERT TUCKER deceased Plaintiffs
Against Re: In Debt
JOHN WILSON and ELDRED FISHER Defendants
This day came the parties by their Attorney's and the Defendant by their Attorney relinquishing their former plea acknowledges the Plaintiffs action for 82 pounds, 15 shillings and 8 pence. Therefore, it is considered that the Plaintiff recover against the said Defendant their debt aforesaid and their costs by them in this behalf expended and the said Defendant in mercy. But this Judgement is to be discharged by the payment of 41 pounds, 7 shillings, 10 pence with interest for the same at the rate of 5% per annum to be computed from April 25, 1768, to the time of payment and the costs.

JAMES LEITCH Plaintiff
Against Re: In Debt
PAUL WATLINGTON and RICHARD BICKERDICK Defendants
This day came the parties by their Attorney's and the Defendant by their Attorney relinquishing their former plea acknowledges the Plaintiffs action for 24 pounds. Therefore, it is considered that the Plaintiff recover against the said Defendant their debt aforesaid and their costs by them in this behalf expended and the said Defendant in mercy. But this Judgement is to be discharged by the payment of 2 pounds, 9 shillings one penny with interest for the same at the rate of 5% per annum to be computed from April 20, 1769, to the time of payment and the costs.

PAGE 27B
EDMOND KEETON Plaintiff
Against Re: In Case for Slander
JAMES MARSHALL Defendant
This day came the parties by their Attorney's and there upon came also a Jury to wit: MASON MILLER, JAMES LEITCH, BARTHOLOMEW THOMPSON, WILLOUGHBY MORGAN, ELDRED FISHER JOEL MOHUN, WILLIAM STEVENSON, CHRISTOPHER RATSEY, WILLIAM IVY, ROGER PIERCE, GEORGE SPARLING and FRANCIS HATTON who being elected tried and sworn the truth to speak upon the issue joined upon their oath do say that the Defendant is not guilty as in pleading he has alleged. Therefore, it is considered that the Plaintiff take nothing by his bill but for his false claims be in mercy. And the Defendant go hence without day and recover against the Plaintiff his costs by him about his defense in this behalf expended.

Order is granted JAMES ATKINSON and JOHN HARDY against EDMOND KEETON for 50 pounds each for 2 days attendance each in his suit against JAMES MARSHALL

This Court rates flour at 12 pounds 6 shillings
This Court is adjourned to Court in Course: GEORGE ABYVON SR. Alderman, TESTE: JOHN BOUSH D.C.

PAGE 28
NORFOLK BOROUGH
At a Hustings Court Held this 20th day of August 1770
PRESENT: CHARLES THOMAS ESQUIRE MAYOR
ANTHONY LAWSON ESQUIRE DEPUTY RECORDER
GENTLEMAN ALDERMEN: GEORGE ABYVON, MAXIMILIAN CALVERT, ARCHIBALD CAMPBELL, JAMES TAYLOR, PAUL LOYALL, CORNELIUS CALVERT, LEWIS HANSFORD

Ordinary License is granted JAMES DUNN, MARY PULLETT and JOHN HARDY on their complying with the law.

WILLIAM SIMPSON against JOHN RUNSBERG by Petition and Summons. Judgement is granted the Plaintiff for 4 pounds, 17 shillings and 8 pence farthing. It is ordered that the Defendant pay the same unto the Plaintiff with costs and fees.

WILLIAM SIMPSON against JOHN RUNSBERG by Petition and Summons. Judgement is granted the Plaintiff for 3 pounds, 19 shillings and 4 pence. It is ordered that the defendant pay the same unto the Plaintiff with costs and fees.

JAMES MARSDEN and SIMON HODGSON against EDWARD GOOD. Dismissed at the Defendants costs.
ROBERT FORESYTHE against JOHN JOHNSON. An Imparlance.
JOHN FIFE against LEWIS HANSFORD Gentleman. Removed by Certiorari

ROBERT GORDON against GEORGE LATHBURY. The Plaintiff by his Attorney moved for Special Bail which is granted. Where upon ROBERT TAYLOR came into Court and entered himself Special Bail for the Defendant and thereon the Defendant by his Attorney prayed an Imparlance.

PAGE 28B
ARCHIBALD WHITE and Company against GEORGE OLDNER. The Plaintiff by his Attorney moved for Special Bail which is granted. Where upon THOMAS MORRIS came into Court and entered himself Special Bail for the Defendant and thereon the Defendant by his Attorney prayed an Imparlance.

STEPHEN TANKARD against RICHARD HOGG. An Imparlance.
RICHARD HOGG against STEPHEN TANKARD. An Imparlance.

WALTER MCCLURG Plaintiff
Against Re: In case
WILLIAM MCCAA Defendant
This day came the parties by their Attorney and the Defendant by his Attorney says that he cannot gainsay the Plaintiff action, nor but that he did assume in manner and form as the Plaintiff against him has declared. Therefore, it is considered that the Plaintiff recover against the said Defendant 258 pounds 19 shillings and 4 pence and his costs by him in this behalf expended and the said Defendant in mercy.

WILLIAM CHISHOLM and LATIMORE HALSTEAD against BAILEY WARREN by Petition and Summons. Judgement is granted the Plaintiff for 4 pounds, 1 shilling and 11 pence farthing. It is ordered that the defendant pay the same unto the Plaintiff with costs and fees.

JAMES DUNLOP against JOHN MACKERROLL. The Plaintiff by his Attorney moved for Special Bail which is granted. Where upon THOMAS BURKE Gentleman came into Court and entered himself Special Bail for the Defendant and thereon the Defendant by his Attorney prayed an Imparlance.

PAGE 29

WILLIAM SIMPSON against SAMUEL BACON Dismissed.

GEORGE KELLY against ARCHIBALD CAMPBELL by Petition and Summons. Judgement is granted the Plaintiff for 2 pounds, 19 shilling and 9 pence. It is ordered that the Defendant pay the same unto the Plaintiff with costs and fees.

WILLIAM MCCAA Plaintiff
Against Re: In Case
NEIL JAMIESON, JAMES TAYLOR, MATTHEW PHRIPP & BASSETT MOSELEY executors of JACOB ELLEGOOD deceased Defendants
This day came as well the Plaintiff by JAMES HOLT Gentleman as BASSET MOSELEY one of the executors of JACOB MOSELEY one of the Executions of JACOB ELLEGOOD deceased in his proper person and says that he cannot gainsay the Plaintiffs action nor but that his testator did assume in manner and form as the Plaintiff has declared. Therefore, it is considered that Plaintiff recover against the said Defendant 6 pounds and 6 pence and his costs by him in this behalf expended. When assets after paying preceding judgements, debts of greater dignity and the Defendants own claims against the estate of the said testator to be levied of the goods and chattels which were of the said Jacob at the time of his death that shall hereafter come to the hands of the said Defendant to be administered and the said Defendants in mercy.

JOHN AUSTIN FINNIE Plaintiff
Against Re: In Case
LEWIS HANSFORD and Company Defendants
This day came the Plaintiff by WILLIAM ROSCOW WILSON CURLE Gentleman his Attorney and the
Plaintiff by his Attorney moved for Special Bail which is granted. Where upon ARCHIBALD CAMPBELL

PAGE 29B

this day came into Court and entered himself Special Bail for the Defendant LEWIS and the said Defendant says that he cannot gainsay the Plaintiffs action nor but that he did assume in manner and form as the Plaintiff against him had declared. Therefore, it is considered that the Plaintiff recover against the said Defendant 25 pounds 7 shillings and his costs by him in this behalf expended and the said Defendant in mercy. And thereon the suit against the other Defendants is continued.

ANTHONY LAWSON Plaintiff
Against Re: In Case
NEIL JAMIESON, JAMES TAYLOR, MATT PHRIPP, BASSET MOSELEY executors of JACOB ELLEGOOD deceased Defendant
This day came as well the Plaintiff by JAMES HOLT Gentleman as BASSET MOSELEY one of the executors of JACOB MOSELEY one of the Executions of JACOB ELLEGOOD deceased in his proper person and says that he cannot gainsay the Plaintiffs action nor but that his testator did assume in manner and form as the Plaintiff has declared. Therefore, it is considered that Plaintiff recover against the said Defendant 6 pounds and his costs by him in this behalf expended. When assets after paying preceding judgements, debts of greater dignity and the defendants own claims against the estate of the said testator to be levied of the goods and chattels which were of the said Jacob at the time of his death that shall hereafter come to the hands of the said Defendant to be administered and the said Defendants in mercy.

BENJAMIN HODGES against ROBERT FORESYTHE Dismissed.

JOHN BAYNES against JOHN MARLEY by Petition and Summons. Judgement is granted the Plaintiff for 1 pound, 10 shilling and 8 pence. It is ordered that the defendant pay the same unto the Plaintiff with costs and fees.

PAGE 30

WILLIAM FARRER Plaintiff
Against Re: In Case
NEIL JAMIESON, JAMES TAYLOR, MATT PHRIPP, BASSET MOSELEY executors of JACOB ELLEGOOD deceased Defendant
This day came as well the Plaintiff by WILLIAM RASCOW WILSON CURLE Gentleman his Attorney as BASSET MOSELEY one of the executors of JACOB ELLEGOOD deceased in his proper person and says that he cannot gainsay the Plaintiffs action nor but that his testator did assume in manner and form as the Plaintiff has declared. Therefore, it is considered that Plaintiff recover against the said Defendant 37 pounds 5 shillings and a half penny and his costs by him in this behalf expended. When assets after paying preceding judgements, debts of greater dignity and the defendants own claims against the estate of the said testator to be levied of the goods and chattels which were of the said Jacob at the time of his death that shall hereafter come to the hands of the said Defendant to be administered and the said Defendants in mercy.

MARY STAUNTON against MATTHEW KELLY and wife dismissed at the Defendants costs.
MATTHEW KELLY who as well against MARY STAUNTON Dismissed.
MATTHEW KELLY and ANN, his wife against FRANCIS CONNER, Imparlance.
MATTHEW KELLY against JOHN MACMULLAN an alias capias.
FRANCIS CONNER against MATTHEW KELLY and ANN his wife. Imparlance.

PAUL LOYALL and MATTHEW PHRIPP against WILLIAM GRAY. This day came the parties by their Attorney's and the Defendant by his Attorney with the assent of the Court, agreed to amend the Capias. Thereupon JAMES MURPHREE came into Court and entered himself Special Bail for the Defendant and the said Defendant pleaded that he did not assume issue joined and referred.

PAGE 30B
MARY SMALLWOOD Plaintiff

Against Re: In Debt for rent

DICKERSON PRIOR and FRANCES his wife administrator of RICHARD FRASIER deceased Defendants

This day came as well the Plaintiff by JAMES HOLT Gentleman as well the Defendants in their proper person and acknowledges the Plaintiffs actions for 10 pounds. Therefore, it is considered that Plaintiff recover against the said defendant her debt aforesaid and her costs by her in this behalf expended. When assets to be levied of the goods and chattels of the said intestate RICHARD, if so, much the said DICKERSON PRIOR and FRANCES his wife have in their hands to be administered and if they have it not then the costs are to be levied of their goods and chattels and the said defendant in mercy.

COATNEY WILDER against CADER COOPER and THOMAS CRATCHET, Imparlance.

GEORGE ABYVON Gentleman against CHARLES JENKINS executor of JOSEPH LOCKHART an Imparlance.

MATHIAS GALE and MARY MOORE complaint against RICHARD ROTHERY, Infant respondent in Chancery. This day came as well the Complainants by THOMAS BURKE Gentleman their Attorney as the said Infant respondent in his proper person and JOHN GREENWOOD is appointed GUARDIAN to the infant to defend him in this suit and leave is given to amend the bill and make JOSEPH MITCHELL, JOHN COX and others Complainants and time is allowed to consider it and ordered that a subpoena be issued against MARY ROTHERY widow who is admitted Defendant with the said infant respondent.

JOHN TAYLOR'S Power of Attorney to JAMES GILCHRIST and ROBERT TAYLOR was proved by the oath of JOHN MCKERROL and ordered to be registered.

PAGE 31
GEORGE PAGAN and Company Plaintiffs

Against Re: In Debt

JOHN WILSON Defendant

This day came the parties by their Attorney's and the Defendant by his Attorney relinquishing his former plea acknowledges the Plaintiff's action for 211 pounds 9 shillings and 8 pence. Therefore, it is considered that the Plaintiff recover against he said Defendant their debt aforesaid and their costs by them in this behalf expended and the said defendant in mercy. But this judgement is to be discharged by the payment of 105 pounds 14 shillings and 10 pence with interest for the same at the rate of 5% per annum to be computed from October 30, 1766, to the time of payment and the costs.

ROBERT TUCKER Plaintiff

Against Re: In Case

WILLIAM MCCAA Defendant

This day came the parties by their Attorney's and there upon came also a Jury to wit: WILLIAM STEVENSON, WILLIAM CORBELL, ROBERT STEAD, WILLIAM GRAY, HARDRESS WALLER, ROBERT HATTON, JOHN CHESHIRE, CHARLES GODFREY, EDMOND KEETON, JAMES MURPHREE, JOHN ARDISS and EDWARD ARCHER who being elected tried and sworn the truth to speak upon the issue joined upon their oath do say that the defendant did assume in manner and form as the Plaintiff against him has declared and do assess the Plaintiff damages by occasion of the non-performance of that assumption to 8 pounds 1 shilling and 3 pence half penny besides his costs. Therefore, it is considered that the Plaintiff recover against the said Defendant his damages aforesaid in form aforesaid assessed and his costs by him about his suit in this behalf expended and the Defendant in mercy.

PAGE 31B
ELIAS ELLERY Plaintiff

Against Re: In Case

NATHANIEL YOUNG and JOHN SMITH Defendants

This day came the parties by their Attorney's and thereupon came also a Jury to wit: JOHN CALVERT, THOMAS PEARSON, WILLIAM BALLARD, THOMAS MORRIS, WILLIAM MCCAA, JONATHAN EILBECK, JOHN MCLEAN, DANIEL HUTCHINGS, CHARLES COOPER, RICHARD BICKERDICK, GEORGE WINKLE and JOHN SELDEN who being elected tried and sworn the truth to speak upon the issue joined upon their oath do say that the Defendants did assume in manner and form as the Plaintiff against him has declared and do assess the Plaintiff damages by occasion of the non-performance of that assumption to 5 pounds 6 shilling and 6 pence farthing besides his costs. Therefore, it is considered that the Plaintiff recover against the said Defendant his damages aforesaid in form aforesaid assessed and his costs by him about his suit in this behalf expended and the Defendant in mercy.

EDMOND BRUCE Plaintiff

Against Re: In Trespass

MATT KELLY & ANN, his wife Defendants

This day came the parties by their Attorney's and thereupon came also a Jury to wit: JOHN CALVERT, THOMAS PEARSON, WILLIAM BALLARD, THOMAS MORRIS, WILLIAM MCCAA, JONATHAN EILBECK, JOHN MCLEAN, DANIEL HUTCHINGS, CHARLES COOPER, RICHARD BICKERDICK, GEORGE WINKLE and JOHN SELDEN who being elected tried and sworn the truth to speak upon the issue joined upon their oath do say that the Defendants are guilty of the Trespass in the declaration mentioned in manner and form as the Plaintiff against him has declared and do assess the Plaintiff damages by occasion thereof to 1 pounds 1 shilling besides his costs. Therefore, it is considered that the Plaintiff recover against the said Defendant his damages aforesaid in form aforesaid assessed and his costs by him about his suit in this behalf expended. This Court being of Opinion that the Trespass was will full and the said Defendants in mercy.

PAGE 32

MATTHEW KELLY and ANN, his wife Plaintiffs
Against Re: In Trespass, Assault & Battery
JUDAH ALLEN Defendant

This day came the parties by their Attorney's and thereupon came also a Jury to wit: JOHN CALVERT, THOMAS PEARSON, WILLIAM BALLARD, THOMAS MORRIS, WILLIAM MCCAA, JONATHAN EILBECK, JOHN MCLEAN, DANIEL HUTCHINGS, CHARLES COOPER, RICHARD BICKERDICK, GEORGE WINKLE and JOHN SELDEN who being elected tried and sworn the truth to speak upon the issue joined upon their oath do say that the Defendants is guilty of the trespass, Assault and Battery in the declaration mentioned in manner and form as the Plaintiff against her has declared and do assess the Plaintiff damages by occasion thereof to 2 pounds. Therefore, it is considered that the Plaintiffs recover against the said Defendant their damages aforesaid in form aforesaid assessed and their costs by them in this behalf expended and the Defendant may be taken.

On the motion of JAMES DIXON* a witness for EDMOND BRUCE against MATTHEW KELLY and ANN his wife, it is ordered that the said BRUCE pay him 25 pounds tobacco for 1 day's attendance in his suit against MATTHEW KELLY and wife.

On the motion of ELIZABETH TAYLOR, a witness for EDMOND BRUCE against MATTHEW KELLY and ANN his wife, it is ordered that the said BRUCE pay him 25 pounds tobacco for 1 day's attendance at this Court in his suit against KELLY and wife.

On the motion of JOHN MCNEIL and MARGARET his wife, witnesses for EDMOND BRUCE against MATTHEW KELLY and ANN his wife, it is ordered that the said BRUCE pay them 25 pounds tobacco each for 1 days each at this Court in his suit against MATTHEW KELLY and Ann his wife.

On the motion of ELIZABETH CROFT, a witness for EDMOND BRUCE against MATTHEW KELLY and ANN his wife, it is ordered that the said BRUCE pay her 25 pounds tobacco for 1 day's attendance at this Court in his suit against MATTHEW KELLY and wife.

PAGE 32B

On the motion of ANN KING a witness for MATTHEW KELLY and ANN his wife against JUDAH ALLEN. It is ordered that the said KELLY and wife pay her 25 pounds tobacco for 1 day's attendance at this Court in their suit against JUDAH ALLEN

JANE MUNROE against JOSEPH GREAR and ALICE his abates by Plaintiff marriage.

WILLIAM MURPHREY Plaintiff
Against Re: In Trespass, Assault & Battery
JOHN MCNEIL and MARGARET, his wife Defendants

This day came the Plaintiff by JAMES HOLT Gentleman his Attorney and there upon came also a Jury to wit: JAMES ARCHDEACON, WILLIAM STEVENS, EDMOND KEETON, ROBERT HATTON, HARDRESS WALLER, JAMES MURPHREE, ROBERT STEED, JOHN CHESHIRE, CHARLES GODFREY, WILLIAM GRAY, JOHN ARDIS and WILLIAM CORBIN who being elected tried and sworn the truth to speak upon the issue joined withdrew and returned and the Plaintiff being solemnly called and not appearing the suit is discontinued.

The Court is adjourned until tomorrow 10 o'clock: CHARLES THOMAS MAYOR, TESTE: JOHN BOUSH D.C.

PAGE 33

NORFOLK BOROUGH
At a Hustings Court Held this 21st day of August 1770
PRESENT: CHARLES THOMAS ESQUIRE MAYOR
GENTLEMAN ALDERMEN: GEORGE ABYVON, MAXIMILIAN CALVERT, ARCHIBALD CAMPBELL, JAMES TAYLOR, LEWIS HANSFORD, CORNELUIS CALVERT

Our Lord the King against JAMES FLETCHER, JOHN GILCHRIST, and JAMES GILCHRIST an ALIAS SCIRE FACIAS against JAMES FLETCHER and JOHN GILCHRIST and the other defendant JAMES pleaded OYER of the record which is granted.

THOMAS NEWTON SR. & JOHN TAYLOR executors of ROBERT TUCKER deceased Plaintiffs
Against Re: In Case
GEORGE BLINN Defendant

This day came the parties by their Attorney's and thereupon came also a Jury to wit: BASSETT MOSELEY, JOHN MACLEAN, WILLIAM BROWN, ELDRED FISHER, JOHN THOMAS, FRANCIS HAYNES, JOHN SMITH, BARTHOLOMEW THOMPSON, ROBERT GILMOUR, ROBERT TAYLOR, JOHN CHESHIRE and ROBERT* who being elected tried and sworn the truth to speak upon the issue joined upon their oath do say that the Defendant did assume in manner and form as the Plaintiff against him have declared and do assess the Plaintiff damages by occasion of the non-performance of that assumption to 24 pounds, 18 shillings and 2 pence half penny besides their costs. Therefore, it is considered that the Plaintiff recover against the said defendant their damages aforesaid in form aforesaid assessed and their costs by them about their suit in this behalf expended and the said Defendant in mercy.

PAGE 33B

THOMAS BYCROFT Plaintiff

Against Re: In Case

JOHN MARNIX* Defendant

This day came the parties by their Attorney's and there upon came also a Jury to wit:

JOHN LEE, EDWARD MITCHELL, JAMES WALKER, JONATHAN GODFREY, EDMOND KEETON, THOMAS MORRIS, CHARLES COOPER, SAMUEL TOMLINSON, THOMAS FARRER, CHARLES COOPER, THOMAS PEARSON and JOHN SHORE who being elected tried and sworn the truth to speak upon the issue joined upon their oath do say that the Defendant is guilty in manner and form as the Plaintiff against him have declared and do assess the Plaintiff damages by occasion of the non-performance of that assumption to 10 pounds, 10 shillings besides his costs. Therefore, it is considered that the Plaintiff recover against the said defendant their damages aforesaid in form aforesaid assessed and their costs by them about their suit in this behalf expended and the said Defendant in mercy. And on motion of the defendant by his Attorney a new trial is granted him.

NEIL JAMIESON and COMPANY against THOMAS NEWTON SR. and JOHN TAYLOR Executors of ROBERT TUCKER deceased. Dismissed.

SARAH CLAYTON against MATTHEW KELLY and ANN his wife. Dismissed.

MOSES LANGLEY against FRANCES MOORE administratrix of JOHN MOORE and EDWARD PARKE. The Plaintiff filed his bill and time is allowed the Defendant to consider it.

WILLIAM SMITH against THOMAS GRANT discontinued at the Plaintiffs costs.

On the motion of JAMES MARSHALL, a witness for THOMAS BYCROFF against JOHN MARNIX. It is ordered that the said BYCROFT pay him 50 pounds of Tobacco for 2 days attendance at this Court in his suit against JOHN MARNIX.

PAGE 34

On the motion of a witness for JOHN MARNIX at the suit of THOMAS BYCROFT it is ordered that the said MARNIX pay him 50 pounds of tobacco for 2 days attendance at this Court in the suit of BYCROFT against him.

WALTER MCCLURG Plaintiff

Against Re: In Debt

CHARLES COOPER Defendant

This day came the parties by their Attorney's and the Defendant by his Attorney acknowledges the Plaintiff's action for 15 pounds, 17 shillings and 6 pence. Therefore, it is considered that the Plaintiff recover against the said Defendant his debt aforesaid and his costs by him in this behalf expended and the said Defendant in mercy. But this judgement is to be discharged by the payment of 7 pounds 18 shillings and 9 pence with interest for the same at the rate of 5% per annum to be computed from June 24th, 1765, to the time of payment and the costs.

HALLCOTT PRIDE Plaintiff

Against Re: In Case

CHARLES COOPER Defendant

This day came the parties by their Attorney's and the defendant by his Attorney says that he cannot gainsay the Plaintiffs action nor but that he did assume in manner and form as the Plaintiff against him has declared. Therefore, it is considered that the Plaintiff recover against the said Defendant 68 pounds 11 shillings and his costs by him in this behalf expended and the said Defendant in mercy.

MARY ROSS against JOHN SMITH. The Defendant pleaded payment issue joined and referred.

PAGE 34B

DUNCAN SHARP Plaintiff

Against Re: In Case

JOHN MCKERROLL Defendant

This day came the parties by their Attorney's and thereupon came also a Jury to wit: JOHN LEE, EDWARD MITCHELL, JAMES WALKER, JONATHAN GODFREY, EDMOND KEETON, THOMAS MORRIS, CHARLES COOPER, SAMUEL TOMLINSON, THOMAS FARRER, CHARLES COOPER, THOMAS PEARSON and JOHN SHORE who being elected tried and sworn the truth to speak upon the issue joined upon their oath do say that the Defendant did assume in manner and form as the Plaintiff against him have declared and do assess the Plaintiff damages by occasion of the non-performance of that assumption to 1 pound, 17 shillings and 6 pence besides their costs. Therefore, it is considered that the Plaintiff recover against the said defendant their damages aforesaid in form aforesaid assessed and their costs by them about their suit in this behalf expended and the said Defendant in mercy.

JOHN MCFARLAN Plaintiff

Against Re: In Case

JOHN MCKERROLL Defendant

This day came the parties by their Attorney's and thereupon came also Jury to wit: BASSET MOSELEY, JOHN MCLEAN, WILLIAM BROWN, ELDRED FISHER, JOHN THOMAS, FRANCIS HAYNES, JOHN SMITH, BARTHOLOMEW THOMPSON, ROBERT GILMOUR, ROBERT TAYLOR, JOHN CHESHIRE and ROBERT STEAD who being elected tried and sworn the truth to speak upon the issue joined upon their oath do say that the Defendant did assume in manner and form as the Plaintiff against him have declared and do assess the Plaintiff damages by occasion of the non-performance of that assumption to 4 pounds, 15 shillings and 11 pence besides their costs. Therefore, it is considered that the Plaintiff recover against the said Defendant their damages aforesaid in form aforesaid assessed and their costs by them about their suit in this behalf expended and the said Defendant in mercy.

<u>PAGE 35</u>
ROBERT SHEDDEN and Company Plaintiffs
Against Re: In Case
ROBERT BRYCE Defendant
This day came the parties by their Attorney's and the Defendant by his Attorney relinquishing his former plea, says that he cannot gainsay the Plaintiff action nor but that he did assume in manner and form as the Plaintiff against him has declared. Therefore, it is considered that the Plaintiff recover against the said Defendant 114 pounds 15 shillings and their costs by them in this behalf expended and the said Defendant in mercy.

On the Motion of PHAROAH FITZPATRICK a witness for JOHN MCKERROLL at the suit of DUNCAN SHARP. It is ordered that the said MCKERROLL pay him 50 pounds tobacco for 2 days attendance at this Court in the suit of SHARP against him.

GEORGE OLDNER against JOHN CHESHIRE a general commission to take the depositions is granted the parties on both sides.

ANDREW MORANO against JOHN DAVEREUX*. The Defendant pleaded that he had tendered to the Plaintiff 8 pounds 19 shillings and 4 pence half penny New York Currency before the commencement of the suit and also that he did not assume the residue.

JONATHAN DYSON and SARAH, his wife against JOHN ASHLEY. The Defendant pleaded that he was not guilty issue joined and referred.

This Court is adjourned to Court in Course: CHARLES THOMAS MAYOR, TESTE: JOHN BOUSH D.C.C.

<u>PAGE 35B</u>
<u>NORFOLK BOROUGH</u>
At a Hustings Court Held this 24th day of September 1770
PRESENT: CHARLES THOMAS ESQUIRE MAYOR
GENTLEMAN ALDERMEN: GEORGE ABYVON, JAMES TAYLOR, ARCHIBALD CAMPBELL, CORNELIUS CALVERT, LEWIS HANSFORD

JOHN CHAPMAN against PETER DALE. On the motion of the Plaintiff by his Attorney a DEDIMUS is granted him to take the depositions of ELIZABETH GOODWIN and ELIZABETH BURCHER giving the Defendant notices.

EDWARD ARCHER Plaintiff
Against Re: In Case
JOHN IVY Defendant
This day came as well the Plaintiff by JAMES HOLT Gentleman his Attorney and the Defendant in his proper person and says that he cannot gainsay the Plaintiffs action nor but that he did assume in manner and form as the Plaintiff against him has declared. Therefore, it is considered that the Plaintiff recover against the said Defendant 5 pounds 4 shillings and 4 pence and his costs by them in this behalf expended. And the said Defendant in mercy.

MATHIAS GALE and MARY MOORE & others against RICHARD ROTHERY and MARY ROTHERY. Time is allowed MARY to consider the Bill.
MAXIMILIAN CALVERT against WILLIAM SKINKER. The Plaintiff by his Attorney moved for Special Bail which is granted. Where upon JOHN SMITH MERCHANT came into Court and entered himself Special Bail for the Defendant and thereon the Defendant by his Attorney prayed an Imparlance.

<u>PAGE 36</u>
RICHARD BASSET against HENRY RITTER an Imparlance.

ROBERT TUCKER against CHRISTOPHER RATSEY. The Plaintiff by his Attorney moved for Special Bail which is granted. Where upon MATTHEW PHRIPP Gentleman came into Court and entered himself Special Bail for the defendant and thereon the Defendant by his Attorney prayed an Imparlance.

CHRISTOPHER RATSEY against ROBER TUCKER an Imparlance

GEORGE LOGAN, ROBERT GILMOUR & CO. against WILLIAM MCCAA. The Plaintiff by his Attorney moved for Special Bail which is granted. Where upon JOHN WILSON this day came into Court and entered himself Special Bail for the Defendant and thereon the Defendant by his Attorney prayed an Imparlance.

WILLIAM MCCAA against GEORGE LOGAN, ROBERT GILMOUR & CO. The Defendant pleaded that they did not assume issue joined and referred.

NATHANIEL YOUNG and JOHN SMITH against JOHN BAYNES by Petition & Summons. Judgement is granted the Plaintiffs for 3 pounds 13 shillings and 9 pence. It is ordered that the Defendant pay the same unto the Plaintiff with costs and fees.

BAILEY WARREN Plaintiff
Against Re: In Case
MATTHEW ROTHERY Defendant
This day came the parties by their Attorney's and their mutual consent submit all matters in difference between them to the determination of JOHN TAYLOR, JOHN GREENWOOD, and BASSET MOSELEY or any two of them and agree that their award there upon should be the Judgement of the Court and the same is ordered accordingly.

PAGE 36B

WILLIAM SIMPSON against THOMAS PEARSON dismissed.

WILLIAM SIMPSON against RICHARD CHESHIRE by Petition & Summons. Judgement is granted the Plaintiffs for 1 pound 13 shillings and 6 pence. It is ordered that the Defendant pay the same unto the Plaintiff with costs and fees.

NATHANIEL YOUNG & JOHN SMITH Plaintiffs
Against Re: In Case
WILLIAM MCCAA Defendant
This day came the parties by their Attorney's and the Defendant by his Attorney says that he cannot gainsay the Plaintiffs actions nor but that he did assume in manner and form as the Plaintiff against him have declared. Therefore, it is considered that the Plaintiff recover against the said Defendant 111 pounds, 11 shillings and 10 pence and their costs by them about their suit in this behalf expended. And the said Defendant in mercy. And the Plaintiff agrees to stay execution one month.

ROBERT WATERS Plaintiff
Against Re: In Case
WILLIAM MCCAA Defendant
This day came the parties by their Attorney's and the Defendant by his Attorney says that he cannot gainsay the Plaintiffs actions nor but that he did assume in manner and form as the Plaintiff against him have declared. Therefore, it is considered that the Plaintiff recover against the said Defendant 142 pounds and 7 pence half penny and their costs by them about their suit in this behalf expended. And the said Defendant in mercy. And the Plaintiff agrees to stay execution one month.

PAGE 37

JOHN STEWART Plaintiff
Against Re: In Case
ROBERT GILMOUR Admin of JAMES GRAY deceased Defendant
This day came as well the Plaintiff by THOMAS BURKE Gentleman his Attorney as the Defendant in his proper person and the said Defendant says that he cannot gainsay the Plaintiffs actions nor but that his intestate did assume in manner and form as the Plaintiff against him have declared. Therefore, it is considered that the Plaintiff recover against the said Defendant 7 pounds, 15 shillings and 9pence and his costs by him in this behalf expended, when assets to be levied of the goods and chattels of the said Intestate if so much the said ROBERT GILMOUR has in his hands to be administered and if he has it not then the costs are to be levied of his proper goods and chattels and the said ROBERT GILMOUR in mercy.

WALTER LYON against WILLIAM BROWN. The Plaintiff by his Attorney moved for Special Bail which is granted. Where upon JOHN IVY this day came into Court and entered himself Special Bail for the defendant and order against the said Defendant.

WILLIAM NIMMO and SAMUEL TENANT Executors of ADAM THOROWGOOD deceased against GEORGE OLDNER. The Plaintiff by his Attorney moved for Special Bail which is granted. Where upon JOHN MCLACHAN came into Court and entered himself Special Bail for the Defendant and thereon the Defendant by his Attorney prayed an Imparlance.

PAGE 37B

DANIEL CURLING against JOSIAH HOFFMIRE and WILLIAM SHIPWASH Defendant JOSIAH has leave to IMPARLE and discontinued against SHIPWASH.

SAMUEL CALVERT and PEGGY, his wife and JOHN ROSS, ALEXANDER ROSS, and ROBERT ROSS infants and by the said SAMUEL their guardian against ANDREW SPROWLE and WILLIAM ORANGE executors of JOHN ROSS in chancery removed by Certiorari

Our Lord the King against JAMES FLETCHER, JOHN GILCHRIST, and JAMES GILCHRIST. The Defendants FLETCHER and JOHN GILCHRIST prayed OYER of the record which is granted them and continued against the other Defendant.

PETER BISER was this day brought before the Court by a Warrant from under the hand and seal of PAUL LOYALL Gentleman and PETER MCNABB having worn the peace against him. It is ordered that the Sergeant take the said PETER BISER and keep him in Custody until he gives bond and security himself in 20 pounds and 2 securities in 10 pounds each for his keeping the peace for 6 months and pay costs.

Order is granted WILLIAM WALKER, WILLIAM BICKERDICK, RICHARD BROWN, and PETER WATSON against PETER MCNABB for 50 pounds tobacco for 2 days attendance each in his complaint against PETER BISER.

ANN WALLACE and NICHOLAS POOLE against SAMUEL MIDDLETON. The suit abates by the Defendants death.

ANN BOUCHER administratrix of DANIEL ROTHERY against MATTHEW ROTHERY on motion of the Plaintiff by her Attorney a DEDIMUS ESTATEM is granted her to take the depositions of WILLIAM SIMPSON giving the Defendant reasonable notice.

PAGE 38

THOMAS TAYLOR Plaintiff
Against Re: In Case
JOHN YOUNG Defendant
This day came the parties by their Attorney's and there upon came also a Jury to wit: JOHN CHESHIRE, MASON MILLER, CHARLES GODFREY, WILLIAM FARRER, RICHARD BROWN, ROBERT STEAD, NATHANIEL BOUSH, FRANCIS HAYNES, JONATHAN DISON, GEORGE WINKLE, PETER DALE and GEORGE BRUCE who being elected tried and sworn the truth to speak upon the issue joined upon their oath do say that the

Defendant did assume in manner and form as the Plaintiff against him has declared and do assess the Plaintiff damages by occasion of the non-performance of that assumption to 18 pounds besides his costs. Therefore, it is considered that the Plaintiff recover against the said Defendant his damages aforesaid in form aforesaid assessed and his costs by him in this behalf expended and the said Defendant in mercy. Where upon the Defendant filed his bill of injunction on his giving security on or before the Next Borough Court is allowed and ALEXANDER BELL who was Special Bail for the said Defendant this day surrendered him up and the Plaintiff on his motion, the said YOUNG is committed in Custody until he shall have satisfied this judgement and the costs.

JOHN AUSTIN FINNIE Plaintiff
Against Re: In Case
LEWIS HANSFORD & CO. Defendants

This day came the parties by their Attorney's and the Defendant EDWARD HACK MOSELEY his Attorney says that he cannot gainsay the Plaintiffs actions nor but that he did assume in manner and form as the Plaintiff against him have declared. Therefore, it is considered that the Plaintiff recover against the said Defendant 25 pounds, 7 shillings and his costs by him in this behalf expended and the said Defendant in mercy.

PAGE 38B
JOHN SMITH Plaintiff
Against Re: In Chancery
WILLIAM CHISHOLM Defendant

This day came the parties by their Attorney's and their mutual consent submit all matters in difference between them to the determination JOHN TAYLOR, JOHN GREENWOOD and JOHN LAWRENCE Gentleman or any two of them and agree that their award there upon be the decree of this Court and the same is ordered accordingly.

Ordinary License is granted JOHN HUNT on his complying with the law.

JOHN SHERLOCK Plaintiff
Against Re: In Case
JOSHUA EDWARDS Defendant

This day came the parties by their Attorney's and there upon came also a Jury to wit: DANIEL HUTCHINGS, BASSET MOSELEY, JOHN CRAMOND, JOHN SMITH, JOHN LIVINGSTON, GEORGE FARRER, JONATHAN MEREDITH, JOHN SELDEN, BAILEY WARREN, SAMUEL BACON, JOHN SHORES and JOSHUA WRIGHT who being elected tried and sworn the truth to speak upon the issue joined upon their oath do say that the Defendant did assume in manner and form as the Plaintiff against him has declared and do assess the Plaintiff damages by occasion of the non-performance of that assumption to 16 pounds, 18 shillings and 9 pence besides his costs. Therefore, it is considered that the Plaintiff recover against the said Defendant his damages aforesaid in form aforesaid assessed and his costs by him in this behalf expended and the said Defendant in mercy.

On the motion of ADAM MCCOY, a witness for JOHN YOUNG Defendant at the suit of THOMAS TAYLOR it is ordered that the said YOUNG pay him 115 pounds tobacco and 3 shillings and a penny half penny for
PAGE 39
One day's attendance at this Court coming 39 miles and returning for ferriages at coming and returning according to law.

THOMAS BYCROFT Plaintiff
Against Re: In Case
JOHN MARNIX Defendant

This day came the parties by their Attorney's and there upon came also a jury to wit:
JOHN CHESHIRE, MASON MILLER, CHARLES GODFREY, WILLIAM FARRER, RICHARD BROWN, ROBERT STEAD, NATHANIEL BOUSH, FRANCIS HAYNES, JONATHAN DISON, GEORGE WINKLE, PETER DALE and GEORGE BRUCE who being elected tried and sworn the truth to speak upon the issue joined, withdrew and not returning any verdict the Cause is Continued.

On the Motion of JOHN FIFE, a witness for JOHN SHERLOCK against JOSHUA EDWARDS. It is ordered that the said SHERLOCK pay him 25 pounds tobacco for 1 day's attendance in his suit JOSHUA EDWARDS.
On the motion of RICHARD BICKERDICK, a witness for JOHN MARNIX at the suit of THOMAS BYCROFT. It is ordered that the said MARNIX pay him 25 pounds of tobacco for 1 day's attendance in his suit against him.

SARAH CANN executrix of JOHN CANN deceased Plaintiff
Against Re: In Debt
WILLIAM MCCAA Defendant

This day came the parties by their Attorney's and the Defendant by his Attorney acknowledges the Plaintiff actions for 117 pounds, 18 shillings and 10 pence.
Therefore, it is considered that the Plaintiff recover against the said Defendant and her debt aforesaid and her costs by her in the behalf expended and the said Defendant in mercy. But this Judgement is to be discharged by the payment of 58 pounds 19 shillings and 5 pence with interest for the same at the rate of 5% per annum to be computed from September 19th, 1770, to the time of payment and costs and agrees to stay execution 1 month.

This Court is adjourned to Court in Course: CHARLES THOMAS MAYOR, TESTE: JOHN BOUSH D.C.C.

PAGE 39B
NORFOLK BOROUGH
At a Hustings Court Held this 25th day of September 1770
PRESENT: CHARLES THOMAS ESQUIRE MAYOR
GENTLEMAN ALDERMEN: GEORGE ABYVON, MAXIMILIAN CALVERT, ARCHIBALD CAMPBELL, PAUL LOYALL, LEWIS HANSFORD, JAMES TAYLOR

THOMAS NEWTON SR., THOMAS NEWTON JR., PAUL LOYALL, THOMAS ROBERTS, and JOHN TUCKER against ROBERT TUCKER attachment for answer.

JOHN DUNN an infant by JOSEPH CALVERT his next friend against WILLIAM MCCAA. The defendant pleaded not guilty issue joined and referred

JOHN MCLACHAN against JAMES DUNN. The defendant pleaded not guilty issue joined and referred.

GEORGE VEALE JR., and NATHANIEL BURGESS executors of HARDRESS deceased against EDWARD VOSS. The Defendant pleaded that he did not assume issue joined and referred.

JOHN MARCOM HERBERT against THOMAS YARD. The former order is set aside, and THOMAS BURKE enters himself Special Bail for the Defendant and pleads that he did not assume issue joined and referred.

PAUL LOYALL against NATHANIEL STROUD. The former order of this Court against him the said Defendant and ROBERT TUCKER his bail be confirmed and a Writ of Inquiry is awarded him for his damages.

JOSHUA WRIGHT against JOHN HARDY. The Defendant pleaded that he did not assume issue joined and referred.
HOWARD POOL against THOMAS THOMPSON. The Defendant pleaded that he did not assume issue joined and referred.

PAGE 40
SEYMOUR POWELL against JOHN COLEMAN. The former order of this Court against him the said Defendant and JOSEPH CALVERT Sergeant his bail be confirmed, and a Writ of Inquiry is awarded him for his damages.

ROBERT BANKS who as well against OWEN CRUMLESS and CATHERINE his wife. The Defendant Pleaded that they do not owe, issue joined and referred.

SAMUEL SAMWAYS* against JOHN ASHLEY. The Defendant pleaded that he did not assume issue joined and referred.
MATTHEW KELLY who as well against JOHN MCNEIL. The Defendant pleaded that he does not woe, issue joined and referred.
MARY ANN THELABALL against JOHN COLVILLE. The Defendant pleaded that he did not assume issue joined and referred.

CHARLES COOPER and CHAPMAN MANSON Plaintiff
Against Re: In Case
GEORGE FARRER Defendant
This day came the parties by their Attorney's and there upon came also a Jury to wit: WILLIAM STEVENSON, JOHN SHORE, ROBERT GILMOUR, JOHN RICHARDSON, BARTHOLOMEW THOMPSON, JOHN OLIVE, RICHARD KELSICK, JAMES MURPHREE, WILLIAM BELL, GEORGE KELLY, RICHARD BICKERDICK and JONATHAN MEREDITH who being elected tried and sworn the truth to speak upon the issue joined upon their oath do say that the Defendant is guilty in manner and form as the Plaintiff against him have declared and do assess the Plaintiff damages by occasion thereof to 16 pounds, 6 shillings and 3 pence besides their costs. Therefore, it is considered that the Plaintiff recover against the said Defendant their damages aforesaid in form aforesaid assessed and their costs by them in this behalf expended. And the said Defendant in mercy. And the Defendant by his Attorney tendered his bill of Injunction was referred.

PAGE 40B
CAPLE and OSGOOD HANBURYS against EDWARD HACK MOSELEY. The Defendant pleaded payment issue joined and referred.
CAPLE and OSGOOD HANBURYS against EDWARD HACK MOSELEY. The Defendant pleaded payment issue joined and referred.
CAPLE and OSGOOD HANBURYS against EDWARD HACK MOSELEY. The Defendant pleaded payment issue joined and referred.

JAMES JOLLIFF against JOHN BRICKELL. The Defendant pleaded not Guilty with leave issue joined and referred.
GEORGE JOSEPH FENWICK against WILLIAM KEETON. The Defendant pleaded that he did not assume issue joined and referred.

THOMAS ROBERTS Plaintiff
Against Re: In Case
ROBERT STEED Defendant
This day came the parties by their Attorney's and there upon came also a Jury to wit:
WILLIAM STEVENSON, JOHN SHORE, ROBERT GILMOUR, JOHN RICHARDSON, BARTHOLOMNEW THOMPSON, JOHN OLIVE, RICHARD KELSICK, JAMES MURPHREE, WILLIAM BELL, GEORGE KELLY, RICHARD BICKERDICK and JONATHAN MEREDITH who being elected tried and sworn the truth to speak upon the issue joined withdrew and not returning any verdict the cause is continued.

MARGARET BANNERMAN Plaintiff against BENJAMIN BANNERMAN Defendant in Chancery. On the Motion of the Plaintiff by WILLIAM RASCOW WILSON CURLE Gentleman her attorney. It is ordered that the Sergeant summon THOMAS VEALE, JAMES MARSDEN*, HUMPHREY ROBERTS, AMOS ETHERIDGE, and ROBERT SHEDDEN SEQUESTRATORS, to appear at the next Court to be held for this Borough to render an account of their proceedings of the said SEQUESTRATION.

PAGE 41

It is ordered that the Sergeant Summon the Constables of this Borough to appear at the Next Court to show cause why they have not destroyed the hogs running at large in this Borough.

JOHN CRAMOND Plaintiff
Against Re: On a SCIRE FACIAS
ELDRED TUCKER Defendant

This day came the parties by their Attorney's and the Defendant by his Attorney says that he is not informed. Therefore, it is considered that the Plaintiff recover against the said Defendant 35 pounds 12 shillings and 6 pence. Also 246 pounds net tobacco and 15 shillings or 150 pounds of tobacco and 1 shilling and 3 pence and his costs by him in this behalf expended and the said Defendant in mercy.

The Court this day rated flour at 12 pounds 6 shillings per hundred
This Court is adjourned to Court in Course: GEORGE ABYVON SR. Alderman, TESTE: JOHN BOUSH D.C.C.

PAGE 41B

NORFOLK BOROUGH
At a Hustings Court Held this 22nd day of October 1770
PRESENT: CHARLES THOMAS ESQUIRE MAYOR
GENTLEMAN ALDERMEN: GEORGE ABYVON, JAMES TAYLOR, MAXIMILIAN CALVERT,

CAPLE and OSGOOD HANBURYS against EDWARD HACK MOSELEY. Dismissed at the Defendants Cost.
CAPLE and OSGOOD HANBURYS against EDWARD HACK MOSELEY and CARY MITCHELL. Dismissed at the Defendants cost.
CAPLE and OSGOOD HANBURYS against EDWARD HACK MOSELEY. Dismissed at the Defendants Cost.

MATTHEW KELLY who as well against JOHN MCNEIL dismissed that the Defendants cost.

WILLIAM ROBINSON this day produced a License from under the hand and seal of JOHN RANDOLPH, JOHN BLAIR SR. and GEORGE WYTHE Gentleman to practice as an Attorney and he having taken the oath to the Government and subscribed the test also the oath of an Attorney is admitted to practice in this Court.

AARON BARBER and JOSIAH HOFFMIRE against JOHN CURLING. Order against the Defendant and DANIEL CURLING his bail.

AARON BARBER and JOSIAH HOFFMIRE against JOSEPH CURLING. Order against the Defendant and JOHN CURLING his bail.
JOHN GREENWOOD against JOHN IVY. Order against the Defendant and SAMUEL LANGLEY his bail.

PAGE 42

ROBERT STEED against HENRY TUCKER and JOHN TAYLOR. The Plaintiff by his Attorney moved for Special Bail which is granted where upon ROBERT TAYLOR came into Court and entered himself Special Bail for the Defendants and there on the Defendants by their Attorney prayed an Imparlance.

GEORGE CARLTON against JOHN TAYLOR an Imparlance and on the motion of the Plaintiff by his Attorney A DEDIMUS is granted him to take the deposition of ROBERT ELLIOT giving notice.

ROBERT NICHOLSON and JOHN BROWN executors of JOHN BROWN against JOHN SMITH and JOSEPH HUTCHINGS. The Plaintiffs by their Attorney moved for Special Bail which is granted. Whereupon SAMUEL PORTLOCK came into Court and entered himself Special Bail for the Defendant JOSEPH HUTCHINGS and Imparlance and attachment is awarded the Defendant JOHN SMITH.

THOMAS ODELL against JOHN HARDY dismissed.
THOMAS ODELL against JOHN HARDY dismissed.

JOHN HARDY & ELIZABETH his wife against THOMAS ODELL dismissed.
JAMES MOORE against NATHANIEL BOUSH an Imparlance.

JAMES MOORE against NATHANIEL BOUSH and FREDERICK BOUSH. The Plaintiff by his Attorney moved for Special Bail which is granted where upon SAMUEL PORTLOCK came into Court and entered himself Special Bail for the Defendant NATHANIEL and thereon, he by his Attorney prayed an Imparlance and OYER and the suit is dismissed against FREDERICK BOUSH the other Defendant.

CHARLES MAYLE against JOHN GREENWOOD an Imparlance.
ALEXANDER CARR against PHILIP OSBURN Dismissed.

PAGE 42B

BENJAMIN JOHNSON and ELIZABETH GODFREY JOHNSON, his wife against JOHN HUNT and ANN HUNT his wife an Imparlance. And on Motion of the Defendants by their Attorney a DEDIMUS is granted them to take the Deposition of JOSHUA WHITE and LOCKWARD WEEKS giving the Plaintiffs legal notice.

JOHN CRAMOND against WILLIAM HANCOCK a Special Imparlance.

ADRIEL MILBY against JOHN WESTCOTT and CHARLES BURTON. Order against the Defendant BURTON and WRIGHT WESTCOTT his bail and attachment against JOHN WESTCOTT the other Defendant.

THOMAS ROBERTS Plaintiff
Against Re: In Case
ROBERT STEED Defendant
This day came the parties by their Attorney's and the Jury that was sworn in this cause at the last Court not returning any verdict are discharged and thereon the cause is continued.

RICHARD BICKERDICK and MATTHEW KELLY were this day appointed as Constables in the room of JAMES ESTHER and RALPH SAUNDERS and they having taken the Oaths to the Government and subscribed the test, also the oath of a Constable of the Borough enter upon the execution of their office.

This Court is adjourned until tomorrow 10 o'clock, TESTE: JOHN BOUSH D.C.C.

PAGE 43
NORFOLK BOROUGH
At a Hustings Court Held this 23rd day of October 1770
PRESENT: CHARLES THOMAS ESQUIRE MAYOR
ANTHONY LAWSON ESQUIRE DEPUTY RECORDER
GENTLEMAN ALDERMEN: GEORGE ABYVON, MAXIMILIAN CALVERT, PAUL LOYALL, JAMES TAYLOR

THOMAS BYCROFT Plaintiff
Against Re: In Case
JOHN MARNIX Defendant
This day came the parties by their Attorney's and the Jury that was sworn in this cause at the last Court being called and not returning any verdict are by the Court discharged.

JOHN CHAPMAN against PETER DALE on motion of the Plaintiff by his Attorney a DEDIMUS is granted the Plaintiff to take the deposition of THOMAS DRUREY giving the Defendant legal notice.

THOMAS BYCROFT Plaintiff
Against Re: In Case
JOHN MARNIX Defendant
This day came the parties by their Attorney's and there upon came also a Jury to wit: NICHOLAS WONYCOTT, JOHN JONES, PAUL HERITER, JOHN DUNN, JAMES DUNN, NICHOLAS POOLE, STEPHEN TANKARD, ELDRED FISHER, HARDRESS WALLER, ROGER PEARCE, JOHN WILLIAMSON and JOHN COLVILLE, who being elected tried and sworn the truth to speak upon the issue joined upon their oath do say that the Defendant is guilty in manner and form as the Plaintiff against him have declared and do assess the Plaintiff damages by occasion thereof to 7 pounds 12 shillings besides his costs. Therefore, it is considered that the Plaintiff recover against the said Defendant his damages aforesaid in form aforesaid assessed and his costs by him in this behalf expended. And the said Defendant in mercy.

PAGE 43B
MARY MALICOTE Plaintiff
Against Re: In Case
CHARLES COOPER Defendant
This day came as well the Plaintiff by WILLIAM RASCOW WILSON CURLE Gentleman his Attorney as the Defendant in his proper person and relinquishing his former plea says that he cannot gainsay the Plaintiffs actions nor but that he did assume in manner and form as the Plaintiff against him have declared. Therefore, it is considered that the Plaintiff recover against the said Defendant 6 pounds, 13 shillings and 10 pence and his costs by him in this behalf expended and the said Defendant in mercy.

MARY ROSS Plaintiff
Against Re: In Debt
JOHN SMITH Defendant
This day came the parties by their Attorney's and there upon came also a Jury to wit: WILLIAM STEVENSON, RICHARD BICKERDICK, WILLIAM SMITH, CHARLES COOPER, GEORGE FARRER, JOHN LEE, SCARBROUGH TANKARD, HODGE MILLER, FRANCIS HAYNES, CHARLES GODFREY, JOSHUA WRIGHT, and GEORGE ALLISON who being elected tried and sworn the truth to speak upon the issue joined upon their oath do say that the Defendant has not paid the debt in the declaration mentioned. Therefore, it is considered that the Plaintiff recover against he said Defendant her debt aforesaid amounting to 20 pounds and her costs by her about her suit in this behalf expended. And the Defendant in mercy. But this judgement is to be discharged by the payment of 10 pounds with interest for the same at the rate of 5% per annum to be computed from August 19, 1767, to the time of payment and costs.

PAGE 44
GEORGE VEALE JR. and NATHANIEL BURGESS Executors of HARDRESS LAMOUNT Deceased Plaintiffs
Against Re: In Case
EDWARD VOSS Defendant
This day came the parties by their Attorney's and there upon came also a Jury to wit: WILLIAM STEVENSON, RICHARD BICKERDICK, WILLIAM SMITH, CHARLES COOPER, GEORGE FARRER, JOHN LEE, SCARBROUGH TANKARD, HODGE MILLER, FRANCIS HAYNES, CHARLES GODFREY, JOSHUA WRIGHT, and GEORGE ALLISON who being elected tried and sworn the truth to speak upon the issue joined upon their oath do say that the Defendant did not assume as in pleading he has alleged. Therefore, it is considered that the Plaintiff take nothing by their bill but

for their false claims be in mercy. And the Defendant go hence without day and recover against the plaintiff his costs by him about his defense in this behalf expended.

JOHN MARKHAM HERBERT Plaintiff
Against Re: In Case
JAMES YARD Defendant
This day came the parties by their Attorney's and there upon came also a Jury to wit: WILLIAM STEVENSON, RICHARD BICKERDICK, WILLIAM SMITH, CHARLES COOPER, GEORGE FARRER, JOHN LEE, SCARBROUGH TANKARD, HODGE MILLER, FRANCIS HAYNES, CHARLES GODFREY, JOSHUA WRIGHT and GEORGE ALLISON who being elected tried and sworn the truth to speak upon the issue joined upon their oath do say that the Defendant did assume in manner and form as the Plaintiff against him has declared and so assess the Plaintiffs damages by occasion of the non-performance of that assumption to 8 pounds, 13 shillings and 6 pence besides his costs.

PAGE 44B
Therefore, it is considered that the Plaintiff recover against the said Defendant his damages aforesaid in form aforesaid assessed his costs by him in this behalf expended and the said Defendant in mercy.
On the motion of CALEB HERBERT, a witness for JOHN MARKHAM HERBERT against JAMES YARD. It is ordered that the said HERBERT pay him 50 pounds tobacco for 2 days attendance at this Court in his suit against the said JOHN MARKHAM HERBERT.

JOSHUA WRIGHT Plaintiff
Against Re: In Case
JOHN HARDIE Defendant
This day came the parties by their Attorney's and there upon came also a Jury to wit: WILLIAM STEVENSON, RICHARD BICKERDICK, WILLIAM SMITH, CHARLES COOPER, GEORGE FARRER, JOHN LEE, SCARBROUGH TANKARD, HODGE MILLER, FRANCIS HAYNES, CHARLES GODFREY, GEORGE ALLISON and THOMAS MORRIS who being elected tried and sworn the truth to speak upon the issue joined upon their oath do say that the Defendant did assume in manner and form as the Plaintiff against him has declared and so assess the Plaintiffs damages by occasion of the non-performance of that assumption to 6 pounds, 9 shillings and 8 pence half penny besides his costs. Therefore, it is considered that the Plaintiff recover against the said Defendant his damages aforesaid in form aforesaid assessed his costs by him in this behalf expended and the said Defendant in mercy.

Order is granted JAMES MARSHALL against THOMAS BYCROFT for 75 pounds tobacco for 3 days attendance in his suit against JOHN MARNIX

Order is granted RICHARD BICKERDICK against JOHN MARNIX for 50 pounds tobacco for 2 days attendance in his suit of THOMAS BYCROFT against him.

PAGE 45
JOHN LEE Plaintiff
Against Re: In Case
FRANCES FRASIER Administratrix of RICHARD FRASIER Deceased who since the commencement of this suit inter married with DICKERSON PRIOR Defendants
This day came the parties by their Attorney's and the Defendants by their Attorney relinquishing their former plea say that they cannot gainsay the Plaintiff's action nor but that their intestate did assume in manner and form as the Plaintiff against them has declared. Therefore, it is considered that the Plaintiff recover against the said Defendant 29 pounds 8 shillings and 6 pence and his costs by him in this behalf expended and the said Defendant in mercy.

JAMES ATKINSON was this day appointed a Constable in the room of REUBEN SHARP and he having taken the oaths to the Government and subscribed the teste also the oath of a Constable of the Borough enters upon

This Court this day rated Flour at 12/6 per hundred
This Court is adjourned to Court in Course: CHARLES THOMAS MAYOR, TESTE: JOHN BOUSH D.C.C.

PAGE 45B
NORFOLK BOROUGH
At a Hustings Court Held this 19TH day of November 1770
PRESENT: CHARLES THOMAS ESQUIRE MAYOR
GENTLEMAN ALDERMEN: GEORGE ABYVON, WILLIAM AITCHESON, ARCHIBALD CAMPBELL, CORNELIUS CALVERT, PAUL LOYALL

JAMES WALLACE against ROBERT COOPER by Petition & Summons. Judgement is granted the Plaintiff for 4 pounds and 8 pence. It is ordered that the Defendant pay the same unto the Plaintiff with costs and fees.

JOHN RANDOLPH Esquire Plaintiff
Against Re: In Case
NEIL JAMIESON, JAMES TAYLOR, MATTHEW PHRIPP and BASSETT MOSELEY executors of JACOB ELLEGOOD deceased Defendants
This day came as well the Plaintiff by WALTER LYON Gentleman his Attorney as BASSET MOSELELY one of the executors of JACOB ELLEGOOD deceased in his proper person and the said Defendant says that he cannot gainsay the Plaintiffs actions nor, but their testator did assume in manner and form as the Plaintiff against him have declared. Therefore, it is considered that the Plaintiff recover against the said Defendant 10 pounds and his costs by him in this behalf expended, when assets after paying preceding judgements, debts of greater dignity with the

defendants own claims against the Estate of the said testator to be levied of the goods and chattels which were of the said JACOB at the time of his death that shall here after come to the hands of the said defendants to be administered and the said defendants in mercy.

Order is granted WILLIAM CONNER against JAMES WALLACE for 25 pounds tobacco for 1 day at this Court in his suit against ROBERT COOPER.

PAGE 46
ALEXANDER BELL against FREDERICK RAMPENDALL Dismissed.

JOHN MCLACHAN against JOHN MADDOX. The Plaintiff by his Attorney moved for Special Bail which is granted where upon STEPHEN TANKARD came into Court and entered himself Special Bail for the Defendants and there on the Defendants by their Attorney prayed an Imparlance.

JAMES MOORE against FREDERICK BOUSH and NATHANIEL BOUSH Special Imparlance & OYER.
DAVID COCKRAN and Co. against ALLISON GIBBS an ALIAS CAPIAS

JAMES BRIDGES against JOSEPH CALVERT. The Plaintiff by his Attorney moved for Special Bail which is granted where upon THOMAS NEWON JR. came into Court and entered himself Special Bail for the Defendants and there on the Defendants by their Attorney prayed an Imparlance.

WILLIAM WEBLY against JAMES WEBB and APHIA his wife. Executrix of WILLIS LANGLEY an Imparlance.

STEPHEN TANKARD against JOHN THOMAS Dismissed.

SAMUEL PORTLOCK against WILLIAM SHIPWASH and JOHN WILSON. Order against the Defendant SHIPWASH and THOMAS STEWART his bail and dismissed against JOHN WILSON.

THOMAS SNALE & ELIZABETH, his wife against JOHN IVY administrator of WILLIAM IVY deceased dismissed.

ADRIEL MILBY against JOHN WESTCOTT and CHARLES BURTON an Alias attachment against JOHN WESTCOTT.

ROBERT NICHOLSON and JOHN BROWN executors of JOHN BROWN Deceased against JOHN SMITH and JOSEPH HUTCHINGS. SAMUEL PORTLOCK and STEPHEN TANKARD came into Court and entered themselves as Special Bail.

PAGE 46B
And thereon the Defendants pleaded payment issue joined and referred.

JOSEPH CALVERT complaint against ARCHIBALD CAMPBELL is rejected.

WILLIAM HARRIS was this day brought before the Court for Breach of the Peace and ELIZABETH PARNAL having sworn the peace against him it is ordered that the Sergeant take him and keep in custody until he gives bond and security himself in 5 pounds and 1 security in 50 shillings for his keeping the peace and being of good behavior for the term of 6 months and pay the costs of this prosecution.

HANNAH O'BRIAN against JAMES OBRIAN dismissed at the Defendants Cost.

This Court is adjourned until tomorrow at 9 o'clock, CHARLES THOMAS MAYOR, TESTE: JOHN BOUSH D.C.C.

NORFOLK BOROUGH
At a Hustings Court Held this 20TH day of November 1770
PRESENT: CHARLES THOMAS ESQUIRE MAYOR
GENTLEMAN ALDERMEN: GEORGE ABYVON, JAMES TAYLOR, ARCHIBALD CAMPBELL, CORNELIUS CALVERT, LEWIS HANSFORD, WILLIAM AITCHESON

WILLIAM SIMPSON against EDWARD HANSFORD by Petition & Summons. Judgement is granted the Plaintiff for 4 pounds, 19 shillings and 11 pence. It is ordered that the Defendant pay the same unto the Plaintiff with costs and fees.

PAGE 47
BAILEY WARREN Plaintiff
Against Re: In Case
MATTHEW ROTHERY Defendant
The parties having mutually submitted all matters in difference between them to the determination of JOHN TAYLOR, JOHN GREENWOOD and BASSET MOSELEY and agreed that their award thereon should be made the Judgement of this Court and they having returned their award in the premises in these words to wit:
In obedience to an order of Norfolk County Court bearing date in September last and also an order of Norfolk Hustings bearing date in September last. We have proceeded to examine and state the accounts between MATTHEW ROTHERY and BAILEY WARREN and find a balance of 31 pounds 11 shillings and 5 pence half penny Virginia Currency due from MATTHEW ROTHERY to BAILEY WARREN (as per a state thereof here unto annexed will appear), MATTHEW ROTHERY charges WARREN with 10 hogs heads of rum short delivered of the cargo as per bill of lading which are accounted for as follows to wit: 7 hogshead are included in the 228 pounds, 15 shillings and half penny advanced BAILEY WARREN by WILLIS WILSON in Grenada, 2 hogs head marked NR N16 and 21 leaked out on board the ship as appears by a surgery of JOHN KELSO and THOMAS SNALE sworn to the 8th of August last before CHARLES THOMAS ESQUIRE and one other hogs head was expended on board the ship and sold the seamen in Grenada by order of MATTHEW ROTHERY. 6 hogs head of rum marked WW N21,13,20,18,25 and

27 which MATTHEW ROTHERY charges BAILEY WARREN with appears to have leaked out on board the ship and are included in the survey of JOHN KELSO and THOMAS SNALE above mentioned. CAPTAIN WALKINSHAW and ROBERT ELLIOTT who were upon a former survey say that they inspected two hogs head of rum which were properly

PAGE 47B

Stowed, but partly out and made their return accordingly and at the same time added in their return which we are told is either lost or mislaid that they observed several hogsheads in the lower tier improperly stowed and there was ballast on the top of some but saw no marks or numbers nor can they tell of the particular hogs heads leaked out were part of them nor do they know but they were stowed being up and bulge free. CAPTAIN THOMAS SNALE who signs the survey declares that he was particular in observing them unstowed these very hogs head he surveyed and that they appeared to him to be old water casks and the hoop worm eaten and rotten which was confirmed by JOHN RICHARDSON the cooper who trimmed many of the full hogshead after they came on shore. One in particular appeared to want only one hoop but in driving the hoop he broke and set 11 although this survey produced to us is not obtained. Strictly speaking in the usual form by an order from a Magistrate to them directed yet we think BAILEY WARREN ought not to be liable to MATTHEW ROTHERY for the rum leaked out until he as an owner of the vessel is obliged to pay it. With regard to a deficiency in salt imported from ALICANS it does not appear to us it was ever exactly measured out and we know that there is not only a considerable difference between the Spanish measure and ours but that all salt except stowed salt loses a very considerable quantity in measure which we have never known CAPTAINS made liable for without proof of it's being *embarrled**. With respect to a deficiency in delivery of the cargo at Grenada amounting to 67 pounds 4 shillings and 1 penny Grenada Currency charged by WILLIS WILSON to MATTHEW ROTHERY as no bill of lading has been produced to us or any other proof relative thereto sufficient to subject MATTHEW ROTHERY to WILLIS WILSON or we can't make WARREN liable to ROTHERY for that sum until such proof is produced or until WILLIS WILSON has recovered it of MATTHEW ROTHERY a suit for which is now depending but are of opinion that BAILEY WARREN should

PAGE 48

Be liable to MATTHEW ROTHERY for whatever sum WILLIS WILSON recovers from him on that Account and Therefore, award that the balance of 31 pounds 11 shillings and a half penny VIRGINIA currency should remain in the hands of said MATTHEW ROTHERY until that suit is determined. Given under our hands at Norfolk this 25th day of October 1770. JOHN GREENWOOD, JOHN TAYLOR, BASSET MOSELEY.

It is there upon considered that the Plaintiff recover against the said Defendant the said 31 pounds 11 shillings and a half penny Virginia Currency and his costs by him in this behalf expended and the execution of this judgement is stayed until the suit brought by the Defendant against WILLIS WILSON in the County Court of Norfolk is determined.

It is ordered that MARY ROSS'S house and lot be added and included in the prison bounds of the Borough.

ROBERT BANKS who as well against OWIN CRUMLESS and CATHERINE his wife agreed dismissed.

JOHN MCLACHAN against JAMES DUNN abates by the Defendants death.

ANN BOUCHER administratrix of DANIEL ROTHERY Deceased Plaintiff

Against Re: In Case

MATTHEW ROTHERY Defendant

This day came the parties by their Attorney's and there upon came also a Jury to wit: JOHN CALVERT, ELDRED FISHER, WILLIAM STEVENSON, JOHN LIVINGSTON, JOHN CHESHIRE, BASSET MOSELEY, PHILIP CARBERY, WILLIAM MARSH, STEPHEN TANKARD, CHARLES COOPER, HARDRESS WALLER and JONATHAN DYSON

PAGE 48B

Who being elected tried and sworn the truth to speak upon the issue joined upon their oath do say that the Defendant did assume in manner and form as the Plaintiff against him has declared and so assess the Plaintiffs damages by occasion of the non-performance of that assumption to 49 pounds, 17 shillings and 6 pence besides her costs. Therefore, it is considered that the Plaintiff recover against the said Defendant her damages aforesaid in form aforesaid assessed her costs by her in this behalf expended and the said Defendant in mercy.

HOWARD POOLE against THOMAS THOMPSON Continued and on motion of the Defendant by his Attorney a DEDIMUS is granted him to take the deposition of HUGH KELLY giving the Plaintiff legal notice.

ANDREW MORANO Plaintiff

Against Re: In Case

JOHN DEVEREUX Defendant

This day came the parties by their Attorney's and there upon came also a Jury to wit: RICHARD TAYLOR, MAXIMILIAN MARLEY, BARTHOLOMEW THOMPSON, JOHN WILLS, HOWARD POOLE, JAMES MURPHREE, JOSEPH GREAR, EDWARD HANSFORD, JAMES ESTHER, THOMAS PEARSON, JOHN WALKER and JOHN WILSON who being elected tried and sworn the truth to speak upon the issue joined upon their oath do say that the defendant tendered to the Plaintiff 8 pounds 19 shillings and 4 pence half penny New York Currency and did assume the residue in manner and form as the Plaintiff against him has declared and do assess the Plaintiff Damages by Occasion of the non-performance of that assumption to 6 pounds 6 shillings and 3 farthings. Therefore, on the prayer of the Defendant it is considered that he recover against the Plaintiff his costs by him in this behalf expended and the Plaintiff for his false claims in mercy.

PAGE 49
MARY ANN THELABALL Plaintiff
Against Re: In Case
JOHN COLVILLE Defendant
This day came the parties by their Attorney's and there upon came also a Jury to wit: WILLIAM MARSH, JONATHAN DYSON, CHARLES COOPER, STEPHEN TANKARD, BASSETT MOSELEY, PHILIP CARBERY, JOHN CALVERT, JOHN CHESHIRE, JOHN LIVINGSTON, ELDRED FISHER, WILLIAM STEVENSON and MATT KELLY who being elected tried and sworn the truth to speak upon the issue joined upon their oath do say that the Defendant did assume in manner and form as the Plaintiff against him has declared and do assess the Plaintiff damages by occasion of the non-performance of that assumption to 1 pound and 1 pound costs. Therefore, it is considered that the Plaintiff recover against the said Defendant her damages in form aforesaid assessed and 1-pound costs by her in this behalf expended and the said Defendant in mercy.

JOHN STEWART against MEARNS JOHN. The Plaintiff by his Attorney moved for Special Bail which is granted where upon JAMES WALKER and JAMES LEITCH came into Court and entered Themselves Special Bail for the Defendant and there on the Defendants by his Attorney prayed an Imparlance.

Order is granted WILLIAM CLARK against EDWARD HANSFORD for 25 pounds of tobacco for 1 day's attendance in WILLIAM SIMPSON suit against him.

PAGE 49B
Order is granted ANN HUBBARD against JOHN COLVILLE for 50 pounds tobacco for 2 days attendance in MARY ANN THELABALLS suit against him.

This Court is adjourned Court in Course, CHARLES THOMAS MAYOR, TESTE: JOHN BOUSH D.C.C.

NORFOLK BOROUGH
At a Hustings Court Held this 24TH day of December 1770
PRESENT: CHARLES THOMAS ESQUIRE MAYOR
ANTHONY LAWSON Esquire Deputy Recorder
GENTLEMAN ALDERMEN: GEORGE ABYVON, LEWIS HANSFORD, ARCHIBALD CAMPBELL, JAMES TAYLOR

JOHN SMITH against JOHN MAYLEIGH Dismissed.
WILLIAM WEBLY against JAMES WEBB and APHIA his wife. By Petition & Summons. Judgement is granted the Plaintiff for 2 pounds, 17 shillings and 11 pence. It is ordered that the Defendant pay the same unto the Plaintiff with costs and fees.

ARCHIBALD WHITE and Company against JOHN TATEM. The Plaintiff by his Attorney moved for Special Bail which is granted where upon SAMUEL PORTLOCK came into Court and entered Themselves Special Bail for the Defendant and there on the Defendants by his Attorney prayed an Imparlance

JOSHUA EDWARDS and MARY, his wife against THOMAS DICKINSON an Imparlance.
WRIGHT WESTCOTT against WILLIS DUNFORD an Imparlance.

PAGE 50
JOHN RAMSAY Plaintiff
Against Re: In Case
NEIL JAMIESON, JAMES TAYLOR, MATTHEW PHRIPP and BASSETT MOSELEY executors of JACOB ELLEGOOD deceased Defendants
This day came as well the Plaintiff by JAMES HOLT Gentleman his Attorney as BASSET MOSELELY one of the defendants in his proper person says that they cannot gainsay the Plaintiffs actions nor, but their testator did assume in manner and form as the Plaintiff against him have declared. Therefore, it is considered that the Plaintiff recover against the said Defendant 5 pounds, 12 shillings and his costs by him in this behalf expended, when assets after paying preceding judgements, debts of greater dignity with the defendants own claims against the Estate of the said testator to be levied of the goods and chattels which were of the said JACOB at the time of his death that shall here after come to the hands of the said NEIL JAMIESON, JAMES TAYLOR, MATT PHRIPP and BASSETT MOSELEY to be administered and the said NEIL JAMIESON, MATT and BASSETT money in mercy.

MICHAEL HAYES against NATHANIEL STANLEY Dismissed.

HENRY CUYLER, BARAUD RENDERS CUYLER and JOHN SMITH executors of HENRY CUYLER late of NEW YORK Merchant against ROBERT TUCKER Special Imparlance and discontinued against GAVIN CORBIN TUCKER. And THOMAS BURKE undertakes for the Plaintiff that he will pay to the Defendant all such damages costs and charges as shall be awarded against him by the Court.

JOHN VAN CORTLANDT against ROBERT TUCKER Heir at law and GAVIN CORBIN TUCKER devise under the will of the late ROBERT TUCKER a Special Imparlance and discontinued against GAVIN CORBIN TUCKER. And also, THOMAS BURKE undertakes for the Plaintiff that he will pay to the Defendant all such damages as shall be awarded against him by the Court.

WILLIAM SIMPSON against JOHN SMITH an Imparlance.

PAGE 50B
NEIL JAMIESON against ROBERT TUCKER heir at law and GAVIN CORBIN TUCKER devisee under the will of the late ROBERT TUCKER Special Imparlance and discontinued against GAVIN CORBIN TUCKER.

DICKERSON PRIOR and FRANCES his wife administratrix of RICHARD FRASIER against THOMAS BUTT an Imparlance.

JOHN GREENWOOD against JOHN TAYLOR JR. and HENRY TUCKER an Imparlance.

MATTHEW KELLY against EDMOND KEETON. By Petition & Summons. Judgement is granted the Plaintiff for 4 pounds, 19 shillings and 9 pence. It is ordered that the Defendant pay the same unto the Plaintiff with costs and fees.

MATTHEW ROTHERY against ANN BOUCHER administratrix of DANIEL ROTHERY time to consider the bill.
JOHN SCOTT and ANN, his wife against PETER BISER a Special Imparlance.
THOMAS HADDON against JOHN ARCHER and THOMAS BAILEY discontinued.

JEREMIAH FOREMAN against AARON BARBER and JOSIAH HOFFMIRE. Attachment against BARBER and discontinued against HOFFMIRE

SAMUEL PORTLOCK against JOHN WILSON Special Imparlance and OYER.
PAUL HERITTER and MARY ANN, his wife against JENNET LONG discontinued.

Order is granted BIRD ROWAND, DINAH GUTTERY and ROSANNAH RITTER against PAUL HERITTER and MARY ANN his wife for 50 pounds tobacco each 2 days attendance each in their suit against JENNET LONG.

DAVID COCKRAN and Company against ALLANSON GIBBS discontinued.
KING against SARAH LONG dismissed.

The King by CHARLES THOMAS Esquire against JOSEPH KENNEDY dismissed.

PAGE 51
ADRIEL MILBY Plaintiff
Against Re: In Debt
JOHN WESTCOTT and CHARLES BURTON Defendant
This day came the Plaintiff by WILLIAM RASCOW WILSON CURLE Gentleman his Attorney and the Defendant JOHN Being dead the suit against him abates and CHARLES the other Defendant being solemnly called and not appearing. Order that the former order of this Court against him the said Defendant CHARLES and WRIGHT WESTCOTT his bail be confirmed. Therefore, it is considered that the Plaintiff recover against him the said Defendant and WRIGHT WESTCOTT his bail aforesaid his debts amounting to 56 pounds and his costs by him about his suit in that behalf expended and the said Defendant in mercy. But this judgement is to be discharged by the payment of 28 pounds with interest for the same at the rate of 5% per annum to be computed from 14th October 1769 to the time of payment and costs.

GEORGE MUTER and Company against ROBERT TUCKER son and heir of the deceased ROBERT TUCKER. GAWIN CORBIN, CORBIN* devisee under the will of the said ROBERT TUCKER deceased and THOMAS NEWTON SR. and JOHN TAYLOR executors of the said ROBERT TUCKER deceased discontinued against CORBIN TUCKER and the other Defendants prayed OYER of the Record which is granted them.

JOHN ESDALE against ROBERT TUCKER heir at law and GAVIN CORBIN TUCKER devisee under the will of the late ROBERT TUCKER deceased and THOMAS NEWTON SR. and JOHN TAYLOR executors of the said ROBERT TUCKER deceased discontinued against CORBIN TUCKER and the other Defendants prayed OYER of the Record which is granted them. .

SAMUEL FARMER against ROBERT TUCKER heir at law and GAVIN CORBIN TUCKER devisee under the will of the late ROBERT TUCKER deceased and THOMAS NEWTON SR. and JOHN TAYLOR executors of the said ROBERT TUCKER deceased discontinued against CORBIN TUCKER and the other Defendants prayed OYER of the Record which is granted them.

PAGE 51B
THOMAS MANN RANDOLPH against ROBERT TUCKER heir at law and GAVIN CORBIN TUCKER devisee under the will of the late ROBERT TUCKER deceased and THOMAS NEWTON SR. and JOHN TAYLOR executors of the said ROBERT TUCKER deceased discontinued against GAVIN CORBIN TUCKER and the other Defendants prayed OYER of the Record which is granted them.

JOSIAH GRANBERRY against ROBERT TUCKER heir at law and GAVIN CORBIN TUCKER devisee under the will of the late ROBERT TUCKER deceased and THOMAS NEWTON SR. and JOHN TAYLOR executors of the said ROBERT TUCKER deceased discontinued against GAVIN CORBIN TUCKER and the other Defendants prayed OYER of the Record which is granted them.

ROBERT DONALD against ROBERT TUCKER heir at law and GAVIN CORBIN TUCKER devisee under the will of the late ROBERT TUCKER deceased and THOMAS NEWTON SR. and JOHN TAYLOR executors of the said ROBERT TUCKER deceased discontinued against GAVIN CORBIN TUCKER and the other Defendants prayed OYER of the Record which is granted them.

FRANCIS WARING against ROBERT TUCKER heir at law and GAVIN CORBIN TUCKER devisee under the will of the late ROBERT TUCKER deceased and THOMAS NEWTON SR. and JOHN TAYLOR executors of the said ROBERT TUCKER deceased discontinued against GAVIN CORBIN TUCKER and the other Defendants prayed OYER of the Record which is granted them.

GEORGE KIPPIN and Company against ROBERT TUCKER heir at law and GAVIN CORBIN TUCKER devisee under the will of the late ROBERT TUCKER deceased and THOMAS NEWTON SR. and JOHN TAYLOR executors of the said ROBERT TUCKER deceased discontinued against GAVIN CORBIN TUCKER and the other Defendants prayed OYER of the Record which is granted them.

JAMES BUCHANAN against ROBERT TUCKER heir at law and GAVIN CORBIN TUCKER devisee under

PAGE 52

the will of the late ROBERT TUCKER deceased, and THOMAS NEWTON SR. and JOHN TAYLOR executors of the said ROBERT TUCKER deceased discontinued against CORBIN TUCKER and the other Defendants prayed OYER of the Record which is granted them.

GARDNER FLEMING against ROBERT TUCKER heir at law and GAVIN CORBIN TUCKER devisee under the will of the late ROBERT TUCKER deceased and THOMAS NEWTON SR. and JOHN TAYLOR executors of the said ROBERT TUCKER deceased discontinued against GAVIN CORBIN TUCKER and the other Defendants prayed OYER of the Record which is granted them.

NATHANIEL LITTLETON SAVAGE against ROBERT TUCKER heir at law and GAVIN CORBIN TUCKER devisee under the will of the late ROBERT TUCKER deceased and THOMAS NEWTON SR. and JOHN TAYLOR executors of the said ROBERT TUCKER deceased discontinued against GAVIN CORBIN TUCKER and the other Defendants prayed OYER of the Record which is granted them.

RICHARD RANDOLPH against ROBERT TUCKER heir at law and GAVIN CORBIN TUCKER devisee under the will of the late ROBERT TUCKER deceased and THOMAS NEWTON SR. and JOHN TAYLOR executors of the said ROBERT TUCKER deceased discontinued against GAVIN CORBIN TUCKER and the other Defendants prayed OYER of the Record which is granted them.

JOHN BOWDOIN against ROBERT TUCKER heir at law and GAVIN CORBIN TUCKER devisee under the will of the late ROBERT TUCKER deceased and THOMAS NEWTON SR. and JOHN TAYLOR executors of the said ROBERT TUCKER deceased discontinued against GAVIN CORBIN TUCKER and the other Defendants prayed OYER of the Record which is granted them.

CHARLES CARTER against ROBERT TUCKER heir at law and GAVIN CORBIN TUCKER devisee under the will of the late ROBERT TUCKER deceased and THOMAS NEWTON SR. and JOHN TAYLOR executors of the said ROBERT TUCKER deceased discontinued against GAVIN CORBIN TUCKER and the other Defendants prayed OYER of the Record which is granted them.

PAGE 52B

ARCHIBALD CARY against ROBERT TUCKER heir at law and GAVIN CORBIN TUCKER devisee under the will of the late ROBERT TUCKER deceased and THOMAS NEWTON SR. and JOHN TAYLOR executors of the said ROBERT TUCKER deceased discontinued against GAVIN CORBIN TUCKER and the other Defendants prayed OYER of the Record which is granted them.

REESE MEREDITH against ROBERT TUCKER heir at law and GAVIN CORBIN TUCKER devisee under the will of the late ROBERT TUCKER deceased and THOMAS NEWTON SR. and JOHN TAYLOR executors of the said ROBERT TUCKER deceased discontinued against GAWIN CORBIN TUCKER, and the other Defendants prayed OYER of the Record which is granted them.

ARCHIBALD RITCHIE against ROBERT TUCKER heir at law and GAVIN CORBIN TUCKER devisee under the will of the late ROBERT TUCKER deceased and THOMAS NEWTON SR. and JOHN TAYLOR executors of the said ROBERT TUCKER deceased discontinued against GAVIN CORBIN TUCKER and the other Defendants prayed OYER of the Record which is granted them.

GEORGE MUTER and COMPANY, JOHN ESDALE, SAMUEL FARMER, THOMAS MANN RANDOLPH, JOSIAH GRANBERY, ROBERT DONALD, FRANCIS WARING, GEORGE KIPPIN and COMPANY, JAMES BUCHANAN and COMPANY, GARDNER FLEMING, NATHANIEL LITTLETON SAVAGE, RICHARD RANDOLPH, JOHN BOWDOIN, CHARLES CARTER, ARCHIBALD CARY, REESE MEREDITH and ARCHIBALD RITCHIE, HENRY CUYLER, BARAUD RENDERS CUYLER and JOHN SMITH executors of HENRY CUYLER late of New York Merchant, JOHN VAN CORTLANDT, and NEIL JAMIESON against THOMAS NEWTON SR. & JOHN TAYLOR executors of the last will and testament of ROBERT TUCKER lately deceased, ROBERT TUCKER son and heir of the said ROBERT TUCKER, GAVIN CORBIN TUCKER devisee under the will of the late ROBERT TUCKER deceased and EDWARD HUNT and THOMAS HUNT. Time is allowed the Defendants THOMAS NEWTON SR. and JOHN TAYLOR executors of the said ROBERT TUCKER deceased and ROBERT TUCKER son and heir of the said ROBERT TUCKER to consider the bill and discontinued against GAVIN CORBIN TUCKER devisee under the will of the said ROBERT TUCKER and EDWARD HUNT and THOMAS HUNT.

PAGE 53

JENNET LONG having this day sworn an oath before the Court. Ordered that she be fined 5 shillings or 50 pounds tobacco and upon failure of immediate payment on security for the same at the laying of the next levy. Ordered that the Sergeant after execution issues take her and give her ten lashes.

KING by JOSEPH NESBITT against ELDRED FISHER and WILLIAM SKINKER dismissed at the Plaintiff's costs.
THOMAS PARSONS administrator of THOMAS WILDS deceased against WILLIAM SMITH an Imparlance.

This Court is adjourned Court in Course. CHARLES THOMAS MAYOR, TESTE: JOHN BOUSH D.C.C.

NORFOLK BOROUGH
At a Hustings Court Held this 21st day of January 1771
PRESENT: CHARLES THOMAS ESQUIRE MAYOR
ANTHONY LAWSON Esquire Deputy Recorder
GENTLEMAN ALDERMEN: GEORGE ABYVON, JAMES TAYLOR, PAUL LOYALL, CORNELIUS CALVERT, LEWIS HANSFORD, WILLIAM AITCHESON, MAXIMILIAN CALVERT.

JAMES ROGERS against WILLIAM WOOD Dismissed.

WRIGHT WESTCOTT administrator of JOHN WESTCOTT deceased against JOHN TATEM and JOSEPH HUTCHINGS, SAMUEL PORTLOCK of this Borough this day came into Court and undertook for the Defendants that in case they shall be cast in this suit they the said Defendants will pay the condemnation of the Court surrender their bodies to prison in execution for the same or that he the said PORTLOCK will pay the condemnation or surrender the bodies of the said Defendants as aforesaid.

PAGE 53B

Whereupon the Defendants by their Attorney prayed and have leave to imparle* here the next Court and then to Plead.

WILLIAM CHISHOLM assignee of WILLIAM KID Plaintiff
Against Re: In Debt
ALEXANDER HAY Defendant

This day came as well the Plaintiff by THOMAS BURKE Gentleman his Attorney as the Defendant in Custody of the Sergeant of this Borough and acknowledges the Plaintiff action for 8 pounds, 6 shillings and 10 pence half penny with interest for the same at the rate of 5% per annum to be computed from October 9, 1769, to the time of payment. Therefore, it is considered that the Plaintiff recover against the said Defendant his debt aforesaid together with his costs by him in this behalf expended and the said Defendant in mercy. And the said Defendant being ruled to give Special Bail and failing so to do. On Motion of the Plaintiff by his Attorney aforesaid the Defendant is continued in Custody of the Sergeant until he shall have satisfied this Judgement and costs.

SIMON PORTLOCK against ABRAHAM WORMINGTON. The Defendant pleaded that he does not detain issue joined and referred.

MICHAEL CHRISTIAN assignee of WILLIAM MCCAA against JOHN SMITH, STEPHEN TANKARD of this Borough this day came into Court and undertook for the Defendant that in case he shall be costs in this suit he the said Defendant will pay the condemnation of the Court or render his body to Prison in execution for the same or that the said TANKARD will pay the condemnation or render the body of the said Defendant as aforesaid. Where upon the Defendants by their Attorney prayed and have leave to IMPARLE here the next Court and then to Plead.

SAMUEL ALLYNE against GEORGE CARLSON, MATT PHRIPP of this Borough this day came into Court and undertook for the Defendant that in case he shall be costs in this suit he the said Defendant will pay the condemnation of the Court or render his body to prison in execution for the same or that he the said PHRIPP will pay the condemnation or render the body of the said defendant as aforesaid. Where upon the Defendant by his Attorney prayed and have leave to IMPARLE here for the next Court and then to Plead.

PAGE 54
PRESENT:
CHARLES THOMAS ESQUIRE MAYOR, MAX CALVERT, CORNELIUS CALVERT & WILLIAM AITCHESON.

HARDRESS WALLER, JOINER.
WILLIAM & JONATHAN SIMPSON, BUTCHERS & PARTNERS
BASSETT & ALEXANDER MOSELEY, MERCHANTS & PARTNERS
PAUL LOYALL, GENTLEMAN
CHARLES GODFREY, MARINER
FRANCIS & GRIFFIN PEART, MERCHANTS & PARTNERS
NICHOLAS WONYCOTT, MERCHANT
EDWARD ARCHER, MERCHANT
LEWIS HANSFORD & COMPANY MERCHANTS
JAMES BALFOUR & DANIEL BARRAUD, MERCHANTS & PARTNERS
JONATHAN DISON, CARPENTER
JOSEPH CALVERT, JOHN WILSON MERCHANTS
JOHN RAMSAY & JAMES TAYLOR PRACTITIONERS OF PHYSICK & PARTNERS
JOHN TAYLOR & THOMAS NEWTON Executors of ROBERT TUCKER Deceased
SAMUEL BOUSH GENTLEMAN
GEORGE GORDON & DAVID CHEVISS & DAVID CROSS MERCHANTS
WILLIAM RASCOW WILSON CURLE GENTLEMAN
WILLIAM CHISHOLM & JOHN BOWNESS MERCHANTS & PARTNERS
WILLIAM BOLDEN & JOHN LAWRENCE & COMPANY MERCHANTS & PARTNERS
ARCHIBALD WHITE & COMPANY MERCHANTS
DUNCAN CAMPBELL, MARINER
JOHN CORRIS, MERCHANT
NEIL MCCOULL, MERCHANT
WILLIAM JACOB, PLANTER
JOHN GAWITH, MARINER
ARCHIBALD CAMPBELL, GENTLEMAN
THOMAS BRESSIE, MERCHANT
JOSEPH MITCHELL, JOHN LEWELLING, WILLIAM STEVENSON, THOMAS THOMPSON, MATT ROTHERY & JOEL MOHUN PARTNERS & GEORGE BRUCE
COMPLAINTS: IN CHANCERY
SARAH WINTERTON, an infant daughter, and heiress of NICHOLAS WINTERTON deceased. ANN WINTERTON widow and GEORGE ABYVON admin of the said NICHOLAS WINTERTON deceased respondents.

PAGE 54B

This day came as well the Plaintiffs by their Attorney's and the Defendant SARAH by her guardian, the Defendant ANN by her Attorney, and the Defendant GEORGE in his proper person and on the Prayer of JOSEPH MITCHELL, JOHN LEWELLING, WILLIAM STEVENSON, THOMAS THOMPSON, MATTHEW ROTHERY & JOEL MOHUN Partners and GEORGE BRUCE by their Attorney they are admitted Plaintiffs. JONATHAN SIMPSON being dead the suit as to him abates, and thereon the Defendants filed their answers. Where upon the cause was heard on the bill and said answers. On consideration where of it is ordered and decreed that MATTHEW PHRIPP, JOHN TAYLOR SR, JOHN LAWRENCE, JOHN GREENWOOD & JAMES MARSDEN Gentleman or any three of them being first sworn meet, state and examine the claims and demands of the Complainants and Respondents GEORGE ABYVON and that they or any three of them meet and set apart the dower of the Defendant ANN in the lands in the Borough of Norfolk in the Bill mentioned and make their report to the next Court to be held for the Borough.

FRANCIS WILLIS JR. assignee of RICHARD DUNBAR against ROBERT TUCKER a DEDIMUS is granted the Plaintiff to take the deposition of MATHIAS SMITH giving notice.

DAVID HARPER Plaintiff
Against Re: In Case
AMOS ETHERIDGE Defendant

This day came as well the Plaintiff by WILLIAM RASCOW WILSON CURLE Gentleman his Attorney as the defendant in his proper person and says that he cannot gainsay the Plaintiffs action nor but that he did assume in manner and form as the Plaintiff against him has declared. Therefore, it is considered that the Plaintiff recover against the said Defendant 13 pounds 13 shillings and 5 pence with interest for the same at the rate of 5% per annum to be computed from March 10th, 1769, to the time of payment and the costs.

JOHN HARDY Plaintiff
Against Re: In Case
JOSHUA WRIGHT Defendants

This day came the parties by their Attorney's and the Defendant prayer and has leave to IMPARLE here until next court and then to plead.

PAGE 55

WILLIAM SIMPSON against MARY SCOTT. By Petition & Summons. Judgement is granted the Plaintiff for 1 pounds, 19 shillings and 4 pence. It is ordered that the Defendant pay the same unto the Plaintiff with costs and fees.

WILLIAM SIMPSON against WILLIAM GRAY. Dismissed.
WILLIAM SIMPSON against JONATHAN DISON. Dismissed.

WILLIAM SIMPSON against PETER MCNABB. By Petition & Summons. Judgement is granted the Plaintiff for 1 pounds, 15 shillings and 1 penny. It is ordered that the Defendant pay the same unto the Plaintiff with costs and fees.

WILLIAM SIMPSON against JOHN SHERLOCK. By Petition & Summons. Judgement is granted the Plaintiff for 2 pounds, 17 shillings and 1 pence. It is ordered that the Defendant pay the same unto the Plaintiff with costs and fees.

WILLIAM SIMPSON against JOHN DALGLEISH. By Petition & Summons. Judgement is granted the Plaintiff for 3 pounds, 4 shillings and 9 pence. It is ordered that the Defendant pay the same unto the Plaintiff with costs and fees.

WILLIAM SIMPSON against WILLIAM ORANGE dismissed at the Plaintiff costs.

NICHOLAS LOYD against ALEXANDER LOVE. CORNELIUS CALVERT Gentleman. This day came into Court and undertook for the Defendant that in Case he shall be costs in this suit he the said Defendant will pay the condemnation of the Court or render his body to prison in execution for the same or that he the said CALVERT will pay the condemnation or render the body of the said defendant as aforesaid. Whereupon the Defendant by his Attorney prays and has leave to IMPARLE here the next Court and then to plead.

Ordinary License is granted ROGER PIERCE on his complying with the law.
JOSEPH GREAR against JOHN LYONS Dismissed.
THOMAS NEWTON against JOHN BAKER Dismissed for want of estate.

PAGE 55B

EDWARD VOSS Plaintiff
Against Re: In Detinue
PETER LONG Defendant

This day came the Parties by their Attorneys and the Defendant pleaded that he does not detain the Negro fellow JACK in the declaration mentioned and agreed the issue should be tried immediately and there upon came also a Jury to wit: WILLIAM BROWN, THOMAS MORRIS, WILLIAM BELL, WILLIAM JENKINSON, CHARLES COOPER, JOHN LIVINGSTON, JOHN GREENWOOD, DANIEL HUTCHINGS, JAMES MARSDEN, BAILEY WARREN, SAMUEL TUMLINSON, and CHARLES GODFREY who being elected tried and sworn the truth to speak upon the issue joined upon their oath do say that the Defendant does detain the said Negro in the declaration mentioned in manner and form as the Plaintiff against him has declared and that the said slave is the value of 100 pounds and they do asses the Plaintiff damages by occasion of the Defendants detaining the said slave to 1 shilling besides his costs. Therefore, it is considered that the Plaintiff recover against the said Defendant the slave aforesaid if to be had or the value of him if not to be had together with his damages aforesaid in form aforesaid assessed and his costs by him in this behalf expended and the said Defendant in mercy.

ALEXANDER KIDD Plaintiff
Against Re: In Case
ALEXANDER HAY Defendant
This day came the parties by their Attorney's and the Defendant by his Attorney says that he cannot gainsay the Plaintiffs action nor but that he did assume in manner and form as the Plaintiff against him has declared. Therefore, it is considered that the Plaintiff recover against the said Defendant 22 pounds and 5 pence 3 farthing and his costs by him in this behalf expended and the said Defendant in mercy.

PAGE 56
MARGARET BANNERMAN Plaintiff
Against Re: In Chancery
BENJAMIN BANNERMAN Defendant
This day came the Plaintiff by WILLIAM RASCOW WILSON CURLE Gentleman her Attorney and the Commissioners appointed to SEQUESTER the Estate of the Defendant his day returned an Account of their proceedings in their words to wit:
Debit the Estate of MR. BEN BANNERMAN his account current with trustees. Credit 1770 September.

	To Cash Paid for 3 padlocks	7/6
	To Stock lock	4/6
Dec. 1770	To the repairs of one Tenement	1.1.9
	to paid vending 2 Negroes	15/
	To Cash Paid MARSDEN & HODGSON for a gown	
	And a Bed Bottom for MRS BANNERMAN	1.15.2
	To Paid advertising the Negroes belonging to the estate	
01.10.1771	Cash Paid for a Memorandum Book	7 1/2
	Balance 8.4.1 1/2 to 12.18.8 on June 1, 1770	
	By Cash received of MRS. HOLS for rent	2.6.8
01.21.1771	By Cash received of JOHN BELL	10.0.0
	By Cash received from SAMUEL PORTLOCK	12.18.8

1771 JANUARY 21 by balance brought down L.8.4. 1 ½ Errors accepted this 20TH January 1771
JAMES MARSDEN, AMOS ETHERIDGE, THOMAS VEALE, HUMPHREY ROBERTS, ROBERT SHEDDEN.

On consideration where of it is ordered and decreed that the balance there in of L.8.4. 1 ½
Be lodged in the Clerk's office for the use of the Plaintiff agreeable to a former decree in this suit made and continued until they can return an account of their further proceedings to the next Court to be held for this Borough.

CHARLES COOPER Plaintiff
Against Re: In Case
WILLIAM FINNIE Defendant
This day came the Defendant by THOMAS BURKE Gentleman his attorney and the Plaintiff the solemnly called came not. But made default nor is his suit further prosecuted. Therefore, on the prayer of the Defendant it is considered that he recover against the Plaintiff 5 shillings current money and his costs by him about his defense in this behalf expended according to the form of the Act of Assembly. And the Plaintiff for his false claims be in mercy.

PAGE 56B
This Court is adjourned until tomorrow at 9 o'clock. CHARLES THOMAS MAYOR, TESTE: JOHN BOUSH D.C.C.

NORFOLK BOROUGH
At a Hustings Court Held this 22nd day of January 1771
PRESENT: CHARLES THOMAS ESQUIRE MAYOR
ANTHONY LAWSON ESQUIRE DEPUTY RECORDER
GENTLEMAN ALDERMEN: GEORGE ABYVON, MAXIMILIAN CALVERT, PAUL LOYALL, JAMES TAYLOR, LEWIS HANSFORD, CORNELIUS CALVERT

THOMAS ROBERTS Plaintiff
Against Re: In Case
ROBERT STEED Defendant
This day came the parties by their Attorney's and there upon came also a Jury to wit:
JONATHAN GODFREY, JOHN CHESHIRE, JOHN CALVERT, FRANCIS HAYNES, CHARLES COOPER, JOHN CRAMOND, WILLIAM IVY, JOHN SMITH, ROBERT CROOKE, JOHN BROWN, JOHN MCLEAN, and NICHOLAS POOLE who being elected tried and sworn the truth to speak upon the issue joined upon their oath do say that the Defendant did assume in manner and form as the Plaintiff against him has declared and do assess the Plaintiff damages by occasion of the non-performance of that assumption in 14 pounds 7 shillings and 7 pence besides his costs. Therefore, it

is considered that the Plaintiff recover against the said Defendant his damages aforesaid in form aforesaid assessed and his costs by him about his in this behalf expended and the said Defendant in mercy.

JAMES GIBSON and Company against NICHOLAS WONYCOTT. Order against the Defendant and JOSEPH CALVERT Sergeant his bail.

PAGE 57

ALEXANDER LOVE & JOHN THOMAS Plaintiff
Against Re: In Case
HENRY COLLINS ESQUIRE Defendant
This day came the Defendant by WILLIAM RASCOW WILSON CURLE Gentleman his Attorney and the Plaintiff though solemnly called came not but made default nor in their suit further prosecuted. Therefore, on the prayer of the Defendant it is considered that he recover against the Plaintiff 5 shillings current money and his costs by him about his defense in this behalf expended according to the form of the act of assembly and the Plaintiffs for their false claims be in mercy.

JEREMIAH FOREMAN against AARON BARBER and JOSIAH HOFFMIRE. This day came the parties by their Attorneys and the Defendant prayed and have cause to IMPARLE here the next court and then to Plead.

WILLIAM WEBLY against RICHARD BROWN and WILLIAM SKINKER executors of JOHN MATTHEWS deceased dismissed.
SEYMOUR POWELL against JOHN COLEMAN Discontinued.

GEORGE OLDNER Plaintiff
Against Re: In Case
JOHN CHESHIRE Defendant
This day came the parties by their Attorney's and there upon came also a Jury to wit:
JOHN MCLEAN, WILLIAM IVY, JOHN LIVINGSTON, JOHN CALVERT, CHARLES COONE, GEORGE COLLINS, JOHN BROWN, WILLIAM STEVENSON, THOMAS PEARSON, EDMOND KEETON, THOMAS THOMPSON and ROBERT CROOKE, who being elected tried and sworn the truth to speak upon the issue joined upon their oath do say that the Defendant did assume in manner and form as the Plaintiff against him has declared and do assess the Plaintiff damages by occasion of the non-performance of that assumption to 25 pounds 19 shillings and 11 pence besides his costs. Therefore, it is considered that the Plaintiff recover against the said Defendant his damages aforesaid in form aforesaid assessed and his costs by him about his suit in this behalf expended and the said Defendant in mercy.

PAGE 57B

Order is granted THOMAS MORRIS and BENNETT BOUSH against GEORGE OLDNER for 250 pounds tobacco each for 10 days attendance each. JONATHAN GODFREY for 150 pounds of tobacco for 6 days attendance and JOHN PEARSON for 100 pounds of tobacco for 4 days attendance in his suit against JOHN CHESHIRE.
Order is granted WILLOUGHBY WILLIAMSON against GEORGE OLDNER for 1225 pounds of tobacco for 13 days attendance in this Court coming and returning 25 miles 12 times in his suit against JOHN CHESHIRE.

JOHN EILBECK and WILLIAM CHALMERS Plaintiff
Against Re: In Case
JONATHAN MEREDITH and ELIZABETH, his wife Defendants.
This day came the parties by their Attorney's and there upon came also a Jury to wit:
JOHN WILSON, RICHARD TALBOT, NICHOLAS POOL, JONATHAN DISON, JONATHAN GODFREY, FRANCIS HAYNES, WRIGHT WESTCOTT, JOHN CHESHIRE, JOHN SMITH, THOMAS SNALE, THOMAS MORRIS and JAMES COOPER who being elected tried and sworn the truth to speak upon the issue joined upon their oath do say that the Defendant did assume in manner and form as the Plaintiff against him have declared and do assess the Plaintiff damages by occasion of the non-performance of that assumption to 129 pounds, 3 shillings and 9 pence half penny besides their costs. Therefore, it is considered that the Plaintiff recover against the said Defendant their damages aforesaid in form aforesaid assessed and their costs by them about their suit in this behalf expended and the said Defendant in mercy.

Order is granted ROBERT FRY against JONATHAN MEREDITH and ELIZABETH his wife for 275 pounds of tobacco for 11 days attendance in the suit of JON EILBECK and WILLIAM CHALMERS against them.

Order is granted MOLLY THURMER and JAMES DISON against JONATHAN MEREDITH

PAGE 58

And ELIZABETH his wife for 275 pounds of tobacco each for 11 days attendance each. FREER ARMISTON for 50 pounds of tobacco for 2 days attendance and JAMES ESTHER for 175 pounds tobacco each for 7 days attendance of his wife in the suit of JOHN EILBECK and WILLIAM CHALMERS against them.

This Court is adjourned Court in Course. CHARLES THOMAS MAYOR, TESTE: JOHN BOUSH D.C.C.

NORFOLK BOROUGH

At a Hustings Court Held this 25th day of February 1771
PRESENT: CHARLES THOMAS ESQUIRE MAYOR
GENTLEMAN ALDERMEN: GEORGE ABYVON, MAXIMILIAN CALVERT, ARCHIBALD CAMPBELL, JAMES TAYLOR, LEWIS HANSFORD, CORNELIUS CALVERT, PAUL LOYALL, WILLIAM AITCHESON

WALTER PETER assignee of SNODGRASS and TEMPLEMAN against JOSIAH BUTT administrator of THOMAS BUTT. This day came the parties by their Attorney's and the Defendants prays and has leave here to IMPARLE until the next Court and then to plead.

EDMOND KEETON against MATT KELLY Dismissed at the Plaintiff Costs.
THOMAS SMITH against HENRY HINTON Dismissed.
THOMAS SMITH against HENRY HINTON Dismissed.

JONATHAN DISON against FREDERICK RAMPENDALL Dismissed.
JOHN TATEM SENIOR against WILLIAM HAYNES Dismissed.

PAGE 58B
DUGAL GILCHRIST against DONALD CAMPBELL. Order against the Defendant and JAMES ROGERS his bail.

JAMES CARMICHAEL against WILLIAM GRAY. JOSEPH HARDING came this day into Court and undertook for the Defendant that in case he shall be cast in in this suit he the said Defendant will pay the condemnation of the Court or render his body to prison in execution for the same or that he the said HARDING will pay the condemnation or render the body of the said Defendant as aforesaid. Where upon the Defendant by his Attorney prays and has leave to IMPARLE here until the next Court and then to plead.

WILLIAM MCKINNIE against WILLIAM SIMPSON and JOHN MCLACHAN. STEPHEN TANKARD came this day into Court and undertook for the Defendant that in case he shall be cast in in this suit he the said Defendant will pay the condemnation of the Court or render his body to prison in execution for the same or that he the said TANKARD will pay the condemnation or render the body of the said Defendant as aforesaid. Where upon the Defendant by his Attorney prays and has leave to IMPARLE here until the next Court and then to plead.

JOSEPH WILLIAMSON against ALEXANDER BELL. JOHN WILSON came this day into Court and undertook for the Defendant that in case he shall be cast in in this suit he the said Defendant will pay the condemnation of the Court or render his body to prison in execution for the same or that he the said WILSON will pay the condemnation or render the body of the said Defendant as aforesaid. Where upon the Defendant prayed an Imparlance?

THOMAS NICHOLSON against CHARLES JENKINS Discontinued.

MATTHEW GODFREY against WILLIAM MCCAA, MARY BROUGH and JOHN WILSON. Discontinued against MCCAA. The Defendant MARY not being arrested. On the motion of the Plaintiff by his Attorney an ALIAS CAPIAS is awarded him against the said Defendants returnable here next Court and ALEXANDER BELL this day came

PAGE 59
Into Court and undertook for the Defendant JOHN WILSON that in case he shall be cast in this suit he the said Defendant will pay the condemnation of the Court or render his body to prison in execution for the same or that he the said BELL will pay the condemnation or render the body of the said Defendant as aforesaid. Where upon the Defendant by his Attorney prays and has leave to IMPARLE here until the next Court and then to plead.

PHILIP CARBERY Plaintiff
Against Re: In Debt
JOHN COLEMAN Defendant
This day came as well the Plaintiff by WILLIAM RASCOW WILSON CURLE Gentleman his Attorney as the Defendant in Custody of the Sergeant of this Borough and acknowledges the Plaintiffs action for 6 pounds, 5 shillings. Therefore, it is considered that the Plaintiff recover against the said Defendant his debt aforesaid and his costs by him about his suit in this behalf expended and the said Defendant in Mercy. And the Defendant being ruled to give special bail and failing so to do. On motion of the Plaintiff by his Attorney aforesaid the said Defendant is continued in Custody of the Sergeant until he shall have satisfied this judgement and costs. But this Judgement is to be discharged by the payment of 3 pounds 2 shillings and 6 pence with interest for the same at the rate of 5% per annum to be computed from August 2nd, 1770, to the time of payment and costs.

ANN MATTHEWS Plaintiff
Against Re: In Debt
JOHN COLEMAN Defendant
This day came as well the Plaintiff by WILLIAM RASCOW WILSON CURLE Gentleman his Attorney as the Defendant in Custody of the Sergeant of this Borough and acknowledges the Plaintiffs action for 10 pounds. Therefore, it is considered that the Plaintiff recover against the said Defendant her debt aforesaid and her costs by her in this behalf expended and the said Defendant in Mercy. And the Defendant being ruled to give special bail and failing so to do. On motion of the Plaintiff by her Attorney aforesaid the said Defendant is continued in Custody of the Sergeant until he shall have satisfied this judgement and costs.

PAGE 59B
But this Judgement is to be discharged by the payment of 5 pounds with interest for the same at the rate of 5% per annum to be computed from June 9, 1770, to the time of payment and costs.

STEPHEN TANKARD against RICHARD HOG. On motion of the Plaintiff by his Attorney a DEDIMUS is granted him to take the Deposition of WILLIAM FINNIE and JAMES PASTEUR giving the defendants reasonable notice.

ALEXANDER BELL against JOSIAH BUTT. On motion of the Plaintiff by his Attorney a DEDIMUS is granted him to take the deposition of HEREKIAH FENTRESS giving the Defendant reasonable notice.

JOHN CHAPMAN against PETER DALE in ejectment. On motion of the Plaintiff by his Attorney to read the deposition of ELIZABETH GOODWIN taken in this suit and upon solemn argument is the opinion of the Court that the same was not taken agreeable to notice given and ought not to be read. And a DEDIMUS is granted the Plaintiff to take the deposition of BENNET KIRBY the said ELIZABETH GOODWIN giving the Defendant reasonable notice.

HARDRESS WALLER and others Plaintiff
Against Re: In Chancery
NICHOLAS WINTERTON'S heiress, widow, and administrator Defendants
By consent of the Plaintiffs and Defendants. JOHN HUTCHINGS and GOODRICH BOUSH Gentleman are appointed Commissioners in the room of JOHN TAYLOR and JOHN LAWRENCE Gentleman who with the other 3 Commissioners in a former decree in this suit made and being first sworn meet, state and examine the claims and demands of the Plaintiffs and Defendant GEORGE ABYVON and that they or any three of them set apart the dower of the Defendant ANN in the Lands of the Borough of Norfolk in the bill mentioned and make their report to the next Court to be held for this Borough

PAGE 60
PAUL LOYALL and MATTHEW PHRIPP Plaintiffs
Against Re: In Case
WILLIAM GRAY Defendant
This day came the parties by their Attorney's and there upon came also a Jury to wit:
JOHN SHAW, GEORGE GORDON, RICHARD TAYLOR, NICHOLAS POOLE, WILLIAM IVY, JOHN WALKER, JOHN LEE, STEPHEN TANKARD, HOWARD POOLE, JAMES MURPHREE, THOMAS THOMPSON and SAMUEL BACON who being elected tried and sworn the truth to speak upon the issue joined upon their oath do say that the Defendant did assume in manner and form as the Plaintiff against him have declared and do assess the Plaintiff damages by occasion of the non-performance of that assumption to 25 pounds 8 shillings and 3 farthing besides their costs. Therefore, it is considered that the Plaintiffs recover against the said Defendant their damages aforesaid in form aforesaid assessed and their costs by them in this behalf expended and the said Defendant in mercy.

JOHN GILMOUR and COMPANY against JOHN TATEM Dismissed.

JOHN SMTIH Plaintiff
Against Re: In Chancery
WILLIAM CHISHOLM Defendant
The parties having mutually submitted all matters in difference between them to the determination of JOHN TAYLOR, JOHN GREENWOOD and JOHN LAWRENCE Gentleman and agreed their award thereupon should be made the decree of the Court and they are having returned their award in the premises in their words to wit. In obedience to an Order of Norfolk Hustings Court to us directed bearing date the 24th September 1770 we the subscribes have met and a Plan of the Land in dispute between JOHN SMITH and WILLIAM CHISHOLM being produced to us, taken by ARTHUR BOUSH Surveyor of this County an examination there of as well of sundry witnesses on Oath together with the Deposition of WILLIAM BOLDEN which was admitted as evidence by the said JOHN SMITH it appears to us that the aforementioned land is not so wide upon the water as on the Street by 36 feet and it being fully proved to us that at the sale the said JOHN SMITH declared that the difference at High Water did not

PAGE 60B
Exceed 15 or 20 feet. We are Therefore, of Opinion that JOHN SMITH as well as WILLIAM CHISHOLM were deceived in the quantity of land then put up for sale for want of a regular plan being produced and that the land ought to remain the property of the said JOHN SMITH. Norfolk 14th February 1771.
JOHN TAYLOR, JOHN GREENWOOD, JOHN LAWRENCE. On consideration where it is ordered and decreed that the suit be dismissed, and that the Plaintiff pay unto the Defendant his costs by him about his defense in this behalf expended.

JONATHAN DISON and SARAH, his wife Plaintiff
Against Re: In Case for Slander
JOHN ASHLEY Defendant
This day came the parties by their Attorney's and there upon came also Jury to wit:
JOHN SHAW, GEORGE GORDON, RICHARD TAYLOR, NICHOLAS POOL, WILLIAM IVY, JOHN WALKER, JOHN LEE, JOHN CRAMOND, HOWARD POOLE, PHILIP CARBERY, THOMAS THOMPSON, and SAMUEL BACON who being elected tried and sworn the truth to speak upon the issue joined upon their oath do say that the Defendant is guilty of speaking the slanderous words in manner and form as in the declaration against him is alleged and do assess the Plaintiff damages by occasion of the speaking of the slanderous words in the declaration mentioned to 100 pounds besides their costs. Therefore, it is considered that the Plaintiff recover against the said Defendant their damages aforesaid inform aforesaid assessed and their costs by them in this behalf expended and the said defendant in mercy.

THOMAS NEWTON SR., THOMAS NEWTON JR., PAUL LOYALL and THOMAS ROBERTS against ROBERT TUCKER answer filed and time to consider it.

JAMES KEMPE and CHARLES WILLIAMSON against JAMES MURDAUGH and JOHN MCLEAN answer filed and time to consider it.
PAUL LOYALL against NATHANIEL STROUD Discontinued.

This Court is adjourned Court in Course, CHARLES THOMAS MAYOR, TESTE: JOHN BOUSH D.C.C.

PAGE 61

NORFOLK BOROUGH

At a Hustings Court Held this 25th day of MARCH 1771

PRESENT: CHARLES THOMAS ESQUIRE MAYOR

GENTLEMAN ALDERMEN: GEORGE ABYVON, JAMES TAYLOR, ARCHIBALD CAMPBELL, CORNELIUS CALVERT, LEWIS HANSFORD, WILLIAM AITCHESON

SUSANNAH DALE against JOHN SOUTHERLAND in Case. This day came the Parties by their Attorney's, and the Defendant prays and has leave to IMPARLE here until the Next Court and then to plead.

JAMES HUNTER against WILLIAM WHITE in case. This day came the Parties by their Attorney's, and the Defendant prays and has leave to IMPARLE here until the Next Court and then to plead.

WILLIS WILSON against MATTHEW ROTHERY in Case. This day came the Parties by their Attorney's, and the Defendant prays and has leave to IMPARLE here until the Next Court and then to plead.

GEORGE WEBB and JOSEPH LANGLEY against JOHN BANES and NANCY ASHLEY time to consider the bill.

WILLIS WILSON & COMPANY against NATHANIEL POYNER. This day came the Plaintiffs by WILLIAM RASCOW WILSON CURLE Gentleman their Attorney and the Defendant being solemnly called and not appearing a conditional order is granted the Plaintiff against the said Defendant and AARON BARBER his bail.

HENRY GREEN against BARNABY CARNEY in Case. This day came the Parties by their Attorney's, and the Defendant prays and has leave to IMPARLE here until the Next Court and then to plead.

ANN MIDDLETON executrix of SAMUEL MIDDLETON against ANN WALLACE and NICHOLAS POOLE. OYER of Record is granted the Defendants.

PAGE 61B

JOHN RAMSAY and JAMES TAYLOR against THOMAS WALKER Dismissed.

MARK TALBOT against WILLIAM and JOHN INGRAM. JOHN BOUSH this day came into Court and undertook for the defendants that in case they should be cast in this suit they the said Defendants will pay the condemnation of the Court or render their bodies to prison in execution for the same or that the said BOUSH will pay the condemnation or render the bodies of the said Defendants as aforesaid where upon the Defendants pray and have leave to IMPARLE here until next court and then plead.

ROBERT BOWREY against JOHN COLVILLE by Petition and SUMMONS. Judgement is granted the Plaintiff for 1 pound, 18 shillings. It is ordered that the Defendant pay the same unto the Plaintiff with costs and fees.

ABRAHAM WORMINGTON against ZACHARIAS HUTCHINGS Dismissed at the Plaintiffs costs.

ELIZABETH HOPKINS Executrix of JOHN HOPKINS against ELDRED FISHER, JOHN MCLEAN this day came into Court and undertook for the Defendant that in case he shall be cast in this suit for the said Defendant will pay the condemnation of the Court or render his body to prison in execution for the same of the said defendant as aforesaid. Where upon the Defendant by his Attorney prayed and has leave to IMPARLE here until the next Court and then to plead.

THOMAS DAVIS Executor of WILLIAM GOODING against JAMES DAWSON in case. This day came the parties by their Attorney's and the said Defendant prays and has leave to IMPARLE here until the next Court and then to plead.

JOHN WILSON against SAMUEL PORTLOCK in case. The parties by their Attorney's and the Defendant prays and has leave to IMPARLE here until the next Court and then to plead.

JOHN WILLIAMSON against JOSEPH CALVERT and ANTHONY FLEMING. This day came the Parties by their Attorney, and the Defendants pray and have leave to Special IMPARLE here until the next Court and then to plead.

PAGE 62

JOHN WILLIAMSON against JOSEPH CALVERT and PAUL HERITTER. This day came the Parties by their Attorney, and the Defendants pray and have leave to IMPARLE Special until the next Court and then to plead.

NATHANIEL YOUNG and JOHN SMITH against JOHN ASHLEY. This day came the Plaintiffs by WILLIAM RASCOW WILSON CURLE Gentleman their Attorney and the Defendant being solemnly called and appearing a conditional order is granted the Plaintiff against the said Defendant and JOHN WILLIAMSON his bail.

NATHANIEL YOUNG and JOHN SMITH against WRIGHT WESTCOTT administrator against JOHN WESTCOTT. This day came the parties and the Defendant pray and have leave to IMPARLE here until the next Court and then to plead.

SAMUEL WILSON against SAMUEL BRESSIE. This day came the Plaintiff by WILLIAM RASCOW WILSON CURLE Gentleman his Attorney and the Defendant being solemnly called and not appearing a conditional order is granted the Plaintiff against the said Defendant and SAMUEL WORMINGTON his bail.

NEIL JAMIESON, JAMES TAYLOR, MATT PHRIPP and BASSET MOSELEY executors of JACOB ELLEGOOD deceased Plaintiffs
Against Re: In Debt.
STEPHEN TANKARD Defendant

This day came the parties by their Attorney's and there upon came also a jury to wit: CHARLES COOPER, JOHN ARDISS, JONATHAN DISON, JOHN WOODSIDES, RICHARD BICKERDICK, THOMAS FARRER, JOHN CRAMOND, WILLIAM IVY, BARTHOLOMEW THOMPSON, ELDRED FISHER, JAMES ESTHER and HARDRESS WALLER who being elected tried and sworn the truth to speak upon the issue joined upon their oath do say that they Defendant does not owe as in pleading by their bill but for the false claims be in mercy and the Defendant go hence without day and recover against the Plaintiff his costs by him about his defense in this behalf expended.

Ordinary License is granted MATT KELLY and JOSEPH GREAR according to law

PAGE 62B
PRESENT:
CHARLES THOMAS ESQUIRE MAYOR,
GENTLEMAN ALDERMAN: LEWIS HANSFORD, WILLIAM AITCHESON, CORNELIUS CALVERT

HARDRESS WALLER, JOINER, WILLIAM and JONATHAN SIMPSON Butchers and Partners
BASSET and ALEXANDER MOSELEY Merchants and Partners
PAUL LOYALL Gentleman
CHARLES GODFREY Mariner
FRANCIS and GRIFFIN PEART Merchants and Partners
NICHOLAS WONYCOTT Merchant
EDWARD ARCHER Merchant
LEWIS HANSFORD and COMPANY Merchants
JAMES BALFOUR and DANIEL BARRAUD Merchants and Partners
JONATHAN DISON Carpenter,
JOSEPH CALVERT, JOHN WILSON Merchants
JAMES RAMSAY and JAMES TAYLOR Practitioners of Physick and Partners
JOHN TAYLOR and THOMAS NEWTON Executors of ROBERT TUCKER deceased
SAMUEL BOUSH Gentleman,
GEORGE GORDON, DAVID CHEVIS, DAVID CROSS, Merchants
WILLIAM RASCOW WILSON CURLE Gentleman,
WILLIAM CHISHOLM, and JOHN BOWNESS Merchants and Partners
WILLIAM BOLDEN and JOHN LAWRENCE and Company Merchants & Partners
ARCHIBALD WHITE and Company Merchants
DUNCAN CAMPBELL Mariner
JOHN CARRIE Merchant
NEIL MCCOUL Merchant
WILLIAM JACOBS Planter
JOHN GAWITH Mariner
ARCHIBALD CAMPBELL Gentleman
THOMAS BRESSIE Merchant
JOSEPH MITCHELL, JOHN LEWELLING, WILLIAM STEVENSON, THOMAS THOMPSON, MATT ROTHERY and JOEL MOHUN Partners and GEORGE

BRUCE Plaintiff
Against Re:
SARAH WINTERTON an infant daughter and heiress of NICHOLAS WINTERTON Deceased ANN WINTERTON widow and GEORGE ABYVON Gentleman admin of the said NICHOLAS WINTERTON Deceased Defendants
This day came as well the Plaintiffs by their Attorney's and the Defendant Sarah by her guardian. The Defendant Ann by her Attorney and the Defendant GEORGE in his proper person and the Commissioners appointed to state and examine the claims and demands of the Plaintiffs and Defendant GEORGE ABYVON and also to set aside the dower of the Defendant ANN in the Land in the Borough of Norfolk in the bill mentioned this day made their report in these words to wit:
Norfolk Borough:
PAGE 63
In Obedience to an Order of the Court in Chancery for Norfolk Borough bearing date the 23rd day of February 1771 and hereto annexed. We the Subscribers being first sworn have examined the claims and demands of the several persons hereafter mentioned and in the said order named against the Estate of the Said NICHOLAS WINTERTON and do find that there is now due from the said Estate to the several persons hereafter named the several and respective sums of money hereafter mentioned that is to say:
To THOMAS BRESSIE due by bond with interest as per bond to which we refer 17 pounds, 4 shillings and 1 penny.
ARCHIBALD CAMPBELL due by bond with interest as per bond to which we refer 39 pounds, 16 shillings and 2 pence.
JONATHAN DISON due by an award on an arbitration bond 24 pounds, 6 shillings and 7 pence.
GEORGE ABYVON administrator balance of his account current money being so much paid in discharging judgements and costs obtained on bonds more than assets came to his hands 22 pounds, 1 shillings and 2 pence.

HARDRESS WALLER due by account 18 pounds, 3 shillings and 3 pence.

WILLIAM SIMPSON surviving partner of JONATHAN SIMPSON due by account 6 pounds 3 shillings.

BASSET and ALEXANDER MOSELEY per account 9 pounds.

PAUL LOYALL per account 16 pounds, 17 shillings and 8 pence.

CHARLES GODFREY per account 19 pounds and 2 pence.

FRANCIS and GRIFFIN PEART per account 8 pounds, 5 shillings and 8 pence.

NICHOLAS WONYCOTT by decree 30 pounds, 7 shillings and 10 pence.

EDWARD ARCHER by decree 40 pounds,18 shillings.

LEWIS HANSFORD and COMPANY by decree no proof.

BALFOUR and BARRAUND by decree 1 pound 9 shillings and 2 pence.

PAGE 63B

JOSEPH CALVERT and JOHN BOWNESS by decree 6 pounds, 8 shillings and 10 pence.

WILLIAM BOLDEN and JOHN LAWRENCE by account 2 pounds, 8 shillings and 11 pence.

ARCHIBALD WHITE and Company by decree 17 pounds, 6 shillings.

DUNCAN CAMPBELL by note and receipt 21 pounds, 8 shillings and 1 penny.

JOHN CARRIE by account 9 pounds, 8 shillings and 10 pence.

NEIL MCCOUL by account 18 pounds, 10 shillings and 3 pence.

WILLIAM JACOBS by account 11 pounds, 19 shillings and 3 pence.

JOHN GAWITH by account 4 pounds and 6 pence.

JOSEPH MITCHELL by account 10 pounds, 12 shillings and 4 pence.

JOHN LEWELLING by account 2 pounds.

WILLIAM STEVENSON by account 5 pounds, 9 shillings and 7 pence.

THOMAS THOMPSON by account 10 pounds, 5 shillings and 3 pence.

MATTHEW ROTHERY and JOEL MOHUN by account 4 pounds, 16 shillings and 8 pence.

GEORGE BRUCE by account 15 pounds, 10 shillings and 3 pence.

GEORGE ABYVON private account 115 pounds, 15 shillings and 1 penny. Amounting in the whole to 567 pounds, 12 shillings and 3 pence. And we have set apart the dower of the Defendant ANN in the land situate in the said Borough in the said order mentioned in manner following that is to say the back rooms of the dwelling house below and above stairs, also the kitchen and smoke house together with so much of the said land as is contained in the following bounds to wit:

Beginning at the southward post of the back door of the said dwelling house and returning hence easterly a straight course to a post at the corner of the back door and garden, thence south westwardly along the paling of the back yard to the street called the Back Street. Thence northwestwardly along the said street to another post of the yard near the southeast corner of the dwelling house thence to the said corner. Thence along the side of the said house to the beginning. And to have the use of the back door and of the passages and stairs to both her said rooms, yard, and kitchen. Unless the heir or person claiming under the said decedent will at their own expense make a back door in the lower room set apart to said ANN and also erect a winding staircase to passage out of said room to her upper room aforesaid and build up the present cellar door which is now in the yard set apart by us to the said ANN WINTERTON.

Given under our hands

PAGE 64

This 20th day of March 1771.

GOODRICH BOUSH, JAMES MARSDEN, and JOHN GREENWOOD.

And it appearing to the Court that the Slaves and personal estate of the Intestate NICHOLAS WINTERTON in the bill named to the amount of 204 pounds, 10 shillings and 9 pence have been applied towards the discharging the debts due from the said Intestate at the time of his death by bonds and other Specialties when with his real estate was chargeable. It is Therefore, ordered and decreed that the dower so as aforesaid set apart be held firm and stable and that GEORGE ABYVON make sale of the other 2/3 of the lot with the appurtenances and the reversion of the other third part and pay the Plaintiff THOMAS BRESSIE 16 pounds, 4 shillings and 1 penny with interest on the same after the rate of 5% per annum to be computed from April 14, 1767 to the day of sale and GEORGE ABYVON retain 22 pounds, 1 shilling and 2 pence being so much over paid in discharging judgements and costs on bonds more than assets came to his hands that he proportion the over plus arising from the sale of the said lot among the other Plaintiffs and himself agreeable to the several demands due by the simple contracts. And it is further ordered and decreed that the said GEORGE ABYVON also make sale of the lot of land in the Town of Fredericksburg in the bill mentioned giving notice of the time and place in the Virginia Gazette. (WILLIAM RASCOW WILSON CURLE Attorney for the Defendant ANN agreeing to accept of a 9th part of the account of sales thereof in lieu of her down. LEWIS HANSFORD one of the Plaintiffs having disclaimed his demand and DAVID CHEVIS claim having been refused by the Commissioners) and that the said GEORGE ABYVON make his report to the Court.

On the Petition of EMANUEL ANTONIO setting forth that he is a free born Subject of his Catholic Majesty and that he is detained in Slavery by JAMES CAMPBELL and Company and prayed that Council might be assigned him to make inquiry thereof. On consideration thereof WILLIAM RASCOW WILSON CURLE Gentleman is assigned Council

PAGE 64B

To take the petitioner to make such inquiry and report the same tomorrow.

TIMOTHY TRYTITLE Lessee of JOHN CHAPMAN Plaintiff
Against Re: In Ejectment
PETER DALE Defendant
This day came the parties by their Attorney's and there upon came also a Jury to wit:
JONATHAN DISON, RICHARD BICKERDICK, RICHARD TAYLOR, THOMAS BUTT, JOHN WOODSIDE, WILLIAM COLLEY, STEPHEN TANKARD, HOWARD POOLE, THOMAS THOMPSON, CHARLES COOPER, JOHN WILSON and JAMES COOPER who being elected tried and sworn the truth to speak upon the issue joined (but before the Jury withdrew the Plaintiff by his Attorney tendered his bill of exceptions the Defendants evidence TIMOTHY TRYTITLE LESSEE of JOHN CHAPMAN before MAXIMILIAN CALVERT ESQUIRE MAYOR, GEORGE ABYVON, PAUL LOYALL, CHARLES THOMAS, LEWIS HANSFORD, JAMES TAYLOR, CORNELIUS CALVERT Gentleman Justices of Our Lord the King of the Court of Hustings for the Borough of Norfolk at the Court house in said Borough prosecuted against HENRY HOLDFAST a certain plea of Trespass and Ejectment by writ of the said Lord the King supposing by his declaration on his writ aforesaid.
(AUTHOR NOTE: LINE IS PARTLY MISSING HERE.)
For that whereas one JOHN CHAPMAN on the first day of May 1768 at the Parish of Elizabeth River and Borough aforesaid had demised granted and to form let to the said TIMOTHY one Messuage, one tenement and a piece or parcel of land with the appurtenances lying and being in the said Borough aforesaid situate on the southside of the Main Street to have and to hold the tenement aforesaid with the appurtenances unto the said TIMOTHY and his assigns from the last day of April then last past unto the full end and term of 10 years thence next following and fully to be completed and end by virtue of which demise the said TIMOTHY into the tenement aforesaid with the appurtenances entered and was there of possessed until the said HENRY afterwards to wit the same first day of May in the year aforesaid with force and arms into the tenements aforesaid with the appurtenances

PAGE 65

And upon the possession of him the said TIMOTHY entered and the said TIMOTHY from his farm aforesaid his term aforesaid not then nor yet ended. Ejected expelled and removed from his possession thereof held out and still does hold out and other enormities to him then and there offered against the Peace of Our Lord the King and to the damages of the said TIMOTHY 10 pounds and therefore, he bring his suit.
WILLIAM RASCOW WILSON CURLE for Plaintiff

JOHN DOE and RICHARD ROE pledges sir you may see by this declaration in Ejectment I am sued for the premises above mentioned being in your possession and to which I have no title. If therefore you claim any there to and intend to defend it, you must appear on Monday the 25th of this instant December at the Courthouse in the Borough aforesaid and make your defense otherwise is hall suffer judgement to pass against me by default and you will be turned out of possession.
Your friend, HENRY HOLDFAST
To MR. PETER DALE. Tenant in possession Norfolk Borough December 4th, 1769
To which said declaration a certain PETER DALE Tenant in possession by JAMES HOLT his Attorney came into the same Court before the said Justices who was admitted Defendant in the room of HENRY HOLDFAST and Defended the force and inquiry when and confessed the lease entry and ouster aforesaid and pleaded that he was not guilty of the trespass and ejectment aforesaid in the declaration aforesaid mentioned and of this he put himself on the Country and the said TIMOTHY like wise.
Now here at the trial of the issue aforesaid between the parties aforesaid by WILLIAM RASCOW WILSON CURLE The Council for the Plaintiff to maintain the issue aforesaid on the part of the Plaintiff and to prove the title of the said TIMOTHY TRYTITLE to the demised premises at the time of the demise aforesaid made were given in evidence to the Jurors aforesaid the deposition of THOMAS DRUREY taken pursuant to a writ issuing out of said Court requiring THOMAS NEWTON JR. and JOHN MATHIAS Gentleman greeting. Know ye that we trusting to your fidelity and provident Circumspection in diligently examined THOMAS DRUREY a witness on behalf of JOHN CHAPMAN Plaintiff against PETER DALE Defendant in a suit of Ejectment in our Hustings Court of Norfolk Borough depending on and undetermined command you or any two or more of you that at such certain days and places as you shall appoint you assemble yourselves and the witness aforesaid before you or any two or more of you, you call

PAGE 65B

And cause to come and diligently examine on the Holy Evangelist of Almighty God
And his examination into our Borough Court of Norfolk distinctly and plainly without delay you shall send and certify enclosed. Returning to us also this writ witness JOHN BOUSH Deputy Clerk of our Said Court at the Courthouse the 26th day of December in the 11th year of our Reign. JOHN BOUSH Deputy Clerk which deposition is in these words to wit:
JOHN CHAPMAN against PETER DALE
The deposition of THOMAS DRUREY aged 75 years and upwards taken on behalf of the Plaintiff.
The said THOMAS DRUREY being sworn upon the Holy Evangelist of Almighty God deposes that he personally knew a certain WILLIAM WISE who lived in Charles Parish in York County and Colony of Virginia that the said WILLIAM WISE had 2 children namely WILLIAM and ELIZABETH and this deponent believes they were by one mother for that so it was always believed, and the contrary was never to his knowledge supposed that he knew not that he can recollect the mother of them.
That the said WILLIAM the son and brother of ELIZABETH had afterwards a son named WILLIAM WISE who removed from the said Parish to Norfolk Town where this deponent has personally seen him and knew that he lived in the said town somewhere near the place where the defendant now lives and that the said WILLIAM as this deponent believes was married to a certain ANN THOMPSON.
That the said ELIZABETH the daughter of WILLIAM the grandfather, Sister of WILLIAM the father and Aunt of WILLIAM the son was married to a certain JOHN CHAPMAN who was to the best of the deponents knowledge her first and only husband having never heard of her having any other that by him she had a son named JOHN who was her eldest and believed she had other children but does not remember to have known any of them.

That the said JOHN CHAPMAN the son of ELIZABETH married ANN ALLAN and never had any other wife to the said Deponents knowledge that he knows the said JOHN and ANN had children believes the Plaintiff maybe one of them but does not know it of his own knowledge and further the said deponent says not THOMAS DRUREY (here spelled with W, DREWREY) sworn before us and took in person of the Defendant and the Plaintiffs Attorney. THOMAS NEWTON JR., JOHN MATTHIAS also the deposition of BENNET KIRBY which was duly taken in these words to wit:

PAGE 66

Deposition of BENNET KIRBY age about 66 years. Taken By virtue of a commission here unto annexed on behalf of JOHN CHAPMAN Plaintiff against PETER DALE Defendant in a Suit in Ejectment now depending in the Hustings Court of Norfolk Borough both parties with their Attorney's being present.

The deponent being first sworn upon the HOLY EVANGELIST deposes and says:

That he personally knew may years a certain WILLIAM WISE of Charles Parish in York County that he had issue his eldest son and heir at law WILLIAM whom he also well knew and that he WILLIAM the son had issue WILLIAM his son and heir at law whom he likewise well knew that the last-mentioned WILLIAM married ANN THOMPSON and moved down to the Borough of Norfolk aforesaid.

That the first mentioned WILLIAM WISE had also issue ELIZABETH sister of the whole blood to WILLIAM the son that the said ELIZABETH intermarried with one JOHN CHAPMAN and had issue JOHN their eldest son and heir at law which said JOHN the son intermarried with a certain ANNE ALLAN and had issue JOHN the Plaintiff their heir at law and further this deponent says not.

BENNET KIRBY sworn to before us this 26th day of February 1771

CHARLES THOMAS, GEORGE ABYVON, GOODRICH BOUSH,

Also, the Deposition of ROBERT WISE which was duly taken in these words. In obedience to a writ from the worshipful the Court of the Borough of Norfolk bearing date the 26th of February in the 11th year of his present Majesty King George the third.

We ROBERT SMITH Gentleman one of his Majesty's Justice of the Peace for the County of York and BENNET KIRBY of the same County Gentleman have accordingly met and have taken the deposition of ROBERT WISE.

The deposition of ROBERT WISE of lawful age being first sworn on the HOLY EVANGELIST OF ALMIGHTY GOD deposes that he does not remember anything relative to his Grandfather WILLIAM WISE but remembers to have been at the house of MR. JOHN CHAPMAN several times and always called the wife of the said JOHN CHAPMAN, Aunt as he had been informed, she was he was so young he could not know himself and being above 7 years of age. And being asked what he knows of his brother WILLIAM WISE his removal from this County to the County of Norfolk says that he remembers and knows his brother WILLIAM did remove from this County to the County of Norfolk at which time he was intermarried with

PAGE 66B

One ANN THOMPSON being asked whether he ever was at Norfolk during the time of his brothers' residence there.

Says that about 12 or 15 months after his said brother had resided in Norfolk, he came over to York County and invited this despondent to return with him, which he did, and that his said brother then lived in the house now in the possession of PETER DALE or in a house situation the same lot of ground now in the possession of the said DALE and in dispute between JOHN CHAPMAN and the said DALE.

ROBERT WISE. The within deposition taken before us this 9th day of March 1771

ROBERT SMITH, BENNET KIRBY

Also attested copy of the will of WILLIAM WISE dated the 13th day of January 1717

In the Name of God Amen this 14th day of January 1717

I WILLIAM WISE of Charles Parish in York County in the Colony of Virginia being of perfect mined and memory thanks be given unto Almighty God do make, ordain this my last will and testament in manner and form following that is to say:

First and chiefly I give my soul into the hands of Almighty God who gave it me and my body I commend unto the earth to be decently buried at the discretion of my executrix here after named not doubting at the general resurrection. I shall receive the same against in manner and form following:

I give and bequeath unto my loving wife SARAH WISE the use of the plantation where on I now dwell during her natural life with all house's orchards all the other appurtenances there unto belonging with privilege to clear what grounds she shall occasion for plant. Also, for firewood, fencing and board timber for her use.

Also, I give unto my loving wife and to her disposal one Negro man named SAM and one Negro woman named EDITH and the labor of one Negro man named WILL during her natural life but after her death, I give the said WILL unto my grandson WILLIAM CHAPMAN son of JOHN CHAPMAN by ELIZABETH his wife. Also, I give and bequeath unto my son WILLIAM WISE the Plantation where on he

PAGE 67

Now dwells with all housing and orchards and all other appurtenances there unto belong. Also, I give unto my said son WILLIAM the plantation where on I now dwell after the decease of my wife all the aforesaid plantations and widens of land. I give unto my said son WILLIAM and to the heirs of his body lawfully begotten, also I give unto my said son my seal ring and still but he not to have it before my wife decease.

Also, I give unto my grandson WILLIAM WISE son of my son WILLIAM, one Negro boy named JAMES and my silver tankard but he not to have that before my wife's death. Also, I give unto my granddaughter MARY WISE daughter of my son WILLIAM one Negro woman named SUSAN. Also, I give and bequeath unto my son in law JOHN CHAPMAN and my daughter ELIZABETH his wife use of all my lands and plantations in York Hampton Parish during both their lives and after both their decease then I give the aforesaid plantation and divides of land unto the two eldest sons JOHN and WILLIAM CHAPMAN my two grandsons and their heirs forever to be equally divided between them. I also give unto my son in law JOHN CHAPMAN and ELIZABETH his wife one Negro man Named ROBIN and all my cattle and sheep that I have upon that plantation where he now dwells. Also, I give unto my grandson WILLIAM CHAPMAN one Negro Boy named JACK and my horse shaver and one good feather bed and furniture. Also, I give unto my granddaughter ANN CHAPMAN, one Negro Boy named DICK.

Also, I give unto my granddaughter FRANCES WISE daughter of my son CHARLES WISE, deceased the plantation and dividend of land in Charles Parish York County, where the widow of SOPER now dwells and to her heirs. Also, I give unto my said Granddaughter one Negro Boy HUMPHREY and one Negro girl named MOLL but if it should please God that my said Granddaughter FRANCES should depart this life before she be one and twenty years of age or married then I give the aforesaid tract of land and planation unto my son WILLIAM WISE and his heirs forever.

Also, I give the aforesaid Negro called HUMPHREY unto my grandson WILLIAM WISE. Also, I give the aforesaid named girl MOLL unto my granddaughter ELIZABETH CHAPMAN, I also give unto my said granddaughter FRANCES WISE one new silver tankard marked F.W. on the bottom and 6 silver spoons marked F.W. but if it shall please God that my said

PAGE 67B

Granddaughter shall depart this life before she be one and twenty years of age or married then I give the aforesaid tankard and spoon unto my son WILLIAM WISE.

Also, I give unto my son in law THOMAS RAY all my wearing clothes, my silver headed cane and for the remainder of my personal estate which I have not disposed of I give the one half of it to my loving wife and the other half of it I give unto my granddaughter FRANCES WISE, but if it should please god that my said Granddaughter FRANCES should depart this world before she comes to the age of one and twenty years or married then I give the same one half of my estate to be divided between my son WILLIAM WISE and my son in law JOHN CHAPMAN and my will is that my wife have the management of my granddaughter FRANCES WISE her estate during her life and after whom she s hall appoint and of this my last will and testament. I make my loving wife SARAH WISE my full and sole executrix and I do hereby utterly disallow and revoke all other wills and testaments, legacies and executors or executrix by me in any wise before this time named ratified and confirm this and one other to be my last will and testament.

In witness whereof I have here unto set my hand and seal the day and year above written. WILLIAM WISE (SEAL), signed, sealed, published, and delivered by me my last will and testament in the presence of ANTHONY BUTTS, CHARLES CALTHROP, EDWARD GRAY, ALEXANDER BARTLETT x his mark.

This last will and testament of WILLIAM WISE deceased was proved in Court by WILLIAM WISE who made oath to it and being proved by the oaths of ANTHONY BUTTS, EDWARD GRAY and ALEXANDER BARTLET witness there to is admitted to record.

TESTE: PHILIP LIGHTFOOT COURT CLERK

Also, the copy of a parish register mentioning the birth of ELIZABETH and FRANCES WISE daughters of WILLIAM WISE by MARY his wife born September 2nd, 1674, in these words to wit:

ELIZABETH & FRANCES (twins) daughters of WILLIAM WISE by MARY his wife born September 2nd, 1674, a copy.

TESTE: JOSEPH DAVENPORT Rector HINDE RUSSELL 68.

Also, another mentioning the Baptism of WILLIAM son of WILLIAM by MARY his wife on the 10th of June 1677 in these words to wit:

PAGE 68

WILLIAM son of WILLIAM WISE by MARY his wife born - Baptized June 10th, 1677, a copy

Teste: JOSEPH DAVENPORT RECTOR HINDE RUSSELL 68

Also, another mentioning the birth of WILLIAM WISE son of WILLIAM by SARAH his wife November 20th, 1708, in their words to wit:

WILLIAM WISE son of WILLIAM by SARAH his wife was born November 20th, 1708, a true copy. JOSEPH DAVENPORT, RECTOR HINDE RUSSELL 68

Also, another mentioning the birth of JOHN CHAPMAN son of JOHN by ELIZABETH his wife January 24th, 1701, in these words to wit:

JOHN CHAPMAN son of JOHN by ELIZABETH his wife was born January 24th, 1701, a true copy.

Teste: JOSEPH DAVENPORT RECTOR HINDE RUSSELL 68

Also, another mentioning of the birth of JOHN CHAPMAN son of JOHN CHAPMAN JR. by ANN his wife in these words to wit:

JOHN CHAPMAN son of JOHN CHAPMAN JR. and ANN his wife born the 11th day of February 1725/26.

JOSEPH STROUD Clerk of York Hampton Parish

Also, an Inventory & Appraisement and account of Sales of the Estate of WILLIAM WISE the younger rendered by JOHN TAYLOR and SAMUEL SMITH administrators in these words and figures to wit:

Pursuant to an Order of Norfolk County Court bearing date the 20th of May 1737

We the subscribers being first sworn have appraised the Estate of WILLIAM WISE deceased as follows to wit:

1 oval table oak 15/, 1 large square table oak 15/	L1.10.0
1 Smaller Table 7/6, 1 dozen Leather Bottom English Chairs old 65/	3.12.6
1 Looking Glass in the Hall	1.10.0
1 Pair Pistols & Holster & Holster Caps	1.10.0
1 Chest lock & key old	0.10.0
1 Bed, Blanket, pair sheets & Rug	5.0.0
1 Bed tick, 17/6, 1 Cross leg table & warming pan 7/	1.4.6

1 Trunk 7/6, 1 Small old trunk 1/3	0.8.9
3 DELPH BOWLS, 1 Pint Decanter, A Salt & Apothecary Medicine Pot	0.4.0

PAGE 68B

1 Bed, Pillow, Pair Sheets, Bedstead & Upstairs & Old Rug Hall chamber	3.0.0
1 Bed, Bedstead, Cord Hyde, pair blankets & Rug in the Parlor Chamber	2.00
22 Plates, 5 Dishes, 2 Brass Candlesticks	1.18.0
3 Iron pots 12/, 1 Brass Skillet 4/ 1 Frying pan & spit 5/6	1.2.6
1 Anchor & some rigging in pledge for a debt to the estate, the anchor 20/ & the rigging 20/	2.0.0
1 Negro Man named COOPER, L30, 1 Negro Man JAMMY L25	55.0.0
1 Old Negro Woman SUE	15.0.0
Part of a lot in Norfolk Town with the buildings thereon	60.0.0
1 Negro girl named NAN L22, 1 Negro Girl named HANAH L15	37.0.0

May 24, 1737, by ROBERT TUCKER, ABEL LEWELLING, PETER MALBONE, JOHN KEEN,
Norfolk Schedule Account Sales of the Estate of WILLIAM WISE deceased auction June 1, 1737, EDWARD MAGEE

2 Large Tables 16/1, 12 leather bottom Chairs 4/2 50/	L3.6.0
1 Large looking glass, 44/6, 1 chest lock & key 6/3	2.10.9
1 bed blanket pair sheets & rug 86/6, 2 old trunks 6/11	4.13.5
1 bed pillow pair sheets 40/7 1 smaller trunk 35/5	3.16.0
3 iron pots 16/3, 1 brass skillet, 1 frying pan & spit 15/2	1.11.5
12 soup plates to ditto 16/3, 5 dishes 10 plates, 2 porringers old 23/11	2.0.0
1 pair money scales	4.2 1/2
ALEXANDER MCPHERSON	L18.2.0
1 Small table 8/3, a parcel of Earthen ware 5/	13.3
1 pine table and warming pan	8.0
MR. JOHN TAYLOR	L1.1.3
1 Small anchor	1.0.0
MR. SAMUEL SMITH, DR. 1 pair pistols holsters & holster caps	1.13.6
MR. ROBERT COOKE, DR. a parcel of old rigging	1.2.0
MR. JOHN KEEN, DR. 1 bed tick	0.12.0
JOSEPH ROBERTS, DR. 2 old rush bottom chairs	0.2.6
MR. PETER DALE, DR. PART OF A LOT & HOUSE	76.2.6

PAGE 69

MR. JOSIAH SMITH, DR. 1 pair brass candlesticks	L. 5.6
	100.1.3

Also, the testimony of MASON MILLER who deposes that he personally knew WILLIAM WISE who died in Norfolk but that he had issue in the deponent's knowledge WILLIAM and MARY. That WILLIAM died in the year 1745 or 1745 and MARY was then about 14 years and that she was married to one DIER in the year 1748 then very young and that she has been dead about 4 years leaving issue an infant daughter who is since dead. The Council for the Defendant to prove that the said TIMOTHY had no Seiren Interest on title in or to the aid land and tenement and that he could not recover possession of the premises in the declaration aforesaid mentioned and that the said PETER was not guilty of the trespass and ejectment aforesaid on the part of the said PETER to the jurors aforesaid in evidence offered on attested copy of the will of WILLIAM WISE late of Norfolk in these words to wit:

In the Name of God Amen: I WILLIAM WISE do make this my last will.

Item: I give and bequeath to my loving wife ANN WISE, a Negro man called CUPER, a Negro Woman called SUE, to her during her natural life and after her decease then to be sold and the money equally divided among my children.

Item: I give and bequeath unto my loving son WILLIAM WISE, a Negro boy called JAMES to him, and his heirs lawfully begotten forever and if he dies without heir to return to the rest of my children and to be sold for ready money and the money to be equally divided among them.

Item: I give and bequeath unto my daughter MARY WISE a Negro Girl called NAN, to her and her heirs forever only the first living child that she shall bear to my son CHARLES WISE to him and his heirs forever.

Item: I give to my loving son JOHN WISE a Negro Girl called HANNAH to him and his heirs lawfully begotten by his body forever.

I give and bequeath to my loving wife ANN WISE all my household goods until my children come of age then to be equally divided amongst them as they come of age.

I leave the use of the lot and house to my loving wife ANN WISE to bring up my children to schooling

PAGE 69B

Provided that she is not forced to sell it to pay my debts.

I also give and bequeath to my loving son WILLIAM WISE one seal ring marked W.W.

I also give and bequeath to my daughter MARY WISE one large ring to her and her heirs forever.

WILLIAM WISE, Signed, and Sealed in presence of us: ABEL LEWELLING, RICHARD DAVIS, ELIZABETH THOMPSON x her mark.

The above will was proved May 20th, 1737

A copy TESTE: JOHN BOUSH D. 68

Also, a Deed of Bargain & sale from JOHN TAYLOR and SAMUEL SMITH administrators with the will of the said WILLIAM annexed to the said PETER DALE the Defendant in these words to wit:

This Indenture made the 17th day of June 1737 between JOHN TAYLOR and SAMUEL SMITH JR. of the Borough of Norfolk Gentleman administrators (testament annexed) of the Estate of WILLIAM WISE late of the Borough of Norfolk aforesaid deceased of the one part and PETER DALE of the aforesaid Borough Ship Carpenter of the other part whereas the said WILLIAM WISE did in his life time by his last will and testament in writing devise among other things part of a lot and house there on situate in Norfolk Town to be sold for the payment of his debts and by the said will did appoint his wife ANN WISE sole executrix of this said will, which said ANN at a Court held for the County of Norfolk in her proper person came into Court and utterly refused to take upon herself the burden of the execution of the said will and whereas the said JOHN TAYLOR and SAMUEL SMITH JR. on application to the said Court and their performing what the law in that case esquire. Administration with the will annexed was granted them as greatest creditors to the said WILLIAM WISE and whereas the said JOHN TAYLOR and SAMUEL SMITH JR. pursuant to the said will on the first day of June last past caused the said land inter alia to be sold after due publication by the way of auction to the highest bidder.

The said PETER DALE for the sum of 76 pounds 2 shillings and 6 pence current money of Virginia.

Now this indenture witnesses that the said JOHN TAYLOR and SAMUEL SMITH JR. for and in consideration of all which recited promises and also in consideration of the sum of 75 pounds 2 shillings

PAGE 70

6 pence current money to them in hand paid before the sealing and delivery of these presents by the said PETER DALE the receipt whereof they do hereby acknowledge and thereof and every part thereof acquit. Exonerate and discharge him the said PETER DALE his heirs executors and administrators have bargained sold aliened and enfeoffed and confirmed and by these presents do bargain, sell, alien, enfeoff and confirm unto the said PETER DALE all the aforementioned piece or part of a lot of land with a small house thereon wherein JOHN YOUNG now dwells situate on the south side of the Main Street of Norfolk Town according to the Bounds there of together with all houses, buildings, gardens, fence, pails privileges advantages hereditaments and appurtenances and all the estate right title interest property claim and demand rents issues and profits of the said land and premises or any part thereof to have and to hold the said piece of land and premises with the appurtenances unto him the said PETER DALE his heirs and assigns forever to the only proper use comfit and behoof of him the said PETER DALE his heirs and assigns forever in fee simple in as full large and ample manner to all intents and purposes as the said JOHN TAYLOR and SAMUEL SMITH JR. in their capacity aforesaid are impowered to make alter, sell, alien and convey unto him the said PETER DALE his heirs and assigns forever.

In witness where of the said JOHN TAYLOR and SAMUEL SMITH JR. have here unto set our hands and seals the day and year first above written.

JOHN TAYLOR and seal, SAMUEL SMITH JR. and sealed and delivered and livery seisin duly made given and received upon the land herein specified by Turf and the latch of the door in the name of the whole, to hold unto the said PETER DALE, his heirs and assigns according to the purpose and true meaning of the above deed in the presence of us SIMON HANCOCK, ABEL LEWELLING, A. MCPHERSON,

I ANN MAGEE late wife of the above-named WILLIAM WISE deceased do by these presents relinquish all my right and title of down of and into the land and premises above mentioned witness my hand this 17th day of June 1737

ANN MAGEE x her mark

Present: SIMON HANCOCK, ABEL LEWELLING, A. MCPHERSON Norfolk County.

At a Court held the 17th day of June 1737. JOHN TAYLOR and SAMUEL SMITH JR. acknowledges the

PAGE 70B

within deed to PETER DALE, also ANN MAGEE acknowledges her relinquishment of her dower in and to the land in said deed specified all which at the motion of the said PETER DALE are admitted to record.

TESTE: SOLO WILSON COURT CLERK.

Also, an attested copy of the said administrators account current of their testator's estate duly admitted and recorded in these words to wit: 1737 DR. The Estate of WILLIAM WISE deceased to administrations CR. June 21st.

TO HENRY GRISTOCK Account by Receipt	L0.11.7
TO SAM SMITH ditto L50.12.7 TO ABEL LEWELLING L1.10.9	52.3.4
TO SOL. WILSON L2.11.6 TO ALEXANDER MCPHERSON 3.8.9	6.0.3
TO JAMES GILESS L5.9.1 TO MAYOR BOUSH L12.10	17.19.1
TO JOHN KEEN L1.9.5 TO SAM POWERS15/ TO NANCY HADDON 8/9	2.13.2
TO JO. SMITH L4.16.5 1/2 TO JOHN TAYLOR L11.0.0	15.16.5 1/2
TO DOCTOR RAMSAY L2.1.10 TO JOHN DRUREY BALANCE 18/6	3.0.4
TO EDWARD MAGEE'S Account L1.16. TO MR. NIMMO FEE 15/	2.11.0
TO ROBERT DIBBS Account paid ABEL LEWELLING	6.3
BALANCE DUE TO THE ESTATE	1.19.9 1/2
1737 JUNE 21ST	L103.1.3
By Sundries sold as by account sales	L100.1.3
Rent Received from YOUNG	3.0.0
Norfolk June 23rd, 1737, errors excepted paid SAM SMITH JR.	L103.1.3

And OLD JOHN TAYLOR This 25th June 1737 audited the account pursuant to an Order of court by us ROBERT TUCKER, ARCHIBALD TAYLOR. Returned July 17, 1737, and order for record and the said WILLIAM RASCOW WILSON CURLE desires the Justices before whom the trial of the issue aforesaid was to inform the Jurors aforesaid and declare to them the law of and upon the premises and that the lease aforesaid to the same Plaintiff made for the reasons aforesaid was valid and that the said TIMOTHY TRYTITLE ought to be restored to the premises aforesaid for the cause as aforesaid. But the same Justices left it indifferently to the Jurors aforesaid to say whether the said matter by the said WILLIAM RASCOW WILSON CURLE in manner and form aforesaid shown was sufficient to restore the said TIMOTHY aforesaid

PAGE 71

To entitle him to his action aforesaid, wherefore the said WILLIAM RASCOW WILSON CURLE because the matter aforesaid by the said WILLIAM RASCOW WILSON CURLE shown and to the Jurors aforesaid in evidence produced and given does not appear nor could in any manner by the verdict of Jurors aforesaid request of the said Justice according to the form of the statue in such case made and provided this present bill which contains in itself the matter aforesaid to the same JURORS by the said WILLIAM RASCOW WILSON CURLE in evidence shown in manner and form aforesaid which said justices aforesaid at the request of the said WILLIAM RASCOW WILSON CURLE to this present bill according to the form of the statue in such case did put their seal in the Kings Court aforesaid this 25th day of March 1771. CHARLES THOMAS and seal, GEORGE ABYVON and seal, ARCHIBALD CAMPBELL and seal, WILLIAM AITCHESON, and seal, upon their oath do say that the Defendant is not guilty of the trespass and ejectment in the declaration mentioned. Therefore, it is considered that the Plaintiff take nothing by his bill but for his false claims be in mercy. And the Defendant go hence without day and recover against the lessor of the Plaintiff his costs by him about his defense in this behalf expended from which Judgement the Plaintiff by his Attorney aforesaid prayed an appeal to the 8th day of the next General Court which on his giving which on his giving bond and security of prosecution on or before the 10th day of April is allowed.

Order is granted MASON MILLER against JOHN CHAPMAN for 50 pounds of tobacco for 2 days attendance in his suit against PETER DALE.

This Court is adjourned until tomorrow 9 O'CLOCK, CHARLES THOMAS MAYOR, TESTE: JOHN BOUSH D.C.C.

PAGE 71B
NORFOLK BOROUGH
At a Hustings Court Held this 26th day of MARCH 1771
PRESENT: CHARLES THOMAS ESQUIRE MAYOR
GENTLEMAN ALDERMEN: GEORGE ABYVON, LEWIS HANSFORD, PAUL LOYALL, JAMES TAYLOR,

Ordinary License is granted JOHN RANSBERG on his complying with the law.
Ordinary License is granted JAMES ATKINSON on his complying with the law.

EMANUEL ANTONIO a Negro Man now in the possession of JAMES CAMPBELL & Company of this Borough on his Petition is allowed to sue for his freedom in forma pauperis and WILLIAM RASCOW WILSON CURLE Gentleman is assigned Guardian and Council to that end, and it is ordered that the said JAMES CAMPBELL & Company do not transport him out of the County of Norfolk and that they treat him humanly during the pending suit.

ADRIEL MILBY Plaintiff
Against Re: In Debt.
WRIGHT WESTCOTT administrator of JOHN WESTCOTT deceased Defendant
This day came as well the Plaintiff by WILLIAM RASCOW WILSON CURLE Gentleman his Attorney as the Defendant in his proper person and the said Defendant acknowledges the Plaintiff action for 56 pounds. Therefore, it is considered that the Plaintiff recover against the said Defendant his debt aforesaid and his costs by him about his suit in this behalf expended to be levied of the goods and chattels of the said Intestate if so, much the said WRIGHT WESTCOTT has in his hands to be administered and if he has it not then the costs are to be levied of his proper goods and chattels and the said Defendant in mercy. But this Judgement is to be discharged by the payment of 28 pounds with interest for the same at the rate of 5% per annum to be computed from October 14, 1769, to the time of payment and costs.

PAGE 72
SAMUEL SAMWAYS Plaintiff
Against Re: In Case
JOHN ASHLEY Defendants
This day came the parties by their Attorney's and there upon came also a Jury to wit: JOHN LIVINGSTON, GEORGE GORDON, JAMES MURPHREE, NICHOLAS POOLE, ELDRED FISHER, DANIEL HUTCHINGS, WILLIAM IVY, STEPHEN TANKARD, JOHN CALVERT, WILLIAM STEVENSON, WRIGHT WESTCOTT and JOHN DISON who being elected tried and sworn the truth to speak upon the issue joined upon their oath do say that the Defendant did assume in manner and form as the Plaintiff against him has declared and do assess the Plaintiff damages by occasion of the non-performance of that assumption to 20 pounds besides his costs.
Therefore, it is considered that the Plaintiff recover against the said Defendant his damages aforesaid in form aforesaid assessed and his cost by him in this behalf expended. And the Defendant in mercy.

HOWARD POOLE, Plaintiff
Against Re: In Case
THOMAS THOMPSON Defendant
This day came the parties by their Attorney's and there upon came also a Jury to wit: RICHARD TAYLOR, JOHN PASTEUR, SIMON PORTLOCK, JOHN LEE, JAMES GILCHRIST, JOSEPH GREAR, EDWARD HANSFORD, JAMES ESTHER, JAMES WALKER, MATTHEW KELLY, RICHARD BICKERDICK and JOHN DUNN who being elected tried and sworn the truth to speak upon the issue joined upon their oath do say that the Defendant did not assume as in pleading he has alleged.
Therefore, it is considered that the Plaintiff take nothing by his bill but for his false claims be in mercy. And the Defendant go hence without day and recover against the Plaintiff his costs by him about his defense in this behalf expended.

Order is granted JOHN RUNSBERG against SAMUEL SAMWAYS for 200 pounds of tobacco for 8 days attendance in his suit against JOHN ASHLEY.

PAGE 72B
Order is granted DINAH GUTTERY against SAMUEL SAMWAYS for 175 pounds of tobacco for 7 days attendance in his suit against JOHN ASHLEY.

JAMES NICHOLSON, WILLIAM NICHOLSON, MATTHEW GODFREY, and DANIEL HUTCHINGS Esquire of JOSHUA NICHOLSON deceased Plaintiff
Against Re: In Debt.
JOHN WILLIAM and JOHN ASHLEY Defendants
This day came as well the Plaintiff by WILLIAM RASCOW WILSON CURLE Gentleman their Attorney as the Defendant JOHN ASHLEY in his proper person. The suit against the other Defendant is discontinued and acknowledges the Plaintiffs action for 59 pounds 13 shillings and 6 pence. Therefore, it is considered that the Plaintiff recover against the said Defendant their Debt aforesaid and their costs by them about their suit in this behalf expended and the said Defendant in mercy. But this Judgement is to be discharged by the payment of 29 pounds 16 shillings and 9 pence with interest for the same at the rate of 5% per annum to be computed from June 10, 1762, to the time of payment and the costs.

MATTHIAS GALE, MARY MOORE, JOSEPH MITCHEL, and JOHN COX complaints against RICHARD ROTHERY an infant and MARY ROTHERY respondents. This day came the complainants by THOMAS BURKE Gentleman their Attorney and leave is given to amend the bill and make GEORGE ABYVON Gentleman executor of HENRY ROTHERY deceased respondent and time is allowed them to consider it.

Order is granted JAMES COOPER against THOMAS THOMPSON for 175 pounds tobacco for 7 days attendance in the suit of HOWARD POOLE against him.

Order is granted GEORGE KELLY against THOMAS THOMPSON for 150 pounds of tobacco for 6 days attendance in the suit of HOWARD POOLE against him.

Order is granted HUGH KELLY against THOMAS THOMPSON for 200 pounds of tobacco for 8 days attendance in the suit of HOWARD POOLE against him.

PAGE 73

Order is granted JOSEPH MITCHELL against THOMAS THOMPSON for 225 pounds tobacco for 9 days attendance in the suit of HOWARD POOLE against him.

Order is granted THOMAS BUTT against HOWARD POOLE for 150 pounds of tobacco for 6 days attendance in the suit of THOMAS THOMPSON against him.

Order is granted CHARLES COOPER against HOWARD POOLE for 200 pounds of tobacco for 8 days attendance in the suit of THOMAS THOMPSON against him.

JAMES GIBSON & Company against NICHOLAS WONYCOTT Dismissed at the Defendants Costs.

JOHN DUNN an infant by JOSEPH CALVERT his next friend Plaintiff
Against Re: In case for slander
WILLIAM MCCAA Defendant
This day came the parties by their Attorney's and there upon came also a Jury to wit: JAMES MURPHREE, MATTHEW KELLY, JAMES WALKER, JAMES ESTHER, WILLIAM IVY, JAMES GILCHRIST, RICHARD BICKERDICK, JOSEPH GREAR, CHARLES COOPER, JOHN PASTEUR, SIMON PORTLOCK and SAMUEL DENBY who being elected tried and sworn the truth to speak upon the issue joined upon their oath do say that the Defendant is guilty of speaking the slanderous words in manner and form as in the declaration against him is alleged and do assess the Plaintiff damages by occasion of the speaking of the slanderous words in the declaration mentioned to 5 pounds besides his costs. Therefore, it is considered that the Plaintiff recover against the said Defendant his damages aforesaid in form aforesaid assessed and his costs by him in this behalf expended and the said Defendant in mercy.

THOMAS NEWTON SR. and JOHN TAYLOR Executors of ROBERT TUCKER deceased Plaintiff
Against Re: In Case
JOSEPH CALVERT Defendant
This day came the parties by their Attorney's and there upon came also a Jury to wit:
JOHN MCLEAN, JOHN DISON, JOEL MOHUN, GEORGE GORDON, NICHOLAS POOLE,

PAGE 73B

WILLIAM STEVENSON, STEPHEN TANKARD, RICHARD TAYLOR, JOHN LIVINGSTON, JOHN LEE, WRIGHT WESTCOTT, and EDWARD HANSFORD who being elected tried and sworn the truth to speak upon the issue joined upon their oath do say that the Defendant did not assume as in pleading he has alleged.
Therefore, it is considered that the Plaintiff take nothing by their bill but for their false claims be in mercy. And the Defendant go hence without day and recover against the Plaintiff his costs by him about his Defense in this Behalf Expended.

Order is granted JOHN LEE against JOHN DUNN an infant by JOSEPH CALVERT his next friend for 175 pounds tobacco for 7 days attendance in his suit against WILLIAM MCCAA.

Order is granted EDWARD HANSFORD against JOHN DUNN an infant by JOSEPH CALVERT his next friend for 175 pounds tobacco for 7 days attendance in his suit against WILLIAM MCCAA.

Order is granted JOHN HICKS against WILLIAM MCCAA for 495 pounds tobacco for 9 days attendance coming and returning 18 miles 5 times and 3 pounds ferriages in the suit of JOHN DUNN an infant by JOSEPH CALVERT his next friend against him.

MATTHEW GODFREY against MARY BROUGH and JOHN WILSON an attachment against the Defendant MARY and the other Defendant pleaded payment issue joined and referred.

PAGE 74

MAXIMILIAN CALVERT against WILLIAM SKINKER Discontinued.

JAMES JOLLIFF SENIOR Plaintiff
Against Re: In Case for Slander
JOHN BIRCKELL Defendant
This day came the parties by their Attorney's and there upon came also a Jury to wit: BASSET MOSELEY, ROBERT TUCKER, THOMAS PRICE, WILLIAM MACKIE, HARDRESS WALLER, JOHN MILLS, DANIEL HUTCHINGS, JOHN HARDY, ANTHONY FLEMING, MASON MILLER, JAMES WALKER and SAMUEL DENBY who being elected tried and sworn the truth to speak upon the issue joined upon their oath do say that the Defendant is not guilty as in pleading he has alleged. Therefore, it is considered that the Plaintiff take nothing by his bill but for his false claims being mercy and the Defendant go hence without day and recover against the Plaintiff his costs by him about his defense in this Behalf expended.

Order is granted JOHN COLLINS against JAMES JOLLIFF SR. for 125 pounds of tobacco for 5 days attendance in his suit against JOHN BRICKELL.

Order is granted BETTY BOLSON alias HOSIER against JAMES JOLLIFF SR. for 100 pounds of tobacco for 4 days attendance in his suit against JOHN BRICKELL.

Order is granted THOMAS ELLIS JR. against JAMES JOLLIFF SR. for 100 pounds of tobacco for 4 days attendance in his suit against JOHN BRICKELL.

Order is granted GEORGE VEALE Gentleman against JOHN BRICKELL for 25 pounds of tobacco for 1 day's attendance in the suit of JAMES JOLLIF SR. against him.

EDWARD HACK MOSELEY against LEWIS HANSFORD Attachment.

JAMES KEMPE and CHARLES WILLIAMSON against JAMES MURDAUGH and JOHN MCLEAN answers filed and time to consider them.

SAMUEL WARNER against EDWARD CANNON. The Defendant pleaded not guilty. Issue joined and referred.

PAGE 74B
MOSES LANGLEY against FRANCES MOORE administratrix of JOHN MOORE deceased and EDWARD PARKE Attachment for answers.

FRANCIS WILLIS JR. Assignee of RICHARD DUNBAR against ROBERT TUCKER plea, issue joined and referred.

RICHARD JOHNSON JR. against MASON MILLER Plea and time.

THOMAS ROBERTS against JOHN ASHLEY. The defendant pleaded not guilty. Issue joined and referred.

LEMUEL ROBERTS against JOHN GUY. The former order of this Court against him the said Defendant and THOMAS TALBOT his bail be confirmed, and a writ of inquiry is awarded him for his damages.

JOHN CRAMOND against SARAH CANN, Executrix of JOHN CANN deceased. The Defendant pleaded that she did not assume issue joined and referred (Notice for books)

WILLIAM SIMPSON against ARCHIBALD OWEN. The Defendant pleaded payment issue joined and referred.

WILLIAM SIMPSON against CHARLES COOPER. The former order of this Court against him the said Defendant and JAMES DUNN his bail be confirmed, and a writ of inquiry is awarded him for his damages.

WILLIAM SIMPSON against JOHN SMITH. The Defendant pleaded that he did not assume issue joined and referred.

MARY ROSS against JOHN COLVILLE. The Defendant pleaded that he did not assume issue joined and referred.

PAGE 75
MALACHI MOUND against CHARLES JENKINS executor of JOSEPH LOCKHART continued.

This Court is adjourned to Court in Course. CHARLES THOMAS MAYOR, TESTE: JOHN BOUSH D.C.C.

NORFOLK BOROUGH
At a Hustings Court Held this 22nd day of APRIL 1771
PRESENT: CHARLES THOMAS ESQUIRE MAYOR
GENTLEMAN ALDERMEN: GEORGE ABYVON, MAXIMILIAN CALVERT, ARCHIBALD CAMPBELL, JAMES TAYLOR, LEWIS HANSFORD

ROBERT TUCKER against CHRISTOPHER RATSEY dismissed at the Defendant's costs.
CHRISTOPHER RATSEY against ROBERT TUCKER dismissed at the Plaintiff costs.

EMANUEL ANTONIO against JAMES CAMPBELL, ARCHIBALD CAMPBELL, WILLIAM AITCHESON, and JAMES PARKER. Special Imparlance as to ARCHIBALD CAMPBELL, WILIAM AITCHESON and JAMES PARKER. And DEDIMUS is granted the Plaintiff to take the depositions of EMANUEL DE ESTRADA and JOSEPH DE VALLAROS giving the Defendants notice and discontinued against JAMES CAMPBELL the other Defendant.

JAMES DUNN against JOHN HARDY Dismissed.

NATHANIEL YOUNG and JOHN SMITH against THOMAS BUTTS an Imparlance.
DUGALL GILCHRIST and SARAH his wife against MARY CROFT an Imparlance.

CHARLES WARREN against MATTHEW ROTHERY by Petition & summons Judgement is granted the Plaintiff for 3 pounds 10 shillings. It is ordered that the Defendant pay the same unto the Plaintiff with costs and fees.

JAMES CAMPBELL & Company against JOSHUA WRIGHT an Imparlance.

PAGE 75B
RICHARD BOOKER assignee of PETER WARREN who was assignee of DANIEL HENDRICKSON against JOSIAH HOFFMIRE. Order against the Defendant and ARRON BARBER his bail.

JOHN GREENWOOD against WILLIAM GRAY Dismissed.
JOHN GREENWOOD against ALEXANDER MARSINGBURG Dismissed.

GEORGE GORDON against JOHN FOWLER Dismissed.
JOHN HUTCHINGS, MATTHEW PHRIPP and SAMUEL BOUSH against ALEXANDER BALL an Imparlance.

JONATHAN DISON and SARAH, his wife against JOHN ASHLEY an Imparlance.

WILLIAM FREEMAN against CHARLES GODFREY. Order against the Defendant and JOSEPH CALVERT Sergeant
THOMAS HEPBURN against JAMES ROGERS. Order against the Defendant and JOSEPH POPE his bail.

JOHN IVY and ELIZABETH his wife against GOODRICH BOUSH & SAMUEL BOUSH an Imparlance.

JAMES CAMPBELL & COMPANY against JOHN RICHARDSON an Imparlance.

RICHARD TEMPLEMAN against JOHN RICHARDSON an Imparlance.

JAMES CAMPBELL and COMPANY against JOHN RICHARDSON by Petition and Summons Judgement is granted the Plaintiff for 5 pounds. It is ordered that the Defendant pay the same unto the plaintiff with costs and fees. And on failure of immediate payment. Ordered that the Sergeant give him 39 lashes on his bare back at the public whipping post.

WILLIAM WESTCOTT against WRIGHT WESTCOTT administrator of JOHN WESTCOTT deceased pleaded not guilty issue joined and referred.

PAGE 76
JAMES GIBSON and COMPANY against EDMUND MORTON JR. Discontinued.

FRANCIS WISHART against JOHN IVY Administrator of WILLIAM IVY deceased an Imparlance.

WILLIAM CHISHOLM and LATTIMER HALSTEAD against JOHN JOY. The Plaintiff by their Attorney moved for Special Bail which is granted. Where upon SAMUEL LANGLEY came into Court and entered himself Special Bail for the Defendant and thereon the Defendant by his Attorney prayed an Imparlance.

ROBERT FRY and MARY his wife against HARDRESS WALLER Dismissed.

HARDRESS WALLER against ROBERT FRY and MARY his wife Dismissed.

Ordinary License is granted LOUISA INMAN and STEPHEN TANKARD ferryman on their complying with the law.

JOHN RICHARDSON against MARK TALBOT. The Plaintiff by his Attorney moved for Special Bail which is granted. Whereupon JOSEPH CALVERT came into Court and entered himself Special Bail for the Defendant and thereon the Defendant by his Attorney prayed an Imparlance.

THOMAS NICHOLSON against CHARLES JENKINS an Imparlance.

WRIGHT WESTCOTT surviving executor of WRIGHT WESTCOTT deceased against JOHN SMITH. Order against the Defendant and JOSEPH CALVERT Sergeant.

MOSES LANGLEY against FRANCES MOORE Administratrix of JOHN MOORE deceased and EDWARD PARK. Answers filed and time to consider them.

GEORGE WEBB and JOSEPH LANGLEY against JOHN BAYNES and NANCY ASHLEY time to consider the bail.

ROBERT NICHOLSON and JOHN BROWN executors of JOHN BROWN deceased Plaintiff
Against Re: In Debt
JOHN SMITH and JOSEPH HUTCHINGS Defendants
This day came the parties by their Attorney's and there upon came also a Jury to wit: JOHN MACLEAN, JAMES DISON, EDWARD PARK, JOHN CALVERT, STEPHEN TANKARD, PHILIP CARBERY, DANIEL HUTCHINGS, ALEXANDER MOSELEY, BARTHOLOMEW THOMPSON, WILLIAM BALLARD, JAMES MURPHREE and JOHN JONES who being elected tried and sworn the truth to speak upon the issue joined upon their oath do say that the Dependents
PAGE 76B
Have not paid the debt in the declaration mentioned. Therefore, it is considered that the Plaintiffs recover against the said Defendants their debt aforesaid amounting to 90 pounds 6 shillings and 6 pence and their costs by them in this behalf expended. And the Defendants in mercy. But this judgement is to be discharged by the payment of 45 pounds 3 shillings and 3 pence with interest for same at the rate of 5% per annum to be computed from February 21, 1769, to the time of payment and the costs.

WILLIAM SIMPSON Plaintiff
Against Re: In Debt
JOHN SMITH Defendant
This day came the parties by their Attorney's and there upon came also a Jury to wit: JOHN MACLEAN, JAMES DISON, EDWARD PARK, JOHN CALVERT, ALEXANDER MC SWEEN, PHILIP CARBERY, DANIEL HUTCHINGS, ALEXANDER MOSELEY, BARTHOLOMEW THOMPSON, WILLIAM BALLARD, JAMES MURPHREE and JOHN JONES who being elected tried and sworn the truth to speak upon the issue joined upon their oath do say that the Dependent have not paid the debt in the declaration mentioned. Therefore, it is considered that the Plaintiffs recover against the said Defendants his debt aforesaid amounting to 42 pounds 9 shillings and 7 pence and his costs by him in this behalf expended. And the Defendant in mercy. But this judgement is to be discharged by the payment of 21 pounds 4 shillings and 9 pence with interest for the same at the rate of 5% per annum to be computed from June 20, 1770, to the time of payment and the costs.

WILLIAM SIMPSON Plaintiff
Against Re: In Case
JOHN SMITH Defendant
This day came the parties by their Attorney's and there upon came also a Jury to wit: JOHN MACLEAN, JAMES DISON, EDWARD PARK, JOHN CALVERT, ALEXANDER MCQUEEN, PHILIP CARBERY, DANIEL HUTCHINGS, ALEXANDER MOSELEY, BARTHOLOMEW THOMPSON, WILLIAM BALLARD, JAMES MURPHREE and JOHN JONES who being elected tried and sworn the truth to speak upon the issue joined upon their oath do say that the Dependent did assume in manner and form as the Plaintiff against him has declared and do assess the Plaintiff damages by occasion of the nonperformance of that assumption to 87 pounds 1 shilling and 7 pence half penny besides his costs. Therefore, it is

considered that the Plaintiffs recover against the said Defendants his damages aforesaid in form aforesaid assessed and his costs by him in this behalf expended. And the Defendant in mercy.

PAGE 77

WILLIAM SIMPSON against CHARLES COOPER Dismissed.

MARY ROSS Plaintiff
Against Re: In Case
JOHN COLVILLE Defendant
This day came the parties by their Attorney's and the Defendant by his Attorney relinquishing his former plea says that he cannot gainsay the Plaintiffs action nor but that he did assume in manner and form as the Plaintiff against him has declared. Therefore, it is considered that the Plaintiff recover against the said Defendant 12 pounds 19 shillings and 2 pence together with her costs by her about her suit in this behalf expended and the said Defendant in mercy.

MATTHEW GODFREY against MARY BROUGH and JOHN WILSON. Discontinued against MARY BROUGH and continued against JOHN WILSON.

Order is granted SAMUEL CALVERT against MARY ROSS for 25 pounds of tobacco for 1 day's attendance in her suit against JOHN COLVILLE.

FRANCIS WILLIS JR. assignee of RICHARD DUNBAR Plaintiff
Against Re: In Case
ROBERT TUCKER Defendant
This day came the parties by their Attorney's and there upon came also a Jury to wit: JOHN MACLEAN, JAMES DISON, EDWARD PARK, JOHN CALVERT, ALEXANDER MCSWEEN, PHILIP CARBERY, DANIEL HUTCHINGS, ALEXANDER MOSELEY, BARTHOLOMEW THOMPSON, WILLIAM BALLARD, JAMES MURPHREE and JOHN JONES who being elected tried and sworn the truth to speak upon the issue joined upon their oath do say that the Dependent did assume in manner and form as the Plaintiff against him has declared and do assess the Plaintiff damages by occasion of the nonperformance of that assumption to 89 pounds 5 shilling besides his costs. Therefore, it is considered that the Plaintiffs recover against the said Defendants his damages aforesaid in form aforesaid assessed and his costs by him in this behalf expended. And the Defendant in mercy.

WILLIAM RONALD and COMPANY Plaintiffs
Against Re: In Case
JOHN LUKE Defendant
This day came as well the Plaintiffs by THOMAS BURKE Gentleman their Attorney as the Defendant in Custody of the Sergeant of this Borough, and the said Defendant says that he cannot gainsay the Plaintiff's action nor but that he did assume in manner and form as the Plaintiff against him have declared. Therefore, it is considered that the Plaintiff

PAGE 77B

Recover against the said Defendant 11 pounds 15 shillings and their costs by them about their suit in this behalf expended and the said Defendant in mercy. And the Plaintiff by their said Attorney agree to allow all just discounts.

THOMAS NEWTON SR., THOMAS NEWTON JR., and PAUL LOYALL, THOMAS ROBERTS, and JOHN TUCKER against ROBERT TUCKER replication and commission.

BENJAMIN BANNERMAN'S MOTION is rejected.

GEORGE ABYVON Gentleman executor of HENRY ROTHERY deceased against MATTHEW ROTHERY Defendant pleaded that he did not assume issue joined and referred.

JAMES KEMPE and CHARLES WILLIAMSON against JAMES MURDAUGH and JOHN MACLEAN replication and commission.

RICHARD JOHNSON JR. against MASON MILLER Replication and issue.

MALACHI MAUND against CHARLES JENKINS executor of JOSEPH LOCKHART Deceased, the Defendant pleaded that his testator did not assume issue joined and referred.

ARCHIBALD WHITE and Company against MARY NICHOLAS. The Defendant pleaded that she is not guilty. Issue joined and referred.

JOHN WOODSIDE against CHARLES JENKINS executor of JOSEPH LOCKHART deceased. The Defendant pleaded that his testator did not assume issue joined and referred.

PHILOMON RUSSELL against ALEXANDER BELL. The Defendant pleaded that he did not assume issue joined and referred.

MATHIAS GALE, MARY MOORE and others against MARY ROTHERY widow and RICHARD ROTHERY infant. Leave is granted the Plaintiffs to take their bill to amend.

ALEXANDER BELL against JOSIAH BUTTS. The Defendant pleaded not guilty. Issue joined and referred.

JOHN CRAMOND Plaintiff
Against Re: In Case
SARAH CANN Executrix of JOHN CANN deceased Defendant
This day came the parties by their Attorney's and there upon came also a Jury to wit:

PAGE 78
DANIEL BARRAUD, JOHN LIVINGSTON, JOHN JONES, WILLIAM BALLARD, ALEXANDER MOSELEY, DANIEL HUTCHINGS, ALEXANDER MC SWEEN, JOHN CALVERT, STEPHEN TANKARD, PHILIP CARBERY, JAMES DISON, and BARTHOLOMEW THOMPSON who being elected tried and sworn the truth to speak upon the issue joined upon their oath do say that the Dependent did not assume as in pleading she has alleged. Therefore, it is considered that the Plaintiffs take nothing by his bill but for his false claims be in mercy. And the Defendants go hence without day and recover against the plaintiff her costs by her about her defense in this behalf expended.

Order is granted ANDREW STEWART against SARAH CANN executrix of JOHN CANN Deceased 61 pounds of tobacco for one day's attendance and returning 12 miles once in the suit of JOHN CRAMOND against her.

Order is granted DUNCAN CAMPBELL against SARAH CANN executrix of JOHN CANN deceased for 25 pounds of tobacco for 1 day's attendance of his wife ANN in the suit of JOHN CRAMOND against her.

Order is granted WILLIAM BELL against SARAH CANN executrix of JOHN CANN deceased for 25 pounds of tobacco for one day attendance in the suit of JOHN CRAMOND against her.

LEMUEL ROBERTS Plaintiff
Against Re: In Case
JOHN GUY Defendant
This day came the Plaintiff by his Attorney and thereupon came also a Jury to wit: JOHN MACLEAN, MATTHIAS CHRISTIAN, NICHOLAS WONYCOTT, RICHARD BICKERDICK, JAMES ESTHER, JOHN CRAMOND, RICHARD TEMPLEMAN, JAMES MURPHREE, RICHARD BASSETTS, JOHN STANHOPE, THOMAS RANDOLPH, and JAMES BAKER who being sworn well and truly to inquire of damages in this suit upon their oath do say that the Plaintiff has sustained damages by occasion of the Breach of Promise in the Declaration mentioned to 1 penny. Therefore, it is considered that the Plaintiff recover against the said Defendant and THOMAS TALBOT his bail his damages aforesaid and one penny costs. And the said Defendant in mercy.

Order is granted JACOB ROACH and JOSIAH TRUSS against JAMES CAMPBELL & COMPANY for 25 pounds of tobacco each for one day's attendance each in their suit against JOHN RICHARDSON.

PAGE 78B
LEMUEL ROBERTS Plaintiff
Against Re: In Trespass
JOHN GUY Defendant
This day came the Plaintiff by his Attorney and thereupon came also a Jury to wit: JOHN MACLEAN, MATTHIAS CHRISTIAN, NICHOLAS WONYCOTT, RICHARD BICKERDICK, JAMES ESTHER, JOHN CRAMOND, RICHARD TEMPLEMAN, JAMES MURPHREE, RICHARD BASSETTS, JOHN STANHOPE, THOMAS RANDOLPH, and JAMES BAKER who being sworn well and truly to inquire of damages in this suit upon their oath do say that the Plaintiff has sustained damages by occasion of the Defendants trespass in the Declaration mentioned to 1 penny. Therefore, it is considered that the Plaintiff recover against the said Defendant and THOMAS TALBOT his bail his damages aforesaid and one penny costs. And the said Defendant in mercy.

Order is granted AMY SIMMONS against JOHN GUY for 46 pounds of Tobacco for one day Attendance coming and retuning 7 miles once in the suit of LEMUEL ROBERTS against him.

Order is granted MARY PEAD against JOHN GUY for 52 pounds of Tobacco for one day Attendance coming and retuning 9 miles once in the suit of LEMUEL ROBERTS against him.

Order is granted MALBONE SHELTON against JOHN GUY for 46 pounds of Tobacco for one day Attendance coming and retuning 7 miles once in the suit of LEMUEL ROBERTS against him.

Order is granted JOHN CHAPMAN against JOHN GUY for 43 pounds of Tobacco for one day Attendance coming and retuning 6 miles once in the suit of LEMUEL ROBERTS against him.

Order is granted THOMAS SNALE against JOHN GUY for 25 pounds of Tobacco for one day Attendance in the suit of LEMUEL ROBERTS against him.

Order is granted JAMES GUY against JOHN GUY for 25 pounds of Tobacco for one day Attendance in the suit of LEMUEL ROBERTS against him.

PAGE 79
Order is granted SOLOMON LAMBERT against JOHN GUY for 25 pounds of Tobacco for one day Attendance in the suit of LEMUEL ROBERTS against him.

Order is granted JOHN WIDDLE against JOHN GUY for 25 pounds of Tobacco for one day Attendance in the suit of LEMUEL ROBERTS against him.

Order is granted JAMES GUY, ELIZABETH GUY, ELIZABETH WIDDLE, JOHN BOGGESS, and JESSE JONES THOMAS SNALE against SAMUEL ROBERTS for 25 pounds of Tobacco each for one day Attendance each in his suit of against JOHN GUY.
This Court is adjourned to Court in Course, CHARLES THOMAS MAYOR, TESTE: JOHN BOUSH D.C.C.

<u>NORFOLK BOROUGH</u>
At a Hustings Court Held this 24TH day of JUNE 1771
PRESENT: GEORGE ABYVON ESQUIRE MAYOR
GENTLEMAN ALDERMEN: ARCHIBALD CAMPBELL, CHARLES THOMAS, LEWIS HANSFORD, JAMES TAYLOR, MAXIMILIAN CALVERT, CORNELIUS CALVERT

Ordinary License is granted PAUL HERRITTER and RICHARD BASSETT on their complying with the law.

SAMUEL SWANN against ALEXANDER MORRISON. On motion of the Plaintiff a DEDIMUS is granted him to take the depositions of NATHANIEL FLEMING giving the Defendant notice.

SAMUEL ALLYNE against GEORGE CARLTON. On motion of the Plaintiff a DEDIMUS is granted him to take the deposition of ALEXANDER CAMPBELL esquire giving the Defendant notice.

PETER MCNABB against JOHN TAYLOR. Dismissed.
MATTHEW ROTHERY against AARON BARBER. An Imparlance.
JOHN LAWRENCE against JOHN GILCHRIST. An Imparlance.

PAGE 79B
ANNA MOORE executrix of FRANCIS MOORE deceased against MARK TALBOT and ELDRED FISHER an Imparlance against MARK TALBOTT and the Defendant ELDRED FISHER pleaded payment issue joined and referred.

MATTHEW ROTHERY and MARY, his wife Plaintiff
Against Re: In Case
ANN BOUCHER Defendant
This day came the Defendant by her Attorney and the Plaintiffs though solemnly called came not but made default nor is their suit further prosecuted. Therefore, on the prayer of the Defendant. It is considered that she recover against the Plaintiffs 5 shillings current money and her costs by her about her defense in this behalf expended according to the form of the Act of Assembly and the Plaintiff for their false claims in mercy.

WILLIAM SHIELDS against FREDERICK BOUSH. Dismissed.

ISAAC ALLWINELE against JOHN GOODRICH by Petition and Summons. Judgement is granted the Plaintiff for 3 pounds 7 shillings and 7 pence. It is ordered that the Defendant pay the same unto the Plaintiff with costs and fees.

Order is granted SOLOMON HODGES against ISAAC ALLWINELE for 25 pounds tobacco for 1 day attendance in his suit against JOHN GOODRICH.

JOHN LEE against JAMES BRIDGER and MARY GRIMES. The Plaintiff by his Attorney moved for Special Bail which is granted. Where upon JOHN LELLO came into Court and undertook for the Defendants and thereon the defendants by their Attorney prayed an Imparlance.

JOHN MCLACHLAN against EDWARD GOOD. Special Imparlance.
MARY PULLETT against RICHARD TALBOTT. Imparlance.

ROBERT PEARCE against WILLIAM WALKER by Petition and Summons. Judgement is granted the Plaintiff for 2 pounds. It is ordered that the Defendant pay the same unto the Plaintiff with costs and fees.
ROBERT FORESYTHE against WILLIAM JOHNSON. Dismissed.

WILLIAM GRAY against JAMES CHAMPION. Order against the Defendant and GEORGE ALLINSON his bail.

PAGE 80
WILLIAM WILKINS Plaintiff
Against Re: In Case
WILLIAM PRICE Defendant
This day came as well the Plaintiff by his Attorney as the Defendant in Custody of the Sergeant of this Borough, and the said Defendant says that he did not assume upon himself in manner and form as the Plaintiff against him has declared. Therefore, the trial of the issue is referred until the next Court and the said Defendant being ruled to give Special Bail and failing so to do is continued in the Custody of the said Sergeant until that time.

HENRY BRESSIE against CHARLES MAYLE. An Imparlance.
TULLY ROBINSON and JOHN CRAMOND against JAMES READ. An attachment
DANIEL RICHARDSON against WILLIAM ROBINSON. An Imparlance.
ELIZABETH MEREDITH against WILLIAM KEETON. Dismissed.
AARON BARBER and JOSIAH HOFFMIRE against SAMUEL BUTT SR. Dismissed at the Defendants cost.
JANE MILLER against AARON BARBER and JOSIAH HOFFMIRE. Dismissed at the Defendants costs.
JOHN CRAMOND against DAVID MCCLENAHAN. An Imparlance.

ADAM STEWART against MARSDEN and HODGSON. The Plaintiff by his Attorney moved for Special Bail which is granted. Whereupon WILLIAM MARSH came into Court and undertook for the Defendant MARSDEN and thereon the said Defendant by his Attorney prayed an Imparlance. And discontinued against HODGSON the other Defendant.

SAMUEL LANGLEY against WILLIAM IVY. Dismissed at the Plaintiffs Costs.

JAMES MOORE against FREDERICK BOUSH and NATHANIEL BOUSH. The Plaintiff by his Attorney moved for Special Bail which is granted. Whereupon SAMUEL PORTLOCK came into Court and undertook for the Defendants and thereon the Defendants by their Attorney prayed an Imparlance and OYER.

JAMES MARSDEN and SIMON HODGSON against THOMAS YOUNG. Dismissed.
JAMES MILLER against ROBEY COKE. Dismissed.

GEORGE LOGAN, ROBERT GILMOUR & COMPANY against WRIGHT WESTCOTT Administrator of
PAGE 80B
JOHN WESTCOTT. An Imparlance.

ALEXANDER GORDON against WRIGHT WESTCOTT and STEPHEN WRIGHT, time to consider the bill.

GEORGE KELLY against EDMOND KEETON by Petition and Summons. Judgement is granted the Plaintiff for 1 pounds, 12 shillings and 6 pence. It is ordered that the Defendant pay the same unto the Plaintiff with costs and fees.

JONATHAN MEREDITH and ELIZABETH, his wife against MATTHEW KELLY and ANN his wife. An Imparlance.

CHARLES SAWYER against JOHN GILCHRIST and THOMAS JACK. Special Imparlance against JOHN
GILCHRIST and discontinued against THOMAS JACK.

SAMUEL SIMMONS against ZACHERIAS MARSINGALE. Imparlance.
MATTHEW ROTHERY and MARY, his wife against GEORGE WATSON and ANN his wife. Special Imparlance.
On the Attachment obtained by JOHN GILCHRIST against the estate of DUGALL GILCHRIST who has privately removed himself or so absconds that the ordinary process cannot be served on him. The Sergeant now making return that by virtue thereof he has attached all the Estate of the said DUGALL GILCHRIST in the hands of WILLIAM RASCOW WILSON CURLE Gentleman who appeared and admitted that he had in his hands 1 pound 17 shillings and 11 pence of the said DUGALL GILCHRIST and the said DUGALL GILCHRIST being called and not appearing nor replevying. Where up on the Plaintiff proved his demand of 14 pounds 3 shillings and 6 pence to be due by his own oath. Therefore, it is considered that the Plaintiff recover the same against the said DUGALL GILCHRIST and his costs by him in this behalf expended and ordered that the garnishee pay the money in his hands to the Plaintiff as far as the same will extend.

JOHN COLES assignee of JOHN HUTCHINGS executor of JOHN TUCKER deceased against JOSEPH CALVERT. This day came as well the Plaintiff by his Attorney as the Defendant in Custody of the Coroner of the County of Norfolk and the said Defendant being ruled to give Special Bail and failing so to do is contained in Custody.

The King & WILLIAM COLLEY against JOHN HARDY. Dismissed at the Plaintiffs costs.

PAGE 81
Order is granted RICHARD BICKERDICK against JOHN HARDY for 25 pounds tobacco for 1 day attendance in the Complaint of WILLIAM COLLEY against him.

Order is granted THOMAS WALMSLEY against JOHN HARDY for 25 pounds tobacco for 1day attendance in the Complaint of WILLIAM COLLEY against him.

Order is granted HUGH KENNY and JOHN HUGHS against WILLIAM COLLEY for 25 pounds tobacco each for 1 day attendance each in his Complaint against JOHN HARDY.

SAMUEL WARNER Plaintiff
Against Re: In Case
EDWARD CANNON Defendant
This day came the Parties by their Attorney's and there upon came also a Jury to wit:
JONATHAN DISON, THOMAS SNALE, ELDRED FISHER, JOHN SHAW, ALEXANDER BELL, JAMES GILCHRIST, JAMES HALSTEAD, WILLIAM IVY, BARTHOLOMEW THOMPSON, THOMAS FARRER, JOHN PASTEUR, and BENJAMIN NEWBOLD who being elected tried and sworn the truth to speak upon the issue joined withdrew and returned and the Plaintiff being solemnly called came not but made default. Therefore, on the prayer of the Defendant. It is considered that he recover against the Plaintiff 5 shillings current money and his costs by him about his defense in this behalf expended according to the form of the act of assembly and the Plaintiff for his false claims be in mercy.

Order is granted THOMAS REYNOLDS WALKER against EDWARD CANNON for 237 pounds of tobacco for 3 days attendance coming and returning 18 miles three times in the suit of SAMUEL WARNER against him.

Order is granted CHARLES CASON against EDWARD CANNON for 291 pounds of tobacco for 3 days attendance coming and returning 24 miles three times in the suit of SAMUEL WARNER against him.

Order is granted JOHN ATTWOOD against EDWARD CANNON for 100 pounds of tobacco for 1 day's attendance coming and returning 25 miles once in the suit of SAMUEL WARNER against him.

Order is granted WILLIAM JAMES against EDWARD CANNON for 200 pounds of tobacco for 2days attendance coming and returning 25 miles twice in the suit of SAMUEL WARNER against him.

<u>PAGE 81B</u>
Order is granted EDWARD ATTWOOD against SAMUEL WARNER for 300 pounds of tobacco for 3 days attendance coming and returning 25 miles three times in his suit against EDWARD CANNON.

Order is granted ROBERT WARD against SAMUEL WARNER for 291 pounds of tobacco for 3 days attendance coming and returning 25 miles three times in his suit against EDWARD CANNON.

Order is granted HILARY CASON against SAMUEL WARNER for 309 pounds of tobacco for 3 days attendance coming and returning 26 miles three times in his suit against EDWARD CANNON.

GEORGE JOSEPH FENWICK Plaintiff
Against Re: In Case
WILLIAM KEETON Defendant
This day came the parties by their Attorney's and there upon came also a Jury to wit: JONATHAN DISON, THOMAS SNALE, ELDRED FISHER, JOHN SHAW, ALEXANDER BELL, JAMES GILCHRIST, JAMES HALSTEAD, WILLIAM IVY, BARTHOLOMEW THOMPSON, THOMAS FARRER, JOHN PASTEUR, and BENJAMIN NEWBOLD who being elected tried and sworn the truth to speak upon the issue joined upon their oath do say that the Defendant did not assume as in pleading he has alleged. And on the motion of the Plaintiff by his Attorney a new trial is granted him.

MATHIAS GALE, ANN MOORE, JOSEPH MITCHELL, and JOHN COX Plaintiffs
Against Re: In Chancery
RICHARD ROTHERY an infant and MARY ROTHERY WIDOW Defendants
This day came the parties by their Attorney's and on a prayer GEORGE ABYVON Executor of HENRY ROTHERY deceased is made a Defendant and THOMAS BUTT admitted as Plaintiff in this suit. Where up on answers were filed and the cause set for hearing.

CHARLES THOMAS ESQUIRE against ROGER PEARCE. Dismissed.

The Court Rates Flour at 12 shillings per hundred.
This Court is adjourned to Court in Course, GEORGE ABYVON MAYOR, TESTE: JOHN BOUSH D.C.C.

<u>PAGE 82</u>
<u>NORFOLK BOROUGH</u>
At a Hustings Court Held this 22nd day of JULY 1771
PRESENT: GEORGE ABYVON ESQUIRE MAYOR
ANTHONY LAWSON ESQUIRE DEPUTY RECORDER
GENTLEMAN ALDERMEN: MAXIMILIAN CALVERT, CHARLES THOMAS, JAMES TAYLOR, CORNELIUS CALVERT

HENRY CUYLER, BARAUD RENDERS CUYLER and JOHN SMITH executors of HENRY CUYLER deceased Plaintiff
Against Re: In Case
ROBERT TUCKER heirs at law of ROBERT TUCKER deceased Defendant
The Plaintiff not further prosecuting on the motion of the Defendant by his Attorney. It is ordered that this suit be discontinued, and that the Plaintiff pay to the Defendant his costs.

JOHN VAN CORTLAND Plaintiff
Against Re: In Case
ROBERT TUCKER heirs at law of ROBERT TUCKER deceased Defendant
The Plaintiff not further prosecuting on the motion of the Defendant by his Attorney. It is ordered that this suit be discontinued, and that the Plaintiff pay to the Defendant his costs.

NEIL JAMIESON Plaintiff
Against Re: In Case
ROBERT TUCKER heirs at law of ROBERT TUCKER deceased Defendant
The Plaintiff not further prosecuting on the motion of the Defendant by his Attorney. It is ordered that this suit be discontinued, and that the Plaintiff pay to the Defendant his costs.

<u>PAGE 82B</u>
GEORGE MUTER and COMPANY, JOHN ESDALE, SAMUEL FARMER, THOMAS MANN RANDOLPH, JOSIAH GRANBERY, ROBERT DONALD, FRANCIS WARING, GEORGE KIPPIN and COMPANY, JAMES BUCHANAN and COMPANY, GARDNER FLEMING, NATHANIEL LITTLETON SAVAGE, RICHARD RANDOLPH, JOHN BOWDOIN, CHARLES CARTER, ARCHIBALD CARY, REESE MEREDITH and ARCHIBALD RITCHIE, Plaintiff
Against Re: <u>An SCIRE FACIAS</u>
ROBERT TUCKER heirs at law of ROBERT TUCKER deceased and THOMAS NEWTON and JOHN TAYLOR executors of the said ROBERT TUCKER Defendants

The Plaintiff not further prosecuting on the motion of the Defendant by their Attorney's. It is ordered that this suit be discontinued and that the Plaintiffs pay to the Defendant their costs.
MEMO: There was a suit by each Plaintiff.

GEORGE MUTER and COMPANY, JOHN ESDALE, SAMUEL FARMER, THOMAS MANN RANDOLPH, JOSIAH GRANBERY, ROBERT DONALD, FRANCIS WARING, GEORGE KIPPIN and COMPANY, JAMES BUCHANAN and COMPANY, GARDNER FLEMING, NATHANIEL LITTLETON SAVAGE, RICHARD RANDOLPH, JOHN BOWDOIN, CHARLES CARTER, ARCHIBALD CARY, REESE MEREDITH, and ARCHIBALD RITCHIE, HENRY CUYLER, BARAUD RENDERS CUYLER, JOHN SMITH executors of HENRY CUYLER, JOHN VAN CORTLAND, and NEIL JAMIESON Plaintiff
Against Re: In Chancery
THOMAS NEWTON & JOHN TAYLOR Executors of ROBERT TUCKER deceased and ROBERT TUCKER SON and heirs at law of the said ROBERT TUCKER Defendant.
The Plaintiff not further prosecuting on the motion of the Defendant by their Attorney's. It is ordered that this suit be discontinued and that the Plaintiffs pay to the Defendant their costs.
MEMO: There was but one suit in Chancery.

GEORGE ABYVON against JOHN SOUTHERLAND Dismissed.

PAGE 83
WILLIAM SIMPSON administrator of FRANCIS CLARKE against SAMUEL SIMMONS. The Defendant pleaded payment issue joined and referred.
JOHN GREENWOOD against WILLIAM CALLIS abates by the Defendants death.

WILLIS WILSON & COMPANY Plaintiffs
Against Re: In Case
SAMUEL SIMMONS Defendant
This day came as well the Plaintiffs by WILLIAM ROSCOW WILSON CURLE Gentleman their Attorney as the Defendant in his proper person and the said Defendant says that he cannot gainsay the Plaintiffs action nor but that he did assume in manner and form as the Plaintiff against him have declared.
Therefore, it is considered that the Plaintiff recover against the said Defendant 6 pounds 15 shillings and 2 pence and their costs by them in this behalf expended, and the said Defendant in mercy.

ZACHERIAS MARSINGALE against CHARLES MANNING. An Imparlance.
MALACHI MAUND against JOHN CHAPMAN Dismissed.
WILLIAM SIMPSON against WILLIAM INGRAM & JOHN INGRAM. Dismissed.

JOSEPH HARDING against CHARLES CASSON. by Petition and Summons. Judgement is granted the Plaintiff for 4 pounds, 12 shillings and 6 pence. It is ordered that the Defendant pay the same unto the Plaintiff with costs and fees.

WILLISON and MCSWEEN against JOHN AUSTIN FINNIE. A Special Imparlance.

HENRY FILKINS against JAMES ARCHDEACON. by Petition and Summons. Judgement is granted the Plaintiff for 1 pounds, 6 shillings. It is ordered that the Defendant pay the same unto the Plaintiff with costs and fees.

JAMES GILCHRIST and ROBERT TAYLOR against JOHN FOWLER and GEORGE FOWLER. The Plaintiffs by their Attorney moved for Special Bail which is granted. Whereupon JOHN BROWN came into Court and undertook for the Defendant GEORGE FOWLER and thereon the said Defendant by his Attorney prayed an Imparlance. And discontinued against JOHN FOWLER the other Defendant.

TULLY ROBINSON against ROBERT SHEDDEN. Special Imparlance.

PAGE 83B
JOHN CRAMOND against PRUDENCE BAYNES. Special Imparlance.
PHILIP CARBERY against NEIL JAMIESON. Imparlance.
THOMAS SNALE and ELIZABETH, his wife against JOHN IVY administrator of WILLIAM IVY Deceased. Time to consider the bill.
FREDERICK BOUSH against WILLIAM GODFREY administrator of JONATHAN GODFREY Deceased. An Imparlance.
GEORGE ABYVON against MARK TALBOT. Order against the Defendant and JOHN EDWARDS his bail.

THOMAS BRESSIE and HENRY BRESSIE Plaintiffs
Against Re: In Debt
ARTHUR BUTT Defendant
This day came the Plaintiff by WILLIAM ROSCOW WILSON CURLE Gentleman their Attorney as the Defendant in his proper person and the said Defendant acknowledges the Plaintiffs action for 27 pounds 1 shilling. Therefore, it is considered that the Plaintiff recover against the said Defendant their debt aforesaid and their costs by them in this behalf expended. And the said Defendant in mercy.
But this Judgement is to be discharged by the payment of 13 pounds 10 shillings and 6 pence with interest for the same at the rate of 5% per annum to be computed from December 8, 1769, to the time of payment and the costs. And the Plaintiffs agree to stay execution of this judgement 7 months.

WILLIS WILSON & Company against PELEGE MILLER. Dismissed.
Ordinary License is granted JOSEPH POPE and NATHANIEL BURGESS on their complying with the law.

Order is granted DAVID JARVIS and WRIGHT BRICKELL against JAMES ARCHDEACON for 25 pounds of tobacco each for 1 day attendance each in the suit of HENRY FILKINS against him.

TULLY ROBINSON and JOHN CRAMOND Plaintiffs
Against Re: In Case
JAMES READE Defendant
This day came the Plaintiffs by WILLIAM ROBINSON Gentleman their Attorney and attachment having been awarded the Plaintiffs against the estate said Defendant

PAGE 84
And the Sergeant now making return that by virtue thereof he has attached a clothing brush and the said Defendant being solemnly called and not appearing nor replevying his said goods whereby the said Plaintiff remain thereof against him undefended. Therefore, it is considered that the Plaintiff recover against the said Defendant their demand of 40 pounds 10 shillings together with their costs by them in this behalf expended and the said Defendant in mercy. And ordered that the sergeant sell the attached effects according to law and apply the money arising thereby in discharge of this judgement and the costs there of as far as the same will extend and that he return an account of his proceedings therein to the next Court.

On the attachment obtained by PAUL LOYALL Plaintiff against the Estate of GEORGE RAMSAY who has privately removed himself or so absconds that the Ordinary process cannot be served on him and the Sergeant now making return that by Virtue thereof he had attached all the Estate of the Said GEORGE RAMSAY in the hands of JOHN MEARNS who appeared and on oath declared that he was indebted to the said GEORGE RAMSAY 8 pounds 17 shillings and 2 pence 3 farthing and the said Defendant being called and not appearing. Whereupon the Plaintiff proved his demand of 13 pounds 1 shilling and 4 pence by his own oath. Therefore, it is considered that the Plaintiff recover the same against the said GEORGE RAMSAY and his costs by him in this behalf expended. And ordered that the garnishee pay the money in his hands to the Plaintiff in discharge of this judgement and the costs as far as the same will extend.

ROBERT NELSON & CATHARINE, his wife Plaintiff
Against Re: In Trespass, Assault & Battery
MATTHEW KELLY and ANN, his wife Defendants
This day came the Defendants by WILLIAM RASCOW WILSON CURLE Gentleman their Attorney and the Plaintiff though solemnly called came not but made default nor is their suit further prosecuted. Therefore, on the prayer of the Defendants by their Attorney. It is considered that they recover against the Plaintiffs 5 shillings current money and their cots by them about their defense in this behalf expended according to the form of the act of assembly and the Plaintiffs for their false claims in mercy.

WILLIAM WILKINS against WILLIAM PRICE. Dismissed.

PAGE 84B
JOHN EILBECK & JONATHAN EILBECK Plaintiffs
Against Re: In Case
WRIGHT WESTCOTT administrator of JOHN WESTCOTT Deceased Defendant
This day came as well the Plaintiffs by WILLIAM RASCOW WILSON CURLE Gentleman their Attorney as the Defendant in his proper person and the said Defendant says that he cannot gainsay the Plaintiffs actions nor but that his intestate did assume in manner and form as the Plaintiff against him have declared. Therefore, it is considered that the Plaintiff recover against the said Defendant 12 pounds, 11 shillings and 8 pence 1 farthing and their costs by them in this behalf expended, when assets after paying preceding judgements, debts of greater dignity with the defendants own claims against the Estate of the said intestate due by simple contract, to be levied of the goods and chattels which were of the said JOHN at the time of his death that shall here after come to the hands of the said WRIGHT to be administered and the said WRIGHT in mercy.

WILLIAM FARRER and THOMAS FARRER Plaintiff
Against Re: In Case
WRIGHT WESTCOTT administrator of JOHN WESTCOTT Deceased Defendant
This day came as well the Plaintiffs by WILLIAM RASCOW WILSON CURLE Gentleman their Attorney as the Defendant in his proper person and the said Defendant says that he cannot gainsay the Plaintiffs actions nor but that his intestate did assume in manner and form as the Plaintiff against him have declared. Therefore, it is considered that the Plaintiff recover against the said Defendant 7 pounds, 4 shillings and 9 pence half penny and their costs by them in this behalf expended, when assets after paying preceding judgements, debts of greater dignity with the Defendants own claims against the Estate of the said intestate due by simple contract, to be levied of the goods and chattels which were of the said JOHN at the time of his death that shall here after come to the hands of the said WRIGHT to be administered and the said WRIGHT in mercy.

On the Attachment obtained by JONATHAN MEREDITH and ELIZABETH his wife against the Estate of WILLIAM KEETON who has privately removed himself or so absconds that the ordinary process cannot be served on him and the Sergeant now making return that by virtue thereof he had attached one large pine chest, one glass corn, 4 tumblers, one pair scales and weights, some strip holland, two jackets, one coat and one pair of breaches and Sundry mariners books and the Defendant being called and not appearing nor replevying: Where upon the Plaintiff proved their Demands of

PAGE 85

2 pounds, 6 shillings and 11 pence 1 farthing to be just. Therefore, it is considered that the Plaintiff recover the same against the said Defendant together their costs by them in this behalf expended. And ordered that the Sergeant sell the attached effects according to the law and apply the money arising thereby in discharge of this judgement and the costs thereof as far as the same will extend and that he return an account of his proceedings where into the next Court.

This Court is adjourned to Court in Course, GEORGE ABYVON MAYOR, TESTE: JOHN BOUSH D.C.C.

NORFOLK BOROUGH
At a Hustings Court Held this 19th day of AUGUST 1771
PRESENT: GEORGE ABYVON ESQUIRE MAYOR
GENTLEMAN ALDERMEN: ARCHIBALD CAMPBELL, CHARLES THOMAS, PAUL LOYALL, MAXIMILIAN CALVERT, LEWIS HANSFORD, JAMES TAYLOR,

ALEXANDER BELL against WILLIAM MALLICOTE. By Petition and Summons. Judgement is granted the Plaintiff for 1 pounds, 9 shillings and 3 pence. It is ordered that the Defendant pay the same unto the Plaintiff with costs and fees.

WILLIAM COOPER and others against PETER ADAMS. Dismissed.
JOHN GREENWOOD against WILLIAM BROOK COTTON. Order against the Defendant.

ROBERT GILCHRIST against BARNABAS LORAIN. Dismissed at the Defendants cost.

PAUL LOYALL against ALLEN WOOD. By Petition and Summons. Judgement is granted the Plaintiff for 2 pounds, 9 shillings and a half penny. It is ordered that the Defendant pay the same unto the Plaintiff with costs and fees.

JOHN MARLEY against JOHN HARDY. An Imparlance.
JOHN MARLEY against JOHN HARDY & ELIZABETH his wife. An Imparlance.

LEMUEL CORNICK JR. against HUMPHREY MARSINGBURG. Dismissed.

PAGE 85B
ISAAC LUKE assignee of EDWARD LOWE against GEORGE BLINN. An Attachment.

ROGER PEARSE against FREDERICK BRACEGIRDLE. Dismissed.

ROGER PEARSE against JOHN VALLENCIER. By Petition and Summons. Judgement is granted the Plaintiff for 3 pounds, 17 shillings and 9 pence. It is ordered that the Defendant pay the same unto the Plaintiff with costs and fees.

WILLIAM PRIESTMAN against JOSHUA WRIGHT. The Plaintiffs by his Attorney moved for Special Bail which is granted. Whereupon SAMUEL DENBY came into Court and undertook for the Defendant and thereon the said Defendant by his Attorney prayed an Imparlance.

JOHN JONES against RICHARD KELSICK. An Imparlance.

JOHN WILSON against WILLIAM GRAY. The Plaintiffs by his Attorney moved for Special Bail which is granted. Whereupon JOHN RICHARDSON came into Court and undertook for the Defendant and thereon the said Defendant by his Attorney prayed an Imparlance.

JOHN WILSON against WILLIAM GRAY. By Petition and Summons. Judgement is granted the Plaintiff for 1 pounds 15 shillings and 3pence. It is ordered that the Defendant pay the same unto the Plaintiff with costs and fees.
JOHN WILSON against SAMUEL WILSON. By Petition and Summons. Judgement is granted the Plaintiff for 3 pounds. It is ordered that the Defendant pay the same unto the Plaintiff with costs and fees.

WILLIAM SIMPSON against WILLIAM COTTON. Dismissed.

EDWARD WRIGHT executor of JOSEPH JONES against JOHN MCLACHLAN. The Plaintiff by his Attorney moved for Special Bail which is granted. Whereupon WILLIAM LIDDLE came into Court and undertook for the Defendant and thereon the said Defendant by his Attorney prayed an Imparlance.

JOSEPH CALVERT against JOHN WILLIAMSON. The Plaintiff by his Attorney moved for Special Bail which is granted. Whereupon SAMUEL BOUSH came into Court and undertook for the Defendant and thereon the said Defendant by his Attorney prayed an Imparlance.

PAGE 86
DAVID JAMIESON against KEMP WHITING. The Plaintiff by his Attorney moved for Special Bail which is granted. Whereupon JOSEPH CALVERT came into Court and undertook for the Defendant and a Judgement is granted the Plaintiff by NIHIL Deceit and a Writ of Inquiry is award the Plaintiff for his damages.
JOSEPH HARDING against JAMES ROGERS. Dismissed at the Defendants cost.

EDMOND KEETON charged in execution of the suit of GEORGE KELLY was this day brought before the Court by warrant under the hand of GEORGE ABYVON Gentleman and he having subscribed and delivered a schedule of his estate and taken the oath agreeable to the Act of Assembly in such cases made and provided. It is ordered that the Sergeant sell the effects contained in the said schedule and that he discharge him out of his custody.

JOHN JONES and PHILISTRIA his wife executrix of JAMES TURNER. Deceased against FRANCIS BUSHWORM. Dismissed at the Plaintiffs costs.

WILLIAM SIMPSON Plaintiff
Against Re: In Debt
ARCHIBALD AVEN Defendant
This day came the parties by their Attorney's and there upon came also a Jury to wit: MASON MILLER, GEORGE JACKSON, JOSEPH HARDING, ELDRED FISHER, NATHANIEL YOUNG, JOHN BALLANTINE, DANIEL PECK, ROBERT HATTON, JOHN SELDEN, JAMES WALKER, ROBERT STEELE and GEORGE WINKLE who being elected tried and sworn the truth to speak upon their issue joined upon their oath do say that the Defendant has not paid the Debt in the declaration mentioned. Therefore, it is considered that the Plaintiff recover against the said Defendant his debt aforesaid amounting to 50 pounds 7 shillings and 6 pence and his costs by him in this behalf expended and the said defendant in mercy. But this judgement is to be discharged by the payment of 25 pounds 3 shillings and 9 pence with interest for the same at the rate of 5% per annum to be computed from June 10th, 1770, to the time of payment and the costs.

WILLIAM LEWELLING Plaintiff against MATTHEW PHRIPP Administrator of JOHN PHRIPP JR. Deceased. In Chancery. It Is ordered that ALEXANDER DIACK, JOHN WILKINS and JOHN SHEDDEN meet, state, and examine the accounts between the parties and make their report to the next Court.

PAGE 86B
MATTHEW GODFREY Plaintiff
Against Re: In Debt
JOHN WILSON Defendant
This day came the parties by their Attorney's and there upon came also a Jury to wit: MASON MILLER, GEORGE JACKSON, JOSEPH HARDING, ELDRED FISHER, NATHANIEL YOUNG, JOHN BALLANTINE, DANIEL PECK, ROBERT HATTON, JOHN SELDEN, JAMES WALKER, ROBERT STEELE and GEORGE WINKLE who being elected tried and sworn the truth to speak upon their issue joined upon their oath do say that the Defendant has not paid the Debt in the declaration mentioned. Therefore, it is considered that the Plaintiff recover against the said Defendant his debt aforesaid amounting to 198 pounds and 11 pence and his costs by him in this behalf expended and the said defendant in mercy. But this judgement is to be discharged by the payment of 106 pounds 18 shillings and 7 pence with interest for the same at the rate of 5% per annum to be computed from January 15th, 1771, to the time of payment and the costs.

RICHARD JOHNSON JR. Plaintiff
Against Re: In Case
MASON MILLER Defendant
This day came the parties by their Attorney's and there upon came also a Jury to wit: JOHN SELDEN, ROBERT STEEL, GEORGE WINKLE, GEORGE JACKSON, JOSEPH HARDING, ELDRED FISHER, NATHANIEL YOUNG, JOHN BALLANTINE, DANIEL PECK, ROBERT HATTON, JAMES WALKER and JAMES CUNNINGHAM who being elected tried and sworn the truth to speak upon the issue joined upon their oath do say that the defendant did not assume in pleading he has alleged.

PAGE 87
Order is granted PAUL WATLINGTON against MASON MILLER for 184 pounds tobacco for 1 day's attendance coming and returning 53 miles once and 14 shillings and 6 pence ferriages in this suit of RICHARD JOHNSON JR. against him.

Order is granted ABRAHAM WORMINGTON against MASON MILLER for 25 pounds tobacco for 1 day attendance in the suit of RICHARD JOHNSON JR. against him.

GEORGE ABYVON Gentleman Executor of HENRY ROTHERY Deceased Plaintiff
Against Re: In Case
MATTHEW ROTHERY Defendant
This day came the parties by their Attorney's and there upon came also a Jury to wit: MASON MILLER, JAMES CUNNINGHAM, DANIEL PECK, ROBERT HATTON, ELDRED FISHER, NATHANIEL YOUNG, JOHN BALLANTINE, JAMES WALKER, GEORGE WINKLE, ROBERT STEELE, JOHN SELDEN and GRIFFIN PEART who being elected tried and sworn the truth to speak upon their oath do say that the Defendant did assume in manner and form as the Plaintiff against him has declared and do asses the Plaintiff damages by occasion of the non-performance of that assumption to 14 pounds 12 shillings and 10 pence 1 farthing besides his costs. Therefore, it is considered that the Plaintiff recover against the said Defendant his damages aforesaid in form aforesaid assessed and his costs by him in this behalf expended and the said Defendant in mercy.

EDWARD HACK MOSELEY against LEWIS HANSFORD. Publication and set for hearing.
EDWARD HACK MOSELEY against ARCHIBALD INGRAM, JAMES INGRAM & COMPANY. On motion of the Defendants by their Attorney a DEDIMUS is granted them to take the depositions of JOHN THOMPSON giving the Plaintiff notice.

SAMUEL SWANN against ALEXANDER MORRISON. The Defendant pleaded not guilty. Issue joined and referred.
ROBERT FORESYTH against JOHN JOHNSON. The Defendant pleaded Not guilty. Issue joined and referred.
ARCHIBALD WHITE & COMPANY against GEORGE OLDNER. The Defendant pleaded payment issue joined and referred.

PAGE 87B
STEPHEN TANKARD against RICHARD HOGG. The Defendant pleaded that he did not assume issue joined and referred.
RICHARD HOGG against STEPHEN TANKARD. The Defendant pleaded that he did not assume issue joined and referred.
JAMES DUNLOP against JOHN MCCARROLL. The Defendant pleaded Not Guilty issue joined and referred.
MATTHEW KELLY and ANN, his wife against FRANCIS CONNER. The Defendant pleaded not guilty issue joined and referred.

FRANCIS CONNER against MATTHEW KELLY and ANN his wife. Dismissed for want of security for costs

CORTNEY WILDER against KEDAR COOPER and THOMAS CRATH Dismissed.

GEORGE ABYVON against CHARLES JENKINS executor of JOSEPH LOCKHART deceased. The Defendant pleaded that his testator did not assume issue joined and referred.

ROBERT GORDON against GEORGE LATHBURY. The Defendant pleaded that he did not assume issue joined and referred.

RICHARD BASSETT against HENRY RITTER. The Defendant pleaded not guilty issue joined and referred.

LOGAN GILMOUR and COMPANY against WILLIAM MCCAA. The Defendant pleaded that he did not assume issue joined and referred.

AARON BARBER and JOSIAH HOFFMIRE against JOHN CURLING. Ordered that the former order of the Court be confirmed, and a Writ of Inquiry is awarded to the Plaintiff for their damages.

AARON BARBER and JOSIAH HOFFMIRE against JOSEPH CURLING. Ordered that the former order of this Court be confirmed, and a Writ of Inquiry is awarded the Plaintiff for their damages.

WALTER LYON against WILLIAM BROWN. The former order of this Court is confirmed, and a Writ of Inquiry is awarded the Plaintiff for his damages.

WILLIAM NIMMO surviving executor of ADAM THOROWGOOD deceased against GEORGE OLDNER. The Defendant pleaded payment issue joined and referred.

PAGE 88

WILLIAM SMITH and RICHARD TEMPLEMAN administrators of ROBERT TUCKER deceased against JOSIAH HOFFMIRE. The Defendant pleaded that he did not assume issue joined and referred.

DANIEL CURLING against JOSIAH HOFFMIRE. The Defendant pleaded that he did not assume issue joined and referred.

JOHN GREENWOOD Plaintiff

Against Re: In Debt

JOHN IVY Defendant

This day came the Plaintiff by JAMES HOLT Gentleman his Attorney and the Defendant being solemnly called and not appearing. Ordered that the former order of this Court against the said Defendant and SAMUEL LANGLEY his bail be confirmed. Therefore, it is considered that the Plaintiff recover against the said Defendant and SAMUEL LANGLEY his bail aforesaid his debt amounting to 103 pounds 8 shillings and 3 pence half penny and his costs by him in this behalf expended and the said Defendant in mercy. But this judgement is to be discharged by the payment of 51 pounds 14 shillings and 1 penny 3 farthings with interest for the same at the rate of 5% per annum to be computed from September 1, 1769, to the time of payment and costs

ROBERT STEED against HENRY TUCKER and JOHN TAYLOR. The Defendant HENRY TUCKER being dead the suit against him abates and JOHN TAYLOR the other Defendant pleaded that he did not assume issue joined and referred.

JAMES MOON against NATHANIEL BOUSH in case. The Defendant pleaded that he did not assume issue joined and referred.

CHARLES MAYLE against JOHN GREENWOOD. The Defendant pleaded that he did not assume issue joined and referred.

BENJAMIN JOHNSON and ELIZABETH, his wife against JOHN HUNT and ANN his wife. The Defendant pleaded not guilty issue joined and referred.

JOHN CRAMOND against WILLIAM HANCOCK. The Defendant pleaded that he did not assume issue joined and referred. (Memo: Notice given for books)

JOHN STEWART against JOHN MEARNS. The Defendant pleaded payment issue joined and referred.

PAGE 88B

JOHN MCLACHLAN against JOHN MADDON. The Defendant pleaded payment issue joined and referred.

JAMES BRIDGER against JOSEPH CALVERT. The Defendant in person pleased that he did not assume issue joined and referred.

WILLIAM WEBLEY against JAMES WEBB and APHIA his wife executrix of WILLIS LANGLEY deceased judgement by default and a writ of inquiry is awarded the Plaintiff for his damages.

SAMUEL PORTLOCK against WILLIAM SHIPWASH. The former order against the Defendant and THOMAS STEWART his bail is confirmed, and time is allowed to assign breaches.

ARCHIBALD WHITE and COMPANY against JOHN TATEM. The Defendant pleaded payment issue joined and referred.

JOHN EDWARDS and MARY, his wife against THOMAS DICKERSON. The Defendant pleaded not guilty issue joined and referred.

WRIGHT WESTCOTT against WILLS DUNFORD. The Defendant pleaded not guilty issue joined and referred.

DICKERSON PRYOR and FRANCES his wife administratrix of RICHARD FRAZIER against THOMAS BUTT. The Defendant pleaded that he did not assume issue joined and referred.

THOMAS PARSONS administrator of THOMAS WILDS SR. deceased against WILLIAM SMITH. The Defendant pleaded that he did not assume issue joined and referred.

WILLIAM SIMPSON against JOHN SMITH. The Defendant pleaded that he did not assume issue joined and referred.

JOHN GREENWOOD against JOHN TAYLOR JR. and TUCKER. The Defendant HENRY TUCKER being dead. The case against him abates. And the other Defendant pleaded that he did not assume issue joined and referred. And on the motion of the said Defendant by his Attorney a DEDIMUS is granted him to take the Depositions of ARTHUR MORSON, SAMUEL BROWN, PHILIP HALL JR. giving the Plaintiff legal notice.

JOHN SCOTT and ANN, his wife against PETER BISER. The Defendant pleaded not guilty issue joined and referred.

Ordinary License is granted SAMUEL PORTLOCK on his complying with the law.
JEREMIAH FOREMAN against AARON BARBER Dismissed.

PAGE 89
SAMUEL PORTLOCK against JOHN WILSON. The Defendant pleaded payment and time allowed to assign breaches.

JAMES HUNTER and ELIZABETH TENANT executors of SAMUEL TENANT deceased against JAMES ARCHDEACON. Special Imparlance.

ARCHIBALD WHITE & COMPANY against MARY NICHOLAS Discontinued.

Order is granted PHILIP CARBERY, ROBERT TUCKER and JOSEPH MITCHELL against MATTHEW ROTHERY for 25 pounds tobacco each for 1 day attendance each in the suit of GEORGE ABYVON Executor of HENRY ROTHERY against him.

This Court is adjourned until tomorrow 9 O'clock, GEORGE ABYVON MAYOR, TESTE: JOHN BOUSH D.C.C.

NORFOLK BOROUGH
At a Hustings Court Held this 20th day of AUGUST 1771
PRESENT: GEORGE ABYVON ESQUIRE MAYOR
GENTLEMAN ALDERMEN: ARCHIBALD CAMPBELL, MAXIMILIAN CALVERT, LEWIS HANSFORD, JAMES TAYLOR,

MOSES LANGLEY against FRANCES MOORE administratrix of MOORE deceased and EDWARD PARK. Replication and commission.

PHILOMON RUSSELL Plaintiff
Against Re: In Case
ALEXANDER BELL Defendant
This day came the parties by their Attorney's and there upon came also a Jury to wit: DANIEL HUTCHINGS, ROBERT MACKIE, JAMES MURPHREE, GEORGE GORDON, JOHN MACLEAN, JAMES DISON, WILLIAM STEPHENSON, JOHN WILSON, JOHN WOODSIDE, SCARBROUGH TANKARD, THOMAS CLARK and JAMES DUNN who being elected tried and sworn the truth to speak upon the issue joined withdrew and not returning any verdict the cause is continued.

Order is granted ROBERT MORRIS against ALEXANDER BELL for 50 pounds tobacco for 2 days attendance in the suit of PHILOMON RUSSELL against him.

PAGE 89B
Order is granted JOEL MOHUN against PHILOMON RUSSELL for 25 pounds tobacco for 1 day attendance in his suit against ALEXANDER BELL.

MALACHI MAUND Plaintiff
Against Re: In Debt
CHARLES JENKINS Executor of JOSEPH LOCKHART deceased Defendant
This day came the parties by Their Attorney and thereupon came also a Jury to wit: MASON MILLER, RICHARD BICKERDICK, NICHOLAS POOLE, ROGER PEARSE, RICHARD KELSICK, ALEXANDER MOSELEY, WRIGHT WESTCOTT, THOMAS FARRER, JOHN CALVERT, ROBERT HATTON, JOEL MOHUN and THOMAS SNALE who being elected tried and sworn the truth to speak upon the issue joined upon their oath do say that the Defendants testator did assume in manner and form as the Plaintiff against him have declared and do assess the Plaintiff damages by occasion of the non-performance of that assumption to 7 pounds 19 shillings and 6 pence half penny besides his costs. Therefore, it is considered that the Plaintiff recover against the said Defendant his damages aforesaid in form aforesaid assessed and his costs by him in this behalf expended and the said defendant in mercy.

Order is granted HENRY BRESSIE against MALACHI MAUND for 125 pounds of tobacco for 5 days attendance in his suit against CHARLES JENKINS executor of JOSEPH LOCKHART deceased.

WILLIAM WESTCOTT Plaintiff
Against Re: In Case
WRIGHT WESTCOTT administrator of JOHN WESTCOTT deceased Defendant
This day came the parties by their Attorney's and thereupon came also a Jury to wit: NICHOLAS POOLE, ALEXANDER MOSELEY, ROGER PEARSE, MASON MILLER, RICHARD BICKERDICK, RICHARD KELSICK, THOMAS SNALE, ROBERT HATTON, THOMAS FRASIER, JOEL MOHUN, JOHN CALVERT, and CHAPMAN MASON who being elected tried and sworn withdrew and not returning any verdict the cause is continued.

This Court is adjourned to Court in Course, GEORGE ABYVON MAYOR, TESTE: JOHN BOUSH D.C.C.

PAGE 90

NORFOLK BOROUGH

At a Hustings Court Held this 23rd day of September 1771

PRESENT: GEORGE ABYVON ESQUIRE MAYOR

GENTLEMAN ALDERMEN: ARCHIBALD CAMPBELL, LEWIS HANSFORD, PAUL LOYALL, CORNELIUS CALVERT, CHARLES THOMAS

Ordinary License is granted JAMES DUNN on his complying with the law.

JOHN GREENWOOD against JOHN IVY. Order against the Defendant and WILLIAM NICHOLSON his bail.

TULLY ROBINSON Plaintiff

Against Re: In Debt

JOHN IVY Defendant

This day came the parties by their Attorney's and the defendant by his Attorney acknowledges the Plaintiff's action for 40 pounds. Therefore, it is considered that the Plaintiff recover against the said Defendant his debt aforesaid and his costs by him in this behalf expended and the said Defendant in mercy. But this judgement is to be discharged by the payment of 20 pounds with interest for the same at the rate of 5% per annum to computed from April 17th, 1765, to the time of payment and costs.

JAMES MARSDEN and SIMON HODGSON against JOHN IVY Discontinued

JAMES MARSDEN and SIMON HODGSON against ALLEN WOOD Discontinued

JAMES MARSDEN and SIMON HODGSON against JONATHAN MEREDITH & ELIZABETH his wife. An attachment against JONATHAN MEREDITH'S ESTATE and continued against his wife.

NATHANIEL CUNNINGHAM against ABRAHAM COOPER Special Imparlance.

JOHN GOODRICH against ALEXANDER MCSWEEN. The Defendant pleaded that he did not assume issue joined and referred.

WILLIAM GODFREY Administrator of JONATHAN GODFREY against HUMPHREY ROBERTS discontinued.

PAGE 90B

JOHN SCOTT against JOHN LELLO and JOHN MORRIS. The Plaintiff by his Attorney moved for Special Bail which is granted. Whereupon EDWARD GOOD and ARTHUR BUTT came into Court and undertook for the Defendant and there on the said Defendants by their Attorney prayed an Imparlance.

GEORGE VEALE, JAMES WEBB, WILLIAM AITCHESON, MATTHEW GODFREY, JOHN HUTCHINGS, THOMAS VEALE, MAXIMILIAN CALVERT, JOSEPH HUTCHINGS, JOHN PORTLOCK, CORNELIUS CALVERT, SAMUEL HAPPER, GOODRICH BOUSH, MALACHI WILSON, MATTHEW PHRIPP, DAVID PORTER, THOMAS NEWTON, JOHN WILSON, and JOHN TAYLOR Gentleman Justices of the peace for Norfolk County at the instance of THOMAS OLD and BARBARA his wife against ANDREW SPROWLE and JOHN SPROWLE and JOHN HUNTER, Imparlance and OYER.

JOHN GILCHRIST against EDWARD HANSFORD. An Imparlance.

NEIL JAMIESON Administrator of HENRY TUCKER deceased against THOMAS SNALE. Order against the Defendant and JOHN WOODSIDE his bail.

NEIL JAMIESON Administrator of HENRY TUCKER deceased against CHARLES GODFREY. Order against the Defendant and JOSEPH CALVERT Sergeant.

SPROWLE & CROOKS against WRIGHT WESTCOTT. Administrator of JOHN WESTCOTT deceased. The Plaintiff CROOKS being dead the suit as to him abates and an Imparlance as to SPROWLE.

ROGER STEWART against JOHN MCNEIL. An Imparlance.

MISTERS LOGAN GILMOUR & Co. against WILLIAM DALE Dismissed.

MISTERS LOGAN, GILMOUR & CO. against WILLIAM B. COTTON Dismissed.

MISTERS LOGAN, GILMOUR & CO. against JONATHAN DISON. The Plaintiff by his Attorney moved for Special Bail which is granted. Whereupon JOSEPH WOODSIDE came into Court and undertook for the Defendant and thereon the defendant by his Attorney prayed an Imparlance.

MISTERS LOGAN, GILMOUR & CO. against THOMAS BUTT. The Plaintiff by his Attorney moved for Special Bail which is granted. Whereupon STEPHEN TANKARD came into Court and undertook for the Defendant and thereon the defendant by his Attorney prayed an Imparlance.

PAGE 91

JAMES ARCHDEACON and ALEXANDER MCSWEEN against JOSIAH MARSINGBURG and DAVID CHAMBERS Dismissed.

ANN SYMONS by ROBERT BANKS her next friends against THOMAS DREWRY. WILLIAM SMITH is appointed guardian to the infant Defendant to defend him in this suit. And thereon the said Defendant by his Attorney prayed a Special Imparlance.

CORNELIUS CALVERT against JONATHAN MEREDITH an Attachment.

KEDAR COOPER against JOSHUA PEED. Special Imparlance.

JONATHAN DISON against ROBERT TUCKER. An Imparlance.

GEORGE RIDDELL against JOHN JONES. Special Imparlance.

GEORGE OLDNER against JOHN NASH. Special Imparlance.

JOHN SHAKELFORD Plaintiff
Against Re: In Case
JAMES MUDIE Defendant
This day came as well the Plaintiffs by WILLIAM ROSCOW WILSON CURLE Gentleman his Attorney as the Defendant in his proper person and the said Defendant says that he cannot gainsay the Plaintiffs action nor but that he did assume in manner and form as the Plaintiff against him has declared. Therefore, it is considered that the Plaintiff recover against the said 5 pounds 14 shillings and his costs by him in this behalf expended and the said Defendant in mercy.

PHILOMON RUSSELL Plaintiff
Against Re: In Case
ALEXANDER BELL Defendant
This day came the parties by their Attorney's and in this cause at the last Court, were this day called and not appearing they are discharged and ordered that the Sergeant summon a new jury to appear at the next Court.

WILLIAM WESTCOTT Plaintiff against WRIGHT WESTCOTT admin of JOHN WESTCOTT deceased Defendant. This day came the parties by their Attorney's and the Jury that was sworn in this cause and returning any verdict are discharged.

PAGE 91B
THOMAS ROBERTS against JOHN ASHLEY agreed dismissed.

JOHN WOODSIDE Plaintiff
Against Re: in Case
CHARLES JENKINS Executor of JOSEPH LOCKHART deceased Defendant
This day came the parties by their Attorney's and there upon came also a Jury to wit: EDWARD HANSFORD, ALEXANDER MASSENBURG, JAMES LEITCH, JAMES MARSDEN, JAMES MURPHREE, STEPHEN TANKARD, JOSEPH LANGLEY, HENRY HALSTEAD, JOHN NASH, WILLIAM NICHOLSON, THOMAS OLD and JAMES HALSTEAD who being elected tried and sworn the truth to speak upon the issue joined upon their oath do say that the Defendants testator did assume in manner and form as the Plaintiff against him has declared and do assess the Plaintiff damages by occasion of the non-performance of that assumption to 11 pounds 9 shillings and 9 pence besides his costs. Therefore, it is considered that the Plaintiff recover against the said Defendant his damages aforesaid in form aforesaid assessed and his costs by him in this behalf expended to be levied of the goods and chattels of the said testator if so, much the said CHARLES JENKINS has in his hands to be administered and if he has it not then the costs are to be levied of his proper goods and chattels and the said Defendant in mercy.

ALEXANDER BELL Plaintiff
Against Re: In Case
JOSIAH BUTT Defendant
This day came the parties by their Attorney's and there upon came also a Jury to wit: EDWARD HANSFORD, ALEXANDER MASSENBURG, JAMES LEITCH, JAMES MARSDEN, JAMES MURPHREE, STEPHEN TANKARD, JOSEPH LANGLEY, HENRY HALSTEAD, JOHNNASH, WILLIAM NICHOLSON, THOMAS OLD and JAMES HALSTEAD who being elected tried and sworn the truth to speak upon the issue joined upon their oath do say that the Defendant is not guilty as in the pleading he has alleged. Therefore, it is considered that the Plaintiff take nothing by his bill but for his false claims.
PAGE 92
Be in mercy. And the Defendant go hence without day and recover against the Plaintiff his costs by him about his defense in this behalf expended.

Order is granted THOMAS CREECH against JOHN WOODSIDE for 25 pounds tobacco for 1 day's attendance in his suit against CHARLES JENKINS executor of JOSEPH LOCKHART deceased.

Order is granted HEREKIAH FENTRESS against ALEXANDER BELL for 150 pounds of tobacco for 6 days attendance in his suit against JOSIAH BUTT.

Order is granted NEHEMIAH FENTRESS against ALEXANDER BELL for 150 pounds of tobacco for 6 days attendance in his suit against JOSIAH BUTT.

Order is granted ELIZABETH WILSON against ALEXANDER BELL for 125 pounds of tobacco for 5 days attendance in his suit against JOSIAH BUTT.

Order is granted MATT GODFREY against JOSIAH BUTT for 175 pounds of tobacco for 7 days attendance in his suit against ALEXANDER BELL against him.

Order is granted BENJAMIN BUTT against JOSIAH BUTT for 175 pounds of tobacco for 7 days attendance in his suit against ALEXANDER BELL against him.

Order is granted MARY SUGGS against JOSIAH BUTT for 100 pounds of tobacco for 4 days attendance in his suit against ALEXANDER BELL against him.

Order is granted SARAH BUTT against JOSIAH BUTT for 75 pounds of tobacco for 3 days attendance in his suit against ALEXANDER BELL against him.

Order is granted WALTER SIKES against JOSIAH BUTT for 25 pounds of tobacco for 1 day's attendance in his suit against ALEXANDER BELL against him.

ISAAC LUKE assignee of EDWARD LOWE against GEORGE BLINN. The former order of this Court against him the said Defendant and

PAGE 92B
ISAAC LUKE assignee of EDWARD LOWE against GEORGE BLINN in debt. This day came the Plaintiff by WILLIAM RASCOW WILSON CURLE Gentleman his Attorney and an attachment having been awarded the Plaintiff against the Estate of the said Defendant and the Sheriff now making return that by virtue thereof he has attached, one silver teaspoon and the said Defendant being solemnly called and not appearing. A writ of Inquiry is awarded to inquire.

The Court rates Flour this day at 14 shillings per centum
This Court is adjourned to Court in Course. GEORGE ABYVON MAYOR, TESTE: JOHN BOUSH D.C.C.

NORFOLK BOROUGH
At a Hustings Court Held this 21st day of October 1771
PRESENT: GEORGE ABYVON ESQUIRE MAYOR
GENTLEMAN ALDERMEN: LEWIS HANSFORD, MAXIMILIAN CALVERT, CHARLES THOMAS, CORNELIUS CALVERT

RICHARD BASSETT against HENRY RITTER abates by the Defendant's death.
SIMON PORTLOCK against ABRAM WORMINGTON abates by the death of the Plaintiff.
JONATHAN DISON and SARAH, his wife against JOHN ASHLEY Abates.
WILLIAM GRAY against JAMES CHAMPION abates by the death of the Plaintiff.
FREDERICK BOUSH against WILLIAM GODFREY admin of JOHN GODFREY dismissed at the Defendant's cost.
JOHN JONES against RICHARD KELSICK. Dismissed at the Defendant's costs.
JOHN WILSON against WILLIAM GRAY. Abates by the death of the parties.
MISTERS LOGAN, GILMOUR against JONATHAN DISON Abates by the Defendants death.
JONATHAN DISON against ROBERT TUCKER abates by the Plaintiff's death.

PAGE 93
JAMES CARMICKHAIL against WILLIAM GRAY abates by the Defendants death.
JOHN STEWART against JOHN MEARNS Dismissed.
ANTHONY LAWSON against JOSHUA WRIGHT. Special Imparlance.

JAMES MARSDEN and SIMON HODGSON against ALEXANDER BELL. The Plaintiff by their Attorney moved for Special Bail which is granted. Whereupon JOHN CRAMOND came into Court and entered himself Special Bail for the Defendant and thereon the Defendant by his Attorney prayed an Imparlance.

BENJAMIN NEWBOLD and JOHN WALKER ELIAS ELLERY. Dismissed.

ARCHIBALD CAMPBELL against JAMES ROGERS. The Plaintiff by his Attorney moved for Special Bail which is granted. Whereupon JOHN MACLACHLAN this day came into Court and entered himself Special Bail for the Defendant and thereon the defendant by his Attorney prayed an Imparlance.

BENJAMIN JOHNSON and ELIZABETH, his wife against JOHN HUNT and ANN his wife abates.
The King by JOHN PURNAL and ELIZABETH his wife against JOHN MEARNS Dismissed.
THOMAS NICHOLSON against CHARLES JENKINS. Discontinued.

JAMES MARSDEN and SIMON HODGSON against JONATHAN MEREDITH and ELIZABETH his wife. The Plaintiffs by their Attorney moved for Special Bail which is granted. Whereupon ALEXANDER BELL this day came into Court and entered himself Special Bail for the Defendant and thereon the defendant by his Attorney prayed an Imparlance.

CORNELIUS CALVERT against JONATHAN MEREDITH. The Plaintiff by his Attorney moved for Special Bail which is granted. Whereupon ALEXANDER BELL this day came into Court and entered himself Special Bail for the Defendant and thereon the defendant by his Attorney prayed an Imparlance.

EDWARD WRIGHT Esquire of JOSEPH JONES deceased against JOHN MCLACHAN discontinued at the Plaintiff's costs with Attorney's fee.

This Court is adjourned to Court in Course. GEORGE ABYVON MAYOR, TESTE: JOHN BOUSH D.C.C.

PAGE 93B
NORFOLK BOROUGH
At a Hustings Court Held this 25th day of November 1771
PRESENT: GEORGE ABYVON ESQUIRE MAYOR
GENTLEMAN ALDERMEN: ARCHIBALD CAMPBELL, JAMES TAYLOR, PAUL LOYALL, CHARLES THOMAS, LEWIS HANSFORD, CORNELIUS CALVERT, MAXIMILIAN CALVERT.

WILLIAM MARSH and COMPANY against ALEXANDER BELL Dismissed.
JOHN MCNEIL against MATTHEW KELLY. An Imparlance.
CHARLES WARREN against MATTHEW ROTHERY. An Imparlance.
LODWICK GRAY by BENJAMIN DINGLEY GRAY his next friend against WILLIAM IVY. An Imparlance.

PHILIP CHAMBERLAIN by PHILIP CARBERY his next friend against WILLIAM IVY. By Petition and Summons. Judgement is granted the Plaintiff for 3 pounds 4 shilling and 5 pence. It is ordered that the Defendant pay the same unto the Plaintiff with costs and fee. And the Plaintiff agrees to stay the execution of this judgement until after next Court.

WILLIAM ORANGE against WILLIAM IVY. Dismissed.

EDWARD WRIGHT and JAMES JONES Executors of JOSEPH JONES against JOHN MCLACHAN. The Plaintiffs by their Attorney moved for Special Bail which is granted. Whereupon ALEXANDER BELL came into Court and entered himself Special Bail for the Defendant and thereon the Defendant by his Attorney prayed an Imparlance.

HENRY FLEMING against JOSHUA WRIGHT. The Plaintiffs by their Attorney moved for Special Bail which is granted. Whereupon WILLIAM BOWEN came into Court and entered himself Special Bail for the Defendant and thereon the Defendant by his Attorney prayed A Special Imparlance.

HENRY FLEMING and COMPANY against JOSHUA WRIGHT. The Plaintiffs by their Attorney moved for Special Bail which is granted. Whereupon WILLIAM BOWEN came into Court and entered himself Special Bail for the Defendant and thereon the defendant by his Attorney prayed A Special Imparlance.

HENRY BRESSIE against AARON BARBER. An Attachment.
ANTHONY LAWSON against ALEXANDER BELL. Dismissed.
TULLY ROBINSON and Company against JOHN WISE. A Special Imparlance.

PAGE 94
JOHN MCLACHLAN against THOMAS WALKER and JOHN VALLENCIER. The Plaintiff by his Attorney moved for Special Bail which is granted. Whereupon STEPHEN TANKARD came into Court and entered himself Special Bail for the Defendant and thereon the defendant by his Attorney prayed An Imparlance.

JOHN CRAMOND against JOHN TATEM. The Plaintiff by his Attorney moved for Special Bail which is granted. Whereupon SAMUEL PORTLOCK came into Court and entered himself Special Bail for the Defendant and thereon the defendant by his Attorney prayed An Imparlance.

ROBERT STEELE against JOHN RUNSBERG. By Petition and Summons. Judgement is granted the Plaintiff for 2 pounds 10 shillings. It is ordered that the Defendant pay the same unto the Plaintiff with costs and fee.
JOHN MEARNS against JOHN MCNEIL. By Petition and Summons. Judgement is granted the Plaintiff for 4 pounds 12 shillings. It is ordered that the Defendant pay the same unto the Plaintiff with costs and fee.

MICHAEL CHRISTIAN assignee of WILLIAM MCCAA against ALEXANDER BELL. The Plaintiff by his Attorney moved for Special Bail which is granted. Whereupon JOHN MCLACHAN came into Court and entered himself Special Bail for the Defendant and thereon the defendant by his Attorney prayed An Imparlance.

MICHAEL CHRISTIAN and LABON JOHNSTON against ALEXANDER BELL. The Plaintiffs by their Attorney moved for Special Bail which is granted. Whereupon JOHN MCLACHAN came into Court and entered himself Special Bail for the Defendant and thereon the defendant by his Attorney prayed An Imparlance.

SAMUEL BRESSIE against MALACHI MAUND. Discontinued at the Plaintiffs Costs.

JAMES DUNN against THOMAS SNALE. By Petition and Summons. Judgement is granted the Plaintiff for 3 pounds 3 shillings and 10 pence. It is ordered that the Defendant pay the same unto the Plaintiff with costs and fee.

MALACHI MAUND assignee of NOAH SUGG against SAMUEL BRESSIE. The Plaintiff by his Attorney moved for Special Bail which is granted. Whereupon HENRY BRESSIE came into Court and entered himself Special Bail for the Defendant and thereon he by his Attorney prayed An Imparlance.

PETER KATZ against JAMES CAMPBELL & COMPANY. An Imparlance.
PETER KATZ against JAMES CAMPBELL & COMPANY. An Imparlance.

HENRY BRESSIE assignee of SAMUEL BRESSIE against THOMAS and MATTHEW CHERRY. Imparlance.
HENRY BRESSIE against JOHN SHIPWASH. Dismissed.

PAGE 94B
MISTERS THOMAS WILSON, WILLIAM WILSON, and ALICE CARR against The Plaintiff by his Attorney moved for Special Bail which is granted. Whereupon JOSEPH CALVERT came into Court and entered himself Special Bail and order against the Defendant.

LOGAN GILMOUR and COMPANY Plaintiff
Against Re: In Case
AMOS WICKERSHAM and ALEXANDER KIDD Administrators of JOHN KIDD deceased Defendant

This day came as well the Plaintiff by THOMAS BURKE Gentleman their Attorney as the defendants in their proper person and say that they cannot gainsay the Plaintiffs action nor but that their intestate did assume in manner and form as the Plaintiff against them have declared. Therefore, it is considered that the Plaintiff recover against the said Defendants 78 pounds 13 shillings and 9 pence and their costs by them about their suit in this behalf expended to be levied of the goods and chattels of the said intestate JOHN KIDD if so, much the said AMOS WICKERSHAM and ALEXANDER KIDD have in their hands to be administered and if they have it not then the costs are to be levied of their proper goods and chattels and the said Defendants in mercy.

JOHN SHEDDEN and Company Plaintiffs
Against Re: In Case
AMOS WICKERSHAM and ALEXANDER KIDD Administrators of JOHN KIDD deceased Defendant
This day came as well the Plaintiff by THOMAS BURKE Gentleman their Attorney as the defendants in their proper person and say that they cannot gainsay the plaintiff's action nor but that their intestate did assume in manner and form as the Plaintiff against them have declared. Therefore, it is considered that the Plaintiff recover against the said Defendants 26 pounds and their costs by them about their suit in this behalf expended to be levied of the goods and chattels of the said intestate JOHN KIDD if so, much the said AMOS WICKERSHAM and ALEXANDER KIDD have in their hands to be administered and if they have it not then the costs are to be levied of their proper goods and chattels and the said Defendants in mercy.

ARCHIBALD BROWN Plaintiff
Against Re: In Case
AMOS WICKERSHAM and ALEXANDER KIDD Administrators of JOHN KIDD deceased Defendant
This day came as well the Plaintiff by THOMAS BURKE Gentleman their Attorney as the Defendant in their proper person and say that they cannot gainsay the Plaintiffs action nor but that their intestate did assume in manner and form as the Plaintiff against them have declared. Therefore, it is considered that the Plaintiff recover against the said Defendants 10 pounds 3 shillings and 6 pence
PAGE 95
and his costs by them about his suit in this behalf expended to be levied of the goods and chattels of the said intestate JOHN KIDD if so, much the said AMOS WICKERSHAM and ALEXANDER KIDD have in their hands to be administered and if they have it not then the costs are to be levied of their proper goods and chattels and the said Defendants in mercy.

JAMES ARCHDEACON Plaintiff
Against Re: In Case
AMOS WICKERSHAM and ALEXANDER KIDD Administrators of JOHN KIDD deceased Defendant
This day came as well the Plaintiff by THOMAS BURKE Gentleman their Attorney as the defendant in their proper person and say that they cannot gainsay the plaintiff's action nor but that their intestate did assume in manner and form as the Plaintiff against them have declared. Therefore, it is considered that the Plaintiff recover against the said Defendants 6 pounds 12 shillings and 6 pence and his costs by them about their suit in this behalf expended to be levied of the goods and chattels of the said intestate JOHN KIDD if so, much the said AMOS WICKERSHAM and ALEXANDER KIDD have in their hands to be administered and if they have it not then the costs are to be levied of their proper goods and chattels and the said Defendants in mercy.

GEORGE LOGAN Plaintiff
Against Re: In Case
AMOS WICKERSHAM and ALEXANDER KIDD Administrators of JOHN KIDD deceased Defendant
This day came as well the Plaintiff by THOMAS BURKE Gentleman their Attorney as the defendant in their proper person and say that they cannot gainsay the plaintiff action nor but that their intestate did assume in manner and form as the Plaintiff against them have declared. Therefore, it is considered that the Plaintiff recover against the said Defendants 17 pounds and his costs by him about his suit in this behalf expended to be levied of the goods and chattels of the said intestate JOHN KIDD if so, much the said AMOS WICKERSHAM and ALEXANDER KIDD have in their hands to be administered and if they have it not then the costs are to be levied of their proper goods and chattels and the said Defendants in mercy.

GEORGE KELLY Plaintiff
Against Re: In Case
AMOS WICKERSHAM and ALEXANDER KIDD Administrators of JOHN KIDD deceased Defendant
This day came as well the Plaintiff by THOMAS BURKE Gentleman their Attorney as the defendant in their proper person and say that they cannot gainsay the plaintiff action nor but that their intestate did assume in manner and form as the Plaintiff against them have declared. Therefore, it is considered that the Plaintiff recover against the said Defendants 19 pounds 4 shillings and 11 pence and his costs
PAGE 95B
by him about his suit in this behalf expended to be levied of the goods and chattels of the said intestate JOHN KIDD if so, much the said AMOS WICKERSHAM and ALEXANDER KIDD have in their hands to be administered and if they have it not then the costs are to be levied of their proper goods and chattels and the said Defendants in mercy.

AMOS WICKERSHAM and ALEXANDER KIDD administrators of JOHN KIDD deceased Power of Attorney to ALEXANDER LOVE and JONATHAN MITCHELL was this day acknowledged and ordered to be registered.

On the motion of ARCHIBALD CAMPBELL Gentleman and GEORGE WILSON administrators of JOHN WILSON deceased setting forth that their intestate died in Custody of the Sergeant of this Borough upon an execution at the suit of MATT GODFREY Gentleman and that afterwards his goods and chattels were taken by another execution and prayed the same might be quashed. The Court on solemn argument are of opinion the said execution ought not to be quashed. From which Judgement the said ARCHIBALD CAMPBELL and GEORGE WILSON Administrators as aforesaid prayed an appeal to the 8th day of the Next General Court which on their giving security of prosecution at or before the next Court is granted them.

ARCHIBALD CAMPBELL Plaintiff
Against Re: In Debt
JAMES ROGERS Defendant
This day came as well the Plaintiff by THOMAS BURKE Gentleman his Attorney as the Defendant in his proper person and acknowledges the Plaintiff's action for 12 pounds 4 shillings and 6 pence current money. Therefore, it is considered that the Plaintiff recover against the said Defendant his Debt aforesaid and his costs by him about his suit in this behalf expended and the said Defendant in mercy.

SAMUEL SWANN Plaintiff
Against Re: In Trespass
ALEXANDER MORRISON Defendant
This day came the parties by their Attorney's and thereupon came also a Jury to wit: ELDRED FISHER, JOSEPH HARDING, JAMES MURPHREE, EDWARD MITCHELL, WILLIAM BALLARD, STEPHEN TANKARD, WILLIAM IVY, ROBERT STEELE, THOMAS HEPBURN, BARTHOLOMEW THOMPSON, THOMAS FARRER and ROBERT TAYLOR who being elected tried and sworn the truth to speak upon the issue joined upon their oath do say that the Defendant is guilty of the Trespass in the declaration mentioned in manner and form as the Plaintiff against him has declared and do assess the Plaintiff damages by occasion thereof to 17 pounds besides his costs.

PAGE 96
Therefore, it is considered that the Plaintiff recover against the said Defendant his damages by the Jurors aforesaid in this verdict assessed and his costs by him in this behalf expended and the said Defendant in mercy.

ANTHONY WARWICK and ARCHIBALD BUCHANAN against JAMES DUNLOP. The Plaintiffs by their Attorney moved for Special Bail which is granted. Whereupon JOHN GILCHRIST came into Court and entered himself Special Bail for the defendant and thereon prayed an Imparlance.

On the Attachment obtained by JONATHAN MEREDITH and ELIZABETH his wife against the Estate of JOHN FIELD and ALICE his wife who have privately removed themselves or so absconds that the Ordinary process cannot be served on them and the Sheriff now making return that by virtue thereof he has levied the same in the hands of JAMES LEITCH who appeared on oath declared he had in his hands 2 pounds 5 shillings and 3 pence and the said Defendant being called and not appearing where upon the Plaintiff proved their account of 2 pounds 5 shillings and 6 pence. Therefore, it is considered that the Plaintiff recover the same against the Defendant and their costs by them in this behalf expended and it is ordered that the garnishee pay the money in his hands to the Plaintiffs in discharge of this judgement and costs and the Sergeant return an account of his proceedings at the next Court.

Order is granted NATHANIEL FLEMING against SAMUEL SWAN for 345 pounds of tobacco for 3 days attendance coming and returning 30 miles 3 times and 1 shilling and 10 pence ferriages in his suit against ALEXANDER MORRISON (tax 2 days)

Order is granted WILLIAM GRANBURY and HENRY BATES against SAMUEL SWAN for 130 pounds tobacco each for 2 days attendance each coming and returning 30 miles twice and 1/3 ferriages each in his suit against ALEXANDER MORRISON.

ROBERT GORDON against GEORGE LATHBURY. Dismissed.

ARCHIBALD WHITE and COMPANY Plaintiff
Against Re: In Debt.
GEORGE OLDNER Defendant
This day came the parties by their Attorney's and the Defendant by his Attorney relinquishing his former plea, acknowledges the Plaintiffs action for 28 pounds 10 shillings and 6 pence. Therefore, it is considered that the Plaintiff recover against the said Defendant in mercy. But this judgement is to be discharged by the payment of 14 pounds 5 shillings and 6 pence with interest for the same at the rate of 5% per annum to be computed from July 15th, 1767, to the time of payment and the costs.

PAGE 96B
WALTER LYON Plaintiff
Against Re: In Case
WILLIAM BROWN Defendant
This day came the Plaintiff by JAMES HOLT Gentleman his Attorney and thereupon came also a Jury to wit: ELDRED FISHER, JOSEPH HARDING, JAMES MURPHREE, EDWARD MITCHELL, WILLIAM BALLARD, STEPHEN TANKARD, WILLIAM IVY, ROBERT STEELE, THOMAS HEPBURN, BARTHOLOMNEW THOMPSON, THOMAS FARRER and ROBERT TAYLOR who being sworn well and truly to inquire of damages in this suit upon their oath do say that the Plaintiff has sustained damages by occasion of the Defendants breach of promise in the declaration mentioned to 11 pounds 9 shillings and 6 pence besides his costs. Therefore, it is considered by the Court that the Plaintiff recover against the said Defendant his damages aforesaid in form aforesaid assessed and his costs by him in this behalf expended and the said Defendant in mercy.

GEORGE ABYVON Plaintiff
Against Re: In Case
CHARLES JENKINS executor of JOSEPH LOCKHART Deceased Defendant

This day came the parties by their Attorney's and thereupon came also a Jury to wit: ELDRED FISHER, JOSEPH HARDING, JAMES MURPHREE, EDWARD MITCHELL, WILLIAM BALLARD, STEPHEN TANKARD, WILLIAM IVY, ROBERT STEELE, THOMAS HEPBURN, BARTHOLOMEW THOMPSON, THOMAS FARRER and ROBERT TAYLOR who being elected tried and sworn the truth to speak upon the issue joined upon their oath do say that the Defendant testator did assume in manner and form as the Plaintiff against him has declared and do assess the Plaintiff damages by occasion of the non-performance of that assumption to 18 pounds, 5 shillings besides his costs. Therefore, it is considered by the Court that the Plaintiff recover against the said Defendant his damages aforesaid in form aforesaid assessed and his costs by him in this behalf expended. To be levied of the goods and chattels of the said Testator if so, much the said CHARLES JENKINS has in his hands to be administered and if he has it not then the costs are to be levied of his proper goods and chattels and the said Defendant in mercy.

WILLIAM NIMMO Surviving executor of ADAM THOROWGOOD Deceased Plaintiff
Against Re: In Debt.
GEORGE OLDNER Defendant

This day came the parties by their Attorney's and there upon came also a Jury to wit:
ELDRED FISHER, JOSEPH HARDING, JAMES MURPHREE, EDWARD MITCHELL, WILLIAM BALLARD, STEPHEN TANKARD, WILLIAM IVY, ROBERT STEELE, THOMAS HEPBURN, BARTHOLOMEW THOMPSON, THOMAS FARRER, and ROBERT TAYLOR who being elected tried and sworn the truth to speak upon the issue joined upon their oath do say that the Defendant has not paid the debt in the declaration mentioned. Therefore, it is considered that the Plaintiff recover against the said Defendant his debt aforesaid amounting to 40 pounds and his costs by him about his suit in this behalf expended. And the said Defendant in mercy.

PAGE 97

But this Judgement is to be discharged by the payment of 20 pounds with interest for the same at the rate of 5% per annum to be computed from January 16, 1768, to the time of payment and the costs.

ARCHIBALD WHITE and COMPANY Plaintiffs
Against Re: In Debt.
JOHN TATEM Defendant

This day came the parties by their Attorney's and the Defendant by his Attorney relinquishes his former plea and acknowledges the Plaintiff's action for 55 pounds 10 shillings and 8 pence half penny. Therefore, it is considered that the Plaintiff recover against the said Defendant his debt aforesaid and their cots by them in this behalf expended and the said Defendant in mercy. But this judgement is to be discharged by the payment of 27 pounds 15 shillings and 4 pence 1 farthing with interest for the same at the rate of 5% per annum to be computed from September 19, 1768, to the time of payment & costs.

This Court is adjourned to Court in Course. GEORGE ABYVON MAYOR. TESTE: JOHN BOUSH D.C.C.

NORFOLK BOROUGH

At a Hustings Court Held this 20th day of January 1772
PRESENT: GEORGE ABYVON ESQUIRE MAYOR
GENTLEMAN ALDERMEN: PAUL LOYALL, MAXIMILIAN CALVERT, LEWIS HANSFORD, CORNELIUS CALVERT

JOHN IVY and ELIZABETH his wife against GOODRICH BOUSH and SAMUEL BOUSH agreed dismissed.
MATTHEW COCKRAN against ROBERT BOYD. Dismissed.

HENRY BRESSIE Plaintiff
Against Re: In Debt
JOHN SHIPWASH Defendant

The Plaintiff not further prosecuting. On the motion of the Defendant by his Attorney. It is ordered that this suit be discontinued, and that the Plaintiff pay the Defendant his costs.

THOMAS LANGLEY SR. against JOHN and JOSEPH HUTCHINGS in DETINUE. This day the Plaintiff by his Attorney as the Defendant JOSEPH in his proper person and prays and has leave to IMPARLE here until the next Court and then to plead.

PAGE 97B

THOMAS LANGLEY SR. Plaintiff against JAMES PASTEUR Defendant in detinue. This day came the parties by their Attorney's and the said Defendant says that he does not detain the slave in manner and form as the Plaintiff against him has declared and of this he puts himself upon the Country and the Plaintiff likewise, Therefore, the issue is referred until the next Court.

WILLISON and MCSWEEN Plaintiffs against JOHN BURNLEY Defendant in debt. This day came the Plaintiffs by THOMAS BURKE Gentleman their Attorney and the Defendant being solemnly called and not appearing. A Conditional order is granted the Plaintiff against the said Defendant and ALEXANDER LOVE his bail.

On the Attachment obtained by WILLIAM IVY against the Estate of PETER ADAMS who has privately removed himself or so absconds that the Ordinary process of law cannot be served on him and the Sheriff now making return that by virtue thereof he has levied the same in the hands of ROGER PIERCE who appeared and on oath declared that he has sufficient in his hands to satisfy the Plaintiffs claim payable the 25th day of April next and the said Defendant being called and not appearing nor replevying his said estate. Where upon the Plaintiff proved his said claim to 19 pounds 5 shillings and 10 pence to be just. Therefore, it is considered that the Plaintiff recover the same against the said Defendant together with his costs by him in this behalf expended and it is ordered that the garnishee pay the money at the time limited for payment.

The King against JOHN DAVID MUNSTER. Dismissed at the Defendant's cost.

HENRY BRESSIE Plaintiff
Against Re: In Case
AARON BARBER Defendant
This day came the Plaintiff by THOMAS BURKE Gentleman his Attorney and an attachment having been awarded the Plaintiff against the estate of the said Defendant and the Sheriff now making return that by virtue thereof he has attached one tea chest and the said Defendant being solemnly called and not appearing. A writ of inquiry is awarded the Plaintiff to inquire of damages in this suit.

JOHN WILLS against JOHN JOHNSON. Dismissed.

ROBERT GILCHRIST against WILLIAM DAVENPORT. By Petition and Summons. Judgement is granted the Plaintiff for 1 pounds 18 shillings and 6 pence. It is ordered that the Defendant pay the same unto the Plaintiff with costs and fee.

PAGE 98

GEORGE JACKSON against ALEXANDER BELL. Dismissed.

JOHN LAWRENCE and MATTHEW PHRIPP Executors of THOMAS THOMPSON deceased against LEMUEL LANGLEY in debt. This day came the Plaintiffs by WILLIAM RASCOW WILSON CURLE Gentleman their attorney and the Defendant being solemnly called and not appearing. A conditional order is granted the Plaintiff against the said Defendant and CADER COOPER his bail.

JOHN LAWRENCE and MATTHEW PHRIPP Executors of THOMAS THOMPSON deceased against LEMUEL LANGLEY in debt. This day came the Plaintiffs by WILLIAM RASCOW WILSON CURLE Gentleman their Attorney and the Defendant being solemnly called and not appearing. A conditional order is granted the Plaintiff against the said Defendant and CADER COOPER his bail.

HENRY FLEMING, HENRY BRAY and ROBERT FISHER against JOSEPH HUTCHINGS ESQUIRE in debt. This day came the parties by their Attorney's and the Defendant prays and has leave to IMPARLE here until the next Court and then to plead.

MALACHI MAUND against SAMUEL and HENRY BRESSIE in case. This day came the parties by their Attorneys and the defendants pray and have leave to IMPARLE here until the next Court and then to plea.

ANDREW MARTIN against ALEXANDER BELL. Dismissed.
JOSHUA WRIGHT against JOHN FROST. Dismissed.

JOHN HARDY against JOHN BAISER. By Petition and Summons. Judgement is granted the Plaintiff for 1 pounds 19 shillings and 2 pence. It is ordered that the Defendant pay the same unto the Plaintiff with costs and fee.

On the Petition of BASSET MOSELEY against PAUL LOYALL and LATIMORE HALSTEAD, Administrators of JONATHAN DISON deceased for 3 pounds 15 shillings and 3 pence 3 farthing said to be due by account. This day came the parties in their proper person and the Plaintiff having provided his demand to be just by his own oath. Therefore, it is considered the course that the Plaintiff recover the same against the said Defendants together with his costs by him in this behalf expended. When assets after satisfying debts of greater dignity and the defendants own claims of equal dignity against the estate of the said intestate to be levied of the good and chattels of the said intestate if so, much the said defendant have in their hands to be administered and if they have it not then the costs are to be levied of their proper good and chattels and the said Defendant in mercy.

DICKERSON PRIOR against AARON BARBER and HOFFMIRE in case. This day came the Plaintiff by THOMAS BURKE Gentleman his Attorney and the defendants being solemnly called and not appearing a conditional order is granted the Plaintiff against the said Defendants and JOHN WOODSIDE their bail.

PAGE 98B

JAMES ROGERS against JAMES CLARKE. By Petition and Summons. Judgement is granted the Plaintiff for 2 pounds 2 shillings and 10 pence. It is ordered that the Defendant pay the same unto the Plaintiff with costs and fee.

Order is granted ROBERT MOORIE against JAMES ROGERS for 25 pounds of tobacco for 1 day's attendance in his suit against JAMES CLARKE.

WILLIAM WILLIS against CHARLES HARVEY PARKER. Dismissed.
JOSEPH MITCHELL against JOHN POOL. Dismissed.

JOSEPH MITCHELL against NICHOLAS POOLE in debt. STEPHEN TANKARD this day came into Court and undertook for the Defendant that in case he shall be cast in this suit he the said Defendant will pay the condemnation of the Court or render his body to prison in execution for the same or the body of the said Defendant aforesaid where upon the Defendant by his Attorney prays and has leave to IMPARLE until the next Court and then to plead.

JOHN WOODSIDE against WILLIAM GODFREY administrators of JONATHAN GODFREY deceased. This day came the parties by their Attorney's and the Defendant prays and has leave to IMPARLE here until the next Court and then to plead.

JOHN CRAMOND against JOHN PARSONS in case. JAMES MOORE of Princess Anne County this day came into Court and undertook for the Defendant that in case he shall be cast in this suit he the said Defendant will pay the Condemnation of the Court or render his body to prison or render the body of the said Defendant as aforesaid. Whereupon the Defendant by his Attorney prays and has leave to IMPARLE here until the next Court and then to plead.

DAVID ETHERIDGE against ELDRED FISHER and EDWARD PARKE in debt. JAMES MARSDEN this day came into Court and undertook for the Defendants that in case they shall be cast in this suit that they said Defendants will pay the condemnation of the Court or render their bodies to prison in execution for the same or that he the said MARSDEN will pay the condemnation of the Court or render the bodies of the said Defendants as aforesaid where upon the Defendants by their Attorney prays and has leave to IMPARLE until the next Court and then to plead.

MISTERS BOUSH and BALLARD against JAMES and EDWARD DAVIS. Dismissed.
GEORGE WATSON against ALICE FIELD by attachment. Dismissed.

Order is granted CHRISTOPHER SHELTON and GEORGE FARRER against ROBERT GILCHRIST for 75 pounds of tobacco for 3 days attendance each in this suit against WILLIAM DAVENPORT.

PAGE 99
On the motion of MATTHEW GODFREY Gentleman by WILLIAM RASCOW WILSON CURLE Gentleman his Attorney. Order that the Clerk deliver him WILLIAM MCCAA and alias bond in his suit against him.

ANDREW STEWART against ALEXANDER BELL in debt. JOHN MCLACHLAN this day came into Court and undertook for the Defendant that in case they shall be cast in this suit he the said Defendants will pay the condemnation of the Court or render his body to prison in execution for the same or that he the said MCLACHLAN will pay the condemnation of the Court or render the body of the said Defendant as aforesaid where upon the Defendant in person prays and has leave to IMPARLE until the next Court and then to plead.

King against JUDY DUNFORD alias FENWICK and ELIZABETH CROFT by warrant dismissed at the defendant's cost.

This Court rates Flour at 15 shillings per centum
This Court is adjourned to Court in Course. GEORGE ABYVON MAYOR, TESTE: JOHN BOUSH D.C.C.

NORFOLK BOROUGH
At a Hustings Court Held this 24th day of February 1772
PRESENT: GEORGE ABYVON ESQUIRE MAYOR
GENTLEMAN ALDERMEN: ARCHIBALD CAMPBELL, JAMES TAYLOR, LEWIS HANSFORD,

JOHN STANHOPE against NATHANIEL BOUSH in case. This day came the parties by their Attorney's and the Defendant prays and has leave to IMPARLE here until the next Court and then to plead.

MATT KELLY and ANN, his wife against THOMAS TAYLOR and ELIZABETH his wife. This day came the parties by their Attorney's and the Defendant prays and has leave to IMPARLE here until the next Court and then plead.

JOHN REISER against PETER DEMOUNT. Dismissed.

MATT KELLY who as well as against MARY STAUNTON in debt. This day came the parties by their Attorneys and the Defendant prays and has leave to IMPARLE here until the next Court and then to plead.

WILLIAM GRAHAM against ROGER PIERCE in case. This day came the parties by their Attorney's and the Defendant prays and has leave to a Special IMPARLE here until the next Court and then to plead.

ROGER PIERCE against WILLIAM GRAHAM in case. This day came the parties by their Attorney's and the Defendant prays and has leave to IMPARLE special here until the next Court and then to plead.

ROBERT DONALD against WILLIAM WOOD. Dismissed.

PAGE 99B
JOHN REISER against ROGER PIERCE in case. RICHARD BROWN this day came into Court and undertook for the Defendant that in case they shall be cast in this suit he the said Defendants will pay the condemnation of the Court or render his body to prison in execution for the same or that he the said BROWN will pay the condemnation of the Court or render the body of the said Defendant as aforesaid where upon the Defendant in person prays and has leave to SPECIAL IMPARLE until the next Court and then to plead.

ROGER PIERCE against JOSEPH TODD in case. This day came the parties by their Attorney's and the defendant prays and has leave to Special IMPARLE here until the next Court and then to plead.

JOHN WILSON against JOHN MCWILLIAMS. Dismissed.
JOHN MCWILLIAMS against JOHN WILSON. Dismissed.

MISTERS YOUNG and SMITH against JAMES ROGERS by Petition and Summons. Judgement is granted the Plaintiff for 1 pounds 12 shillings and 9 pence. It is ordered that the Defendant pay the same unto the Plaintiff with costs and fee.

MISTERS YOUNG and SMITH against WILLIAM MINETREE. By Petition and Summons. Judgement is granted the Plaintiff for 2 pounds 2 shillings. It is ordered that the Defendant pay the same unto the Plaintiff with costs and fee.
JOSEPH NISBIT against RICHARD BROWN. Dismissed.

NICHOLAS BROWN SEABROOK against AARON BARBER in Case. HENRY SINGLETON this day came into Court and undertook for the Defendant that in case they shall be cast in this suit he the said Defendants will pay the condemnation of the Court or render his body to prison in execution for the same or that he the said SINGLETON will pay the condemnation of the Court or render the body of the said Defendant as aforesaid where upon the Defendant in person prays and has leave to SPECIAL IMPARLE until the next Court and then to plead.

JOHN CRAMOND against JONATHAN JACKSON in debt. This day came the parties by their Attorney's and the defendant prays and has leave to IMPARLE here until the next Court and then to plead.

WILLIAM SIMPSON Administrator of FRANCIS CLARKE deceased Plaintiff
Against Re: In Case
JONATHAN JACKSON Defendant
This day came as well the Plaintiff by WILLIAM RASCOW WILSON CURLE Gentleman his Attorney as the defendant in their proper person and says that he cannot gainsay the plaintiff's action nor but that he did assume in manner and form as the Plaintiff has declared. Therefore, it is considered that the Plaintiff recover against the said Defendant 8 pounds 11 shillings and 2 pence with interest thereon after at the rate of 5% per annum to be computed from December 24, 1770, to the time of payment and costs.

PAGE 100
LEMUEL LANGLEY against ARCHIBALD CAMPBELL admin of JOHN DALGLEISH deceased. Time.

GEORGE KELLY against MATTHEW PHRIPP and JOHN LAWRENCE executors of THOMAS THOMPSON in case. This day came as well the Plaintiff by his Attorney as MATT PHRIPP one of the Defendants in his proper person and prays and has leave to IMPARLE until the next Court and then to plead.

WILLS COWPER against JOHN POLLOCK in case. This day came the parties and their Attorney's, and the Defendant prays and has leave to IMPARLE here until the next Court and then to plead.

WILLS COWPER against ABRAHAM PATEON dismissed.

BENJAMIN CROOKER having obtained a license under the hands and seal of JOHN RANDOLPH, ROBERT CARTER NICHOLAS and GEORGE WYTHE Gentleman to practice as an Attorney and he having taken the oaths to the government and subscribed the test also the oath of an attorney's and admitted to practice in this Court.

ANDREW RONALD this day produced a license under the hands and seals of JOHN RANDOLPH and GEORGE WYTHE Gentleman to practice as an Attorney and he having taken the oaths to the Government and subscribed the test also the oath of an Attorney as admitted to practice in this Court.

WILLIAM WEBLY against JAMES WEBB and APHIA his wife. Executrix of WILLIS LANGLEY deceased dismissed at the Defendants costs.

ANNA MOORE executrix of FRANCIS MOORE deceased against MARK TALBOT and ELDRED FISHER in debt. This day came the parties by their attorneys and the Defendants TALBOT pleaded payment in manner and form as the plaintiff against him has declared and of this he puts himself upon the country and the Plaintiff likewise Therefore, the trial of the issue is referred until the next Court and continue against the other Defendant.

ISAAC LUKE assignee of EDWARD LOWE Plaintiff
Against Re: In Debt.
GEORGE BLINN Defendant
This day came the Plaintiff by WILLIAM RASCOW WILSON CURLE Gentleman his Attorney and there upon came also a Jury to wit: RICHARD BROWN, JOHN WILKINS, THOMAS FARRER, JAMES WALKER, JAMES DISON, GRIFFIN PEART, DICKERSON PRYOR, ROGER PIERCE, JAMES DUNN, JOHN SMITH, PAUL PROBY and JOSEPH NISBIT who being sworn well and truly to inquire of damages in this suit upon their oath do say that the Plaintiff has sustained damages by occasion of the Defendants breach of promise in the declaration mentioned to 15 pounds 16 shillings and 6 pence 3 farthings sterling besides his costs. Therefore, it is considered by the Court that the Plaintiff recover against the said Defendant his damages aforesaid in form aforesaid assessed and his costs by him in this behalf expended and the said Defendant in mercy. And the Court says the said sterling money may be discharged in current money at 25% difference of exchange.

PAGE 100B
And it is ordered that the Sergeant sell the attached effects according to law and apply the money arising thereby in discharging of this judgement and the costs and also return an accounting of his proceedings thereon at the next Court.

This Court rates Flour at 15 shillings per centum
This Court is adjourned to Court in Course, GEORGE ABYVON MAYOR, TESTE: JOHN BOUSH D.C.C.

NORFOLK BOROUGH
At a Hustings Court Held this 23rd day of March 1772
PRESENT: GEORGE ABYVON ESQUIRE MAYOR
GENTLEMAN ALDERMEN: ARCHIBALD CAMPBELL, MAXIMILIAN CALVERT, PAUL LOYAL, JAMES TAYLOR, LEWIS HANSFORD, CORNELIUS CALVERT

JOHN MEARNS against JOHN WALKINSHAW. Dismissed.
WILLIAM LIDDLE against JOHN CAMPBELL. Dismissed.

CHARLES RUDDER against JAMES DAWSON. By Petition and Summons. Judgement is granted the Plaintiff for 2 pounds. It is ordered that the Defendant pay the same unto the Plaintiff with costs and fee. And on failure of immediate payment, it is ordered the Sergeant give him 39 lashes on his bare back well laid on at the whipping post.

MISTERS YOUNG and SMITH against JOHN FROST. Dismissed.

CHARLES MAYLE against SAMUEL BRESSIE in debt. This day came the parties by their Attorney's and the Defendant prays and has leave to Special IMPARLE here until next Court and then to plead and OYER of the bond is granted.

CHARLES MAYLE against SAMUEL BRESSIE in case. This day came the parties by their Attorney's and the Defendant says that he did not assume upon himself in manner and form as the Plaintiff against him has declared and of this he puts himself upon the country and the plaintiff likewise. Therefore, the trial of the issue is referred until next Court.

ROBERT SHEDDEN and Company against BRYAN CROSBIE. This day JOHN GREENWOOD came into Court and undertook for the Defendant that in case he shall be cast in this suit he the said Defendant will pay the condemnation of the Court or render his body to prison in execution for the same or that he the said GREENWOD will pay the condemnation of the Court or render the body of the said Defendant as aforesaid.

PAGE 101

Where upon the defendant by his Attorney prays and has leave to special IMPARLE here until the next Court and then to plead.

WILLIAM SIMPSON against MATTHEW PHRIPP and JOHN LAWRENCE executors of THOMAS THOMPSON deceased in case. This day came the Plaintiff by his Attorney as MATTHEW PHRIPP one of the Defendants in his proper person and prays and has leave to IMPARLE here until the next Court and then to plead.

MICHAEL CHRISTIAN and JOHN HARMANSON against ALEXANDER MCSWEEN in case. This day came the parties by their Attorney's and the Defendant prays and has leave to IMPARLE here until next Court and then to plead.

CHARLES WARREN against MATTHEW ROTHERY abates by the Defendants death.

JAMES DAVIDSON against JAMES YOUNG and ANDREW MILLER and COMPANY in case. Discontinued against YOUNG and ROBERT GILMOUR this day came unto Court and undertook for the Defendants that in case they shall be cast in this suit that they said Defendants will pay the condemnation of the Court or render their bodies to prison in execution for the same or that he the said GILMOUR will pay the condemnation of the Court or render the bodies of the said Defendants as aforesaid where upon the Defendants by their Attorney's pray and have leave to IMPARLE here until the next Court and then to plead. And JOHN LAWRENCE undertakes for the Plaintiff that he will pay the Defendants all such damages costs and charges as shall be awarded against him by the Court.

CASPER HERITTER Plaintiff
Against Re: In Case
LUAN CLEMONS Defendant.
This day came as well the Plaintiff by WILLIAM RASCOW WILSON CURLE Gentleman his Attorney as the Defendant in custody of the Sergeant and says that he cannot gainsay the Plaintiffs action nor but that he did assume in manner and form as the Plaintiff against him has declared. Therefore, it is considered that the Plaintiff recover against the said Defendant 5 pounds 5 shillings and 1 penny and his costs by him about his suit in this behalf expended and the said Defendant in mercy and no Comitatus being prayed he is discharged.

MATT ROTHERY against ANN BOUCHER admin of DANIEL ROTHERY abates by the Plaintiffs death.
WILLIS WILSON against MATTHEW ROTHERY abates by the Defendants death.
FRANCIS WISHART against JOHN IVY administrator of WILLIAM IVY deceased abates the Plaintiff's death.
MATTHEW ROTHERY against AARON BARBER abates the by the Plaintiff's death.

PAGE 101B

GEORGE JOSEPH FENWICK against WILLIAM KEETON. Dismissed at Plaintiff's costs for want of payment at former trial.

ROBERT FORESYTHE Plaintiff
Against Re: In case
JOHN JOHNSON Defendant
This day came the Defendant by JAMES HOLT Gentleman his Attorney and the Plaintiff though solemnly called came not but made default nor is his suit further prosecuted. Therefore, on the prayer of the Defendant it is considered that he recover against the Plaintiff 5 shillings current money and his costs by him about his defense in this behalf expended according to the form of the act of assembly and the plaintiff for his false claims be in mercy.

ANNA MOORE Executrix of FRANCIS MOORE Deceased Plaintiff
Against Re: In Case
MARK TALBOT and ELDRED FISHER Defendants
This day came the parties by their Attorneys and there upon came also a Jury to wit: JOHN GILCHRIST, JOEL MOHUN, JOHN RICHARDSON, PAUL PROBY, WILLIAM STEVENSON, WILLIAM FREEMAN, JAMES DISON, ROBERT TAYLOR, RICHARD TALBOT, DICKERSON PRIOR, STEPHEN TANKARD and HENRY BRESSIE who being elected tried and sworn the truth to speak upon the issue joined upon their oath do say that the defendant have not paid the debt in the declaration mentioned Therefore, it is considered that the Plaintiff recover against the said Defendants her debt aforesaid amounting to 14 pounds 4 shillings and her costs by her in this behalf expended and the said Defendant in

mercy. But this judgement is to be discharged by the payment of 7 pounds 2 shillings with interest for the same at the rate of 5 % per annum to be computed from September 29, 1770, to the time of payment and the costs.

AARON BARBER and JOSIAH HOFFMIRE Plaintiff
Against Re: In Case
JOHN CURLING Defendant
This day came the Plaintiff by JAMES HOLT Gentleman their Attorney and there upon came also a Jury to wit: JOHN GILCHRIST, JOEL MOHUN, JOHN RICHARDSON, PAUL PROBY, WILLIAM STEVENSON, JAMES DISON, ROBERT TAYLOR, RICHARD TALBOT, DICKERSON PRIOR, STEPHEN TANKARD, HENRY BRESSIE and WILLIAM FREEMAN who being sworn well and truly to inquire of damages in this suit upon their oath do say that the Plaintiff have sustained damages by occasion of the Defendants breach of promise in the Declaration mentioned to 16 pounds 16 shillings besides their costs. Therefore, it is considered by the Court that the Plaintiff recover against the Defendant and DANIEL CURLING his bail their damages aforesaid in form aforesaid and their costs by them about their suit in this behalf expended and the said Defendant in mercy.

PAGE 102
MATTHEW KELLY and ANN, his wife Plaintiff
Against Re: In Trespass Assault and Battery
FRANCIS CONNER Defendant
This day came the Defendant by JAMES HOLT Gentleman his Attorney and the Plaintiff called came not but made default nor is their suit further prosecuted. Therefore, on the prayer of the Defendant it is considered that he recover against the Plaintiff 5 shillings current money and his costs by him about his Defense in this behalf expended according to the form of the Act of Assembly and the Plaintiff for their false claims be in mercy.

AARON BARBER and JOSIAH HOFFMIRE Plaintiff
Against Re: in Case
JOSEPH CURLING Defendants
This day came the Plaintiff by JAMES HOLT Gentleman their Attorney and there upon came also a Jury to wit: JOHN GILCHRIST, JOEL MOHUN, JOHN RICHARDSON, PAUL PROBY, WILLIAM STEVENSON, WILLIAM FREEMAN, JAMES DISON, ROBERT TAYLOR, RICHARD TALBOT, DICKERSON PRIOR, STEPHEN TANKARD, and HENRY BRESSIE who being sworn well and truly to inquire of damages in this suit upon their oath do say that the Plaintiff have sustained damages by occasion of the Defendants Breach of Promise in the Declaration mentioned to 27 pounds 16 shillings and 10 pence besides their costs. Therefore, it is considered by the Court that the Plaintiff recover against the Defendant and JOHN CURLING his bail their damages aforesaid in form aforesaid and their costs by them about their suit in this behalf expended and the said Defendant in mercy.

WILLIAM SMITH and RICHARD TEMPLEMAN administrators of ROBERT TUCKER deceased Plaintiffs
Against Re: In Case
JOSIAH HOFFMIRE Defendant
This day came the parties by their Attorney's and there upon came also a Jury to wit: JOHN GILCHRIST, JOEL MOHUN, JOHN RICHARDSON, PAUL PROBY, WILLIAM STEVENSON, WILLIAM FREEMAN, JAMES DISON, ROBERT TAYLOR, RICHARD TALBOT, DICKERSON PRIOR, STEPHEN TANKARD, and HENRY BRESSIE who being elected tried and sworn the truth to speak upon the issue joined upon their oath do say that the Defendant did assume in manner and form as the Plaintiffs against him has declared and do assess the Plaintiffs damages by occasion of the non-performance of that assumption to 8 pounds, and 3 pence besides their costs. Therefore, it is considered that the Plaintiff recover against the said Defendant their damages aforesaid in form aforesaid assessed and their costs by them about their suit in this behalf expended. And the said Defendant in mercy.

PAGE 102B
Order is granted NATHANIEL RAINES against AARON BARBER and JOSIAH HOFFMIRE for 25 pounds of tobacco for 1 day's attendance in their suit against JOHN CURLING.

Order is granted NATHANIEL RAINES against AARON BARBER and JOSIAH HOFFMIRE for 25 pounds of tobacco for 1 day's attendance in their suit against JOHN CURLING. (Listed 2x)

DANIEL CURLING Plaintiff
Against Re: In Case
JOSIAH HOFFMIRE Defendant
This day came the parties by their Attorney's and the Defendant by his Attorney relinquishes his former plea says that he cannot gainsay the Plaintiffs action nor but that he did assume in manner and form as the Plaintiff against him has declared. Therefore, it is considered that the Plaintiff recover against the said Defendant 3 pounds 11 shillings and 9 pence and his costs by him in this behalf expended and the said Defendant in mercy.

SAMUEL PORTLOCK against WILLIAM SHIPWASH. Breaches assigned and a Writ of Inquiry.
WRIGHT WESTCOTT administrator of JOHN WESTCOTT deceased against JOHN TATEM and JOSEPH HUTCHINGS This day came the parties by their Attorney's and the Defendant pleaded payment n manner and form as the Plaintiff against them have declared and of this they put themselves upon the County and the Plaintiff likewise Therefore, the trial of the issue is referred until the next Court.

JAMES MOORE Plaintiff

Against Re: In Case

NATHANIEL BOUSH Defendant

This day came the parties by their Attorney's and there upon came also a Jury to wit: : JOHN GILCHRIST, JOEL MOHUN, JOHN RICHARDSON, PAUL PROBY, WILLIAM STEVENSON, WILLIAM FREEMAN,JAMES DISON, ROBERT TAYLOR, RICHARD TALBOT, DICKERSON PRIOR, STEPHEN TANKARD, and HENRY BRESSIE who being elected tried and sworn the truth to speak upon the issue joined upon their oath do say that the Defendant did assume in manner and form as the Plaintiffs against him has declared and do assess the Plaintiffs damages by occasion of the non-performance of that assumption to 64 pounds, 8 shillings and 6 pence besides their costs.

Therefore, it is considered that the Plaintiff recover against the said Defendant their damages aforesaid in form aforesaid assessed and their costs by them about their suit in this behalf expended. And the said Defendant in mercy.

Order is granted FREDERICK BOUSH against JAMES MOORE for 116 pounds of tobacco for 2 days attendance coming and returning 11 miles twice in his suit against NATHANIEL BOUSH.

PAGE 103

JOHN MCLACHLAN Plaintiff

Against Re: In Debt.

JOHN MADDOX Defendant

This day came the parties by their Attorney's and there upon came also a Jury to wit: JOHN GILCHRIST, JOEL MOHUN, JOHN RICHARDSON, PAUL PROBY, WILLIAM STEVENSON, WILLIAM FREEMAN, JAMES DISON, ROBERT TAYLOR, RICHARD TALBOT, DICKERSON PRIOR, STEPHEN TANKARD, HENRY BRESSIE and SAMUEL BRESSIE who being elected tried and sworn the truth to speak upon the issue joined upon their oath do say that the Defendant has not paid the debt in the declaration mentioned. Therefore, it is considered that the Plaintiff recover against he said Defendant his debt aforesaid amounting to 8 pounds 13 shillings and his costs by him in this behalf expended and the said Defendant in mercy.

JAMES BRIDGER Plaintiff

Against Re: In Case

JOSEPH CALVERT Defendant

This day came the parties by their Attorney's and there upon came also a Jury to wit: JOHN GILCHRIST, JOEL MOHUN, JOHN RICHARDSON, PAUL PROBY, WILLIAM STEVENSON, WILLIAM FREEMAN,JAMES DISON, ROBERT TAYLOR, RICHARD TALBOT, DICKERSON PRIOR, STEPHEN TANKARD, and HENRY BRESSIE who being elected tried and sworn the truth to speak upon the issue joined upon their oath do say that the Defendant did assume in manner and form as the Plaintiffs against him has declared and do assess the Plaintiffs damages by occasion of the non-performance of that assumption to 12 pounds, 16 shillings besides his costs. Therefore, it is considered that the Plaintiff recover against the said Defendant their damages aforesaid in form aforesaid assessed and their costs by them about their suit in this behalf expended. And the said Defendant in mercy.

WRIGHT WESTCOTT Plaintiff

Against Re: In Trespass

WILLIS DUNFORD Defendant

This day came the Defendant by JAMES HOLT Gentleman his Attorney and the plaintiff solemnly called came not but made default nor is his suit further prosecuted. Therefore, on the prayers of the Defendant. It is considered that he recover against the Plaintiff 5 shillings current money and his costs by him about his defense in this behalf expended according to the form of the Act of Assembly and the Plaintiff for his false claims be in mercy.

Order is granted JAMES ATKINSON against CHARLES RUDDER for 100 pounds of tobacco for 4 days attendance at this Court as a witness in his suit against JAMES DAWSON.

PAGE 103B

JOSHUA EDWARDS and MARY, his wife Plaintiffs

Against Re: In Trespass Assault and Battery

THOMAS DICKERSON Defendants

This day came the parties by their Attorney's and there upon came also a Jury to wit: JOHN GILCHRIST, JOEL MOHUN, JOHN RICHARDSON, PAUL PROBY, WILLIAM STEVENSON, WILLIAM FREEMAN, JAMES DISON, ROBERT TAYLOR, RICHARD TALBOT, DICKERSON PRIOR, STEPHEN TANKARD, and HENRY BRESSIE who being elected tried and sworn the truth to speak upon the issue joined upon their oath do say that the Defendant is not guilty as in pleading he has alleged. Therefore, it is considered that the Plaintiff take nothing by their bill but for their false claims be in mercy and the Defendant go hence without day and recover against the Plaintiffs his costs by him about his Defense in this behalf expended.

DICKERSON PRIOR and FRANCES his wife administratrix of RICHARD FRASIER deceased Plaintiff

Against Re: In Case

THOMAS BUTT Defendant

This day came the parties by their Attorney's and there upon came also a Jury to wit: JOHN MCLEAN, THOMAS DICKERSON, WILLIAM BICKERDICK, JOHN MARLEY, JOHN WALKER, JOHN SHEDDEN, REUBEN SHARP, SAMUEL BRESSIE, SAMUEL TOMLINSON, JOSEPH HARDING, PETER EDWARDS, and ROBERT GILMOUR who being elected tried and sworn the truth to speak upon the issue joined upon their oath do say that the Defendant did not assume as in pleading he has alleged. Therefore, it is considered that the Plaintiff take nothing by their bill but for their false claims be in mercy and the Defendant go hence without day and recover against the Plaintiffs his costs by him about his Defense in this behalf expended.

PAUL HERITRER against PETER REISER by warren dismissed at the Defendants cost.

PAGE 104

Order is granted GEORGE FARRER against THOMAS DICKERSON for 150 pounds tobacco for 6 days attendance of his wife JUDAH in the suit of JOSHUA EDWARDS and MARY his wife against him.

Order is granted BAILEY WARREN against THOMAS DICKERSON for 150 pounds tobacco for 6 days attendance of his wife ELIRA in the suit of JOSHUA EDWARDS and MARY his wife against him.

Order is granted JONATHAN HOPKINS against JOHN PARSONS administrator of THOMAS WILD deceased for 366 pounds of tobacco for 6 days attendance coming and returning 12 miles 6 times in his suit against WILLIAM SMITH.

Order is granted JOHN MURDEN against JOHN PARSONS administrator of THOMAS WILD deceased for 330 pounds of tobacco for 6 days attendance at this Court, coming and returning 10 miles 6 times in his suit against WILLIAM SMITH.

Order is granted JAMES WHITEHURST against JOHN PARSONS administrator of THOMAS WILD deceased for 448 pounds of tobacco for 7 days attendance at this Court, coming and returning 13 miles 7 times in his suit against WILLIAM SMITH.

Order is granted GEORGE WILLIAMS against JOHN PARSONS administrator of THOMAS WILD deceased for 448 pounds of tobacco for 7 days attendance at this Court coming and returning 13 miles 7 times in his suit against WILLIAM SMITH.

Order is granted THOMAS GODFREY against JOHN PARSONS administrator of THOMAS WILD deceased for 448 pounds of tobacco for 7 days attendance of his wife SARAH GODFREY at this Court coming and returning 13 miles 7 times in his suit against WILLIAM SMITH.

Order is granted JONATHAN MEREDITH against WILLIAM SMITH 25 pounds of tobacco for 1 day's attendance in the suit of JONATHAN PARSONS administrator of THOMAS WILDS deceased against him.

Order is granted WILLOUGHBY WEBLIN against WILLIAM SMITH for 427 pounds of tobacco for 7 days attendance at this Court coming and returning 12 miles 7 times in the suit of JOHN PARSONS admin of THOMAS WILDS deceased against him.

Order is granted WILLIAM KAYS against WILLIAM SMITH for 448 pounds of tobacco for 7 days attendance at this Court coming and returning 13 miles 7 times. WILLIAM WHITEHURST against WILLIAM SMITH for 448 pounds of tobacco for 7 days attendance at this Court coming and returning 13 miles 7 times. TULLY MOSELEY against WILLIAM SMITH for 402 pounds of tobacco for 6 days attendance at this Court coming and returning 14 miles 6 times in the suit of JOHN PARSONS Administrator of THOMAS WILDS deceased against him.

Our Lord the King against JAMES FLETCHER, JOHN GILCHIRST and JAMES GILCHRIST dismissed.

PAGE 104B

WILLIAM LEWELLING Plaintiff

Against Re: In Chancery

MATTHEW PHRIPP Administrator of JOHN PHRIPP JR. Deceased Defendant

This day came the Plaintiff by WILLIAM RASCOW WILSON CURLE Gentleman his Attorney as the Defendant in his proper person and the Commissioners appointed to meet, state, and examine the account between the parties this day made their report in these words to wit: DR. The Estate MR. JOHN PHRIPP in account with the estate of RICHARD LEWELLING CR.

06.26.1762	To Cash Received ABEL LEWELLING sale of land per receipt	L50.0.0
12.13.1762	To WILLIAM ORANGES Account	1.10.0
1763 APR	To AITCHESON & PARKER for their Account against MRS. WALKE	1.4.0
	To Interest on L50 FROM 0.24.1762 UNTIL 03.18.1772	24.6.3
		77.0.3
1761 JAN	By Sundries	2.3.4
1762 JAN	By Cash paid MR. BOUSH for Clerk's fees	4.1.0
MARCH 9	By Cash paid MRS. NISBIT	0.4.0
JUNE 17	By cash paid ARCHIBALD WHITE his account	10.4.1
JUNE 29	By Cash paid SAMUEL FARMER his account	1.12.4 1/2
	By Interest on L15.10.9 1/2 From March 18, 1762, until March 18, 1772, 10 YEARS	7.15.4 1/2
		L26.0.2
	By Balance due the Estate of R. LEWELLING	51.0.1
		L77.0.3

In Obedience to the Order of the worshipful Court of Norfolk we the subscribed have examined the accounts between the Estate of JOHN PHRIPP and the Estate of RICHARD LEWELLING both deceased and do find the above balance of 51 pounds and 1 penny due from the former to the later ALEXANDER DIACK, JOHN WILKINS JR., JOHN SHEDDEN. On Consideration whereof it is ordered and decreed that the Defendant pay unto the Plaintiff the said 51 pounds and one penny and his costs by him about his suit in this behalf expended.

JOHN SCOTT and ANN, his wife Plaintiffs
Against Re: In Case for Slander
PETER BEISER Defendant

This day came the parties by their Attorney's and there upon came also a Jury to wit: JOHN MCLEAN, THOMAS DICKERSON, WILLIAM FARRER, JOHN WALKER, JOHN SHEDDEN, REUBEN SHARP E, BARTHOLOMEW THOMPSON, SAMUEL TOMLINSON, JOSEPH HARDING, PETER EDWARD, ROBERT GILMOUR and HENRY SINGLETON who being elected tried and sworn the truth to speak upon the issue joined upon their oath do say that the Defendant is guilty of speaking the slanderous words in manner and form as in the declaration against him is alleged.

PAGE 105

And do assess the Plaintiffs damages by occasion of the Speaking of the Slanderous words in the declaration mentioned to 35 pounds besides their costs. Therefore, it is considered that the plaintiff recover against the said Defendant their damages aforesaid in form aforesaid assessed and their costs by them in this behalf expended and the said Defendant in mercy.

Order is granted JOHN HARDY against JOHN SCOTT and ANN his wife for 325 pounds of tobacco for 13 days attendance in their suit against PETER BEISER.

Order is granted JOHN MARLEY against JOHN SCOTT and ANN his wife for 325 pounds of tobacco for 13 days attendance in their suit against PETER BEISER.

Order is granted WILLIAM BICKERDICK against JOHN SCOTT and ANN his wife for 200 pounds of tobacco for 8 days attendance in their suit against PETER BEISER.

JOHN HARDY against JOSHUA WRIGHT in case. This day came the Parties by their Attorney's as Defendant says that he did not assume upon himself in manner and form as the Plaintiff against him has declared and this he puts himself upon the country and the Plaintiff likewise, Therefore, the trial of the issue is referred until the next Court.

NICHOLAS LOYD against ALEXANDER LOVE in case. This day came the Parties by their Attorney's as Defendant says that he did not assume upon himself in manner and form as the Plaintiff against him has declared and of this he puts himself upon the country and the Plaintiff likewise, Therefore, the trial of the issue is referred until the next Court.

JOSEPH WILLIAMSON against ALEXANDER BELL. Judgement by default & Writ of Inquiry.
SUSANNAH DALE against JOHN SOUTHERLAND. Judgement by default & Writ of Inquiry.

MICHAEL CHRISTIAN assignee of WILLIAM MCCAA against JOHN SMITH. This day came the Parties by their Attorney's as Defendant pleaded payment in manner and form as the Plaintiff against him has declared and of this, he puts himself upon the country and the Plaintiff likewise, Therefore, the trial of the issue is referred until the next Court.

JAMES HUNTER against WILLIAM WHITE. The Defendant pleaded Plaintiff deceased? Issue joined and referred.
WILLIS WILSON & COMPANY against NATHANIEL POINER. The former order of this Court against him the said defendant and AARON BARBER his bail be confirmed, and a Writ of Inquiry is awarded the Plaintiff for his damages to be as curtained at the next Court.

PAGE 105B

ANN MIDDLETON Executrix of SAMUEL MIDDLETON against ANN WALLACE and NICHOLAS POOLE. This day came the parties by their Attorney's and the Defendant pleaded payment in manner and form as the Plaintiff against him has declared and of this they put themselves upon the Country and the Plaintiff likewise. Therefore, the trial of the issue is referred until the next Court.

MARK TALBOT against WILLIAM & JOHN INGRAM. This day came the Parties by their Attorney's as Defendant says that they did not assume upon themselves in manner and form as the Plaintiff against them have declared and this they put themselves upon the Country and the Plaintiff likewise, Therefore, the trial of the issue is referred until the next Court.

This Court rates Flour at 15 shillings per centum
This Court is adjourned to Court in Course, GEORGE ABYVON MAYOR, TESTE: JOHN BOUSH D.C.C.

NORFOLK BOROUGH

At a Hustings Court Held this 20th day of April 1772
PRESENT: GEORGE ABYVON ESQUIRE MAYOR
GENTLEMAN ALDERMEN: ARCHIBALD CAMPBELL, JAMES TAYLOR, PAUL LOYAL, CHARLES THOMAS, LEWIS HANSFORD, CORNELIUS CALVERT, MAXIMILIAN CALVERT

PATIENCE NICHOLSON Plaintiff
Against Re: In Case
JOHN WILLS Defendant

This day came as well the Plaintiff by WILLIAM RASCOW WILSON CURLE Gentleman Attorney as the Defendant in his proper person and says that he cannot gainsay the Plaintiff's action nor but that he did assume in manner and form as the Plaintiff against him has declared.

Therefore, it is considered that the Plaintiff recover against the said Defendant 6 pounds and her costs by her about her suit in this behalf expended and the said Defendant in mercy.

SUSANNA DALE against JOHN SOUTHERLAND abates by the Defendants death.
IRBY BESSIE against JOHN SOUTHERLAND abates by the Defendants death.

PAGE 106
WILLIAM FREEMAN against CHARLES GODFREY Dismissed at the Plaintiff's Cost.

JOHN HUNT against CRISTIES STEWART. By Petition and Summons. Judgement is granted the Plaintiff for 1 pounds 10 shillings. It is ordered that the Defendant pay the same unto the Plaintiff with costs and fee.
CHARLES MAYLE assignee of ANNIS PORTLOCK against SAMUEL BRESSIE. Dismissed at Plaintiffs cost.

CUMMING WARWICK and Company Plaintiff against DANIEL PECK Defendant in Case. This day came the parties by their Attorney's and the Defendant prays and has leave to IMPARLE here until the next Court and then to plead.

WILLIAM BICKERDICK Plaintiff against WILLIAM PRIESTMAN Defendant in Trespass, Assault & Battery.
JOHN LAWRENCE this day came into Court and undertook for the Defendant that in case he shall be cast in this suit, he the said Defendant will pay the condemnation of the Court or render his body to prison in execution for the same or that he the said LAWRENCE will pay the condemnation to the Court or render the body of the said Defendant as aforesaid where upon the defendant by his Attorney prays and has leave to IMPARLE here until the next Court and then to plead.

WILLIAM FARRER against JOHN HUNT and SARAH his wife Dismissed.

JOHN HARDY Plaintiff against WILLIAM LEWELLING Defendant in Case. SAMUEL BOUSH undertook for the Defendant that in case he shall be cast in this suit, he the said Defendant will pay the condemnation of the Court or render his body to prison in execution for the same or that he the said BOUSH will pay the condemnation to the Court or render the body of the said Defendant as aforesaid where upon the defendant by his Attorney prays and has leave to IMPARLE here until the next Court and then to plead.

PHILIP CARBERY Plaintiff against THOMAS DICKERSON Defendant. By Petition and Summons. Judgement is granted the Plaintiff for 5 pounds. It is ordered that the Defendant pay the same unto the Plaintiff with costs and fee. And on failure of immediate payment. Ordered that the Sergeant give him 39 lashes on his bare back at the public whipping post.

JOHN HARRIS Plaintiff against MAX CALVERT Defendant in Trespass. This day came the parties by their Attorney's and the Defendant prays and has leave to IMPARLE here until the next Court and then to Plead.

ALEXANDER MCSWEEN against WILLIAM INGRAM, ARCHIBALD CAMPBELL Gentleman undertakes for the Plaintiff that he will pay to the Defendant and all such damages, costs and charges as shall be awarded against him by the Court.

ALEXANDER MCSWEEN against WILLIAM INGRAM dismissed at the Plaintiff's Costs.

PAGE 106B
WILLIAM SIMPSON Plaintiff
Against Re: In Case
PAUL LOYALL & LATIMORE HALSTEAD administrators of JONATHAN DISON Deceased Defendants
This day came the parties by their Attorney's and the Defendants by their Attorney says that they cannot gainsay the Plaintiffs action nor but that their intestate did assume in manner and form as the Plaintiff against them have declared. Therefore, it is considered that the Plaintiff recover against the said Defendants 10 pounds 10 shillings and 11 pence farthing and his costs by him about his suit in this behalf expended. When assets after paying preceding judgements, debts of greater dignity and the Defendants own claims of equal dignity against the Estate of the said intestate to be levied of the goods and chattels which were of the said JONATHAN at the time of his death that shall here after come to the hands of the said PAUL LOYALL and LATIMORE HALSTEAD to be administered and the said PAUL and LATIMORE in mercy.

WILLIAM SIMPSON Plaintiff
Against Re: In Debt
PAUL LOYALL & LATIMORE HALSTEAD administrators of JONATHAN DISON Deceased Defendants
This day came the parties by their Attorney's and the Defendants by their Attorney acknowledges the Plaintiffs action for 38 pounds, 17 shillings and 10 pence. Therefore, it is considered that the Plaintiff recover against the said Defendants his debt aforesaid and his costs by him about his suit in this behalf expended. When assets after paying preceding judgements, debts of equal dignity and the Defendants own claims of equal dignity against the Estate of the said intestate to be levied of the goods and chattels which were of the said JONATHAN at the time of his death that shall here after come to the hands of the said PAUL LOYALL and LATIMORE HALSTEAD to be administered and the said PAUL and LATIMORE in mercy. But this judgement is to be discharged by the payment of 14 pounds 8 shillings and 7 pence with interest for the same at the rate of 5% per annum to be computed from JANUARY 20, 1769, to the time of payment and the costs.

RICHARD TALBOT Plaintiff
Against Re: In Case
PAUL LOYALL & LATIMORE HALSTEAD administrators of JONATHAN DISON Deceased Defendants
This day came the parties by their Attorney's and the Defendants by their Attorney says that they cannot gainsay the Plaintiffs action nor but that their intestate did assume in manner and form as the Plaintiff against them have declared. Therefore, it is considered that the

Plaintiff recover against the said Defendants 11 pounds 2 shillings and 9 pence and his costs by him about his suit in this behalf expended. When assets after paying preceding judgements, debts of greater dignity and the Defendants own claims of equal dignity against the Estate of the said intestate to be levied of the

PAGE 107

goods and chattels which were of the said JONATHAN at the time of his death that shall here after come to the hands of the said PAUL LOYALL and LATIMORE HALSTEAD to be administered and the said PAUL and LATIMORE in mercy.

Order is granted JOHN STANHOPE against PHILIP CARBERY for 25 pounds tobacco for 1 day's attendance at this Court in his suit against THOMAS DICKERSON.

Order is granted MATTHEW KELLY against PHILIP CARBERY for 25 pounds tobacco for 1 day's attendance at this Court in his suit against THOMAS DICKERSON.

Ordinary license is granted ANN BREITHWAIT on her complying with the law.

BENJAMIN LEWELLING against DEMSEY VEALE in Trespass, Assault, and Battery. This day came the parties by Their Attorneys and the defendant prays and has leave to IMPARLE here until the next Court and then to Plead.

EDWIN STRONG against JAMES ARCHDEACON. Dismissed.

JOHN WOODSIDE Plaintiff against JONATHAN IVY and THOMAS TALBOT defendants in debt. This day the Plaintiff by WILLIAM ROBINSON Gentleman his Attorney and the Defendant THOMAS being called, the suit against the other Defendant is discontinued and not appearing. A conditional order is granted the Plaintiff against the said Defendant THOMAS and JOHN MACLEAN his bail.

PATIENCE NICHOLSON Plaintiff against WILLIAM LEWELLING Defendant in Case. SAMUEL BOUSH undertook for the Defendant that in case he shall be cast in this suit, he said Defendant will pay the condemnation of the Court or render his body to prison in execution for the same or that he the said BOUSH will pay the condemnation to the Court or render the body of the said Defendant as aforesaid where upon the Defendant by his Attorney prays and has leave to IMPARLE here until the next Court and then to plead.

GEORGE KELLY Plaintiff against GEORGE WILSON and ARCHIBALD CAMPBELL administrators of JOHN WILSON deceased Defendants in case. This day the parties by their Attorney's and the Defendant pray and have been leave to IMPARE here until the next Court and then to plead.

JOHN HARRIS Plaintiff against GEORGE WILSON and ARCHIBALD CAMPBELL administrators of JOHN WILSON Deceased Defendants in case. This day came the parties by their Attorney's and the Defendant pray and have leave to IMPARLE here until the next Court and then to Plead.

JOSEPH HARDING Against JAMES ROGERS Dismissed.
NATHANIEL BURGESS against JAMES ROGERS Dismissed.
King by PHILIP CARBERY against THOMAS DIXON by warrant Dismissed.

PAGE 107B
GEORGE WILSON & ARCHIBALD CAMPBELL administrators of JOHN WILSON Deceased Plaintiff
Against Re: In Case
LEMUEL ROBERTS Defendant
This day came as well the Plaintiff by ANDREW RONALD Gentleman their Attorney as the Defendant in his proper person and says that he cannot gainsay the Plaintiffs action nor but that he did assume in manner and form as the Plaintiff against him have declared. Therefore, it is considered that the Plaintiff recover against the said Defendant 11 pounds 7 shillings and 6 pence and their costs by them about their suit in this behalf expended and the said Defendant in mercy.

GEORGE WILSON and ARCHIBALD CAMPBELL administrators of JOHN WILSON deceased Plaintiffs against SAMUEL CALVERT in case. This day came the parties by their Attorney's and the Defendant prays and has leave to IMPARLE here until the next court and then to plead.

GEORGE WILSON and ARCHIBALD CAMPBELL administrators of JOHN WILSON deceased Plaintiffs against JONATHAN CALVERT in case. This day came the parties by their Attorney's and the Defendant prays and has leave to IMPARLE here until the next Court and then to plead.

MALBONE SHELTON against LEMUEL ROBERTS in Case. This day came the parties by their Attorney's and the Defendant prays and has leave to IMPARLE here until the next Court and then to plead.

JAMES CAMPBELL and Company Plaintiff against BARNABY CARNEY Defendant in case. WRIGHT WESTCOTT this day came into Court and undertook for the Defendants that in case he shall be cast in this suit, he the said Defendant will pay the condemnation of the Court or render his body to prison in execution for the same or that he the said WESTCOTT will pay the condemnation to the Court or render the body of the said Defendant as aforesaid where upon the Defendant by his Attorney prays and has leave to IMPARLE here until the next Court and then to plead.

ALEXANDER MASSENBURG Plaintiff against LOUISA INMAN Defendant in case. This day came the parties by their Attorneys and the Defendant prays and has leave to IMPARLE here until the next Court and then to Plead.

KING against JOHN CAMPBELL by warrant dismissed at Defendants Costs.

JUDY FENWICK, JOHN DAVIS, ROGER PIERCE, and JAMES BARKER being summoned to attend this Court as witnesses in our Complaint against JOHN CAMPBELL and being solemnly called and not appearing. It is ordered that for such their contempt they be fined 350 pounds of tobacco each unless they appear at the next Court to be held for this Borough to show cause.

Ordinary License is granted ROBERT POMEROY on his complying with the law.

PAGE 108

PHILOMON RUSSELL Plaintiff
Against Re: In Case
ALEXANDER BELL Defendant
This day came the parties by their Attorney's and there upon came also a Jury to wit: WILLIAM JUNKERSON, PAUL PROBY, THOMAS POOLE, WILLIAM IVY, JAMES CUNNINGHAM, JOHN HURT, WILLIAM INGRAM, JOHN RICHARDSON, EDWARD MITCHELL, JAMES LEITCH, JAMES WALKER, and ROBERT STEEL who being elected tried and sworn the truth to speak upon the issue joined upon their oath do say that the Defendant did assume in manner and form as the Plaintiff against him has declared and do assess the Plaintiff damages by occasion of the non-performance of that assumption to 8 pounds 7 shillings and 10 pence half penny besides his costs. Therefore, it is considered that the Plaintiff recover against the said Defendant his damages aforesaid in form aforesaid assessed and his costs by him about his suit in this behalf expended and the said Defendant in mercy.

WILLIAM WESTCOTT Plaintiff
Against Re: In Case
WRIGHT WESTCOTT Administrator of JOHN WESTCOTT deceased defendant
This day came the parties by their attorney's and there upon came also a jury to wit: JOHN BROWN, THOMAS TERRY, ROBERT RAY, WILLIAM STEVENSON, NICHOLAS WONYCOTT, NATHANIEL BOUSH, JOHN NASH, CHARLES GODFREY, ELDRED FISHER, PHILOMON RUSSELL, WILLIAM BICKERDICK, and EDMOND ALLMON who being elected tried and sworn the truth to speak upon the issue joined upon their oath do say that the Defendant is guilty in manner and form as the Plaintiff against him has declared and do assess the Plaintiff damages by occasion thereof to 60 pounds besides his costs. Therefore, it is considered that the Plaintiff recover against the said Defendant his damages aforesaid in form aforesaid assessed and his costs by him about his suit in this behalf expended. To be levied of the goods and chattels of the said intestate JONATHAN WESTCOTT if so, much the said WRIGHT WESTCOTT has in his hands to be administered and if he has it not then the costs to be levied of his proper goods and chattels and the said Defendant in mercy.

THOMAS NEWTON SR. & JOHN TAYLOR Executors of ROBERT TUCKER Deceased Plaintiff
Against Re: In Case
PAUL LOYALL Defendant
This day came the parties by their Attorney's and there upon came also a Jury to wit: JOHN GREENWOOD, WILLIAM FARRER, WILLIAM JUNKERSON, JOHN SHAW, HENRY BRESSIE, JOHN SHEDDEN, WILLIAM INGRAM, JOHN HURT, THOMAS MCCULLOCH, WILLIAM CORBIT, ROBERT TAYLOR and CHARLES GODFREY who being elected tried and sworn the truth to speak upon the issue joined upon their oath do say that the Defendant did assume in manner and form as the Plaintiff against him has declared and do assess the Plaintiff damages by occasion of the non-performance of that assumption to 236 pounds 9 shillings and 2 pence half penny besides his costs.

PAGE 108B

Therefore, it is considered that the Plaintiff recover against the said Defendant his damages aforesaid in form aforesaid assessed and his costs by him about his suit in this behalf expended and the said Defendant in mercy.

CHARLES MAYLE Plaintiff
Against Re: In Case
SAMUEL BRESSIE Defendant
This day came the parties by their Attorney's and by their mutual consent submit all matters in difference between them to the determination of JOHN WILSON and ABRAHAM WORMINGTON and agree that their award there upon be made by the Judgement of the Court and the same is ordered accordingly.

CHARLES MAYLE against SAMUEL BRESSIE in debt. Dismissed at the Plaintiffs costs.

STEPHEN TANKARD Plaintiff
Against Re: In Case
RICHARD HOGG Defendant
This day the parties by their attorney's and the Defendant by his Attorney relinquishing his former plea says that he cannot gainsay the Plaintiff's action nor but that he did assume in manner and form as the Plaintiff against him has declared. Therefore, it is considered that the Plaintiff recover against the said Defendant 18 pounds 15 shillings and his costs by him about his suit in this behalf expended and the said Defendant in mercy. And the Plaintiff agrees to stay the execution of this judgement 3 months.

RICHARD HOGG against STEPHEN TANKARD Dismissed.

Order is granted MARGARET RIVERS against PHILOMON RUSSELL for 150 pounds of tobacco for 6 days attendance in his suit against ALEXANDER BELL.

Order is granted WILLIAM FARRER against PHILOMON RUSSELL for 25 pounds of tobacco for 1 day's attendance at this Court in his suit against ALEXANDER BELL.

Order is granted JOHN MARNIX against ALEXANDER BELL for 200 pounds of tobacco for 8 days attendance in his suit against PHILOMON RUSSELL against him.

It is ordered the Clerk register JOHN MACDUFF receipts to PAUL LOYALL and on the motion of the said LOYALL leave is given him to have the said receipts when registered.

This Court is adjourned until tomorrow at 10 o'clock, GEORGE ABYVON MAYOR, TESTE: JOHN BOUSH D.C.C.

PAGE 109
NORFOLK BOROUGH
At a Hustings Court Held this 21st day of April 1772
PRESENT: GEORGE ABYVON ESQUIRE MAYOR
GENTLEMAN ALDERMEN: ARCHIBALD CAMPBELL, MAXIMILIAN CALVERT, PAUL LOYAL, JAMES TAYLOR, CHARLES THOMAS, CORNELIUS CALVERT,

On the motion of PAUL LOYALL Gentleman. It is ordered that the Clerk deliver him the accounts granted ROBERT TUCKER which is lodged in the suit of THOMAS NEWTON JR. and JOHN TAYLOR executors of the said ROBERT TUCKER deceased against him.

WRIGHT WESTCOTT Administrators of JOHN WESTCOTT Deceased Plaintiff
Against Re: In Debt.
JOHN TATEM and JOSEPH HUTCHINGS Defendant
This day came the parties by their Attorney's and the Defendant by their Attorney relinquishing their former plea acknowledges the Plaintiffs action for 215 pounds 4 shillings. Therefore, it is considered that the Plaintiff recover against the said Defendants his debt aforesaid and his costs by him in this behalf expended and the said Defendant in mercy. But this judgement is to be discharged by the payment of 107 pounds 12 shillings with interest for the same at the rate of 5% per annum to be computed from September 29, 1769, to the time of payment and the costs.

JOHN CRAMOND Plaintiff
Against Re: In Case
WILLIAM HANCOCK Defendant
This day came the parties by their Attorney's and thereupon came also a Jury to wit: HECTOR MCCALLISTER, WILLIAM CORBIT, ROBERT TAYLOR, JAMES DUNN, EDWARD MOSELEY, HENRY FLEMING, WILLIAM IVY, RICHARD TALBOT, JOHN WALKER, STEPHEN TANKARD, GEORGE BOWNESS, and JOHN LEE who being elected tried and sworn the truth to speak upon the issue joined upon their oath do say that the Defendant did not assume as in pleading he has alleged. Therefore, it is considered that the Plaintiff take nothing by his bill but for his false claims be in mercy. And the Defendant go hence without day and recover against the Plaintiff his costs by him about his defense in this behalf expended.

WILLIS WILSON & COMPANY against NATHANIEL POYNER agreed dismissed.
JAMES KEMP and CHARLES WILLIAMSON against JAMES MURDAUGH and JOHN MACLEAN. Set for hearing on the bill, answers, replication, and depositions.

PAGE 109B
WILLIAM SIMPSON Admin of FRANCIS CLARK deceased Plaintiff
Against Re: In Debt
SAMUEL SIMMONS Defendant
This day came the parties by their Attorney's and hereupon came also a Jury to wit: JOHN MACLEAN, NATHANIEL BOUSH, WILLIAM INGRAM, ELDRED FISHER, RICHARD LANGLEY, WRIGHT WESTCOTT, FREER ARMISTON, RICHARD BROWN, SAMUEL TOMLINSON, JOHN SMITH, RICHARD BASSET and ALEXANDER MASSENBURG who being elected tried and sworn the truth to speak upon the issue joined upon their oath do say that the Defendant has paid the debt as in pleading he has alleged. Therefore, it is considered that the Plaintiff take nothing by his bill but for his false claims be in mercy. And the Defendant go hence without day and recover against the Plaintiff his costs by him about his Defense in this behalf expended.

Order is granted THOMAS OLD against SAMUEL SIMMONS for 871 pounds of tobacco for 10 days attendance at this Court coming and returning 23 miles 9 times and 3 shillings and 9 pence ferriages in the suit of WILLIAM SIMPSON administrator of FRANCIS CLARK deceased against him.

Order is granted WILLIAM WALLACE against SAMUEL SIMMONS for 175 pounds of tobacco for 10 days attendance at this Court in the suit of WILLIAM SIMPSON administrator of FRANCIS CLARK deceased against him.

CHARLES MAYLE Plaintiff
Against Re: In Case
JOHN GREENWOOD Defendant
This day came the parties by their Attorney's and there upon came also a Jury to wit: JONATHAN SHEDDEN, JOHN LEE, HENRY FLEMING, WILLIAM CORBIT, RICHARD TALBOT, JOHN WALKER, STEPHEN TANKARD, ROBERT TAYLOR, WILLIAM IVY, GEORGE BOWNESS, DANIEL HUTCHINGS and JAMES DUNN who being elected tried and sworn the truth to speak upon the issue joined upon their oath do say that the Defendant did assume in manner and form as the Plaintiff against him has declared and do assess the Plaintiff Damages by occasion of the non-performance of that assumption to 8 pounds 15 shillings besides his costs. Therefore, it is considered that the Plaintiff recover against

86

the said Defendant his damages aforesaid in form aforesaid assessed and his costs by him in this behalf expended and the said Defendant in mercy.

JAMES MOORE against NATHANIEL BOUSH plea filed and time and costs
SAMUEL PORTLOCK against JOHN WILSON breaches assigned and time to consider them.

PAGE 110
ROBERT STEED Plaintiff
Against Re: In Case
JOHN TAYLOR Defendant
This day came the parties by their Attorney's and there upon came also a Jury to wit: JOHN LEE, RICHARD TALBOT, STEPHEN TANKARD, DANIEL HUTCHINGS, JOHN MACLEAN, JOHN SHEDDEN, JOHN WALKER, WILLIAM CORBIT, GEORGE BOWNESS, HENRY FLEMING, WILLIAM IVY and WILLIAM FARRER who being elected tried and sworn the truth to speak upon the issue joined upon their oath do say that the Defendant did assume in manner and form as the Plaintiff against him has declared and do assess the Plaintiff Damages by occasion of the non-performance of that assumption to 45 pounds 11 shillings and 3 pence besides his costs. Therefore, it is considered that the Plaintiff recover against the said Defendant his damages aforesaid in form aforesaid assessed and his costs by him in this behalf expended and the said Defendant in mercy.

WILLIAM TABB Plaintiff
Against Re: In Chancery
JOHN TABB Defendant
This day came as well the Plaintiff by WILLIAM RASCOW WILSON CURLE Gentleman his Attorney as the Defendant by JOHN MCLEAN Gentleman who was appointed guardian to the Defendant to defend him in this suit. And the Commissioners appointed to make equal partition and division between the parties of the following tract or planation of land, situate lying and being on the SAPONY CREEK in the County of Dinwiddie containing about 1150 acres in the bill mentioned.
This day made their report in these words to wit:
Pursuant to a decree of the Court of Hustings of Norfolk Borough bearing date the 21st day of August 1769 and by virtue of a Commission to us directed we have carefully vied the land mentioned in the said decree and do make equal partition and division between the parties in manner and form following: We do allot and assign to the Plaintiff WILLIAM TABB 602 acres at the upper end of the tract which is bounded as follows: beginning at a gum on the south side SAPPONY CREEK thence south 24 degrees west. 176 poles to Hickory Sapling thence north 88 degrees west, 10 poles to a shrub oak, thence north 30 degrees west, 399 poles to 2 white oaks near WILLIAMS REISERS thence north 70 degrees east 20 poles to the creek, thence north 62 degrees east along the old back line to a new dividing line thence along the new line south 60 degrees east to Sappony Creek thence up the creek as it tends to the beginning.
We also allot and assign the Defendant JOHN TABB 710 acres at the lower end of the said tract and bounded as follows: Beginning at the end of the new dividing line where

PAGE 110B
It comes to the old back line, thence along the old line north 62 degrees east to the Red lick Branch and down the Branch as it tends to SAPPONY CREEK thence up the creek as it meanders to the new line aforesaid along the new line north by 30 degrees west to the beginning as witness our hands and seals this 27th day of April 1774.
JOHN MANSON & SEAL, WILLIAM RIVES & SEAL, PHILIP JONES & SEAL, ROBERT WALKER & SEAL
On consideration whereof it is ordered and decreed that the partition and division so as aforesaid made behold firm and stable between the parties their heirs and assigns forever and that the costs of this suit be equally borne by both parties.

WILLIAM MCKINNIE against WILLIAM SIMPSON and JOHN MCLACHLAN. This day came the parties by their Attorney's and the Defendants pleaded payment in manner and form as the Plaintiff against them has declared and of this he puts himself upon the Country and the Plaintiff likewise. Therefore, the trial of the issue referred until the next Court.

HENRY GREEN against BARNABY CARNEY. This day came the parties by their Attorneys and the Defendant says that he did not assume upon himself in manner and form as the Plaintiff against him has declared and of this he puts himself upon the Country and the Plaintiff likewise. Therefore, the trial of the issue is referred until the next Court.

ELIZABETH HOPKINS Executrix of JOHN HOPKINS against ELDRED FISHER. This day came the parties by their Attorneys and the Defendant pleaded he does not detain in manner and form as the Plaintiff against him has declared and of this he puts himself upon the Country and the Plaintiff likewise. Therefore, the trial of the issue is referred until the next Court.

THOMAS DAVIS Executors of WILLIAM GOODING Deceased against JAMES DAWSON. This day came the parties by their Attorneys and the Defendant says that he did not assume upon himself in manner and form as the Plaintiff against him has declared and of this he puts himself upon the Country and the Plaintiff likewise. Therefore, the trial of the issue is referred until the next Court.

JOHN WILLIAMSON against JOSEPH CALVERT and ANTHONY FLEMING in Trespass. This day came the parties by their Attorneys and the Defendant pleaded not guilty severally in manner and form as the Plaintiff against him has declared and of this he puts himself upon the Country and the Plaintiff likewise. Therefore, the trial of the issue is referred until the next Court.

JOHN WILLIAMSON against JOSEPH CALVERT and PAUL HERITTER in DETINUE. This day came the parties by their Attorneys and the Defendants pleaded they do not detain severally in manner and form as the Plaintiff against him has declared and of this he puts himself upon the Country and the Plaintiff likewise. Therefore, the trial of the issue is referred until the next Court.

DOUGALL GILCHRIST against DONALD CAMPBELL. Dismissed.

PAGE 111
EDWARD HACK MOSELEY Complainant
Against Re: In Chancery
LEWIS HANSFORD Respondent
This Course was this day heard on the bill, answer, replication and depositions and the arguments of the Council on both sides. On consideration where of it is ordered and degreed that JOHN TAYLOR, JOHN GREENWOOD, JOHN LAWRENCE, and JAMES PARKER or any three of them meet, state, and examine the accounts between the complainant and respondent and it is further ordered and decreed that the said respondents lay before the Commissioners all books of accounts relating to the co-partnership and that he also answer upon oath unto every matter and thing concerning the same and their award to be the decree of the Court.

JOHN WILSON against SAMUEL PORTLOCK Dismissed at the Plaintiff Costs.

This Court rates Flour at 16/8 per hundred
This Court is adjourned to Court in Course, GEORGE ABYVON MAYOR, TESTE: JOHN BOUSH D.C.C.

NORFOLK BOROUGH
At a Hustings Court Held this 25th day of MAY 1772
PRESENT: GEORGE ABYVON ESQUIRE MAYOR
GENTLEMAN ALDERMEN: ARCHIBALD CAMPBELL, MAXIMILIAN CALVERT, PAUL LOYALL, CHARLES THOMAS, LEWIS HANSFORD

JOHN WILSON JR. against ELDRED FISHER. Dismissed.
GEORGE WILSON JR. against ELDRED FISHER. Dismissed.
JOHN NAIRNEY against JOHN JONES. By Petition and Summons. Judgement is granted the Plaintiff for 3 pounds 14 shillings and 9 pence. It is ordered that the Defendant pay the same unto the Plaintiff with costs.

THOMAS TAULSON against PETER THOMAS and ISAAC HOLDEN. Dismissed.

PAGE 111B
JOHN LAWRENCE and JOHN GREENWOOD against HARDRESS WALLER. Dismissed at the Defendants Cost.
JOHN LAWRENCE and JOHN GREENWOOD against THOMAS WALKER and STEPHEN TANKARD. Dismissed against WALKER. Order against TANKARD and SAMUEL PORTLOCK his bail.

JOHN MCNEIL against JOHN MEARNS in case. This day came the parties by their Attorney's and the Defendant by his Attorney prays and has leave to IMPARLE here until the next Court and then to plead.

ANDREW SPROWLE administrator of JOHN SPROWLE and ROBERT CROOKS deceased against GEORGE COLLINS in case. This day came the parties by their Attorney's and the Defendant prays and has leave to IMPARLE here until the next Court and then to plead.

FREDERICK AUGUSTUS DOEBER Plaintiff
Against Re: In Case
WILLIAM GEORGE Defendant
This day came as well the Plaintiff by WILLIAM RASCOW WILSON CURLE Gentleman his Attorney as the Defendant in his proper person and the said Defendant having surrendered himself up in discharge of his bail says that he cannot gainsay the Plaintiff against him has declared. Therefore, it is considered that the Plaintiff recover against the said Defendant 19 pounds 10 shillings and 10 pence and his costs by him in this behalf expended and the said Defendant in mercy. And the said Defendant being ruled to give Special Bail and failing so to do. On the motion of the Plaintiff by his Attorney, the said Defendant is continued in Custody of the Sergeant until he shall satisfy this judgement and the costs.

ROBERT STEEL Plaintiff
Against Re: In Case
GEORGE WILSON & ARCHIBALD CAMPBELL admin of JOHN WILSON Deceased Defendants
This day came as well the Plaintiff by WILLIAM RASCOW WILSON CURLE Gentleman his Attorney and ARCHIBALD CAMPBELL one of the Defendants in his proper person and says that they cannot gainsay the Plaintiff's action nor but that their intestate did assume in manner and form as the Plaintiff against them has declared.
Therefore, it is considered that the Plaintiff recover against the said Defendant 16 pounds and his costs
PAGE 112
By him about his suit in this behalf expended. When assets after paying preceding judgements, debts of greater dignity and the Defendants own claims of equal dignity against the Estate of the said intestate to be levied of the goods and chattels which were of the said JOHN at the time of his death that shall here after come to the hands of the said GEORGE and ARCHIBALD to be administered and the said Defendants in mercy.

SUSANNAH ESTHER against ELDRED FISHER in case. This day Came the parties by their Attorneys and the Defendant prays and has leave to IMPARLE here until the next Court and then to plead.

AITCHESON and PARKER against ALEXANDER BELL in debt. This day came the parties by their Attorneys and the Defendant prays and has leave to IMPARLE here until the next Court and then to plead.

MARY ROTHERY and others executors of MATTHEW ROTHERY against GEORGE WATSON and ANN his wife administratrix of RICHARD BOUCHER in chancery. Time to consider bill.

MARY ROTHERY and others executors of MATTHEW ROTHERY against DOROTHY ROTHERY administratrix of HENRY ROTHERY in case. This day Came the parties by their Attorneys and the Defendant prays and has leave to IMPARLE here until the next Court and then to plead.

MARY ROTHERY and other executors of MATTHEW ROTHERY against THOMAS PREESON in case. This day Came the parties by their Attorneys and the Defendant prays and has leave to Special IMPARLE here until the next Court and then to plead.

THOMAS NEWTON against JOSHUA WRIGHT Dismissed at the Defendants costs.

WILLIAM GODFREY against THOMAS DREWRY in T.A.B. This day Came the parties by their Attorneys and the Defendant prays and has leave to IMPARLE here until the next Court and then to plead.
WILLIAM GODFREY against WILLIAM SMITH in T.A.B. This day Came the parties by their Attorneys and the Defendant prays and has leave to IMPARLE here until the next Court and then to plead.

MATTHEW KELLY against HENRY LUG. *Dismissed.

JAMES EDMUNDSON administrator of WILLIAM RAMSAY deceased against ANTHONY FLEMING in debt. This day came the parties by their Attorney's and the Defendant prays and has leave to IMPARLE here until the next Court and then to plead.

GEORGE SPARLING & COMPANY against JOHN MCLACHLAN. Dismissed at the Defendants Costs.

PAGE 112B
JOSEPH MITCHELL Plaintiff
Against Re: In Debt for rent
RICHARD TALBOT Defendant
This day came as well the Plaintiff by WILLIAM RASCOW WILSON CURLE Gentleman his Attorney and the Defendant in his proper person and the said Defendant acknowledges the Plaintiffs action for 7 pounds 4 shillings and 6 pence. Therefore, it is considered that the Plaintiff recover against the said Defendant his debt aforesaid and his costs by him in his suit in this behalf expended and the said Defendant in mercy.

SAMUEL CAHOON Plaintiff
Against Re: In Case
ALEXANDER MASSENBURG Defendant
This day came as well the Plaintiff by BENJAMIN CROOKER Gentleman his Attorney and the Defendant in his proper person and the said Defendant having surrendered himself up in discharge of his bail says that he cannot gainsay the Plaintiff's action nor but that he did assume in manner and form as the Plaintiff against him has declared. Therefore, it is considered that the Plaintiff recover against the said Defendant 6 pounds, 17 shillings and 3 pence and his costs by him in this behalf expended. And the said Defendant in Mercy. And the said Defendant being ruled to give Special Bail and failing so to do. On the Motion of the Plaintiff by his Attorney aforesaid the Defendant is continued in Custody of the said Sergeant until he shall have satisfied this judgement and the costs.

DANIEL SANDFORD who as well on behalf of our Sovereign Lord the King as himself against MALACHI MAUND. This day came the parties by their Attorney's and the Defendant pleaded not guilty in manner and form as the plaintiff against him has declared and of this he puts himself upon the Country and the Plaintiff likewise. Therefore, the issue is referred.

MAXIMILIAN CALVERT against STEPHEN TANKARD in case. This day came the Plaintiff by WILLIAM RASCOW WILSON CURLE his Attorney and the Defendant being solemnly called and not appearing. A conditional order is granted the Plaintiff against the said Defendant.

JOHN SHEPHERD against GEORGE WILSON and ARCHIBALD CAMPBELL administrators of JOHN WILSON deceased in case. This day came the parties by their Attorney's and the Defendant prays and have leave to IMPARALE here until next Court and then to plead.

JOHN LAWRENCE and JOHN GREENWOOD against ALEXANDER BELL. Discontinued.

PAGE 113
PRISCILLA JOHNSON against MALACHI MAUND in chancery. Time is allowed to consider the bill.

GEORGE VEALE JR. against JOHN LELLO in T.A.B. This day came the parties by their Attorney's and the Defendant prays and has leave to IMPARLE here until the next Court and then to plead.

CALEB HANBURY against ALEXANDER BELL in case. This day came the parties by their Attorney's and the Defendant prays and has leave to IMPARLE here until the next Court and then to plead.

WILLIAM MOSELEY against ALEXANDER BELL in debt. This day came the parties by their Attorney's and the Defendant prays and has leave to IMPARLE here until the next Court and then to plead.

JAMES BALFOUR and DANIEL BARRAUD against JOHN HEATON in case. This day came the Plaintiffs by BENJAMIN CROOKER Gentleman their Attorney and the Defendant being solemnly called and not appearing a conditional order is granted the Plaintiff against the said defendant and JOHN SMITH his bail.

JAMES BALOUR and DANIEL BARRAUD against JOHN JONES in case. This day came the parties by their Attorney's and the Defendant prays and has leave to IMPARLE here until the next Court and then to plead.

JOHN CALVERT against BARNABY CARNEY in case. NICHOLAS GAUTIER this day came into Court and undertook for the Defendant that in case he shall be cast in this suit he the said Defendant will pay the condemnation of the Court or render his body to Prison in execution for the same or that the said GAUTIER will pay the condemnation of the Court or render the body of the said Defendant as aforesaid. Where upon the Defendants by their Attorney prays and have leave to IMPARLE here until the next Court and then to Plead.

JAMES MUDIE against THOMAS TILLIDGE in case. SETH POINTER this day came into Court and undertook for the Defendant that in case he shall be cast in this suit he the said Defendant will pay the condemnation of the Court or render his body to Prison in execution for the same or that the said POINTER will pay the condemnation of the Court or render the body of the said Defendant as aforesaid. Where upon the Defendants by their Attorney prays and have leave to IMPARLE here until the next Court and then to Plead.

CORNELIUS CALVERT against JOHN SMITH in case. JOSEPH HUTCHINGS Gentleman this day came into Court and undertook for the Defendant that in case he shall be cast in this suit he the said Defendant will pay the condemnation of the Court or render his body to Prison in execution for the same or that the said HUTCHINGS will pay the condemnation of the Court.

PAGE 113B

or render the body of the said Defendant as aforesaid. Where upon the Defendants by their Attorney prays and have leave to IMPARLE here until the next Court and then to Plead.

ALEXANDER BELL against MALACHI MAUND in T.A.B. This day came the parties by their Attorney's and the defendant prays and has leave to Special IMPARLE here until the next Court and then to plead.

THOMAS MURGOTROID against AMOS WICKERSHAM and ALEXANDER KIDD admin of JOHN KIDD deceased. Dismissed.

MARGARET BANNERMAN against BENJAMIN BANNERMAN. On motion of the Plaintiff by WILLIAM RASCOW WILSON CURLE Gentleman her Attorney. It is ordered that the Sergeant summon THOMAS VEALE, JAMES MARSDEN, HUMPHREY ROBERTS, AMOS ETHERIDGE, and ROBERT SHEDDEN *Sequestrators to appear at the next Court to be held for this Borough to render an account of their proceedings of their sequestration.

JAMES DUNLOP Plaintiff
Against Re: In Case
JOHN MCKERROLL Defendant
This day came the parties by their Attorney's and GEORGE GORDON in the room of THOMAS BURKE came into Court and undertook for the Defendant that in case he shall be cast in this suit he the said Defendant will pay the condemnation of the Court or render his body to Prison in execution for the same or that the said GORDON will pay the condemnation of the Court or render the body of the said Defendant as aforesaid. And there upon came also a Jury to wit: WILLIAM STEVENSON, ROBERT POMEROY, WILLIAM SMITH, WILLIAM IVY, JONATHAN BARROT, JOHN LEE, JAMES LEITCH, JOHN HARRIS, JOHN EDWARDS, JOHN OLIFFE, HENRY FLEMING, and GRIFFIN PEART who being elected tried and sworn the truth to speak upon the issue joined upon their oath do say that the Defendant is guilty in manner and form as the Plaintiff against him has declared and do assess the Plaintiff Damages by occasion thereof to 59 pounds 3 shillings and 10 pence besides his costs. Therefore, it is considered that the Plaintiff recover against the said Defendant his damages aforesaid in form aforesaid assessed and his costs by him in this behalf expended and the said Defendant in mercy.

Order is granted ANTHONY WARWICK against JAMES DUNLOP for 460 pounds of tobacco for 4 days attendance, coming and returning 30 miles 4 times and 15 shillings ferriages in this suit against JOHN MCKERROLL

PAGE 114

Order is granted BENJAMIN CROOKER against JAMES DUNLOP for 611 pounds of tobacco for 4 days attendance coming and returning 28 miles 4 times 5 shillings ferriages in his suit against JOHN MCKERROLL

JAMES KEMPE and CHARLES WILLIAMSON Plaintiff
Against Re: In Junction in Chancery
JAMES MURDAUGH and JOHN MACLEAN Defendants
This cause was this day heard on the bill and answer and the arguments of the council on both sides. On consideration where of it is ordered and decreed that the injunction be dissolved and that the Plaintiffs pay unto the Defendants their costs by them about their defense in his behalf expended.

JAMES MURDAUGH guardian of ANNE WALKE and assignee of EDWARD WRIGHT who was her late guardian against JOHN MACLEAN in debt. This day the parties by their Attorney's and the Defendant pleaded payment in manner and form as the Plaintiff against him has declared and of this he puts himself upon the Country and the Plaintiff likewise Therefore, the trial of the issue is referred until the next Court.

WILLIAM CALVERT this day took the oaths to the government and subscribed the test also the oath of Deputy Sergeant of the said Borough enters on the execution of his office in the room of SAMUEL PORTLOCK.

The King against JULIET a Negro. Dismissed. WILLIAM BOOKER her master paying costs.

DAVID JAMIESON against KEMPE WHITING. Dismissed. At the Defendants Costs.

WILLIAM SIMPSON Plaintiff
Against Re: In Case
JOHN SMITH Defendant
This day came the parties by their Attorney's and there upon came also a Jury to wit: WILLIAM STEVENSON, ROBERT POMEROY, WILLIAM SMITH, WILLIAM IVY, JONATHAN BARROT, PHILIP CARBERY, JAMES LEITCH, JOHN HARRIS, JOHN EDWARDS, JOHN OLIFFE, HENRY FLEMING, and JOHN MACLEAN who being elected tried and sworn the truth to speak upon the issue joined upon their oath do say that the Defendant did assume in manner and form as the Plaintiff against him has declared and do assess the Plaintiffs damages

PAGE 114B
by occasion of the non-performance of that assumption to 10 pounds 1 shillings besides his costs. Therefore, it is considered that the Plaintiff recover against the said Defendant his damages aforesaid in form aforesaid assessed and his costs by him in this behalf expended and the said Defendant in mercy.

JOHN GOODRICH against ALEXANDER MCSWEEN on motion of the Plaintiff by his Attorney a DEDIMUS is granted the Plaintiff to take the Deposition of JOHN GOODRICH SR. giving notice and continued.

LOGAN GILMOUR and Company Plaintiffs
Against Re: In case
WILLIAM MCCAA Defendants
This day came the parties by their Attorney's and there upon came also a Jury to wit: WILLIAM STEVENSON, WILLIAM IVY, ROBERT POMEROY, WILLIAM SMITH, JONATHAN BARROT, PHILIP CARBERY, JAMES LEITCH, JOHN HARRIS, JOHN EDWARDS, JOHN OLIFFE, HENRY FLEMING and JOHN MACLEAN who being elected tried and sworn the truth to speak upon the issue joined upon their oath do say that the Defendant did assume in manner and form as the Plaintiff against him has declared and do assess the Plaintiffs damages by occasion of the non-performance of that assumption to 20 pounds 4 shillings and 1 farthing besides his costs. Therefore, it is considered that the Plaintiff recover against the said Defendant his damages aforesaid in form aforesaid assessed and his costs by him in this behalf expended and the said Defendant in mercy.

WILLIAM MCCAA Plaintiff
Against Re: In Case
GEORGE LOGAN, ROBERT GILMOUR, and COMPANY Defendants
This day came the Plaintiff by WALTER LYON Gentleman his Attorney and there upon came also a Jury to wit: WILLIAM STEVENSON, WILLIAM IVY, ROBERT POMEROY, WILLIAM SMITH, JONATHAN BARROT, PHILIP CARBERY, JAMES LEITCH, JOHN HARRIS, JOHN EDWARDS, JOHN OLIFFE, HENRY FLEMING, and JOHN MACLEAN who being elected tried and sworn the truth to speak upon the issue joined, withdrew, and returned. And the Plaintiff though solemnly called came not but made default nor is his suit further prosecuted. Therefore, on the prayer of the Defendants it is considered that they recover against the Plaintiff 5 shillings and their costs by them about their defense in behalf expended, according to the form of Act of Assembly and the Plaintiff for his false claims be in mercy.

PAGE 115
MOSES LANGLEY against FRANCIS MOORE admin of JOHN MOORE deceased and EDWARD PARKE. Replication of the Depositions and suit thereon is set for hearing.

JOHN GREENWOOD Plaintiff
Against Re: In Case
JOHN TAYLOR Defendant
This day came the parties by their Attorney's and there upon came also a Jury to wit:
BARTHOLOMEW THOMPSON, WILLIAM CORBIT, EDWARD PARKE, GRIFFIN PEART, STEPHEN WRIGHT, ROBERT GILMOUR, JOHN SHEDDEN, JOHN GILCHRIST, ELDRED FISHER, JAMES MUPHREE, GEORGE GORDON, and JAMES WALKER who being elected tried and sworn the truth to speak upon the issue joined upon their oath do say that the Defendant did not assume as in pleading he has alleged. Therefore, it is considered that the Plaintiff take nothing by his bill but for his false claims be in mercy. And the Defendant go hence without day and recover against the said Plaintiff his costs by him about his defense in this behalf expended.

HENRY BRESSIE Plaintiff
Against Re: In Case
AARON BARBER Defendant
This day came the Plaintiff by WILLIAM RASCOW WILSON CURLE Gentleman his Attorney and by consent of the said Plaintiff by his Attorney aforesaid, the Defendant is admitted to appear in person and thereon says that he cannot gainsay the Plaintiff's action nor but that he did assume in manner and form as the Plaintiff against him has declared. Therefore, it is considered that the Plaintiff recover against the said Defendant 35 pounds 17 shillings and his costs by him about his suit in this behalf expended and the said Defendant in mercy and it is ordered that the Sergeant restore to the Defendant the attached effects and Plaintiff agrees to stay the execution of this judgement until the first day of October next.

This Court is adjourned until tomorrow 9 o'clock, GEORGE ABYVON MAYOR, TESTE: JOHN BOUSH D.C.C.

PAGE 115B
NORFOLK BOROUGH
At a Hustings Court Held this 26th day of MAY 1772
PRESENT: GEORGE ABYVON ESQUIRE MAYOR
GENTLEMAN ALDERMEN: ARCHIBALD CAMPBELL, CHARLES THOMAS, LEWIS HANSFORD, CORNELIUS CALVERT

It is ordered that the Sergeant summon RICHARD BICKERDICK to appear at the next Court to be held for this Borough to answer the complaint of RACHEL RICHARDSON.

SAMUEL PORTLOCK Plaintiff
Against Re: In Debt.
WILLIAM SHIPWASH Defendant
This day came the Plaintiff by WALTER LYON Gentleman his Attorney and there upon came also a Jury to wit: FRANCIS PEART, THOMAS FERRY, JOHN MACLEAN, THOMAS FARRER, WILLIAM FREEMAN, JAMES DUNN, DANIEL HUTCHINGS, WILLIAM IVY, EDWARD ARCHER, JOHN OLIFFE, JAMES GILCHRIST and PHILIP CARBERY who being sworn well and truly to inquire of damages upon their oath do say that the Plaintiff has sustained damages by occasion of the Defendants breaking the condition of the writing obligatory in the declaration mentioned to 445 pounds 18 shillings and 10 pence half penny besides his costs. Therefore, it is considered by the Court that the Plaintiff recover against the said Defendant and THOMAS STEWART his bail, the 1000-pound debt in the said declaration mentioned together with his damages aforesaid in form aforesaid assessed and his costs by him in this behalf expended and the said Defendant in mercy. But this Judgement the costs excepted is to be discharged by the payment of the said damages and costs.

THOMAS LANGLEY SR. Plaintiff
Against Re: In Detinue for a negro slave
JAMES PASTEUR Defendant
This day came the parties by their Attorney's and there upon came also a Jury to wit: JAMES MURPHREE, SAMUEL MURRAY, JAMES LEITCH, RICHARD BICKERDICK, BARTHOLOMEW THOMPSON, JAMES HALDANE, JOHN WOODSIDE, EDWARD MITCHELL, DICKERSON PRIOR, JOHN SHEDDEN, GEORGE GORDON, and JOHN WILKINS who being elected tried and sworn the truth to speak upon the issue joined upon their oath do say that the Defendant does detain the said Negro in the declaration mentioned in manner and form as the Plaintiff

PAGE 116
Against him has declared and that the said slave is of the value of 60 pounds, and they do assess the damages of the Plaintiff by Occasion of the detaining of the salve to 1 shilling besides his costs.
Therefore, it is considered that the Plaintiff recover against the said Defendant the slave aforesaid if to be had or the value of him if not to be had together with his damages aforesaid in form aforesaid assessed and his costs by him in this behalf expended and the said defendant in mercy. And where upon the Defendant filed his reasons in arrest of Judgement in these words to wit: LANGLEY against PASTEUR reasons in arrest of Judgement that whereas the said THOMAS LANGLEY is heir at law of LEMUEL LANGLEY the devisor who by his last will and testament in these words to wit: devised the reversion in the Negro Slave LUCY from whom the said Negro Slave REBECCA in the said declaration mentioned is descended and all the rest and residue of his estate not before devised or given away from his heir at law to MARY LANGLEY his wife, who conveyed the same to MARY LANGLEY by deed in these words to wit: From whom the said Defendant claims thereon the cause is continued until the next Court for the matters of law arising thereon to be argued.

MICHAEL CHRISTIAN Assignee of WILLIAM MCCAA Plaintiff
Against Re: In Debt
JOHN SMITH Defendant
This day came the parties by their Attorney's and there upon came also a Jury to wit: JOHN MACLEAN, JOHN OLIFF, JAMES DAWSON, JAMES DUNN, THOMAS FERRY, GRIFFIN PEART, EDWARD ARCHER, DANIEL HUTCHINGS, WILLIAM IVY, WILLIAM FREEMAN, THOMAS FARRER and PHILIP CARBERY who being elected tried and sworn the truth to speak upon the issue joined upon their oath do say that the Defendant has not paid the debt in the declaration mentioned. Therefore, it is considered that the Plaintiff recover against the said Defendant his debt amounting to 72 pounds 7 shillings and 4 pence and his costs by him in this behalf expended and the said defendant in mercy. But this Judgement is to be discharged by the payment of 6 pounds 17 shillings and 8 pence with interest there on at the rate of 5% per annum to be computed from January 22, 1770, to the time of payment and costs.

Order is granted JOHN GODFREY against JAMES PASTEUR for 50 pounds tobacco for 2 days attendance in the suit of THOMAS LANGLEY against him.

PAGE 116B
Order is granted THOMAS MARSHALL against THOMAS LANGLEY SR. for 200 pounds of tobacco for 8 days attendance of himself and ELIZABETH his wife at this Court in his suit against JAMES PASTEUR.

WALTER PETER assignee of SNODGRASS and TEMPLEMAN Plaintiffs
Against Re: In Debt.
JOSIAH BUTT administrator of THOMAS BUTT deceased Defendant
This day came the parties by their Attorney's and there upon came also a Jury to wit:
JOHN MACLEAN, JOHN OLIFF, JAMES DAWSON, JAMES DUNN, THOMAS FERRY, GRIFFIN PEART, EDWARD ARCHER, DANIEL HUTCHINGS, WILLIAM IVY, WILLIAM FREEMAN, THOMAS FARRER and PHILIP CARBERY who being elected tried and sworn the truth to speak upon the issue joined upon their oath do say that the Defendant intestate has not paid the debt in the declaration mentioned. Therefore, it is

considered that the Plaintiff recover against the said Defendant his debt amounting to 40 pounds and his costs by him in this behalf expended to be levied of the goods and chattels of the said intestate if so, much of the said JOSIAH BUTT has in his hands to be administered and if he has it not then the costs to be levied of his proper goods and chattels and the said Defendant in mercy.

But this Judgement is to be discharged by the payment of 20 pounds 17 shillings and 4 pence with interest there on at the rate of 5% per annum to be computed from June 21, 1769, to the time of payment and costs.

JOSEPH WILLIAMSON Plaintiff
Against Re: In Case
ALEXANDER BELL Defendant

This day came the Plaintiff by WILLIAM RASCOW WILSON CURLE Gentleman his Attorney and there upon came also a Jury to wit:

This day came the parties by their Attorney's and there upon came also a Jury to wit: JOHN MACLEAN, JOHN OLIFF, JAMES DAWSON, JAMES DUNN, THOMAS FERRY, GRIFFIN PEART, EDWARD ARCHER, DANIEL HUTCHINGS, WILLIAM IVY, WILLIAM FREEMAN, THOMAS FARRER, and PHILIP CARBERY who being sworn well and truly to inquire of damages in this suit upon their oath do say that the Plaintiff has sustained damages by occasion of the Breach of Promise in the Declaration mentioned to 34 pounds 9 shillings besides his costs. Therefore, it is considered by the Court that the Plaintiff recover against the said Defendant his damages aforesaid in form aforesaid assessed and his costs by him in this behalf expended and the said Defendant in mercy.

PAGE 117

ANN MIDDLE Executrix of SAMUEL MIDDLETON Deceased Plaintiff
Against Re: On a Writ of SCIRE FACIAS
ANN WALLACE and NICHOLAS POOL Defendant

This day came the parties by their Attorney's and the Defendant by their Attorney relinquishing their former plea acknowledges the Plaintiff's action for 133 pounds 6 shillings and 8 pence. Also 212 pounds of net tobacco 15 shillings or 150 pounds of tobacco and 1 shilling and 3 pence. Therefore, it is considered that the Plaintiff recover against the said Defendant her debts aforesaid and her cost by her in this behalf expended and the said Defendant in mercy. But this Judgement is to be discharged by the payment of 60 pounds 13 shillings and 4 pence with interest thereon after the rate of 5 % per annum to be computed from June 20, 1767, to the time of payment and costs.

This Court is adjourned to Court in Course, GEORGE ABYVON MAYOR, TESTE: JOHN BOUSH D.C.C.

NORFOLK BOROUGH

At a Hustings Court Held this 22ⁿᵈ day of JUNE 1772
PRESENT: GEORGE ABYVON ESQUIRE MAYOR
GENTLEMAN ALDERMEN: ARCHIBALD CAMPBELL, JAMES TAYLOR, PAUL LOYALL, CHARLES THOMAS, LEWIS HANSFORD, CORNELIUS CALVERT, MAXIMILIAN CALVERT

JOHN DAVIS against JOHN VALLENCIER. Dismissed.
JOHN DAVIS against JOHN VALLENCIER. Dismissed.
SAMUEL BOUSH against ANDREW ESTAVE. Dismissed.

PAGE 117B

MISTERS JOHN and THOMAS GILCHRIST against BARNABY CARNEY in case. This day ABRAHAM WORMINGTON came into Court and undertook for the Defendant that in case he shall be casts in this suit he the said Defendant will pay the condemnation of the Court or render his body to Prison in execution for the same or that the said WORMINGTON will pay the condemnation of the Court or render the body of the said Defendant as aforesaid. Where upon the Defendants by their Attorney prayed and have leave to IMPARLE here the next Court and then to Plead.

MARTHA LAWRENCE and JOHN LAWRENCE executors of JOHN LAWRENCE against JOHN GILCHRIST in case. This day came the parties by their Attorneys and the Defendant prays and has leave to IMPARLE here until the next Court and then to plead.

EDWARD ARCHER Executor of EDWARD ARCHER against JONATHAN MEREDITH and ELIZABETH his wife in case. This day came the parties by their Attorneys and the Defendant prays and has leave to IMPARLE here until the next Court and then to plead.

MESSIEURS WILLIAM and JOHN BROWN against ALEXANDER BELL in case. JOHN MCLACHLAN this day came into Court and undertook for the Defendant that in case he shall be casts in this suit he the said Defendant will pay the condemnation of the Court or render his body to Prison in execution for the same or that the said MCLACHLAN will pay the condemnation of the Court or render the body of the said Defendant as aforesaid. Where upon the Defendants by their Attorney prayed and have leave to IMPARLE here the next Court and then to Plead.

MESSIEURS INGLES and LONG Plaintiffs
Against Re: In Case
EDWARD HANSFORD Defendant

This day came as well the Plaintiffs by ANDREW RONALD Gentleman their Attorney. As the Defendant in their proper person and the said Defendant having surrendered himself up in discharge of his bail, says that he cannot gainsay the plaintiff's action nor but that he did assume in manner and form as the Plaintiff has declared. Therefore, it is considered that the Plaintiff recover against the said Defendant 17 pounds 13 shillings and 9 pence and their costs by them about their suit in this behalf expended and the said Defendant in mercy and the Plaintiff did not pray a COMMITTITUR of the said Defendant.

PAGE 118

FRANCES ROBERTSON against JOHN SMITH in debt. JOSEPH HUTCHINGS Gentleman this day came into Court and undertook for the Defendant that in case he shall be casts in this suit he the said Defendant will pay the condemnation of the Court or render his body to Prison in execution for the same or that the said HUTCHINGS will pay the condemnation of the Court or render the body of the said Defendant as aforesaid. Where upon the Defendants by their Attorney prayed and have leave to IMPARLE here the next Court and then to Plead.

GEORGE WILSON and ARCHIBALD CAMPBELL admin of JOHN WILSON deceased Plaintiff
Against Re: In Case
JOHN SMITH Defendant
This day came as well the Plaintiff BY ANDREW RONALD GENTLEMAN their Attorney as the Defendant in his proper person and the Said Defendant acknowledges the Plaintiff actions for 24 pounds 10 shillings and 10 pence. Therefore, it is considered that the Plaintiff recover against the said Defendant their debt aforesaid and their costs by them in this behalf expended and the said Defendant in mercy. But this judgement is to be discharged by the payment of 7 pounds 6 shillings and 2 pence with interest thereon after the rate of 5% per annum to be computed from March 20th, 1771, to the time of payment and the costs and the Plaintiff agrees to stay the execution of this judgement 6 months.

GEORGE WILSON and ARCHIBALD CAMPBELL administrators of JOHN WILSON deceased against ELDRED FISHER in case. WRIGHT WESTCOTT this day came into Court and undertook for the Defendant that in case he shall be casts in this suit he the said Defendant will pay the condemnation of the Court or render his body to Prison in execution for the same or that the said WESTCOTT will pay the condemnation of the Court or render the body of the said Defendant as aforesaid. Where upon the Defendants by their Attorney prayed and have leave to IMPARLE here the next Court and then to Plead.

JOSEPH NORTHRUP against ABRAM PATEON in Trespass. This day came the parties by their Attorneys and the Defendant prays and has leave to Special IMPARLE here until the next Court and then to plead.
JOSEPH NORTHRUP against ABRAM PATEON in Trespass. This day came the parties by their Attorneys and the Defendant prays and has leave to Special IMPARLE here until the next Court and then to plead.

WILLIAM and JOHN BROWN against HARDRESS WALLER. Dismissed.

PAGE 118B

THOMAS NEWTON assignee of JOHN SMITH against WILLIAM SMITH in debt for rent. This day RICHARD TEMPLEMAN came into Court and undertook for the Defendant that in case he shall be cast in this suit he the said Defendant will pay the condemnation of the Court or render his body to Prison in execution for the same or that the said TEMPLEMAN will pay the condemnation of the Court or render the body of the said Defendant as aforesaid. Where upon the Defendant pleaded, he does not owe in manner and form as the Plaintiff against him has declared and of this he puts himself upon the Country and the Plaintiff likewise Therefore, the trial of the issue is referred until the next Court.

JOSHUA WRIGHT against JOHN ASHLEY by Petition and summons. Judgement is granted the Plaintiff for 2 pounds 11 shillings and 4 pence. It is ordered that the Defendant pay the same unto the Plaintiff with costs and fee.

JOHN SHAW and MARY, his wife executors of JAMES ARNOT deceased against JAMES BAYNES Dismissed.

THOMAS LANGLEY against JAMES WEBB in debt. This day came the parties by their Attorneys and the Defendant prays and has leave to IMPARLE here until the next Court and then to plead.

REDERICK AUGUSTUS DOEBER assignee of JOSEPH CALVERT against WILLIAM GEORGE and JAMES LEITCH. This day came the parties by their Attorney's and the defendants pleaded not guilty in manner and form as the Plaintiff against them has declared and of this they put themselves upon the Country and the Plaintiff likewise. Therefore, trial of the issue is referred until the next Court.

JOSHUA WRIGHT against WILLIAM DAVIS. Dismissed.
ALEXANDER BELL against MALACHI MAUND. Dismissed.

CHARLES GODFREY and ANN, his wife against EDWARD ARCHER acting executor of EDWARD ARCHER deceased this day came as well the Plaintiffs by their Attorney as the Defendants in person and prays and has leave to IMPARLE here until the next Court and then to plead.

JOHN GOODRICH against SOLOMON SHEPHERD JR. This day came the parties by their Attorneys and the Defendant prays and has leave to IMPARLE here until the next Court and then to plead.

JOHN LAWRENCE against JOHN GILCHRIST abates by the Plaintiffs death.
JAMES PATRICK against ABRAM SIMPSON By warrant. Dismissed at the Plaintiffs costs.

PAGE 119
HARDRESS WALLER, JOINER.
WILLIAM & JONATHAN SIMPSON, BUTCHERS & PARTNERS
BASSETT & ALEXANDER MOSELEY, MERCHANTS & PARTNERS
PAUL LOYALL, GENTLEMAN

CHARLES GODFREY, MARINER
FRANCIS & GRIFFIN PEART, MERCHANTS & PARTNERS
NICHOLAS WONYCOTT, MERCHANT
EDWARD ARCHER, MERCHANT
LEWIS HANSFORD & COMPANY MERCHANTS
JAMES BALFOUR & DANIEL BARRAUD, MERCHANTS & PARTNERS
JONATHAN DISON, CARPENTER
JOSEPH CALVERT, JOHN WILSON MERCHANTS
JOHN RAMSAY & JAMES TAYLOR PRACTITIONERS OF PHYSICK & PARTNERS
JOHN TAYLOR & THOMAS NEWTON Executors of ROBERT TUCKER Deceased
SAMUEL BOUSH GENTLEMAN
GEORGE GORDON & DAVID CHEVIS & DAVID CROSS MERCHANTS
WILLIAM RASCOW WILSON CURLE GENTLEMAN
WILLIAM CHISHOLM & JOHN BOWNESS MERCHANTS & PARTNERS
WILLIAM BOLDEN & JOHN LAWRENCE & COMPANY MERCHANTS & PARTNERS
ARCHIBALD WHITE & COMPANY MERCHANTS
DUNCAN CAMPBELL, MARINER
JOHN CORRIS, MERCHANT
NEIL MCCOULL, MERCHANT
WILLIAM JACOB, PLANTER
JOHN GAWITH, MARINER
ARCHIBALD CAMPBELL, GENTLEMAN
THOMAS BRESSIE, MERCHANT
JOSEPH MITCHELL, JOHN LEWELLING, WILLIAM STEVENSON, THOMAS THOMPSON, MATT ROTHERY & JOEL MOHUN PARTNERS & GEORGE BRUCE

COMPLAINTS: IN CHANCERY

SARAH WINTERTON, an infant daughter, and heiress of NICHOLAS WINTERTON deceased. ANN WINTERTON widow and GEORGE ABYVON admin of the said NICHOLAS WINTERTON deceased Defendants.

This day came as well the Plaintiffs by their Attorney's and the Defendant SARAH by her guardian, the Defendant ANN by her Attorney, and the Defendant GEORGE in his proper person, who was appointed Commissioner to make sale of the 2/3 of the lands in the Borough of Norfolk in the bill mentioned and the reversion of the other 1/3 portion thereof. And also, to make sale of the lot of land in the Town of Fredericksburg in the said bill mentioned after giving notice, of the time and place in the Virginia Gazette this day made his report in these words to wit:

PAGE 119B

1772 Dr. the Estate of NICHOLAS WINTERTON deceased in account with GEORGE ABYVON Trustee CR.

To Cash paid THOMAS BRESSIE his debts due by specialty with interest by decree	17.18.10
To Cash paid Doctor ARCHIBALD CAMPBELL his debt due by specialty with interest by decree	47.14.11
To my claim as Administrator retained as by decree	22.1.2.
To Cash paid the widow for her 9th part of the land in Fredericksburg as by decree	2.13.8
	90.8.7
To my commissions on the amount of the sale of the land being L155.5.0	7.15.3
	90.3.10
Balance to pay costs of suit and be divided among the simple contract creditors	57.1.2
	155.5.0
By the amount of sales of 2/3 of the lot of land in Norfolk Borough and the reversion of the other 1/3 thereof after the widows death sold at public sale to MR. SAMUEL BOUSH	130.0.0
By amount of the sales of the lot of land in Fredericksburg sold at Vendue to MR. GEORGE HILL	25.5.0
	155.5.0

In obedience to a decree of the Hustings Court of Norfolk Borough Bearing date the 25th day of March 1771 to me directed. I have sold at public sale to SAMUEL BOUSH Gentleman 2/3 of the lot of land late belonging to the said NICHOLAS WINTERTON in the said decree mentioned situate in the said Borough and the reversion of the other 1/3 part thereof after the said WINTERTON'S Widow's death for 130 pounds current money. And have also sold at public auction sale to GEORGE HILL the other lot of land in the said decree mentioned, also late belonging to the said NICHOLAS WINTERTON situate in the Town of Fredericksburg for 25 pounds 5 shillings current money. And out of the proceeds of the sales of the lots of land. I have paid as above mentioned that is to say:

To THOMAS BRESSIE his debt & interest due by specialty	17.18.10

To Dr. ARCHIBALD CAMPBELL his debt & interest due by specialty	47.14.11
And have retained my own claim as administrator according to the said decree	22.1.2
And have per ANN WINTERTON widow for her 9th part of the sales of the land in Fredericksburg	2.13.8
And have retained my hands my commission on the sales of the lands at 5%	7.15.3
All which sums amount in the whole to:	90.3.10
which leaves a balance in my hands to pay costs & divided among the simple contractors	57.1.2
	155.5.0

PAGE 120

Which balance I have in my hands ready to pay as in the said decree is mentioned. Given in my hand this 22nd day of June 1772. GEORGE ABYVON

On consideration where of it is ordered and decree that the sales so as aforesaid made be held firm and stable that the purchasers be quieted in profession thereof and that the infant Defendant SARAH WINTERTON daughter and heiress of said intestate within 6 months after her arrive to the age of 21 years by good sufficient deed or deeds convey unto the purchasers of the said lands with the appurtenances in the fee simple thereof unless she the said SARAH WINTERTON shall within that time show cause to the contrary and it is further ordered and decree that the Defendant GEORGE after deducting 3 pounds for the widow and infant Defendants Attorney's fees and the Clerk and Sergeants fees out of the balance in the said report mentioned that he proportion the remainder among the simple contract creditors agreeable to their several claims which are mentioned in a former directed order.

MATHIAS GALE, ANN MOORE, JOSEPH MITCHELL, JOHN COX & THOMAS BUTT Plaintiff
Against Re: In Chancery
RICHARD ROTHERY an infant son and heir of HENRY ROTHERY deceased, MARY ROTHERY widow and GEORGE ABYVON executor of the said HENRY ROTHERY deceased Defendants.
This cause was this day heard on the bill and answers and the arguments of the council on both sides. On consideration where of it is ordered and decreed that MATTHEW PHRIPP, JOHN LAWRENCE, JAMES ARCHDEACON, BASSET MOSELEY and JOHN GILCHRIST Gentleman or any three of them being first sworn before any magistrate of this county meet state and examine the claims and demands of the Plaintiff and Defendant GEORGE ABYVON and that they or any three of them meet and separate the dower of the Defendant MARY in the two parcels of land in the Borough of Norfolk in the bill mentioned and make their report to the next Court to be held for this Borough.

JUDAY* FENWICK alias DUNFORD, JOHN DAVIS, ROGER PIERCE and JAMES BARKER being summoned to attend this Court as witnesses in our Complaint against JOHN CAMPBELL were at Court held the 20th day of April last fined 350 pounds of tobacco each unless they appeared and show cause why. Ordered the said fine be confirmed and that they part costs.

PAGE 120B

WILLIAM KEATON was this day brought before the Court by warrant for misbehavior and the same being proved. It is ordered that the Sergeant take and keep him in Custody until he gives bond and security himself in 20 pounds and 2 securities in 10 pounds each for his being of good behavior for 6 months and pay the costs of this prosecution.

JOHN STANHOPE this day took the oaths to the Government and subscribed the test also the oath of a Constable of this Borough enters upon the execution of his office.

The King against DANIEL BARBER dismissed at the Defendants Costs.

WILLIAM MCKENNA Plaintiff
Against Re: In Debt
WILLIAM SIMPSON and JOHN MCLACHLAN Defendants
This day came the parties by their Attorney's and thereupon came also a Jury to wit: SAMUEL BACON, JAMES GILCHRIST, WILLIAM WALKER, ROBERT ALLAN, BASSET MOSELEY, WILLIAM STEVENSON, THOMAS ROBERTS, STEPHEN WRIGHT, ANDREW MARTIN, JOHN WELLS, JAMES MURPHREE, and RICHARD BICKERDICK who being elected tried and sworn the truth to speak upon the issue joined upon their oath do say that the Defendants have not paid the Debt in the declaration mentioned. Therefore, it is considered that the Plaintiff recover against the said Defendants his debt amount to 220 pounds and his costs by him in this behalf expended and the said Defendants in mercy. But this judgement is to be discharged by the payment of 110 pounds with interest thereon after the rate of 5% per annum to be computed from February 20, 1770, to the time of payment and costs.

EDWARD HACK MOSELEY against ARCHIBALD INGRAM, JAMES INGRAM, and Company in case. This day came the Parties by their Attorney's, and the Defendants say that they did not assume upon themselves and that within 5 years in manner and form as the Plaintiff against them has declared and of this they put themselves upon the Country and the Plaintiff likewise Therefore, the trial of the issue is referred until the next Court.

GEORGE CARLTON against JOHN TAYLOR not guilty issue joined and referred.

<u>PAGE 121</u>
SAMUEL PORTLOCK against JOHN WILSON replication and issue.

DANIEL SANFORD who as well on behalf of our Sovereign Lord the King as himself Plaintiff
Against Re: In Debt.
MALACHI MAUND Defendant
This day came the parties by their Attorney's and thereupon came also a Jury to wit:
SAMUEL BACON, JAMES GILCHRIST, WILLIAM WALKER, ROBERT ALLAN, BASSET MOSELEY, WILLIAM STEVENSON, THOMAS ROBERTS, STEPHEN WRIGHT, ANDREW MARTIN, JOHN WELLS, JAMES MURPHREE, and RICHARD BICKERDICK who being elected tried and sworn the truth to speak upon the issue joined upon their oath do say that the Defendant is not guilty in manner and form as the Plaintiff against him have declared. Therefore, it is considered that the Plaintiff take nothing by his bill but for his false claims be in mercy. And the Defendant go hence without day and recover against the Plaintiff his costs by him about his defense in this behalf expended.

JOHN WILLIAMSON Plaintiff
Against Re: In Trespass
JOSEPH CALVERT and ANTHONY FLEMING Defendants
This day came the parties by their Attorney's and thereupon came also a Jury to wit: SAMUEL BACON, JAMES GILCHRIST, WILLIAM WALKER, ROBERT ALLAN, BASSET MOSELEY, WILLIAM STEVENSON, THOMAS ROBERTS, STEPHEN WRIGHT, ANDREW MARTIN, JOHN WELLS, JAMES MURPHREE, and RICHARD BICKERDICK who being elected tried and sworn the truth to speak upon the issue joined upon their oath do say that the Defendants are not guilty of the trespass in manner and form as the Plaintiff against him have declared. Therefore, it is considered that the Plaintiff take nothing by his bill but for his false claims be in mercy. And the Defendant go hence without day and recover against the Plaintiff his costs by him about his defense in this behalf expended.

JOHN WILLIAMSON Plaintiff
Against Re: In Detinue for Negro Wench SARAH
JOSEPH CALVERT & PAUL HERITTER Defendants
This day came the parties by their Attorney's and thereupon came also a Jury to wit: SAMUEL BACON, JAMES GILCHRIST, WILLIAM WALKER, ROBERT ALLAN, BASSET MOSELEY, WILLIAM STEVENSON, THOMAS ROBERTS, STEPHEN WRIGHT, ANDREW MARTIN, JOHN WELLS, JAMES MURPHREE, and RICHARD BICKERDICK who being elected tried and sworn the truth to speak upon the issue joined upon their oath do say that the Defendants do detain the said Negro SARAH in the declaration mentioned in manner and form as the Plaintiff against them have declared and that the said Negro is of the value of 10 pounds. Therefore, it is considered that the Plaintiff recover against the said Defendants the slave aforesaid if to be had or the value of her if not to be had and
<u>PAGE 121B</u>
His costs by him in this behalf expended and the said Defendants in mercy.

JAMES MOORE against NATHANIEL BOUSH and FREDERICK BOUSH replication and time.
JAMES MOORE against FREDERICK BOUSH and NATHANIEL BOUSH plea and time.

NATHANIEL YOUNG and JOHN SMITH against JOHN ASHLEY the former order of this Court against him the said Defendant and JOHN WILLIAMSON his bail be confirmed, and a writ of inquiry is rewarded the Plaintiff for his damages.

SAMUEL WILSON against SAMUEL BRESSIE. the former order of this Court against him the said Defendant and SAMUEL WORMINGTON his bail be confirmed, and a writ of inquiry is rewarded the Plaintiff for his damages.

NATHANIEL YOUNG and JOHN SMITH against THOMAS BUTT. The Defendant pleaded that he did not assume issue joined and referred.

DUGAL GILCHRIST and SARAH his wife against MARY CROSS. Dismissed.
JAMES CAMPBELL & COMPANY against JOSHUA WRIGHT the Defendant pleaded not guilty issue joined and referred.

RICHARD BOOKER assignee of PETER WARREN who was assignee of DANIEL HENDERICKSON Plaintiff
Against Re: In Debt.
JOSIAH HOFFMIRE Defendant
This day came the Plaintiff by WILLIAM RASCOW WILSON CURLE Gentleman his Attorney and the Defendant being solemnly called and not appearing ordered that the former order of this Court against him the said Defendant and AARON BARBER his bail be confirmed. Therefore, it is considered that the Plaintiff recover against the said Defendant and AARON BARBER his bail aforesaid his debt amounting to 36 pounds and his costs by him in this behalf expended and the said Defendant in mercy. But this Judgement is to be discharged by the payment of 13 pounds 10 shillings with interest thereon after the rate of 5% per annum to be computed from October 10th, 1763, to the time of payment and costs.

Order is granted ANTHONY FLEMING against JOSEPH CALVERT and PAUL HERITTER for 75 pounds of tobacco for 3 days attendance in the suit of JOHN WILLIAMSON against them.

PAGE 122
JOHN HUTCHINGS, MATTHEW PHRIPP and SAMUEL BOUSH against ALEXANDER BELL the Defendant pleaded he did not assume issue joined and referred.

THOMAS HEPBURN against JAMES ROGERS the former order of this Court against him the said Defendant and JOSEPH POPE his bail be confirmed, and a writ of inquiry is awarded the Plaintiff for his damages.

JAMES CAMPBELL & COMPANY against JOHN RICHARDSON in case. The Defendant pleaded not guilty issue joined and referred.

RICHARD TEMPLEMAN against JOHN RICHARDSON in case the Defendant pleaded not guilty issue joined and referred.

WILLIAM CHISHOLM and LATIMORE HALSTEAD against JOHN IVY the Defendant pleaded he did not assume issue joined and referred.
JOHN RICHARDSON against MARK TALBOT. The Defendant pleaded payment issue joined and referred.

WRIGHT WESTCOTT surviving executor of WRIGHT WESTSCOTT deceased against JOHN SMITH,
JOSEPH CALVERT Sergeant enters himself Special Bail, Judgement by defaults and writ of inquiry.

JOHN LEE against JAMES BRIDGER and MARY GRIMES. The Defendant pleaded payment issue joined and referred.

MARY PULLET against RICHARD TALBOT. The Defendant pleaded that he did not assume issue joined and referred.
HENRY BRESSIE against CHARLES MAYLE. The Defendant pleaded that he did not assume issue joined and referred.
JOHN CRAMOND against DAVID MACCLENAHAN. The Defendant pleaded not guilty issue joined and referred.

ADAM STEWART against JAMES MARSDEN. The Defendant pleaded payment issue joined and referred.

JOHN COLES assignee of JOHN HUTCHINGS executor of JOHN TUCKER deceased against JOSEPH CALVERT. The Defendant pleaded payment issue joined and referred.

PAGE 122B
JAMES MOORE against FREDERICK BOUSH and NATHANIEL BOUSH. The Defendant pleaded payment issue joined and referred.

JAMES CAMPBELL and COMPANY against GEORGE WILSON & ARCHIBALD CAMPBELL administers of JONATHAN WILSON deceased. The Defendants pleaded they did not assume issue joined and referred.

This Court is adjourned to Court in Course, GEORGE ABYVON MAYOR, TESTE: JOHN BOUSH D.C.C.

NORFOLK BOROUGH
At a Hustings Court Held this 20TH day of JULY 1772
PRESENT: PAUL LOYALL ESQUIRE MAYOR
GENTLEMAN ALDERMEN: GEORGE ABYVON, MAXIMILIAN CALVERT, ARCHIBALD CAMPBELL, JAMES TAYLOR, LEWIS HANSFORD, CORNELIUS CALVERT,

ROGER STEWART against JOHN MCNEIL abates by the Defendants death.
JOHN MCNEIL against MATTHEW KELLY abates by the Plaintiff's death.

JOHN LAWRENCE and MATTHEW PHRIPP executors of THOMAS THOMPSON deceased against LEMUEL LANGLEY abates by the Defendants death.

JOHN LAWRENCE and MATTHEW PHRIPP executors of THOMAS THOMPSON deceased against LEMUEL LANGLEY abates by the Defendants death.

LEMUEL LANGLEY against ARCHIBALD CAMPBELL administrator of JONATHAN DALGLEISH deceased. Abates by the Plaintiff's death.
JOHN MCNEIL against JOHN MEARNS abates by the Plaintiff's death

THOMAS BURKE against JOHN RODMAN by Petition and summons. Judgement is granted the Plaintiff for 1 pound 10 shillings. Ordered that the Defendant pay the same unto the Plaintiff with costs and fees.
JOHN SHAW and MARY, his wife executors of JAMES ARNOT deceased against JAMES BAYNES in case. Order against the Defendant and JOSEPH CALVERT Sergeant his bail.

PAGE 123
WILLIAM HARDY against JOHN EDWARDS. Dismissed.
MISTERS JOHN & WILLIS WILSON against MARY ROTHERY executrix of MATTHEW ROTHERY deceased. Imparlance.
WILLIAM RASCOW WILSON CURLE against JOHN COLVILLE. Dismissed.

WILLIAM RASCOW WILSON CURLE against EDMOND KEATON by Petition and summons. Judgement is granted the Plaintiff for 1 pound 9 shillings. Ordered that the Defendant pay the same unto the Plaintiff with costs and fees.
WILLIAM RASCOW WILSON CURLE against BAILEY WARREN. Dismissed.
JOHN CHESHIRE against RICHARD BROWN. An Imparlance.
HARDRESS WALLER against JAMES GILCHRIST by Petition and summons. Judgement is granted the Plaintiff for 3 pounds 4 shillings and 10 pence. Ordered that the Defendant pay the same unto the Plaintiff with costs and fees.

MATTHEW HOLT Plaintiff
Against Re: In Case
WILLIAM WILLISS Defendant
This day came as well the Plaintiff by ANDREW RONALD Gentleman his Attorney, as the Defendant in his proper person and the said Defendant says that he cannot gainsay the Plaintiffs action nor but that he did assume in manner and form as the Plaintiff against him has declared. Therefore, it is considered that the Plaintiff recover against the said Defendant 17 pounds 10 shillings and 5 pence and his costs by him in this behalf expended and the said Defendant in mercy.

TALBOT THOMPSON against JOHN DAY admin of THOMAS DAY. Imparlance.
JOHN ARDIS against JAMES HARRISON. Dismissed.
JAMES MUDIE against THOMAS MELLET. Dismissed.
JOHN ARDIS against THOMAS HARRISON. JOHN LAWRENCE this day came into Court and undertook for the Defendant that in case he shall be casts in this suit he the said Defendant will pay the condemnation of the Court or render his body to Prison in execution for the same or that the said LAWRENCE will pay the condemnation of the Court or render the body of the said Defendant as aforesaid. Where upon the Defendants by their Attorney prayed and have leave to IMPARLE here the next Court and then to Plead.

PAGE 123B
ROBERT GILMOUR administrator of the Estate of WILLIAM GRAY Deceased Plaintiff
Against Re: In Case
JOHN RICHARDSON Defendant
The parties by their Attorney's and the Defendant brought into Court and tendered to the Plaintiff 7 pounds and his costs by him in this behalf has expended as amends for damages which the Plaintiff has sustained by occasion of the non-performance of the promise in the declaration supposed which the Plaintiff refused to accept. Where upon the said Defendant says that he did not assume and filed his plea. Therefore, the trial of the issue is referred until the next Court. Ordered that unless more damages shall be assessed by the Jury at the trial that what the Defendant has tendered the Plaintiff shall pay all costs hereafter accordingly in this suit.

ROBERT GILMOUR admin of the Estate of WILLIAM GRAY Deceased against BAILEY WARREN. Imparlance.
ROBERT GILMOUR admin of the Estate of WILLIAM GRAY Deceased against JONATHAN MEREDITH. Dismissed.
ROBERT GILMOUR admin of the Estate of WILLIAM GRAY Deceased against GEORGE BLIN. Dismissed.
ROBERT GILMOUR admin of the Estate of WILLIAM GRAY Deceased against NICHOLAS WONYCOTT. Dismissed.
ROBERT GILMOUR admin of the Estate of WILLIAM GRAY Deceased against LOUISA INMAN. Dismissed.
ROBERT GILMOUR admin of the Estate of WILLIAM GRAY Deceased against WRIGHT BRICKELL Dismissed.
ROBERT GILMOUR admin of the Estate of WILLIAM GRAY Deceased against JOHN RUNSBERG. Dismissed.
STEPHEN TANKARD against JOHN RANSBERG. Dismissed at the Plaintiffs costs.
EDWARD ARCHER against JAMES EWELL. Dismissed.

SAMUEL BOUSH against RICHARD FRYER, JAMES WALKER this day came into and undertook for the Defendant that in case he shall be Cast in this suit he the said Defendant will pay the condemnation of the Court or render his body to Prison in execution for the same or that the said LAWRENCE* will pay the condemnation of the Court or render the body of the said Defendant as aforesaid. Where upon the Defendant by his Attorney prays and has leave to IMPARLE here until next Court and then to plead.
JOHN SHAW against HUMPHREY ROBERTS. Dismissed.

PAGE 124
ROBERT SHEDDEN & Company against WILLIAM CONNOR admin of WILLIAM C. CONNOR deceased Order against Defendant & CHARLES CONNOR his bail.

MATTHEW PHRIPP Plaintiff
Against Re: In Case
ROBERT GILMOUR admin of WILLIAM GRAY Deceased Defendant
This day came the parties in their proper persons and the Defendant acknowledges the Plaintiff debt for 20 pounds 6 shillings and 6 pence. Therefore, it is considered that the Plaintiff recover against the said Defendant his debt aforesaid and his costs by him in this behalf expended when assets to be levied of the goods and chattels which were of the said WILLIAM at the time of his death if so much the said ROBERT has in his hands to be administered and if he has it not then the costs are to be levied of his proper goods and chattels and the said defendant in mercy. But this judgement is to be discharged by the payment of 6 pounds and 11 pence with interest thereon after the rate of 5% per annum to be computed from October 25, 1771, to the time of payment and the costs.

WILLIAM ORANGE against GEORGE ALLANSON. Dismissed.

SAMUEL CASTLETON alias MCCASTLETON was this day brought before the Court for misbehavior and the same being proved it is ordered that the Sergeant take and keep him in custody until he gives bond and security himself in 20 pounds and 2 securities in 10 pounds each for his being of good behavior for 6 months and pay the costs of this prosecution.

MARGARET BANNERMAN against BENJAMIN BANNERMAN in Chancery. The Sequestrator this day brought into Court and lodged with the Clerk 11 pounds 10 shillings and 5 ½ pence, ordered he pay the same after deducting his fees to the Plaintiff and thereon the said Sequestrators are discharged, and BENJAMIN CROOKER Gentleman is appointed Sequestrator in their room.

DANIEL HUTCHINGS against MATTHEW PHRIPP and JONATHAN LAWRENCE Executors of THOMAS THOMPSON by Petition and summons. Judgement is granted the Plaintiff for 1 pound 16 shillings and 3 pence. Ordered that the Defendant pay the same unto the Plaintiff with costs and fees.

Order is granted JOHN CARTER and WILLIAM BEVAN against HARDRESS WALLER for 25 pounds of tobacco for 1 day's attendance each in his suit against JAMES GILCHRIST.

PAGE 124B

Order is granted JAMES COOPER and RICHARD TAYLOR against JAMES GILCHRIST for 25 pounds of tobacco each for 1 day's attendance each in the suit of HARDRESS WALLKER against him.

JOHN HOPKINS executors against ELDRED FISHER continued to be tried next Court.

THOMAS DAVIS Executor of WILLIAM GOODING Plaintiff
Against Re: In Case
JAMES DAWSON Defendant
This day came the parties by their Attorney's and there upon came also a Jury to wit: JAMES LEITCH, ROBERT STEEL, JOHN GARDNER, ANDREW MARTIN, WILLIAM CALDERHEAD, ROBERT TAYLOR, ELDRED FISHER, JOHN RICHARDSON, RICHARD BASSET, GRIFFIN PEART, SAMUEL BACON and RICHARD TAYLOR who being elected tried and sworn the truth to speak up on the issue joined upon their oath do say. That the Defendant did assume in manner and form as the Plaintiff against him has declared and assess the Plaintiffs damages by occasion of the non-performance of that assumption to 6 pounds 19 shillings and 8 pence half penny besides his costs. Therefore, it is considered that the Plaintiff recover against the said Defendant his damages aforesaid in form aforesaid and his costs by him about his suit in this behalf expended. And the Defendant in mercy.

SAMUEL PORTLOCK Plaintiff
Against Re: In Debt
JOHN WILSON Gentleman Defendant
This day came the parties by their Attorney's and there upon came also a Jury to wit: JAMES LEITCH, ROBERT STEEL, JOHN GARDNER, ANDREW MARTIN, WILLIAM CALDERHEAD, ROBERT TAYLOR, ELDRED FISHER, JOHN RICHARDSON, RICHARD BASSET, GRIFFIN PEART, SAMUEL BACON and RICHARD TAYLOR who being elected tried and sworn the truth to speak up on the issue joined upon their oath do say. That the Defendant has not performed the conditions of the writing obligatory in the declaration mentioned but the same has broken as the Plaintiff in his replication has alleged and do assess the damages of the Plaintiff by occasion thereof besides his costs to 509 pounds 18 shillings and 9 pence. Therefore, it is considered that the Plaintiff recover against the said Defendant his debt amounting to 1000 pounds and his damages aforesaid in form aforesaid assessed together with costs by him in this behalf expended and the said Defendant in mercy. But this judgement is to be discharged by the payment of the said damages and costs only.

PAGE 125

NATHANIEL YOUNG and JOHN SMITH Plaintiff
Against Re: In Case
JOHN ASHLEY Defendant
This day came the Plaintiff by WILLIAM RASCOW WILSON CURLE Gentleman their Attorney and there upon came a Jury to wit: JAMES LEITCH, ROBERT STEEL, JOHN GARDNER, ANDREW MARTIN, WILLIAM CALDERHEAD, ROBERT TAYLOR, ELDRED FISHER, JOHN RICHARDSON, RICHARD BASSET, GRIFFIN PEART, SAMUEL BACON and RICHARD TAYLOR who being sworn well and truly to inquire of damages in this suit upon their oath do say that the Plaintiff has sustained damages by occasion of the Breach of Promise in the Declaration mentioned to 7 pounds 6 shillings and 6 pence besides their cost . Therefore, it is considered by the Court that the Plaintiff recover against the said Defendant and JOHN WILLIAMSON his bail their damages aforesaid and their costs by them in this behalf expended. And the said Defendant in mercy.

SAMUEL WILSON Plaintiff
Against Re: In Case
SAMUEL BRESSIE Defendant
This day came the Plaintiff by WILLIAM RASCOW WILSON CURLE Gentleman their Attorney and there upon came a Jury to wit: JAMES LEITCH, ROBERT STEEL, JOHN GARDNER, ANDREW MARTIN, WILLIAM CALDERHEAD, ROBERT TAYLOR, ELDRED FISHER, JOHN RICHARDSON, RICHARD BASSET, GRIFFIN PEART, SAMUEL BACON and RICHARD TAYLOR who being sworn well and truly to inquire of damages in this suit upon their oath do say that the Plaintiff has sustained damages by occasion of the Breach of Promise in the Declaration mentioned to 6 pounds 17 shillings and 7 pence besides his cost. Therefore, it is considered by the Court that the Plaintiff recover against the said Defendant and SAMUEL WORMINGTON his bail their damages aforesaid and their costs by them in this behalf expended. And the said Defendant in mercy.

NATHANIEL YOUNG and JOHN SMITH Plaintiff
Against Re: In Case
THOMAS BUTT Defendant
This day came the parties by their Attorney's and there upon came also a Jury to wit: JAMES LEITCH, ROBERT STEEL, JOHN GARDNER, ANDREW MARTIN, WILLIAM CALDERHEAD, ROBERT TAYLOR, ELDRED FISHER, JOHN RICHARDSON, RICHARD BASSET, GRIFFIN PEART, SAMUEL BACON and RICHARD TAYLOR who being elected tried and sworn the truth to speak up on the issue joined upon their oath do say.

That the Defendant did assume in manner and form as the Plaintiff against him has declared and assess the Plaintiffs damages by occasion of the non-performance of that assumption to 21 pounds 7 shillings and 2 pence farthing besides their costs. Therefore, it is considered that the Plaintiff recover against the said Defendant his damages aforesaid in form aforesaid and his costs by him about his suit in this behalf expended. And the Defendant in mercy.

<u>PAGE 125B</u>

WILLIAM CHISHOLM and LATIMORE HALSTEAD Plaintiffs

Against Re: In Case

JOHN IVY Defendant

This day came the parties by their Attorney's and there upon came also a Jury to wit: JAMES LEITCH, ROBERT STEEL, JOHN GARDNER, ANDREW MARTIN, WILLIAM CALDERHEAD, ROBERT TAYLOR, ELDRED FISHER, JOHN RICHARDSON, RICHARD BASSET, GRIFFIN PEART, SAMUEL BACON and RICHARD TAYLOR who being elected tried and sworn the truth to speak up on the issue joined upon their oath do say. That the Defendant did assume in manner and form as the Plaintiff against him has declared and assess the Plaintiffs damages by occasion of the non-performance of that assumption to 33 pounds 7 shillings and 8 pence half penny besides their costs. Therefore, it is considered that the Plaintiff recover against the said Defendant his damages aforesaid in form aforesaid and their costs by them about this suit in this behalf expended. And the Defendant in mercy.

JOHN RICHARDSON Plaintiff

Against Re: In Debt

MARK TALBOT Defendant

This day came the parties by their Attorney's and there upon came also a Jury to wit: DANIEL HUTCHINGS, HARDRESS WALLER, JOHN CRAMOND, JOHN OLIFFE, EDWARD PARKE, WILLIAM GEORGE, EDMOND KEATON, JOHN WOODSIDE, FREER ARMISTON, WILLIAM FREEMAN, ALEXANDER MASSENBURG and THOMAS PEARSON who being elected tried and sworn the truth to speak up on the issue joined upon their oath do say that the Defendant has not paid the debt in the declaration mentioned. Therefore, it is considered that the Plaintiff recover against the said Defendant his debt amounting to 23 pounds 4 shillings and 6 pence and his costs by him in this behalf expended and the said Defendant in mercy. But this judgement is to be discharged by the payment of 11 pounds 12 shillings and 3 pence with interest thereon after the rate of 5% per annum to be computed from March 25th, 1771, to the payment and the costs.

WRIGHT WESTCOTT surviving executor of WRIGHT WESTCOTT deceased Plaintiff

Against Re: In Case

JOHN SMITH Defendant

This day came the parties by their Attorney's and there upon came also a Jury to wit:

DANIEL HUTCHINGS, HARDRESS WALLER, JOHN CRAMOND, JOHN OLIFFE, EDWARD PARKE, WILLIAM GEORGE, EDMOND KEATON, JOHN WOODSIDE, FREER ARMISTON, WILLIAM FREEMAN, ALEXANDER MASSENBURG and THOMAS PEARSON

<u>PAGE 126</u>

who being elected tried and sworn the truth to speak upon the issue joined upon their oath do say. That the Defendant did assume in manner and form as the Plaintiff against him has declared and assess the Plaintiffs damages by occasion of the non-performance of that assumption to 7 pounds 8 shillings and 9 pence besides his costs. Therefore, it is considered that the Plaintiff recover against the said Defendant his damages aforesaid in form aforesaid and his costs by him about his suit in this behalf expended. And the Defendant in mercy.

JOHN LEE Plaintiff

Against Re: In Debt

JAMES BRIDGER and MARY GRIMES Defendants

This day came the parties by their Attorney's and there upon came also a Jury to wit: DANIEL HUTCHINGS, HARDRESS WALLER, JOHN CRAMOND, JOHN OLIFFE, EDWARD PARKE, WILLIAM GEORGE, EDMOND KEATON, JOHN WOODSIDE, FREER ARMISTON, WILLIAM FREEMAN, ALEXANDER MASSENBURG and THOMAS PEARSON who being elected tried and sworn the truth to speak up on the issue joined upon their oath do say that the Defendant has not paid the debt in the declaration mentioned. Therefore, it is considered that the Plaintiff recover against the said Defendant his debt aforesaid amounting to 36 pounds 6 shillings and 11 pence and his costs by him in this behalf expended and the said Defendant in mercy. But this judgement is to be discharged by the payment of 18 pounds 3 shillings and 5 pence half penny with interest thereon after the rate of 5% per annum to be computed from September 29th, 1770, to the payment and the costs.

MARY PULLET Plaintiff

Against Re: In Case

RICHARD TALBOT Defendant

This day came the parties by their Attorney's and there upon came also a Jury to wit:

DANIEL HUTCHINGS, HARDRESS WALLER, JOHN CRAMOND, JOHN OLIFFE, EDWARD PARKE, WILLIAM GEORGE, EDMOND KEATON, JOHN WOODSIDE, FREER ARMISTON, WILLIAM FREEMAN, ALEXANDER MASSENBURG and THOMAS PEARSON who being elected tried and sworn the truth to speak upon the issue joined upon their oath do say. That the Defendant did assume in manner and form as the Plaintiff against him has declared and assess the Plaintiffs damages by occasion of the non-performance of that assumption to 10 pounds 15 shillings besides his costs. Therefore, it is considered that the Plaintiff recover against the said Defendant her damages aforesaid in form aforesaid and her costs by her about her suit in this behalf expended. And the Defendant in mercy.

ADAM STEWART against JAMES MARSDEN. The suit is dismissed for want of the Plaintiffs costs and also for want of appearance.

PAGE 126B

JOHN CRAMOND Plaintiff

Against Re: In Trespass Assault and Battery

DAVID MCCLANAHAN Defendant

This day came the parties by their Attorney's and there upon came also a Jury to wit:
DANIEL HUTCHINGS, HARDRESS WALLER, JOHN SMITH, JOHN OLIFFE, EDWARD PARKE, WILLIAM GEORGE, ALEXANDER MASSENGBURG, THOMAS PEARSON, EDMOND KEATON, JOHN WOODSIDE, FREER ARMISTON, and WILLIAM FREEMAN who being elected tried and sworn the truth to speak upon the issue joined upon their oath do say. That the Defendant is guilty of the Trespass, Assault and Battery in the declaration mentioned in manner and form as the Plaintiff against him has declared and assess the Plaintiffs damages by occasion thereof to 1 shillings and 6 pence besides his costs. Therefore, it is considered that the Plaintiff recover against the said Defendant his damages aforesaid in form aforesaid and his costs by him about his suit in this behalf expended. And the said Defendant maybe taken.

NICHOLAS LOYD Plaintiff

Against Re: In Case

ALEXANDER LOVE Defendant

This day came the parties by their Attorney's and there upon came also a Jury to wit: GRIFFIN PEART, RICHARD TAYLOR, ROBERT STEEL, JAMES LEITCH, JOHN RICHARDSON, ELDRED FISHER, JOHN GARDNER, RICHARD BASSET, SAMUEL BACON, JOHN CRAMOND, WILLIAM LIDDLE, and WILLIAM SKINKER who being elected tried and sworn the truth to speak upon the issue joined upon their oath do say that the Defendant did not assume as in pleading he has alleged. Therefore, it is considered that the Plaintiff take nothing by his bill but for his false claims be in mercy. And the defendant go hence without day and recover against the said Plaintiff his costs by him about his defense in this behalf expended.

SAMUEL HUNTER Plaintiff

Against Re: In Case

WILLIAM WHITE Defendant

This day came the parties by their Attorney's and there upon came also a Jury to wit: JAMES LEITCH, ROBERT STEEL, JOHN GARDNER, ANDREW MARTIN, WILLIAM CALDERHEAD, ROBERT TAYLOR, ELDRED FISHER, JONATHAN RICHARDSON, RICHARD BASSET, GRIFFIN PEART, SAMUEL BACON and RICHARD TAYLOR who being elected tried and sworn the truth to speak upon the issue joined upon their oath do say that the Plaintiff is dead as the Defendant in his pleading has alleged. Therefore, it is considered that the Plaintiff take nothing by his bill but for his false claims be in mercy.

PAGE 127

And the Defendant go hence without day and recover against the Plaintiff his costs by him about his defense in this behalf expended.

Order is granted WILLIAM FREEMAN against NICHOLAS LOYD for 125 pounds of tobacco for 7 days attendance in his suit against ALEXANDER LOVE.

Order is granted WILLIAM JENKINSON against NICHOLAS LOYD for 125 pounds of tobacco for 7 days attendance in his suit against ALEXANDER LOVE.

Order is granted EDWARD MOSELEY against DAVID MCCLANAHAN for 25 pounds tobacco for 1 day's attendance in the suit of JOHN CRAMOND against him.

Order is granted ISAAC JACOBS against JOHN CRAMOND for 88 pounds of tobacco for 1 day attendance coming and returning 21 miles in his suit against DAVID MCCLANAHAN.

ZACHERIAS MARSINGALE against CHARLES MANNING. The Defendant pleaded that he did not assume issue joined and referred until the next Court.

WILLISON and MCSWEEN against JOHN AUSTIN FINNIE the Defendant pleaded that he did not assume issue joined and referred until next Court.

JAMES GILCHRIST and ROBERT TAYLOR against JOHN FOWLER and GEORGE FOWLER. The Defendants pleaded that they did not assume issue joined and referred.

SAMUEL ALLYNE against GEORGE CARLTON the Defendant pleaded that the did not assume issue joined and referred until the next Court.

NATHANIEL YOUNG and JOHN SMITH against WRIGHT WESTCOTT admin of JOHN WESTCOTT deceased. The Defendant pleaded that his intestate did not assume issue joined and referred.

JOHN MCLACHLAN against EDWARD GOOD. The Defendant pleaded that he did not assume issue joined and referred.

LOGAN GILMOUR and Company against WRIGHT WESTCOTT admin of JOHN WESTCOTT deceased the Defendant pleaded that his intestate did not assume issue joined and referred.

JONATHAN MEREDITH and ELIZABETH, his wife against MATT KELLY and ANN his wife abates

CHARLES SAWYER against JOHN GILCHRIST. The Defendant pleaded not guilty issue joined and referred.

PAGE 127B

SAMUEL SIMMONS against ZACHERIAS MARSINGALE. The Defendant pleaded that he did not assume issue joined and referred until the next Court.

TULLY ROBINSON against ROBERT SHEDDEN. The Defendant pleaded that he did not assume issue joined and referred until the next Court.

PHILIP CARBERY against NEIL JAMIESON. The Defendant pleaded that he did not assume issue joined and referred until the next Court.

GEORGE ABYVON against MARK TALBOT. The former order of this Court against him the said Defendant and JOHN EDWARDS his bail be confirmed, and a writ of inquiry is awarded the Plaintiff for his damages.

JOHN GREENWOOD against WILLIAM B. COTTON. The former order of this Court against him the said Defendant is confirmed, and a writ of inquiry is awarded the Plaintiff for his damages.

JOHN MARLEY against JOHN HARDY and ELIZABETH his wife. The Defendant pleaded not guilty issue joined and referred until the next Court.

JOHN MARLEY against JOHN HARDY and ELIZABETH his wife. The Defendant pleaded not guilty issue joined and referred until the next Court.

WILLIAM PRIESTMAN against JOSHUA WRIGHT. The Defendant pleaded payment issue joined and referred until the next Court.

JOSEPH CALVERT against JOHN WILLIAMSON. The Defendant pleaded payment issue joined and referred until the next Court.

JAMES HUNTER and ELIZABETH Tenant Executors of SAMUEL TENANT deceased against JAMES ARCHDEACON. Defendant pleaded he did not assume issue joined and referred.

JOHN GREENWOOD against JOHN IVY. The former order of this Court against him the said Defendant and WILLIAM NICHOLSON his bail be confirmed, and a writ of inquiry is awarded the Plaintiff for is damages in this suit.

JAMES MARSDEN and SIMON HODGSON against JONATHAN MEREDITH and ELIZABETH his wife. The Defendants pleaded that they did not assume issue joined and referred.

PAGE 128

NATHANIEL CUNNINGHAM against ABRAM COOPER. The Defendant pleaded he does not detain. Issue joined and referred.
JOHN SCOTT against JOHN LELLO and JOHN MORRIS. The Defendant pleaded payment issue joined and referred.

This Court this day rates flour at 6/8 per cent
This Court is adjourned to Court in Course. PAUL LOYALL MAYOR. TESTE: JOHN BOUSH D.C.C.

NORFOLK BOROUGH

At a Hustings Court Held this 24TH day of August 1772
PRESENT: PAUL LOYALL ESQUIRE MAYOR
GENTLEMAN ALDERMEN: GEORGE ABYVON, JAMES TAYLOR, ARCHIBALD CAMPBELL, CORNELIUS CALVERT, LEWIS HANSFORD

BARNABY CARNEY against HENRY GREEN in case. RICHARD CARNEY this day came into Court and undertook for the Defendant that in case he shall be Cast in this suit he the said Defendant will pay the condemnation of the Court or render his body to Prison in execution for the same or that the said RICHARD will pay the condemnation of the Court or render the body of the said Defendant as aforesaid. Where upon the Defendant by his Attorney prays and has leave to IMPARLE here until next Court and then to plead.

JOHN SHAW against HUMPHREY ROBERTS Dismissed.

RICHARD BASSET against JOHN HARWOOD in debt. WILLIAM CALVERT undertakes for the Defendant that in case he shall be Cast in this suit he the said Defendant will pay the condemnation of the Court or render his body to Prison in execution for the same or that the said CALVERT will pay the condemnation of the Court or render the body of the said Defendant as aforesaid. Where upon the Defendant by his Attorney prays and has leave to IMPARLE here until next Court and then to plead.

RICHARD BASSET against JOHN POLLOCK in debt. JOHN MCLACHLAN. This day came into Court and undertook for the Defendant that in case he shall be Cast in this suit he the said Defendant will pay the condemnation of the Court or render his body to Prison in execution for the same or that the said MCLACHLAN will pay the condemnation of the Court or render the body of the said Defendant as aforesaid. Where upon the Defendant by his Attorney prays and has leave to IMPARLE here until next Court and then to plead.

PAGE 128B

RICHARD BASSET against DANIEL PECK and JOSEPH HARDING. Dismissed.

MISSIEURS BUCHANAN and HASTIE merchants of Great Britain against ROBERT MACKIE, ROBERT GILMOUR undertakes for the Defendant that in case he shall be Cast in this suit he the said Defendant will pay the condemnation of the Court or render his body to Prison in execution for the same or that the said GILMOUR will pay the condemnation of the Court or render the body of the said Defendant as aforesaid. Where upon the Defendant by his Attorney prays and has leave to IMPARLE here until next Court and then to plead.

WILLIAM HARDY against JOHN EDWARDS. An Imparlance.
PETER LONG against WILLIAM BRITT. Special Imparlance.

ROBERT GILMOUR administrator of WILLIAM GRAY Deceased Plaintiff

Against Re: In Case

WILLIAM GEORGE Defendant

This day came as well the Plaintiff by ANDREW RONALD Gentleman his Attorney as the Defendant in his proper person and the said Defendant says that he cannot gainsay the Plaintiff's action nor but that he did assume in manner and form as the Plaintiff against him has declared. Therefore, it is considered that the Plaintiff recover against the said Defendant 7 pounds 6 shillings and 1 penny half penny and his costs by him about his suit in this behalf expended and the said Defendant in mercy.

MISSIEURS SAMUEL INGLES and PETER LONG against WILLIAM LIDDLE in case. JOHN MCLACHLAN this day came into and undertook for the Defendant that in case he shall be Cast in this suit he the said Defendant will pay the condemnation of the Court or render his body to Prison in execution for the same or that the said MCLACHLAN will pay the condemnation of the Court or render the body of the said Defendant as aforesaid. Where upon the Defendant by his Attorney prays and has leave to IMPARLE here until next Court.

RICHARD KELSICK against NATHANIEL BOUSH in debt SAMUEL BOUSH undertakes for the Defendant that in case he shall be Cast in this suit he the said Defendant will pay the condemnation of the Court or render his body to Prison in execution for the same or that the said SAMUEL will pay the condemnation of the Court or render the body of the said Defendant as aforesaid. Where upon the Defendant by his Attorney prays and has leave to IMPARLE here until next Court and then to plead.

PAGE 129

NICHOLAS WONYCOTT against THOMAS WALKER in case. STEPHEN TANKARD this day came into Court and undertook for the Defendant that in case he shall be Cast in this suit he the said Defendant will pay the condemnation of the Court or render his body to Prison in execution for the same or that the said TANKARD will pay the condemnation of the Court or render the body of the said Defendant as aforesaid. Where upon the Defendant by his Attorney prays and has leave to IMPARLE here until next Court and then to plead.

GEORGE ABYVON Plaintiff

Against Re: In Debt

GEORGE WEBB Defendant

This day came as well the Plaintiff by BENJAMIN CROOKER Gentleman his Attorney as the Defendant in his proper person and the said Defendant acknowledges the Plaintiff action for 35 pounds.

Therefore, it is considered that the Plaintiff recover against the said Defendant his debt aforesaid and his costs by him about his suit in this behalf expended and the said Defendant in mercy. But this Judgement is to be discharged by the payment of 17 pounds 18 shillings and 4 pence with interest for the same at the rate of 5% per annum to be computed from May 14, 1771, to the time of payment and costs.

TULLY ROBINSON and JOHN CRAMOND against JONATHAN MEREDITH. An Attachment.

JAMES MILLS & COMPANY against RICHARD BROWN and JOHN CHESHIRE. Imparlance.

JOHN CHESHIRE and RICHARD BROWN against JAMES MILLS and GEORGE LEDIMORE. Plea & time to consider.

MISSIEURS GILCHRIST and TAYLOR against JONATHAN MEREDITH. Dismissed.

THOMAS NASH JR. executor of NATHANIEL TATEM against TALBOT THOMPSON Dismissed.

JOHN GILCHRIST against JONATHAN MEREDITH. DISMISSED.

SAMUEL BLEWS against ANDREW STEVENSON and ANN his wife. Imparlance.

JAMES HEALEY against ANDREW STEVENSON and ANN his wife. Imparlance.

MISTERS GILCHRIST and TAYLOR against JONATHAN MEREDITH. By Attachment. Dismissed.

PAGE 129B

JOSEPH LANGLEY against JOHN MCLACHLAN in case. WILLIAM LIDDLE this day came into Court and undertook for the Defendant that in case he shall be Cast in this suit he the said Defendant will pay the condemnation of the Court or render his body to Prison in execution for the same or that the said LIDDLE will pay the condemnation of the Court or render the body of the said Defendant as aforesaid. Where upon the Defendant by his Attorney prays and has leave to IMPARLE here until next Court and then to plead.

CUMMING WARWICK & Company against ROBERT MACKIE in case. ROBERT GILMOUR this day came into Court and undertook for the Defendant that in case he shall be Cast in this suit he the said Defendant will pay the condemnation of the Court or render his body to Prison in execution for the same or that the said GILMOUR will pay the condemnation of the Court or render the body of the said Defendant as aforesaid. Where upon the Defendant by his Attorney prays and has leave to IMPARLE here until next Court and then to plead.

MISSIEURS JOHN RAMSAY and JAMES TAYLOR against JOHN CRAMOND admin of MARY ROBERTSON deceased. Imparlance.

ELDRED FISHER against GEORGE ALLANSON by Attachments dated April 1772 Dismissed.

JAMES MURDAUGH guardian of ANNE WALKE and assignee of EDWARD WRIGHT who was her late guardian against JOHN MACLEAN the suit is dismissed.

EDWARD HACK MOSELEY Gentleman Plaintiff

Against Re: In Case

JAMES INGRAM Defendant

This day came the parties by their Attorneys and there upon came also a Jury to wit: ROBERT GILMOUR, BENJAMIN NEWBOLD, BARTHOLOMEW THOMPSON, THOMAS FARRER, LATIMORE HALSTEAD, JOHN RICHARDSON, JAMES GLASSFORD, HENRY CORNICK, DANIEL HUTCHINGS, ROGER PIERCE, WILLIAM STEVENSON, and JACOB BISHOP who being elected tried and sworn the truth to speak upon the issue joined upon their oath do say that the Defendant did assume in manner and form as the Plaintiff against him has declared and assess the Plaintiffs damages by occasion of the non-performance of that assumption to 3 pounds 14 shillings and 3 pence besides his costs. Therefore, it is considered that the Plaintiff recover against the said Defendant her damages aforesaid in form aforesaid and her costs by her about her suit in this behalf expended. And the Defendant in mercy. The Plaintiff having agreed to stay the Execution of this Judgement for 2 months.

PAGE 130
ROBERT GILMOUR against ROBERT POMEROY. Continued.
RAMSAY and TAYLOR against ROBERT POMEROY. Discontinued.

ELIZABETH HOPKINS executrix of JOHN HOPKINS Deceased Plaintiff
Against Re: In detinue for 2 Negroes
ELDRED FISHER Defendant
This day came the parties by their Attorney's and there upon came also a Jury to wit: DUNCAN CAMPBELL, JOHN WALKER, GRIFFIN PEART, GEORGE WILSON, WILLIAM CHISHOLM, PAUL PROBY, ALEXANDER MOSELEY, WILLIAM INGRAM, THOMAS SNALE, JOHN MCLACHLAN, JAMES DUNN, and CHARLES GODFREY who being elected tried and sworn the truth to speak upon the issue joined upon their oath do say. That the Defendant does not detain the said Negroes in manner and form as the Plaintiff against him has declared. Therefore, it is considered that the Plaintiff take nothing by her bill but for her false claims be in mercy. And the defendant go hence without day and recover against the said Plaintiff his costs by him about his defense in this behalf expended.

JAMES MOORE Plaintiff against NATHANIEL BOUSH Defendant. The demurer of the Defendant to the Plaintiff's suit was this day argued and adjudged good. Therefore, it is considered that the suit be dismissed, and that the Plaintiff pay unto the Defendant his costs by him about his defense in this behalf expended.

JAMES MOORE against NICHOLAS BOUSH. Dismissed at the Plaintiff's costs.

The King by SAMUEL BLEWS against ANDREW STEVENSON by warrant. Dismissed at the Defendants Costs.

ANDREW STEVENSON was this day brought before the Court by warrant for breach of the Peace the same being proved it is ordered that the Sergeant take and keep him in custody until he gives bond and security himself in 20 pounds and 2 securities in 10 pounds each for his keeping the peace 6 months and pay the costs of this prosecution. Where upon the STEVENSON with his securities came into Court and entered into recognizance.

Order is granted PETER BEISER against SAMUEL BLEWS for 25 pounds of tobacco for 1 day's attendance in his Complaint against ANDREW STEVENSON.

PAGE 130B
Order is granted WILLIAM WEBLIN against ELIZABETH HOPKINS executrix of JOHN HOPKINS deceased for 192 pounds of tobacco for 3 days attendance coming and returning 13 miles 3x in her suit against ELDRED FISHER.

Order is granted ADAM PRICE against ELIZABETH HOPKINS executrix of JOHN HOPKINS deceased for 273 pounds of tobacco for 3 days attendance coming and returning 22 miles 3x in her suit against ELDRED FISHER.

Order is granted ELIZABETH MURDEN against ELIZABETH HOPKINS executrix of JOHN HOPKINS deceased for 165 pounds of tobacco for 3 days attendance coming and returning 10 miles 3x in her suit against ELDRED FISHER.

Order is granted JOHN BEISER against ELIZABETH HOPKINS executrix of JOHN HOPKINS deceased for 25 pounds of tobacco for 1 day's attendance in her suit against ELDRED FISHER.

Order is granted WILLIAM SMITH and SARAH his wife against ELDRED FISHER for 25 pounds of tobacco for 1 day's attendance each in the suit of ELIZABETH HOPKINS executrix of JOHN HOPKINS deceased against him.

Order is granted PETER BEISER against JAMES HEALEY for 25 pounds of tobacco for 1 day's attendance in his Complaint against ANDREW STEVENSON.

MATHIAS GALE, ANN MOORE, JOSEPH MITCHELL, JOHN COX, and THOMAS BUTT against RICHARD ROTHERY an infant son and heir of HENRY ROTHERY Deceased, MARY ROTHERY widow and GEORGE ABYVON executor of the said HENRY ROTHERY Deceased.
The Plaintiff MATHIAS being dead the suit as to him abates and JOHN HUNT, RICHARD ASTON, JOHN HENDERSON and WILLIAM FISHER executors of the said MATHIAS GALE deceased are at liberty on their motion to be inserted into the bill as Plaintiffs and the suit is discontinued against THOMAS BUTT one of the Plaintiffs there upon it is ordered and decreed that the Commissioners appointed in former decree and order do state, examine the claims and demands and make report to the next Court to be held for this Borough.

This Court is adjourned until tomorrow 9 o'clock, PAUL LOYALL MAYOR, TESTE: JOHN BOUSH D.C.C.

PAGE 131
NORFOLK BOROUGH
At a Hustings Court Held this 25TH day of August 1772
PRESENT: PAUL LOYALL ESQUIRE MAYOR
GENTLEMAN ALDERMEN: GEORGE ABYVON, JAMES TAYLOR, ARCHIBALD CAMPBELL, CORNELIUS CALVERT, LEWIS HANSFORD

JOHN HUTCHINGS, MATTHEW PHRIPP and SAMUEL BOUSH Plaintiff
Against Re: In Case
ALEXANDER BELL Defendant
This day came the parties by their Attorneys and there upon came also a Jury to wit:
JOHN MACLEAN, ELDRED FISHER, JOHN SMITH, HENRY FLEMING, JOHN WILKINS, STEPHEN TANKARD, JAMES MURPHREE, JOHN JONES, WILLIAM INGRAM, BENJAMIN NEWBOLD, WILLIAM JAQUES and JOHN GILCHRIST who being elected tried and sworn the truth to speak upon the issue joined upon their oath do say that the Defendant did assume in manner and form as the Plaintiff against him has declared and assess the Plaintiffs damages by occasion of the non-performance of that assumption to 7 pounds 7 shillings and 11pence besides his costs. Therefore, it is considered that the Plaintiff recover against the said Defendant her damages aforesaid in form aforesaid and their costs by them about their suit in this behalf expended. And the Defendant in mercy.

THOMAS HEPBURN Plaintiff
Against Re: In Case
JAMES ROGERS Defendant
This day came the Plaintiff by THOMAS BURKE Gentleman and there upon came also a Jury to wit: JOHN MACLEAN, ELDRED FISHER, JOHN SMITH, HENRY FLEMING, JOHN WILKINS, STEPHEN TANKARD, JAMES MURPHREE, JOHN JONES, WILLIAM INGRAM, BENJAMIN NEWBOLD, WILLIAM JAQUES and JOHN GILCHRIST who being sworn well and truly to inquire of damages in this suit upon their oath do say that the Defendant* has sustained damages by occasion of the Defendants Breach of Promise in the Declaration mentioned to 21 pounds, 8 shillings and 10 pence besides his costs. Therefore, it is considered by the Court that the Plaintiff recover against the said Defendant and JOSEPH POPE his bail his damages aforesaid and his costs by him about his suit in this behalf expended. And the said Defendant in mercy.

PAGE 131B
JOHN COLES assignee of JOHN HUTCHINGS executor of JOHN TUCKER Deceased Plaintiff
Against Re: In Case
JOSEPH CALVERT Defendant
This day came the Plaintiff by his Attorney as the Defendant in his proper person and there up on came also a Jury to wit: JOHN MACLEAN, ELDRED FISHER, JOHN SMITH, HENRY FLEMING, JOHN WILKINS, STEPHEN TANKARD, JAMES MURPHREE, JOHN JONES, WILLIAM INGRAM, BENJAMIN NEWBOLD, WILLIAM JAQUES and JOHN GILCHRIST who being elected tried and sworn the truth to speak upon the issue joined upon their oath do say that the Defendant has not paid the debt in the declaration mentioned. Therefore, it is considered that the Plaintiff recover against the said Defendant his debt aforesaid amounting to 274 pounds and 8 pence and his costs by him in this behalf expended. And the said Defendant in mercy. But this judgement is to be discharged by the payment of 137 pounds and 4 pence with interest there on at the rate of 5% per annum to be computed from June 10th, 1769, to the time of payment and costs.

THOMAS NEWTON assignee of JOHN SMITH Plaintiff
Against Re: In Debt for rent
WILLIAM SMITH Defendant
This day came the parties by their Attorney's and there upon came also a Jury to wit: JOHN MACLEAN, ELDRED FISHER, JOHN SMITH, HENRY FLEMING, JOHN WILKINS, STEPHEN TANKARD, JAMES MURPHREE, JOHN JONES, WILLIAM INGRAM, BENJAMIN NEWBOLD, WILLIAM JAQUES and JOHN GILCHRIST who being elected tried and sworn the truth to speak upon the issue joined upon their oath do say that the Defendant does owe the debt in the declaration mentioned. Therefore, it is considered that the Plaintiff recover against the said Defendant his debt aforesaid amounting to 35 pounds and his costs by him about his suit in this behalf expended and the said Defendant in mercy.

FREDERICK AUGUSTUS DOEBER assignee of JOSEPH CALVERT Plaintiff
Against Re: In Debt
WILLIAM GEORGE and JAMES LEITCH Defendants
This day came the parties by their Attorney's and there upon came also a Jury to wit: THOMAS HEPBURN, JOHN WALKER, JOHN BROWN, JOHN POLLOCK, JAMES CARMICKHAIL, JOHN MCLACHLAN, THOMAS SNALE, WILLIAM CHISHOLM, JOHN WOODSIDE, DICKERSON PRIOR, JAMES WALKER and JOHN RICHARDSON who being elected tried and sworn the truth to speak upon the issue joined upon their oath do say that the Defendants are not guilty in manner and form as the Plaintiff against him has declared. Therefore, it is considered that the Plaintiff take nothing by his bill but for his false claims be in mercy. And the Defendant go hence without day and recover against the Plaintiff their costs by them about their defense in this behalf expended.

PAGE 132
CHARLES GODFREY and ANNA, his wife Plaintiffs
Against Re: In Case
EDWARD ARCHER acting executor of EDWARD ARCHER Deceased Defendant
This day came as well the Plaintiffs by BENJAMIN CROOKER Gentleman his Attorney as the defendant in his proper person and the said Defendant says that he cannot gainsay the Plaintiff's action nor but that he did assume in manner and form as the Plaintiff against him have declared. Therefore, it is considered that the Plaintiff recover against the said Defendant 125 pounds 18 shillings and 9 pence half penny and their costs by them in this behalf expended and the said Defendant in mercy.

JAMES CAMPBELL and Company Plaintiff
Against Re: In Case
JOSHUA WRIGHT Defendant
This day came the parties by their Attorney's and there upon came also a Jury to wit: JOHN MCLACHLAN, JOHN POLLOCK, JAMES CARMICKHAIL, JOHN RICHARDSON, JOHN WOODSIDE, THOMAS SNALE, WILLIAM CHISHOLM, JOHN WALKER, THOMAS HEPBURN, DICKERSON PRIOR, JOHN BROWN and JAMES WALKER who being elected tried and sworn the truth to speak upon the issue joined upon their oath do say that the Defendant is guilty in manner and form at the Plaintiff against him have declared and do assess the Plaintiff damages by occasion thereof to 9 pounds 4 shillings besides their costs. Therefore, it is considered that the Plaintiff recover against the said Defendants their damages aforesaid in form aforesaid assessed and their costs by them in this behalf expended and the said Defendant in mercy.

SAMUEL ALLYN Plaintiff
Against Re: In Case
GEORGE CARLSON Defendant
This day came the parties by their Attorney's and there upon also a Jury to wit: PETER TAYLOR, ANDREW MARK, ROBERT WALLER, RICHARD BICKERDICK, GEORGE WILSON, MATTHEW MCVIE, JOHN SHAW, WILLIAM SKINKER, JOHN SHEDDEN, WILLIAM GEORGE, JAMES LEITCH, and ANDREW BALLINGALD who being elected tried and sworn the truth to speak upon the issue joined upon their oath do say that the Defendant did not assume as in pleading he has alleged. Therefore, it is considered that the Plaintiff take nothing by his bill but for his false claims be in mercy. And the Defendant go hence without day and recover against the Plaintiff his costs by him about his defense in this behalf expended.

PAGE 132B
JOHN MCLACHLAN Plaintiff
Against Re: In Case
EDWARD GOOD Defendant
This day came the parties by their Attorneys and there upon came also a Jury to wit:
JOHN GILCHRIST, WILLIAM JAQUES, JOHN INGRAM, JOHN RICHARDSON, JAMES MURPHREE, STEPHEN TANKARD, JOHN WILKINS, HENRY FLEMING, JOHN SMITH, ELDRED FISHER, BENJAMIN NEWBOLD and WILLOUGHBY MORGAN who being elected tried and sworn the truth to speak upon the issue joined upon their oath do say that the Defendant did assume in manner and form as the Plaintiff against him has declared and assess the Plaintiffs damages by occasion of the non-performance of that assumption to 14 pounds 6 shillings and 5 pence besides his costs. Therefore, it is considered that the Plaintiff recover against the said Defendant her damages aforesaid in form aforesaid and their costs by them about their suit in this behalf expended. And the Defendant in mercy.

Order is granted SAMUEL PORTLOCK against JOHN HUTCHINGS, MATT PHRIPP and SAMUEL BOUSH for 100 pounds of tobacco for 4 days attendance in their suit against ALEXANDER BELL.

Order is granted SAMUEL BACON against JOHN HUTCHINGS, MATT PHRIPP and SAMUEL BOUSH for 100 pounds of tobacco for 4 days attendance in their suit against ALEXANDER BELL.

Order is granted ROBERT WALLER against WILLIAM SMITH for 75 pounds of tobacco for 3 days attendance in the suit against THOMAS NEWTON assignee of JOHN SMITH against him.

Order is granted WILLIAM CHISHOLM against WILLIAM SMITH for 75 pounds of tobacco for 3 days attendance in the suit against THOMAS NEWTON assignee of JOHN SMITH against him.

Order is granted ALEXANDER DIACK against FREDERICK AUGUSTUS DOEBER for 75 pounds of tobacco for 3 days attendance in the suit against WILLIAM GEORGE and JAMES LEITCH.

Order is granted SARAH MASSENBURG against FREDERICK AUGUSTUS DOEBER for 75 pounds of tobacco for 3 days attendance in the suit against WILLIAM GEORGE and JAMES LEITCH.

PAGE 133
Order is granted ROBERT FRY against WILLIAM GEORGE and JAMES LEITCH for 75 pounds of tobacco for 3 days attendance of his wife in the suit of FREDERICK AUGUSTUS DOEBER against them.

Order is granted SUSANNA ESTHER against WILLIAM GEORGE and JAMES LEITCH for 75 pounds of tobacco for 3 days attendance in the suit of FREDERICK AUGUSTUS DOEBER against them.

Order is granted RICHARD BICKERDICK against JAMES CAMPBELL & Company for 75 pounds of tobacco for 3 days attendance in their suit against JOSHUA WRIGHT.

Order is granted EDWARD PARKER against JAMES CAMPBELL & Company for 50 pounds of tobacco for 2 days attendance in their suit against JOSHUA WRIGHT.

EDWARD ARCHER executor of EDWARD ARCHER Deceased against JONATHAN MEREDITH and ELIZABETH his wife. Dismissed.

JAMES MARSDEN and SIMON HODGSON against JONATHAN MEREDITH and ELIZABETH his wife. Dismissed.
JOHN SCOTT against JOHN LELLO and JOHN MORRIS. Dismissed.

JAMES CAMPBELL & Company Plaintiff
Against Re: In Case
GEORGE WILSON and ARCHIBALD CAMPBELL Admins of JOHN WILSON Deceased Defendant
This day came the parties by their Attorney's and there upon came also a Jury to wit: JAMES CARMICKHAIL, PETER TAYLOR, WILLIAM GEORGE, MATTHEW MCVIE, THOMAS SNALE, RICHARD BICKERDICK, CHARLES GODFREY, DICKERSON PRIOR, JOHN POLLOCK, JAMES LEITCH, WILLIAM LIDDLE and WILLIAM SKINKER who being elected tried and sworn the truth to speak upon the issue joined upon their oath do say that the Defendants intestate did assume in manner and form as the Plaintiff against them have declared and do assess the Plaintiff damages by occasion of the nonperformance of that assumption to 382 pounds 3 shillings and 3 pence half penny besides their costs. Therefore, it is considered that the Plaintiff recover against the said Defendant their damages aforesaid in form aforesaid assessed and their costs by them in this behalf expended when assets to be levied of the goods and chattels of the said intestate if so much the said GEORGE WILSON and ARCHIBALD CAMPBELL have in their hands to be administered and if they have it not then the costs are to be levied of their proper goods and chattels and the said Defendants in mercy. And the parties have agreed to release errors if any should appear in the addition of their accounts.

PAGE 133B

GEORGE CARLSON against JOHN TAYLOR dismissed at the Defendants costs.

Order is granted JOHN PEAD, JOHN HAWKS, GEORGE HAMOT, HENRY HOLMS, and THOMAS PEBWORTH against GEORGE WILSON and ARCHIBALD CAMPBELL admin of JOHN WILSON deceased for 50 pound of tobacco each for 2 days attendance in the suit of JAMES CAMPBELL and Company against them.

This Court is adjourned until tomorrow 10 o'clock, PAUL LOYALL MAYOR, TESTE: JOHN BOUSH D.C.C.

NORFOLK BOROUGH

At a Hustings Court Held this 26TH day of August 1772
PRESENT: PAUL LOYALL ESQUIRE MAYOR
GENTLEMAN ALDERMEN: GEORGE ABYVON, MAXIMILIAN CALVERT, ARCHIBALD CAMPBELL, JAMES TAYLOR, LEWIS HANSFORD

Ordinary License is granted SAMUEL PORTLOCK and JAMES ATKINSON on their complying with the law.

JOHN GREENWOOD Plaintiff
Against Re: In Debt
WILLIAM B. COTTON Defendant
This day came the Plaintiff by WILLIAM RASCOW WILSON CURLE Gentleman his Attorney and thereupon came also a Jury to wit: SAMUEL BACON, WILLIAM JAQUES, JOHN EDWARDS, GRIFFIN PEART, JOHN BARRET, BASSET MOSELEY, DANIEL HUTCHINGS, JOHN RICHARDSON, JOHN LIVINGSTON, CHARLES GODFREY, MASON MILLER and JAMES DUNN who being sworn well and truly to inquire of damages upon their oath do say that the Plaintiff has sustained damages by occasion of the Defendants Breaking the condition of the writing obligatory in the declaration mentioned to 18 pounds 6 shillings besides his costs. Therefore, it is considered by the Court that the Plaintiff recover against the said Defendant the 36 pounds 12 shillings debt in the declaration mentioned together with his damages aforesaid in form aforesaid assessed and his costs by him in this behalf expended and the said Defendant in mercy.

PAGE 134

But this judgement is to be discharged by the Payment of the said damages with interest there on at the rate of 5% per annum to be computed from MARCH 14, 1768, to the time of payment and costs.

GEORGE ABYVON Plaintiff
Against Re: In Case
MARK TALBOT Defendant
This day came the Plaintiff by WILLIAM RASCOW WILSON CURLE Gentleman his Attorney and there upon came also a Jury to wit: SAMUEL BACON, WILLIAM JAQUES, JOHN EDWARDS, GRIFFIN PEART, JOHN BARRET, BASSET MOSELEY, DANIEL HUTCHINGS, JOHN RICHARDSON, JOHN LIVINGSTON, CHARLES GODFREY, MASON MILLER and JAMES DUNN who being sworn well and truly to inquire of damages upon their oath do say that the Plaintiff has sustained damages by occasion of the Defendants Breach of Promise to 7 pounds 10 shillings and 3 pence besides his costs. Therefore, it is considered that the Plaintiff recover against the said Defendant and JOHN EDWARDS his bail his damages aforesaid in form aforesaid assessed and his costs by him in this behalf expended and the said Defendant in mercy.

GEORGE LOGAN, ROBERT GILMOUR, and Company Plaintiff
Against Re: In Case
WRIGHT WESTCOTT admin of JOHN WESTCOTT Defendant
This day came the parties by their Attorney's and there upon came also a Jury to wit: This day came the Plaintiff by WILLIAM RASCOW WILSON CURLE Gentleman his Attorney and there upon came also a Jury to wit: SAMUEL BACON, WILLIAM JAQUES, JOHN EDWARDS, GRIFFIN PEART, JOHN BARRET, BASSET MOSELEY, DANIEL HUTCHINGS, JOHN RICHARDSON, JOHN LIVINGSTON, CHARLES GODFREY, MASON MILLER and JAMES DUNN who being elected tried and sworn the truth to speak upon the issue joined upon their oath do say that the Defendants intestate did assume in manner and form as the Plaintiff against him have declared and do assess the Plaintiff damages by occasion of the nonperformance of that assumption to 13 pounds 2 shillings and 1 penny besides their costs. Therefore, it is considered that the Plaintiff recover against the said Defendant his damages aforesaid in form aforesaid assessed and their costs by them in this behalf

expended when assets to be levied of the goods and chattels of the said intestate JOHN if so much the said WRIGHT has in his hands to be administered and if they have it not then the costs are to be levied of his proper goods and chattels and the said Defendants in mercy.

WILLIAM DAVIS this day produced a license form under the hand and seal of JOHN RANDOLPH and GEORGE WYTHE Gentleman to practice as an Attorney and he having taken the oath to the government and subscribed the test, also the oath of an Attorney is admitted to practice as an Attorney in this Court.

PAGE 134B

WILLIAM PRIESTMAN Plaintiff
Against Re: In Case
JOSHUA WRIGHT Defendant

This day came the parties by their Attorney's and there upon came also a Jury to wit: SAMUEL BACON, WILLIAM JAQUES, JOHN EDWARDS, GRIFFIN PEART, JOHN BARRET, BASSET MOSELEY, DANIEL HUTCHINGS, JOHN RICHARDSON, JOHN LIVINGSTON, CHARLES GODFREY, MASON MILLER, and JAMES DUNN who being elected tried and sworn the truth to speak upon the issue joined upon their oath do say that the Defendant has not paid the debt in the declaration mentioned. Therefore, it is considered that the Plaintiff recover against the said Defendant his debt amounting to 56 pounds 13 shillings and 3 pence and his costs by him about his suit in this behalf expended. And the said Defendants in mercy.

JOHN GREENWOOD Plaintiff
Against Re: In Case
JOHN IVY Defendant

This day came the Plaintiff by WILLIAM RASCOW WILSON CURLE Gentleman his Attorney and there upon came also a Jury to wit: SAMUEL BACON, WILLIAM JAQUES, JOHN EDWARDS, GRIFFIN PEART, JOHN BARRET, BASSET MOSELEY, DANIEL HUTCHINGS, JOHN RICHARDSON, JOHN LIVINGSTON, CHARLES GODFREY, MASON MILLER and JAMES DUNN who being sworn well and truly to inquire of damages upon their oath do say that the Plaintiff has sustained damages by occasion of the Defendants Breach of Promise to 16 pounds 17 shillings and 3 pence half penny besides his costs. Therefore, it is considered that the Plaintiff recover against the said Defendant and WILLIAM NICHOLSON his bail his damages aforesaid in form aforesaid assessed and his costs by him in this behalf expended and the said Defendant in mercy.

JOSEPH CALVERT against JOHN WILLIAMSON. Dismissed at Plaintiff's costs.

JAMES HUNTER and ELIZABETH TENANT executors of SAMUEL TENANT Plaintiff
Against Re: In Case
JAMES ARCHDEACON Plaintiff

This day came the parties by their Attorney's and there upon came also a Jury to wit: SAMUEL BACON, WILLIAM JAQUES, JOHN EDWARDS, GRIFFIN PEART, JOHN BARRET, BASSET MOSELEY, DANIEL HUTCHINGS, JOHN RICHARDSON, JOHN LIVINGSTON, CHARLES GODFREY, MASON MILLER and JAMES DUNN who being elected tried and sworn the truth to speak upon the issue joined upon their oath do say that the Defendant did assume in manner and form as the Plaintiff against him has declared and do assess the Plaintiff damages by occasion of the nonperformance of that assumption to 47 pounds 15 shillings and 4 pence besides their costs.

PAGE 135

Therefore, it is considered that the Plaintiff recover against the said Defendant their damages aforesaid in form aforesaid assessed and their costs by them in this behalf expended. And the said Defendants in mercy.

MATTHEW ROTHERY & MARY, his wife against GEORGE WATSON and ANN his wife the suit as to the Plaintiff MATTHEW abates by his death and continued against the Defendants.

JOHN CRAMOND against BRUDENCE BAYNES. The Defendant she did not assume, and notice given for the books issue joined and referred.

JOHN GILCHRIST against EDWARD HANSFORD. The Defendant pleaded he did not assume issue joined and referred.

Order is granted WILLIAM HUNTER against JAMES HUNTER and ELIZABETH TENANT Executors of SAMUEL TENANT for 165 pounds of tobacco for 3 days attendance coming and returning 10 miles 3 times in their suit against JAMES ARCHDEACON.

EMANUEL ANTONIO against JAMES CAMPBELL, ARCHIBALD CAMPBELL, WILLIAM AITCHESON, and JAMES PARKER removed by certiorari.

TULLY ROBINSON Plaintiff
Against Re: In Case
ROBERT SHEDDEN Defendant

This day came the parties by their Attorney's and there upon came also a Jury to wit: SAMUEL BACON, WILLIAM JAQUES, JOHN EDWARDS, GRIFFIN PEART, JOHN BARRET, BASSET MOSELEY, DANIEL HUTCHINGS, JOHN RICHARDSON, JOHN LIVINGSTON, CHARLES GODFREY, MASON MILLER and JAMES DUNN who being elected tried and sworn the truth to speak upon the issue joined upon their oath do say that the Defendant did assume in manner and form as the Plaintiff against him has declared and do assess the Plaintiff damages by occasion of the nonperformance of that assumption to 6 pounds 8 shillings and 8 pence besides his costs. Therefore, it is considered that the Plaintiff recover against the said Defendant his damages aforesaid in form aforesaid assessed and his costs by him in this behalf expended. And the said Defendants in mercy.

PAGE 135B

NEIL JAMIESON administrator of HENRY TUCKER deceased against CHARLES GODFREY, GEORGE ABYVON Gentleman this day came into Court and undertook for the Defendant that in case he shall be casts in this suit he the said Defendant will pay the condemnation of the Court or render his body to Prison in execution for the same or that the said ABYVON will pay the condemnation or render the body of the said Defendant as aforesaid. Where upon the Defendant pleaded payment. Therefore, ordered that the judgement obtained by the Plaintiff against the said Defendant and GEORGE ABYVON Gentleman his bail be set aside.

NEIL JAMIESON Administrator of HENRY TUCKER Deceased Plaintiff
Against Re: In Debt
THOMAS SNALE Defendant

This day came the parties by their Attorney's and by consent the Judgement obtained by the said Plaintiff against the said Defendant and JOHN WOODSIDE his bail is set aside and there upon the Defendant by his Attorney acknowledges the Plaintiffs action for 30 pounds 3 shillings and 6 pence. Therefore, it is considered that the Plaintiff recover against the said Defendant his debt aforesaid and his costs by them in this behalf expended and the said Defendant in mercy. This Judgement is to be discharged by the payment of 3 pounds 15 shillings and 6 pence without any further interest and the Plaintiff agrees to stay execution of this Judgement 3 months.

SPROWLE and CROOKS against WRIGHT WESTCOTT administrator of JOHN WESTCOTT deceased. The suit abates by the Plaintiff's death.

MISSIEURS LOGAN GILMOUR & COMPANY against THOMAS BUTT. The Defendant pleaded payment issue joined and referred to next Court.

ANN SYMONS by ROBERT BANKS her next friend against THOMAS DREWREY. The Defendant pleaded not guilty issue joined and referred to next Court.

CORNELIUS CALVERT against JONATHAN MEREDITH. Dismissed at the Plaintiff's cost.
KEDAR COOPER against JOSHUA PEAD. The Defendant pleaded that he does not detain the Negro slave. Issue joined and referred.
ANTHONY LAWSON against JOSHUA WRIGHT. The Defendant pleaded not guilty issue joined and referred.

PAGE 136

JAMES MARSDEN and SIMON HODGSON against ALEXANDER BELL. The Defendant pleaded he did not assume, issue joined and referred.

LODOWICK GRAY by BENJAMIN DINGLEY, GRAY next friend against WILLIAM IVY. The Defendant pleaded he did not assume issue joined and referred.

EDWARD WRIGHT and JAMES JONES executor of JOSEPH JONES against JOHN MCLACHLAN. The Defendant pleaded he did not assume issue joined and referred.

HENRY FLEMING and Company against JOSHUA WRIGHT. The Defendant pleaded payment issue joined and referred until next Court.

JOHN MCLACHLAN against THOMAS WALKER and JOHN VALLENCIER. The Defendant pleaded they did not assume issue joined and referred.

JOHN CRAMOND against JOHN TATEM. The Defendant pleaded issue joined and referred.

MISSIEURS TULLY ROBINSON and JOHN CRAMOND against JOHN WISE. The Defendant pleaded not guilty issue joined and referred until next Court.

MICHAEL CHRISTIAN assignee of WILLIAM MCCAA against ALEXANDER BELL. The Defendant pleaded payment issue joined and referred.
MICHAEL CHRISTIAN and LABON JOHNSTON against ALEXANDER BELL. The Defendant pleaded payment issue joined and referred.
MALACHI MAUND assignee of NOAH SUGG against SAMUEL BRESSIE. The Defendant pleaded payment issue joined and referred.
MALACHI MAUND against SAMUEL and HENRY BRESSIE. The Defendant pleaded they did not assume issue joined and referred until next Court.

PAGE 136B

PETER KATZ against JAMES CAMPBELL and Company. The Defendant pleaded they did not assume issue joined and referred to the Next Court.

PETER KATZ against JAMES CAMPBELL and Company. The Defendant pleaded they did not assume issue joined and referred to the Next Court.

HENRY BRESSIE assignee of SAMUEL BRESSIE against THOMAS and MATTHEW CHERRY. The defendants pleaded payment issue joined and referred.

THOMAS WILSON & Company against THOMAS POLLOCK. Order the former order of this Court against the said Defendant be confirmed and a writ of inquiry is awarded the Plaintiff for his damages.

THOMAS LANGLEY SR. against JOHN and JOSEPH HUTCHINGS. The Defendant plead they do not detain. Issue joined and referred.

MISTERS WILLISON and MCSWEEN against JOHN BURNLEY order the former order of this Court against the said Defendant and ALEXANDER LOVE his bail be confirmed and a Writ of Inquiry is awarded the Plaintiff for their damages.

HENRY FLEMING, HENRY BRAG and ROBERT FISHER against JOSEPH HUTCHINGS Esquire, the Defendant pleaded payment issue joined and referred.

This Court this day rated flour at 16/8 per centum

This Court is adjourned to Court in Course, PAUL LOYALL MAYOR, TESTE: JOHN BOUSH D.C.C.

PAGE 137

NORFOLK BOROUGH

At a Hustings Court Held this 21st day of September 1772

PRESENT: PAUL LOYALL ESQUIRE MAYOR

GENTLEMAN ALDERMEN: GEORGE ABYVON, CHARLES THOMAS, LEWIS HANSFORD, JAMES TAYLOR, MAXIMILIAN CALVERT

WRIGHT WESTCOTT against THOMAS RASCOE. Order against the Defendant and JOHN TATEM Gentleman his bail.

JAMES E. COLLEY against JOSMITH BELT. Dismissed.

JAMES INGRAM against PETER MCNABB. An Imparlance.

GEORGE WILSON and ARCHIBALD CAMPBELL administrators of JOHN WILSON Deceased against ABRAM WORMINGTON. An Imparlance.

GEORGE WILSON and ARCHIBALD CAMPBELL administrators of JOHN WILSON Deceased against JOHN INGRAM dismissed at the Plaintiffs costs.

HENRY TUCKER and SON Plaintiffs

Against Re: In Case

ARCHIBALD CAMPBELL admin of GEORGE COOPER Deceased Defendants

This day came as well the Plaintiffs by ANDREW RONALD Gentleman their Attorney as the Defendant in his proper person and says that he cannot gainsay the Plaintiffs action nor but that his intestate did assume in manner and form as the Plaintiff against him have declared. Therefore, it is considered that the Plaintiff recover against the said Defendant 86 pounds 7 shillings and 6 pence and their costs by them in this behalf expended when assets to be levied of the goods and chattels of the said Intestate if so much the said ARCHIBALD CAMPBELL has it in his hands to be administered and if he has it not then the costs are to be levied of his proper goods and chattels and the said Defendant in mercy.

GEORGE KELLY against EDWARD DAVIS by Petition and summons. Judgement is granted the Plaintiff for 4 pounds 2 shilling and 9 pence. It is ordered that the Defendant pay the same unto the Plaintiff with costs and fee.

WILLIAM HOLT against DANIEL PECK. The suit is dismissed.

PAGE 137B

JAMES DUNLAP against JOHN WALKINSHAW Dismissed at Defendants costs.

JOHN PLUMBER against ELDRED FISHER. An Imparlance.

GEORGE FRITH Plaintiff

Against Re: In Case

JAMES EWELL Defendant

This day came as well the Plaintiff by BENJMAIN CROOKER Gentleman his Attorney. As the Defendant in Custody of the Sergeant of this Borough and says that he cannot gainsay the Plaintiff's action nor but that he did assume in manner and form as the Plaintiff against him have declared. Therefore, it is considered that the Plaintiff recover against the said Defendant 30 pounds and his costs by him in this behalf expended and the said Defendant in mercy. And the said Defendant being ruled to give Special Bail and failing so to do. On the Motion of the Plaintiff by his Attorney aforesaid the Defendant is continued in Custody of the said Sergeant until he shall have satisfied this judgement and the costs.

WILLIAM KEATON against CORNELIUS CALVERT. An Imparlance.

SARAH LANGLEY and JOSEPH LANGLEY executors of LEMUEL LANGLEY deceased against ARCHIBALD CAMPBELL administrator of JOHN DALGLEISH deceased. Time is allowed to consider a bill.

JOHN HAMILTON and Company Plaintiff

Against Re: In Case

JAMES EWELL Defendants

This day came as well the Plaintiff by BENJMAIN CROOKER Gentleman his Attorney. As the Defendant in Custody of the Sergeant of this Borough and says that he cannot gainsay the Plaintiff's action nor but that he did assume in manner and form as the Plaintiff against him have declared. Therefore, it is considered that the Plaintiff recover against the said Defendant 10 pounds and his costs by him in this behalf expended and the said Defendant in mercy. And the Plaintiff Attorney did not pray a COMMITTITUR of the said Defendant.

FRENCH MISTERS BALFOUR and BARRAUD against DANIEL DIXON in debt dismissed.

FRENCH MISTERS BALFOUR and BARRAUD against DANIEL DIXON by petition dismissed.

PAGE 138

ANDREW SPROWLE administrator of MISTERS SPROWLE and CROOKS Deceased Plaintiff

Against Re: In Case

WRIGHT WESTCOTT administrator of JOHN WESTCOTT deceased Defendant

This day came the parties by their Attorney's and the Defendant by his Attorney says that he cannot gainsay the Plaintiffs action nor but that his testator did assume in manner and form as the Plaintiff has declared. Therefore, it is considered that Plaintiff recover against the said Defendant 31 pounds 11 shillings and 7 pence and his costs by him in this behalf expended. When assets after paying preceding judgements, debts of greater dignity and the defendants own claims against the estate of the said testator to be levied of the goods and chattels which were of the said JOHN at the time of his death that shall hereafter come to the hands of the said WRIGHT to be administered and the said Defendants in mercy.

CHARLES THOMAS against JOHN AUSTIN FINNIE. Dismissed

KING by JOSEPH PHIDALL against JOHN MEARNS. Dismissed at Defendants cost.

YOUNG and SMITH against WRIGHT WESTCOTT administrator of JOHN WESTCOTT continued at the Defendants cost.

CHARLES SAWYER against JOHN GILCHRIST discontinued for want of security for the costs of the suit.

SAMUEL SIMMONS against ZACHERIAS MARSINGALE Discontinued for want of Security for the costs of security.

MARK TALBOT Plaintiff
Against Re: In Case
WILLIAM INGRAM and JOHN INGRAM Defendants
This day came the parties by their Attorney's and thereupon came also a jury to wit: WILLIAM BICKERDICK, ROBERT ALLAN, PHILIP CARBERY, JOHN BARRET, FREER ARMISTON, ABRAHAM PATEON, JAMES WALKER, PAUL PROBY, JOHN CARMOUNT*, CHARLES GODFREY, WILLIAM JAQUES and EDWARD ARCHER who being elected tried and sworn the truth to speak upon the issue joined upon their oath do say that the Defendants did assume in manner and form as the Plaintiff against him has declared and do assess the Plaintiff damages by occasion of the non-performance of that assumption to 4 pounds 16 shillings and 8 pence besides his costs. Therefore, it is considered that the Plaintiff recover against the said Defendant his damages aforesaid in form aforesaid assessed and his costs by him in this behalf expended. And the Said Defendant in mercy.

PAGE 138B
JAMES CAMPBELL and Company Plaintiffs
Against Re: In Case
JOHN RICHARDSON Defendant
This day came the parties by their Attorney's and thereupon came also a Jury to wit: JOSEPH POPE, THOMAS TERRY, JOHN MARLEY, JOSEPH LANGLEY, JOHN MEARNS, RICHARD BICKERDICK, JAMES LANGLEY, JOEL MOHUN, SAMUEL BLEWS, KEDAR COOPER, JAMES ARCHDEACON and JOHN CRAMOND who being elected tried and sworn the truth to speak upon the issue joined upon their oath do say that the Defendant is guilty in manner and form as the Plaintiffs against him have declared and do assess the Plaintiff damages by occasion thereof to 20 pounds besides their costs. Therefore, it is considered that the Plaintiff recover against the said defendant their damages aforesaid in form aforesaid assessed and their costs by them in this behalf expended and the said Defendant in mercy.

RICHARD TEMPLEMAN Plaintiff
Against Re: In Case
JOHN RICHARDSON Defendants
This day came the parties by their Attorney's and thereupon came also a Jury to wit: JOSEPH POPE, THOMAS TERRY, JOHN MARLEY, JOSEPH LANGLEY, JOHN MEARNS, RICHARD BICKERDICK, JAMES LANGLEY, JOEL MOHUN, SAMUEL BLEWS, KEDAR COOPER, JAMES ARCHDEACON and JOHN CRAMOND who being elected tried and sworn the truth to speak upon the issue joined upon their oath do say that the Defendant is guilty in manner and form as the Plaintiff against him has declared and do assess the Plaintiff damages by occasion thereof to 40 pounds besides their costs. Therefore, it is considered that the Plaintiff recover against the said defendant his damages aforesaid in form aforesaid assessed and his costs by him about his suit in this behalf expended and the said Defendant in mercy.

Order is granted JACOB ROACH against JAMES CAMPBELL & Company for 75 pounds to tobacco for 3 days attendance in their suit against JOHN RICHARDSON.

JOSEPH POPES Motion for Ordinary license was rejected.

PAGE 139
Order is granted JACOB ROACH against RICHARD TEMPLEMAN for 75 pounds tobacco for 3 days attendance in his suit against JOHN RICHARDSON.

WILLISON and MCSWEEN against JOHN AUSTIN TINNIE. Continued at the Plaintiffs costs.

JAMES GILCHRIST and ROBERT TAYLOR against JOHN FOWLER and GEORGE FOWLER on the motion of the Plaintiff by his Attorney a DEDIMUS is granted them to take the depositions of JOHN CHESHIRE and HUMPHREY MASSINGBURG Gentleman and the defendants reasonable notice of the time and place.

PHILIP CARBERY Plaintiff
Against Re: In Case
NEIL JAMIESON Defendant
This day came the parties by their Attorney's and there upon came also a Jury to wit: JOSEPH POPE, THOMAS TERRY, JOHN MARLEY, JOSEPH LANGLEY, JOHN MEARNS, JOHN CRAMOND*, RICHARD BICKERDICK, JAMES LANGLEY, JOEL MOHUN, SAMUEL BLEWS, KEDAR COOPER, and JAMES ARCHDEACON who being elected tried and sworn the truth to speak upon the issue joined upon their oath do say that the Defendant

did assume in manner and form as the Plaintiff against him has declared and do assess the Plaintiff damages by occasion of the non-performance of that assumption to 19 pounds 18 shillings and 4 pence besides his costs. Therefore, it is considered that the Plaintiff recover against the said defendant his damages aforesaid in form aforesaid assessed and his costs by him about his suit in this behalf expended and the said Defendant in mercy.

Order is granted DAVID OSHEAL against NEIL JAMIESON for 97 pounds of tobacco for 1 day's attendance in this Court, coming and returning 24 miles once and 1 shilling and 3 pence ferriages in the suit of PHILIP CARBERY against him.

Order is granted ROBERT ALLAN against PHILIP CARBERY for 25 pounds of tobacco for 1 day's attendance in his suit against NEIL JAMIESON.

On the complaint of JOSEPH TYSON setting forth that JOHN RICHARDSON detains him in service and the said JOHN RICHARDSON proving that the said TYSON is a convict and that he had bought him it is ordered that he return to his said master's service.

PAGE 139B

JOHN HUNT, RICHARD AYTON, JOHN HENDERSON, and WILLIAM FISHER executors of MATHIAS GALE deceased, ANN MOORE, JOSEPH MITCHEL, JOHN COX and MISSEURIERS JOHN RAMSAY and TAYLOR Plaintiff
Against Re: In Chancery
RICHARD ROTHERY an infant son and heir of HENRY ROTHERY deceased, MARY ROTHERY widow, and GEORGE ABYVON executor of the said HENRY deceased Defendants
This day came as well the Plaintiffs by their Attorney's as the Defendants RICHARD ROTHERY by his guardian the Defendants MARY and GEORGE by their Attorney and the Commissioners appointed to state and examine the claims and demands of the Plaintiffs and Defendant GEORGE ABYVON and also to set apart the dower of the Defendant MARY in the 2 parcels of land in the Borough of Norfolk in the bill mentioned this day made by their report in these words to wit:
"In obedience to the annexed decree of the Worshipful the Court of Chancery for the Borough of Norfolk. We the subscribers being first duly sworn on the Holy Evangelist of Almighty God met together and have laid off the dower of MARY ROTHERY widow of HENRY ROTHERY deceased in the real estate of the said HENRY and have adjusted and as curtained the claims of the several Plaintiffs in a bill in the said Worshipful Court of Chancery exhibited against the heir the widow and the executor of the said HENRY in manner and form following to wit: Dower in the tenement unfinished we have laid off as follows: the lower and upper rooms and one half of the passage on the southside of the house, the widow being to have no part of the cellar, kitchen or garrets nor of the stair case down in the land from back of the house to the southern boundary of the lot on the lane between that and the land of COLONEL JOHN WILLOUGHBY and in width 16 and half feet from said lane and in the water lot after laying of a lane 11 feet wide between the land of CORNELIUS CALVERT Gentleman and the late HENRY ROTHERY and a back lane 11 feet wide between the land of CORNELIUS CALVERT Gentleman and the late HENRY ROTHERY and a back lane between the land of the said HENRY and HODGE MILLER 10 feet wide. We allot to the widow 12 feet in said water lot from the lane aforesaid adjoining CORNELIUS CALVERT Gentleman and running from said back lane to the southern boundary. And we find due and owing from the estate of said HENRY ROTHERY to the several claimants interest to this day included to the widow MARY MOORE of Whitehaven 91 pounds 19 shillings sterling exchange 25% by bond 114 pounds 18 shillings and 9 pence. To the executors of MATHIAS GALE of London 104 pounds sterling exchange 25% 130 pounds. To JOSEPH MITCHEL, 18 pounds, 19 shillings. TO JOHN COX of New York City

PAGE 140

7 pounds 14 shillings and 6 pence. To RAMSAY and TAYLOR 16 pounds 7 shillings and 9 pence. 328 pounds. * We also find due from said estate GEORGE ABYVON Gentleman executor of said ROTHERY 2 pounds and 7 pence half penny. 330 pounds and 7 pence half penny*. Given under our hands in the Borough of Norfolk. This 19th day of September 1772
JOHN GILCHRIST, JAMES ARCHDEACON, BASSET MOSELEY and the executor of the said MATHIAS GALE deceased allow 17/3 ½ to be deducted out of their claim being compound interest. And it appearing to the Court that the slaves and personal estate of the testator HENRY ROTHERY in the bill mentioned to the amount of 162 pounds 12 shillings and 6 pence exclusive of the Defendant's GEORGE'S pocket expenses have been applied towards the discharging the debt due from the said testator at the time of his death by bonds and other specialties where with his real estate was chargeable. Therefore, it is ordered and decreed that the dower so as aforesaid set apart be held firm and stable. And that JOHN GREENWOOD Gentleman after giving convenient notice in the Virginia Gazette sell at Public Auction and for 3 months credit the other 2/3 of the said lands with the appurtenances and the reversion of the other third part of the said land and appurtenances situate on the main street in the Borough aforesaid and in case of a deficiency to satisfy the Plaintiff and Defendant GEORGE ABYVON claims. That the said JOHN GREENWOOD under the like conditions sell so much of the other piece or parcel of land situate on Elizabeth River in the said bill mentioned as will satisfy the said claims and make his report to the next Court to be held for this Borough.

JAMES MOORE Plaintiff
Against Re: In Case
FREDERICK BOUSH and NATHANIEL BOUSH Defendants
This day came the parties by their Attorney's and there upon came also a Jury to wit: JOSEPH POPE, THOMAS TERRY, JOHN MARLEY, JOSEPH LANGLEY, JOHN MEARNS, JOHN CRAMOND, RICHARD BICKERDICK, JAMES LANGLEY, JOEL MOHUN, SAMUEL BLEWS, KEDAR COOPER, and JAMES ARCHDEACON who being elected tried and sworn the truth to speak upon the issue joined upon their oath do say that the Defendants have not paid the debt in the declaration mentioned. Therefore, it is considered that the Plaintiff recover against the said Defendants his debt amounting to 266 pounds and his costs by him about his suit in this behalf expended. And the said Defendant in mercy. But this Judgement is to be discharged by the payment of 100 pounds with interest there on of the after the rate of 5% per annum to be computed from June 30, 1772, to the time of payment and the costs. Also interest on 66 pounds 13 shillings and 5 pence after the rate of 5% per annum to be computed from October 31, 1770, to the time of payment and the costs. And also interest on 100 pounds after the rate of 5 % per annum to be computed from April 30th, 1771, to the time of payment and the costs and the Plaintiff rebases 13/4

<u>PAGE 140B</u>
This Court is adjourned until tomorrow 10 o'clock, PAUL LOYALL MAYOR, TESTE: JOHN BOUSH D.C.C.

<u>NORFOLK BOROUGH</u>
At a Hustings Court Held this 22nd day of September 1772
PRESENT: PAUL LOYALL ESQUIRE MAYOR
GENTLEMAN ALDERMEN: GEORGE ABYVON, CHARLES THOMAS, ARCHIBALD CAMPBELL, JAMES TAYLOR, MAXIMILIAN CALVERT

JOHN GOODRICH against ALEXANDER MCSWEEN. On the motion of the Plaintiff by his Attorney at DEDIMUS is granted him to take the depositions of JOHN ARCHER giving the Defendant reasonable notice.

Monsieur LOGAN GILMOUR & Company Plaintiffs
Against Re: In Debt
THOMAS BUTT Defendant
This day came the parties by their Attorney's and there upon came also a Jury to wit: THOMAS TERRY, HENRY FLEMING, JOHN SMITH, WILLIAM WALKER, HARDRESS WALLER, JOHN CALVERT, ALEXANDER MOSELEY, EDWARD ARCHER, JOHN CARMOUNT*, EDWARD MITCHELL, JOHN WILLS, and WILLIAM BICKERDICK who being elected tried and sworn the truth to speak upon the issue joined upon their oath do say that the Defendant has not paid the debt in the declaration mentioned. Therefore, it is considered that the Plaintiff recover against the said Defendant their Debt amounting to 44 pounds and their costs by them in this behalf expended and the said Defendant in mercy. But this Judgement is to be discharged by the payment of 22 pounds with interest thereon after the rate of 5% per annum to be computed from August 2nd, 1770, to the time of payment and the costs.

<u>PAGE 141</u>
ANN SYMONS by ROBERT BANKS her next friend against THOMAS DREWREY. The suit is dismissed at the Defendants costs.

ANTHONY LAWSON Plaintiff
Against Re: In Case
JOSHUA WRIGHT Defendant
This day came the parties by their Attorney's and there upon came also a Jury to wit: THOMAS TERRY, HENRY FLEMING, JOHN SMITH, WILLIAM WALKER, HARDRESS WALLER, JOHN CALVERT, ALEXANDER MOSELEY, EDWARD ARCHER, JOHN CARMOUNT, EDWARD MITCHELL, JOHN WILLS, and WILLIAM BICKERDICK who being elected tried and sworn the truth to speak upon the issue joined upon their oath do say that the Defendant is guilty in manner and form as the Plaintiff against him has declared and do assess the Plaintiff damages by occasion thereof to 8 pounds besides his costs. Therefore, it is considered that the Plaintiff recover against the said Defendant his damages aforesaid in form aforesaid assessed and his costs by him about his suit in this behalf expended and the said Defendant in mercy.

Order is granted JAMES SCOTT alias ANDERSON against ANTHONY LAWSON for 50 pounds of tobacco for 2 days attendance in his suit against JOSHUA WRIGHT.

JOHN GILCHRIST Plaintiff
Against Re: in Case
EDWARD HANSFORD Defendant
This day came the parties by their Attorney's and there upon came also a Jury to wit:
ANDREW BALLINGALD, JOSEPH PEAD, JONATHAN MEREDITH, KEDAR COOPER, JOHN MCLACHLAN, JAMES CARMICHAEL, ROBERT ALLAN, JAMES MURPHREE, JOHN SHEDDEN, DANIEL HUTCHINGS, BARTHOLOMEW THOMPSON, and WILLIAM SKINKER who being elected tried and sworn the truth to speak upon the issue joined upon their oath do say that the Defendant did assume in manner and form as the Plaintiff against him has declared and do assess the Plaintiff damages by occasion of the non-performance of that assumption to 20 pounds 8 shillings and 1 penny farthing besides his costs. Therefore, it is considered that the Plaintiff recover against the said Defendant his damages aforesaid in form aforesaid and his costs by him about his suit in this behalf expended and the said defendant in mercy.

<u>PAGE 141B</u>
NEIL JAMIESON Admin of HENRY TUCKER Plaintiff
Against Re: In Debt for rent
CHARLES GODFREY Defendant
This day came the parties by their Attorney's and there upon came also a Jury to wit: THOMAS TERRY, HENRY FLEMING, JOHN SMITH, WILLIAM WALKER, HARDRESS WALLER, JOHN CALVERT, ALEXANDER MOSELEY, EDWARD ARCHER, JOHN CARMOUNT*, EDWARD MITCHELL, JOHN WILLS, and WILLIAM BICKERDICK who being elected tried and sworn the truth to speak upon the issue joined upon their oath do say that the Defendant has not paid the debt in the declaration mentioned. Therefore, it is considered that the Plaintiff recover against the said Defendant his debt amounting to 4 pounds 4 shillings. Therefore, on the prayer of the Defendant it is considered that he recover against the Plaintiff 5 shillings current money and his costs by him in this behalf expended according to the form of the Act of Assembly and the Plaintiff for his false claims be in mercy.

MISTERS JAMES MARSDEN and SIMON HODGSON Plaintiff
Against Re: In Case
ALEXANDER BELL Defendant
This day came the parties by their Attorney's and there upon came also a Jury to wit:

ANDREW BALLINGALD, JOSEPH PEAD, JONATHAN MEREDITH, KEDAR COOPER, JOHN MCLACHLAN, JAMES CARMICHAEL, ROBERT ALLAN, JAMES MURPHREE, JOHN SHEDDEN, DANIEL HUTCHINGS, BARTHOLOMEW THOMPSON, and WILLIAM SKINKER who being elected tried and sworn the truth to speak upon the issue joined upon their oath do say that the Defendant did assume in manner and form as the Plaintiffs against him have declared and do assess the Plaintiffs damages by occasion of the non-performance of that assumption to 11 pounds 11 shillings and 3 pence besides their costs. Therefore, it is considered that the Plaintiff recover against the said Defendant their damages aforesaid in form aforesaid and his costs by them about their suit in this behalf expended and the said Defendant in mercy.

LODWICK GRAY by BENJAMIN DINGLEY GRAY his next friend Plaintiff
Against Re: In Case
WILLIAM IVY Defendant
This day came the parties by their Attorney's and there upon came also a Jury to wit:
ANDREW BALLINGALD, JOSEPH PEAD, JONATHAN MEREDITH, KEDAR COOPER, JOHN MCLACHLAN, JAMES CARMICHAEL, ROBERT ALLAN, JAMES MURPHREE, JOHN SHEDDEN, DANIEL HUTCHINGS, BARTHOLOMEW THOMPSON, and WILLIAM SKINKER who being elected tried and sworn the truth to speak upon the issue joined upon their oath do say that the Defendant did assume in manner and form as the Plaintiff against him has declared and do assess the Plaintiffs damages by occasion of the non-performance of that assumption to 7 pounds 6 pence farthing besides his costs.

PAGE 142

Therefore, it is considered that the Plaintiff recover against the said Defendant their damages aforesaid in form aforesaid and his costs by them about their suit in this behalf expended and the said Defendant in mercy.

EDWARD WRIGHT and JAMES JONES Executors of JOSEPH JONES Plaintiff
Against Re: In Case
JOHN MCLACHLAN Defendant
This day came the parties by their Attorney's and there upon came also a Jury to wit: THOMAS TERRY, HENRY FLEMING, JOHN SMITH, WILLIAM WALKER, HARDRESS WALLER, JOHN CALVERT, ALEXANDER MOSELEY, EDWARD ARCHER, JOHN CARMOUNT, EDWARD MITCHELL, JOHN WILLS, and WILLIAM BICKERDICK who being elected tried and sworn the truth to speak upon the issue joined upon their oath do say that the Defendant did assume in manner and form as the Plaintiff against him has declared and do assess the Plaintiffs damages by occasion of the non-performance of that assumption to 23 pounds 11 pence half penny besides their costs. Therefore, it is considered that the Plaintiff recover against the said Defendant their damages aforesaid in form aforesaid and their costs by them about their suit in this behalf expended and the said defendant in mercy.

HENRY FLEMING Plaintiff
Against Re: In Debt
JOSHUA WRIGHT
This day came the parties by their Attorney's and the Defendant by his Attorney relinquishes his former plea and acknowledges the Plaintiffs action for 46 pounds 14 shillings and 6 pence sterling with interest thereon after the rate of 5% per annum to be computed from August 15, 1771, to the time of payment. Therefore, it is considered that the Plaintiff recover against the said Defendant his debt aforesaid together with his costs by him in this behalf expended and the said Defendant in mercy. And the Court says that the sterling money may be discharged in current money at 25% difference of exchange. And the Plaintiff has agreed to stay the execution of this Judgement 3 months.

HENRY FLEMING & Company Plaintiff
Against Re: In Debt
JOSHUA WRIGHT Defendant
This day came the parties by their Attorney's and the Defendant by his Attorney relinquishes his former plea and acknowledges the Plaintiffs action for 49 pounds 4 shillings and 1 pence sterling.

PAGE 142B

Therefore, it is considered that the Plaintiff recover against the said Defendant their debt aforesaid and their costs by them in this behalf expended and the said Defendant in mercy. But this judgement is to be discharged by the payment of 24 pounds 12 shillings and 5 pence half penny sterling with interest thereon after the rate of 5% per annum to be computed from June 5, 1771, to the time of payment with costs. And the Court says that the Sterling money may be discharged in current money at 25% difference of exchange and the Plaintiffs have agreed to stay the execution of this Judgement 3 months.

KEDAR COOPER Plaintiff
Against Re: In Detinue for Negro CAMBRIDGE
JOSHUA PEAD Defendant
This day came the parties by their Attorney's and thereupon came also a Jury to wit: JAMES CARMICHAEL, ROBERT ALLAN, ANDREW BALLENGALD, JOHN MCLACHLAN, JONATHAN MEREDITH, JAMES MURPHREE, DANIEL HUTCHINGS, CHARLES GODFREY, JAMES MARSDEN, WILLIAM SKINKER, BARTHOLOMEW THOMPSON, and JOHN MALLET who being elected tried and sworn the truth to speak upon the issue joined upon their oath do say that the Defendant has detain the said Negro CAMBRIDGE in the declaration mentioned in manner and form as the Plaintiff against him has declared and that the said slave is the value of 30 pounds and they do assess the damages of the Plaintiff by occasion of the Defendants detaining the slave to 1 penny besides his costs. Therefore, it is considered that the Plaintiff recover against the said Defendant the slave aforesaid if to be had or the Value of him if not to be had together with his damages aforesaid in form aforesaid assessed and his costs by him in this behalf expended and the said Defendant in mercy.

MICHAEL CHRISTIAN assignee of WILLIAM MCCAA Plaintiff
Against Re: In Debt
ALEXANDER BELL Defendant
This day came the parties by their Attorney's and there upon came also a Jury to wit: THOMAS TERRY, HENRY FLEMING, JOHN SMITH, WILLIAM WALKER, HARDRESS WALLER, JOHN CALVERT, ALEXANDER MOSELEY, EDWARD ARCHER, JOHN CARMOUNT, EDWARD MITCHELL, JOHN WILLS, and WILLIAM BICKERDICK who being elected tried and sworn the truth to speak upon the issue joined upon their oath do say that the Defendant has not paid the debt in the declaration mentioned. Therefore, it is considered that the Plaintiff recover against the said Defendant his debt amounting to 41 pounds 13 shillings and 9 pence and his costs by him in this behalf expended and the said Defendant in mercy.

PAGE 143

But this judgement is to be discharged by the payment of 20 pounds 16 shillings and 4 pence half penny with interest thereon after the rate of 5% per annum to be computed from June 13, 1770, to the time of payment and the costs.

MICHAEL CHRISTIAN and LABON JOHNSTON Plaintiff
Against Re: In Debt
ALEXANDER BELL Defendant
This day came the parties by their Attorney's and there upon came also a Jury to wit: THOMAS TERRY, HENRY FLEMING, JOHN SMITH, WILLIAM WALKER, HARDRESS WALLER, JOHN CALVERT, ALEXANDER MOSELEY, EDWARD ARCHER, JOHN CARMOUNT, EDWARD MITCHELL, JOHN WILLS, and WILLIAM BICKERDICK who being elected tried and sworn the truth to speak upon the issue joined upon their oath do say that the Defendant has not paid the debt in the declaration mentioned. Therefore, it is considered that the Plaintiff recover against the said Defendant their debt amounting to 9 pounds 12 together with their costs by them in this behalf expended and the said Defendant in mercy.

JOHN CRAMOND Plaintiff
Against Re: In Debt
JOHN TATEM Defendant
This day came the parties by their Attorney's and the Defendant by his Attorney relinquishes his former plea, acknowledges the Plaintiff's action for 59 pounds 14 shillings and 2 pence with interest there on after the rate of 5% per annum to be computed from October 23, 1771, to the time of payment. Therefore, it is considered that the Plaintiff recover against the said Defendant his damages aforesaid and his costs by him about his suit in this behalf expended and the said Defendant in mercy.

Order is granted PEGGY WHRITING* against KEDAR COOPER for 50 pounds of tobacco for 2 days attendance at this Court in his suit against JOSHUA PEAD.

Order is granted WILLIS BRAMBLE against JOSHUA PEED for 50 pounds of tobacco for 2 days attendance at this Court in the suit of KEDAR COOPER against him.

JOHN MCLACHLAN against JOHN VALLENICER and THOMAS WALKER continued at Defendants costs.

PAGE 143B

Order is granted MASON COOPER against JOSHUA PEED for 50 pounds tobacco for 2 days attendance in the suit of KEDAR COOPER against him.

DANIEL RICHARDSON against WILLIAM ROBINSON dismissed at the Defendants Costs.
MARY ROTHERY against GEORGE WATSON and ANN his wife. The Defendants pleaded not guilty issue joined and referred.

GEORGE VEALE, JAMES WEBB, WILLIAM AITCHESON, MATTHEW GODFREY, JOHN HUTCHINGS, THOMAS VEALE, MAXIMILIAN CALVERT, JOSEPH HUTCHINGS, JOHN PORTLOCK, CORNELIUS CALVERT, SAMUEL HAPPER, GOODRICH BOUSH, MALACHI WILSON, MATTHEW PHRIPP, DAVID PORTER, THOMAS NEWTON, JOHN WILSON, and JOHN TAYLOR Gentleman Justices of the Peace for Norfolk County at the instance of THOMAS OLD and BARBARA his wife against ANDREW SPROWLE and JOHN HUNTER time is allowed to assign breaches.

GEORGE OLDNER against JOHN NASH. The Defendant pleaded not guilty issue joined and referred.
DICKERSON PRIOR against AARON BARBER and HOFFMIRE. Order that the former order of this Court against the said Defendants and JOHN WOODSIDE their bail be confirmed, and a writ of inquiry is awarded the Plaintiff for his damages.

JOSEPH MITCHEL against NICHOLAS POOLE. The Defendant pleaded payment issue joined and referred.

JOHN WOODSIDE against WILLIAM GODFREY administrator of JONATHAN GODFREY deceased the Defendant plead he did not assume issue joined and referred.

WILLIAM KEATON against CORNELIUS CALVERT, RICHARD BICKERDICK undertakes for the Plaintiff that he will pay to the defendant all such damages costs and charges as shall be awarded against him by the Court.

JOHN CRAMOND against JOHN PASSONS. The Defendant pleaded that he did not assume and act of limitations and notice for the books issue joined and referred.

DAVID ETHERIDGE against ELDRED FISHER and EDWARD PARKE. The Defendant pleaded payment issue joined and referred to next Court.

PAGE 144

ANDREW STEWART against ALEXANDER BELL. The Defendant pleaded payment issue joined and referred.

JOHN STANHOPE against NATHANIEL BOUSH. The Defendant pleaded that he did not assume issue joined and referred.
MATTHEW KELLY and ANN, his wife against THOMAS TAYLOR and ELIZABETH his wife the Defendants pleaded not guilty issue joined and referred.

MATTHEW KELLY who as well against MARY STAUNTON. The Defendant pleaded that she does not owe issue joined and referred.
ROGER PIERCE against JOSEPH TODD. The Defendant pleaded he is not guilty issue joined and referred.

NICHOLAS BROWN SEABROOK against AARON BARBER. The Defendant pleaded he did not assume issue joined and referred to next Court.
JOHN CRAMOND against JONATHAN JACKSON. The Defendant plead payment issue joined and referred.

WILLIS COWPER against JOHN POLLOCK. The Defendant pleaded he did not assume issue joined and referred to next Court.
ROBERT SHEDDEN and Company against BRYAN CROSBIE. The Defendant pleads payment issue joined and referred.
MICHAEL CHRISTIAN and JOHN HARMANSON against ALEXANDER MCSWEEN. The Defendant pleaded he did not assume issue joined and referred.

CUMMING WARWICK and Company against DANIEL PECK. The Defendant pleaded he did not assume issue joined and referred until next Court.

WILLIAM BICKERDICK against WILLIAM PRIESTMAN. The Defendant pleaded not guilty in justification issue joined and referred.
WILLIAM MCDOUGALL against HUMPHREY ROBERTS. The Defendant pleaded he did not assume issue joined and referred.
JOHN HARDIE against WILLIAM LEWELLING dismissed at the Defendants costs.

PAGE 144B

JOHN HARRIS against MAX CALVERT. The Defendant pleaded not guilty. Issue joined and referred.
BENJAMIN LEWELLING against DEMPSEY VEALE. The Defendant pleaded not guilty issue joined and referred.
PATIENCE NICHOLSON against WILLIAM LEWELLING. Dismissed at the Defendants costs.

GEORGE KELLY against ARCHIBALD CAMPBELL admin of JOHN WILSON deceased. The defendant pleaded they did not assume issue joined and referred.

JOHN HARRIS against GEORGE WILSON and ARCHIBALD CAMPBELL administrators of JOHN WILSON Deceased. The Defendants pleaded they did not assume issue joined and referred.

GEORGE WILSON and ARCHIBALD CAMPBELL administrators of JOHN WILSON Deceased against SAMUEL CALVERT. The Defendant pleaded he did not assume issue joined and referred.

GEORGE WILSON and ARCHIBALD CAMPBELL administrators of JOHN WILSON Deceased against JOHN CALVERT. The Defendant pleaded he did not assume issue joined and referred.

MALBONE SHELTON against LEMUEL ROBERTS. The Defendant pleaded he did not assume issue joined and referred.
JAMES CAMPBELL and Company against BARNABY CARNEY. The Defendant pleaded he did not assume issue joined and referred.
ALEXANDER MASSENBURG against LOUISA INMAN. The Defendant pleaded not guilty issue joined and referred.

MISTERS THOMAS WILSON, WILLIAM WILSON, and ALICE CARR Plaintiff
Against Re: In Case
THOMAS POLLOCK Defendant
This day came the Plaintiffs by WILLIAM RASCOW WILSON CURLE Gentleman their Attorney and there upon came also a Jury to wit: THOMAS TERRY, HENRY FLEMING, JOHN SMITH, WILLIAM WALKER, HARDRESS WALLER, JOHN CALVERT, ALEXANDER MOSELEY, EDWARD ARCHER, JOHN CARMOUNT, EDWARD MITCHELL, JOHN WILLS, and WILLIAM BICKERDICK who being sworn well and truly to inquire of damages in this suit upon their oath do say that the Plaintiffs have sustained damages by occasion of the Defendants Breach of Promise in the Declaration mentioned to 40 pounds 8 shillings and 11 pence sterling besides their costs.

PAGE 145

Therefore, it is considered that the Plaintiff recover against the said Defendant their damages aforesaid in form aforesaid assessed and their costs by them in this behalf expended and the said Defendant in mercy. And the Court says that the said sterling money may be discharged in current money at 25% difference of exchange.

MISTERS WILLSON* and MCSWEEN Plaintiff
Against Re: In Debt
JOHN BURNLEY Defendant
This day came the Plaintiffs by THOMAS BURKE Gentleman their Attorney and thereupon came also a Jury to wit: THOMAS TERRY, HENRY FLEMING, JOHN SMITH, WILLIAM WALKER, HARDRESS WALLER, JOHN CALVERT, ALEXANDER MOSELEY, EDWARD ARCHER, JOHN CARMOUNT, EDWARD MITCHELL, JOHN WILLS, and WILLIAM BICKERDICK who being sworn well and truly to inquire of damages in this suit upon their oath do say that the Plaintiffs have sustained damages by occasion of the defendants Breach of Promise in the Declaration mentioned to 1 penny sterling besides their costs. Therefore, it is considered that the Plaintiff recover against the said Defendant and ALEXANDER LOVE his bail, their damages aforesaid in form aforesaid assessed and their costs by them in this behalf expended and the said Defendant in mercy.

HENRY FLEMING, HENRY BRAG and ROBERT FISHER Plaintiff
Against Re: In Debt
JOSEPH HUTCHINGS Esquire Defendant
This day came the parties by their Attorney's and there upon came also a Jury to wit: JAMES ARCHDEACON, JAMES CUNINGHAM, ROBERT ALLAN, JAMES MARSDEN, JAMES MELLET, JOHN MCLACHLAN, JAMES MURPHREE, JOHN LIVINGSTON, CADER COOPER, WILLIAM SKINKER, BARTHOLOMEW THOMPSON and SAMUEL TOMLINSON who being elected tried and sworn the truth to speak upon the issue joined upon their oath do say that the Defendant has not paid the debt in the declaration mentioned. Therefore, it is considered that the Plaintiff recover against the said Defendant their debt amounting to 400 pounds and their costs by them about their suit in this behalf expended and the said Defendant in mercy. But this judgement is to be discharged by the payment of 200 pounds with interest thereon after the rate of 5% per annum to be computed from December 22, 1770, to the time of payment and costs.

Order that the County prison and yard be included in the Borough Prison Bounds.

PAGE 145B
JOHN WOODSIDE Plaintiff
Against Re: In Case
THOMAS TALBOT Defendant
This day came the Plaintiff by WILLIAM ROBINSON Gentleman this Attorney and the Defendant being solemnly called and not appearing. Ordered that the former order of this Court against him the said Defendant and JOHN MACLEAN his bail be confirmed. Therefore, it is considered that the Plaintiff recover against the said Defendant and JOHN MACLEAN his bail aforesaid his debt amounting to 545 pounds 15 shillings and 4 pence and his costs by him about his suit in this behalf expended and the said Defendant in mercy. But this judgement is to be discharged by the payment of 80 pounds 19 shillings and 10 pence farthing with interest there on after the rate of 5% per annum to be computed from this day to the time of payment and costs.

The Court this day rated flour at 16/8 per centum
This Court is adjourned to Court in Course, PAUL LOYALL MAYOR, TESTE: JOHN BOUSH D.C.C.

PAGE 146
NORFOLK BOROUGH
At a Hustings Court Held this 19TH day of October 1772
PRESENT: PAUL LOYALL ESQUIRE MAYOR
GENTLEMAN ALDERMEN: MAXIMILIAN CALVERT, GEORGE ABYVON, CHARLES THOMAS, ARCHIBALD CAMPBELL, JAMES TAYLOR, LEWIS HANSFORD, CORNELIUS CALVERT

THOMAS CLAIBORNE this day produced a Certificate from under the hand of JOHN QUARLES Deputy Clerk of the County of King William that he had obtained a license to practice as an Attorney and had qualified to same and he having taken the oath to the Government and subscribed the test also the oath of an Attorney is admitted to practice in this Court.

JOHN BOUSH was this day appointed Clerk of the said Borough and he having taken the oath to the Government and subscribed the teste also the oath of Town Clerk enters on the execution of his office in the room of SAMUEL BOUSH who has resigned.

It is ordered that the Sergeant summon HENRY FLEMING to appear at the Next Court to answer the Complaint of MARGARET DOBSON his servant and that in the meantime not to misuse her and suffer her to appear at Court.

JOHN HARDY against JOSHUA WRIGHT dismissed.

MISTERS ARCHDEACON and INGRAM against WILLIAM DONALDSON in case.
This day came the parties by their Attorney's and the Defendant prays and has leave to IMPARLE here until the next Court and then to plead.

WILLIAM TREBELL and ROBERT NICHOLSON executors of JOSEPH SCRIVENER deceased Plaintiffs against GEORGE JOSEPH FENWICK Defendant in case. This day came the Plaintiffs by BENJAMIN CROOKER Gentleman their Attorney and the Defendant being called and not appearing. A conditional order is granted the Plaintiff against the said Defendant and JOHN WILLS his bail.

PETER KATZ against JAMES CAMPBELL and Company. The Plaintiff not further prosecuting his suit the same is discontinued. (2X)

PAGE 146B
WILLIAM FARRER against EDWARD HANSFORD by Petition and summons. Judgement is granted the Plaintiff for 1 pounds 13 shilling. It is ordered that the Defendant pay the same unto the Plaintiff with costs and fee.

WILLIAM and THOMAS FARRER against JOHN RANSBERG by Petition and summons. Judgement is granted the Plaintiff for 3 pounds 10 shilling and 6 pence half penny. It is ordered that the Defendant pay the same unto the Plaintiff with costs and fee.

WILLIAM and THOMAS FARRER against RICHARD TALBOT by Petition and summons. Judgement is granted the Plaintiff for 2 pounds 13 shilling and 4 pence. It is ordered that the Defendant pay the same unto the Plaintiff with costs and fee.

JOHN MACLEAN against RICHARD TALBOT by Petition and summons. Judgement is granted the Plaintiff for 3 pounds. It is ordered that the Defendant pay the same unto the Plaintiff with costs and fee.

HESLOP and BLAIR against MISTERS ELIAS BOYER and PETER KATZ in case. This day came the Plaintiffs by BENJAMIN CROOKER Gentleman their Attorney and the defendant being called and not appearing. A conditional order is granted the Plaintiff against the said Defendant and JAMES LEITCH their bail.

JOHN RANSBERG Plaintiff
Against Re: In Case
JOSHUA GOUGH Defendant
WILLIAM SMITH/COOPER* undertakes for the Defendant that in case he shall be Cast in this suit he the said Defendant will pay the condemnation of the Court or render his body to Prison in for the same or that the said SMITH will pay the condemnation of the Court or render the body of the said Defendant as aforesaid. Where upon the Defendant by his Attorney prays and has leave to IMPARLE here until next Court and then to plead

JAMES DUNLOP & CHRISTOPHER ROBERTS Plaintiffs
Against Re: In Case
DANIEL PECK Defendant
This day came as well the Plaintiff by BENJAMIN CROOKER Gentleman their Attorney, as the Defendant in his proper person and says that he cannot gainsay the Plaintiffs action nor but that he did assume in manner and form as the Plaintiff against him has declared Therefore, it is considered that the Plaintiff

PAGE 147

Recover against the said Defendant 15 pounds 5 shillings and 5 pence and their costs by them in their suit in this behalf expended. And the said Defendant in mercy. And the Plaintiff by his Attorney aforesaid agrees to wait the execution of this judgement until the first of December Next.

JOHN and THOMAS GILCHRIST against JOHN KENNEDY. The Plaintiff not further prosecuting their suit the same as dismissed.

ANDREW SPROWLE admin of MISTERS SPROWLE and CROOKS Deceased Plaintiff
Against Re: In Debt
THOMAS ROBERTS Defendant
PAUL LOYALL Gentleman here in Court undertakes for the Defendant that in case he shall be Cast in this suit he the said Defendant will pay the condemnation of the Court or render his body to Prison in execution for the same or that the said LOYALL will pay the condemnation of the Court or render the body of the said Defendant as aforesaid. Where upon the Defendant by his Attorney prays and has leave to IMPARLE here until next Court and then to plead

ANDREW SPROWLE admin of MISTERS SPROWLE and CROOKS Deceased Plaintiff
Against Re: In Debt
ALEXANDER BELL Defendant
JOHN MCLACHLAN here in Court undertakes for the Defendant that in case he shall be Cast in this suit he the said Defendant will pay the condemnation of the Court or render his body to Prison in execution for the same or that the said MCLACHLAN will pay the condemnation of the Court or render the body of the said Defendant as aforesaid. Where upon the Defendant by his Attorney prays and has leave to IMPARLE here until next Court and then to plead.

ANDREW SPROWLE admin of MISTERS SPROWLE and CROOKS Deceased Plaintiff
Against Re: In Debt
ARTHUR BUTT Defendant
STEPHEN TANKARD here in Court undertakes for the Defendant that in case he shall be Cast in this suit he the said Defendant will pay the condemnation of the Court or render his body to Prison in execution for the same or that the said TANKARD will pay the condemnation of the Court or render the body of the said Defendant as aforesaid. Where upon the Defendant by his Attorney prays and has leave to IMPARLE here until next Court and then to plead.

PAGE 147B
JOHN PHRIPP Gentleman Plaintiff
Against Re: In Debt for rents
JOHN LAWRENCE and MATT PHRIPP Executors of THOMAS THOMPSON deceased Defendant
This day came as well the Plaintiff by JAMES HOLT Gentleman his Attorney as the Defendant MATTHEW in his proper person acknowledges the Plaintiffs action for 69 pounds 8 shillings and half penny. Therefore, it is considered that the Plaintiff recover against the said Defendant his debt aforesaid and his costs by him in this behalf expended. And to be levied of the goods and chattels of the said testator THOMAS THOMPSON if so, much the said JOHN LAWRENCE and MATT PHRIPP have in their hands to be administered and if they have it not then the costs to be levied of their proper goods and chattels and the said Defendants in mercy.

MARSDIN* and HODGSON Plaintiff against WILLIAM CONNER Defendant in Case. This day came the parties by their Attorney's and the Defendant prays and has leave to IMPARLE here until the next Court and then to plead

TULLY ROBINSON and JOHN CRAMOND Plaintiffs against JONATHAN MEREDITH Defendant in case. The Defendant being called and not appearing. On the motion of the Plaintiff by their Attorney an alias Attachment is awarded them against the estate of the said Defendant for 40 pounds and costs returnable here the next Court.

ELDRED TUCKER against GEORGE ALLANSON. Attachment against WILLIAM IVY. The Garnishee.

ZACHERIAS MARSINGALE against CHARLES MANNING. Dismissed for want of security for the costs.

HENRY BRESSIE Plaintiff
Against Re: In Case
CHARLES MAYLE Defendant
This day came the parties by their Attorney's and there upon came also a Jury to wit: ROBERT TAYLOR, THOMAS TERRY, THOMAS HEPBURN, WILLIAM BICKERDICK, JAMES CARMICHAEL, JOHN MARLEY, ALEXANDER MOSELEY, PHILIP CARBERY, MORTO BRYAN, JOSHUA GOUGH, ANDREW BALLENTINE, and CONSTANTINE RIDDICK who being tried and sworn the truth to speak upon the issue joined upon their oath do says that the Defendant did assume in manner and form as the Plaintiff against him have declared and do assess the Plaintiff damages by occasion of the non-performance of that assumption to 5 pounds 18 shillings and 10 pence half penny besides his costs.
PAGE 148
Therefore, it is considered that the Plaintiff recover against the said Defendant his damages aforesaid in form aforesaid assessed and his costs by him in this behalf expended and the said Defendant in mercy.

SARAH LANGLEY and JOSEPH LANGLEY executors of SAMUEL LANGLEY deceased Plaintiff
Against Re: In Chancery
ARCHIBALD CAMPBELL admin of JOHN DALGLEISH Deceased Defendant
On the motion of the Plaintiff by their Attorney for a decretal order in this Cause the same is granted and ordered that the Surveyor of this County survey the land in the bill mentioned and make report to the next Court to be held for this Borough.

WILLISON and MCSWEEN Plaintiffs against JOHN AUSTIN FINNIE Defendant in case HECTOR MCALLISTER undertakes for the Plaintiff that he will pay to the Defendant all such damages costs and charges as shall be awarded against them by the Court.

WILLISON and MCSWEEN Plaintiff
Against Re: In Case
JOHN AUSTIN FINNIE Defendant
This day came the parties by their Attorney's and there upon came also a Jury to wit:
ROBERT TAYLOR, THOMAS TERRY, THOMAS HEPBURN, WILLIAM BICKERDICK, JAMES CARMICHAEL, JOHN MARLEY, ALEXANDER MOSELEY, PHILIP CARBERY, MORTO BRYAN, JOSHUA GOUGH, ANDREW BALLENTINE, and CONSTANTINE RIDDICK who being tried and sworn the truth to speak upon the issue joined upon and returned and the Plaintiff being called came not but made default. Therefore, on the prayers of the Defendant it is considered that he recover against the Plaintiff 5 shillings current money and his costs by him about his defense in this behalf expended according to the form of the Act of Assembly and the Plaintiff for his false claims be in mercy.

JOHN CRAMOND Plaintiff
Against Re: In Case
PRUDENCE BAYNES Defendant
This day came the parties by their Attorney's and the Defendant in her proper person and says that she cannot gainsay the Plaintiffs action nor but that she did assume in manner and form as the Plaintiff against her has declared.
PAGE 148B
Therefore, it is considered that the Plaintiff recover against the said Defendant 6 pounds 7 shillings and 6 pence and his costs by him about his suit in this behalf expended. And the said Defendant in mercy.

NATHANIEL CUNNINGHAM Plaintiff
Against Re: In Detinue for a Negro Slave named EMANUEL
ABRAHAM COOPER Defendant
This day came the parties by their Attorney's and there upon came also a Jury to wit:
ROBERT TAYLOR, THOMAS TERRY, THOMAS HEPBURN, WILLIAM BICKERDICK, JAMES CARMICHAEL, JOHN MARLEY, ALEXANDER MOSELEY, PHILIP CARBERY, MORTO BRYAN, JOSHUA GOUGH, ANDREW BALLENTINE, and CONSTANTINE RIDDICK who being tried and sworn the truth to speak upon the issue joined upon, withdrew, and returned and the Plaintiff being called came not but made default. Therefore, on the prayers of the Defendant it is considered that he recover against the Plaintiff 5 shillings current money and his costs by him about his defense in this behalf expended according to the form of the Act of Assembly and the Plaintiff for his false claims be in mercy.

JOHN MCLACHLAN Plaintiff
Against Re: In Case
THOMAS WALKER and JOHN VALLENTINE Defendants
This day came the parties by their Attorney's and there upon came also a Jury to wit: ROBERT TAYLOR, THOMAS TERRY, THOMAS HEPBURN, WILLIAM BICKERDICK, JAMES CARMICHAEL, JOHN MARLEY, ALEXANDER MOSELEY, PHILIP CARBERY, MORTO BRYAN, JOSHUA GOUGH, ANDREW BALLENTINE, and CONSTANTINE RIDDICK who being tried and sworn the truth to speak upon the issue joined upon their oath do says that the Defendant did assume in manner and form as the Plaintiff against him have declared and do assess the Plaintiff damages by occasion of the non-performance of that assumption to 3 pounds 16 shillings and 6 pence besides his costs.
Therefore, it is considered that the Plaintiff recover against the said Defendant his damages aforesaid in form aforesaid assessed and his costs by him in this behalf expended and the said Defendant in mercy.

MISTERS BUCHANAN and HASTIE Merchants of Great Britain Plaintiffs
Against Re: In Case
ROBERT MACKIE Defendant
This day came the parties by their Attorney's and the Defendant in Custody of the Sergeant by this Attorney and relinquishing his former plea says that he cannot gainsay the Plaintiff's action nor but that he did assume in manner and form as the Plaintiff against him have declared. Therefore, it is considered that the Plaintiff

<u>PAGE 149</u>
Recover against the said Defendant 126 pounds 4 shillings and 10 pence and his costs by them in this behalf expended and the said Defendant in mercy. And the said Defendant being ruled to give Special Bail and failing so to do. On the motion of the Plaintiff by their Attorney, the said Defendant is continued in Custody of the said Sergeant until he shall have satisfied this judgement and the costs.

CUMMING WARWICK and Company Plaintiff
Against Re: In Case
ROBERT MACKIE Defendant
This day came the parties by their Attorney's and the Defendant in Custody of the Sergeant by his Attorney relinquishing his former plea says that he cannot gainsay the Plaintiff's action nor but that he did assume in manner as the Plaintiff against him have declared. Therefore, it is considered that the Plaintiff recover against the said Defendant 24 pounds 4 shillings and 9 pence half penny and their costs by them in this behalf expended and the said Defendant in mercy.

ANDREW STEWART Plaintiff
Against Re: In Case
ALEXANDER BELL Defendant
This day came the parties by their Attorney's and the Defendant by his Attorney relinquishing his former plea acknowledges the Plaintiffs action for 14 pounds 14 shillings and 10 pence with interest thereon after the rate of 5% per annum to be computed form August 20, 1770, to the time of payment. Therefore, it is considered that the Plaintiff recover against the said Defendant his debt aforesaid and his costs by him about his suit in this behalf expended and the said Defendant in mercy.

MISTERS TULLY ROBINSON and JOHN CRAMOND Plaintiff
Against Re: In Case
JOHN WISE Defendant
This day came the parties by their Attorney's and there upon came also a Jury to wit: CONSTANTINE RIDDICK, ANDREW BALLENTINE, JOSHUA GOUGH, PHILIP CARBERY, ALEXANDER MOSELEY, JOHN MARLEY, JAMES CARNEY, WILLIAM BICKERDICK, THOMAS HEPBURN, ROBERT TAYLOR, THOMAS TERRY and JOHN MACLEAN who being elected tried and sworn the truth to speak upon the issue joined upon their oath do say that the Defendant is guilty in manner and form as the Plaintiff against him have declared and do assess the Plaintiff damages by occasion thereof to 2 pounds 10 shillings besides their costs. Therefore, it is considered that the Plaintiff recover against the said Defendant their damages aforesaid in form aforesaid assessed and their costs by them in in about their suit in this behalf expended and the said Defendant in mercy.

<u>PAGE 149B</u>
Ordinary License is granted JAMES DUNN on his complying with the law.

GEORGE RIDDELL against JOHN JONES. The Plaintiff is not further prosecuting his suit. The same is dismissed.

BENJAMIN LEWELLING against DEMPSEY VEALE. The Plaintiff is not further prosecuting his suit. The same is dismissed.

WRIGHT WESTCOTT Plaintiff
Against Re: (Blank)
THOMAS RASCOE Defendant
JOHN TATEM Gentleman and ENOCH EASTWOOD here in Court undertake for the Defendant that in case he shall be Cast in this suit he the said Defendant will pay the condemnation of the Court or render his body to Prison in execution for the same or that the said TATEM and EASTWOOD will pay the condemnation of the Court or render the body of the said Defendant as aforesaid. Where upon the Defendant by his Attorney pleaded general issue not guilty. Therefore, ordered that the judgement obtained at the last court against him, and JOHN TATEM Gentleman be set aside.

MALACHI MAUND assignee of NOAH SUGG against SAMUEL BRESSIE continued at the Defendants costs.
MALACHI MAUND against SAMUEL and HENRY BRESSIE continued at the Defendants costs.

HENRY BRESSIE assignee of SAMUEL BRESSIE Plaintiff
Against Re: In Debt
THOMAS and MATTHEW CHERRY Defendants
This day came the parties by their Attorneys and there upon came also a Jury to wit:
CONSTANTINE RIDDICK, ANDREW BALLENTINE, JOSHUA GOUGH, PHILIP CARBERY, ALEXANDER MOSELEY, JOHN MARLEY, JAMES CARNEY, WILLIAM BICKERDICK, THOMAS HEPBURN, ROBERT TAYLOR, THOMAS TERRY, and JOHN MACLEAN who being elected tried and sworn the truth to speak upon the issue joined upon their oath do say that the Defendants have not paid the debt in the declaration mentioned. Therefore, it is considered that the Plaintiff recover against the said Defendant 45 pounds and his costs by him about his suit in this behalf expended and the said Defendant in mercy.

But this judgement is to be discharged by the payment of 22 pounds 10 shillings with interest after the rate of 5% per annum to be computed from September 3, 1770, to the time of payment and the costs.

ROBERT SHEDDEN and Company Plaintiff
Against Re: In Debt
BRYAN CROSBIE Defendant
This day came the parties by their Attorney's and the Defendant by his Attorney relinquishing his former plea acknowledges the Plaintiff's action for 82 pounds 4 shillings and 3 pence. Therefore, it is considered that the Plaintiff recover against the said Defendant their debt aforesaid and their costs by them in this behalf expended. And the said Defendant in mercy. But this judgement is to be discharged by the payment of 41 pounds 2 shillings and 1 penny half penny. With interest thereon after the rate of 5% per annum to be computed from March 20, 1771, to the time of payment and the costs.

JOSEPH MITCHELL Plaintiff
Against Re: In Debt
NICHOLAS POOLE Defendant
This day came the parties by their Attorney's and the Defendant by his Attorney relinquishing his former plea acknowledges the Plaintiff's action for 58 pounds 4 shillings. Therefore, it is considered that the Plaintiff recover against the said Defendant their debt aforesaid and his costs by him in this behalf expended. And the said Defendant in mercy. But this judgement is to be discharged by the payment of 29 pounds 2 shillings with interest thereon after the rate of 5% per annum to be computed from November 14, 1771, to the time of payment and the costs.

DAVID ETHERIDGE Plaintiff
Against Re: In Debt
ELDRED FISHER and EDWARD PARKE Defendants
This day came the parties by their Attorney's and the Defendant by their Attorney relinquishing their former plea acknowledges the Plaintiff's action for 100 pounds. Therefore, it is considered that the Plaintiff recover against the said Defendant their debt aforesaid and their costs by them in this behalf expended. And the said Defendant in mercy.

But this judgement is to be discharged by the payment of 41 pounds 2 shillings and 1 penny half penny. With interest thereon after the rate of 5% per annum to be computed from June 20, 1771, to the time of payment and the costs.

JOHN WOODSIDE Plaintiff
Against Re: In Case
WILLIAM GODFREY administrator of JONATHAN GODFREY deceased Defendant
This day came the parties by their Attorney's and there upon came also a Jury to wit: CONSTANTINE RIDDICK, ANDREW BALLENTINE, JOSHUA GOUGH, PHILIP CARBERY, ALEXANDER MOSELEY, JOHN MARLEY, JAMES CARNEY, WILLIAM BICKERDICK, THOMAS HEPBURN, ROBERT TAYLOR, THOMAS TERRY and JOHN MACLEAN who being elected tried and sworn the truth to speak upon the issue joined upon their oath do say that the Defendant intestate did assume in manner and form as the Plaintiff against him have declared and do assess the Plaintiff damages by occasion of the non-performance of that assumption to 11 pounds 15 shillings and 4 pence half penny besides his costs. Therefore, it is considered that the Plaintiff recover against the said Defendant his damages aforesaid in form aforesaid assessed and his costs by him in in about their suit in this behalf expended. To be levied of the goods and chattels of the said Intestate JONATHAN GODFREY if so, much the said WILLIAM GODFREY has in his hands to be administered and if he has it not then the costs are to be levied of his proper goods and chattels and the said defendant in mercy.

JOHN STANHOPE against NATHANIEL BOUSH continued at Defendants costs.

MATTHEW KELLY Plaintiff
Against Re: In Trespass, Assault and Battery
THOMAS TAYLOR and ELIZABETH, his wife Defendants
This day came the parties by their Attorney's and there upon came also a Jury to wit: CONSTANTINE RIDDICK, ANDREW BALLENTINE, JOSHUA GOUGH, PHILIP CARBERY, ALEXANDER MOSELEY, JOHN MARLEY, JAMES CARNEY, WILLIAM BICKERDICK, THOMAS HEPBURN, ROBERT TAYLOR, THOMAS TERRY and JOHN MACLEAN who being elected tried and sworn the truth to speak upon the issue joined upon their oath do say that the Defendants are not guilty of the trespass, assault and battery in the declaration mentioned as the Plaintiff against him have declared. Therefore, it is considered that the Plaintiff take nothing by his bill but for his false claims be in mercy. And the Defendants go hence without day and recover against the Plaintiff their costs by them about their Defense in this behalf expended.

Order is granted SAMUEL DAVIS MACASTLETON against THOMAS TAYLOR and ELIZABETH his wife for 50 pounds tobacco for 2 days attendance in the suit of MATTHEW KELLY against them.

Order is granted LUCRETIA TAYLOR against THOMAS TAYLOR and ELIZABETH his wife for 25 pounds tobacco for 1 day's attendance in the suit of MATTHEW KELLY against them.

Order is granted ELEANOR STAUNTON against THOMAS TAYLOR and ELIZABETH his wife for 25 pounds tobacco for 1 day's attendance in the suit of MATTHEW KELLY against them.

Order is granted HANNAH BRIAN against MATTHEW KELLY for 25 pounds tobacco for 1 day's attendance in his suit against THOMAS TAYLOR and ELIZABETH his wife.

MARY ROTHERY against GEORGE WATSON and ANN his wife dismissed at the Plaintiff's costs.

Order is granted TULLY ROBINSON against ROBINSON and CRAMOND for 165 pounds of tobacco for 3 days attendance and returning 10 miles 3x in their suit against JOHN WISE.

DICKERSON PRIOR against AARON BARBER and HOFFMIRE continued at Plaintiff's cost.

Order is granted CHARLES CAMPBELL against WILLISON and MCSWEEN for 55 pounds of tobacco for 1 day's attendance coming and returning 10 miles once in their suit against JOHN AUSTIN FINNIE

This Court is adjourned until tomorrow at 9 o'clock, PAUL LOYALL MAYOR, TESTE: JOHN BOUSH D.C.

PAGE 151B
NORFOLK BOROUGH
At a Hustings Court Held this 20TH day of October 1772
PRESENT: PAUL LOYALL ESQUIRE MAYOR
GENTLEMAN ALDERMEN: GEORGE ABYVON, MAXIMILLIAN CALVERT, ARCHIBALD CAMPBELL, CHARLES THOMAS, LEWIS HANSFORD,

WILLIAM GRAHAM Plaintiff against ROGER PIERCE. Defendant ANDREW RONALD undertakes for the Plaintiff that he will pay to the Defendant all such damages costs and charges as shall be awarded against him by the Court.

WILLIAM GRAHAM Plaintiff against ROGER PIERCE. This day came the parties by their Attorney's and the Defendant pleaded not guilty in manner and form as the Plaintiff against him has declared and of this he puts himself upon the Country and the Plaintiff likewise. Therefore, the trail of the issue is referred until the next Court.

JOHN BEISER against ROGER PIERCE in Case. This day came the parties by their Attorney's and the Defendant says that he did not assume upon himself in manner and form as the Plaintiff against him has declared and of this he puts himself upon the Country and the Plaintiff likewise. Therefore, the trail of the issue is referred until the next Court.

ROGER PIERCE against WILLIAM GRAHAM in Case. This day came the parties by their Attorney's and the Defendant pleaded not guilty in manner and form as the Plaintiff against him has declared and of this he puts himself upon the Country and the Plaintiff likewise. Therefore, the trail of the issue is referred until the next Court.

GEORGE WEBB and JOSEPH LANGLEY Plaintiff against JOHN BAYNES and NANCY ASHLEY Defendants. The Plaintiffs by their Attorney filed their bill and time is allowed the Defendants to consider it.

WILLS COWPER Plaintiff
Against Re: In Case.
JOHN POLLOCK Defendant
This day came the parties by their Attorney's and there upon came also a Jury to wit:
THOMAS TERRY, JOHN WELLS, WILLIAM BICKERDICK, GEORGE WINKLE, DANIEL HUTCHINGS, SCARBROUGH TANKARD, ALEXANDER MOSELEY, WRIGHT WESTCOTT,
PAGE 152
PETER BEISER, JOHN HARRIS, ROBERT ALLEN, and WILLIAM WALKER who being elected tried and sworn the truth to speak upon the issue joined upon their oath do say that the Defendant did assume in manner and form as the Plaintiff against him has declared and do assess the Plaintiff's damages by occasion of the non-performance of that assumption to 8 pounds 19 shillings and 7 pence besides his costs. Therefore, it is considered that the Plaintiff recover against the said Defendant his damages aforesaid in form aforesaid assessed and his costs by him about his suit in this behalf expended and the said Defendant in mercy.

NICHOLAS BROWN SEABROOK Plaintiff
Against Re: In Case
AARON BARBER Defendant
This day came the parties by their Attorney's and there upon came also a Jury to wit:
THOMAS TERRY, JOHN WELLS, WILLIAM BICKERDICK, GEORGE WINKLE, DANIEL HUTCHINGS, SCARBROUGH TANKARD, ALEXANDER MOSELEY, WRIGHT WESTCOTT,PETER BEISER, JOHN HARRIS, ROBERT ALLEN, and WILLIAM WALKER who being elected tried and sworn the truth to speak upon the issue joined upon their oath do say that the Defendant did assume in manner and form as the Plaintiff against him has declared and do assess the Plaintiff's damages by occasion of the non-performance of that assumption to 2 pounds 8 shillings and 8 pence. Therefore, on the prayer of the Defendant. It is considered that he recover against the Plaintiff 5 shillings current money and his costs by him about his defense in this behalf expended according to the form of the Act of Assembly and the Plaintiff for his false claims be in mercy.

JOHN LAWRENCE and JOHN GREENWOOD Plaintiff
Against Re: In Debt.
STEPHEN TANKARD Defendant
This day came as well the Plaintiff by BENJAMIN CROOKER Gentleman their Attorney as the Defendant in his proper person and the said Defendant acknowledges the Plaintiffs action for 16 pounds 15 shillings. Therefore, it is considered that the Plaintiff recover against the said Defendant their debt aforesaid and their costs by them in this behalf expended and the said Defendant in mercy.
But this judgement is to be discharged by the payment of 8 pounds 7 shillings and 6 pence with interest thereon at the rate of 5% per annum to be computed from October 25, 1771, until the time of payment and the costs.

ANDREW SPROWLE admin of JOHN SPROWLE and ROBERT CROOKS deceased. Plaintiff against GEORGE COLLINS Defendant in case. This day came the parties by their Attorney's and the Defendant says that he did not

PAGE 152B

Assume upon himself in manner and form at the Plaintiff against him has declared and of this he puts himself upon the Country and the Plaintiff likewise Therefore, the trial of the issue is referred until the next Court.

AITCHESON and PARKER Plaintiffs against ALEXANDER BELL Defendant. In Debt. This day came the parties by their Attorney's and the Defendant pleaded payment in manner and form as the Plaintiff against him has declared and of this he puts himself upon the Country and the Plaintiff likewise Therefore, the trial of the issue is referred until the next Court.

MARY ROTHERY and other executors of MATTHEW ROTHERY Plaintiffs against DOROTHY ROTHERY admin of HENRY ROTHERY Defendant. In Case. This day came the parties by their Attorney's and the Defendant says that her intestate did not assume upon himself and pleads the act of limitations in manner and form as the Plaintiff against her has declared and of this she puts herself upon the Country and the Plaintiff likewise Therefore, the trial of the issue is referred until the next Court.

MARY ROTHERY and other executors of MATTHEW ROTHERY Plaintiffs against THOMAS PEARSON, Defendant. In Case. This day came the parties by their Attorney's and the Defendant says that he did not assume upon himself and pleads the act of limitations in manner and form as the Plaintiff against her has declared and of this he puts himself upon the Country and the Plaintiff likewise Therefore, the trial of the issue is referred until the next Court.

WILLIAM GODFREY Plaintiff against THOMAS DREWREY Defendant. In T.A.B. This day came the parties by their Attorney's and the Defendant says that he is not guilty in manner and form as the Plaintiff against him has declared and of this he puts himself upon the Country and the Plaintiff likewise Therefore, the trial of the issue is referred until the next Court.

WILLIAM GODFREY Plaintiff against WILLIAM SMITH Defendant. In T.A.B. This day came the parties by their Attorney's and the Defendant says that he is not guilty in manner and form as the Plaintiff against him has declared and of this he puts himself upon the Country and the Plaintiff likewise Therefore, the trial of the issue is referred until the next Court.

Page 153

JAMES EDMUNDSON admin of WILLIAM RAMSAY Deceased Plaintiff against ANTHONY FLEMING Defendant. In Debt. This day came the parties by their Attorney's and the Defendant pleaded payment in manner and form as the Plaintiff against him has declared and of this he puts himself upon the Country and the Plaintiff likewise Therefore, the trial of the issue is referred until the next Court.

ROGER PIERCE Plaintiff
Against Re: In Case for Slander
JOSEPH TODD Defendant
This day came the parties by their Attorney's and there upon came also a Jury to wit: JOHN MACLEAN, JOHN SMITH, JOHN WALKER, JOHN LIVINGSTON, WILLIAM BALLARD, STEPHEN TANKARD, WILLIAM FREEMAN, JAMES LEITCH, SAMUEL BACON, JOHN GRIFFIN, HENRY FLEMING and JAMES DUNN who being elected tried and sworn the truth to speak upon the issue joined upon their oath do say that the Defendant is guilty of speaking the slanderous words in manner and form as in the declaration against him is alleged and do assess the Plaintiff damages by occasion of the speaking of the slanderous words in the declaration mentioned to 3 pounds 15 shillings besides his costs. Therefore, it is considered that the Plaintiff recover against the said Defendant his damages aforesaid in form aforesaid assessed and his costs by him about his suit in this behalf expended in mercy.

GEORGE VEALE JUNIOR Plaintiff against JOHN LELLO Defendant. In T.A.B. This day came the parties by their Attorney's and the Defendant pleaded not guilty in manner and form as the Plaintiff against him has declared and of this he puts himself upon the Country and the Plaintiff likewise Therefore, the trial of the issue is referred until the next Court.

WILLIAM MOSELEY Plaintiff against ALEXANDER BELL Defendant. In Debt. This day came the parties by their Attorney's and the Defendant pleaded payment in manner and form as the Plaintiff against him has declared and of this he puts himself upon the Country and the Plaintiff likewise Therefore, the trial of the issue is referred until the next Court.

JAMES BALFOUR and DANIEL BARRAUD Plaintiffs against JOHN HEATON in Case. This day came the Plaintiff by BENJAMIN CROOKER Gentleman their Attorney and the Defendant not appearing. Ordered that the suit be entered for the Plaintiff against him the said Defendant and JOHN SMITH his bail for what damages the Plaintiffs have sustained to be ascertained at the next Court upon a writ of Inquiry.

JOHN CALVERT Plaintiff against BARNABY CARNEY Defendant. In Case. This day came the parties by their Attorney's and the Defendant says that he did not assume upon himself in manner and form as the Plaintiff against him has declared and of this he puts himself upon the Country and the Plaintiff likewise Therefore, the trial of the issue is referred until the next Court.

JAMES MUDIE Plaintiff against THOMAS TILLIDGE Defendant. In Case. This day came the parties by their Attorney's and the Defendant pleaded not guilty in manner and form as the Plaintiff against him has declared and of this he puts himself upon the Country and the Plaintiff likewise Therefore, the trial of the issue is referred until the next Court.

MISTERS JOHN and THOMAS GILCHRIST Plaintiffs against BARNABY CARNEY Defendant. In Case. This day came the parties by their Attorney's and the Defendant says that he did not assume upon himself in manner and form as the Plaintiff against him has declared and of this he puts himself upon the Country and the Plaintiff likewise Therefore, the trial of the issue is referred until the next Court.

MISTERS WILLIAM and JOHN BROWN Plaintiffs against ALEXANDER BELL Defendant. In Case. This day came the parties by their Attorney's and the Defendant says that he did not assume upon himself in manner and form as the Plaintiff against him has declared and of this he puts himself upon the Country and the Plaintiff likewise Therefore, the trial of the issue is referred until the next Court.

FRANCIS ROBERTSON Plaintiff against JOHN SMITH Defendant. In Debt. This day came the parties by their Attorney's and the Defendant pleaded payment in manner and form as the Plaintiff against him has declared and of this he puts himself upon the Country and the Plaintiff likewise Therefore, the trial of the issue is referred until the next Court.

WILLIAM BICKERDICK Plaintiff
Against Re: In Trespass, Assault, & Battery
WILLIAM PRIESTMAN Defendant
This day came the parties by their Attorneys and there upon came also a Jury to wit: WILLIAM WALKER, ROBERT ALLAN, JOHN HARRIS, PETER BEISER, WRIGHT WESTCOTT, ALEXANDER MOSELEY, SCARBROUGH TANKARD, DANIEL HUTCHINGS, JOHN WILLS, THOMAS TERRY, GEORGE WINKLE and MARLO BRYAN who being elected tried and sworn the truth to speak upon the issue joined upon their oath do say that the Defendant is guilty of the trespass, assault and battery in the declaration mentioned in manner and form as the Plaintiff against him have declared and do assess the Plaintiff damages by occasion thereof to 3 pounds. Therefore, it is considered that the Plaintiff recover against the said Defendant his damages aforesaid in form aforesaid assessed and his costs by him about his suit in this behalf expended and the said Defendant may be taken.

GEORGE WILSON and ARCHIBALD CAMPBELL administrators of JOHN WILSON deceased Plaintiff against ELDRED FISHER Defendant in case. This day came the parties by their attorney's and the defendant says that he did not assume upon himself in manner and form as the Plaintiff against him have declared and of this he puts himself upon the Country and the Plaintiff likewise Therefore, the trial of the issue is referred until the next Court.

JOSEPH NORTHRUP Plaintiff against ABRAHAM PATEON Defendant in Trespass. This day came the parties by their Attorney's and the Defendant pleaded not guilty in manner and form as the Plaintiff against him has declared and of this he puts himself upon the Country and the Plaintiff likewise Therefore, the trial of the issue is referred until the next Court.

JOSEPH NORTHRUP Plaintiff against ABRAHAM PATEON Defendant. In Case. This day came the parties by their Attorney's and the Defendant pleaded not guilty in manner and form as the Plaintiff against him has declared and of this he puts himself upon the Country and the Plaintiff likewise Therefore, the trial of the issue is referred until the next Court.

THOMAS LANGLEY Plaintiff against JAMES WEBB Defendant. In Detinue. This day came the parties by their Attorney's and the Defendant pleaded that he does not detain the Negro Slave named DAVID in manner and form as the Plaintiff against him has declared and of this he puts himself upon the Country and the Plaintiff likewise Therefore, the trial of the issue is referred until the next Court.

On the motion of JAMES DISON, a witness for ROGER PIERCE against JOSEPH TODD. It is ordered that the said PIERCE pay him 75 pounds of tobacco for 3 days attendance at this Court according to law.

On the motion of GRIFFIN PEART a witness for ROGER PIERCE against JOSEPH TODD. It is ordered that the said PIERCE pay him 75 pounds of tobacco for 3 days attendance at this Court according to law.

On the motion of WILLIAM MINETREE, a witness for WILLIAM BICKERDICK against WILLIAM PRIESTMAN. It is ordered that the said BICKERDICK pay him 50 pounds of tobacco for 2 days attendance at this Court according to law.

Order is granted FRANCIS DISON against WILLIAM PRIESTMAN for 50 pounds of tobacco for 2 days attendance at this court in the suit of WILLIAM BICKERDICK against him.

MALBONE SHELTON Plaintiff
Against Re: In Case
LEMUEL ROBERTS Defendant
This day came the parties by their Attorney's and there upon came also a Jury to wit: JOHN MACLEAN, JOHN SMITH, JOHN WALKER, JOHN LIVINGSTON, WILLIAM BALLARD, STEPHEN TANKARD, WILLIAM FREEMAN, JAMES LEITCH, SAMUEL BACON, JOHN GRIFFIN, HENRY FLEMING and JAMES DUNN who being elected tried and sworn the truth to speak upon the issue joined upon their oath do say that the Defendant did

assume in manner and form as the Plaintiff against him has declared and do assess the Plaintiff damages by occasion of the speaking of the non-performance of that assumption to 7 pounds 14 shillings and 5 pence besides his costs. Therefore, it is considered that the Plaintiff recover against the said Defendant his damages aforesaid in form aforesaid assessed and his costs by him about his suit in this behalf expended in mercy.

PAGE 155

JAMES CAMPBELL and Company Plaintiffs
Against In Case.
BARNABY CARNEY Defendant

This day came the parties by their Attorney's and the Defendant by his Attorney relinquishing his former plea says that he cannot gainsay the Plaintiffs action nor but that he did assume in manner and form as the Plaintiff against him has declared. Therefore, it is considered that the Plaintiff recover against the said Defendant 88 pounds 16 shillings and 5 pence and their costs by them about their suit in this behalf expended and the said Defendant in mercy.

GEORGE KELLY Plaintiff
Against Re: In Case
GEORGE WILSON and ARCHIBALD CAMPBELL admin of JOHN WILSON deceased Defendant

This day came the parties by their Attorney's and the Defendants by their Attorney relinquishing their former plea says that they cannot gainsay the Plaintiffs action nor but that their intestate did assume in manner and form as the Plaintiff against them has declared. Therefore, it is considered that the Plaintiff recover against the said Defendants 10 pounds 10 shillings and his costs by him about his suit in this behalf expended to be levied of the goods and chattels of the said intestate JOHN WILSON if so much the said GEORGE and ARCHIBALD have in their hands to be administered and if they have it not then the costs are to be levied of their proper goods and chattels and the said Defendants in mercy.

JOHN CRAMOND Plaintiff
Against Re: In Debt
JONATHAN JACKSON Defendant

This day came the parties by their Attorney's and there upon came also a Jury to wit: JOHN MACLEAN, JOHN SMITH, JOHN WALKER, JOHN LIVINGSTON, WILLIAM BALLARD, STEPHEN TANKARD, WILLIAM FREEMAN, JAMES LEITCH, SAMUEL BACON, JOHN GRIFFIN, HENRY FLEMING and JAMES DUNN who being elected tried and sworn the truth to speak upon the issue joined upon their oath do say that the Defendant has not paid the debt in the declaration mentioned. Therefore, it is considered that the Plaintiff recover against the said Defendant his debt amounting to 62 pounds and his costs by him in this behalf expended and the said Defendant in mercy. But this judgement is to be discharged by the payment of L.17.9.4 *with interest thereon after the rate of 5% per annum to be computed from October 15, 1772, until the time of payment and the costs.

PAGE 155B

GEORGE OLDNER Plaintiff
Against Re: In Case for Slander
JOHN NASH Defendant

This day came the parties by their Attorney's and there upon came also a Jury to wit: JAMES DUNN, HENRY FLEMING, JOHN GRIFFIN, SAMUEL BACON, JAMES LEITCH, WILLIAM FREEMAN, WILLIAM BALLARD, JOHN LIVINGSTON, JOHN WALKER, JOHN SMITH, JOHN MACLEAN and BASSET MOSELEY who being elected tried and sworn the truth to speak upon the issue upon their oath do say that the Defendant is guilty of speaking the slanderous words in manner and form as the declaration against him is alleged and do assess the Plaintiff damages by occasion of the speaking of the slanderous words in the declaration mentioned to 5 pounds his costs. Therefore, it is considered that the Plaintiff recover against the said Defendant his damages aforesaid in form aforesaid assessed and his costs by him about his suit in this behalf expended and the said Defendant in mercy.

On the motion of HENRY KNIGHT, a witness for GEORGE OLDNER against JOHN NASH. It is ordered that the said OLDNER pay him 290 pounds of tobacco and 14 shillings and 6 pence for 2 days attendance at this Court coming 80 miles and returning for the ferriages according to law.

On the motion of WILLIAM WILKINS, a witness for GEORGE OLDNER against JOHN NASH. It is ordered that the said OLDNER pay him 290 pounds of tobacco and 14 shillings and 6 pence for 2 days attendance at this Court coming 80 miles and returning for the ferriages according to law. But only 25 pounds of tobacco to be taxed in the bill of costs against Defendant.

MATTHEW KELLY who as well Plaintiff
Against Re: In Debt for selling liquor without License
MARY STAUNTON Defendant

This day came the parties by their Attorney's and there upon came also a Jury to wit: JOHN MACLEAN, JOHN SMITH, JOHN WALKER, JOHN LIVINGSTON, WILLIAM BALLARD, STEPHEN TANKARD, WILLIAM FREEMAN, JAMES LEITCH, SAMUEL BACON, JOHN GRIFFIN, HENRY FLEMING and JAMES DUNN who being elected tried and sworn the truth to speak upon the issue joined upon their oath do say that the Defendant does owe the said Debt in the declaration mentioned in manner and form as the Plaintiff against him has declared. Therefore, it is considered that the Defendant forfeit and pay 10 pounds 1 moiety thereof to our Lord the King his heirs for and towards the better support of this Government. And the other moiety to the informer together with his costs by him about his suit in this behalf expended and the said Defendant in mercy.

PAGE 156

Order is granted CONSTANTINE RIDDICK against MATTHEW KELLY who as well for 50 pounds of tobacco for 2 days attendance at this Court in his suit against MARY STAUNTON.

This Court this day rated flour at 16/8 per centum weight
This Court is adjourned until Court in Course: PAUL LOYALL MAYOR. TESTE: JOHN BOUSH D.C.

NORFOLK BOROUGH

At a Hustings Court Held this 21st day of December 1772
PRESENT: PAUL LOYALL ESQUIRE MAYOR
GENTLEMAN ALDERMEN: GEORGE ABYVON, CHARLES THOMAS, ARCHIBALD CAMPBELL, JAMES TAYLOR, LEWIS HANSFORD, CORNELIUS CALVERT, MAXIMILIAN CALVERT

JOHN MARLEY Plaintiff against JOHN HARDY Defendant. In Trespass, Assault and Battery. The Plaintiff not further prosecuting. On the motion of the Defendant by his Attorney it is ordered that the suit be dismissed, and that the Plaintiff pay to the Defendants his costs.

JOHN MARLEY Plaintiff against JOHN HARDY and ELIZABETH his wife Defendant. In Trespass, Assault and Battery. The Plaintiff not further prosecuting. On the motion of the Defendant by his Attorney it is ordered that the suit be dismissed, and that the Plaintiff pay to the Defendants his costs.

MARGARET DOBSON Plaintiff against HENRY FLEMING Defendant by complaint. The Plaintiff not further prosecuting. On the motion of the Defendant by his Attorney it is ordered that the Complaint be dismissed, and that the Plaintiff pay to the Defendants his costs.

PAGE 156B

JAMES TATE Plaintiff against NATHANIEL WILSON Defendant. In Trespass, assault and Battery and false imprisonment. The Plaintiff not further prosecuting on the motion of the Defendant by his Attorney it is ordered that the suit is discontinued.

JOHN MCLACHLAN against JOHN VALLENCIER by Petition and summons. Judgement is granted the Plaintiff for 1 pounds 9 shilling and 2 pence. It is ordered that the Defendant pay the same unto the Plaintiff with costs and fee.

SAMUEL PORTLOCK against WILLIAM WYNHALL Defendant. The Plaintiff not further prosecuting his suit. The same is dismissed.

It is ordered that the Sergeant summon REUBEN SHARP to appear at the next Court to be held for this Borough to answer the Complaint of his apprentice THOMAS NELSON.

JOSHUA GOUGH administrator of all and singular the goods and chattels and credits which were of JAMES GOUGH, MARINER, Deceased, not administered by JOSHUA WRIGHT late administrator Plaintiff against JOSIAH HODGES Defendant in Case. This day came the parties by their Attorney's and the Defendant prays and has leave to IMPARLE here until the next Court and then to Plead. On the motion of the Plaintiff by his attorney a DEDIMUS is granted him to take the depositions of JOHN PEARSON giving the Defendant notice.

EDWARD WRIGHT Plaintiff against JOHN MCLACHLAN Defendant in case. This day came the parties by their Attorney's and the Defendant prays and has leave to IMPAREL here until the next Court and then to plead.

PETER B. WHITING Plaintiff against EDWARD DAVIS Defendant in case. This day came the parties by their Attorney's and the Defendant prays and has leave to IMPAREL here until the next Court and then to plead.

JUDITH DUNFORD Plaintiff against GEORGE J. FENWICK Defendant in case. This day came the parties by their Attorney's and the Defendant prays and has leave to IMPAREL here until the next Court and then to plead.

JAMES HUNTER and ELIZABETH TENANT executors of SAMUEL TENANT Plaintiffs against WILLIAM SIMPSON executor of FRANCIS CLARK Deceased Defendant. In Debt. This day came the parties by their Attorney's and the Defendant prays and has leave to IMPAREL here until the next Court and then to plead.

PAGE 157

MATTHEW PHRIPP Gentleman Plaintiff
Against Re: In Debt.
WILLIAM STEVENSON Defendant
This day came as well the Plaintiff by WILILAM RASCOW WILSON CURLE Gentleman his Attorney as the Defendant in his proper person and acknowledges the Plaintiff action for 28 pounds 1 shillings and 8 pence.
Therefore, it is considered that the Plaintiff recover against the said Defendant his debt aforesaid and his costs by him about his suit in this behalf expended and the said Defendant in mercy. But this Judgement is to be discharged by the payment of 7 pounds 19 shillings and 2 pence with interest for the same at the rate of 5% per annum to be computed from August 24, 1772, to the time of payment and costs.

JAMES CARMICHAEL Plaintiff against JOHN GARRICK and ELIZABETH his wife Defendants. In Case. This day came as well the Plaintiff by ANDREW RONALD Gentleman his Attorney as the Defendants in Custody of the Sergeant of this Borough, and the said Defendants say that they did not assume upon themselves in manner and form as the Plaintiff against them have declared and of this they put themselves upon the County and the Plaintiff likewise. Therefore, by Consent the trial of the issue is referred until tomorrow and the said Defendant being ruled to give Special Bail and failing so to do, are continued in the custody of the said Sergeant until that time.

LOGAN GILMOUR & Company Plaintiffs against JOHN GARRICK and ELIZABETH his wife Defendants. In Case. This day came as well the Plaintiff by ANDREW RONALD Gentleman his Attorney as the Defendants in Custody of the Sergeant of this Borough, and the said Defendants say that they did not assume upon themselves in manner and form as the Plaintiff against them have declared and of this they put themselves upon the County and the Plaintiff likewise. Therefore, by Consent the trial of the issue is referred until tomorrow and the said Defendant being ruled to give Special Bail and failing so to do, are continued in the custody of the said Sergeant until that time.

GUSTAVUS HAMILTON an infant by BARNABAS LORAIN Plaintiff against MALCOMB BROWN Defendant. T.A.B. The Plaintiff not further prosecuting his suit the same is dismissed.

JOHN VALLENCIER against THOMAS WALKER dismissed at the Defendants costs.

PAGE 157B

RALPH ELLIOTT Plaintiff against JOHN POLLOCK Defendant. In Case. The Plaintiff not further prosecuting his suit the same is dismissed.

PETER SINGLETON Plaintiff against MISTERS ROGER PIERCE and MORTO BRIAN Defendants. This Plaintiff not further prosecuting his suit against PIERCE, the same is discontinued. And ALEXANDER GAUTIER came into Court and undertook for the Defendant that in case he shall be costs in this suit he the said Defendant will pay the condemnation of the Court or render his body to Prison in execution for the same or that the said GAUTIER will pay the condemnation or render the body of the said Defendant as aforesaid. Where upon the Defendants by their Attorney prayed and have leave to IMPARLE here the next Court and then to Plead.

NEWCOMB DODD Plaintiff against THOMAS RASCOE and LEAH his wife executors of SUSANNAH LAMOUNT Deceased Defendant. In case. This day came the parties by their Attorney's and the Defendant prays and has leave to IMPAREL here until the next Court and then to plead.

JAMES CARMICHAEL Plaintiff against HARDRESS WALLER Defendant. In Trespass. This day came the parties by their Attorney's and the Defendant prays and has leave to IMPAREL here until the next Court and then to plead.

JAMES CARMICHAEL Plaintiff against JOHN GARRICK Defendant. In Trespass. This day came the parties by their Attorney's and the Defendant prays and has leave to IMPAREL here until the next Court and then to plead.

JAMES BALFOUR and DANIEL BARRAUD Plaintiff against JOHN JONES Defendant. In Case. On the motion of the Defendant by his Attorney a DEDIMUS is granted him to take the deposition of GEORGE WRAY, JOHN HUNTER, ZACHERIAH BEAN, and WILLIAM DAVIS JR. giving the Plaintiff reasonable notice of the time and place.

JOHN HARMANSON Plaintiff against WILLIAM PIGOT Defendant. In Case. The Plaintiff not further prosecuting his suit. The same is dismissed.

JOHN SMITH assignee of WILLIAM FLOOD Plaintiff against MARY WILSON and GEORGE WILSON Defendants. In Debt. JAMES LEITCH and JAMES CARMICHAEL came into Court and undertook for the Defendant that in case he shall be casts in this suit he the said Defendant will pay the condemnation of the Court or render his body to Prison in execution for the same or that they said LEITCH or CARMICHAEL will pay the condemnation or render the body of the said Defendant as aforesaid. Where upon the Defendants by their Attorney prayed and have leave to IMPARLE here the next Court and then to Plead.

PAGE 158

LOGAN GILMOUR and Company Plaintiff against JOHN VALLENCIER Defendant. The Plaintiff not further prosecuting his suit. The same is dismissed.

WILLIAM HOLT against DANIEL PECK by Petition and summons. Judgement is granted the Plaintiff for 3 pounds 16 shilling and 11 pence. It is ordered that the Defendant pay the same unto the Plaintiff with costs and fee.

JOHN GARRICK JR. Plaintiff against JAMES CARMICHAEL Defendant. In Case. This day came the parties by their Attorney's and the Defendant prays and has leave to IMPAREL here until the next Court and then to plead.

MATTHEW PHRIPP Gentleman Plaintiff against NATHANIEL BOUSH Defendant. In Debt. SAMUEL BOUSH this day came into Court and undertook for the Defendant that in case he shall be casts in this suit he the said Defendant will pay the condemnation of the Court or render his body to Prison in execution for the same or that the said BOUSH will pay the condemnation or render the body of the said Defendant as aforesaid. Where upon the Defendant by his Attorney prayed and have leave to IMPARLE here the next Court and then to Plead.

JOHN WILSON Plaintiff against SAMUEL PORTLOCK Defendant. Injunction in Chancery. The Plaintiff by his Attorney filed his Bill of Injunction and time is allowed the Defendant to consider it. And ordered that the Plaintiff give Bond and Security in the Clerk's Office.

ROBERT TUCKER Plaintiff against THOMAS VEALE Gentleman and FRANCIS HATTON executors of DAVID HARPER Deceased Defendants. In Case. This day came the parties by their Attorney's and the Defendant prays and has leave to IMPAREL here until the next Court and then to plead.

HENRY BRESSIE Plaintiff
Against Re: In Debt
NATHANIE POINER Defendant
This day came as well the Plaintiff by THOMAS CLAIBORNE Gentleman his Attorney as the Defendant in his proper person and acknowledges the Plaintiff action for 326 pounds 6 shillings. Therefore, it is considered that the Plaintiff recover against the said Defendant his debt aforesaid and his costs by him about his suit in this behalf expended and the said Defendant in mercy.

PAGE 158B

But this Judgement is to be discharged by the payment of 164 pounds with interest thereon after the of 5% per annum to be computed from April 24, 1772, to the time of payment and costs.

NEAL BROWN Plaintiff against JAMES ALLISON Defendant. In T.A.B. This day came the parties by their Attorney's and the Defendant prays and has leave to IMPAREL here until the next Court and then to plead.

JOHN GARRICK Plaintiff against JAMES CARMICHAEL Defendant. In Trespass. This day came the parties by their Attorney's and the Defendant prays and has leave to IMPAREL here until the next Court and then to plead.

ELDRED FISHER against GEORGE ALLANSON. Attachment abates by the Plaintiff's death.

JOHN HUTCHINGS and EDWARD CHAMPION TRAVIS surviving executors of JOHN TUCKER Deceased Plaintiffs against WILLIAM LIDDLE and EDWARD GOOD Defendant. In Debt. The Plaintiffs not further prosecuting their suit the same is dismissed.

SUSANNAH ESTHER against ELDRED FISHER. The suit abates by the Defendants death.

GEORGE WILSON and ARCHIBALD CAMPBELL administrators of JOHN WILSON Deceased against ELDRED FISHER. The suit abates by the Defendants death.

JOHN PLUMBER against ELDRED FISHER. The suit abates by the Defendants death.

JAMES RATTERY was this day brought before the Court by warrant from under the hand of JAMES TAYLOR Gentleman for being a person of lewd life and conversation and common disturber of the peace and the same being proved to the Court. It is ordered that the Sergeant take and keep him in Custody until he gives bond and security himself in 10 pounds and 2 securities in 5 pounds each for keeping the peace and being of good behavior for 3 months and pay the costs of this prosecution.

WILLIAM WALKER Plaintiff against SAMUEL SUAN* Defendant. In Case. This day came the parties by their Attorney's and the Defendant prays and has leave to IMPAREL here until the next Court and then to plead.

PETER SINGLETON Plaintiff against ROGER PIERCE and MORTO BRYAN. Defendant. In Case. The Plaintiff not further prosecuting. On the motion of the Defendants by their Attorney it is ordered that the suit be dismissed, and that the Plaintiff pay to the Defendants their costs.

PAGE 159

THOMAS NEWTON assignee of JOHN SMITH Plaintiff against WILLIAM SMITH. Defendant. In Debt. JOHN WILSON Gentleman this day came into Court and undertook for the Defendant that in case he shall be casts in this suit he the said Defendant will pay the condemnation of the Court or render his body to Prison in execution for the same or that he the said WILSON will pay the condemnation or render the body of the said Defendant as aforesaid. Where upon the Defendants by their Attorney prayed and have leave to IMPARLE here the next Court and then to Plead.

JOSEPH HUTCHINGS Gentleman Trustee in Trust for JOHN SMITH Plaintiff against RICHARD BROWN Defendant. In Case. This day came the parties by their Attorney's and the Defendant prays and has leave to Special IMPAREL here until the next Court and then to plead.

BARNABAS LORAIN Plaintiff against NATHANIEL WILSON Defendant. In Case. This day came the parties by their Attorney's and the Defendant prays and has leave to Special IMPAREL here until the next Court and then to plead.

ALEXANDER GRAHAM Plaintiff against WILLIAM FEARSON Defendant. In Case. The Plaintiff not further prosecuting. On the motion of the Defendants by their Attorney it is ordered that the suit be dismissed, and that the Plaintiff pay to the Defendants their costs.

JOHN WILLIAMSON Plaintiff against ROBERT SHEDDEN Defendant. In Detinue. This day came the parties by their Attorney's and the Defendant prays and has leave to Special IMPAREL here until the next Court and then to plead.

PATRICK TELFER Plaintiff against JOHN CRAMOND Defendant. In Case. ANDREW RONALD undertakes for the Plaintiff that he shall will pay to the Defendant all such damages, costs and charges as shall be awarded against him by the Court and there upon HENRY BRESSIE came into Court and undertook for the Defendant that in case he shall be casts in this suit he the said Defendant will pay the condemnation of the Court or render his body to Prison in execution for the same or that he the said BRESSIE will pay the condemnation or render the body of the said Defendant as aforesaid. Where upon the Defendant by his Attorney prayed and have leave to IMPARLE here the next Court and then to Plead.

JAMES ARCHDEACON Plaintiff against WILLIAM WRIGHT Defendant. In Case. The Plaintiff not further prosecuting. On the motion of the Defendants by their Attorney it is ordered that the suit be dismissed, and that the Plaintiff pay to the Defendants their costs.

PAGE 159B

Ordinary License is granted ANDREW STEVENSON on his complying with the law.

ALEXANDER GORDON Plaintiff against ALEXANDER PURDIE and JOHN DIXON Defendants. This day came the parties by their Attorney's and the Defendant PURDIE prays and has leave to Special IMPAREL here until the next Court and then to plead. And the Plaintiff not further his suit against DIXON. The same is dismissed.

CHRISTOPHER CALVERT Plaintiff against FREDERICK BOUSH Defendant. In Case. BENJAMIN CROOKER undertakes for the Defendant that in case he shall be casts in this suit he the said Defendant will pay the condemnation of the Court or render his body to Prison in execution for

129

the same or that the said CROOKER will pay the condemnation or render the body of the said Defendant as aforesaid. Where upon the Defendant by his Attorney prayed and have leave to IMPARLE here the next Court and then to Plead.

ANDREW SPROWLE admin of MISTERS SPROWLE and CROOKS Deceased Plaintiffs
Against Re: In Debt.
DANIEL PECK Defendant
This day came as well the Plaintiff by WILLIAM RASCOW WILSON CURLE Gentleman his Attorney as the Defendant in Custody of the Sergeant of this Borough and acknowledges the Plaintiffs action for 13 shillings and 4 pence. Therefore, it is considered that the Plaintiff recover against the said Defendant his debt aforesaid and his costs by him about his suit in this behalf expended. And the said Defendant in Mercy. And the said Defendant being ruled to give Special Bail and failing so to do. On the Motion of the Plaintiff by his Attorney aforesaid the Defendant is continued in Custody of the said Sergeant until he shall have satisfied this judgement and the costs. But this judgement is to be discharged by the payment of 33 pounds 6 shillings and 8 pence with interest thereon after the rate of 5% per annum to be computed from October 25, 1771, to the time of payment and the costs.

JAMES BERRY Plaintiff against ALEXANDER MURRAY Defendant in Debt. This day came the parties by their Attorney's and the Defendant prays and has leave to IMPAREL here until the next Court and then to plead.

WILLIAM SKINKER Plaintiff against MISTERS PAUL LOYALL, NEWTON, and Company Defendants. In Case. This day came the parties by their Attorney's and the Defendant prays and has leave to IMPAREL here until the next Court and then to plead.

PAGE 160

MATTHEW LATCHWELL against BRYAN and PIERCE. Dismissed at the Plaintiffs costs.

JOHN BARRET Plaintiff against ROBERT FRY Defendant in Trespass. This day came the parties by their Attorney's and the Defendant prays and has leave to IMPAREL here until the next Court and then to plead.

HENRY FLEMING and Company Plaintiffs against NATHANIEL BOUSH Defendant. In Case. JOSEPH CALVERT undertakes for the Defendant that in case he shall be casts in this suit he the said Defendant will pay the condemnation of the Court or render his body to Prison in execution for the same or that the said CALVERT will pay the condemnation or render the body of the said Defendant as aforesaid. Where upon the Defendant by his Attorney prayed and have leave to IMPARLE here the next Court and then to Plead.

JAMES HUNTER assignee of DANIEL DALE Plaintiff
Against Re: In Debt.
JOHN POLLOCK Defendant
This day came as well the Plaintiff by BENJAMIN CROOKER Gentleman his Attorney as the Defendant in Custody of the Sergeant of this Borough, in his proper person, and acknowledges the Plaintiffs action for 19 pounds 2 shillings and 6 pence. Therefore, it is considered that the Plaintiff recover against the said Defendant his debt aforesaid and his costs by him about his suit in this behalf expended. And the said Defendant in Mercy. And the said Defendant being ruled to give Special Bail and failing so to do. On the Motion of the Plaintiff by his Attorney aforesaid the Defendant is continued in Custody of the said Sergeant until he shall have satisfied this judgement and the costs. But this judgement is to be discharged by the payment of 9 pounds 11 shillings with interest thereon after the rate of 5% per annum to be computed from April 25, 1772, to the time of payment and the costs.

RALPH ELLIOT Plaintiff
Against Re: In Case
JOHN POLLOCK Defendant
This day came as well the Plaintiff by WILLIAM RASCOW WILSON CURLE Gentleman his Attorney as the Defendant in Custody of the Sergeant of this Borough, in his proper person, and says that he cannot gainsay the Plaintiffs actions nor but that he did assume in manner and form as the Plaintiff against him has declared.
PAGE 160B
Therefore, it is considered that the Plaintiff recover against the said Defendant 9 pounds 3 shillings and his costs by him about his suit in this behalf expended. And the said Defendant in Mercy. And the Defendant being ruled to give Special Bail and failing so to do. On the Motion of the Plaintiff by his Attorney aforesaid the Defendant is continued in Custody of the said Sergeant until he shall have satisfied this judgement and the costs.

JOHN COLVILLE against ANN BREITHWAIT. The suit is Dismissed at the Defendants Costs.

PHILIP CARBERY Plaintiff against STEWART HOLT Defendant. In Case. This day came the Plaintiff by WILLIAM RASCOW WILSON CURLE Gentleman his Attorney and the Defendant being called and not appearing a conditional order is granted the Plaintiff against the said Defendant and DOUGLASS WILLET his bail.

GIBSON GRANBERY & Company against ROGER PIERCE by attachment. Dismissed.

This Court is adjourned until tomorrow 10 o'clock, PAUL LOYALL MAYOR, TESTE: JOHN BOUSH D.C.

NORFOLK BOROUGH
At a Hustings Court Held this 22nd day of December 1772
PRESENT: PAUL LOYALL ESQUIRE MAYOR
GENTLEMAN ALDERMEN: GEORGE ABYVON, CHARLES THOMAS, LEWIS HANSFORD, CORNELIUS CALVERT,

On the Attachment obtained by DANIEL HUTCHINGS against the Estate of ROGER PIERCE who has privately removed or so absconds that the ordinary process cannot be served on him and the Sergeant now making return that by virtue thereof he has attached a Negro girl called MULLER, a hogshead of rum and a servant man, and also in the hands SAMUEL PORTLOCK, SARAH MASSENBURG, ELIZABETH STEEL and ELIZABETH BRICKLE and the Defendant being solemnly called and not appearing nor replevying his said estate. Where upon the Plaintiff proved his demand of 8 pounds 12 shillings by his own oath.

PAGE 161

Therefore, it is considered that the Plaintiff recover the same against the said Defendant together with his costs by him in this behalf expended. And it is ordered that the Sergeant sell the attached effects to wit: the hogshead of rum and apply the money arising thereby in discharge of this judgement and the costs and that he return an account of his proceedings to the next court and discontinued against the garnishes and other attached effects.

ROBERT GILMOUR administrator of the estate of WILLIAM GRAY deceased Plaintiff against JOHN RICHARDSON Defendant in case. The Plaintiff not further prosecuting. On the motion of the Defendant by his Attorney it is ordered that the suit be dismissed, and that the Plaintiff pay to the Defendant his costs.

Order is granted ROBERT STEEL against JOHN RICHARDSON for 100 pounds of tobacco for 4 days attendance in the suit of ROBERT GILMOUR admin of the Estate of WILLIAM GRAY deceased against him.

Order is granted JAMES CARMICHAEL against JOHN RICHARDSON for 100 pounds of tobacco for 4 days attendance in the suit of ROBERT GILMOUR admin of the Estate of WILLIAM GRAY deceased against him.

JAMES BALFOUR and DANIEL BARRAUD Plaintiff
Against Re: In Case
JOHN HEATON Defendant
This day came the Plaintiff by BENJAMIN CROOKER Gentleman their Attorney and there upon came also a Jury to wit: BARTHOLOMEW THOMPSON, GEORGE RAE, JOHN HARRIS, JAMES HALDANE, STEPHEN WRIGHT, SCARBROUGH TANKARD, JOHN BALLENTINE, WRIGHT WESTCOTT, GEORGE GORDON, JAMES BALLENTINE, JACOB BISHOP and JAMES MURPHREE who being sworn well and truly to inquiry of damages in this suit upon their oath do day that the Plaintiff have sustained damages by occasion of the Defendants Breach of Promise in the declaration mentioned to 24 pounds besides their costs. Therefore, it is considered by the Court that the Plaintiffs recover against the said Defendant and JOHN SMITH his bail their damages aforesaid in form aforesaid assessed and their costs by them in this behalf expended. And the said Defendants in mercy.

HENRY BRESSIE against ROGER PIERCE. Dismissed.
JAMES MARSDEN against ROGER PIERCE. Dismissed.
JOSEPH NORTHRUP against ABRAHAM PATEON. In Case. Dismissed at the Defendants costs.

PAGE 161B

JOSEPH NORTHRUP against ABRAHAM PATEON. In Trespass. Dismissed at the Defendants costs.

JOHN HARRIS Plaintiff
Against Re: In case on a note of hand
GEORGE NELSON and ARCHIBALD CAMPBELL admin of JOHN WILSON Deceased Defendant
This day came the parties by their Attorney's and the Defendants by their Attorney relinquishing their former plea say that they cannot gainsay the Plaintiffs action nor but that their intestate did assume in manner and form as the Plaintiff against them have declared. Therefore, it is considered that the Plaintiff recover against the said Defendant 13 pounds 3 shillings and 5 pence and his costs by him in this behalf expended when assets after paying proceeding judgements debts of greater dignity and the Defendants owns claims of equal dignity against the estate of the said intestate, to be levied of the goods and chattels which were of the said JOHN at the time of his death that shall hereafter come to the hands of the said GEORGE and ARCHIBALD to be administered and the said Defendants in mercy.

WRIGHT WESTCOTT Plaintiff
Against Re: In Trespass
THOMAS RASCOE Defendant
This day came the parties by their attorney's and there upon came also a Jury to wit: ROBERT STEEL, JOSHUA WILLIAMSON, EDWARD PARKE, SAMUEL CALVERT, THOMAS HEPBURN, JOHN CRAMOND, JAMES LEITCH, JOHN STANHOPE, WILLIAM GODFREY, SAMUEL BLEWS, WILLIAM CORBIT and ROBERT BARON who being elected tried and sworn the truth to speak upon the issue joined upon their oath do say that the Defendant is not guilty of the trespass in the declaration mentioned in manner and form as the Plaintiff against him has declared. Therefore, it is considered that the Plaintiff take nothing by this bill but for his false claims to be in mercy. And the said Defendant go hence without day and recover against the Plaintiff his costs by him about his Defendant in this behalf expended.

WILLIAM GODFREY Plaintiff
Against Re: In Trespass, Assault, Battery
THOMAS BREWREY Defendant
This day came the parties by their Attorney's and there upon came also a Jury to wit: BARTHOLMEW THOMPSON,

PAGE 162

GEORGE RAE, JOHN HARRIS, JAMES HALDANE, SCARBROUGH TANKARD, JOHN BALLENTINE, WRIGHT WESTCOTT, GEORGE GORDON, JAMES BALLENTINE, JACOB BISHOP, JAMES MURPHREE and WILLIAM STEVENSON who being elected tried and sworn the truth to speak upon the issue joined upon their oath do say that the Defendant is guilty of the Trespass and Battery in the declaration mentioned in manner and form as the Plaintiff against him has declared and do assess the Plaintiff damages by the occasion there of to 8 pounds besides his costs. Therefore, it is considered that the Plaintiff recover against the said Defendant his damages aforesaid in form aforesaid assessed and his costs by him in his suit in this behalf expended and the said Defendant may be taken.

WILLIAM GODFREY Plaintiff
Against Re: In Trespass, Assault and Battery
WILLIAM SMITH Defendant
This day came the parties by their Attorney's and there upon came also a Jury to wit: BARTHOLMEW THOMPSON, GEORGE RAE, JOHN HARRIS, JAMES HALDANE, SCARBROUGH TANKARD, JOHN BALLENTINE, WRIGHT WESTCOTT, GEORGE GORDON, JAMES BALLENTINE, JACOB BISHOP, JAMES MURPHREE and WILLIAM STEVENSON who being elected tried and sworn the truth to speak upon the issue joined upon their oath do say that the Defendant is guilty of the Trespass, assault and Battery in the declaration mentioned in manner and form as the Plaintiff against him has declared and do assess the Plaintiff damages by the occasion there of to 2 pounds besides his costs. Therefore, it is considered that the Plaintiff recover against the said Defendant his damages aforesaid in form aforesaid assessed and his costs by him in his suit in this behalf expended and the said Defendant may be taken.

JACOB ALLAN assignee of JOHN GREENWOOD who was assignee of WILLIAM ASBURN Plaintiff against JOSHUA WRIGHT Defendant in Debt. This day came the Plaintiff by BENJAMIN CROOKER Gentleman his Attorney and the Defendant being called and not appearing. A conditional order is granted the Plaintiff against the defendant.

Order is granted GEORGE MELONY against WRIGHT WESTCOTT for 75 pounds tobacco for 3 days attendance at the Court in this suit against THOMAS RASCOE.

Order is granted BENJAMIN HAYNE against WRIGHT WESTCOTT for 75 pounds tobacco for 3 days attendance at the Court in this suit against THOMAS RASCOE.

PAGE 162B
Order is granted JOHN CULPEPER against WRIGHT WESTCOTT for 75 pounds tobacco for 3 days attendance at the Court in this suit against THOMAS RASCOE.

Order is granted ENOS EASTWOOD against WRIGHT WESTCOTT for 75 pounds tobacco for 3 days attendance at the Court in this suit against THOMAS RASCOE.

Order is granted JUDITH EASTWOOD against WRIGHT WESTCOTT for 75 pounds tobacco for 3 days attendance at the Court in this suit against THOMAS RASCOE.

Order is granted STEPHEN WRIGHT against WRIGHT WESTCOTT for 75 pounds tobacco for 3 days attendance at the Court in this suit against THOMAS RASCOE.

Order is granted WILLIAM BOOKER against THOMAS RASCOE for 75 pounds tobacco for 3 days attendance at the Court in the suit of WRIGHT WESTCOTT against him.

JOHN CRAMOND Plaintiff
Against Re: In Case
JOHN PARSONS Defendant
This day came the parties by their Attorney's and there upon came also a Jury to wit: ROBERT STEEL, JOSHUA WILLIAMSON, THOMAS DREWREY, EDWARD PARKE, SAMUEL BACON, THOMAS HEPBURN, JAMES LEITCH, JOHN STANHOPE, SAMUEL BLEWS, WILLIAM CORBIT, JAMES CARMICHAEL, and ROBERT BARON, who being elected tried and sworn the truth to speak upon the issue joined upon their oath do say that the Defendant did assume in manner and form as the Plaintiff against him has declared and do assess the Plaintiff Damages by Occasion of the non-performance of that assumption to 10 pounds besides his costs. Therefore, it is considered that the Plaintiff recover against the said Defendant his damages aforesaid in form aforesaid assessed and his costs by him in this behalf expended and the said Defendant in mercy.

Order is granted JOHN RAMSAY against WILLIAM GODFREY for 50 pounds of tobacco for 2 days attendance at this Court in his suit against THOMAS DREWREY.

Order is granted RICHARD COLLINS against WILLIAM GODFREY for 50 pounds of tobacco for 2 days attendance at this Court in his suit against THOMAS DREWREY.

PAGE 163
Order is granted BALTIS ECHERD against WILLIAM GODFREY for 50 pounds of tobacco for 2 days attendance at this Court in his suit against THOMAS DREWREY.

Order is granted JOHN CARTER against WILLIAM GODFREY for 50 pounds of tobacco for 2 days attendance at this Court in his suit against THOMAS DREWREY.

Order is granted THOMAS BRITON against WILLIAM GODFREY for 50 pounds of tobacco for 2 days attendance at this Court in his suit against THOMAS DREWREY.

Order is granted HENRY PALMER against WILLIAM GODFREY for 50 pounds of tobacco for 2 days attendance at this Court in his suit against THOMAS DREWREY.

Order is granted ELIZABETH BUCKLER against THOMAS DREWREY for 50 pounds of tobacco for 2 days attendance at this Court in the suit of WILLIAM GODFREY against him.

Order is granted JAMES BALLARD against THOMAS DREWREY for 50 pounds of tobacco for 2 days attendance at this Court in the suit of WILLIAM GODFREY against him.

Order is granted ANTHONY PAYNE against THOMAS DREWREY for 50 pounds of tobacco for 2 days attendance at this Court in the suit of WILLIAM GODFREY against him.

Order is granted JOHN RAMSAY against WILLIAM GODFREY for 50 pounds of tobacco for 2 days attendance at this Court in the suit against WILLIAM SMITH.

Order is granted RICHARD COLLINS against WILLIAM GODFREY for 50 pounds of tobacco for 2 days attendance at this Court in the suit against WILLIAM SMITH.

Order is granted BALTIS ECHORD against WILLIAM GODFREY for 50 pounds of tobacco for 2 days attendance at this Court in the suit against WILLIAM SMITH.

Order is granted JOHN CARTER against WILLIAM GODFREY for 50 pounds of tobacco for 2 days attendance at this Court in the suit against WILLIAM SMITH.

PAGE 163B
Order is granted THOMAS BRITON against WILLIAM GODFREY for 50 pounds of tobacco for 2 days attendance at this Court in the suit against WILLIAM SMITH.

Order is granted HENRY PALMER against WILLIAM GODFREY for 50 pounds of tobacco for 2 days attendance at this Court in the suit against WILLIAM SMITH.

Order is granted ELIZABETH BUCKLER against WILLIAM SMITH for 50 pounds of tobacco for 2 days attendance at this Court in the suit of WILLIAM GODFREY against him.

Order is granted JAMES BALLARD against WILLIAM SMITH for 50 pounds of tobacco for 2 days attendance at this Court in the suit of WILLIAM GODFREY against him.

Order is granted ANTHONY PANE against WILLIAM SMITH for 50 pounds of tobacco for 2 days attendance at this Court in the suit of WILLIAM GODFREY against him.

Order is granted TULLY ROBINSON against JOHN CRAMOND for 165 pounds of tobacco for 3 days attendance at this Court coming and returning 10 miles 3 times in his suit against JOHN PARSONS.

Order is granted CHRISTOPHER WHITEHURST against JOHN CRAMOND for 256 pounds of tobacco for 4 days attendance at this Court coming and returning 13 miles 4 times in his suit against JOHN PARSONS.

Order is granted SAMUEL GWIN against JOHN CRAMOND for 100 pounds of tobacco for 4 days attendance at this Court in his suit against JOHN PARSONS.

Order is granted JOHN EVANS against JOHN PARSONS for 220 pounds of tobacco for 4 days attendance at this Court coming and returning 10 miles 4 times in this suit of JOHN CRAMOND against him.
PAGE 164
JAMES CARMICHAEL Plaintiff
Against Re: In Case
JOHN GARRICK and ELIZABETH, his wife Defendants
This day came the parties by their Attorney's and there upon came also a Jury to wit: WILLIAM WALKER, WILLIAM STEVENSON, JOHN BALLENTINE, WRIGHT WESTCOTT, JOHN HARRIS, SCARBROUGH TANKARD, JACOB BISHOP, JAMES BALLENTINE, GEORGE GORDON, JAMES MURPHREE, GEORGE RAE, and WILLIAM LIDDLE who being elected tried and sworn the truth to speak upon the issue joined upon their oath do say that the Defendants did not assume as in pleading they have alleged. Therefore, it is considered that the Plaintiff take nothing by this bill but for his false claims be in mercy. And the Defendants go hence without day and recover against the Plaintiff their costs by them about their Defense in this Behalf Expended.

LOGAN GILMOUR and Company Plaintiffs
Against Re: In Case
JOHN GARRICK and ELIZABETH, his wife Defendants
This day came the parties by their Attorney's and the Defendants in Custody by their Attorney say that they cannot gainsay the Plaintiffs action nor but that they did assume in manner and form as the Plaintiff against him have declared. Therefore, it is considered that the Plaintiff recover against the said Defendant 33 pounds 2 shillings and 8 pence and their costs by them in this behalf expended and the Defendants in mercy. And the Plaintiffs by their Attorney did not pray a COMMITTITUR of the Defendants.

Order is granted JAMES DAVIS, JAMES HALDANE, ROBERT STEEL and ANTHONY FLEMING against JOHN GARRICK and ELIZABETH his wife for 25 pounds of tobacco each for 1 day's attendance each in the suit of JAMES CARMICHAEL against them.

This Court this day rated flour at 16/8 per centum

This Court is adjourned to Court in Course, PAUL LOYALL MAYOR, TESTE: JOHN BOUSH D.C.

PAGE 164B

NORFOLK BOROUGH

At a Hustings Court Held this 25th day of January 1773

PRESENT: PAUL LOYALL ESQUIRE MAYOR

GENTLEMAN ALDERMEN: GEORGE ABYVON, MAXIMILIAN CALVERT, ARCHIBALD CAMPBELL, JAMES TAYLOR, LEWIS HANSFORD, WILLIAM AITCHESON

WILLIAM RASCOW WILSON CURLE Plaintiff

Against Re: In Case

JAMES MARSDEN, and JONATHAN EILBECK executors of ELDRED FISHER deceased defendants

This day came as well the Plaintiff in his proper person and the Defendant by their Attorney's, and the said Defendants say that they cannot gainsay the Plaintiffs action nor but that their testator did assume in manner and form as the Plaintiff against them have declared. Therefore, it is considered that the Plaintiff recover against the said Defendants 6 pounds 2 shillings and 6 pence half penny and his costs by him about his suit in this behalf expended when assets after paying debts of greater dignity and the defendants own claims of equal dignity against the estate of the said testator, to be levied of the goods and chattels which were of the said ELDRED at the time of his death that shall hereafter come to the hands of the said JAMES and JONATHAN to be administered and the said Defendants in mercy.

MISTERS JOHN RAMSAY and JAMES TAYLOR Plaintiffs against JAMES MARSDEN and JONATHAN EILBECK executors of ELDRED FISHER deceased Defendants. In Case. This day came the parties by their Attorney's and the Defendants pray and have leave to IMPARLE here until the next Court and then to plead.

WILLIAM and THOMAS FARRER Plaintiffs against JAMES MARSDEN and JONATHAN EILBECK executors of ELDRED FISHER deceased Defendants. In Case. This day came the parties by their Attorney's and the Defendants pray and have leave to IMPARLE here until the next Court and then to plead.

JOHN SHEPHERD Plaintiffs against JAMES MARSDEN and JONATHAN EILBECK executors of ELDRED FISHER deceased Defendants. In Case. This day came the parties by their Attorney's and the Defendants pray and have leave to IMPARLE here until the next Court and then to plead.

GEORGE WILSON and ARCHIBALD CAMPBELL administrators of JOHN WILSON Deceased Plaintiffs against JAMES MARSDEN and

PAGE 165

JONATHAN EILBECK executors of ELDRED FISHER deceased Defendants. In Case. This day came the parties by their Attorney's and the Defendants pray and have leave to IMPARLE here until the next Court and then to plead.

JAMES HALDANE Plaintiffs against JAMES MARSDEN and JONATHAN EILBECK executors of ELDRED FISHER deceased Defendants. In Case. This day came the parties by their Attorney's and the Defendants pray and have leave to IMPARLE here until the next Court and then to plead.

Misters LOGAN GILMOUR and Company Plaintiffs against ARCHIBALD BUCHANAN Defendant. This day came the Plaintiffs by their Attorney and the Defendant being called and not appearing. A conditional order is granted the Plaintiff against the said Defendants and JAMES INGRAM his bail.

BARNABY CARNEY against JOSEPH CULPEPER. The Plaintiff not further prosecuting his suit the same is dismissed.

JOHN RICHARDSON against WILLIAM HERBERT Defendant. In Trespass. This day came the parties by their Attorney's and the Defendants pray and have leave to IMPARLE here until the next Court and then to plead.

CHRISTOPHER WRIGHT Plaintiff against WILLIAM WISHART Defendant. In Case. This day came the parties by their Attorney's and the Defendants pray and have leave to IMPARLE here until the next Court and then to plead.

ANN BREITHWAIT against JOHN COLVILLE. Dismissed at the Plaintiff's costs.

ANN BREITHWAIT against JOHN COLVILLE. by Petition and summons. Judgement is granted the Plaintiff for 4 pounds 7 shilling and 8 pence. It is ordered that the Defendant pay the same unto the Plaintiff with costs and fee.

JOHN GARRICK Plaintiff against JAMES CARMICHAEL Defendant. In Trespass, Assault & Battery, and false imprisonment. This day came the parties by their Attorney's and the Defendants pray and have leave to IMPARLE here until the next Court and then to plead.

ROBERT HATTON against SOLOMON EDY. Dismissed at the Defendants costs.

EDWARD DAVIS Plaintiff against WILLIAM COCKIN Defendant. The Plaintiff not further prosecuting his suit and the same is Dismissed.

<u>PAGE 165B</u>

WILLS COWPER Plaintiff against WRIGHT WESTCOTT Defendant. In Debt. JOSEPH CALVERT undertakes for the Defendant that in case he shall be casts in this suit he the said Defendant will pay the condemnation of the Court or render his body to Prison in execution for the same or that the said CALVERT will pay the condemnation or render the body of the said Defendant as aforesaid. Where upon the Defendant by his Attorney prayed and have leave to IMPARLE here the next Court and then to Plead.

JOHN GREENWOOD against SAMUEL WILLIAMS. The Plaintiff not further prosecuting his suit. The same is Dismissed.

STEPHEN TANKARD, ROBERT STEED and MARY POOLE executors of NICHOLAS POOL deceased Plaintiffs against JAMES HALDANE Defendant in debt. JAMES LEITCH this day came into Court and undertook for the Defendant that in case he shall be casts in this suit he the said Defendant will pay the condemnation of the Court or render his body to Prison in execution for the same or that the said LEITCH will pay the condemnation or render the body of the said Defendant as aforesaid. Where upon the Defendant by his Attorney prayed and have leave to IMPARLE here the next Court and then to Plead.

SAMUEL HOSIER Plaintiff against JOHN HARDY Defendant. In T.A.B. This day came the parties by their Attorney's and the Defendant prays and have leave to IMPARLE here until the next Court and then to plead.

ALEXANDER KIDD and AMOS WICKERSHAM admin of JOHN KIDD Deceased Plaintiffs against THOMAS WALKER, JOHN VALLENCIER and STEPHEN TANKARD Defendants. In Debt. CHRISTOPHER CALVERT this day came into Court and undertook for the Defendants that in case they shall be casts in this suit that the said Defendants will pay the condemnation of the Court or render their bodies to Prison in execution for the same or that the said CALVERT will pay the condemnation or render the bodies of the said Defendants as aforesaid. Where upon the Defendants by their Attorney prayed and have leave to IMPARLE here the next Court and then to Plead.

JOHN COLINS Plaintiff against MARTIN MURPHREY Defendant. In T.A.B. This day came the Plaintiff by WILLIAM DAVIS Gentleman his Attorney and the defendant being called and not appearing. A conditional order is granted the Plaintiff against the said Defendant and JAMES ARCHDEACON his bail and a DEDIMUS is granted to take depositions on both sides.

JOHN EDWARDS against JAMES KNIGHT the Plaintiff not further prosecuting his suit the same is dismissed.

<u>PAGE 166</u>

JAMES WILLS and COUPLAND WHITFIELD assignee of JOHN HARWOOD Plaintiff

Against Re: In Debt

DANIEL PECK Defendant

This day came as well the Plaintiffs by BENJAMIN CROOKER Gentleman their Attorney's and the Defendant in his proper person and acknowledges the Plaintiffs action for 20 pounds. Therefore, it is considered that the Plaintiff recover against he said Defendant their debt aforesaid and their cost by them in this behalf expended. And the said Defendant in mercy. But this judgement is to be discharged by the payment of 10 pounds with interest thereon after the rate of 5% per annum to be computed from July 30th, 1772, to the time of payment and the costs

SCARBROUGH TANKARD Plaintiff

Against Re: In Debt.

THOMAS WARD Defendant

This day came as well the Plaintiff in his proper person as the Defendant by his Attorney and acknowledges the Plaintiffs action for 15 pounds 1 shilling and 7 pence half penny with interest thereon at the rate of 5% per annum to be computed from August 21, 1772, to the time of payment. Therefore, it is considered that the Plaintiff recover against the said Defendant his debt aforesaid together with his costs by him about his suit in this behalf expended. And the said defendant in mercy.

JOHN EDWARDS Plaintiff against JOHN KNIGHT Defendant. In Case. This day came the Plaintiff by WALTER LYON Gentleman his Attorney and the Defendant being called and not appearing. A conditional order is granted the Plaintiff against the said Defendant and HECTOR MCALLISTER his bail.

WILLIAM WAGER Plaintiff against JOHN RANSBERG Defendant. In Case. This day came the parties by their Attorney's and the Defendants prays and have leave to IMPARLE here the next Court and then to Plead.

ROBERT GILMOUR admin of WILLIAM GRAY Plaintiff against JOHN GARRICK Defendant. In Case.
JOSEPH CALVERT undertakes for the Defendant that in case he shall be casts in this suit he the said Defendant will pay the condemnation of the Court or render his body to Prison in execution for the same or that the said CALVERT will pay the condemnation or render the body of the said Defendant as aforesaid. Where upon the Defendant by his Attorney prayed and have leave to IMPARLE here the next Court and then to Plead.

<u>PAGE 166B</u>

On the motion of the Plaintiff by his Attorney a DEDIMUS is granted him to take the depositions of WILLIAM BUDDIN giving the Defendant reasonable notice of the time and place.

JOHNSTON and BURGESS and Company against WILLIAM WALKER by Petition and summons. Judgement is granted the Plaintiff for 1 pounds 9 shilling and 9 pence. It is ordered that the Defendant pay the same unto the Plaintiff with costs and fee.

WILLIAM WALKER against THOMAS MORRIS. Dismissed.

WILLIAM WALKER against HENRY WELLS by Petition and summons. Judgement is granted the Plaintiff for 1 pounds 11 shilling and 6 pence. It is ordered that the Defendant pay the same unto the Plaintiff with costs and fee.

WILLIAM WALKER against WILLIAM IVY by Petition and summons. Judgement is granted the Plaintiff for 1 pounds 14 shilling and 6 pence. It is ordered that the Defendant pay the same unto the Plaintiff with costs and fee.

HENRY FLEMING and Company against ALEXANDER BELL. Dismissed.

JOSEPH CALVERT Plaintiff against THOMAS DICKERSON Defendant. In Case. This day came the parties by their Attorney's and the Defendants prays and have leave to IMPARLE here the next Court and then to Plead.

JOHN EDWARDS against CHARLES COOPER by Petition and summons. Judgement is granted the Plaintiff for 1 pounds 19 shilling and 11 pence half penny. It is ordered that the Defendant pay the same unto the Plaintiff with costs and fee.

ALEXANDER KEITH against WILLIAM LIDDLE. In Case. JAMES LEITCH this day came into Court and undertook for the Defendant that in case he shall be casts in this suit he the said Defendant will pay the condemnation of the Court or render his body to Prison in execution for the same or that the said LEITCH will pay the condemnation or render the body of the said Defendant as aforesaid. Where upon the Defendant by his Attorney prays and have leave to IMPARLE here the next Court and then to Plead.

PAGE 167
JAMES HALDANE Plaintiff against JOHN BRUCE Defendant. In Case. This day the parties came by their Attorney's and the Defendant says he did not assume upon himself in manner and form as the Plaintiff against him has declared and of this he puts himself upon the Country and the Plaintiff likewise. Therefore, the trail of the issue is referred until the next Court. And on the motion of the Defendant by his Attorney a DEDIMUS is granted to take the depositions of ROBERT HUTCH giving the Plaintiff reasonable notice of time and place.

WILLIAM FITCHBOURNE Plaintiff against THOMAS WALKER, ROBERT BARRON* and HENRY BRESSIE. In Debt. JOHN WILSON Gentlemen, this day came into Court and undertook for the Defendants BARON* and BRESSIE and CHARLES COOPER, Bricklayer for WALKER that in case they shall be casts in this suit they the said Defendants will pay the condemnation of the Court or render their bodies to Prison in execution for the same or that the said WILSON and COOPER will pay the condemnation or render the bodies of the said Defendants as aforesaid. Where upon the Defendants by his Attorney prayed an imparlance.

ALEXANDER MARTIN Plaintiff against JOHN MEARNS Defendant. In Case. This day came the parties by their Attorney's and the Defendants prays and have leave to IMPARLE here the next Court and then to Plead.

PHILIP CARBERY Plaintiff against JOHN SCOTT Defendant. In Case. The Defendant being called and not appearing. On the motion of the Plaintiff by his Attorney an Attachment is awarded him against the estate of the said Defendant for 12 pounds and costs returnable here the next Court.

JOHN HAMILTON and Company Plaintiffs against JOHN MCLACHLAN Defendant. In Case. WRIGHT WESTCOTT and WILLIAM SIMPSON this day came into Court and undertook for the Defendant that in case he shall be casts in this suit he the said Defendant will pay the condemnation of the Court or render his body to Prison in execution for the same or that the said WESTCOTT and SIMPSON will pay the condemnation or render the body of the said Defendant as aforesaid. Where upon the Defendant by his Attorney prays and have leave to IMPARLE here the next Court and then to Plead.

JOHN MCNEIL against THOMAS STEWART. The Plaintiff not further prosecuting his suit the same is dismissed.

ROBERT SHEDDEN and Company Plaintiffs against ABRAM GIBSON Defendant in Case. GEORGE COLLINS this day came into Court and undertook for the Defendant that in case he shall be casts in this suit he the said Defendant will pay the condemnation of the Court or render his body to Prison in execution for the same or that the said COLLINS will pay the condemnation or render the body of the said Defendant as aforesaid. Where upon the Defendant by his Attorney prays and have leave to IMPARLE here the next Court and then to Plead.

PAGE 167B
JAMES MAXWELL against ALEXANDER BELL. The Plaintiff not further prosecuting his suit the same is dismissed.
TULLY ROBINSON and JOHN CRAMOND against JONATHAN MEREDITH discontinued.

JACOB ALLAN assignee of JOHN GREENWOOD who was assignee of WILLIAM ASHBURN* Plaintiff against JOSHUA WRIGHT Defendant. In Debt. The Defendant being called and not appearing on the motion of the Plaintiff by his Attorney an Attachment is awarded him against the Estate of the said Defendant for 50 pounds Sterling and costs returnable here the next Court.

THOMAS DICKERSON was this day brought before the Court by warrant for being a person of lewd life and conversation and the same being proved. It is ordered that the Sergeant take and keep him in Custody until he gives bond with security to wit himself in 50 pounds and 2 securities in 25 pounds each for the said DICKERSON being of good behavior for 12 months and pay costs.

MISTERS GILSON, GRANBERY and Company Plaintiffs against WILLIAM ROUNDTREE Defendant. In Case. The Plaintiff not further prosecuting. On the motion of the Defendant, it is ordered that the suit be dismissed and that the Plaintiffs pay to the Defendant his costs.

JAMES CARMICHAEL Plaintiff against JOHN GARRICK in Trespass. On the motion of the Plaintiff by his Attorney a DEDIMUS is granted him to take the deposition of WILLIAM BUDDIN and JOHN POWELL giving the Defendant reasonable notice of the time and place.

JAMES CARMICHAEL Plaintiff against HARDRESS WALLER Defendant. In Trespass. On the motion of the Plaintiff by his Attorney a DEDIMUS is granted him to take the deposition of WILLIAM BUDDIN and JOHN POWELL giving the Defendant reasonable notice of the time and place.

JAMES CAMPBELL and Company Plaintiff against JAMES MARSDEN and JONATHAN EILBECK executors of ELDRED FISHER deceased Defendants in Debt. This day came the parties by their Attorney's and the Defendants prays and has leave to IMPARLE here until the next Court and then to plead.

PAGE 168
JAMES CAMPBELL and Company Plaintiff against JAMES MARSDEN and JONATHAN EILBECK executors of ELDRED FISHER deceased Defendants. In Case. This day came the parties by their Attorney's and the Defendants prays and has leave to IMPARLE here until the next Court and then to plead.

GABRIEL MAUPIN Plaintiff against JAMES MARSDEN and JONATHAN EILBECK executors of ELDRED FISHER deceased Defendants in Debt. This day came the parties by their Attorney's and the Defendants prays and has leave to IMPARLE here until the next Court and then to plead.

WILLIAM BUTT Plaintiff against JAMES MARSDEN and JONATHAN EILBECK executors of ELDRED FISHER deceased Defendants in Debt. This day came the parties by their Attorney's and the Defendants prays and has leave to IMPARLE here until the next Court and then to plead.

STEPHEN TANKARD, ROBERT STEED and MARY POOL executors of NICHOLAS POOL Deceased Plaintiff against JAMES MARSDEN and JONATHAN EILBECK executors of ELDRED FISHER deceased Defendants in Debt. This day came the parties by their Attorney's and the Defendants pray and has leave to IMPARLE here until the next Court and then to plead.

ROBERT CARTWRIGHT Plaintiff against JAMES MARSDEN and JONATHAN EILBECK executors of ELDRED FISHER deceased Defendants in Case. This day came the parties by their Attorney's and the Defendants prays and has leave to IMPARLE here until the next Court and then to plead.

JOHN LAWRENCE and MATTHEW PHRIPP Executors of THOMAS THOMPSON deceased Plaintiffs against JAMES MARSDEN and JONATHAN EILBECK executors of ELDRED FISHER deceased Defendants. In Case. This day came the parties by their Attorney's and the Defendants prays and has leave to IMPARLE here until the next Court and then to plead.

JOHN FISHER Plaintiff against JAMES MARSDEN and JONATHAN EILBECK executors of ELDRED FISHER deceased Defendants. In Case. This day came the parties by their Attorney's and the Defendants prays and has leave to IMPARLE here until the next Court and then to plead.

PAGE 168B
EDWARD STABLER Plaintiff
Against Re: In Debt.
JAMES MARSDEN and JONATHAN EILBECK executors of ELDRED FISHER deceased Defendants
This day came the parties by their Attorney's and the Defendants by their Attorney acknowledges the Plaintiff actions for 219 pounds 11 shillings. Therefore, it is considered that the Plaintiff recover against the said Defendants his debt aforesaid and his costs by him about his suit in this behalf expended. When assets after paying debts of superior dignity and the Defendants own claims of equal dignity against the estate of the said testator, to be levied of the goods and chattels which were of the said ELDRED at the time of his death that shall hereafter come to the hands of the said JAMES and JONATHAN to be administered and the said Defendants in mercy. But this judgement is to be discharged by the Payment of 109 pounds 15 shillings and 6 pence with interest thereon after the rate of 5% per annum to be computed from May 10, 1772, to the time of payment and the costs.

JOHN SHEDDEN Plaintiff against JAMES MARSDEN and JONATHAN EILBECK executors of ELDRED FISHER deceased Defendants. In Case. This day came the parties by their Attorney's and the Defendants prays and has leave to IMPARLE here until the next Court and then to plead.

THOMAS NEILSON against REUBEN SHARP E by Complaint. Dismissed at Defendants Costs.
JAMES MOORE against JONATHAN HOPKINS on a motion continued.
The King against JAMES BELL by warrant dismissed at the Defendants Costs.

This Court is adjourned to Court in Course, PAUL LOYALL MAYOR, TESTE: JOHN BOUSH D.C.

PAGE 169
NORFOLK BOROUGH
At a Hustings Court Held this 22nd day of March 1773
PRESENT: PAUL LOYALL ESQUIRE MAYOR
GENTLEMAN ALDERMEN: GEORGE ABYVON, CHARLES THOMAS, ARCHIBALD CAMPBELL, CORNELIUS CALVERT, LEWIS HANSFORD,

This Court is adjourned until tomorrow at 9 o'clock, PAUL LOYALL MAYOR, TESTE: JOHN BOUSH D.C.

NORFOLK BOROUGH
At a Hustings Court Held this 23rd day of March 1773
PRESENT: PAUL LOYALL ESQUIRE MAYOR
GENTLEMAN ALDERMEN: GEORGE ABYVON, CHARLES THOMAS, ARCHIBALD CAMPBELL, JAMES TAYLOR, LEWIS HANSFORD, CORNELIUS CALVERT

JOHN PLUMMER Plaintiff against JAMES MARSDEN and JONATHAN EILBECK executors of ELDRED FISHER deceased Defendants. In Case. This day came the parties by their Attorney's and the Defendants prays and has leave to IMPARLE here until the next Court and then to plead.

FREDERICK BOUSH against JAMES MOORE. In Chancery. Time to consider the bill.

AARON WHITEHURST against SAMUEL CALVERT. In Detinue. This day came the parties by their Attorney's and the Defendants prays and has leave to IMPARLE here until the next Court and then to plead.

BARNABY CARNEY against JAMES MARSDEN and JONATHAN EILBECK executors of ELDRED FISHER deceased Defendants. In Case. This day came the parties by their Attorney's and the Defendants prays and has leave to IMPARLE here until the next Court and then to plead.

JOHN SHEDDEN and Company against MAXIMILIAN CALVERT. Dismissed.

PAGE 169B

MISTERS MCKEAND and BUCHANAN against ROBERT TUCKER. In Case. JOSEPH CALVERT this day came into Court and undertook for the Defendant that in case he shall be casts in this suit he the said Defendant will pay the condemnation of the Court or render his body to Prison in execution for the same or that the said CALVERT will pay the condemnation or render the body of the said Defendant as aforesaid. Where upon the Defendant by his Attorney prays and have leave to IMPARLE here the next Court and then to Plead.

ARCHIBALD GOVAN against THOMAS CLAIBORNE. In Case. BENJAMIN CROOKER here in Court undertakes for the Defendant that in case he shall be cast in this suit he the said Defendant will pay the condemnation of the Court or render his body to Prison in execution for the same or that the said CROOKER will pay the condemnation or render the body of the said Defendant as aforesaid. Where upon the Defendant says that he did not assume upon himself in manner and form as the Plaintiff against him has declared and of this he puts himself upon the Country and the Plaintiff likewise. Therefore, the trial of the issue is referred until the next Court.

MISTERS GEORGE and JOHN BOWNESS against JAMES MARSDEN and JONATHAN EILBECK executors of ELDRED FISHER deceased Defendants. In Case. This day came the parties by their Attorney's and the Defendants prays and has leave to IMPARLE here until the next Court and then to plead.

FREDERICK AUGUSTUS DOEBER against RICHARD TALBOT. In Debt. JOSEPH CALVERT this day came into Court and undertook for the Defendant that in case he shall be casts in this suit he the said Defendant will pay the condemnation of the Court or render his body to Prison in execution for the same or that the said CALVERT will pay the condemnation or render the body of the said Defendant as aforesaid. Where upon the Defendant by his Attorney prays and have leave to IMPARLE here the next Court and then to Plead.

JAMES LEITCH against CHARLES MILLER. Dismissed at the Plaintiff's costs.

THOMAS RASCOE against WRIGHT WESTCOTT. This day came the parties by their Attorney's and the Defendants prays and has leave to IMPARLE here until the next Court and then to plead.

PHILIP CARBERY against JOHN WILLIAMS. In Case. This day came the parties by their Attorney's and the Defendants prays and has leave to IMPARLE here until the next Court and then to plead.

PAGE 170

JAMES CRAMBIE against JAMES WALKER surviving partner of WALKER and MCROB. In Case. This day came the parties by their Attorney's and the Defendant says that he did not assume upon himself in manner and form as the Plaintiff against him has declared and of this he puts himself upon the Country and the Plaintiff likewise. Therefore, the trial of the issue is referred until the next Court.

JOHN FLAHERTY against CHARLES HILL. In Debt. The Defendant being called and not appearing. On the motion of the Plaintiff by his Attorney an Attachment is awarded him against the estate of the said Defendant for 27 pounds and costs returnable here the next Court.

JOHN CRAMOND against HARDRESS WALLER. In Case. This day came the parties by their Attorney's and the Defendant prays and has leave to IMPARLE here until the next Court and then to plead.

CHRISTOPHER CALVERT against PAUL LOYALL. In Debt. This day came the Plaintiff by BENJAMIN CROOKER Gentleman his Attorney and the Defendant being called and not appearing. A conditional order is granted the Plaintiff against the said Defendant and JOSEPH CALVERT his bail.

PHILIP CARBERY against JOHN SCOTT. In Case. WILLIAM WEBLY this day came into Court and undertook for the Defendant that in case he shall be casts in this suit he the said Defendant will pay the condemnation of the Court or render his body to Prison in execution for the same or that the said WEBLY will pay the condemnation or render the body of the said Defendant as aforesaid. Where upon the Defendant by his Attorney prays and have leave to IMPARLE here the next Court and then to Plead.

STEPHEN TANKARD Plaintiff against EDWARD BOOKER Defendant. In Case. WILLIAM BOOKER came into Court and undertook for the Defendant that in case he shall be casts in this suit he the said Defendant will pay the condemnation of the Court or render his body to Prison in execution for the same or that the said WILLIAM BOOKER will pay the condemnation or render the body of the said Defendant as aforesaid. Where upon the Defendant by his Attorney prays and have leave to IMPARLE here the next Court and then to Plead.

JOHN and WILLIS WILSON against CHARLES CASSON. Dismissed.

<u>PAGE 170B</u>

JACOB ALLAN Assignee of JOHN GREENWOOD who was assignee of WILLIAM ASBURN Plaintiff

Against Re: In Debt.

JOSHUA WRIGHT Defendant

This day came the Plaintiff by BENJAMIN CROOKER Gentleman his Attorney. And an Attachment having been awarded the Plaintiff against the estate of the said Defendant and the Sergeant now making return that by virtue thereof he has attached a tobacco box and the said Defendant being solemnly called and not appearing nor replevying his said effects whereby the said Plaintiff remains thereof against him undefended. Therefore, it is adjudged by the Court that the Plaintiff do recover against the said Defendant his debt amounting to 88 pounds 16 shillings and 8 pence sterling and his costs by him in this behalf expended and the said Defendant in mercy. And the Plaintiff by his Attorney Aforesaid releases the attached effects. But this Judgement is to be discharged by the payment of 44 pounds 8 shillings and 4 pence sterling with interest thereon after the rate of 5% per annum to be computed from June 19, 1772, to the time of payment and the Costs. And the Court says the sterling money may be discharged in current money at a 25% difference of exchange.

EDWARD JONES against JAMES HALDANE. In Case. JAMES LEITCH this day came into Court and undertook for the Defendant that in case he shall be casts in this suit he the said Defendant will pay the condemnation of the Court or render his body to Prison in execution for the same or that the said LEITCH will pay the condemnation or render the body of the said Defendant as aforesaid. Where upon the Defendant by his Attorney prays and have leave to IMPARLE here the next Court and then to Plead.

JAMES CAMPBELL and Company against JAMES MARSDEN and JAMES MAXWELL administrators of JAMES PATTERSON. In Case. This day came the parties by their Attorney's and the Defendant prays and has leave to IMPARLE here until the next Court and then to plead.

ALEXANDER SKINNER against JAMES MARSDEN and JAMES MAXWELL administrators of JAMES PATTERSON. In Case. This day came the parties by their Attorney's and the Defendant prays and has leave to IMPARLE here until the next Court and then to plead.

HUGH MCPHILIMY* against WILLIAM POOLE. Dismissed at the Plaintiff costs for want of security for the costs.

<u>PAGE 171</u>

THOMAS STEWART against JAMES MARSDEN and JAMES MAXWELL administrators of JAMES PATTERSON. In Case. This day came the parties by their Attorney's and the Defendant prays and has leave to IMPARLE here until the next Court and then to plead.

MISTERS RAMSAY and TAYLOR against JAMES MARSDEN and JAMES MAXWELL administrators of JAMES PATTERSON. In Case. This day came the parties by their Attorney's and the Defendant prays and has leave to IMPARLE here until the next Court and then to plead.

WILLIAM MILES against JAMES MARSDEN and JAMES MAXWELL administrators of JAMES PATTERSON. In Case. This day came the parties by their Attorney's and the Defendant prays and has leave to IMPARLE here until the next Court and then to plead.

JOSIAH COOKE against WILLIAM POOLE. Dismissed.

On the petition of ISAAC THOMPSON against JAMES MARSDEN and JAMES MAXWELL admin of JAMES PATTERSON deceased for 3 pounds 17 shillings. Due by account this day came the parties by their Attorney's and the Plaintiff having proved his demanded to be just by his own oath. Therefore, it is considered by the Court that the Plaintiff recover the same against the said Defendants together with his costs by him in this behalf expended when assets after paying proceeding judgements debts of greater dignity and the defendants own claims of equal dignity against the estate of the said intestate to be levied of the goods and chattels which were of the said JAMES at the time of his death that shall hereafter come to the hands of the said Defendants to be administered and the Defendants in mercy.

ISAAC THOMPSON against MATTHEW PHRIPP and JOHN LAWRENCE executors of THOMAS THOMPSON deceased. In Debt. This day came the parties by their Attorney's and the Defendant prays and has leave to IMPARLE here until the next Court and then to plead.

On the petition of SAMUEL BOUSH against JAMES MARSDEN and JONATHAN EILBECK executors of ELDRED FISHER deceased for 1 pound 18 shillings and 4 pence half penny due by account. This day came as well the Plaintiff in his proper person as the Defendants by their Attorney and Plaintiff proved his demand to be just by his own oath. Therefore, it is considered by the Court

<u>PAGE 171B</u>

That the Plaintiff recover the same against the said Defendants together with his costs by him in this behalf expended when assets after paying preceding judgements debts of greater dignity and the Defendants own claims of equal dignity against the estate of the said testator to be levied of the goods and chattels which were of the said ELDRED at the time of his death that shall hereafter come to the hands of the said Defendants to be administered and the said Defendants in mercy.

GEORGE ABYVON against WILLIAM LIDDLE. Dismissed.

GEORGE JACKSON against JOHN MARKHAM HERBERT. Dismissed.

On the petition of JOHN TYLER against JAMES MARSDEN and JAMES MAXWELL admin of JAMES PATTERSON deceased for 2 pounds 13 shillings due by account. This day came the parties by their Attorney's and the Plaintiff having proved his demanded to be just by his own oath. Therefore, it is considered by the Court that the Plaintiff recover the same against the said Defendants together with his costs by him in this behalf expended when assets after paying proceeding judgements debts of greater dignity and the defendants own claims of equal dignity against the estate of the said intestate to be levied of the goods and chattels which were of the said JAMES at the time of his death that shall hereafter come to the hands of the said Defendants to be administered and the Defendants in mercy

On the petition of CHRISTOPHER CALVERT against JAMES MARSDEN and JONATHAN EILBECK executors of ELDRED FISHER deceased for 1 pounds 18 shillings and 4 pence due by account. This day came the parties by their Attorney's and the Plaintiff having proved his demanded to be just by his own oath. Therefore, it is considered by the Court that the Plaintiff recover the same against the said Defendants together with his costs by him in this behalf expended when assets after paying proceeding judgements debts of greater dignity and the defendants own claims of equal dignity against the estate of the said intestate to be levied of the goods and chattels which were of the said ELDRED at the time of his death that shall hereafter come to the hands of the said Defendants to be administered and the Defendants in mercy.

WILLIAM DONALDSON against JAMES MARSDEN and JAMES MAXWELL administrators of JAMES PATTERSON. In Case. This day came the parties by their Attorney's and the Defendant prays and has leave to IMPARLE here until the next Court and then to plead.

PAGE 172

WILLIAM BELL against WILLIAM SIMPSON. In Debt. JOHN MCLACHLAN this day came into Court and undertook for the Defendant that in case he shall be casts in this suit he the said Defendant will pay the condemnation of the Court or render his body to Prison in execution for the same or that the said MCLACHLAN will pay the condemnation or render the body of the said Defendant as aforesaid. Where upon the Defendant by his Attorney prays and have leave to IMPARLE here the next Court and then to Plead.

WILLIAM BELL against WILLIAM SIMPSON admin of FRANCIS CLARK deceased. In Debt. This day came the parties by their Attorney's and the Defendant prays and has leave to IMPARLE here until the next Court and then to plead.

WILLIAM BELL against WILLIAM SIMPSON admin of FRANCIS CLARK deceased. In Debt. This day came the parties by their Attorney's and the Defendant prays and has leave to IMPARLE here until the next Court and then to plead.

RICHARD BROWN against EDWARD DAVIS by Petition and summons. Judgement is granted the Plaintiff for 2 pounds 15 shilling and 4 pence half penny. It is ordered that the Defendant pay the same unto the Plaintiff with costs and fee.

On the petition of JOHN MCLACHLAN against JAMES MARSDEN and JAMES MAXWELL admin of JAMES PATTERSON deceased for 4 pounds 19 shillings and 4 pence half penny due by account. This day came the parties by their Attorney's and the Plaintiff having proved his demanded to be just by his own oath. Therefore, it is considered by the Court that the Plaintiff recover the same against the said Defendants together with his costs by him in this behalf expended when assets after paying proceeding judgements debts of greater dignity and the Defendants own claims of equal dignity against the estate of the said intestate to be levied of the goods and chattels which were of the said JAMES at the time of his death that shall hereafter come to the hands of the said Defendants to be administered and the Defendants in mercy.

On the petition of BOLDEN and LAWRENCE and COMPANY against JAMES MARSDEN and JONATHAN EILBECK executors of ELDRED FISHER deceased for 3 pounds 6 shillings and 6 pence due by account. This day came the parties by their Attorney's and the Plaintiff having proved their demanded to be just by their own oath. Therefore, it is considered by the Court that the Plaintiff recover the same against the said Defendants together with their costs by them in this behalf expended when assets after paying proceeding judgements debts of greater dignity and the defendants own claims of equal dignity against the estate of the said intestate to be levied of the goods and chattels which were of the said ELDRED at the time of his death that shall hereafter come to the hands of the said Defendants to be administered and the Defendants in mercy.

PAGE 172B

JOHN BOWNESS Attorney in fact for MISTERS HALL, FLETCHER and LITTLE DALE Merchants in WHITEHAVEN against JOHN LAWRENCE and MATTHEW PHRIPP executors of THOMAS THOMPSON Deceased. In Debt. This day came the parties by their Attorney's and the Defendant prays and has leave to IMPARLE here until the next Court and then to plead.

JOHN BOWNESS Attorney in fact for MISTERS HALL, FLETCHER and LITTLE DALE Merchants in WHITEHAVEN against JOHN LAWRENCE and MATTHEW PHRIPP executors of THOMAS THOMPSON Deceased. In Debt. This day came the parties by their Attorney's and the Defendant prays and has leave to IMPARLE here until the next Court and then to plead.

THOMAS CARTWRIGHT and SUSANNAH, his wife against JAMES MARSDEN and JONATHAN EILBECK executors of ELDRED FISHER deceased. In Case. This day came the parties by their Attorney's and the Defendant prays and has leave to IMPARLE here until the next Court and then to plead.

PATRICK BYRN against JOHN MANNEN. Dismissed.
PATRICK BYRN against WENTWORTH DOWN. Dismissed.

JOHN CRAMOND against SAMUEL GWIN. In Case. This day came the parties by their Attorney's and the Defendant says he did not assume upon himself in manner and form as the Plaintiff against him has declared and of this he puts himself upon the Country and the Plaintiff likewise. Therefore, the trail of the issue is referred until the next Court to be held for the Borough.

JOHN CRAMOND against WILLIAM ROBINSON. In Case. JOSEPH CALVERT here in Court undertakes for the Defendant that in case he shall be casts in this suit he the said Defendant will pay the condemnation of the Court or render his body to Prison in execution for the same or that the said CALVERT will pay the condemnation or render the body of the said Defendant as aforesaid. Where upon the Defendant by his Attorney prays and have leave to IMPARLE here the next Court and then to Plead.

JOHN CRAMOND against WILLIAM ROBINSON. In Case. BENJMAIN CROOKER here in Court and undertakes for the Defendant that in case he shall be casts in this suit he the said Defendant will pay the condemnation of the Court or render his body to Prison in execution for the same or that the said CROOKER will pay the condemnation or render the body of the said Defendant as aforesaid. Where upon the Defendant by his Attorney prays and have leave to IMPARLE here the next Court and then to Plead.

PAGE 173

MARY ROBINSON executrix of TULLY ROBINSON deceased against JOHN CRAMOND. Continued for the bill.

JOHN TATEM against ALEXANDER GORDON surviving Obligor of JOHN WILSON deceased. This day came the parties by their Attorney's and the Defendant prays and has leave to IMPARLE here until the next Court and then to plead.

CHRISTOPHER CALVERT against BENJAMIN LEIGH. Dismissed.
ROBERT BARON against THOMAS WALKER. Dismissed.

WALTER LYON against ROBERT BARRS. In Case. This day came the parties by their Attorney's and the Defendant prays and has leave to IMPARLE here until the next Court and then to plead.

JAMES MARSDEN and JONATHAN EILBECK executors of ELDRED FISHER deceased against GEORGE WILSON and ARCHIBALD CAMPBELL administrators of JOHN WILSON deceased. Dismissed at Plaintiff's costs.

WILLIS DEANS and LYDIA his wife against WILLIAM WHITE dismissed.
GEORGE VEALE JR. against JOHN LELLO. Abates by the Plaintiffs death.

Ordinary License is granted STEPHEN TANKARD ferry keeper on his complying with the law.
JOHN COLINS against MARTIN MURPHY dismissed at the Plaintiff's cost for want of security for the costs.

The King by JOHN HUNT against WILLIAM SHEPHERD by warrant. Dismissed at the Defendants costs.

JAMES GILCHRIST and ROBERT TAYLOR Plaintiffs against GEORGE FOWLER Defendant. In Case. This day the parties by their Attorney's and there upon came also a Jury to wit: WILLIAM WALKER, HUGH MILLER, CHAPMAN MANSON, ANDREW STEVENSON, WILLIAM SKINKER, THOMAS HEPBURN, STEPHEN TANKARD, RICHARD BICKERDICK, JAMES CUNNINGHAM, WILLIAM BICKERDICK, JOHN STANHOPE, and WILLIAM CORBIT who being elected tried and sworn the truth to speak upon the issue joined with drew and not returning any verdict in this cause. The same is postponed.

PAGE 173B

SAMUEL PORTLOCK Plaintiff
Against Re: In Case
CHRISTOPHER CALVERT Defendant
This day came as well the Plaintiff by THOMAS CLAIBORNE Gentleman his Attorney, as the Defendant in his proper person and says that he cannot gainsay the Plaintiffs action nor but that he did assume in manner and form as the Plaintiff against him has declared. Therefore, it is considered that the Plaintiff recover against the said defendant 99 pounds 18 shillings and 3 pence and his costs by him in this behalf expended and the said Defendant in mercy.

JOHN SHEDDEN and Company Plaintiffs
Against Re: In Case
MAXIMILIAN GRIMES Defendant
This day came as well the Plaintiffs by ANDREW RONALD Gentleman their Attorney as the Defendant, in his proper person and says that he cannot gainsay the Plaintiffs action nor but that he did assume in manner and form as the Plaintiff against him has declared. Therefore, it is considered that the Plaintiff recover against the said defendant 6 pounds and 1 penny and their costs by them in this behalf expended and the said Defendant in mercy. And the Plaintiffs have agreed to stay the execution of this Judgement 2 months.

The King by JOHN HURT against WILLIAM HUGHS, THOMAS EDGE, EDMOND ARCHDEACON, EDWARD RUSHAM and PETER TURBIT by warrant. Dismissed at the Defendants costs.

Order is granted JOHN CHESHIRE against JOHN GILCHRIST and ROBERT TAYLOR for 100 pounds of tobacco for 4 days attendance in their suit against GEORGE FOWLER.

Order is granted WILLIAM FORRESTER against GEORGE FOWLER for 525 pounds of tobacco for 4 days attendance, coming and returning 20 miles twice and 1 pound 9 shillings ferriages in the suit of JAMES GILCHRIST and ROBERT TAYLOR against him.

PAGE 174

MALACHI MAUND Assignee of NOAH SUGG Plaintiff
Against Re: In Debt.
SAMUEL BRESSIE Defendant
This day came the parties by their Attorney's and there upon came also a Jury to wit: PAUL WATLINGTON, JACOB WILLIAMS, JOHN TODD, JOHN CARSE, THOMAS PEARSON, JOHN EDWARDS, GEORGE JACKSON, ABRAHAM PEATON, JOHN CARMOUNT, GEORGE GORDON, JOHN CHESHIRE, and JOHN BALLENTINE who being elected tried and sworn the truth to speak upon the issue joined upon their oath do say that the Defendant has not paid the debt in the declaration mentioned. Therefore, it is considered that the Plaintiff recover against the said Defendant his debt aforesaid amounting to 172 pounds and his costs by him in this behalf expended and the said Defendant in mercy. But this judgement is to be discharged by the payment of 42 pounds 11 shillings and 1 penny farthing with interest thereon after the rate of 5% per annum to be computed from this day to the time of payment and the costs.

MISTERS JOHN RAMSAY and JAMES TAYLOR Plaintiff
Against Re: In Case.
JAMES MARSDEN and JONATHAN EILBECK executors of ELDRED FISHER deceased defendants
This day came the parties by their Attorney's and the Defendant by their Attorney says that they cannot gainsay the Plaintiff action nor but that their testator did assume in manner and form as the Plaintiff against them have declared. Therefore, it is considered that the Plaintiff recover against the said Defendants 53 pounds 4 shillings and 6 pence half penny and their costs by them in this behalf expended when assets after paying preceding judgements. Debts of greater dignity and the Defendants own claims of equal dignity against the estate of the said Testator to be levied of the goods and chattels which were of the said ELDRED at the time of his death that shall hereafter come to the hands of the said Defendants to be administer and the said Defendants in mercy.

THOMAS LANGLEY Senior Plaintiff
Against Re: In Detinue
JOHN HUTCHINGS and JOSEPH HUTCHINGS Defendants.
This day came the parties by their Attorney's and thereupon came also a Jury to wit: JOHN HARRIS, WILLIAM INGRAM, ROBERT TUCKER, WILLIAM CALDERHEAD, GEORGE KELLY, WILLIAM FREEMAN, RICHARD BROWN, RALPH ELLIOT, THOMAS ROBERTS, JAMES MARSDEN, JOHN STONY, and JAMES LEITCH and WILLIAM CORBIT who being elected tried and sworn the truth to speak upon the issue joined with drew and not returning any verdict in this cause. The same is postponed.

PAGE 174B
THOMAS LANGLEY Plaintiff
Against Re: In Detinue
JAMES WEBB Defendant
This day came the parties by their Attorney's and thereupon came also a Jury to wit: JOHN HARRIS, WILLIAM INGRAM, ROBERT TUCKER, WILLIAM CALDERHEAD, GEORGE KELLY, WILLIAM FREEMAN, RICHARD BROWN, RALPH ELLIOT, THOMAS ROBERTS, JAMES MARSDEN, JOHN STONY, and JAMES LEITCH and WILLIAM CORBIT who being elected tried and sworn the truth to speak upon the issue joined with drew and not returning any verdict the cause is postponed.

JOHN SHEPHERD Plaintiff
Against Re: In Case
JAMES MARSDEN and JONATHAN EILBECK executors of ELDRED FISHER deceased Defendants
This day came the parties by their Attorney's and the Defendant by their Attorney says that they cannot gainsay the Plaintiff action nor but that their testator did assume in manner and form as the Plaintiff against them have declared. Therefore, it is considered that the Plaintiff recover against the Defendants 25 pounds 10 shillings and 6 pence and his costs by him in this behalf expended, when assets after paying preceding judgements, debts of greater dignity and the Defendants own claims of equal dignity against the estate of the said Testator to be levied of the goods and chattels which were of the said ELDRED at the time of his death that shall hereafter come to the hands of the said Defendants to be administer and the said Defendants in mercy.

MISTERS WILLIAM and JOHN BROWN Plaintiff
Against Re: In Case
ALEXANDER BELL Defendant
This day came the parties by their Attorney and the Defendant by his Attorney relinquishing his former plea says that he cannot gainsay the Plaintiffs action nor but that he did assume in manner and form as the Plaintiff against him has declared. Therefore, it is considered that the Plaintiff recover against the said Defendant 28 pounds 7 shillings and 2 pence half penny and their costs by them about their suit in this behalf expended and the said Defendant in mercy.

Order is granted RICHARD PAYNE against GEORGE FOWLER for 650 pounds of tobacco for 2 days attendance at this Court and coming and returning 100 miles 2x and 1 pound 11 shillings ferriages in the suit of JAMES GILCHRIST and ROBERT TAYLOR against him.

Ordinary License is granted ROBERT BRITT on his complying with the law.

PAGE 175
JOHN HUNT, RICHARD AYTON, JOHN HENDERSON & WILLIAM FISHER executors of MATHIAS GALE deceased, ANN MOORE, JOSEPH MITCHELL, JOHN COX & Misters JOHN RAMSAY, and JOHN TAYLOR
Plaintiffs
Against Re: In Chancery
RICHARD ROTHERY an infant son and heir of HENRY ROTHERY deceased MARY ROTHERY widow and GEORGE ABYVON executor of the said HENRY ROTHERY deceased Defendants
This day came as well the Plaintiffs by their Attorney's as the Defendant Richard by his guardian, The defendants and GEORGE by their Attorney and it appearing to the Court that MARY MOORE in the Original Process is the real Plaintiff but by the misprision of her Attorney in the subsequent proceedings she is called ANN MOORE and by of the Court the said MARY MOORE is at liberty to be inserted in the Bill and Answers as Plaintiff and the Commissioner appointed to make sale of the other 2/3 of the land with the appurtenances and the reversion of the other third part of the same with its appurtenances situate on the main street in the Borough aforesaid as in the bill mentioned and also so much of the other piece or parcel of land situate on Elizabeth river in the said bill mentioned, this day made his report in these words to wit:
Sales of 2 lots land by orders of Norfolk Borough Court the Estate of the late HENRY ROTHERY deceased.

Date to whom sold Amount a lot on Main Street with a new erected 2 story house, subject to the widow's dower. October 17, 1772. MAXIMILIAN CALVERT ESQUIRE L300.0.0		300.0.0
Deduct GEORGE KELLY'S Commission 1.1.6, Cash Paid for Punch 1.11.3, Cash paid Advertising 10/ Cash paid Postage 2 Letters 1/3	3.4.0	296.16.0
A lot on the water with which this widow sells her dower to benefit the sale. January 1, 1773, MAXIMILIAN CALVERT ESQUIRE		200.0.0
Deduct GEORGE KELLY'S Commission 1.1.6, Cash Paid for Punch 2.2.6	3.4.0	196.16.0
Deduct widow ROTHERY'S dower on the lot 1/9 of the net proceeds of the sale		21.17.4
		174.18.8
My Commission for sales		10.0.0
Net Proceeds Sales		461.14.8

Error's excepted Norfolk February 22nd, 1773. JOHN GREENWOOD. On Consideration where of it is decreed and ordered that the said Commissioner pay unto the Claimants their several and respective claims. That the sales so as aforesaid made be held firm and stable. That the purchaser be quieted in the possession thereof. And that they infant Defendant RICHARD ROTHERY within 6 months after his arrival to the age of 21 years by good and sufficient deed or deeds convey unto the purchaser of the said lands with the appurtenances the fees simple thereof unless he can within that time show error in this decree. And it is further decreed and ordered that the said Commissioner pay unto the Defendant MARY ROTHERY 1/9th part of the net proceeds of the sales of the lot situated on Elizabeth River, and the overplus he retain in his hands for the use of the said Defendant RICHARD that his costs be borne by the said Commissioner out of the sales which are retained in his hands for the use of the Defendant RICHARD ROTHERY SON and heir at law of HENRY ROTHERY Deceased.

PAGE 175B
MOSES LANGLEY Plaintiff
Against Re: In Chancery
FRANCES MOORE administratrix of JOHN MOORE deceased and EDWARD PARKE Defendants
This cause was this day heard on the bill and answers, replication and deposition and the arguments of the Council on both sides. On consideration whereof it is decreed and ordered that the sale of the Negro wench in the bill mentioned be null and void. That the Plaintiff on or before the 15th of April next pay unto the Defendants 9 pounds 18 shillings and 10 pence and in case of failure it is further decreed and ordered that the Defendants make sale of the said Negro wench and return the above sum and restore the overplus to the said Plaintiff and that the Defendants pay unto the Plaintiff his costs by him about his suit in this behalf expended. From which decree the Defendants by their Attorney prayed an Appeal to the 6th day of the Next General Court which on their giving security of prosecution at or before the Next Court is allowed.

This Court is adjourned until tomorrow at 10 o'clock, PAUL LOYALL MAYOR, TESTE: JOHN BOUSH D.C.

NORFOLK BOROUGH
At a Hustings Court Held this 24th day of March 1773
PRESENT: PAUL LOYALL ESQUIRE MAYOR
GENTLEMAN ALDERMEN: GEORGE ABYVON, CHARLES THOMAS, ARCHIBALD CAMPBELL, JAMES TAYLOR, LEWIS HANSFORD, CORNELIUS CALVERT

On the petition of GEORGE KELLY against JAMES MARSDEN and JONATHAN EILBECK executors of ELDRED FISHER deceased for 5 pounds due by account. This day came the parties by their Attorney's and the Plaintiff having proved his demanded to be just by his own oath. Therefore, it is considered by the Court that the Plaintiff recover the same against the said Defendants together with his costs by him in this behalf expended when assets after paying proceeding judgements debts of greater dignity and the defendants own claims of equal dignity against the estate of the said intestate to be levied of the goods and chattels which were of the said ELDRED at the time of his death that shall hereafter come to the hands of the said Defendants to be administered and the Defendants in mercy

PAGE 176
WILLIAM and THOMAS FARRER Plaintiff
Against Re: In Case
JAMES MARSDEN and JONATHAN EILBECK executors of ELDRED FISHER deceased Defendants
This day came the parties by their Attorney's and the Defendants by their Attorney says that they cannot gainsay the Plaintiff action nor but that their testator did assume in manner and form as the Plaintiff against them have declared. Therefore, it is considered that the Plaintiff recover against the Defendants 35 pounds 4 shillings and 1 penny half penny and their costs by them in this behalf expended, when assets after paying preceding judgements, debts of greater dignity and the Defendants own claims of equal dignity against the estate of the said Testator to be levied of the goods and chattels which were of the said ELDRED at the time of his death that shall hereafter come to the hands of the said Defendants to be administer and the said Defendants in mercy.

GABRIEL MAUPIN Plaintiff
Against Re: In Case
JAMES MARSDEN and JONATHAN EILBECK executors of ELDRED FISHER deceased Defendants
This day came the parties by their Attorney's and the Defendant by their Attorney says that they cannot gainsay the Plaintiff action nor but that their testator did assume in manner and form as the Plaintiff against them have declared. Therefore, it is considered that the Plaintiff recover against the Defendants 33 pounds and 6 pence and his costs by him in this behalf expended, when assets after paying preceding judgements, debts of greater dignity and the Defendants own claims of equal dignity against the estate of the said Testator to be levied of the goods and chattels which were of the said ELDRED at the time of his death that shall hereafter come to the hands of the said Defendants to be administer and the said Defendants in mercy.

JOHN LAWRENCE and MATTHEW PHRIPP executors of THOMAS THOMPSON deceased Plaintiff
Against Re: In Case
JAMES MARSDEN and JONATHAN EILBECK executors of ELDRED FISHER deceased Defendants
This day came the parties by their Attorney's and the Defendants by their Attorney says that they cannot gainsay the Plaintiff action nor but that their testator did assume in manner and form as the Plaintiff against them have declared. Therefore, it is considered that the Plaintiff recover against the Defendants 29 pounds 18 shillings and their costs by them in this behalf expended, when assets after paying preceding judgements,

PAGE 176B
debts of greater dignity and the Defendants own claims of equal dignity against the estate of the said Testator to be levied of the goods and chattels which were of the said ELDRED at the time of his death that shall hereafter come to the hands of the said Defendants to be administer and the said Defendants in mercy.

On the petition of ISAAC THOMPSON against MATTHEW PHRIPP and JOHN LAWRENCE executors of THOMAS THOMPSON deceased for 3 pounds 8 shillings and 10 pence half penny due by account. This day came the parties by their Attorney's and the Plaintiff having proved his demanded to be just by his own oath. Therefore, it is considered by the Court that the Plaintiff recover the same against the said Defendants together with his costs by him in this behalf expended when assets after paying proceeding judgements debts of greater dignity and the Defendants own claims of equal dignity against the estate of the said intestate to be levied of the goods and chattels which were of the said THOMAS at the time of his death that shall hereafter come to the hands of the said Defendants to be administered and the Defendants in mercy

JOHN GOODRICH Plaintiff
Against Re: In Case
ALEXANDER MCSWEEN Defendant
This day came the parties by their Attorney's and there upon came also a Jury to wit: WILLIAM STEVENSON, JOHN LEE, GEORGE JACKSON, CHARLES BOUSHNELL, JOHN MACLEAN, ALEXANDER MOSELEY, ROBERT BARON, SAMUEL TOMLINSON, WILLIAM GEORGE, JOHN RICHARDSON, WILLOUGHBY MORGAN, and JAMES WALKER who being elected tried and sworn the truth to speak upon the issue joined upon their oath do say that the Defendant did assume in manner and form as the Plaintiff against him has declared and do assess the Plaintiff Damages by Occasion of the non-performance of that assumption to 8 pounds 2 shillings and 10 pence besides his costs. Therefore, it is considered that the Plaintiff recover against the said Defendant his damages aforesaid in form aforesaid assessed and his costs by him in this behalf expended and the said Defendant in mercy.

On the petition of JAMES TAYLOR surviving partner of JOHN TAYLOR against JAMES MARSDEN and JONATHAN EILBECK executors of ELDRED FISHER deceased for 1 pound 5 shillings and 7 pence half penny due by account. This day came the parties by their Attorney's and the Plaintiff having proved his demanded to be just by his own oath. Therefore, it is considered by the Court that the Plaintiff recover the same against the said Defendants together with his costs by him in this behalf expended when assets after paying proceeding judgements debts of greater dignity and the defendants own claims of equal dignity against the estate of the said intestate to be levied of the goods and chattels which were of the said ELDRED at the time of his death that shall hereafter come to the hands of the said Defendants to be administered and the Defendants in mercy

PAGE 177
AARON WHITEHURST against SAMUEL CALVERT by Petition and summons. Judgement is granted the Plaintiff for? pounds 15 shilling. It is ordered that the Defendant pay the same unto the Plaintiff with costs and fee.   (? # In Fold)

Order is granted HENRY WHITEHURST against AARON WHITEHURST for 147 pounds of tobacco for 3 days attendance coming and returning 12 miles 2x in his suit against SAMUEL CALVERT

ROBERT GILMOUR Administrator of WILLIAM GRAY Plaintiff
Against Re: In Case
ELIZABETH GRAY Defendant
This day came as well the Plaintiff by ANDREW RONALD Gentleman his Attorney and the Defendant in her proper person says that she cannot gainsay the Plaintiffs action nor but that she did assume in manner and form as the Plaintiff against her has declared. Therefore, it is considered that the Plaintiff recover against the said Defendant 31 pounds 15 shillings and 9 pence half penny and his costs by him about his suit in this behalf expended and the said Defendant in mercy.

HENRY GREEN Plaintiff
Against Re: In Case
BARNABY CARNEY Defendant
This day came the parties by their Attorney's and there upon came also a Jury to wit: ADAM BENNET, DICKERSON PRIOR, WRIGHT WESTCOTT, JOHN GILCHRIST, JOHN BROWN, MORTO BRIAN, GEORGE WILSON, JAMES MURPHREE, JOHN BISER, JOHN BOGGESS, PAUL PROBY and JAMES CARMICHAEL
who being elected tried and sworn the truth to speak upon the issue joined upon their oath do say that the Defendant did assume in manner and form as the Plaintiff against him has declared and do assess the Plaintiff Damages by Occasion of the non-performance of that assumption to 10 pounds besides his costs. Therefore, it is considered that the Plaintiff recover against the said Defendant his damages aforesaid in form aforesaid assessed and his costs by him in this behalf expended and the said Defendant in mercy.

JOHN STANHOPE Plaintiff
Against Re: In Case
NATHANIEL BOUSH Defendant
This day came the parties by their Attorney's and there upon came also a Jury to wit: WILLIAM STEVENSON, JOHN LEE, GEORGE JACKSON, CHARLES BOUSHNELL, JOHN MACLEAN, ALEXANDER MOSELEY, ROBERT BARON, SAMUEL TOMLINSON, WILLIAM GEORGE, JOHN RICHARDSON, WILLOUGHBY MORGAN, and JAMES WALKER who being elected tried and sworn the truth to speak upon the issue joined upon their oath do say that the Defendant did assume in manner and form as the Plaintiff against him has declared and do assess the Plaintiff Damages by Occasion of the non-performance of that assumption to 10 pounds besides his costs.
PAGE 177B
Therefore, it is considered that the Plaintiff recover against the said Defendant his damages aforesaid in form aforesaid assessed and his costs by him in this behalf expended and the said Defendant in mercy.

JAMES MOORE Plaintiff
Against Re: On a motion upon an execution
JONATHAN HOPKINS Defendant
This day came the parties by their Attorney's and the Defendant having had notice agreeable to the Act of Assembly. It is Therefore, considered that the Plaintiff recover against the said Defendant 10 pounds 11 shillings and 3 pence and his costs by him about his suit in this behalf expended and the said Defendant in mercy.

WILLIAM POOLE against HUGH MCPHILIMY. Order against the Defendant.
WILLIAM POOLE against HUGH MCPHILIMY. Order against the Defendant.
GEORGE CARLTON against THOMAS HUGHS. JOSEPH CALVERT enters himself Special Bail and order against Defendant.

Order is granted JOHN AVIS against HENRY GREEN for 275 pounds of tobacco for 11 days attendance at this Court in his suit against BARNABY CARNEY.

Order is granted WILLIS EASTWOOD against HENRY GREEN for 300 pounds of tobacco for 12 days attendance at this Court in his suit against BARNABY CARNEY.

Order is granted THOMAS RASCOE against HENRY GREEN for 300 pounds of tobacco for 12 days attendance at this Court in his suit against BARNABY CARNEY.

Order is granted THOMAS WARD against HENRY GREEN for 125 pounds of tobacco for 5 days attendance at this Court in his suit against BARNABY CARNEY.

Order is granted RICHARD EASTWOOD against BARNABY CARNEY for 75 pounds of tobacco for 3 days attendance at this Court in the Suit of HENRY GREEN against him.

SARAH CANN executrix of JOHN CANN against WILLIAM NICHOLSON by Petition and summons. Judgement is granted the Plaintiff for 2 pounds. It is ordered that the Defendant pay the same unto the Plaintiff with costs and fee.

JOHN TATEM against ALEXANDER GORDON the suit is dismissed.

PAGE 178
Order is granted THOROWGOOD KEELING against SARAH CANN executrix of JOHN CANN deceased for 164 pounds of tobacco for 2 days attendance at this Court coming and returning 16 miles 2x in her suit against WILLIAM NICHOLSON.

JOHN BEISER Plaintiff
Against Re: In Case
ROGER PEARSE Defendant
This day came the parties by their Attorney's and there upon came also a Jury to wit: WILLIAM STEVENSON, JOHN LEE, GEORGE JACKSON, CHARLES BOUSHNELL, JOHN MACLEAN, ALEXANDER MOSELEY, ROBERT BARON, SAMUEL TOMLINSON, WILLIAM GEORGE, JOHN RICHARDSON, WILLOUGHBY MORGAN, and JAMES WALKER who being elected tried and sworn the truth to speak upon the issue joined upon their oath do say that the Defendant did assume in manner and form as the Plaintiff against him has declared and do assess the Plaintiff Damages by Occasion of the non-performance of that assumption to 100 pounds besides his costs. Therefore, it is considered that

the Plaintiff recover against the said Defendant his damages aforesaid in form aforesaid assessed and his costs by him in this behalf expended and the said Defendant in mercy.

Order is granted LORAINA DARBY against JOHN BEISER for 175 pounds of tobacco for 7 days attendance in this Court in his suit against ROGER PEARSE.

Order is granted MARY WILLIAMS against JOHN BEISER for 125 pounds of tobacco for 5 days attendance in this Court in his suit against ROGER PEARSE.

Order is granted PETER BEISER against JOHN BEISER for 125 pounds of tobacco for 5 days attendance in this Court in his suit against ROGER PEARSE.

Order is granted CHRISTIANA FRITSON against JOHN BEISER for 100 pounds of tobacco for 4 days attendance in this Court in his suit against ROGER PEARSE.

Order is granted RICHARD BICKERDICK against ROGER PEARSE for 225 pounds of tobacco for 9 days attendance in this Court in the suit of JOHN BEISER against him.

Order is granted JACOB WILLIAMS against ROGER PEARSE for 125 pounds of tobacco for 5 days attendance in this Court in the suit of JOHN BEISER against him.

Order is granted BARNABAS LORAIN against ROGER PEARSE for 225 pounds of tobacco for 9 days attendance in this Court in the suit of JOHN BEISER against him.

PAGE 178B
MISTERS RAMSAY and TAYLOR against JOHN CRAMOND administrator of FRANCES ROBINSON. On the motion of the Plaintiff by their Attorney a DEDIMUS is granted them to take the depositions of WILLIAM ORR giving the Defendant reasonable notice.

JOHN HARRIS Plaintiff
Against Re: In Trespass
MAXIMILIAN CALVERT Defendant
This day came the parties by their Attorney's and there upon came also a Jury to wit: WILLIAM STEVENSON, JOHN LEE, GEORGE JACKSON, CHARLES BOUSHNELL, JOHN MACLEAN, ALEXANDER MOSELEY, ROBERT BARON, SAMUEL TOMLINSON, WILLIAM GEORGE, JOHN RICHARDSON, WILLOUGHBY MORGAN, and JAMES WALKER who being elected tried and sworn the truth to speak upon the issue joined upon their oath do say that the Defendant is guilty of the trespass in the declaration mentioned in manner and form as the Plaintiff against him has declared and do assess the Plaintiff Damages by Occasion thereof to 5 pounds besides his costs.
Therefore, it is considered that the Plaintiff recover against the said Defendant his damages aforesaid in form aforesaid assessed and his costs by him in this behalf expended and the said Defendant in mercy.

JAMES HUNTER surviving partner of TENANT and HUNTER against WILLIAM KAYS. In Case.
JOHN CRAMOND this day came into Court and undertook for the Defendant that in case he shall be casts in this suit he the said Defendant will pay the condemnation of the Court or render his body to Prison in execution for the same or that the said CRAMOND will pay the condemnation or render the body of the said Defendant as aforesaid. Where upon the Defendant by his Attorney prays and have leave to IMPARLE here the next Court and then to Plead.

The King by ATKINSON against JAMIMA HUTTON by warrant. Dismissed.

This Court this day rated flour at 16/8 per centum weight
This Court is adjourned to Court in Course, PAUL LOYALL MAYOR, TESTE: JOHN BOUSH D.C.

PAGE 179
NORFOLK BOROUGH
At a Hustings Court Held this 24th day of May 1773
PRESENT: PAUL LOYALL ESQUIRE MAYOR
GENTLEMAN ALDERMEN: GEORGE ABYVON, CHARLES THOMAS, ARCHIBALD CAMPBELL, JAMES TAYLOR, LEWIS HANSFORD, CORNELIUS CALVERT

Ordinary License is granted JOHN RANSBERG, ROBERT BANKS, JOSEPH POPE, SCARBROUGH TANKARD, RICHARD BROCK, Trustees of TERESA PEARSE and JOHN HARDY on their complying with the law.

JAMES CUNNINGHAM against GEORGE JOSEPH FENWICK by Petition and summons. Judgement is granted the Plaintiff for 1 pounds 3 shillings. It is ordered that the Defendant pay the same unto the Plaintiff with costs and fee.

JOHN WYATT against TIMOTHY IVES. Conditional order against Defendant and FRANCIS HATTON his bail.
GEORGE JACKSON against GEORGE WILSON and ARCHIBALD CAMPBELL administrator of JOHN WILSON deceased this suit is dismissed.
SAMUEL PORTLOCK against ROBERT STEELE. Dismissed.
THOMAS BRYAN against SAMUEL GWIN. An Imparlance.

On the Attachment obtained by THOMAS NEWTON against the Estate of ROGER PEARSE who has private removed himself so absconds that the ordinary process cannot be served on him and the Sergeant now making return that by virtue thereof he has attached one hogshead rum, a Negro Girl called MILLY and a servant man which I have ready to satisfy the same, also summoned MR. SAMUEL PORTLOCK, SARAH MASSENBURG, ELIZABETH STEEL and ELIZABETH BRICKELL to answer as garnishes after satisfying DANIEL HUTCHINGS and the said Defendant being solemnly called and not appearing no replevying his said effects. Where upon the Plaintiff proved his demand of 9 pounds 2 shillings and 6 pence to be just by his own oath. Therefore, it is considered by the Court that the Plaintiff recover the same against the said Defendant together with his costs by him in this behalf expended. And it is ordered that the Sergeant sell sufficient of the said attached effects except the Negro girl MILLY and pay to the Plaintiff his demand aforesaid after satisfying DANIEL HUTCHINGS demand and that the return an account of this proceedings thereupon at the next Court. And the Attachment against the garnishes is discontinued.

THOMAS APPLEWHAIT against THOMAS WILLIAMSON. An Imparlance.

MALACHI MAUND against ALEXANDER BELL. An Imparlance.

PAGE 179B

On the Attachment by GEORGE KELLY against the Estate of ROGER PEARSE who has privately removed himself or so absconds that the ordinary process cannot be served on him. And the Sergeant now making return that by virtue thereof he has attached one hogshead rum, one Negro Girl called MILLY and a servant man which I have ready after satisfying ELDRED FISHER, also summoned SAMUEL PORTLOCK, SARAH MASSENBURG, ELIZABETH STEEL and ELIZABETH BRICKELL to answer as garnishees upon which the said ELIZABETH BRICKLE appeared and on oath declared she was indebted to the said Defendant 2 shillings and 10 pence 3 farthings and the Defendant being solemnly called and not appearing nor replevying his said effects. Where upon the Plaintiff proved by his demand of 39 pounds 17 shillings to be just. Therefore, it is considered by the Court that the Plaintiff recover the same against the said Defendant together with his costs by him in this behalf expended and it is ordered that ELIZABETH BRICKELL the garnishee pay the money in her hands to the Plaintiff and that the Sergeant sell the attached effects except the Negro girl MILLY and pay to the Plaintiff the balance of his claim after satisfying DANIEL HUTCHINGS. Judgement and costs as the attachment of ELDRED FISHER against the said Defendant is dismissed and that he also return an account of his proceedings at the Next Court and the Attachment against the garnishees is continued.

THOMAS HOWARD and WILLIAM WHITE executors of JOSEPH WRIGHT deceased against JOHN TATEM Senior and JOHN TATEM Junior. In Debt. WRIGHT WESTCOTT this day came into Court and undertook for the Defendants that in case they shall be casts in this suit they the said Defendants will pay the condemnation of the Court or render their bodies to Prison in execution for the same or that the said WESTCOTT will pay the condemnation or render the bodies of the said Defendants as aforesaid. Where upon the Defendants by their Attorney prays and have leave to IMPARLE here the next Court and then to Plead.

THOMAS HOWARD and WILLIAM WHITE executors of JOSEPH WRIGHT deceased against JOHN TATEM Senior and FRANCIS WRIGHT. In Debt. WRIGHT WESTCOTT this day came into Court and undertook for the Defendant that in case they shall be casts in this suit they the said Defendants will pay the condemnation of the Court or render their bodies to Prison in execution for the same or that the said WESTCOTT will pay the condemnation or render the bodies of the said Defendants as aforesaid. Where upon the Defendant by their Attorney prays and have leave to IMPARLE here the next Court and then to Plead.

MARY GRIFFIN Executrix of SAMUEL GRIFFIN against TIMOTHY IVES. In Debt. MALACHI MAUND of this County this day came into Court and undertook for the Defendant that in case he shall be casts in this suit he the said Defendant will pay the condemnation of the Court or render his body to Prison in execution for the same or that the said MAUND will pay the condemnation or render the body of the said Defendant as aforesaid. Where upon the Defendant prays and have leave to IMPARLE here the next Court and then to Plead.

PAGE 180

GEORGE KELLY Plaintiff

Against Re: In Case

MATTHEW PHRIPP and JOHN LAWRENCE executors of THOMAS THOMPSON deceased Defendants

This day came the parties by their Attorney's and the Defendants by their Attorney say that they cannot gainsay the Plaintiff action nor but that their testator did assume in manner and form as the Plaintiff against them have declared. Therefore, it is considered that the Plaintiff recover against the Defendants 32 pounds 16 shillings and 8 pence half penny and his costs by him in this behalf expended when assets after paying preceding judgements debts of greater dignity and the Defendants own claims of equal dignity against the estate of the said Testator to be levied of the goods and chattels which were of the said THOMAS at the time of his death that shall hereafter come to the hands of the said Defendants to be administer and the said Defendants in mercy.

RAMSAY and TAYLOR Plaintiff

Against Re: In Case

JOHN LAWRENCE and MATTHEW PHRIPP executors of THOMAS THOMPSON deceased Plaintiff

This day came the parties by their Attorney's and the Defendants by their Attorney say that they cannot gainsay the Plaintiff action nor but that their testator did assume in manner and form as the Plaintiff against them have declared. Therefore, it is considered that the Plaintiff recover against the Defendants 11 pounds and 3 pence and their costs by them in this behalf expended, when assets after paying preceding judgements, debts of greater dignity and the Defendants own claims of equal dignity against the estate of the said Testator to be levied of the goods and chattels which were of the said THOMAS at the time of his death that shall hereafter come to the hands of the said JOHN and MATTHEW to be administered and the said JOHN and MATTHEW in mercy.

WILLIAM SKINKER and wife against JAMES MARSDEN and JONATHAN EILBECK executors of ELDRED FISHER deceased. Dismissed.

LOGAN GILMOUR and Company against JOHN VALLENCIER by Petition and summons. Judgement is granted the Plaintiff for? pounds 10 shillings and 9 pence half penny. It is ordered that the Defendant pay the same unto the Plaintiff with costs and fee. (? # in fold)

WILLIAM BUTT against JAMES MARSDEN and JONATHAN EILBECK executors of ELDRED FISHER deceased. The Defendants plead that their testator did not assume issue joined and referred.

YOUNG and SMITH against ROBERT TUCKER. by Petition and summons. Judgement is granted the Plaintiff for 4 pounds 17 shillings and 10 pence. It is ordered that the Defendant pay the same unto the Plaintiff with costs and fee.

PAGE 180B
JOHN WILSON and Company against EPHRAIM BALLANCE. * Order against Defendant and SAMUEL BALL ANCE* his bail. (Author note: the surname had two L, word kept changing to Balance.)

On the Attachment obtained by JAMES HALDANE against the estate of ROGER PEARSE who has privately removed himself or so absconds that the ordinary process cannot be served on him and the Sergeant now making return that by virtue thereof he has attached SUNDRY goods to wit:
Two feather beds, 10 white stone dishes, one dozen blue and white China plates, 7 red and white plates, one large mahogany tea table, 3 poplar bedstead, one bed cord, 8 leather bottom chairs, four check, bottom chairs, one pair fire tongs, one coffee pot cooper, one large black walnut table, 3 mahogany tea boards, 5 cotton blankets, 2 green plain blankets, 2 cotton counter pane, one calico counterpane, one pair thread stockings, one iron pot, one frying pan one blue painted chest, 14 stone plates, one India picture, one pot olives, a box with four and half pounds tallow candles, 5 pounds pig tail tobacco, two and half pounds cut tobacco, one basket, one mahogany tea chest, one tub butter, 139 pounds, gross twenty pounds, tare 24 pounds cheese, a set of red and white cross barred curtains, two empty beer barrels, one barrel with some beer, two bed mats, one set calico curtains, one calico counter pane, 5 sheets, 5 pounds pricks tobacco , two feather beds, weight 76 pounds, one bed guilty , 4 sheets, 3 blankets, 2 suit curtains, 2 bed stead, 10 black walnut chairs, one black walnut desk and book case, one 4 foot table, 1 looking glass, 1 brass mortar and pestle, one warming pan, two case bottles, one glass lantern, stamp cotton and sundries for a bed quilt, 3 stone dishes, 11 China plates, 2 large China bowls, 14 black walnut chairs, 2 four foot black walnut tables, one billiard table and sundries thereto belonging 1 three and half foot black walnut table, one 3 and half foot tea table, one 3 and half foot stand, one mahogany stand, one feather bed, 3 blankets, 1 quilt and 2 sheets, 2 pair blankets, one piece stripped stuff, one piece chintz , a trunk with sundries, which was taken away by WILLIAM GEORGE after distrained and attacked and returned the next day with part of the goods taken out, one pair shoes, 2 remnants calico, a blanket, a quadrant, 2 shirts, one pair trousers, one powder horn, one trunk which I have ready after satisfying SARAH CANN house rent all which good have been claimed by SARAH WESTON, ANDREW STEVENSON, JAMES CARMICHAEL, RICHARD BROWN, JOHN WILLON and JOHN YOUNG and delivered excepting those claimed by WILLIAM GEORGE for want of security and two feather beds which I keep believing them not be the property of SARAH WESTON, the claimant. The said SARAH CANN having agreed to postpone the sale thereof to satisfy her rent until the determination of the said Court to which the said attachments are returnable, and they having given bond to abide by the determination of said Court. Also distrained and attached, one feather bed, two pillows, one keg with some barley, 2 carpets, 7 bacon hams, two copper tea kettles, a small trunk, one tin pot, one jar with some reasons, 15 China coffee cups, one China butter boat, nine blue and white China plates, 4 China bowls, one bottle capons, one cannister with some tea, 8 China dishes, 13 China plates, 14 saucers, 15 pots with preserves, and pickles, 8 decanters, one stone water jug, two images, 8 empty jams and jugs, a firkin of dirty grease, one stone dish, two stone plates,
PAGE 181
7 brass candlesticks, one pair back gammon tables, 12 vials, two dice boxes, one padlock, one German flute, one iron, one hand bell, one pair lime squeezers, two stone punch strainers, 4 black jacks, two mustard crusts, two pair tin scales and weights, one funnel, one pint pot, three boxes with some soap, one tub , 4 pewter dishes, 7 case of 50 empty bottles, a paper with hartshorn, two barrels, one hatchet, one water pail, a bag with some hops, one oil lamp, a bag with split peas, one pewter plate, one salver, tin, one empty barrel, one ditto keg, one barrel with flour, a harness tub, with some beef, two ditto and a barrel with pork, 53 bottles of wine, arrack, beer, one tray 40 tin saucers, 2 empty cases, three old bird cages, a box with green wax candles, a pair of wooden scales, a basket and cannisters, with some garden seed three tin pans, one earthen bowl, two stone tea pots, four pewter plates, 2 cakes tallow*, a broken China bowl, with salt two stone saucers, two ditto tea cups, nine China tea cups, four ditto saucers, one washing tub, one scrubbing brush, one stand one ax, one wood saw a parcel iron hooks, one glass lantern, a bundle of paper, two candle benches, half gallon peter pot, one wash bason, one basket with some cards, 105 wine, beer, and jelly glasses, 2 horse whips, one ink stand, a glass (blank), 12 patty pans, one stone fruit dish, one stone tureen, one salver, 3 table matts, one pine? (in fold) 4 empty cannisters, one wash hand bason, one mahogany knife, box, 2 ditto with knives and forks, one pair candlestick, one hammer, one past comb, one pint pewter measure, one piece white dimity, a remnant ditto, 10 wash balls, two horse girts, four cards mettle buttons three pair of sheets 8 pillow cases, on syringe, one broad cloth, one search, one coal and west coat, one cloth jacket, and breeches, 10 shirts, 7 pairs men's pants and brown holland breeches, 3 linen and two gingham jackets, one fustian coat, one straw bed, two punch ladle, one book, a barrel with some rum, a barrel with some beer, a barrel flour, a stand of shelves, one empty beer barrel, two wheel barrows, one dripping stone and frame, a hogshead with some rum, two pair bellows, one grate, one floor cloth, one fish kettle, two large tea kettles, one Dutch oven, one coffee mill, one cullender, one pewter chamber pot, one table bell, one copper saucepan, one brass shallot, one chaffing dish, one pair shovels, and tongs, one tin lantern, one pewter funnel , one pair steel yards, one cooper coffee pot, one earthen chamber pot, one chest, one hair broom, one flat iron, one candle box, one pot rack, two jars with cranberries, and one hundred lemons and green Windsor chairs, one corner cupboard, 9 silver table spoons, 6 table salts, and the shovels for ditto, one cream pot, 5 table tea spoons, one pair ditto tongs, one ditto tea strainer, a book of accounts and sundry papers, one copper coffee pot, which I have already also after satisfying the said SARAH CANN the house rent aforesaid and summoned RICHARD BROWN, SARAH WESTON, ANDREW STEVENSON, JAMES CARMICHAEL, ROBERT ALLAN and WILLIAM GEORGE to appear and answer as garnishees

and the said Defendant being solemnly called and not appearing nor replevying his said effects where upon the Plaintiff proved his demand of 11 pounds 4 shillings and 4 pence half penny to be just by his own oath.

Therefore, it is considered by the Court that the Plaintiff recover the same against the said Defendant together with his costs by him in this behalf expended. And it is ordered that the Sergeant deliver to SARAH CANN the articles contained in her schedule to wit: One hominy* pestle, one large iron pot with hooks and rack, one cooling tub, one pair stake tongs, one pair hand irons, 4 irons, backs, one large delph bowl and one quart decanter, ten tin pans, 6 syllabub glasses,

PAGE 181B

To RICHARD BROWN: The articles contained in his schedule to wit: one billiard table with sundries, thereto belong one square walnut table, one tea table, one stand, one mahogany table,

To ANDREW STEVENSON: The articles contained in his schedule to wit: two beds and furniture, 3 stone dishes and one dozen soup China plates, two large China bowls, one warming pan and pestle and mortar, one dozen leather bottom chairs, one 4-foot table, one glass lantern, one desk and one bookcase, one large looking glass, stamp cotton and sundries for bed quilts.

To SARAH WESTON: one bedstead, one ditto, 5 leather bottom chairs, 5 ditto, 5 calico ditto, tongs, shovels, and dogs, one coffee pot, one tea table, three salvers, one tea chest, 7 China plates, one large oval table, and

To JAMES TAYLOR Gentleman: some bedding and make sale of the rest of the articles contained in the said schedule and out of which first pay unto SARAH CANN her demand of 19 pounds for house rent and then the Plaintiff his above claim and costs and that he also return an account of his proceedings and thereupon at the next Court to be held for this Borough and the attachment against the garnishees is continued

JOHN SYME against JAMES HALDANE. JAMES LEITCH this day came into Court and undertook for the Defendant that in case he shall be casts in this suit he the said Defendant will pay the condemnation of the Court or render his body to Prison in execution for the same or that the said LEITCH will pay the condemnation or render the body of the said Defendant as aforesaid. Where upon the Defendant by his Attorney prays and have leave to IMPARLE here the next Court and then to Plead.

MATTHEW PHRIPP and JOSEPH HUTCHINGS who as well on behalf of our Sovereign Lord the King as for themselves against RICHARD DAVIS. Dismissed.

MATTHEW PHRIPP and JOSEPH HUTCHINGS who as well on behalf of our Sovereign Lord the King as for themselves against MORTO BRYAN. Special Imparlance

JAMES MARSDEN and JONATHAN EILBECK executors of ELDRED FISHER deceased against WILLIAM SISSON. DOCTOR WILLIAM SHEPHERD this day came into Court and undertook for the Defendant that in case he shall be casts in this suit he the said Defendant will pay the condemnation of the Court or render his body to Prison in execution for the same or that the said SHEPHERD will pay the condemnation or render the body of the said Defendant as aforesaid. Where upon the Defendant by his Attorney prays and have leave to IMPARLE here the next Court and then to Plead.

PAGE 182

JAMES MARSDEN and JONATHAN EILBECK executors of ELDRED FISHER deceased against JOHN GILCHRIST. The suit is dismissed at the Plaintiff's cost.

JAMES MARSDEN and JONATHAN EILBECK executors of ELDRED FISHER deceased against THOMAS WALKER, A Conditional order against the Defendant and CHARLES COOPER his bail.

JAMES MARSDEN and JONATHAN EILBECK executors of ELDRED FISHER deceased against JONATHAN DAVIS by Petition and summons. Judgement is granted the Plaintiff for 4 pounds 1 shilling and 3 pence. It is ordered that the Defendant pay the same unto the Plaintiff with costs and fee.

JAMES MARSDEN and JONATHAN EILBECK executors of ELDRED FISHER deceased against HARDRESS WALLER. Dismissed.

JAMES MARSDEN and JONATHAN EILBECK executors of ELDRED FISHER deceased against THOMAS ROBERTS by Petition and summons. Judgement is granted the Plaintiff for 3 pounds 9 shilling and 6 pence. It is ordered that the Defendant pay the same unto the Plaintiff with costs and fee.

JAMES MARSDEN and JONATHAN EILBECK executors of ELDRED FISHER deceased against EDWARD DAVIS. The suit is Dismissed.

DICKERSON PRIOR against JAMES DAWSON. The suit is dismissed.

MATTHEW PHRIPP and JOSEPH HUTCHINGS who as well on behalf of our Sovereign Lord the King as for themselves against JOHN LEWIS. An Alias Capias is awarded the Plaintiffs.

MATTHEW PHRIPP and JOSEPH HUTCHINGS who as well on behalf of our Sovereign Lord the King as for themselves against WILLIAM MURRAY. An Alias Capias is awarded the Plaintiffs.

MATTHEW PHRIPP and JOSEPH HUTCHINGS who as well on behalf of our Sovereign Lord the King as for themselves against WILLIAM NEWTON. An Alias Capias is awarded the Plaintiffs.

WILLIAM ROBINSON against JOSHUA WRIGHT. Special Imparlance.

PAGE 182B

MATTHEW PHRIPP and JOSEPH HUTCHINGS who as well on behalf of our Sovereign Lord the King as for themselves against JOHN BOGGESS. Special Imparlance.

MATTHEW PHRIPP and JOSEPH HUTCHINGS who as well on behalf of our Sovereign Lord the King as for themselves against JOSEPH POPE. An Imparlance.

MATTHEW PHRIPP and JOSEPH HUTCHINGS who as well on behalf of our Sovereign Lord the King as for themselves against JACOB WILLIAMS. An Imparlance.

MATTHEW PHRIPP and JOSEPH HUTCHINGS who as well on behalf of our Sovereign Lord the King as for themselves against MATTHEW KELLY. An Imparlance.

MATTHEW PHRIPP and JOSEPH HUTCHINGS who as well on behalf of our Sovereign Lord the King as for themselves against GEORGE JOSEPH FENWICK. Order against Defendant and PETER KATZ his bail.

MATTHEW PHRIPP and JOSEPH HUTCHINGS who as well on behalf of our Sovereign Lord the King as for themselves against GEORGE ATKINSON. An Imparlance.

MATTHEW PHRIPP and JOSEPH HUTCHINGS who as well on behalf of our Sovereign Lord the King as for themselves against JOHN BYSER. An Imparlance.

MATTHEW PHRIPP and JOSEPH HUTCHINGS who as well on behalf of our Sovereign Lord the King as for themselves against JUDITH DUNFORD. An Imparlance.

JOHN MCLACHLAN against ALEXANDER BELL. In Debt. PAUL LOYALL and THOMAS NEWTON SR. this day came into Court and undertook for the Defendant that in case he shall be casts in this suit he the said Defendant will pay the condemnation of the Court or render his body to Prison in execution for the same or that the said LOYALL and NEWTON will pay the condemnation or render the body of the said Defendant as aforesaid. Where upon the Defendant by his Attorney prays and have leave to IMPARLE here the next Court and then to Plead.

BARTHOLOMEW TAYLOR against MISTERS NATHANIEL YOUNG and POOK. Special Imparlance

PAGE 183

On the petition of JOHN GILCHRIST against JAMES MARSDEN and JONATHAN EILBECK executors of ELDRED FISHER deceased for 3 pound 8 pence due by account. This day came the parties by their Attorney's and the Plaintiff having proved his demanded to be just by his own oath. Therefore, it is considered by the Court that the Plaintiff recover the same against the said Defendants together with his costs by him in this behalf expended when assets after paying proceeding judgements debts of greater dignity and the defendants own claims of equal dignity against the estate of the said intestate to be levied of the goods and chattels which were of the said ELDRED at the time of his death that shall hereafter come to the hands of the said Defendants to be administered and the Defendants in mercy.

THOMAS MORGAN against THOMAS EDWARDS JR. An Imparlance.
GEORGE KELLY against DUGALD GILCHRIST. The suit is dismissed.
JOHN FLAHERTY against CHARLES HILL. The suit is dismissed.
The King by BAILEY WARREN and wife against MORRIS BUCKLEY. Dismissed at the Defendants costs.

BETTY a Negro woman belonging to ELIZABETH DAVIS was this day brought before the Court by warrant under the hands of PAUL LOYALL and CHARLES THOMAS for being a person of lewd life and a common disturber of the peace. And the same being proved it is ordered that the Sergeant take and keep her in Custody until her said Mistress enters into bond and one security in 50 pounds for keeping the peace and being of good behavior for 12 months.

The King by MARY TRACEY against CATHERINE LEWIS. Dismissed.
GEORGE KELLY against JAMES HALDANE. Dismissed.

RICHARD COLLINS against THOMAS HUGHS. In T.A.B. WILLIAM PLUME this day came into Court and undertook for the Defendant that in case he shall be casts in this suit he the said Defendant will pay the condemnation of the Court or render his body to Prison in execution for the same or that the said PLUME will pay the condemnation or render the body of the said Defendant as aforesaid. Where upon the Defendant by his Attorney prays and have leave to IMPARLE here the next Court and then to Plead.

JAMES NORRIS against THOMAS ALEXANDER. The suit is Dismissed.
JOHN TATEM against JAMES ROGERS and JOHN JOHNSON. Dismissed.
MCKEAND and BUCHANAN against EDWARD GOOD. An Imparlance.

PAGE 183B

JOHN MACLEAN, THOMAS TALBOT and HENRY LAMOUNT against JOHN WILSON and JOHN MEARNS. In Debt. The suit is discontinued against JOHN WILSON and JOHN CRAMOND came into Court and undertook for the Defendant that in case he shall be casts in this suit he the said Defendant will pay the condemnation of the Court or render his body to Prison in execution for the same or that the said CRAMOND will pay the condemnation or render the body of the said Defendant as aforesaid. Where upon the Defendant by his Attorney prays and have leave to IMPARLE here the next Court and then to Plead.

PETER MCCARE against JOHN FORESYTH. The Suit is Dismissed.
PETER MCCARE against ANDREW FAIREY. The Suit is Dismissed.

RACHAEL RICHARDSON against ANN BREITHWAIT. An Imparlance.
JAMES CARMICHAEL against RICHARD JARVIS. An Imparlance.

RICHARD BROWN Trustee of TERESA PEARSE against PETER RANDOL. The Suit is Dismissed.
AMELIA SOPHIA LEONORA FELTHAM against BARNABAS LORAIN. An Imparlance.

WILLIAM and THOMAS FARRERS against WILLIAM BRETT. Order against Defendant and ROBERT BRITT his bail.

JOHN DUNN against GEORGE WINKLE and ELIZABETH his wife. An Imparlance.
MISTERS JOHN and JOSEPH HUTCHINGS against JOSHUA WRIGHT. The suit is Dismissed.

WALTER PETER against JOHN STRATTON. An Imparlance.
GEORGE KELLY against MATTHEW MCVIE. Dismissed.

GEORGE KELLY against ZACHERIAH BOLITHO by Petition and summons. Judgement is granted the Plaintiff for 4 pounds 14 shilling and 9 pence. It is ordered that the Defendant pay the same unto the Plaintiff with costs and fee.

JOHN MEARNS against JAMES ROGERS Dismissed.

ARETAS AKERS and ROBERT HOUSTON against JAMES MARSDEN and JAMES MAXWELL administrators of JAMES PATTERSON deceased. Imparlance.
ANDREW STEVENSON against JOHN MEARNS. An Imparlance

PAGE 184
TRAVIS TUCKER an infant by JOHN COLE his guardian against NEIL JAMIESON admin of HENRY TUCKER Deceased. The Defendant by his intestate did not assume issue joined and referred.

CHRISTOPHER WRIGHT against WILLIAM WISHART. On the motion of the Defendant by his Attorney a DEDIMUS is granted him to take the Depositions of LEMUEL RIDDICK and ANTHONY HOLIDAY DE BENE ESSE and giving notice.

This Court is adjourned until tomorrow at 9 o'clock, PAUL LOYALL MAYOR, TESTE: JOHN BOUSH D.C.

NORFOLK BOROUGH
At a Hustings Court Held this 25th day of May 1773
PRESENT: PAUL LOYALL ESQUIRE MAYOR
GENTLEMAN ALDERMEN: GEORGE ABYVON, CHARLES THOMAS, ARCHIBALD CAMPBELL, JAMES TAYLOR, LEWIS HANSFORD, CORNELIUS CALVERT

ARCHIBALD GOVAN Plaintiff
Against Re: In Case
THOMAS CLAIBORNE Defendant
This day came as well the Plaintiff by ANDREW RONALD Gentleman their Attorney as the Defendant in his proper person and says that he cannot gainsay the Plaintiff action nor but that he did assume in manner and form as the Plaintiff against him has declared. Therefore, it is considered that the Plaintiff recover against the said Defendant 118 pounds 1 shillings and 2 pence 3 farthing and his costs by him about his suit in this behalf expended and the said Defendant in mercy.

THOMAS LANGLEY SR. against JOHN HUTCHINGS and JOSEPH HUTCHINGS. This day came the parties by their Attorney's and the Jury not returning any verdict in this cause, they are discharged.

JAMES GILCHRIST and ROBERT TAYLOR against GEORGE FOWLER. This day the parties by their Attorney's and the Jury not returning any verdict in this cause they are discharged.

THOMAS LANGELY against JAMES WEBB. Jury discharged.

PAGE 184B
CHARLES MAYLE Plaintiff
Against Re: In Case
SAMUEL BRESSIE Defendant
The partings having mutually submitted all matters in difference between them to the determination of JOHN WILSON and ABRAM WORMINGTON and agreed that their award thereupon should be made the judgement of this Court and they having returned their award on the promises in these words to wit: Obedient to an Order of the worshipful Court of Norfolk setting we have examined in the case depending between DOCTOR CHARLES MAYLE and SAMUEL BRESSE of Norfolk County and find that the said SAMUEL BRESSIE stands justly indebted by his own consent unto DOCTOR CHARLES MAYLE the sum of 15 pounds 5 shillings and 11 pence Virginia Currency with costs.

Signed by JOHN WILSON and ABRAM WORMINGTON. It is there upon considered that the Plaintiff recover against the said Defendant the said 15 pounds 5 shillings and 11 pence and his costs by him in this behalf expended.

ARCHIBALD CAMPBELL and GEORGE WILSON admins of JOHN WILSON deceased Plaintiff
Against Re: In Case
JOHN CALVERT MARINER Defendant
This day came the parties by their Attorney's and there upon came also a Jury to wit: JOHN MACLEAN, WILLIAM NORTH, PHILIP CARBERY, ANDREW STEVENSON, WILLIAM INGRAM, THOMAS ROBERTS, STEPHEN TANKARD, JOHN BOGUS, WRIGHT BRICKLE, ROBERT FRY, THOMAS TERRY and ROBERT GILMOUR who being elected tried and sworn the truth to speak upon the issue joined upon their oath do say that the Defendant did assume in manner and form as the Plaintiff's against him have declared and do assess the Plaintiff damages by occasion of the non-performance of that assumption to 17 pounds 5 shillings and 3 pence besides their costs. Therefore, it is considered that the Plaintiff recover against the said Defendant damages in form aforesaid and assessed and their costs by them in this behalf expended and the said Defendant in mercy.

ARCHIBALD CAMPBELL and GEORGE WILSON admins of JOHN WILSON deceased Plaintiff
Against Re: In Case
SAMUEL CALVERT MARINER Defendant
This day came the parties by their Attorney's and there upon came also a Jury to wit: JOHN SMITH, JAMES HALDANE, DANIEL HUTCHINGS, JOHN CRAMOND, WRIGHT WESTCOTT, JAMES GILCHRIST, WILLIAM FREEMAN, JOHN CARMOUNT, JOHN TODD, JOHN LELLO, GEORGE GORDON, and EDWARD ARCHER who being elected tried and sworn the truth to speak upon the issue joined upon their oath do say that the Defendant did assume in manner and form as the Plaintiff's against him have declared and do assess the Plaintiff damages by occasion of the non-performance of that assumption to 7 pounds 12 shillings besides their costs. Therefore, it is considered that the Plaintiff recover against the said Defendant damages in form aforesaid and assessed and their costs by them in this behalf expended and the said Defendant in mercy.

PAGE 185
ANDREW SPROWLE Admins of JOHN SPROWLE and ROBERT CROOKS deceased Plaintiff
Against Re: In Case
GEORGE COLLINS Defendant
This day came the parties by their Attorney's and there upon came also a Jury to wit: JOHN SMITH, JAMES HALDANE, DANIEL HUTCHINGS, JOHN CRAMOND, WRIGHT WESTCOTT, JAMES GILCHRIST, WILLIAM FREEMAN, JOHN CARMOUNT, JOHN TODD, JOHN LELLO, GEORGE GORDON, and EDWARD ARCHER who being elected tried and sworn the truth to speak upon the issue joined upon their oath do say that the Defendant did not assume as in pleading he has alleged. Therefore, is it considered that the Plaintiff take nothing by his bill but for his false claims be in mercy. And the Defendant go hence without day and recover against the Plaintiff his costs by him about his defense in this behalf expended.

AITCHESON and PACKER Plaintiff
Against Re: In Case
ALEXANDER BELL Defendant
This day came the parties by their Attorney's and there upon came also a Jury to wit: JOHN SMITH, JAMES HALDANE, DANIEL HUTCHINGS, JOHN CRAMOND, WRIGHT WESTCOTT, JAMES GILCHRIST, WILLIAM FREEMAN, JOHN CARMOUNT, JOHN TODD, JOHN LELLO, GEORGE GORDON, and EDWARD ARCHER who being elected tried and sworn the truth to speak upon the issue joined upon their oath do say that the Defendant has not paid the debt in the declaration mentioned. Therefore, it is considered that the Plaintiff recover against the said Defendant their debt amounting to 17 pounds 4 shillings and 10 pence and their costs by them in this behalf expend and the said Defendant in mercy. But this judgement is to be discharged by the payment of 8 pounds 12 shillings and 5 pence with interest thereon after the rate of 5 % per annum to be computed from July 5, 1771, to the time of payment and costs.

MARGARET BANNERMAN against BENJMAIN BANNERMAN in Chancery. GEORGE VEALE and MAXIMILIAN CALVERT Gentleman are appointed Sequestrators to the Plaintiff in the room of BENJAMIN CROOKER who has resigned.

Order is granted THOMAS EDWARDS JR. against GEORGE COLLINS for 200 pounds of tobacco for 8 days attendance in the suit of ANDREW SPROWLE admin of SPROWLE and CROOKS against him.

MATTHEW ROTHERY executors against HENRY ROTHERY'S Administratrix. On the motion of the Plaintiff by their Attorney a DEDIMUS is granted them to take the deposition of JAMES THOMPSON giving the defendant reasonable notice.

MATTHEW ROTHERY executors against THOMAS PEARSON. On the motion of the Plaintiff by their Attorney a DEDIMUS is granted them to take the deposition of JAMES THOMPSON giving the defendant reasonable notice.

JOHN CALVERT against BARNABY CARNEY abates by the Defendant's death.
MISTERS JOHN and THOMAS GILCHRIST against BARNABY CARNEY abates by the Defendants death.

PAGE 185B
JAMES EDMUNDSON admin of WILLIAM RAMSAY Deceased Plaintiff
Against Re: In Debt
ANTHONY FLEMING Defendant

This day came the parties by their Attorney's and the Defendant by his Attorney relinquishes his former plea, acknowledges the Plaintiff's action for 7 pounds 3 shillings. Therefore, it is considered that the Plaintiff recover against the said Defendant his debt aforesaid and his costs by him in this behalf expended and the said Defendant in mercy.

BARNABY CARNEY against HENRY GREEN abates by the Defendants death.

BARNABY CARNEY against JAMES MARSDEN & JOHN EILBECK executors of ELDRED FISHER abates by the Plaintiff's death.

WILLIAM POOLE against HUGH MCPHILIMY Dismissed. (2X)

JOHN TUCKER Plaintiff

Against Re: In Case

JAMES MARSDEN & JOHN EILBECK executors of ELDRED FISHER deceased Defendants

This day came the parties by their Attorney's and the Defendants by their Attorney say that they cannot gainsay the Plaintiff action nor but that their testator did assume in manner and form as the Plaintiff against them have declared. Therefore, it is considered that the Plaintiff recover against the

Defendants 18 pounds 9 shillings and 9 pence half penny and his costs by him in this behalf expended, when assets after paying preceding judgements, debts of greater dignity and the Defendants own claims of equal dignity against the estate of the said Testator to be levied of the goods and chattels which were of the said ELDRED at the time of his death that shall hereafter come to the hands of the said Defendants to be administered and the said Defendants in mercy.

JAMES MUDIE Plaintiff

Against Re: In Case

THOMAS TILLIDGE Defendant

This day came the parties by their Attorney's and there upon came also a Jury to wit: JOHN SMITH, JAMES HALDANE, DANIEL HUTCHINGS, JOHN CRAMOND, WRIGHT WESTCOTT, JAMES GILCHRIST, WILLIAM FREEMAN, JOHN CARMOUNT, JOHN TODD, JOHN LELLO, GEORGE GORDON, and EDWARD ARCHER who being elected tried and sworn the truth to speak upon the issue joined upon their oath do say that the Defendant did not assume as in pleading he has alleged. Therefore, is it considered that the Plaintiff take nothing by his bill but for his false claims be in mercy. And the Defendant go hence without day and recover against the Plaintiff his costs by him about his defense in this behalf expended.

PAGE 186

MICHAEL CHRISTIAN and JOHN HARMANSON Plaintiff

Against Re: In Case

ALEXANDER MCSWEEN Defendant

This day came the parties by their Attorney's and there upon came also a Jury to wit: JOHN MCLEAN, WILLIAM NORTH, PHILIP CARBERY, WILLIAM INGRAM, THOMAS ROBERT, STEPHEN TANKARD, JOHN BOGUS, WRIGHT BRICKLE, ROBERT FRY, THOMAS TERRY, ROBERT GILMOUR, and WILLIAM FREEMAN who being elected tried and sworn the truth to speak upon the issue joined upon their oath do say that the Defendant did not assume as in pleading he has alleged. Therefore, is it considered that the Plaintiff take nothing by his bill but for his false claims be in mercy. And the Defendant go hence without day and recover against the Plaintiff his costs by him about his defense in this behalf expended.

Order is granted JOHN WEST against THOMAS TILLIDGE for 125 pounds of tobacco for 5 days attendance at this Court as a witness in the suit of JAMES MUDIE against him.

MARSDEN and HODGSON against WILLIAM CONNER. On the motion of the Plaintiff by their Attorney a DEDIMUS is granted them to take the depositions of JOHN PHRIPP DE BENE ESSE giving notice of the time and place to the Defendant

WILLIAM MOSELEY Plaintiff

Against Re: In Debt

ALEXANDER BELL Defendant

This day came the parties by their Attorney's and there upon came also a Jury to wit: JAMES HALDANE, DANIEL HUTCHINGS, JOHN CRAMOND, WRIGHT WESTCOTT, JAMES GILCHRIST, WILLIAM FREEMAN, JOHN CARMOUNT, JOHN TODD, JOHN LELLO, GEORGE GORDON, EDWARD ARCHER and ANDREW STEVENSON who being elected tried and sworn the truth to speak upon the issue joined upon their oath do say that the Defendant has not paid the debt in the declaration mentioned. Therefore, it is considered that the Plaintiff recover against the said Defendant his debt amounting to 8 pounds 5 shillings 8 pence 3 farthings with interest thereon after the rate of 5% per annum to be computed from February 17th, 1772, to the time of payment and the costs and the said Defendant in mercy.

(Note in Margin) SCIRE FACIAS issued by errors March 3, 1774)

FRANCIS ROBINSON Plaintiff

Against Re: In Debt

JOHN SMITH Defendant

This day came the parties by their Attorney's and there upon came also a Jury to wit: JAMES HALDANE, DANIEL HUTCHINGS, JOHN CRAMOND, WRIGHT WESTCOTT, JAMES GILCHRIST, WILLIAM FREEMAN, JOHN CARMOUNT, JOHN TODD, JOHN LELLO, GEORGE GORDON, EDWARD ARCHER and ANDREW STEVENSON who being elected tried and sworn the truth to speak upon the issue joined upon their oath do say that the Defendant has not paid the debt in the declaration mentioned. Therefore, it is considered that the Plaintiff recover against the said Defendant his debt amounting to 523 pounds 12 shillings 8 pence and her costs by her in this behalf expended. and the said Defendant in mercy. But this Judgement is to be discharged by the payment of 228 pounds 6 shillings and 3 pence farthing with interest thereon after the rate of 5% per annum to be computed from November 1, 1766, to the time of payment and the costs.

PAGE 186B
CORNELIUS CALVERT Defendant
Against Re: In Case
JOHN SMITH Defendant
This day came the parties by their Attorney and the Defendant by his Attorney relinquishing his former plea says that he cannot gainsay the Plaintiffs action nor but that he did assume in manner and form as the Plaintiff against him has declared. Therefore, it is considered that the Plaintiff recover against the said Defendant 12 pounds 10 shillings and his costs by him in this behalf expended and the said Defendant in mercy.

HYNDMAN LANCASTER and Company Plaintiff
Against Re: In Case
ARCHIBALD CAMPBELL admin of JOHN DALGLEISH Defendant
This day came as well the Plaintiffs by ANDREW RONALD Gentleman their Attorney as the Defendant in his proper person and says that he cannot gainsay the Plaintiffs action nor but that his intestate did assume in manner and form as the Plaintiff against him have declared. Therefore, it is considered that the Plaintiff recover against the said Defendant 189 pounds 4 shillings and 10 pence sterling and their costs by them in this behalf expended. When assets after paying preceding judgements, debts of equal dignity and the Defendants own claim of equal dignity against the estate of the said intestate to be levied of the goods and chattels which were of the said JOHN at the time of this death, that shall hereafter come into the hands of the said Defendant to be administered and the said Defendant in mercy and the Court says the sterling money may be discharged in Current money at 25% difference of exchange.

Order is granted BARNABAS LORAIN against ROGER PEARSE for 100 pounds of tobacco for 4 days attendance at this Court in the Attachment of JAMES HALDANE against him.

Ordered the Sergeant summon ABRAM PEATON, WILLIAM WALKER, and WILLIAM MICHIE to appear at the next Court to be sworn constables for this Borough

This Court this day rated flour at 16/8 per centum
This Court is adjourned to Court in Course, PAUL LOYALL MAYOR, TESTE: JOHN BOUSH D.C.

PAGE 187
NORFOLK BOROUGH
At a Hustings Court Held this 21st day of June 1773
PRESENT: PAUL LOYALL ESQUIRE MAYOR
GENTLEMAN ALDERMEN: GEORGE ABYVON, LEWIS HANSFORD, ARCHIBALD CAMPBELL, CHARLES THOMAS

JOHN MEARNS against ANDREW STEVENSON. Imparlance.

GEORGE GORDON assignee of JOHN TATEM against ARCHIBALD CAMPBELL and GEORGE WILSON administrators of JOHN WILSON deceased An Imparlance

DAVID CROSS Plaintiff against JAMES MARSDEN and JONATHAN EILBECK Executors of ELDRED FISHER deceased Defendant. In Case. Imparlance

ALEXANDER GRAHAM against JAMES RANKIN. The suit is Dismissed at the Plaintiff's costs.

JAMES HOLT Plaintiff
Against Re: In Case
CHRISTOPHER HERBERT Defendant
This day came the parties in their proper persons and the Defendant says that he cannot gainsay the Plaintiff action nor but that he did assume in manner and form as the Plaintiff against him has declared. Therefore, it is considered that the Plaintiff recover against the said Defendant 35 pounds 1 shillings and 4 pence with interest thereon after the rate of 5% per annum to be computed from August 8, 1764, to the time of payment and the costs.

BENJAMIN ARTHUR against GEORGE GEARY. The suit is dismissed.
ANN SYMONS an infant by ROBERT BANKS her next friend against SAMUEL MCCASTLETON and ABBY his wife. Dismissed.

ROBERT TUCKER against JOHN LAWRENCE and MATTHEW PHRIPP executors of THOMAS THOMPSON deceased. Imparlance.
THOMAS GREEN against JOHN WILLIAMSON. An Imparlance.

MORTO BYRAN against ROGER PEARCE. In Case. The Defendant pleaded he did not assume, issue joined and referred until the next Court to be held for this Borough

MORTO BRYAN against ROGER PEARCE. In Covenant. JAMES LEITCH entered himself special bail for the Defendant and then to pleaded Covenants performed and agreed the suit to be tried on merits of issue joined and referred until next Court.

PAGE 187B
WILLIAM SIMPSON Plaintiff
Against Re: In Debt.
THOMAS BULL Defendant
This day came as well the Plaintiff by WILLIAM ROBINSON Gentleman his Attorney as the Defendant in his proper person and acknowledges the Plaintiffs action for 24 pounds. Therefore, it is considered that the Plaintiff recover against the said Defendant his debt aforesaid and his costs by him about his suit in this behalf expended and the said Defendant in mercy. But judgement is to be discharged by the payment of 12 pounds with interest thereon after the rate of 5% per annum to be computed from January 10th, 1771, to the time of payment and the costs. And the Plaintiff by his Attorney has agreed to stay execution of this Judgement until the first of December next.

JOHN and JONATHAN EILBECK against JOSHUA WRIGHT, JOSEPH CALVERT came into Court and entered himself Special Bail for the Defendant and a conditional order is granted the Plaintiff against the said Defendant.

FREDERICK BOUSH against WILLIAM SIMPSON by Petition and summons. Judgement is granted the Plaintiff for 5 pounds. It is ordered that the Defendant pay the same unto the Plaintiff with costs and fee.

PHILIP HAYNES against JOHN WILLIAMS. Conditional order against Defendant and JOHN GREENWOOD his bail.

JOHN RICHARDSON against THOMAS PEARSON Dismissed.
JOHN RICHARDSON against GEORGE JOSEPH FENWICK by Petition and summons. Judgement is granted the Plaintiff for 2 pounds 1 shillings. It is ordered that the Defendant pay the same unto the Plaintiff with costs and fee.

JOHN RICHARDSON against WILLIAM IVY by Petition and summons. Judgement is granted the Plaintiff for 15 shillings. It is ordered that the Defendant pay the same unto the Plaintiff with costs and fee.

JOSEPH NORTHRUP against SAMUEL MCCASTLETON Dismissed.

JAMES MARSDEN and JONATHAN EILBECK executors of ELDRED FISHER deceased against HOWARD POOLE. Dismissed.

WILLIAM SIMPSON against THOMAS PEARSON by Petition and summons. Judgement is granted the Plaintiff for 2 pounds 5 shillings and 7 pence half penny. It is ordered that the Defendant pay the same unto the Plaintiff with costs and fee.

SIMON BROWNE and Company against JOHN CRAMOND. In Case. WILLIAM SIMPSON. This day came into Court and undertook for the Defendant that in case he shall be casts in this suit he the said Defendant will pay the condemnation of the Court or render his body to Prison in execution for the same or that the said SIMPSON will pay the condemnation or render the body of the said Defendant as aforesaid. Where upon the Defendant by his Attorney prays and have leave to IMPARLE here the next Court and then to Plead.

PAGE 188
WILLIAM SIMPSON Plaintiff
Against Re: In Case
ROGER PEARCE Defendant
This day came the Plaintiff by WILLIAM ROBINSON Gentleman his Attorney as the Defendant in his proper person says that he cannot gainsay the Plaintiff action nor but that he did assume in manner and form as the Plaintiff against him has declared. Therefore, it is considered that the Plaintiff recover against the said Defendant 13 pounds 6 shillings and his costs by him about his suit in this behalf expended and the said Defendant in mercy.

SAMUEL PORTLOCK against ARCHIBALD CAMPBELL. An Imparlance.
ROBERT HATTON against SOLOMON EDY. Dismissed at the Plaintiff's costs.

JAMES MARSDEN and JONATHAN EILBECK executors of ELDRED FISHER deceased against RICHARD BASSET by Petition and summons. Judgement is granted the Plaintiff for 2 pounds 1 shillings. It is ordered that the Defendant pay the same unto the Plaintiff with costs and fee.
MATTHEW PHRIPP and JOSEPH HUTCHINGS who as well on behalf of our Sovereign Lord the King as for themselves against JOHN LEWIS, JAMES VICKERS, WILLIAM MURRAY, and WILLIAM NEWTON Attachments.

JOHN MEARNS against ELISHA REY by Petition and summons. Judgement is granted the Plaintiff for 2 pounds 4 shillings. It is ordered that the Defendant pay the same unto the Plaintiff with costs and fee.

JAMES ROGERS against JAMES ANDERSON Dismissed.
ALEXANDER GORDON against WRIGHT WESTCOTT and STEPHEN WRIGHT demurer filed and time.

ANTHONY WARWICK and ARCHIBALD BUCHANAN against JAMES DUNLOP. In Case. The Defendant by his Attorney pleaded not guilty with leave issue joined and referred.

MARY ROTHERY and others executors of MATTHEW ROTHERY against GEORGE WATSON and ANN his wife. Admin of RICHARD BOUCHER bill filed and time to consider it.

MAXIMILIAN CALVERT against STEPHEN TANKARD. The former order of the Court against the Defendant be confirmed, and a writ of inquiry is awarded the Plaintiff to inquire of damages.

CALEB HANBURY against ALEXANDER BELL. The Defendant pleaded not guilty. Issue joined and referred until the next Court to be held for this Borough.

PAGE 188B

ALEXANDER BELL against MALACHI MAUND. In T.A.B. The suit is dismissed at the Plaintiff's costs.

JOHN GOODRICH against SOLOMON SHEPHERD JR. The suit is dismissed at the Plaintiff's cost.

JOHN SHAW and MARY, his wife executors of JAMES ARNOT deceased, against JAMES BAYNES. The former order of the Court against the said Defendant and JOSEPH CALVERT Sergeant his bail is confirmed, and a writ of inquiry is award the Plaintiff to inquire.

JOHN CHESHIRE against ROBERT BROWN. The Defendant pleaded he did not assume with leave issue joined and referred until the next Court to be held for this Borough.

TALBOT THOMPSON against JOHN DAY admin of THOMAS DAY deceased. The Defendant pleaded he did not assume issue joined and referred until the next Court to be held for this Borough.

JOHN ARDIS against THOMAS HARRISON. The Defendant pleaded not guilty issue joined and referred until the next Court.

ROBERT GILMOUR admin of the Estate of WILLIAM GRAY deceased against BAILEY WARREN. The said Defendant pleaded he did not assume issue joined and referred.

SAMUEL BOUSH against RICHARD FRYER. The Defendant pleaded payment issue joined and referred until next Court.

ROBERT SHEDDEN and Company against WILLIAM CONNER admin of WILLIAM C. CONNER deceased. The former order of the Court against the said Defendant and CHARLES CONNER his bail be confirmed, and a writ of inquiry is awarded the Plaintiff's to inquire of damages in this suit.

RICHARD BASSET against JOHN HARWOOD. The Defendant pleaded payment issue joined and referred until the next Court.

RICHARD BASSET against JOHN POLLOCK. The Defendant pleaded payment issue joined and referred until the next Court.

WILLIAM HARDY against JOHN EDWARDS. The Defendant pleaded he did not assume issue joined and referred until the next Court.

PETER LONG against WILLIAM BRITT. The Defendant pleaded not guilty issue joined and referred until the next Court.

MISTERS SAMUEL INGLES and PETER LONG against WILLIAM LIDDLE. The Defendant pleaded he did not assume issue joined and referred until the next Court.

RICHARD KELSICK against NATHANIEL BOUSH. The Defendant by his Attorney pleaded payment issue joined and referred until the next Court.

PAGE 189

NICHOLAS WONYCOTT against THOMAS WALKER. The Defendant pleaded he did not assume issue joined and referred

JAMES MILLS and Company against RICHARD BROWN and JOHN CHESHIRE. The Defendant pleaded not guilty issue joined and referred until the next Court.

JOSEPH LANGLEY against JOHN MCLACHLAN. The Defendant pleaded he did not assume issue joined and referred

SAMUEL BLEWS against ANDREW STEVENSON and ANN his wife. The Defendant pleaded not guilty issue joined and referred until the next Court.

JAMES HEALY against ANDREW STEVENSON and ANN his wife. The Defendant pleaded not guilty issue joined and referred until the next Court.

MISTERS JOHN RAMSAY and JAMES TAYLOR against JOHN CRAMOND admin of MARY ROBINSON. The Defendant pleaded that his intestate did not assume issue joined and referred

WILLIAM and THOMAS FARRERS against WILLIAM BRITT. ROBERT BRITT this day came into Court
and undertook for the Defendant that in case he shall be cast in this suit he the said Defendant will pay the condemnation of the Court or render his body to Prison in execution for the same or that the said ROBERT will do it for him. And there upon the Judgement in the last Court obtained by the Plaintiff against the said Defendant and bail is set aside and thereon the Defendant pleading payment issue joined and referred.

NATHANIEL YOUNG and JOHN SMITH Plaintiff
Against Re: In Case
WRIGHT WESTCOTT admin of JOHN WESTCOTT Defendant
This day came the parties by their Attorney's and the Defendant by his Attorney says that he cannot gainsay the Plaintiffs action nor but that his intestate did assume in manner and form as the Plaintiff against him have declared. Therefore, it is considered that the Plaintiff recover against the said Defendant 59 pounds 2 shillings and 1 penny half penny and their costs by them in this behalf expended when assess after paying preceding judgements, debts of greater dignity and the Defendants own claim of equal dignity against the estate of the said intestate to be levied of the goods and chattels which were of the said JOHN at the time of his death that shall hereafter come to the hands of the said Defendant to be administered and the said Defendant in mercy.

WILLIAM MCDOUGAL against HUMPHREY ROBERTS. Discontinued at the Plaintiff's costs.

Order is granted LABON GOFFIGAN against HUMPHREY ROBERTS for 50 pounds of tobacco for 2 days attendance in the suit of WILLIAM MCDOUGAL against him.

PAGE 189B
MALACHI MAUND Plaintiff
Against Re: In Case
SAMUEL and HENRY BRESSIE Defendants
This day came the parties by their Attorney's and there upon came also a Jury to wit: JOHN MACLEAN, GEORGE WILSON, WILLIAM STEVENSON, THOMAS HEPBURN, CHRISTOPHER CALVERT, HENRY FLEMING, LATIMORE HALSTEAD, WILLIAM IVY, DANIEL HUTCHINGS, WRIGHT WESTCOTT, GRIFFIN PEART, and JAMES LEITCH who being elected tried and sworn the truth to speak upon the issue joined upon their oath do day that the Defendants did assume in manner and form as the Plaintiff against them has declared and do assess the Plaintiff damages by occasion of the non-performance of that assumption to 6 pounds besides his costs. Therefore, it is considered that the Plaintiff recover against the said Defendant his damages aforesaid in form aforesaid assessed and his costs by him in this behalf expended and the said Defendants in mercy.

WILLIAM GRAHAM Plaintiff
Against Re: In Case
ROGER PEARCE Defendant
This day came the parties by their Attorney's and there upon came also a Jury to wit: JOHN MACLEAN, GEORGE WILSON, WILLIAM STEVENSON, THOMAS HEPBURN, CHRISTOPHER CALVERT, HENRY FLEMING, LATIMORE HALSTEAD, WILLIAM IVY, DANIEL HUTCHINGS, WRIGHT WESTCOTT, GRIFFIN PEART, and JAMES LEITCH who being elected tried and sworn the truth to speak upon the issue joined upon their oath do day that the Defendants is guilty in manner and form as the Plaintiff against them has declared and do assess the Plaintiff damages by occasion thereof to 15 pounds besides his costs. Therefore, it is considered that the Plaintiff recover against the said Defendant his damages aforesaid in form aforesaid assessed and his costs by him in this behalf expended and the said Defendants in mercy.

ROGER PEARCE Plaintiff
Against Re: In Case
WILLIAM GRAHAM Defendant
This day came the parties by their Attorney's and there upon came also a Jury to wit: JOHN MACLEAN, GEORGE WILSON, WILLIAM STEVENSON, THOMAS HEPBURN, CHRISTOPHER CALVERT, HENRY FLEMING, LATIMORE HALSTEAD, WILLIAM IVY, DANIEL HUTCHINGS, WRIGHT WESTCOTT, GRIFFIN PEART, and JAMES LEITCH who being elected tried and sworn the truth to speak upon the issue joined upon their oath do day that the Defendant is not guilty as in pleading he has alleged. Therefore, it is considered that the Plaintiff take nothing by his bill but for his false claims be in mercy. And the Defendant go hence without day and recover against the Plaintiff his costs by him about his defense in this behalf expended.

CHRISTOPHER WRIGHT against WILLIAM WISHART. On the motion of the Plaintiff by his Attorney a DEDIMUS is granted him to take the depositions of EDWARD WRIGHT and THOMAS HOLIDAY giving the Defendant reasonable notice.

Order is granted WILLIAM IVY against WILLIAM GRAHAM for 150 pounds of tobacco for 6 days attendance at this Court in his suit against ROGER PEARCE.

ABRAM PEYTON, WILLIAM WALKER, and WILLIAM MICHIE were this day appointed Constables of this Borough and they having first taken the oath to the Government and subscribed the test also the oath of a constable of the enter on the execution of their office.

PAGE 190
JOHN SHEPHERD
Against Re: In Case
GEORGE WILSON and ARCHIBALD CAMPBELL admin of JOHN WILSON deceased Defendants
This day came the parties by their Attorney's and the Defendants by their Attorney say that they cannot gainsay the Plaintiff's actions nor but that their intestate did assume in manner and form as the Plaintiff against them have declared. Therefore, it is considered that the Plaintiff recover against the said Defendants 8 pounds 11 shillings and 3 pence and his costs by him in this behalf expended. when assess after paying preceding judgements, debts of greater dignity and the Defendants own claim of equal dignity against the estate of the said intestate to be levied of the goods and chattels which were of the said JOHN at the time of his death that shall hereafter come to the hands of the said Defendant to be administered and the said Defendant in mercy

On the Attachment obtained by RALPH ELLIOTT against the Estate of ROGER PEARCE who has privately removed himself or so absconds that the ordinary process cannot be served on him and the Sergeant now making return that by virtue thereof he has attached sundries as per schedule annexed to JAMES HALDANE attachment which I have ready after paying SARAH CANNS house rent and said JAMES HALDANE and the Defendant being called and not appearing where upon the Plaintiff proved his demand of 14 pounds 2 shillings and 6 pence to be just. Therefore, it is considered by the Court that the Plaintiff recover the same against the said Defendant together with his costs by him in this behalf expended and ordered the Sergeant pay unto the Plaintiff his demand and costs out of the sales of the attached effects theretofore sold and return an account thereof to the Court.

On the Attachment obtained by EILBECK ROSS and Company against the Estate of ROGER PEARCE who has privately removed himself or so absconds that the ordinary process cannot be served on him and the Sergeant now making return that by virtue thereof he has attached sundries as per schedule annexed to JAMES HALDANE attachment which I have ready after satisfying RALPH ELLIOT and the Defendant being called and not appearing where upon the Plaintiffs proved their demand of 11 pounds 10 shillings and 1 penny to be just. Therefore, it is considered by the Court that the Plaintiff recover the same against the said Defendant together with their costs by them in this behalf expended and ordered the Sergeant pay unto the Plaintiff their demand and costs of the sales of the attached effects heretofore sold and return an account thereof to the Court.

On the Attachment obtained by WILLIAM and THOMAS FARRER against the Estate of ROGER PEARCE who has privately removed himself or so absconds that the ordinary process cannot be served on him and the Sergeant now making return that by virtue thereof he has attached sundry goods as per schedule annexed to JAMES HALDANE attachment which I have ready after satisfying EILBECK, ROSS and Company and the Defendant being called and not appearing where upon the Plaintiffs proved their demand of 37 pounds 2 shillings and 7 penny to be just.

PAGE 190B

Therefore, it is considered by the Court that the Plaintiff recover the same against the said Defendant together with their costs by them in this behalf expended and ordered the Sergeant pay unto the Plaintiff their demand and costs of the sales of the attached effects heretofore sold.

THOMAS WALKER was this day brought before the Court by warrant for being a person of lewd life and conversation and a common disturber of the peace and the same being proved. It is ordered the Sergeant take and keep in Custody until he gives bond and security himself in 50 pounds and 2 securities in 25 pounds each for keeping the peace 12 months and pay the costs of this prosecution.

PETER BUER was this day brought before the Court by warrant for being a person of lewd life and conversation and a common disturber of the peace and the same being proved. It is ordered the Sergeant take and keep in Custody until he gives bond and security himself in 100 pounds and 2 securities in 10 pounds each for keeping the peace 12 months and pay the costs of this prosecution. Where upon JOHN BUER and RICHARD JARVIS came into Court and acknowledged themselves in debt with PETER agreeable to the order.

This Court is adjourned to Court in Course, PAUL LOYALL MAYOR, TESTE: JOHN BOUSH D.C.

NORFOLK BOROUGH

At a Hustings Court Held this 19th day of July 1773
PRESENT: CHARLES THOMAS ESQUIRE MAYOR
GENTLEMAN ALDERMEN: GEORGE ABYVON, MAXIMILIAN CALVERT ARCHIBALD CAMPBELL, PAUL LOYALL, LEWIS HANSFORD, JAMES TAYLOR

SAMUEL BOUSH was this day appointed Deputy Clerk of the said Borough and he having taken the oaths to the Government and subscribed the test. Also, the oath of Deputy Clerk of the Borough aforesaid enters on the Execution of his office.

WILLIAM and JOHN BROWN against NICHOLAS BROWN SEABROOK and CHARLES COBURN. An Attachment against SEABROOK and discontinued against COLBURN.

JAMES CARMICHAEL against GEORGE JOSEPH FENWICK. The suit is dismissed.
RICHARD BROWN against FRANCIS BRIGHT a conditional order against Defendant and SAM TARRANT his bail.

PAGE 191

JAMES CAMPBELL and Company against JOSHUA WRIGHT. An Imparlance
JAMES WILSON against RICHARD BASSET. An Imparlance.

JOHN HARRIS against CHRISTOPHER HERBERT. In Chancery. Time to Consider on a Bill

JOHN LAWRENCE and JOHN GREENWOOD against ARCHIBALD CAMPBELL and GEORGE WILSON. Administrators of JOHN WILSON. Deceased. An Imparlance.

JOHN CRAMOND against ISAAC EDMONDS. The Suit is Dismissed.

JOHN CRAMOND Plaintiff
Against Re: In Case
LEMUEL PORTLOCK Defendant
This day came as well the Plaintiff by THOMAS CLAIBORNE Gentleman his Attorney as the Defendant in his proper person says that he cannot gainsay the Plaintiff's action nor but that he did assume in manner and form as the Plaintiff against him has declared. Therefore, it is considered that the Plaintiff recover against the said Defendant 40 pounds 5 shillings and 7 pence and his costs by him in this behalf expended and the said Defendant in mercy. And the Plaintiff agrees to stay the execution of this Judgement 6 months.

WILLIAM GOODCHILD against RICHARD COLLINS. Dismissed.
JOHN SHEPHERD against THOMAS PEARSON. Dismissed.

FRANCES MOORE administratrix of JOHN MOORE Deceased. Against CHARLES CAMPBELL and ANNA his wife executors of the last will and testament of FRANCIS MOORE deceased. The Defendants pleaded their testator did not assume issue joined and referred.

ZACHERIAH HUTCHINGS and DINAH his wife against JOHN BARRET. An Imparlance.
JACOB SIKES against JOSIAH SIKES and JESSE SIKES executors of JESSE SIKES. Deceased. Imparlance.

JAMES JOLLIFF admin of SAMUEL SMITH deceased against TIMOTHY IVES. This suit is dismissed.

JOSEPH MITCHELL against JOHN HARDY. An Imparlance.
HENRY GREEN against CELIA SOUTHERLAND admin of JOHN SOUTHERLAND deceased. An Imparlance.

JOHN CRAMOND against WALTER SCOTT. Dismissed.

PAGE 191B
WALTER FRANKLIN and Company Merchants and Partners Plaintiffs
 Against Re: In Debt
JOHN YOUNG Defendant
This day came as well the Plaintiffs by THOMAS CLAIBORNE Gentleman their Attorney and as the Defendant in Custody of the Sergeant in his proper person and acknowledges the Plaintiffs action for 96 pounds which the said Attorney accepted. Therefore, it is considered that the Plaintiff recover against the said Defendant their debt aforesaid together with their costs by them about their suit in this behalf expended and the said Defendant in mercy. And the said Defendant being ruled to give Special Bail and failing so to do. On the motion of the Plaintiff by their Attorney aforesaid, the said Defendant is continued in custody of the Sergeant until he shall have satisfied this Judgement and costs.

SAMUEL DAVIS MCCASTLETON against WILLIAM SIMPSON. Imparlance.

WILLIAM and JOHN BROWN against WILLIAM SIMPSON and VICTOR THOMPSON. JOHN CRAMOND this day came into Court and undertook for the Defendants that in case they shall be casts in this suit they the said Defendant will pay the condemnation of the Court or render their bodies to prison in execution for the same or that the said CRAMOND will do it for them whereupon the Defendants pray and have leave to IMPARLE here the next Court and then to Plead.

SUSANNAH MEADE executor and RICHARD RANDOLPH, GEORGE WALKER, and JOHN DRIVER executors of DAVID MEADE deceased against JOHN LAWRENCE and MATTHEW PHRIPP executors of THOMAS THOMPSON Deceased. Imparlance.

THOMAS FLEMING against ANTHONY FLEMING. An Imparlance.
CHARLES COOPER against ANN BREITHWAIT. An Imparlance.

WILLIAM and JOHN BROWNE Plaintiff
Against Re: In Debt.
CHARLES COOPER JR. Defendant
This day came as well the Plaintiffs by BENJAMIN CROOKER Gentleman their Attorney and as the Defendant in his proper person and acknowledges the Plaintiffs action for 37 pounds 10 shillings. Therefore, it is considered that the Plaintiff recover against the said Defendant their debt aforesaid and their costs by them this behalf expended and the said Defendant in mercy. But this judgement is to be discharged by the payment of 18 pounds 15 shillings with interest thereon after the rate of 5% per annum to be computed from April 22nd, 1773, to the time of payment and the costs. And the Plaintiffs have agreed to stay the execution of this Judgement until November 1, 1773

THOMAS APPLEWHAITE against THOMAS WILLIAMSON. On the motion of the Plaintiff by his Attorney a DEDIMUS is granted him to take depositions of witnesses in BARBADOS giving Defendant reasonable notice.

PAGE 192
JAMES GILCHRIST and ROBERT TAYLOR Plaintiffs
Against Re: In Case
GEORGE FOWLER Defendant
This day came the parties by their Attorney's and there upon came also a Jury to wit: HENRY BRESSIE, BASSET MOSELEY, WILLIAM INGRAM, PHILIP CARBERY, JOHN SELDEN, JOHN BARRET, GEORGE WILSON, PAUL WATLINGTON, JAMES WALKER, WILLIAM GOODRICH, GEORGE GORDON, and JAMES LEITCH who being elected tried and sworn the truth to speak upon the issue joined upon their oath do say that the Defendant did not assume as in pleading he has alleged. Therefore, it is considered that the Plaintiff take nothing by their bill but for their false claims be in mercy. And the Defendant go hence without day and recover against the Plaintiff his costs by him about his defense in this behalf expended.

WARNER LEWIS against ALEXANDER LOVE. A conditional order against Defendant and JOSEPH CALVERT Sergeant his bail.

Ordered the Clerk to deliver to EDWARD PARK and FRANCES MOORE admin of JOHN MOORE deceased papers filed in the suit in Chancery MOSES LANGLEY Against them.

ALEXANDER MASSENBURG against LOUISA INMAN dismissed.

CUMMING WARWICK and Company Plaintiff
Against Re: In Case
DANIEL PECK Defendant
This day came the parties by their Attorney's and there upon came also a Jury to wit: JOHN MACLEAN, DANIEL BARRAUD, JAMES MURPHREE, JAMES DUNN, WILLIAM SKINKER, STEPHEN WRIGHT, STEPHEN TANKARD, GEORGE KELLY, WILLIAM HARWOOD, EDWARD PARK, ANDREW STEVENSON, and JACOB WILLIAMS who being elected tried and sworn the truth to speak upon the issue joined upon their oath do say that the Defendant did assume in manner and form as the Plaintiff against him have declared and do assess the Plaintiff damages by occasion of the non-performance of that assumption to 16 pounds 12 shillings besides their costs. Therefore, it is considered that the

Plaintiff recover against the said Defendant their damages aforesaid in form aforesaid assessed and their costs by them about their suit in this behalf expended and the said Defendant in mercy.

ROBERT SHEDDEN and Company Plaintiff
Against Re: In Case
WILLIAM CONNOR admin of WILLIAM CRAWFORD CONNER Defendant
This day came the Plaintiff by BENJAMIN CROOKER Gentleman their Attorney's and there upon came also a Jury to wit: JOHN MACLEAN, DANIEL BARRAUD, JAMES MURPHREE, JAMES DUNN, WILLIAM SKINKER, STEPHEN WRIGHT, STEPHEN TANKARD, GEORGE KELLY, WILLIAM HARWOOD, EDWARD PARK, ANDREW STEVENSON, and JACOB WILLIAMS who being sworn well and truly to inquire of damages in this suit upon their oath do say that the Plaintiff have sustained damages to 11 pounds 1 shilling and 1 penny farthing besides their costs. Therefore, it is considered by the Court that the Plaintiff recover against the said Defendant and CHARLES CONNOR his bail, their damages aforesaid in form aforesaid assessed and their costs by them about their suit in this behalf expended and the said Defendant in mercy.

PAGE 192B
SAMUEL BLEWS against ANDREW STEVENSON and ALICE his wife. Dismissed agreed.
JAMES HEALY against ANDREW STEVENSON and ALICE his wife. Dismissed agreed.
PETER LONG against WILLIAM BRITT. Agreed Dismissed each party paying his own cost.

EDMOND KEETON was this day brought before the Court for Breach of Peace and the same being proved. It is ordered that the Sergeant take him and keep him in Custody until he gives bond and Security himself in 20 pounds and 2 securities in 10 pounds each for his keeping the peace and being of good behavior for 6 months and pay the costs of this prosecution.

The King against ROGER PEARSE. Dismissed.

CHRISTOPHER WRIGHT against WILLIAM WISHART. In Case. A DEDIMUS is granted to take depositions on both sides DE BENE ESSE giving each other reasonable notice of the time and place.

JOHN CHESHIRE against RICHARD BROWN. The parties mutually submit all matters in difference between them to the determination of JOHN LAWRENCE, WRIGHT WESTCOTT, and WILLIAM CHISHOLM and agree that their award there upon be made the judgement of the Court and the same is ordered accordingly.

PETER SINGLETON against MORTO BRIAN. The suit is dismissed.

THOMAS LANGLEY SR. against JOHN and JOSEPH HUTCHINGS. In Detinue. This day came the parties by their Attorney's and there upon came also a Jury to wit: WILLIAM SKINKER, STEPHEN TANKARD, DANIEL BARRAUD, JAMES DUNN, EDWARD PARKE, WILLIAM HARVEY, CHRISTOPHER CALVERT, EDWARD DAVIS, JOHN BOGGESS, FREER ARMSTON, PAUL PROBY and JOHN MACLEAN who being elected tried and sworn the truth to speak upon the issue joined, withdrew and not returning any verdict the cause is postponed.

THOMAS LANGLEY SR. Against JAMES WEBB. In Detinue. This day came the parties by their Attorney's and there upon came also a Jury to wit: WILLIAM SKINKER, STEPHEN TANKARD, DANIEL BARRAUD, JAMES DUNN, EDWARD PARKE, WILLIAM HARVEY, CHRISTOPHER CALVERT, EDWARD DAVIS, JOHN BOGGESS, FREER ARMSTON, PAUL PROBY and JOHN MACLEAN who being elected tried and sworn the truth to speak upon the issue joined, withdrew and not returning any verdict the cause is postponed.

PAGE 193
Order is granted RICHARD PAYNE against GEORGE FOWLER for 650 pounds of tobacco for 2 days attendance at this Court, coming and returning 100 miles 2x and 2 pounds 19 shillings ferriages in the suit of JAMES GILCHRIST and ROBERT TAYLOR against him.

Order is granted WILLIAM FORRESTER against GEORGE FOWLER for 260 pounds of tobacco for 1 days attendance at this Court, coming and returning 70 miles and 14 shillings and 6 pence ferriages in the suit of JAMES GILCHRIST and ROBERT TAYLOR against him.

Order is granted JAMES EDMUNDSON against GEORGE FOWLER for 331 pounds of tobacco for 1 days attendance at this Court, coming and returning 102 miles and 14 shillings and 6 pence ferriages in the suit of JAMES GILCHRIST and ROBERT TAYLOR against him.

Order is granted NATHANIEL YOUNG against GEORGE FOWLER for 355 pounds of tobacco for 1 days attendance at this Court, coming and returning 110 miles and 5 shillings ferriages in the suit of JAMES GILCHRIST and ROBERT TAYLOR against him.

SAMUEL BOUSH Plaintiff
Against Re: In Debt for rent
RICHARD FRYER Defendant
This day came the parties by their Attorney's and the Defendant by his Attorney relinquishes his former plea, acknowledges the Plaintiff's action for 6 pounds 13 shillings and 10 pence. Therefore, it is considered that the Plaintiff recover against the said Defendant his debt aforesaid and his costs by him in this behalf expended and the said Defendant in mercy.

This Court is adjourned until tomorrow 9 o'clock, CHARLES THOMAS MAYOR, TESTE: JOHN BOUSH D.C.

PAGE 193B
NORFOLK BOROUGH
At a Hustings Court Held this 20th day of July 1773
PRESENT: CHARLES THOMAS ESQUIRE MAYOR

GENTLEMAN ALDERMEN: GEORGE ABYVON, MAXIMILIAN CALVERT, ARCHIBALD CAMPBELL, LEWIS HANSFORD, CORNELIUS CALVERT, JAMES TAYLOR

Order is granted RICHARD PAYNE against GEORGE FOWLER for 1 pound 8 shillings, additional expenses in the suit of JAMES GILCHRIST and ROBERT TAYLOR against him.

RACHAEL RICHARDSON against ANN BREITHWAITE. On motion of the Plaintiff by her Attorney a DEDIMUS is granted her to take the Deposition of CATHERINE DENNY DE BENE ESSE giving reasonable notice.

EDWARD ARCHER executor of EDWARD ARCHER deceased against PAUL LOYALL and LATIMORE HALSTEAD administrators of JONATHAN DISON deceased, JONATHAN DISON son and heir at law of JONATHAN DISON deceased and GEORGE ABYVON. In Chancery. This day came the Plaintiff by WILLIAM DAVIS his Council and SARAH DISON is appointed guardian to the Defendant JONATHAN who is an infant to defend in this suit and time is allowed the Defendants to consider.

JAMES HALDANE against JOHN BRUCE. This day came the parties by their Attorney's and there upon came also a Jury to wit: JAMES WALKER, JOHN BRIGGS, SAMUEL SANDS, ROBERT FRY, JONATHAN RICHARDSON, ANDREW MACKIE, JAMES MURPHREE, JOHN WOODSIDE, JONATHAN EILBECK, EDWARD MITCHELL, PAUL WATLINGTON and JOHN WALKER who being elected tried and sworn the truth to speak upon the issue joined withdrew and not returning any verdict in the premises the suit is continued.

THOMAS LANGLEY SR. Plaintiff
Against Re: In Detinue for a Negro Slave
JOHN HUTCHINGS and JOSEPH HUTCHINGS Defendants
This day came the parties by their Attorney's and there upon came also a Jury to wit: WILLIAM SKINKER, STEPHEN TANKARD, DANIEL BARRAUD, JAMES DUNN, EDWARD PARKE, WILLIAM HARVEY, CHRISTOPHER CALVERT, EDWARD DAVIS, JOHN BOGGESS, FREER ARMSTON, PAUL PROBY and JOHN MACLEAN who being elected tried and sworn the truth to speak upon the issue joined, now returned a Special Verdict in these words to wit: We the Jury do find that LEMUEL LANGLEY made his will in writing in these words to wit: In the name of God Amen and to which we refer. We find that the Plaintiff is heir at law of the LEMUEL LANGLEY. We find that the Negro CADER in the declaration mentioned is a descendant from the Mulattoes woman LUCY in the will mentioned. We find that the Defendant are bona fide purchases for a valuable consideration and claim under the widow and relict of the said LEMUEL LANGLEY. Upon the whole of the law be for the Plaintiff

PAGE 194
We find for the Plaintiff the Negro CADER if to be had, if not find 70 pounds 1shilling damages, other ways we find for the Defendant and the cause is continued until the next Court for the matters of law arising thereon to be continued.

THOMAS LANGLEY Plaintiff
Against Re: In Detinue for a Negro Slave named DAVID
JAMES WEBB Defendant
This day came the parties by their Attorney's and there upon came also a Jury to wit: WILLIAM SKINKER, STEPHEN TANKARD, DANIEL BARRAUD, JAMES DUNN, EDWARD PARKE, WILLIAM HARVEY, CHRISTOPHER CALVERT, EDWARD DAVIS, JOHN BOGGESS, FREER ARMSTON, PAUL PROBY and JOHN MACLEAN who being elected tried and sworn the truth to speak upon the issue joined, now returned a Special Verdict in these words to wit: We the Jury do find that LEMUEL LANGLEY made his will in writing in these words to wit: In the name of God Amen and to which we refer. We find that the Plaintiff is heir at law of the LEMUEL LANGLEY. We find that the Negro DAVID in the declaration mentioned is a descendant from the Mulattoes woman LUCY in the will mentioned. We find that the Defendant are bona fide purchases for a valuable consideration and claim under the widow and relict of the said LEMUEL LANGLEY. Upon the whole of the law be for the Plaintiff we find for the Plaintiff the Negro DAVID if to be had, if not find 70 pounds 1shilling damages, other ways we find for the Defendant and the cause is continued until the next Court for the matters of law arising thereon to be argued.

MARY ROTHERY and others executors of MATTHEW ROTHERY Plaintiff
Against Re: In Case
DOROTHY ROTHERY admin of HENRY ROTHERY Defendant
This day came the parties by their Attorney's and there upon came also a Jury to wit: JOHN BROWN, JAMES CARMICHAEL, JACOB WILLIAMS, ROBERT GRAY, JAMES MARSDEN, JOHN EDWARDS, THOMAS HEPBURN, ANDREW STEVENSON, MORTO BRIAN, JOHN TODD, JOSEPH LANGLEY and THOMAS WALKE who being elected tried and sworn the truth to speak upon the issue joined upon their oath do say that the defendant intestate did not assume as in pleading she has alleged. Therefore, it is considered that the Plaintiffs take nothing by their bill but for their false claims be in mercy and the defendant go hence without day and recover against the Plaintiff her costs by her about her defense in this behalf expended.

JAMES INGRAM against PETER MCNABB. The suit is dismissed at the Defendants costs.

THOMAS NEWTON SR., THOMAS NEWTON JR. and PAUL LOYAL, THOMAS ROBERTS and JOHN TUCKER against ROBERT TUCKER. The cause is continued until August Court for the Defendant to take depositions and ordered to receive hearing at September Court.

PAGE 194B
JAMES CRAMBIE Plaintiff
Against Re: In Case
JAMES WALKER Surviving partner of WALKER and MCROB Defendant
This day came the parties by their Attorney and there upon came also a Jury to wit: JAMES DUNN, FREER ARMSTON, EDWARD PARKE, STEPHEN TANKARD, CHRISTOPHER CALVERT, PAUL PROBY, DANIEL BARRAUD, WILLIAM HARVEY, EDWARD DAVIS, JOHN BOGUS, WILLIAM SKINKER and JOHN MACLEAN who being elected tried and sworn the truth to speak upon the issue joined upon their oath do day that the Defendants did assume in manner and form as the Plaintiff against them has declared and do assess the Plaintiff damages by occasion of the non-performance of that assumption to 48 pounds, 6 shillings and 11 pence half penny sterling besides his costs. Therefore, it is considered that the Plaintiff recover against the said Defendant his damages aforesaid in form aforesaid assessed and his costs by him in this behalf expended and the said Defendants in mercy. And the Court says the sterling money may be discharged in current money at 25% difference of exchange.

Order is granted JOSEPH MITCHEL against MARY ROTHERY and others executors of MATTHEW ROTHERY for 50 pounds of tobacco for 2 days attendance at this Court in their suit against DOROTHY ROTHERY admin of HENRY ROTHERY Deceased.

MARY ROTHERY and others executors of MATTHEW ROTHERY deceased against THOMAS PEARSON. This day came the parties by their Attorney's and thereupon came also a Jury to wit: JOSEPH LANGLEY, JOHN TODD, MORTO BRYAN, ANDREW STEVENSON, JOHN EDWARDS, JAMES MARSDEN, ROBERT GRAY, JAMES CARMICHAEL, THOMAS WALKE, JOHN BROWN, JOSIAH TRUSS, and THOMAS FARRER who being elected tried and sworn the truth to speak upon the issue joined, withdrew and not returning any verdict in the premises the cause is continued.

WILLIAM BUTT Plaintiff
Against Re: In Case
JAMES MARSDEN and JONATHAN EILBECK executors of ELDRED FISHER deceased Defendant
This day came the parties by their Attorney's and there upon came also a Jury to wit: JAMES DUNN, FREER ARMSTON, STEPHEN TANKARD, EDWARD PARKE, CHRISTOPHER CALVERT, PAUL PROBY, DANIEL BARRAUD, WILLIAM HARVEY, EDWARD DAVIS, JOHN BOGUS, WILLIAM SKINKER and JOHN MCLEAN who being elected tried and sworn the truth to speak upon the issue joined upon their oath do say that the Defendant testator did assume in manner and form as the Plaintiff against him has declared and do assess the Plaintiff damages by occasion of the non-performance of that assumption to 50 pounds, 16 shillings and 3 pence half penny besides his costs. Therefore, it is considered by the Court that the Plaintiff recover against the said Defendant his damages aforesaid in form aforesaid assessed and his costs by him in this behalf expended. To be levied of the goods and chattels of the said Testator if so, much the said Defendants have in their hands to be administered and if they have it not then the costs are to be levied of their proper goods and chattels and the said Defendants in mercy.

PAGE 195
Order is granted ROBERT GILCHRIST against JAMES CRAMBIE for 50 pounds of tobacco for 2 days attendance at this Court in his suit against JAMES WALKER surviving partner of WALKER and MCROB

Order is granted ROBERT WALLER against WILLIAM BUTT for 50 pounds of tobacco for 2 days attendance at this Court in his suit against JAMES MARSDEN and JONATHAN EILBECK executors of ELDRED FISHER deceased.

The Court this day rated Flour at 16/8 per centum weight,
This Court is adjourned to Court in Course, CHARLES THOMAS MAYOR, TESTE: JOHN BOUSH D.C.

NORFOLK BOROUGH
At a Hustings Court Held this 23rd day of August 1773
PRESENT: CHARLES THOMAS ESQUIRE MAYOR
GENTLEMAN ALDERMEN: GEORGE ABYVON, PAUL LOYALL, ARCHIBALD CAMPBELL, JAMES TAYLOR, LEWIS HANSFORD,

RICHARD SPENCER against JOHN FIELD. In Debt. BENJAMIN CROOKER Gentleman this day came into Court and undertook for the Defendant that in case he shall be costs in this suit he the said Defendant will pay the condemnation of the Court or render his body to Prison in execution for the same or that the said CROOKER will do it for him where upon the Defendants by his Attorney prays and has leave to IMPARLE here the next Court and then to Plead.

RICHARD SPENCER against JOHN FIELD. In Case. The suit is dismissed at the Plaintiff's cost.
HENRY YOUNG against WILLIAM POOLE. An Imparlance.

RICHARD WOES against JAMES MARSDEN. THOMAS CLAIBORNE Gentleman this day came into Court and undertook for the Defendant that in case he shall be costs in this suit he the said Defendant will pay the condemnation of the Court or render his body to Prison in execution for the same or that the said CLAIBORNE will do it for him where upon the Defendants by his Attorney prays and has leave to IMPARLE here the next Court and then to Plead.

PAGE 195B
MATTHEW ANDERSON Plaintiff
Against Re: In Case
ARCHIBALD CAMPBELL admin of ALEXANDER DALGLEISH deceased Defendant

This day came as well the Plaintiff by ANDREW RONALD Gentleman his Attorney as the Defendant in his proper person and says that he cannot gainsay the Plaintiff's action nor but that his intestate did assume in manner and form as the Plaintiff against him has declared. Therefore, it is considered that the plaintiff recover against the said Defendant 15 pounds and his costs by him in this behalf expended when assets after paying preceding judgements debts of greater dignity and the Defendants own claim of equal dignity against the estate of the said intestate to be levied of the goods and chattels which were of the said ALEXANDER at the time of his death that shall hereafter come to the hands of the said Defendants to be administered and the said Defendant in mercy.

MISTERS LOGAN GILMOUR and Company against JAMES WOOD. The suit is dismissed.
MISTERS LOGAN GILMOUR and Company against HARDRESS WALLER. The suit is dismissed at the Defendants costs.
MISTERS LOGAN GILMOUR and Company against WILLIAM IVY admin of ALICE IVY deceased Imparlance.
MISTERS LOGAN GILMOUR and Company against THOMAS NASH JR. executor of NATHANIEL TATEM. The suit is dismissed.
GEORGE DIXON against JOSEPH YOWART. In T.A.B. Imparlance

GEORGE DIXON against JOSEPH YOWART. In Case. This day came the parties by their Attorney's and the Defendant by his Attorney tendered to the Plaintiff 6 pounds 10 shillings and 2 pence half penny which he received, and the parties have submitted the costs of the suit to the Court's determination.

JAMES HALDANE against ANDREW STEVENSON and ALICE his wife. The suit is dismissed.

JAMES HALDANE against JOHN BRUCE. This day came the parties by their Attorneys and the Jury was sworn in this Cause at the last not returning any verdict in the premises they are by the Court discharged.

MARY ROTHERY and other executors of MATTHEW ROTHERY against THOMAS PEARSON. This day came the parties by their Attorney's and the Jury was sworn in this Cause at the last Court not returning any verdict in the premises they are by the Court discharged.

PAGE 196
WILLIAM SIMPSON Plaintiff
Against Re: *On a writ of SCIRE FACIAS to have execution of a Judgement obtained in this Court by the said Plaintiff against the said Defendant for 10 pounds 1 shilling, also 301 pounds tobacco and 15 shillings or 150 pounds of tobacco and 2 shillings and 6 pence.*
JOHN SMITH Defendant
This day came the Plaintiff by BENJAMIN CROOKER Gentleman his Attorney and the Defendant being duly warranted and not appearing ordered that the Judgement be entered up for the Plaintiff against the said Defendant that he have execution according to the form and effect of the recovery aforesaid and also for the costs of suing forth and prosecuting this suit.

FREDERICK BOUSH Plaintiff
Against Re: Injunction in Chancery
JAMES MOORE Defendant
On the motion of the Plaintiff by council leave is given to file his bill of injunction and time is allowed the Defendant until the next to consider the same and ordered the Plaintiff at or before the next Court give bond and security in the Clerk's office.

JOHN JACKSON and MARTIN JUQIEZ Plaintiff
Against Re: In Debt
JAMES HALDANE Defendant
This day came the parties by their Attorney's and the Defendant by his Attorney acknowledges the Plaintiffs action for 400 pounds Pennsylvania money. Therefore, it is considered that the Plaintiff recover against the said Defendant their debt aforesaid and their costs by them about their suit in this behalf expended and the said Defendant in mercy. But this judgement is to be discharged by the payment of 222 pounds 15 shillings and 8 pence farthing Pennsylvania money with interest thereon after the rate of 5% per annum to be computed from this day to the time of payment and the costs. And the Plaintiff by their Attorney have agreed to stay execution of this Judgement 6 months for the one half and 6 months longer for the other half. And the Court says the said money may be discharged in Virginia money at 33 1/3% difference of exchange.

ANN BREITHWAITE against JOHN COOPER JR. ALIAS CAPIAS
JAMES CARMICHAEL against SAMUEL BLEWS. Dismissed at the Plaintiff's costs.

JAMES CARMICHAEL against WILLIAM WILKINS by Petition and summons. Judgement is granted the Plaintiff for 1 pounds 10 shillings with interest thereon after the rate of 5% per annum to be computed from JANUARY 21ST, 1772 to the time of payment and costs.

WILLIAM WILKINS against JAMES JARVIS. Dismissed at the Plaintiff's costs.
JAMES TRISTRAM against WILLIAM CALVERT. Dismissed at the Plaintiff's cost.

PAGE 196B
Order is granted MARY PARROT, EDWARD DAVIS, and WILLIAM LIDDLE against JAMES JARVIS for 25 pounds of tobacco each for 1 day's attendance at this Court for each in the suit of WILLIAM WILKINS against him.

HARDRESS WALLER against PAUL LOYALL and LATIMORE HALSTEAD admin of JONATHAN DISON deceased Imparlance.

DUGAL GILCHRIST against JOHN SCOTT. In Case. JOHN BROWN merchant this day came into Court and undertook for the Defendant that in case he shall be cast in this suit he the said Defendant will pay the condemnation of the Court or render his body to prison in execution for the same or that he the said BROWN will do it for him where upon the Defendant by his Attorney prays and has leave to IMPARLE here until the next Court and then to plead.

CELIA SOUTHERLAND admin of JOHN SOUTHERLAND Deceased Plaintiff
Against Re: In Debt
SARAH CARNEY and JOHN TATEM executors of BARNABY CARNEY Deceased Defendants

CELIA SOUTHERLAND admin of JOHN SOUTHERLAND Deceased Plaintiff
Against Re: In Case
SARAH CARNEY and JOHN TATEM executors of BARNABY CARNEY Deceased Defendants

SAMUEL FARMER Plaintiff
Against Re: In Case
WRIGHT WESTCOAT Defendant
This day came the parties by their Attorney's and the Defendants pray and have leave to IMPARLE here until the next Court and then to plead.

ANDREW STEVENSON against ROBERT RAY. The suit is dismissed.
WILLIAM and JOHN BROWN against NICHOLAS BROWN SEABROOK. The suit is dismissed.
JAMES MARSDEN and JONATHAN EILBECK executors of ELDRED FISHER deceased against RICHARD BROWN. The suit is dismissed.

MATTHEW PHRIPP and JOSEPH HUTCHINGS who as well in behalf of our Sovereign Lord the King as for themselves against WILLIAM MURRAY, WILLIAM NEWTON, JAMES VICKERS, and JOHN LEWIS, Alias Capias.

MISTERS SAMUEL INGLES and PETER LONG against WILLIAM LIDDLE. The suit is dismissed.
RALPH ELLIOTT against ROGER PEARCE by attachment. Dismissed.

PAGE 197
CHRISTOPHER WRIGHT against WILLIAM WISHART. On the motion of his Attorney a DEDIMUS is granted him to take the deposition of EDWARD WRIGHT and THOMAS HOLIDAY giving the Defendant reasonable notice of the time and place.

WILLIAM and THOMAS FARRER against ROGER PEARCE by attachment dismissed.

NICHOLAS WONYCOTT Plaintiff
Against Re: In Case
THOMAS WALKER Defendant
This day came the parties by their Attorney's and the Defendant by his Attorney relinquishes his former plea says that he cannot gainsay the Plaintiffs action nor but that he did assume in manner and form as the Plaintiff against him has declared. Therefore, it is considered that the Plaintiff recover against the said Defendant 10 pounds 15 shillings and 4 pence and his costs by him about his suit in this behalf expended and the said Defendant in mercy.

Order is granted ANTHONY FLEMING against WILLIAM CALVERT for 24 pounds of tobacco for 1 day's attendance in this Court in the suit of JAMES TRISTRAM against him.

Order is granted JOHN STANHOPE against WILLIAM CALVERT for 24 pounds of tobacco for 1 day's attendance in this Court in the suit of JAMES TRISTRAM against him.

MISTERS JOHN RAMSAY and JAMES TAYLOR Plaintiffs
Against Re: In Case
JOHN CRAMOND admin of MARY ROBERTSON Deceased Defendant
This day came the parties by their Attorney's and the Defendant by his Attorney relinquishes his former plea says that he cannot gainsay the Plaintiffs action nor but that he did assume in manner and form as the Plaintiff against him has declared. Therefore, it is considered that the Plaintiff recover against the said Defendant 54 pounds 19 shillings and 10 pence half penny and his costs by him about his suit in this behalf expended to be levied of the goods and chattels of the said intestate if so much the Defendant has in his hands to be administered and if he has it not then the costs are to be levied of his proper goods and chattels and the said defendant in mercy.

ANTHONY WARWICK and ARCHIBALD BUCHANAN Plaintiff
Against Re: In Case
JAMES DUNLOP Defendant
This day came the parties by their Attorney's and there upon came also a Jury to wit: EDWARD ARCHER, ADAM BENNET, RALPH ELLIOT, WILLIAM IVY, JOSEPH LANGLEY, JOHN CRAMOUNT, GRIFFIN PEART, JOHN SHAW, WILLIAM CORBIT, SAMUEL CALVERT, ROBERT STEELE, and JAMES BALLENTINE who being elected tried and sworn the truth to speak upon the issue joined upon their oath do say that the Defendant is guilty in manner and form as the Plaintiff against him
PAGE 197B
Has declared and do assess the Plaintiff damages by occasion thereof to 500 pounds besides their costs Therefore, it is considered that the Plaintiff recover against the said Defendant their damages aforesaid in form aforesaid assessed and their costs by them about their suit in this behalf expended and the said Defendant in mercy.

ALEXANDER SKINNER Plaintiff
Against Re: In Case
JAMES MARSDEN & JAMES MAXWELL admin of JAMES PATTERSON Defendant
This day came the parties by their Attorney's and the Defendants by their Attorney say that they cannot gainsay the Plaintiff's action nor but that their intestate did assume in manner and form as the Plaintiff against them has declared. Therefore, it is considered that the plaintiff recover against the said Defendant 26 pounds 16 shillings and 6 pence and his costs by him in this behalf expended when assets after paying preceding judgements debts of greater dignity and the Defendants own claim of equal dignity against the estate of the said intestate to be levied of the goods and chattels which were of the said JAMES PATTERSON at the time of his death that shall hereafter come to the hands of the said Defendants to be administered and the said Defendants in mercy.

On the Attachment obtained by MISTERS LOGAN GILMOUR and Company against the ESTATE OF ROBERT POMEROY whose has privately removed himself or so absconds that the ordinary process cannot be served on him and the Sergeant now making return that by virtue thereof he has levied the same in the hands of JAMES ATKINSON who appeared and on oath declared he had in his hands 3 pounds 5 shillings and 3 pence the balance of the attached effects where upon the Plaintiff proved their demand of 22 pounds 3 shillings and 9 pence half penny to be just. Therefore, it is considered that the plaintiff recover the same against the said Defendant together with their costs by them in this behalf expended and ordered that the garnishee pay to the Plaintiffs money in his hands towards discharging this judgement and the costs.

JAMES MARSDEN and JONATHAN EILBECK executors of ELDRED FISHER deceased against ROGER PEARCE. On the motion of the defendant by his Attorney a DEDIMUS is granted him to take the deposition of GEORGE BELL, ROBERT PETERS, and LUCY ORME giving the Plaintiffs notice.

Order is granted JOHN TAYLOR against SAMUEL BLEWS for 25 pounds of tobacco for 1 day's attendance at this Court in the suit of JAMES CARMICHAEL against him.

This Court is adjourned until tomorrow 10 o'clock, CHARLES THOMAS MAYOR, TESTE: JOHN BOUSH D.C.

PAGE 198
NORFOLK BOROUGH
At a Hustings Court Held this 24th day of August 1773
PRESENT: CHARLES THOMAS ESQUIRE MAYOR
GENTLEMAN ALDERMEN: GEORGE ABYVON, PAUL LOYALL, MAXIMILIAN CALVERT, JAMES TAYLOR,

GEORGE WEBB and JOSEPH LANGLEY Plaintiffs
Against Re: In Chancery
JOHN BAYNES and NANCY ASHLEY Defendants
This day still failing to answer the bill of the Plaintiff. On their motion an Attachment is award against them for such their contempt returnable here to the next Court.

ALEXANDER GORDON against WRIGHT WESTCOAT and STEPHEN WRIGHT. Joinder in demur filed and set for arguments.
THOMAS SNALE and ELIZABETH, his wife JOHN IVY order of WILLIAM IVY. Filed and time for the Defendants.

THOMAS OLD and wife by the Justices Against ANDREW SPROWLE and JOHN HUNTER Breaches assigned and time.

WILLIAM SIMPSON Plaintiff
Against Re: In case
MATTHEW PHRIPP and JOHN LAWRENCE executors of THOMAS THOMPSON deceased Defendants
This day came the parties by their Attorney's and the Defendants by their Attorney say that they cannot gainsay the Plaintiff's action nor but that their testator did assume in manner and form as the Plaintiff against them has declared. Therefore, it is considered that the Plaintiff recover against the said Defendant 37 pounds 18 shillings and 5 pence farthing and his costs by him in this behalf expended when assets after paying preceding judgements debts of greater dignity and the Defendants own claim of equal dignity against the estate of the said testator to be levied of the goods and chattels which were of the said THOMAS at the time of his death that shall hereafter come to the hands of the said Defendants to be administered and the said Defendants in mercy.

MARY ROTHERY and other executors of MATTHEW ROTHERY Plaintiff
Against Re: In Chancery
GEORGE WATSON and ANN, his wife admin of RICHARD BOUCHER Defendants
The Plaintiffs not further prosecuting on motion of the Defendants by their Attorney it is ordered that the suit be dismissed, and that the Plaintiff pay to the Defendants their costs.

WILLIAM KEATING against CORNELIUS CALVERT the Defendant pleaded he did not assume issue joined and referred.
ARCHDEACON and INGRAM against WILLIAM DONALDSON. the Defendant pleaded he did not assume issue joined and referred.

PAGE 198B
PRISCILLA JOHNSON Plaintiff
Against Re: In Chancery
MALACHI MAUND Defendant
The Plaintiff not further prosecuting on motion of the Defendants by his Attorney it is ordered that the suit be dismissed, and that the Plaintiff pay to the Defendants his costs.

MISTERS JOHN and WILLIS WILSON Plaintiffs
Against Re: In Case
MARY ROTHERY Executrix of MATTHEW ROTHERY Defendant
The parties by their Attorney's mutually submit all matters in Difference between them to the determination of JOHN GREENWOOD and JOHN LAWRENCE Gentleman and if they disagree to choose an umpire and agree that their award there upon be made the judgement of the Court and the same is ordered accordingly

GEORGE WILSON and ARCHIBALD CAMPBELL admin of JOHN WILSON deceased against ABRAM WORMINGTON. The Defendant pleaded he did not assume issue joined and referred until next Court.

WILLIAM TREBELL and ROBERT NICHOLSON executors of JOSEPH SCRIVENER decease GEORGE JOSEPH FENWICK the Defendant not appearing. Ordered that Judgement be entered for the Plaintiffs against him the said Defendant and JOHN WILLS his bail for what damages the Plaintiffs have sustained to be ascertained at the next Court upon a writ of Inquiry

HESLOP and BLAIR against MISTERS ELIAS BOYER and PETER KATZ. The Defendants not appearing. Ordered that Judgement be entered for the Plaintiffs against him the said Defendant and JAMES LEITCH their bail for what damages the Plaintiffs have sustained to be ascertained at the next Court upon a writ of Inquiry.

JOHN RANSBERG against JOSHUA GOUGH the Defendant pleaded he did not assume issue joined and referred.

ANDREW SPROWLE admin of MISTERS SPROWLE and CROOKS deceased against THOMAS ROBERTS. The Defendants pleaded payment issue joined and referred until next Court.

ANDREW SPROWLE admin of MISTERS SPROWLE and CROOKS deceased against ARTHUR BUTT. The Defendants pleaded payment issue joined and referred until the next Court.

MARSDIN and HODGSON against WILLIAM CONNER. The Defendant pleaded he did not assume issue joined and referred until the next Court.

PAGE 199

JOSHUA GOUGH admin of JAMES GOUGH against JOSIAH HODGES. The Defendant pleaded he did not assume issue joined and referred.

EDWARD WRIGHT against JOHN MCLACHLAN. The Defendant pleaded he did not assume issue joined and referred.
PETER B. WHITING against EDWARD DAVIS. The Defendant pleaded he did not assume issue joined and referred until next Court.

JUDITH DUNFORD against GEORGE JOSEPH FENWICK. The Defendant pleaded not guilty issue joined and referred until next Court.

JAMES HUNTER and ELIZABETH TENANT Executor of SAMUEL TENANT against WILLIAM SIMPSON executor of FRANCIS CLARKE Defendant pleaded that his testator has paid the debt issue joined and referred.

NEWCOMB DODD against THOMAS RASCOE and LEAH his wife executors of SUSANNAH LAMOUNT. The Defendant pleaded not guilty issue joined and referred until the next Court.

JAMES CARMICHAEL against HARDRESS WALLER. The Defendant pleaded not guilty issue joined and referred until the next Court.
JAMES CARMICHAEL against JOHN GARRICK. In Trespass. The suit is Dismissed.

JOHN SMITH assignee of WILLIAM FLOOD against MARY WILSON and GEORGE WILSON. The Defendant pleaded payment issue joined and referred until the next Court.

JOHN GARRICK against JAMES CARMICHAEL. In Case. The Suit is dismissed.

ROBERT TUCKER against THOMAS VEALE Gentleman and FRANCIS HATTON executors of DAVID HARPER. The Defendant pleaded their testator did not assume issue joined and referred until next Court.

MATTHEW PHRIPP against NATHANIEL BOUSH. The Defendant pleaded he did not assume issue joined and referred.
NEAL BROWN against JAMES ALLISON. The Defendant pleaded not guilty issue joined and referred until the next Court.
JOHN GARRICK against JAMES CARMICHAEL. In Trespass. The suit is Dismissed.

JOHN CHESHIRE and RICHARD BROWN against JAMES MILLS and GEORGE LEDIMORE. The Defendant Attorney offered to file their plea in abatement to the Plaintiff writ which was refused as the defendants were not in their proper persons to swear to their plea, where upon they pleaded, they did not assume issue joined and referred. And on motion of the Plaintiff by their Attorney a DEDIMUS is granted them to take the depositions of JOHN PEARSON giving the defendants reasonable notice of the time and place.

PAGE 199B

TRAVIS TUCKER an infant by JOHN COLE his guardian Plaintiff
Against Re: In Case
NEIL JAMIESON Admin of HENRY TUCKER Deceased Defendant
This day came the parties by their Attorney's and there upon came by a JURY to wit. JOHN CARMICHAEL, JOSEPH LANGLEY, GEORGE WEBB, WRIGHT BRICKELL, SAMUEL BACON, JOHN WILLS, WILLIAM IVY, CHRISTOPHER CALVERT, ROBERT FRY, WILLIAM INGRAM, JOHN MCLACHLAN and JOHN EDWARDS who being elected tried and sworn the truth to speak upon the issue joined upon their oath do say that the Defendants intestate did assume in manner and form as the Plaintiff against him has declared and do assess the Plaintiff damages by occasion of thereof

to 19 pounds, 7 shillings and 11 pence besides his costs. Therefore, it is considered that the Plaintiff recover against the said Defendant his damages aforesaid in form aforesaid assessed and his costs by him in this behalf expended. To be levied of the goods and chattels of the said intestate if so, much the said Defendants have in their hands to be administered and if they have it not then the costs are to be levied of their proper goods and chattels and the said Defendants in mercy.

TALBOT THOMPSON Plaintiff
Against Re: In Case
JOHN DAY admin of THOMAS DAY deceased Defendant
This day came the parties by their Attorney's and there upon came also a Jury to wit: JOHN MACLEAN, ANDREW STEVENSON, JOHN ROSS, JOHN STONEY, ROBERT HATTON, JOHN LEE, STEPHEN TANKARD, THOMAS WALKER, GRIFFIN PEART, GEORGE GORDON, JAMES CARMICHAEL and WILLIAM SISSON who being elected tried and sworn the truth to speak upon the issue joined upon their oath do say that the Defendant intestate did assume in manner and form as the Plaintiff against him has declared and do assess the Plaintiff damages by occasion of the non-performance of that assumption to 5pounds, 15 shillings and 6 pence half penny besides his costs. Therefore, it is considered that the Plaintiff recover against the said Defendant his damages aforesaid in form aforesaid assessed and his costs by him in this behalf expended. To be levied of the goods and chattels of the said intestate if so, much the said Defendants have in their hands to be administered and if they have it not then the costs are to be levied of their proper goods and chattels and the said Defendants in mercy.

MAXIMILIAN CALVERT Plaintiff
Against Re: In Case
STEPHEN TANKARD Defendant
This day came the Plaintiff by his Attorney and thereupon came also a Jury to wit: WILLIAM SISSON, JAMES CARMICHAEL, GEORGE GORDON, GRIFFIN PEART, THOMAS WALKER, JOHN MEARNS, JOHN LEE, ROBERT HATTON, JOHN STONEY, JOHN ROSS, ANDREW STEVENSON, and JOHN MACLEAN who being sworn well and truly to inquire of damages in this suit upon their oath do say that the Plaintiff has sustained damages by occasion of the Defendants Breach of Promise to 1 pound 12 shillings and 6 pence besides his costs. Therefore, it is considered the Plaintiff recover against the said Defendants his damages aforesaid in form aforesaid assessed and his cots by him about his suit in this behalf expended and the Defendants in mercy.

PAGE 200
ROBERT GILMOUR admin of the Estate of WILLIAM GRAY Deceased Plaintiff
Against Re: In Debt.
BAILEY WARREN Defendant
This day came the Plaintiff by his Attorney and thereupon came also a Jury to wit: WILLIAM SISSON, JAMES CARMICHAEL, GEORGE GORDON, GRIFFIN PEART, THOMAS WALKER, JOHN MEARNS, JOHN LEE, ROBERT HATTON, JOHN STONEY, JOHN ROSS, ANDREW STEVENSON, and JOHN MACLEAN who being elected tried and sworn the truth to speak upon the issue joined upon their oath do says that the Defendant did assume in manner and form as the Plaintiff against him has declared and do assess the Plaintiff damages by occasion of the non-performance of that assumption to 8 pounds with interest thereon after the rate of 5% per annum to be computed from October 1, 1771, to the time of payment and costs. Therefore, it is considered that the Plaintiff recover against the said Defendant his damages aforesaid in form aforesaid assessed and his costs by him in this behalf expended and the said Defendants in mercy.

RICHARD BASSET Plaintiff
Against In Debt.
JOHN POLLOCK Defendant
This day came the Plaintiff by his Attorney and thereupon came also a Jury to wit: WILLIAM SISSON, JAMES CARMICHAEL, GEORGE GORDON, GRIFFIN PEART, THOMAS WALKER, JOHN MEARNS, JOHN LEE, ROBERT HATTON, JOHN STONEY, JOHN ROSS, ANDREW STEVENSON, and JOHN MACLEAN who being elected tried and sworn the truth to speak upon the issue joined upon their oath do says that the Defendant has not paid the Debt in the declaration mentioned. Therefore, it is considered that the Plaintiff recover against the said Defendant his debt amounting to 20 pounds 11 shillings and 6 pence and his costs by him about his suit in this behalf expended and the said Defendant in mercy. But this judgement is to be discharged by the payment of 10 pounds 5 shillings and 9 pence with interest thereon after the rate of 5% per annum to be computed from July 10th, 1772, to the time of payment and the costs

JOHN ARDIS Plaintiff
Against Re: In Trespass and Battery
THOMAS HARRISON Defendant
This day came the Plaintiff by his Attorney and thereupon came also a Jury to wit: WILLIAM SISSON, JAMES CARMICHAEL, GEORGE GORDON, GRIFFIN PEART, THOMAS WALKER, JOHN MEARNS, JOHN LEE, ROBERT HATTON, JOHN STONEY, JOHN ROSS, ANDREW STEVENSON, and JOHN MACLEAN who being elected tried and sworn the truth to speak upon the issue joined upon their oath do says that the Defendant is guilty of the trespass assault and battery in the declaration mentioned in manner and form as the Plaintiff against him has declared. And do assess the Plaintiff damages by occasion thereof to 20 pounds besides his costs. Therefore, it is considered that the Plaintiff recover against the said Defendant his damages aforesaid in form aforesaid assessed and his costs by him in this behalf expended and the said Defendant may be taken.

Order is granted EDWARD DAVIS against JOHN ARDIS for 125 pounds of tobacco for 5 days attendance at this Court in his suit against THOMAS HARRISON.

PAGE 200B

WILLIAM HARDY against JOHN EDWARD. JOHN PRESTON undertakes for the Plaintiff that he will pay to the Defendant all such damages costs and charges as shall be awarded against him by the Court.

WILLIAM HARDY Plaintiff
Against Re: In Case
JOHN EDWARDS Defendant

This day came the parties by their Attorney's and thereupon came also a Jury to wit: JOHN MACLACHLAN*, JOHN CARMOUNT, WRIGHT BRICKELL, ROBERT FRY, JOSEPH LANGLEY, WILLIAM IVY, CHRISTOPHER CALVERT, SAMUEL BACON, THOMAS POOLE, GEORGE WEBB, JOHN WILLS and SCARBROUGH TANKARD. who being elected tried and sworn the truth to speak upon the issue joined upon their oath do says that the Defendant did assume in manner and form as the Plaintiff against him has declared and do assess the Plaintiff damages by occasion of the non-performance of that assumption to 5 pounds 19 shillings and 9 pence besides his costs. Therefore, it is considered that the plaintiff recover against the said Defendant his damages aforesaid in form aforesaid assessed and his costs by him in this behalf expended and the said Defendants in mercy.

CALEB HANBURY Plaintiff
Against Re: In Case
ALEXANDER BELL Defendant

This day came the parties by their Attorney's and there upon came also a Jury to wit: WILLIAM INGRAM, JOHN ROSS, ANDREW STEVENSON, JAMES CARMICHAEL, ROBERT HATTON, JOHN LEE, JOHN STONEY, THOMAS WALKER, GRIFFIN PEART, GEORGE GORDON, JOHN MEARNS and JOHN MACLEAN who being elected tried and sworn the truth to speak upon the issue joined upon their oath do say that the Defendant is not guilty as in pleading he has alleged. Therefore, it is considered that the plaintiff take nothing by his bill but for his false claims to be in mercy and the Defendant go hence without day and recover against the Plaintiff his costs by him about his defense in this behalf expended.

Order is granted HILLERY HODGES against CALEB HANBURY for 100 pounds of tobacco for 4 days attendance at this Court in his suit against ALEXANDER BELL.

Order is granted THOMAS SHIPWASH against ALEXANDER BELL for 75 pounds of tobacco for 3 days attendance at this Court in the suit of CALEB HANBURY against him.

Order is granted AMBROS SHIPWASH against ALEXANDER BELL for 75 pounds of tobacco for 3 days attendance at this Court in the suit of CALEB HANBURY against him.

Order is granted JOHN INGLES against ALEXANDER BELL for 75 pounds of tobacco for 3 days attendance at this Court in the suit of CALEB HANBURY against him.

PAGE 201

Order is granted JAMES JOLLIFF against ALEXANDER BELL for 50 pounds of tobacco for 2 days attendance at this Court in the suit of CALEB HANBURY against him.

Order is granted WILLIAM DALTON against ALEXANDER BELL for 50 pounds of tobacco for 3 days attendance at this Court in the suit of CALEB HANBURY against him.

The Court this day rated Flour at 16/8 per centum weight
This Court is adjourned to Court in Course, CHARLES THOMAS MAYOR, TESTE: JOHN BOUSH D.C.

NORFOLK BOROUGH

At a Hustings Court Held this 20TH day of September 1773
PRESENT: CHARLES THOMAS ESQUIRE MAYOR
GENTLEMAN ALDERMEN: GEORGE ABYVON, JAMES TAYLOR, LEWIS HANSFORD, CORNELIUS CALVERT

HARDRESS WALLER against ROBERT GILMOUR administrator of WILLIAM GRAY deceased. By petition and summons Judgement is granted the Plaintiff for 4 pounds 8 shillings and 9 pence. It is ordered the Defendants pay the same with costs.

EILBECK ROSS and Company against JOHN WHIDDEN. A conditional order is granted the Plaintiffs against the Defendant and JOHN WILSON Gentleman his bail

MALACHI MAUND against ALEXANDER BELL. In Debt. Imparlance
MALACHI MAUND against JOHN CHERRY. Dismissed.

JAMES GRAHAM against JOHN CRAMOND. In Debt. JAMES GRAHAM against JOHN CRAMOND. In Case. HENRY BRESSIE and THOMAS CLAIBORNE this day came into Court and undertook for the Defendant that in case he shall be cast in this suit, he the said Defendant will pay the condemnation of the court or render his body to prison in execution for the same or that the said HENRY and THOMAS will do it for him whereupon the defendant by his Attorney prays and has leave to IMPARLE here until the next Court and then to plead.

PAGE 201B

JEREMIAH FOREMAN against MISTERS BARBER and HOFFMIRE and NATHANIEL POYNER. JOSEPH CALVERT this day came into Court and undertook for the Defendants BARBER and HOFFMIRE that in case they shall be cast in this suit, they the said Defendants will pay the condemnation of the Court or render his body to prison in execution for the same or that the said CALVERT will do it for them whereupon the Defendant's by their Attorney prays and has leave to IMPARLE here until the next Court and then to plead. And the suit against NATHANIEL POYNER is dismissed.

JOHN CRAMOND against NEWCOMB DODD an alias capias awarded.
JOHN CRAMOND against LEMUEL ROBERTS. The suit is dismissed.
RICHARD BASSET against PHILIP CARBERY. Time is allowed to consider bill.

PETER SHEWSBERY against JUAN alias JAMES MCMELIN, THOMAS CLAIBORNE undertakes for the Plaintiff that he will pay to the Defendant all such damages costs and charges as shall be awarded against him by the Court. And JOHN GILCHRIST this day come into Court and undertook for the Defendant that in case he shall be cast in this suit he the said Defendant will pay the condemnation of the Court or render his body to prison in execution for the same or that he the said GILCHRIST will do it for him. Whereupon the Defendant by his Attorney prays and has leave to IMPARLE here until the next Court and then to plead and a DEDIMUS is granted him to take the deposition of JOHN FORD and GILES STANTON giving the Plaintiff reasonable notice of the time and place.

BARTLET GOODRICH against JAMES TRISTRAM. The suit is dismissed.
STEPHEN HART against JOSEPH NORTHRUP the suit is dismissed at the Plaintiffs costs.

NATHANIEL BURGESS against FRANCIS WILLIAMSON and NEIL SNODGRASS, ABRAHAM WORMINGTON this day came into Court and undertook for the Defendant that in case they shall be cast in this suit they the said Defendant will pay the condemnation of the Court or render their bodies to prison in execution for the same or that the said WORMINGTON will do it for them. Whereupon the Defendants by their Attorney prayed an Imparlance.

MASON MILLER QUI TAM against CHRISTOPHER WILSON. Continued and on motion of the Defendant by his Attorney A DEDIMUS is granted to take the depositions of JOHN BOYD, ROBERT ERRICK and RICHARD LETTY giving the Plaintiff reasonable notice.

SAMUEL SMITH against THOMAS LEAH. The suit is dismissed.
JOHN CRAMOND against THOMAS TAYLOR. Order is against the Defendant.

PAGE 202
JAMES MURDAUGH Plaintiff
Against Re: In Case
LOGAN GILMOUR & Company Defendants
HUGH WYLER Plaintiff
Against Re: In Case
ARCHIBALD CAMPBELL admin of JOHN DALGLEISH

MISTERS EILBECK ROSS & Company
Against Re: In Case
WILLIAM SAVAGE
This day came the parties by their Attorney's and the Defendants pray and have leave to IMPARLE here until the next Court and then to plead.

JAMES LEITCH against THOMAS BURKE. ANDREW RONALD this day came into Court and undertook for the Defendant that in case he shall be cast in this suit he the said Defendant will pay the condemnation of the Court or render his body to prison in execution for the same or that the said RONALD will do it for him. Whereupon the Defendants by his Attorney prays and has leave to IMPARLE here until the next Court and then to plead.

MATTHEW PHRIPP and JOSEPH HUTCHINGS against LEWIS NEWTON, VICKERS, and MURRAY attachment.
ANN BREITHWAIT against JOHN COOPER JR. Imparlance.

JAMES MCMELIN was this day brough before the Court by warrant for being a person of lewd life and conversation and a common disturber of the peace and the same being proved. It is ordered the Sergeant take and him in Custody until he gives bond and security himself in 20 pounds and 2 securities in 10 pounds each for keeping the peace 3 months and pay the costs of this prosecution.

The King by JOSEPH NORTHRUP against STEPHEN HART. Dismissed at the Defendants cost.

JOHN HANNON was this day brought before the Court for having CONTEMNED the Court authority and the same being proved it is ordered that the Sergeant take and keep him in his Custody until he gives bond and security himself in 50 pounds in 2 securities in 25 pounds each for his being of good behavior for 3 months and pay the costs of this prosecution.

EDWARD WRIGHT against JOHN MCLACHLAN. On the motion of the Plaintiff by his Attorney a DEDIMUS is granted him to take the deposition of MARGARET JONES De Bene Esse giving the Defendant reasonable notice.

PAGE 202B
JAMES ARCHDEACON against MARTIN MURPHY. PHILIP CARBERY this day came into Court and undertook for the Defendant that in case he shall be cast in this suit he the said Defendant will pay the condemnation of the Court or render his body to prison in execution for the same or that the said CARBERY will do it for him. Whereupon the Defendants by his Attorney prays and has leave to IMPARLE here until the next Court and then to plead.

JAMES HALDANE Plaintiff
Against Re: In Case
JOHN BRUCE Defendant
This day came the parties by their Attorney's and there upon came also a Jury to wit: JOHN BEGG, JAMES CARMICHAEL, THOMAS HEPBURN, JOHN LEE, JOHN STANHOPE, WILLIAM GOODCHILD, GEORGE WEBB, JOSIAH HODGES, JOHN BAYNES, RICHARD BASSET and JOHN CARMOUNT who being elected tried and sworn the truth to speak upon the issue joined upon their oath do say that the Defendant did not assume as in pleading he has alleged. Therefore, it is considered that the Plaintiff take nothing by his bill but for this false claims be in mercy and the Defendant go hence without day and recover against the plaintiff his costs by him about his defense in the behalf expended.

Order is granted SAMUEL DAVIS MCCASTLETON against JAMES HALDANE for 25 pounds of tobacco for 1 day's attendance at this Court in his suit against JOHN BRUCE.

Order is granted RICHARD BICKERDICK against JAMES HALDANE for 25 pounds of tobacco for 1 day's attendance at this Court in his suit against JOHN BRUCE.

Order is granted CHARLES MCCASTLETON against JAMES HALDANE for 50 pounds of tobacco for 2 days attendance at this Court in his suit against JOHN BRUCE.

Order is granted JOHN ADAMS against JAMES HALDANE for 50 pounds of tobacco for 2 days attendance at this Court in his suit against JOHN BRUCE.

FREDERICK BOUSH against JAMES MOORE. The Defendant filed his answer and time is allowed the Plaintiff to consider it.

Order is granted JAMES DAVIS against JOHN BRUCE for 100 pounds of tobacco for 4 days attendance at this Court. WILLIAM BRADDIN 75 pounds of tobacco for 3 days attendance and ROBERT ROWIN 25 pounds of tobacco for 1 day's attendance at this Court in the suit of JAMES HALDANE against him.

This Court is adjourned until tomorrow at 9 o'clock, CHARLES THOMAS MAYOR, TESTE: JOHN BOUSH D.C.

PAGE 203
NORFOLK BOROUGH
At a Hustings Court Held this 21st day of September 1773
PRESENT: CHARLES THOMAS ESQUIRE MAYOR
GENTLEMAN ALDERMEN: GEORGE ABYVON, PAUL LOYALL, LEWIS HANSFORD, CORNELIUS CALVERT

GEORGE WEBB and JOSEPH LANGLEY against JOHN BAYNES and NANCY ASHLEY. Demurer filed and set for argument.
RICHARD COLLINS against THOMAS HUGHS. The suit is dismissed.

JOSEPH LANGLEY Plaintiff
Against Re: In Case
JOHN MCLACHLAN Defendant
This day came the parties by their Attorney's and thereupon came also a Jury to wit: THOMAS TERRY, JOHN BEGG, HUGH MILLER, PHILIP CARBERY, SAMUEL SANDS, ROBERT MACKIE, WILLIAM JAQUIS, JOHN CHESHIRE, JOSIAH HODGES, WILLIAM WILL, JOHN SHEDDEN and JAMES CARMICHAEL who being elected tried and sworn the truth to speak upon the issue joined upon their oath do say that the Defendant did assume in manner and form as the Plaintiff against him has declared and do assess the Plaintiff damages by occasion of the non-performance of that assumption to 68 pounds 17 shillings and 2 pence besides his costs. Therefore, it is considered that the Plaintiff recover against the said Defendant his damages aforesaid in form aforesaid assessed and his costs by him in this behalf expended and the said Defendant in mercy.

MARY ROTHERY and others executors of MATTHEW ROTHERY Plaintiff
Against Re: In Case
THOMAS PEARSON Defendant
This day came the parties by their Attorney's and there upon came also a Jury to wit: JOHN STANHOPE, ANDREW STEVENS, JAMES HALDANE, JOHN RICHARDSON, GEORGE WILSON, GEORGE KELLY, JAMES LEITCH, BASSET MOSELEY, GILBERT GREENSON, GEORGE WEBB, ALEXANDER MARSENBURG and JOHN MEARNS who being elected tried and sworn the truth to speak upon the issue joined upon their oath do say that the Defendant did not assume as in pleading he has alleged. Therefore, it is considered that the Plaintiff take nothing by their bill but for their false claims be in mercy. And the Defendant go hence without day and recover against the Plaintiff his costs by him in this behalf expended.

JOHN CRAMOND against SAMUEL GWIN. This day came the parties by their Attorney's and thereupon came a Jury to wit: JOHN STANHOPE, ANDREW STEVENS, JAMES HALDANE, JOHN RICHARDSON, GEORGE WILSON, GEORGE KELLY, JAMES LEITCH, BASSET MOSELEY, GILBERT GREENSON, GEORGE WEBB, ALEXANDER MARSENBURG and JOHN MEARNS who being elected tried and sworn the truth to speak upon the issue joined. By the mutual consent of the parties and with the assent of the Court, JOHN STANHOPE one of the Jurors was withdrawn and thereupon the rest of the Jurors from giving any verdict in premises are by the Court Discharged and thereon the Cause is continued until the next Court at the Defendants costs.

PAGE 203B

RICHARD KELSICK Plaintiff

Against Re: In Debt

NATHANIEL BOUSH Defendant

This day came the parties by their Attorney's and thereupon came a Jury to wit: JOHN STANHOPE, ANDREW STEVENS, JAMES HALDANE, JOHN RICHARDSON, GEORGE WILSON, GEORGE KELLY, JAMES LEITCH, BASSET MOSELEY, GILBERT GREENSON, GEORGE WEBB, ALEXANDER MARSENBURG and JOHN MEARNS who being elected tried and sworn the truth to speak upon the issue joined upon their oath do says that the Defendant has not paid the Debt in the declaration mentioned. Therefore, it is considered that the Plaintiff recover against the said Defendant his debt amounting to 260 pounds and his costs by him about his suit in this behalf expended and the said Defendant in mercy. But this judgement is to be discharged by the payment of 130 pounds with interest thereon after the rate of 5% per annum to be computed from October 21, 1771, to the time of payment and the costs

RICHARD BASSET Plaintiff

Against Re: In Debt

JOHN HARWOOD Defendant

This day came the parties by their Attorney's and thereupon came a Jury to wit: JOHN STANHOPE, ANDREW STEVENS, JAMES HALDANE, JOHN RICHARDSON, GEORGE WILSON, GEORGE KELLY, JAMES LEITCH, BASSET MOSELEY, GILBERT GREENSON, GEORGE WEBB, ALEXANDER MARSENBURG and JOHN MEARNS who being elected tried and sworn the truth to speak upon the issue joined upon their oath do says that the Defendant has not paid the Debt in the declaration mentioned. Therefore, it is considered that the Plaintiff recover against the said Defendant his debt amounting to 26 pounds 10 shillings and his costs by him about his suit in this behalf expended and the said Defendant in mercy. But this judgement is to be discharged by the payment of 130 pounds with interest thereon after the rate of 5% per annum to be computed from February 30*, 1772 to the time of payment and the costs

WILLIAM and THOMAS FARRERS Plaintiff

Against Re: In Debt

WILLIAM BRITT Defendant

This day came the parties by their Attorney's and thereupon came a Jury to wit: JOHN STANHOPE, ANDREW STEVENS, JAMES HALDANE, JOHN RICHARDSON, GEORGE WILSON, GEORGE KELLY, JAMES LEITCH, BASSET MOSELEY, GILBERT GREENSON, GEORGE WEBB, ALEXANDER MARSENBURG and JOHN MEARNS who being elected tried and sworn the truth to speak upon the issue joined upon their oath do says that the Defendant has not paid the Debt in the declaration mentioned. Therefore, it is considered that the Plaintiff recover against the said Defendant his debt amounting to 21 pounds, 11 shillings and one penny and their costs by them about this suit in this behalf expended and the said Defendant in mercy. But this judgement is to be discharged by the payment of 10 pounds, 15 shillings and 6 pence with interest thereon after the rate of 5% per annum to be computed from January 1, 1771, to the time of payment and the costs

Order is granted MARGARET MARSHALL against JOSEPH LANGLEY for 125 pounds of tobacco for 5 days attendance at this Court in his suit against JOHN MCLACHLAN.

Order is granted SARAH LANGLEY against JOSEPH LANGLEY for 125 pounds of tobacco for 5 days attendance at this Court in his suit against JOHN MCLACHLAN.

PAGE 204

WILLIAM TREBELL and ROBERT NICHOLSON executors of JOSEPH SCRIVENER Deceased Plaintiff

Against Re: In Case

GEORGE JOSEPH FENWICK

This day came the Plaintiff by BENJAMIN CROOKER Gentleman their Attorney and thereupon came also a Jury to wit: JOHN STANHOPE, ANDREW STEVENS, JAMES HALDANE, JOHN RICHARDSON, GEORGE WILSON, GEORGE KELLY, JAMES LEITCH, BASSET MOSELEY, GILBERT GREENSON, GEORGE WEBB, ALEXANDER MARSENBURG and JOHN MEARNS who being sworn well and truly to inquire of damages in this suit upon their oath do say that the Plaintiff has sustained damages by occasion of the Defendants Breach of Promise to 11 pounds 9 shillings and 9 pence besides their costs. Therefore, it is considered by the Court that the Plaintiff recover against the said Defendants and JOHN WILLS his bail, their damages aforesaid in form aforesaid assessed and his cots by him about his suit in this behalf expended and the Defendants in mercy.

WILLIAM KEATING Plaintiff

Against Re: In Case

CORNELIUS CALVERT Defendant

This day came the parties by their Attorney's and thereupon came a Jury to wit: JOHN STANHOPE, ANDREW STEVENS, JAMES HALDANE, JOHN RICHARDSON, GEORGE WILSON, GEORGE KELLY, JAMES LEITCH, BASSET MOSELEY, GILBERT GREENSON, GEORGE WEBB, ALEXANDER MARSENBURG and JOHN MEARNS who being elected tried and sworn the truth to speak upon the issue joined withdrew and not returning a verdict in the premises the Cause is continued until the next Court.

Order is granted DICKERSON PRIOR against JOSEPH LANGLEY for 125 pounds of tobacco for 5 days attendance of his wife FRANCES at this Court in his suit against JOHN MCLACHLAN.

Order is granted ANDREW STEVENSON against JOSEPH LANGLEY for 125 pounds of tobacco for 5 days attendance at this Court in his suit against JOHN MCLACHLAN.

Order is granted CHARLES RUDDER against JOHN MCLACHLAN for 100 pounds of tobacco for 4 days attendance at this Court in the suit of JOSEPH LANGLEY against him.

Order is granted GEORGE WEBB against JOHN MCLACHLAN for 100 pounds of tobacco for 4 days attendance at this Court in the suit of JOSEPH LANGLEY against him.

Order is granted THOMAS MARSHALL against JOHN MCLACHLAN for 75 pounds of tobacco for 3 days attendance at this Court in the suit of JOSEPH LANGLEY against him.

Order is granted ARTHUR DENBY against JOHN MCLACHLAN for 100 pounds of tobacco for 4 days attendance at this Court in the suit of JOSEPH LANGLEY against him.

GRAHAM against CRAMOND. In Debt & Case. On the motion of the Plaintiff by his Attorney a DEDIMUS is granted him to take depositions of JAMES ORR in each suit giving the Defendant reasonable notice of the time and place.

PAGE 204B
HESLOP and BLAIR Plaintiff
Against Re: In Case
MISTERS ELIAS BOYER and PETER KATZ Defendants
This day came the Plaintiff by BENJAMIN CROOKER Gentleman their Attorney and thereupon came also a Jury to wit: JOHN SHEDDEN, WILLIAM WILLIS, JOSIAH HODGES, JOHN CHESHIRE, WILLIAM JAQUES, PAUL PROBY, SAMUEL LANDS, PHILIP CARBERY, HUGH MILLER, THOMAS TERRY, JOHN BEGG and JAMES CARMICHAEL who being sworn well and truly to inquire of damages in this suit upon their oath do say that the Plaintiff has sustained damages by occasion of the Defendants Breach of Promise to 9 pounds 3 shillings and 3 pence besides their costs. Therefore, it is considered by the Court that the Plaintiff recover against the said Defendants and JAMES LEITCH his bail, their damages aforesaid in form aforesaid assessed and his costs by him about his suit in this behalf expended and the Defendants in mercy.

MISTERS ARCHDEACON and INGRAM Plaintiff
Against Re: In Case
WILLIAM DONALDSON Defendant
This day came the parties by their Attorneys and thereupon came also a Jury to wit: JOHN SHEDDEN, WILLIAM WILLIS, JOSIAH HODGES, JOHN CHESHIRE, WILLIAM JAQUES, PAUL PROBY, SAMUEL LANDS, PHILIP CARBERY, HUGH MILLER, THOMAS TERRY, JOHN BEGG and JAMES CARMICHAEL who being elected tried and sworn the truth to speak upon the issue joined upon their oath do say that the Defendants did assume in manner and form as the Plaintiff against him have declared and do assess the Plaintiff damages by occasion of the non-performance of that assumption to 9 pounds 3 shillings and 4 pence besides their costs. Therefore, it is considered that the Plaintiff recover against the said Defendant their damages aforesaid in form aforesaid assessed and their costs by them in this suit in this behalf expended and the said Defendant in mercy.

JAMES MILLS and Company Plaintiff
Against Re: In Case
RICHARD BROWN and JOHN CHESHIRE Defendants
This day came the Defendants by their Attorney and the Plaintiff though solemnly called came not but made default nor is their suit further prosecuted. Therefore, on the prayer of the Defendant it is considered that they recover against the Plaintiffs 5 shillings current money and their costs by them about their defendant in this behalf expended according to the form of the Act of assembly and the Plaintiff for their false claims be in mercy.

WILLIAM ROBINSON against JOSHUA WRIGHT. On the motion of the Plaintiff by his Attorney a DEDIMUS is granted him to take the depositions of WILLIAM HENRY MACKIE DE BENE ESSE and THOMAS MACKIE of ANTIGUA giving the Defendant reasonable notice of the time and place.

STEPHEN TANKARD, ROBERT STEAD and MARY POOLE, Executors of NICHOLAS POOLE deceased against JAMES HALDANE. The Suit is dismissed at the Defendants Costs.

PAGE 205
JOHN RANSBERG Plaintiff
Against Re: In Case
JOSHUA GOUGH Defendant
This day came the parties by their Attorneys and thereupon came also a Jury to wit: JOHN SHEDDEN, WILLIAM WILLIS, JOSIAH HODGES, JOHN CHESHIRE, WILLIAM JAQUES, PAUL PROBY, SAMUEL LANDS, PHILIP CARBERY, HUGH MILLER, THOMAS TERRY, JOHN BEGG and JAMES CARMICHAEL who being elected tried and sworn the truth to speak upon the issue joined upon their oath do say that the Defendant did assume in manner and form as the Plaintiff against him has declared and do assess the Plaintiff damages by occasion of the non-performance of that assumption to 13 pounds 13 shillings with interest thereon after the rate of 5% per annum to be computed from November 4th 1771 to the time of payment and the costs. Therefore, it is considered that the Plaintiff recover against the said Defendant his damages aforesaid in form aforesaid assessed and his costs by them in this suit in this behalf expended and the said Defendant in mercy.

ANDREW SPROWLE admin of MISTERS SPROWLE and CROOKS deceased Plaintiff

Against Re: In Debt

THOMAS ROBERTS … DISTILLER…. Defendant

This day came the parties by their Attorneys and thereupon came also a Jury to wit: JOHN SHEDDEN, WILLIAM WILLIS, JOSIAH HODGES, JOHN CHESHIRE, WILLIAM JAQUES, PAUL PROBY, SAMUEL LANDS, PHILIP CARBERY, HUGH MILLER, THOMAS TERRY, JOHN BEGG and JAMES CARMICHAEL who being elected tried and sworn the truth to speak upon the issue joined upon their oath do say that the Defendant has not paid the debt in the declaration mentioned. Therefore, it is considered that the Plaintiff recover against the said Defendant his debt amounting to 25 pounds 11 shillings and his costs by him in this behalf expended and the said Defendant in mercy. But this judgement is to be discharged by the payment of 12 pounds 10 shillings and 5 pence half penny with interest thereon after the rate of 5% per annum to be computed from May 1771* to the time of payment and the costs.

ANDREW SPROWLE admin of MISTERS SPROWLE and CROOKS deceased Plaintiff

Against Re: In Debt

ARTHUR BUTT Defendant

This day came the parties by their Attorneys and thereupon came also a Jury to wit: JOHN SHEDDEN, WILLIAM WILLIS, JOSIAH HODGES, JOHN CHESHIRE, WILLIAM JAQUES, PAUL PROBY, SAMUEL LANDS, PHILIP CARBERY, HUGH MILLER, THOMAS TERRY, JOHN BEGG and JAMES CARMICHAEL who being elected tried and sworn the truth to speak upon the issue joined upon their oath do say that the Defendant has not paid the debt in the declaration mentioned. Therefore, it is considered that the Plaintiff recover against the said Defendant his debt amounting to 18 pounds 5 shillings and his costs by him in this behalf expended and the said Defendant in mercy.

But this judgement is to be discharged by the payment of 9 pounds 2 shillings and 6 pence with interest thereon after the rate of 5% per annum to be computed from May 6th, 1767, to the time of payment and the costs.

Order is granted THOMAS PEARSON against RICHARD BROWN and JOHN CHESHIRE for 75 pounds of tobacco for 3 days attendance at this Court in the Suit of JAMES MILLS and Company against them.

JUDITH DUNFORD against GEORGE JOSEPH FENWICK. The suit is dismissed.

PAGE 205B

ANDREW SPROWLE admin of MISTERS SPROWLE and CROOKS deceased Plaintiff

Against Re: In Debt

ALEXANDER BELL Defendant

This day came the parties by their Attorneys and thereupon came also a Jury to wit: JOHN SHEDDEN, WILLIAM WILLIS, JOSIAH HODGES, JOHN CHESHIRE, WILLIAM JAQUES, PAUL PROBY, SAMUEL LANDS, PHILIP CARBERY, HUGH MILLER, THOMAS TERRY, JOHN BEGG and JAMES CARMICHAEL who being elected tried and sworn the truth to speak upon the issue joined upon their oath do say that the Defendant has not paid the debt in the declaration mentioned. Therefore, it is considered that the Plaintiff recover against the said Defendant his debt amounting to 27 pounds 3 pence and his costs by him in this behalf expended and the said Defendant in mercy. But this judgement is to be discharged by the payment of 13 pounds 10 shillings and 1 penny half penny with interest thereon after the rate of 5% per annum to be computed from May 25, 1772, to the time of payment and the costs.

This Court this day rated flour at 16/8 per hundred weight

This Court is adjourned until Court in Course, CHARLES THOMAS MAYOR, TESTE: JOHN BOUSH D.C.

NORFOLK BOROUGH

At a Hustings Court Held this 25th day of October 1773

PRESENT: CHARLES THOMAS ESQUIRE MAYOR

GENTLEMAN ALDERMEN: GEORGE ABYVON, PAUL LOYALL, MAXIMILIAN CALVERT

THOMAS STEWART against JOHN LELLO. An Imparlance.

SAMUEL DAVIS against THOMAS LANGSTON. The suit is dismissed.

MARY ROSS against WILLIAM PENN. JOHN WALKER this day came into Court and undertook for the Defendant in case he shall be cast in this suit he the said Defendant and shall pay the condemnation of the Court or render his body to prison in execution for the same or that he the said WALKER will do it for him. Whereupon the Defendant by his Attorney prays and has leave to IMPARLE here until the next Court and then to plead.

MAXIMILIAN CALVERT against ANDREW STEVENSON. JACOB WILLIAMS this day came into Court and undertook for the Defendant in case he shall be cast in this suit he the said Defendant and shall pay the condemnation of the Court or render his body to prison in execution for the same or that he the said WILLIAMS will do it for him. Whereupon the Defendant by his Attorney prays and has leave to IMPARLE here until the next Court and then to plead.

PAGE 206

JOHN CALVERT against T.M. WILLIAMS. In Case. Imparlance

RICHARD COLLINS and ELIZABETH, his wife against JAMES CARMICHAEL. Imparlance.

RICHARD COLLINS against JAMES CARMICHAEL. Imparlance.

HENRY TILKINS against JOHN HUGHS and JOHN JONES By petition and summons dismissed against HUGHS and Judgement is granted the Plaintiff against the other Defendant JONES for 4 pounds 10 shillings with interest after the rate of 5% per annum to be computed from July 24, 1773, to the time of payment and costs.

ALEXANDER HODGE and wife against JAMES CARMICHAEL. Imparlance.
ANDREW STEVENSON and ALICE, his wife against JOHN HARDY. Imparlance.

(Author's Note: Names are listed 3x, but the info is only listed 1x, so apparently there are 3 cases)
CORNELIUS CALVERT Plaintiff
Against Re: In Debt
JOHN SMITH Defendant
This day came the parties by their Attorneys and the Defendant by this Attorney prays and has leave to Special IMPARLE here until the next Court and then to plead.

CHRISTOPHER WILSON against THOMAS TAYLOR. In Case. Imparlance.
JOHN WILSON against ANDREW STEVENSON. In Debt. The Defendants pleaded he owed nothing. Issue joined and referred until next Court.
JOHN WILSON against ANDREW STEVENSON. CASE. Imparlance

PAGE 206B
BALFOUR and BARRAUD against AARON BARBER. JONATHAN EILBECK this day came into Court and undertook for the Defendant in case he shall be cast in this suit he the said Defendant and shall pay the condemnation of the Court or render his body to prison in execution for the same or that he the said EILBECK will do it for him. Whereupon the Defendant by his Attorney prays and has leave to IMPARLE here until the next Court and then to plead.

HUGH MORIARTY against PATRICK ROBERTSON. An Imparlance.

LOVE MITCHELL & Company against GEORGE ATKINSON by Petition and summons. Judgement is granted the Plaintiff for 5 pounds. It is ordered that the Defendant pay the same unto the Plaintiff with costs and fee.

JACOB ELLEGOOD Plaintiff
Against Re: In Case
PETER KATZ Defendant
This day came as well the Plaintiff by ANDREW RONALD Gentleman his Attorney as the Defendant in his proper person and says that he cannot gainsay the Plaintiff's action nor but that he did assume in manner and form as the Plaintiff against him has declared. Therefore, it is considered that the Plaintiff recover against the said Defendant 7 pounds 6 pence and his costs by him about his suit in this behalf expended and the said Defendant in mercy.

JOSEPH MITCHELL against ROGER PEARCE. Dismissed.

JOHN SHAW against ROSANNA RITTER, JOHN RICHARDSON TAYLOR* this day came into Court and undertook for the Defendant in case he shall be cast in this suit he the said Defendant and shall pay the condemnation of the Court or render his body to prison in execution for the same or that he the said RICHARDSON will do it for him. Whereupon the Defendant by his Attorney prays and has leave to IMPARLE here until the next Court and then to plead.

PHILIP CARBERY against STAFFORD SAYBOURN. The suit is discontinued

THOMAS BRESSIE admin of JAMES IVY deceased against WILLIAM SMITH. The Defendant pleaded he did not assume issue joined and referred until the next Court.

GEORGE FARRER against JOANNA LEWIS by Petition and summons. Judgement is granted the Plaintiff for 1 pounds 12 shillings and 10 pence half penny. It is ordered that the Defendant pay the same unto the Plaintiff with costs and fee.

PAGE 207
MATTHEW PHRIPP and JOSEPH HUTCHINGS & CO. against WILLIAM MURRAY. The suit is dismissed.
MATTHEW PHRIPP and JOSEPH HUTCHINGS & CO. against JOHN LEWIS. The suit is discontinued.
MATTHEW PHRIPP and JOSEPH HUTCHINGS & CO. against WILLIAM NEWTON. The suit is discontinued.
MATTHEW PHRIPP and JOSEPH HUTCHINGS & CO. against JAMES VICKERS. The suit is discontinued.

JOHN CRAMOND against NEWCOMB DODD. The suit is discontinued.
WILLIAM SIMPSON against AARON BARBER. Dismissed.

Ordinary License is granted JAMES DUNN and WILLIAM SMITH on their complying with the law.

MARTHA LAWRENCE and JOHN LAWRENCE executors of JOHN LAWRENCE deceased against JOHN GILCHRIST. The suit abates by the Defendants death.

ROBERT ROBERTSON against ROGER PIERCE. The attachment abates by the Plaintiffs death.

JOSHUA GOUGH admin of JAMES GOUGH deceased against JOSIAH HODGES. The suit abates by the Plaintiff's death.

Ordered that the Ordinary License granted RICHARD BROWN TRUSTEE of TERESA PEARCE be suppressed.

JOHN and JONATHAN EILBECK against JOSHUA WRIGHT. The suit is dismissed.

WILLIAM KEATING Plaintiff
Against Re: In Case
CORNELIUS CALVERT Gentleman Defendant
This day came the parties by their Attorney's and the Jury that was at the last Court elected tried and sworn the truth to speak upon the issue joined, not returning any verdict was this day solemnly called but came not but by consent of the parties by their Attorney's they agreed to receive the verdict which being in the possession of LEWIS HANSFORD Sergeant is brought into Court and is in these words to wit: We of the Jury find for the Plaintiff the sum of 10 pounds 19 shillings and 3 pence besides his costs. Therefore, it is considered that the Plaintiff recover against the said Defendant his damages aforesaid in form aforesaid assessed and his costs by him about his suit in this behalf expended and the said Defendant in mercy.

Order is granted ROBERT ALLAN against LOVE MITCHELL and Company for 25 pounds of tobacco for 1 day's attendance at this Court in their suit against GEORGE ATKINSON.

PAGE 207B
THOMAS SNALE and ELIZABETH, his wife Plaintiff
Against Re: In Chancery
JOHN IVY admin of WILLIAM IVY Deceased Defendant
The Defendant still failing to answer the bill of the Plaintiff. On their motion an Attachment is awarded against him for such his contempt returnable here the next Court.

JAMES BALFOUR and DANIEL BARRAUD Plaintiff against JOHN JONES Defendant. The Defendant pleaded he did not assume with leave issue joined and referred until next Court.

WILLIAM WALKER against SAMUEL SWANN. In Case. The Defendant pleaded he did not assume with leave issue joined and referred until next Court.

JOSEPH HUTCHINGS Gentleman Trustee in Trust for JOHN SMITH against RICHARD BROWN. The Defendant pleaded he did not assume with leave issue joined and referred until next Court.

PATRICK TELFER Plaintiff against JOHN CRAMOND Defendant. In Case. The Defendant pleaded he did not assume with leave issue joined and referred until next Court.

CHRISTOPHER CALVERT against FREDERICK BOUSH. In Case. The Defendant pleaded he did not assume with leave issue joined and referred until next Court.

JAMES BERRY Plaintiff against ALEXANDER MURRAY Defendant. In Debt. The Defendant pleaded payment issue joined and referred until next Court.

WILLIAM SKINKER against MISTERS PAUL LOYALL, NEWTON, and Company. In Case. The Defendants pleaded they did not assume with leave issue joined and referred until next Court.

HENRY FLEMING and Company against NATHANIEL BOUSH. In Case. The Defendant pleaded he did not assume with leave issue joined and referred until next Court.

JOHN BARRET against ROBERT FRY. The Defendant pleaded he was not guilty issue joined and referred until next Court.

PHILIP CARBERY Plaintiff against STEWARD HOLT Defendant. The Defendant not appearing. Ordered that Judgement be entered for the Plaintiff against him the said Defendant and DOUGLAS WILLIS his bail for what damages the Plaintiff sustained to be ascertained at the next Court upon a writ of inquiry.

PAGE 208
JOHN WILSON against WILLIAM KIDD. The suit is dismissed.

JOHN SHAW and MARY, his wife executors of JAMES ARNOT Deceased Plaintiffs
Against Re: In Case
JAMES BAYNES Defendant
This day came the Plaintiff by BENJAMIN CROOKER Gentleman their Attorney and there upon came also a Jury to wit: THOMAS HEPBURN, WILLIAM GOODCHILD, JOHN RICHARDSON, JOSEPH HARDING, JOHN MEARNS, JAMES PASTEUR, HARDRESS WALLER, THOMAS ROBINSON, ARCHIBALD CARY, WILLIAM SISSON, EDWARD JONES, and WILLIAM SKINKER who being sworn well and truly to inquire of damages in this suit upon their oath do say that the Plaintiff has sustained damages by occasion of the Defendants Breach of Promise to 9 pounds 9 shillings and 1 penny besides their costs. Therefore, it is considered that the Plaintiff recover against the said Defendants and JOSEPH CALVERT Sergeant his bail, their damages aforesaid in form aforesaid assessed and his costs by him about his suit in this behalf expended and the Defendants in mercy.

MARSDIN and HODGSON Plaintiff
Against Re: In Case
WILLIAM CONNER Defendant
This day came the Parties by their Attorney's and there upon came also a Jury to wit: THOMAS HEPBURN, WILLIAM GOODCHILD, JOHN RICHARDSON, JOSEPH HARDING, JOHN MEARNS, JAMES PASTEUR, HARDRESS WALLER, THOMAS ROBINSON, ARCHIBALD CARY, WILLIAM SISSON, EDWARD JONES, and WILLIAM SKINKER who being elected tried and sworn the truth to speak upon the issue joined upon their oath do say that the Defendant did assume as in manner and form as the plaintiff against him have declared. And do assess the Plaintiff damages by occasion of the non-performance of that assumption to 19 pounds 3 shillings besides their costs. Therefore, it is considered that the Plaintiff recover against the said Defendant their damages aforesaid in form aforesaid assessed and the costs by them about their suit in this behalf expended and the said Defendant in mercy.

JAMES HUNTER and ELIZABETH TENANT executors of SAMUEL TENANT Plaintiffs
Against Re: In Debt.
WILLIAM SIMPSON executor of FRANCIS CLARKE Deceased Defendant
This day came the Parties by their Attorney's and there upon came also a Jury to wit: THOMAS HEPBURN, WILLIAM GOODCHILD, JOHN RICHARDSON, JOSEPH HARDING, JOHN MEARNS, JAMES PASTEUR, HARDRESS WALLER, THOMAS ROBINSON, ARCHIBALD CARY, WILLIAM SISSON, EDWARD JONES, and WILLIAM SKINKER who being elected tried and sworn the truth to speak upon the issue joined upon their oath do say that the Defendants testator has not paid the debt in the declaration mentioned Therefore, it is considered that the Plaintiff recover against the said Defendant their debt amounting to 63 pounds and their costs by them in his behalf expended. And the said Defendants in mercy. But this judgement is to be discharged by the payment of 6 pounds 13 shillings and 4 pence half penny with interest thereon after the rate of 5% per annum to be computed from this day until the time of payment and the costs.

Order is granted BARNABAS LORAIN against WILLIAM KEATING for 75 pounds of tobacco for 3 days attendance at this Court in this suit against CORNELIUS CALVERT

PAGE 208B
JAMES CARMICHAEL Plaintiff
Against Re: In Trespass
HARDRESS WALLER Defendant
This day came the parties by their Attorney's and thereupon came also a Jury to wit: JOHN BAYNES, GEORGE REY, SAMUEL, SANDS, JOSEPH NORTHRUP, CHARLES COOPER, CHAPMAN MASON, GEORGE ROGERS, EDWARD WONYCOTT, HENRY BRESSIE, WILLIAM HARGRAVES, PAUL PROBY and GEORGE FARRER, who being elected tried and sworn the truth to speak upon the issue joined upon their oath do say that the Defendant is not guilty as in pleading he has alleged. Therefore, it is considered that the Plaintiff take nothing by his bill but for his false claims to be in mercy. And the Defendant go hence without day and recover against the Plaintiff his costs by him about his Defense in this behalf expended.

Order is granted WILLIAM WILLIS against JAMES CARMICHAEL for 75 pounds of tobacco for 3 days attendance at this Court in his suit against HARDRESS WALLER.

Order is granted JOHN RICHARDSON against JAMES CARMICHAEL for 75 pounds of tobacco for 3 days attendance at this Court in his suit against HARDRESS WALLER.

Order is granted ANTHONY FLEMING against HARDRESS WALLER for 25 pounds of tobacco for 1 day's attendance at this Court in the suit of JAMES CARMICHAEL against him.

This Court this day rated flour at 16/8 per hundred weight
This Court is adjourned until Court in Course, CHARLES THOMAS MAYOR, TESTE: JOHN BOUSH D.C.

PAGE 209
NORFOLK BOROUGH
At a Hustings Court Held this 20th day of December 1773
PRESENT: CHARLES THOMAS ESQUIRE MAYOR
GENTLEMAN ALDERMEN: GEORGE ABYVON, MAXIMILIAN CALVERT, ARCHIBALD CAMPBELL, CORNELIUS CALVERT, PAUL LOYALL

PETER SHEWSBERY against JOHN HANNON. The suit is Dismissed.

PHILIP CARBERY against STAFFORD LIGHTBOURNE. In T.A.B. GEORGE KELLY this day came into Court and undertook that in case he shall be cast in this suit he the said Defendant will pay the condemnation of the Court or render his body to prison in execution for the same or that he the said KELLY will do it for him. Whereupon the Defendant by his Attorney prays and has leave to IMPARLE here until the next Court and then to plead.

WARNER LEWIS against SAMUEL ALLYN. In Case. A conditional order against the Defendant and WRIGHT WESTCOTT his bail.
THOMAS WALKER against CHARLES COOPER JR. The suit is dismissed at the Plaintiff's costs.

JAMES INGRAM against GEORGE WILSON and JAMES CARMICHAEL. The suit is dismissed at the Plaintiffs costs.
SAMUEL HOLLOWELL against WILLIAM PLUME. Dismissed.

EDWARD MITCHELL against ROBERT TUCKER by Petition and summons. Judgement is granted the Plaintiff for 1 pounds 12 shillings and 10 pence half penny. It is ordered that the Defendant pay the same unto the Plaintiff with costs and fee.

LOGAN GILMOUR and Company against EDWARD SPRIGG. A conditional order against the Defendant and A. SKINNER his bail.

ANDREW STEVENSON against JOHN WILSON. Imparlance.

WILLIAM JAQUES Plaintiff
Against Re: In Case
GEORGE and MATTHEW JACKSON Defendants
This day came the parties by their Attorney's and by their mutual consent submit all maters in difference between them to the determination of MATTHEW PHRIPP, JOHN GREENWOOD and JOHN LAWRENCE Gentleman IMPARLE on Friday the last day of this month and agree that their award thereupon shall be made the judgement of the Court and the same is ordered accordingly.

ROGER PIERCE against WILLIAM OVE by Petition and summons. Judgement is granted the Plaintiff for 3 pounds 2 shillings and 3 pence. It is ordered that the Defendant pay the same unto the Plaintiff with costs and fee.
JOHN POOL against JOHN BAYNES by petition and summons. Dismissed.

PAGE 209B
WILLIAM SMITH Shopkeeper Plaintiff
Against Re: In Debt
JAMES HALDANE Defendant
AND
MARY POOL and STEPHEN TANKARD executors of NICHOLAS POOLE Deceased Plaintiff
Against Re: In Debt
JAMES HALDANE
JAMES BALLENTINE this day came into Court and undertook for the Defendant that in case he shall be cast in their suits for the said Defendant will pay the condemnation of the Court or render his body to prison in execution for the same or that he the said BALLENTINE will pay the condemnation of the Court or render the Body of the said Defendant and whereupon the Defendant by his Attorney' prays and has leave to IMPARLE here until the next Court and then to plead.

NEIL JAMIESON and Co. against JOHN TATEM JR. & SARAH CARNEY executor of BARNABY CARNEY deceased in case. Imparlance.

MASON MILLER QUI TAM against CHRISTOPHER WILSON. In Debt. The Defendant by his Attorney prayed a special imparlance.

MAXIMILIAN CALVERT against JOHN SCOTT by Petition and summons. Judgement is granted the Plaintiff for 3 pounds. It is ordered that the Defendant pay the same unto the Plaintiff with costs and fee.

HARGRAVES and ORANGE against WILLIAM CASTLE. The suit is dismissed.
ANDREW WATSON against JAMES WILSON. The suit is dismissed.

JAMES SOUTHERLAND against BAILEY WARREN. In Case. GEORGE ATKINSON undertakes for the Plaintiff that he will pay to the defendant all such damages costs and charges as shall be awarded against him by the Court and Imparlance. And on the motion of the Defendant A DEDIMUS is granted him to take the depositions of LEWIS MACLEAN, ANDREW STEAD, and AARON WHITEHURST giving Plaintiff notice.

HENRY HANNAL against JOHN HARDY. The suit is dismissed.
ALEXANDER BELL against MALACHI MAUND. The suit dismissed.

THOMAS CLAIBORNE against ROGER PEARCE. In Debt. The Defendant by his Attorney prayed an Imparlance.

JOHN GARDNER against RICHARD TALBOT by Petition and summons. Judgement is granted the Plaintiff for 2 pounds 15 shillings. It is ordered that the Defendant pay the same unto the Plaintiff with costs and fee.

JAMES LEITCH against ROBERT MCCULLOCH. Dismissed.
MISTERS YOUNG and POOL against MISTERS JOSIAH HOFFMIRE, JOHN SMITH & Company. The suit is dismissed.

PAGE 210

HENRY BRESSIE	Plaintiff	JOHN BOWNESS	Plaintiff	JOSEPH MITCHELL	Plaintiff
Against Re: In Case		Against Re: In Case		Against Re: In Case	
BRISTOL BROWN	Defendant	THOMAS TALBOT	Defendant	WILLIAM NICHOLSON SR.	Defendant

This day came the Parties by their Attorney's, and the Defendants pray and have leave to Special IMPARLE here until the next Court and them to plead.

SMITH and JAMIESON against EDWARD DAVIS. Attachment

ROGER PEARCE was this day brought before the Court by warrant under the hands of CHARLES THOMAS for being a person of (in fold) fame and a violator of the laws of his Country as well as a disturber of the peace in continuing to keep a tippling house contrary to the order of the Court of this Borough and the same being proved it is ordered that the Sergeant take and keep him in custody until he gives bond and security himself in 100 pounds and 2 securities in 25 pounds each for being of good behavior not keeping a tippling house and 12 months and pay the costs of this prosecution.

On the Complaint of PARNELL CHAMBERLAYNE an infant by PHILIP CARBERY her next friend against JAMES ARCHDEACON her next for MESSUAGE. Order that she be discharged from her said master's service and that he pay her costs by her about her complaint in this behalf expenses

JAMES BALFOUR and DANIEL BARRAUD against JOHN JONES. The suit is continued and on the motion of the Defendant by his Attorney a DEDIMUS is granted him to take the deposition of GEORGE JOHNSON giving the Plaintiff's reasonable notice of the time and place.

FREDERICK BOUSH against JAMES MOORE. In Chancery. On the motion of the Defendant by his Attorney a commission is granted him to take the depositions of GEORGE JAMIESON giving the Plaintiff reasonable notice.

FREDERICK BOUSH against JAMES MOORE. In Junction. On the motion of the Defendant by his Attorney a commission is granted him to take the depositions of JONATHAN HOPKINS giving the Plaintiff reasonable notice.

THOMAS NEWTON SR., THOMAS NEWTON JR. , PAUL LOYALL, THOMAS ROBERTS, and JOHN TUCKER against ROBERT TUCKER. In Chancery. Publication of the Depositions and set for hearing.
GEORGE WILSON and ARCHIBALD CAMPBELL. Administrators of JOHN WILSON deceased against ABRAM WORMINGTON. The suit is dismissed.

PAGE 210B
JOHN CRAMOND Plaintiff
Against Re: In Case
SAMUEL GWYNN Defendant
This day came the parties by their Attorney's and there upon came also a Jury to wit: GEORGE GORDON, JAMES MURPHREE, JOHN CALVERT, WILLIAM FARRER, JOHN LIVINGSTON, PHILIP CARBERY, JOHN BOWNESS, ROBERT MACKIE, ROBERT FRY, JOHN BEGG, WILLIAM GOODCHILD and JOHN MACLEAN who being elected tried and sworn the truth to speak upon the issue joined upon their oath do say that the Defendant did not assume as in pleading he has alleged Therefore, it is considered that the Plaintiff take nothing by his bill but for his false claims be in mercy. And the defendant go hence without day and recover against the Plaintiff his costs by him about his defense in this behalf expended.

JOHN SMITH assignee of WILLIAM FLOOD Plaintiff
Against Re: In Debt
MARY WILSON and GEORGE WILSON Defendants
This day came the parties by their Attorney's and there upon came also a Jury to wit: GEORGE GORDON, JAMES MURPHREE, JOHN CALVERT, WILLIAM FARRER, JOHN LIVINGSTON, PHILIP CARBERY, JOHN BOWNESS, ROBERT MACKIE, ROBERT FRY, JOHN BEGG, WILLIAM GOODCHILD, and JOHN MACLEAN who being elected tried and sworn the truth to speak upon the issue joined upon their oath do say that the Defendants have not paid the debt in this declaration mentioned. Therefore, it is considered that the Plaintiff recover against the said Defendants his debt amounting to 40 pounds and his costs by him in this behalf expended and the said Defendants in mercy. But this judgement is to be discharged by the payment of 20 pounds with interest thereon after the rate of 5% per annum to be computed from April 25, 1772, to the time of payment and the costs.

Order is granted JAMES HOLMS against JOHN CRAMOND for 220 pounds of tobacco for 4 days attendance at this Court coming and returning 5 miles 8 times in his suit against SAMUEL GWIN.

The King against MARTIN MURPHY by warrant. Dismissed.
JOHN SYME against JAMES HALDANE. The suit is Dismissed.

This Court this day rated flour at 16/8 per hundred weight
This Court is adjourned until tomorrow 9 o'clock, CHARLES THOMAS MAYOR, TESTE: JOHN BOUSH D.C.

PAGE 211
NORFOLK BOROUGH
At a Hustings Court Held this 21st day of December 1773
PRESENT: CHARLES THOMAS ESQUIRE MAYOR
GENTLEMAN ALDERMEN: GEORGE ABYVON, MAXIMILIAN CALVERT, PAUL LOYALL

HENRY BRESSIE against BRISTOL BROWN. On the motion of the Plaintiff by his Attorney a DEDIMUS is granted him to take the deposition of JOHN BROWN giving the Defendant reasonable notice of the time and place.

Order is granted GEORGE JOHNSON against BALFOUR and BARRAUD for 79 pounds of tobacco for 1 day's attendance, coming and returning 18 miles once and 12 shillings and 6 pence for ferriages in their suit against JONE JONES.

MATTHEW PHRIPP Gentleman Plaintiff
Against Re: In Debt
NATHANIEL BOUSH Defendant
This day came the parties by their Attorney's and there upon came also a Jury to wit: THOMAS MORRIS, JAMES LEITCH, WILLIAM GOODCHILD, PAUL WATLINGTON, FREER ARMSTON, ALEXANDER MOSELEY, JOHN MEARNS, JOHN SHAW, JONATHAN EILBECK, JAMES CARMICHAEL, JOHN BOGUS* and GEORGE GORDON who being elected tried and sworn the truth to speak upon the issue joined upon their

oath do say that the Defendant has not paid the debt in the declaration mentioned. Therefore, it is considered that the Plaintiff recover against the said Defendant their debt amounting to 144 pounds 12 shillings and his costs by him in this behalf expended. And the said Defendants in mercy. But this judgement is to be discharged by the payment of 72 pounds 6 shillings with interest thereon after the rate of 5% per annum to be computed from April 25, 1772, to the time of payment and the costs.

MORTO BRIAN Plaintiff
Against Re: In Covenant
ROGER PEARCE Defendant
This day came the parties by their Attorney's and by their mutual consent submit all matters in difference between them to the determination of JOHN SHAW, JONATHAN EILBECK, BASSET MOSELEY and ALEXANDER MOSELEY Gentleman or any three of them agree that their award there upon shall be made the judgement of the Court and the same is ordered accordingly.

MORTO BRIAN Plaintiff
Against Re: In Case
ROGER PEARCE Defendant
This day came the parties by their Attorney's and by their mutual consent submit all matters in difference between them to the determination of JOHN SHAW, JONATHAN EILBECK, BASSET MOSELEY and ALEXANDER MOSELEY Gentleman or any three of them agree that their award there upon shall be made the judgement of the Court and the same is ordered accordingly.

EDWARD JONES against JAMES HALDANE. The suit is dismissed at the Plaintiff's costs.
Ordinary License is granted JAMES ATKINSON on his complying with the law.

PAGE 211B
STEPHEN TANKARD and MARY POOLE surviving executor of NICHOLAS POOLE deceased Plaintiff
Against Re: In Case
JAMES MARSDEN and JONATHAN EILBECK executors of ELDRED FISHER deceased Defendants
This day came the Parties by their Attorney's and the Defendants by their Attorney say that they cannot gainsay the Plaintiffs actions nor but that their testator did assume in manner and form as the Plaintiff has declared. Therefore, it is considered that the Plaintiffs recover against the said Defendants 8 pounds 18 shillings and 10 pence half penny and their costs by them in this declaration expended. When assets after paying proceeding judgements, debts of greater dignity and the Defendants own claims of equal dignity against the estate of the said testator to be levied of the goods and chattels were of the said Testator at the time of his death that shall here after come to the hands of the said Defendants to be administered and the said Defendants in mercy.

JOHN WILSON Plaintiff
Against Re: In debt for entertaining seamen.
ANDREW STEVENSON Defendant
This day came the parties by their Attorney's and there upon came also a Jury to wit: THOMAS MORRIS, JAMES LEITCH, WILLIAM GOODCHILD, PAUL WATLINGTON, FREER ARMSTON, ALEXANDER MOSELEY, JOHN MEARNS, JOHN SHAW, JONATHAN EILBECK, JAMES CARMICHAEL, JOHN BOGUS and GEORGE GORDON who being elected tried and sworn the truth to speak upon the issue joined upon their oath do say that the Defendant does his owe the debt in manner and form as the Plaintiff has declared. Therefore, it is considered that the Plaintiff recover against the said Defendant his debt amounting to 2 pounds 10 shillings and his costs by him in this behalf expended. And the said Defendants in mercy.

PATRICK TELFER Plaintiff
Against Re: In Case
JOHN CRAMOND Defendant
This day came the parties by their Attorney's and there upon came also a Jury to wit: GEORGE KELLY, JOHN SOMMERVILLE, JAMES ATKINSON, WILLIAM BEVAN, JAMES MURPHY, PREESON BOWDOIN, JOHN MACLEAN, SETH POINTER, JAMES MAXWELL, GEORGE JACKSON, DICKERSON PRIOR and FRANCIS HATTON who being elected tried and sworn the truth to speak upon the issue joined upon their oath do say that the Defendant did assume in manner and form as the Plaintiff against him has declared and do assess the Plaintiff damages by occasion of the nonperformance of that assumption to 34 pounds and 4 pence sterling besides his costs. Therefore, it is considered that the Plaintiff recover against the said Defendant his damages aforesaid in form aforesaid assessed and his costs by him about his suit in this behalf expended and the said Defendant in mercy. And the Court says the sterling money may be discharged in current money at 30% difference of exchange.

JAMES BERRY Plaintiff
Against Re: In Debt
ALEXANDER MURRAY Defendant
This day came the parties by their Attorney's and there upon came also a Jury to wit: THOMAS MORRIS, JAMES LEITCH, WILLIAM GOODCHILD, PAUL WATLINGTON, FREER ARMSTON, ALEXANDER MOSELEY, JOHN MEARNS, JOHN SHAW, JONATHAN EILBECK, JAMES CARMICHAEL, JOHN BOGUS and GEORGE GORDON who being elected tried and sworn the truth to speak upon the issue joined upon their oath do say that the Defendant has not paid the debt. Therefore, it is considered that the Plaintiff recover against the said Defendant his debt amounting to 50 pounds and his costs by him in this behalf expended and the said Defendant in mercy. But this judgement is to be discharged by the payment of 7 pounds 19 shillings Pennsylvania Currency with interest thereon after the rate of 5% per annum to be

computed from this day to the time of payment and the costs and the Court says the Pennsylvania currency may be discharged in Virginia money at 25% for the difference in exchange.

PAGE 212

JOHN BARRET Plaintiff
Against Re: In Trespass
ROBERT FRY Defendant
This day came the parties by their Attorney's and by their mutual consent all matters in differences between them to the determination of BENJAMIN CROOKER and THOMAS CLAIBORNE Gentleman and agree that their award there upon shall be made the judgement of the Court and the same is ordered accordingly.

HENRY FLEMING and Company Plaintiff
Against Re: In Case
NATHANIEL BOUSH Defendant
This day came the parties by their Attorney's and the Defendant by his Attorney relinquishing his former plea says that he cannot gainsay the Plaintiff's action nor but that he did assume in manner and form as the Plaintiffs have declared. Therefore, it is considered that the Plaintiff recover against the said Defendant 22 pounds 3 shillings Virginia currency and their costs by them about their suit in this behalf expended and the said Defendant in mercy.

WILLIAM WALKER Plaintiff
Against Re: In Case
SAMUEL SWANN Defendant
This day came the parties by their Attorney's and there upon came also a Jury to wit: GEORGE KELLY, JOHN SOMMERVILLE, JAMES ATKINSON, WILLIAM BEVAN, JAMES MURPHY, PREESON BOWDOIN, JOHN MACLEAN, SETH POINTER, JAMES MAXWELL, GEORGE JACKSON, DICKERSON PRIOR and FRANCIS HATTON who being elected tried and sworn the truth to speak upon the issue joined upon their oath do say that the Defendant did assume in manner and form as the Plaintiff against him has declared and do assess the Plaintiff damages by occasion of the nonperformance of that assumption to 5 pounds and 10 shillings besides his costs. Therefore, it is considered that the Plaintiff recover against the said Defendant his damages aforesaid in form aforesaid assessed and his costs by him about his suit in this behalf expended and the said Defendant in mercy.

Order is granted DAVID GWIN against WILLIAM WALKER for 140 pounds of tobacco for 2 days attendance at this Court as a witness coming and returning 30 miles once and 1 shilling and three pence for ferriages in his suit against SAMUEL SWANN

This Court is adjourned to Court in Course, CHARLES THOMAS MAYOR, TESTE: JOHN BOUSH D.C.

PAGE 212B

NORFOLK BOROUGH
At a Hustings Court Held this 21st day of February 1774
PRESENT: CHARLES THOMAS ESQUIRE MAYOR
GENTLEMAN ALDERMEN: GEORGE ABYVON, MAXIMILIAN CALVERT, PAUL LOYALL
EDWARD WRIGHT against JOHN MCLACHLAN. The suit abates by the death of the Defendant.
JOHN HAMILTON and Company against JOHN MCLACHLAN. The suit abates by the death of the Defendant.

JAMES HUNTER surviving partner of TENANT and HUNTER against WILLIAM HAYS. The suit abates by the death of the Plaintiff.

JOHN MCLACHLAN against ALEXANDER BELL. The suit abates by the death of the Plaintiff.
JOHN HARRIS against CHRISTOPHER HERBERT. The suit abates by the death of the Defendant.

PETER SHEWSBERY against JOHN HANNON. The suit is dismissed.
PREESON BOWDOIN against PHILIP CARBERY. An Imparlance.

JOHN EDWARDS against WILLIAM GREEN. In Case. THOMAS HEPBURN. This day came into Court and Undertook for the Defendant that in case he shall be cast in this suit he the said Defendant will pay the condemnation of the Court or render his body to prison in execution for the same or that he the said HEPBURN will do it for him. Whereupon the Defendant by his Attorney prays and has leave to IMPARLE here until the next Court and then to plead.

STAFFORD LIGHBURN* against PHILIP CARBERY. Imparlance.

CHARLES CONNER against EDWARD ARCHER. In Case. MAXIMILIAN CALVERT This day came into Court and Undertook for the Defendant that in case he shall be cast in this suit he the said Defendant will pay the condemnation of the Court or render his body to prison in execution for the same or that he the said CALVERT will do it for him. Whereupon the Defendant by his Attorney prays and has leave to IMPARLE here until the next Court and then to plead.

YOUNG SMITH and Company against WILLIAM IVY admin of ALICE IVY deceased. Dismissed.

YOUNG and POOL against THOMAS WILLIAMSON by Petition and summons. Judgement is granted the Plaintiff for 1 pounds 16 shillings and 11 pence. It is ordered that the Defendant pay the same unto the Plaintiff with costs and fee.

YOUNG SMITH and Company against WILLIAM IVY. Imparlance.

PAGE 213

JAMES COWPER against WRIGHT WESTCOTT. In Debt. HENRY BRESSIE this day came into Court and Undertook for the Defendant that in case he shall be cast in this suit he the said Defendant will pay the condemnation of the Court or render his body to prison in execution for the same or that he the said BRESSIE will do it for him. Whereupon the Defendant by his Attorney prays and has leave to IMPARLE here until the next Court and then to plead.

ANDREW RONALD against ROBERT YOUNG. Dismissed.
HENRY WHITEHURST against MAXIMILIAN CALVERT. Imparlance.

GRIEVE, LOUDON and ROBB against JAMES AGNEW admin of ANDREW MCCAA. The suit is dismissed.
JAMES YOUNG against JAMES AGNEW admin of ANDREW MCCAA. This suit is dismissed.

FRANCIS ROBERTSON against JOHN SMITH, THOMAS TALBOT and JOSEPH HUTCHINGS, discontinued against SMITH and TALBOT and HUTCHINGS Time is allowed him

GEORGE KELLY against JOHN JOHNSON. The suit abates by the death of the Defendant.
HERCULES ROSS against RICHARD TALBOT order against the Defendant and ANDREW MARTIN his bail.

PHILIP CARBERY against HENRY WALKER. The suit is dismissed.
BENJAMIN CROOKER as Secretary of the Independent Company against GEORGE RAE. An Imparlance.

JAMES NICHOLSON assignee of AMY HALL against JOHN CRAMOND. JOHN MEARNS this day came into Court and Undertook for the Defendant that in case he shall be cast in this suit he the said Defendant will pay the condemnation of the Court or render his body to prison in execution for the same or that he the said MEARNS will do it for him. Whereupon the Defendant by his Attorney prays and has leave to IMPARLE here until the next Court and then to plead.

ALEXANDER BELL against MALACHI MAUND. Special Imparlance.
ALEXANDER SKINNER against JEREMIAH MATTHEWS. A conditional order is granted the Plaintiff against the Defendant.
LOGAN GILMOUR and Company against ROBERT TUCKER. Dismissed.
JOHN IVY admin of WILLIAM IVY against THOMAS SNALE. Defendant in person pleaded not guilty issue joined and referred until next Court.

PAGE 213B

MALACHI MAUND against SAMUEL CALVERT. WILLIAM CALVERT This day came into Court and Undertook for the Defendant that in case he shall be cast in this suit he the said Defendant will pay the condemnation of the Court or render his body to prison in execution for the same or that he the said WILLIAM CALVERT will do it for him. Whereupon the Defendant by his Attorney prays and has leave to IMPARLE here until the next Court and then to plead.

GRIEVE, LOUDEN and ROBB Plaintiffs
Against Re: In Debt
JAMES AGNEW administrator of ANDREW MCCAA Defendant

GRIEVE, LOUDON and ROBB Plaintiffs
Against Re: In Case
JAMES AGNEW administrator of ANDREW MCCAA Defendant

JAMES YOUNG Plaintiff
Against Re: In Case
JAMES AGNEW administrator of ANDREW MCCAA Defendant
This day came the parties by their Attorney's and the Defendant by his Attorney prays and has leave to IMPARLE here until next Court and then to plead.

(Author's note LISTED 2X)
JAMES and ROBERT DONALD and Company Plaintiffs
Against Re: In Debt
RICHARD TEMPLEMAN Defendant
JOHN WILSON Gentleman this day came into Court and Undertook for the Defendant that in case he shall be cast in this suit he the said Defendant will pay the condemnation of the Court or render his body to prison in execution for the same or that he the said WILSON will do it for him. Whereupon the Defendant by his Attorney prays and has leave to IMPARLE here until the next Court and then to plead.

THOMAS GILCHRIST surviving partner of JOHN and THOMAS GILCHRIST against SARAH CARNEY and JOHN TATEM JR. executors of BARNABY CARNEY deceased. This day came the parties by their Attorney's and the Defendant pray and have leave to IMPARLE here until the next Court and then to plead.

Ordinary License is granted JAMES HALDANE and PAUL WATLINGTON on their complying with the law.

PETER BEVERLY WHITING against EDWARD DAVIS. On motion of the Plaintiff by his Attorney a DEDIMUS is granted him to take the deposition of JASPER CLAYTON giving the Defendant reasonable notice.

PAGE 214

CASPER HERITTER Plaintiff
Against Re: In Trespass
JOHN ATTWOOD Defendant

This day came as well the Plaintiff by THOMAS CLAIBORNE Gentleman his Attorney as the Defendant in his proper person and says he cannot gainsay the Plaintiffs action nor but that he is guilty of the trespass and that the Plaintiff has sustained damages by occasion thereof to 15 pounds besides his costs. Therefore, with the Plaintiffs consent it is considered that he recover against the said Defendant his damages aforesaid and his costs by him in this behalf expended and the said Defendant in mercy. And the Plaintiff by his Attorney have agreed to stay the execution of this Judgement 3 months.

JOHN MORRIS and THOMAS STEWART Plaintiff
Against Re: In Debt
EDWARD WILLIAMS Defendant

This day came the parties in their proper persons and the Defendant acknowledges the Plaintiffs action for 24 pounds 15 shillings and 2 pence. Therefore, it is considered that the Plaintiff recover against the said Defendant their debt aforesaid and their costs by them in this behalf expended and the said Defendant in mercy. But this judgement is to be discharged by the payment of 12 pounds 7 shillings and 7 pence with interest therein after the rate of 5% per annum to be computed from September 17, 1772, to the time of payment and costs. And the Plaintiffs have agreed to stay execution of this judgement 2 months.

SMITH and JAMIESON Plaintiff
Against Re: In Debt.
EDWARD DAVIS Defendant

This day came the Plaintiffs by BENJAMIN CROOKER Gentleman their Attorney and an Attachment having been awarded the Plaintiff against the estate of the Defendant and the Sergeant now making return that by virtue thereof he has attached 1 silver teaspoon, and the Defendant being solemnly called and not appearing nor replevying his said effects, whereby the Plaintiff remain thereof against him undefended. Therefore, it is adjudged by the Court that the Plaintiff do recover against the said Defendant their debt amounting to 15 pounds 16 shillings and 7 pounds and their costs by them in this behalf expended and the said Defendant in mercy. And the Plaintiffs by their Attorney release the attached effects. But this judgement is to be discharged by the payment of 7 pounds 18 shillings and 3 pence half penny with interest thereon after the rate of 5% per annum to be computed from April 4, 1771, to the time of payment and costs.

WILLIAM JAQUES Plaintiff
Against Re: In Case
GEORGE and MATHEW JACKSON Defendants

The parties having mutually submitted all matters in difference between them to the determination of MATTHEW PHRIPP, JOHN GREENWOOD and JONATHAN LAWRENCE Gentleman and agreed that their award thereupon should be made the judgement of the Court. They having returned their award on the Premises in these words to wit: In obedience to an order of the Norfolk Borough Court bearing date the 20$^{th of}$ December last to us directed and here unto annexed. We have stated accounts between GEORGE JACKSON, MATTHEW JACKSON, and WILLIAM JAQUES as joint partners, also between GEORGE JACKSON and WILLIAM JAQUES

PAGE 214B

Private account and on a final settlement of all their accounts we find a balance of 11 pounds 6 shillings and 8 pence half penny current money due to GEORGE JACKSON from WILLIAM JAQUIS. Given under our hands this 22nd day of January 1774. JOHN GREENWOOD, JOHN LAWRENCE, and MATTHEW PHRIPP. It is thereupon considered that the suit to be dismissed and that the Plaintiff pay unto the Defendants their costs by them about their Defense in this behalf expended.

JOHN WILSON against SAMUEL PORTLOCK. In Chancery. The Defendant by his Attorney filed his answer to the bill of the Plaintiff and time is allowed him to consider it.

FRANCES MOORE admin of JOHN MOORE Deceased Plaintiff
Against Re: In Case
CHARLES CAMPBELL and ANNA, his wife executors of FRANCIS MOORE deceased Defendants

This day came the parties by their Attorney's and there upon came also a Jury to wit: WILLIAM INGRAM, DANIEL HUTCHINGS, GEORGE JACKSON, ALEXANDER MOSELEY, PHILIP CARBERY, JONATHAN CALVERT, WRIGHT WESTCOAT, JAMES CARMICHAEL, PREESON BOWDOIN, JAMES LEITCH, JONATHAN LEE, and PAUL WATLINGTON who being elected tried and sworn the truth to speak upon the issue joined upon their oath do say that the Defendant testator did assume in manner and form as the Plaintiff has declared and do assess the Plaintiff damages by occasion of the non-performance of that assumption to 28 pounds 11 shillings and 8 pence besides her costs. Therefore, it is considered that the Plaintiff recover against the said Defendant her damages aforesaid in form aforesaid assessed and her costs by her in this behalf expended to be levied of the goods and chattels of the said Testator FRANCIS MOORE if so, much the said Defendants have in their hands to be administered and if they have it not, then the costs to be levied of their proper goods and chattels and the said Defendant in mercy.

ROBERT TUCKER Plaintiff

Against Re: In Case

THOMAS VEALE Gentleman and FRANCIS HATTON executor of DAVID HARPER Deceased Defendants

This day came the parties by their Attorney's and there upon came also a Jury to wit: EDWARD PARKE, WILLIAM GOODCHILD, RICHARD WILKERSON, JONATHAN SMITH, HENRY BRESSIE, JAMES PASTEUR, JAMES HALDANE, WILLIAM SKINKER, WILLIAM JAQUES, JOHN CARMOUNT, JOHN EDWARDS, JONATHAN MEREDITH who being elected tried and sworn the truth to speak upon the issue joined upon their oath do say that the Defendant testator did assume in manner and form as the Plaintiff has declared and do assess the Plaintiff damages by occasion of the non-performance of that assumption to 24 pounds 3 shillings and 8 pence besides his costs. Therefore, it is considered that the Plaintiff recover against the said Defendant his damages aforesaid in form aforesaid assessed and his costs by him in this behalf expended to be levied of the goods and chattels of the said Testator DAVID HARPER if so, much the said Defendants have in their hands to be administered and if they have it not, then the costs to be levied of their proper goods and chattels and the said Defendant in mercy.

JAMES HALDANE Plaintiff against JOHN JACKSON and MARTIN JUQIEZ* Defendant. Injunction. In Chancery. On the motion of the Plaintiff by his Council leave is given him to file his bill of injunction and time is allowed the Defendant until the Next Court to consider the same and ordered the Plaintiff at or before the next Court give bond and security in the Clerk's office.

PAGE 215

Order is granted JOHN STEWART against ROBERT TUCKER for 255 pounds of tobacco for 3 days attendance at this Court coming and Returning 30 miles twice and 7 shillings and 6 pence for ferriages in his suit against THOMAS VEALE Gentleman and FRANCIS HATTON executors of DAVID HARPER deceased.

Order is granted THOMAS CHERRY JR. against ROBERT TUCKER for 25 pounds of tobacco for 1 day's attendance at this Court in his suit against THOMAS VEALE Gentleman and FRANCIS HATTON executors of DAVID HARPER deceased.

JOHN CHESHIRE and RICHARD BROWN Plaintiffs

Against Re: In Case

JAMES MILLS and GEORGE LEDIMORE Defendants

This day came the parties by their Attorney's and the Defendants by their Attorney relinquishing their former plea, day that they cannot gainsay the Plaintiff's action nor but that they did assume in manner and form as the Plaintiff against them have declared. Therefore, it is considered that the Plaintiff recover against the said Defendant 6 pounds 17 shillings and their costs by them in this behalf expended and the Defendants in mercy.

JAMES BALFOUR and DANIEL BARRAUD Plaintiff

Against Re: In Case

JOHN JONES Defendant

This day came the parties by their Attorney's and thereupon came also a Jury to wit: JOHN EDWARDS, JOHN CARMOUNT, WILLIAM JAQUES, WILLIAM SKINKER, JAMES HALDANE, JAMES PASTEUR, HENRY BRESSIE, JONATHAN SMITH, RICHARD WILKERSON, WILLIAM GOODCHILD, ROBERT TUCKER and GEORGE KELLY who being elected tried and sworn the truth to speak upon the issue joined withdrew and not returning any verdict in the pre mises the cause is post ponded until tomorrow.

Order is granted JAMES HOLT against FRANCES MOORE admin of JOHN MOORE deceased for 50 pounds of tobacco for 2 days attendance at this Court in her suit against CHARLES CAMPBELL and ANNA his wife executors of FRANCIS MOORE deceased

Order is granted THOMAS EASTHER against FRANCES MOORE admin of JOHN MOORE deceased for 75 pounds of tobacco for 3 days attendance at this Court in her suit against CHARLES CAMPBELL and ANNA his wife executors of FRANCIS MOORE deceased

Order is granted IVY LANGLEY against FRANCES MOORE admin of JOHN MOORE deceased for 75 pounds of tobacco for 3 days attendance at this Court in her suit against CHARLES CAMPBELL and ANNA his wife executors of FRANCIS MOORE deceased

Order is granted JOHN DODD against CHARLES CAMPBELL and ANNA his wife executors of FRANCIS MOORE deceased for 50 pounds of tobacco for 2 days attendance at this Court in the suit of FRANCES MOORE admin of JOHN MOORE deceased against them.

Order is granted EDWARD PARKE against CHARLES CAMPBELL and ANNA his wife executors of FRANCIS MOORE deceased for 50 pounds of tobacco for 2 days attendance at this Court in the suit of FRANCES MOORE admin of JOHN MOORE deceased against them.

Order is granted JOHN PEARSON against JOHN CHESHIRE and RICHARD BORWN for 50 pounds of tobacco for 2 days attendance at this Court in their suit against JAMES MILLS and GEORGE LEDIMORE.

PAGE 215B

Order is granted ALEXANDER HARVEY against CHARLES CAMPBELL and ANNA his wife executors of FRANCIS MOORE deceased for 104 pounds of tobacco for 2 days attendance at this Court, coming and returning 9 miles twice in the suit of FRANCES MOORE admin of JOHN MOORE deceased against them.

Order is granted WILLIAM WISHART against FRANCES MOORE admin of JOHN MOORE deceased for 52 pounds of tobacco for 1 day's attendance at this Court, coming and returning 9 miles once in her suit against CHARLES CAMPBELL and ANNA his wife executors of FRANCIS MOORE deceased

Order is granted GEORGE JOHNSON against BALFOUR and BARRAUD for 79 pounds of tobacco for 1 day's attendance coming and returning 18 miles once and 12 shillings and 6 pence for ferriages in their suit against JOHN JONES

This Court is adjourned until tomorrow 9 o'clock, CHARLES THOMAS MAYOR, TESTE: JOHN BOUSH D.C.

<u>NORFOLK BOROUGH</u>
At a Hustings Court Held this 22nd day of February 1774
PRESENT: CHARLES THOMAS ESQUIRE MAYOR
GENTLEMAN ALDERMEN: GEORGE ABYVON, MAXIMILIAN CALVERT, PAUL LOYALL

JAMES DAVIDSON against ANDREW MILLER and Company. The Defendants by their Attorney filed their plea in abatement to the Plaintiff writ, and time is allowed the Plaintiff to consider it.

CHRISTOPHER CALVERT Plaintiff
Against Re: In Case
FREDERICK BOUSH Defendant
This day came the parties by their Attorney's and the Defendant by his Attorney relinquishes his former plea, says that he cannot gainsay the Plaintiffs action nor but that he did assume in manner and form as the Plaintiff against him has declared. Therefore, it is considered that the Plaintiff recover against the said Defendant 11 pounds 13 shillings and 4 pence and his costs by him about his suit in this behalf expended and the said Defendant in mercy.

PHILIP CARBERY against STEWART HOLT. On the motion of the Plaintiff by his Attorney a DEDIMUS is granted him to take the Depositions of JOHN CHESHIRE giving the Defendant reasonable notice.

THOMAS NEWTON assignee of JOHN SMITH against WILLIAM SMITH. The Defendant pleaded that he owes nothing issue joined and referred until the next Court.

PAGE 216
ALEXANDER GORDON against ALEXANDER PURDIE. The Defendant by his Attorney pleaded not guilty with leave issue joined and referred until next Court.

GEORGE WILSON and ARCHIBALD CAMPBELL admin of JOHN WILSON deceased against JAMES MARSDEN and JONATHAN EILBECK executors of ELDRED FISHER deceased. The Defendants by their Attorney pleaded their testator did not assume and had fully administered issue joined and referred.

MISTERS LOGAN GILMOUR and Company against ARCHIBALD BUCHANAN. JAMES INGRAM this day came into Court and Undertook for the Defendant that in case he shall be cast in this suit he the said Defendant will pay the condemnation of the Court or render his body to prison in execution for the same or that he the said INGRAM will do it for him. Thereupon the Judgement obtained by the Plaintiff against the said Defendant and his bail is set aside and the Defendant by his Attorney pleaded he did not assume issue joined and referred.

JAMES HALDANE against JAMES MARSDEN and JONATHAN EILBECK executors of ELDRED FISHER deceased. The Defendants by their Attorney's pleaded that their testator did not assume and had fully administered issue joined and referred.

JAMES CAMPBELL and Company against JAMES MARSDEN and JONATHAN EILBECK executors of ELDRED FISHER deceased in debt. The Defendant by their Attorney pleaded payment and had fully administered issue joined and referred.

JAMES CAMPBELL and Company against JAMES MARSDEN and JONATHAN EILBECK executors of ELDRED FISHER deceased in case. The Defendant by their Attorney pleaded their testator did not assume and had fully administered issue joined and referred.

JOHN RICHARDSON against WILLIAM HERBERT. The Defendant pleaded not guilty with leave issue joined and referred.
CHRISTOPHER WRIGHT against WILLIAM WISHART. The Defendant pleaded not guilty issue joined and referred.

JOHN GARRICK against JAMES CARMICHAEL in T.A.B. The suit is dismissed.

WILLS COWPER against WRIGHT WESTCOAT. The Defendant pleaded payment issue joined and referred until next Court.
SAMUEL HOSIER against JOHN HARDY. The Defendant pleaded not guilty issue joined and referred until next Court.

ROBERT CARTWRIGHT against JAMES MARSDEN and JONATHAN EILBECK executors of ELDRED FISHER deceased in debt. The Defendants pleaded that their Testator did not assume and that they had fully administered. WILLIAM ROBINSON undertakes for the Plaintiff that he will pay to the Defendants all such damages, costs, and charges as shall be awarded against him by the Court and on a motion of the Plaintiff by his Attorney a DEDIMUS is granted him to take the depositions of witnesses giving the Defendant reasonable notice of the time and place.

JOHN EDWARDS against JOHN KNIGHT. The Defendant pleaded that he did not assume issue joined and referred until the next Court.

PAGE 216B
WILLIAM WAGER against JOHN RANSBERG. The Defendant pleaded that he did not assume issue joined and referred until the next Court.

ROBERT GILMOUR admin of WILLIAM GRAY against JOHN GARRICK. In Case. The suit is dismissed at the Defendants Costs.

JOSEPH CALVERT against THOMAS DICKERSON. The Defendants Attorney says he is not informed, and a writ of inquiry is awarded the Plaintiff to inquire of damages in this suit.

ALEXANDER KEITH and WILLIAM LIDDLE. The Defendant pleaded that he did not assume issue joined and referred until the next Court.

WILLIAM LITCHBOURNE against THOMAS WALKER, ROBERT BARRON, and HENRY BRESSIE. The Defendant pleaded payment issue joined and referred until the next Court.

ANDREW MARTIN against JOHN MEARNS. The Defendant pleaded that he did not assume issue joined and referred until the next Court.

PHILIP CARBERY against JOHN SCOTT. The Defendant pleaded that he did not assume issue joined and referred until the next Court.

JOHN SHEDDEN against JAMES MARSDEN and JONATHAN EILBECK executors of ELDRED FISHER deceased. The Defendants pleased that their testator did not assume and that they had fully administered issue joined and referred.

JOHN SHEPHERD against JAMES MARSDEN and JONATHAN EILBECK executors of ELDRED FISHER deceased. The Defendants pleased that their testator did not assume and that they had fully administered issue joined and referred.

ROBERT SHEDDEN and Co. against ABRAM GIBSON. The Defendant pleaded that he did not assume issue joined and referred until the next Court.

Order is granted HENRY KING against BALFOUR and BARRAUD for 262 pounds of tobacco for 4 days attendance coming and returning 18 miles 3x and 1 pound 16 shillings for ferriages in their suit against JOHN JONES.

Order is granted JOHN BURGESS against BALFOUR and BARRAUD for 150 pounds of tobacco for 2 days attendance coming and returning 36 miles once and 12 shillings for ferriages in their suit against JOHN JONES.

Order is granted JOHN WEBB against BALFOUR and BARRAUD for 104 pounds of tobacco for 2 days attendance coming and returning 18 miles once and 12 shillings for ferriages in their suit against JOHN JONES.

Order is granted WILLIAM CUNNINGHAM against BALFOUR and BARRAUD for 104 pounds of tobacco for 2 days attendance coming and returning 18 miles once and 12 shillings for ferriages in their suit against JOHN JONES.

Order is granted BARTRAM PROBY against BALFOUR and BARRAUD for 150 pounds of tobacco for 2 days attendance coming and returning 18 miles once and 12 shillings for ferriages in their suit against JOHN JONES.

PAGE 217

Order is granted GEORGE WRAY against JOHN JONES for 260 pounds of tobacco for 4 days attendance coming and returning 18 miles 3x and 1 pound 16 shillings for ferriages in the suit of BALFOUR and BARRAUD against him.

JAMES BALFOUR and DANIEL BARRAUD Plaintiff
Against Re: In Case.
JOHN JONES Defendant

This day came the parties by their Attorney's and thereupon came also a Jury to wit: JOHN EDWARDS, JOHN CARMOUNT, WILLIAM JAQUES, WILLIAM SKINKER, JAMES HALDANE, JAMES PASTEUR, HENRY BRESSIE, JONATHAN SMITH, RICHARD WILKERSON, WILLIAM GOODCHILD, ROBERT TUCKER and GEORGE KELLY who being elected tried and sworn the truth to speak upon the issue joined upon their oath do now say that the Defendant did not assume with leave as in pleading he has alleged. Therefore, it is considered that the Plaintiff take nothing by their bill but for their false claims be in mercy. And the Defendant go hence without day and recover against the Plaintiff his costs by him about his Defense in this behalf expended.

The Deputy Sergeant agreeable to an Order of the Mayor waited on LEWIS HANSFORD Gentleman one of the Aldermen of the said Borough the 24th of last month being HUSTINGS COURT DAY and desire his attendance at the said Court who answered he would not or could attend while JOSEPH CALVERT was Sergeant.

The Sergeant agreeable to an Order of the Mayor yesterday waited on LEWIS HANSFORD and CORNELIUS CALVERT Gentleman two of the Aldermen of the said Borough being HUSTINGS COURT DAY to desire their attendance at the said Court. Whom the Sergeant informed there was a cause coming on in which one of the sitting alderman was concerned. To which CORNELIUS CALVERT answered we hear you and LEWIS HANSFORD answered very well.

The Sergeant agreeable to an Order of the Mayor yesterday waited on WILLIAM AITCHESON Gentleman one of the Aldermen of the said Borough being HUSTINGS COURT DAY to desire his attendance at the said Court. Whom the Sergeant informed there was a cause coming on in which one of the sitting Alderman was concerned. To which he answered he would not attend and after added he thought he was turned out the last Hall.

The Sergeant agreeable to an Order of the Mayor yesterday waited on JAMES TAYLOR Gentleman one of the Aldermen of the said Borough being HUSTINGS COURT DAY to desire his attendance at the said Court. Whom the Sergeant informed there was a cause coming on in which one of the sitting Alderman was concerned. To which he answered he was too unwell and could not possibly sit.

The Sergeant agreeable to an Order of the Mayor yesterday waited on ARCHIBALD CAMPBELL Gentleman one of the Aldermen of the said Borough being HUSTINGS COURT DAY to desire his attendance at the said Court. Whom the Sergeant informed there was a cause coming on in which one of the sitting Alderman was concerned. To which he answered he would come presently.

The Sergeant agreeable to an Order of the Mayor yesterday waited on ARCHIBALD CAMPBELL, LEWIS HANSFORD, JAMES TAYLOR, CORNELIUS CALVERT, and WILLIAM AITCHESON Gentleman Alderman to desire their attendance at the Hustings Court. Whom the Deputy Sergeant informed there was some business coming on in Court in which one of the sitting Alderman was concerned.

PAGE 217B

And could not be tried without another Alderman to which ARCHIBALD CAMPBELL answered very well. The said LEWIS HANSFORD answered I cannot help it my business must not be left undone. The said JAMES TAYLOR answered I have been very unwell since Saturday last and am not so unwell I think it would be dangerous to sit in a cold Court house. The said CORNELIUS CALVERT answered I do not care to go on the BENCH again in case I should be treated as I have been before, and the said WILLIAM AITCHESON answered he could not attend.

On Complaint being made to the Court that the Business of the Court is delayed through the absence of Aldermen. Ordered that the mayor be requested to summon a Common Hall to know of the said ARCHIBALD CAMPBELL, LEWIS HANSFORD, JAMES TAYLOR, CORNELIUS CALVERT and WILLIAM AITCHESON their reasons for their nonattendance at the Court of Hustings and that the Sergeant be directed to as quaint every Corporator the Business that will be laid before them.

This Court this day rated flour at 16/8 per centum weight
This Court is adjourned to Court in Course, CHARLES THOMAS MAYOR, TESTE: JOHN BOUSH D.C.

NORFOLK BOROUGH

At a Hustings Court Held this 21ST day of March 1774
PRESENT: CHARLES THOMAS ESQUIRE MAYOR
GENTLEMAN ALDERMEN: GEORGE ABYVON, MAXIMILIAN CALVERT, PAUL LOYALL

GEORGE TANKARD against WILLIAM AYLES. HENRY BRESSIE this day came into Court and undertook for the Defendant that in case he shall be cast in this suit he the said Defendant will pay the condemnation of the Court or render his body to Prison in execution for the same or that the said BRESSIE will do it for him. Where upon the Defendants by their Attorney prays and has leave to IMPARLE here the next Court and then to Plead

JOSEPH CALVERT against JAMES ASHLEY. Dismissed at the Plaintiff costs.

WILLIAM BLACK against WILLIAM MEREDITH. ROBERT TUCKER this day came into Court and undertook for the Defendant that in case he shall be cast in this suit he the said Defendant will pay the condemnation of the Court or render his body to Prison in execution for the same or that the said TUCKER will do it for him. Where upon the Defendants by his Attorney prays and has leave to IMPARLE here the next Court and then to Plead

JAMES DAVIS against WILLIAM MEREDITH Dismissed.

PAGE 218

THOMAS NEWTON SR. against CHARLES COOPER and CARY SELDEN. CHAPMAN MANSON and JAMES BAKER this day came into Court and undertook for the Defendant COOPER that in case he shall be cast in this suit he the said Defendant COPPER will pay the condemnation of the Court or render his body to Prison in execution for the same or that the said MANSON and BAKER will do it for him. Where upon the Defendants by their Attorney prays and has leave to IMPARLE here until the next Court and then to Plead. And the suit against the other Defendant SELDEN is discontinued.

EDWARD MOSELEY. BETTY MOSELEY and LEMUEL THOROWGOOD executors of WILLIAM MOSELEY against ALEXANDER BELL. Alias Scire Facias

WILLIAM MCCORMICK and Company against SAMUEL TUCKER. THOMAS ROBERTS of this Borough this day came into Court and undertook for the Defendant that in case he shall be cast in this suit he the said Defendant will pay the condemnation of the Court or render his body to Prison in execution for the same or that the said ROBERTS will do it for him. Where upon the Defendant by his Attorney pleaded, he did not assume issue joined and referred until the next Court.

MATTHEW PHRIPP and JOSEPH HUTCHINGS Church wardens of E.R. PARISH against ABRAM WORMINGTON. Imparlance.

WILLIAM NICHOLSON SR. against PAUL HERITTER. by Petition and summons. Judgement is granted the Plaintiff for 3 pounds. It is ordered that the Defendant pay the same unto the Plaintiff with costs and fee.

JAMES LEITCH against JAMES HALDANE. JOHN MEARNS this day came into Court and undertook for the Defendant COOPER that in case he shall be cast in this suit he the said Defendant will pay the condemnation of the Court or render his body to Prison in execution for the same or that the said MEARNS will do it for him. Where upon the Defendants by their Attorney prays and has leave to IMPARLE here until the next Court and then to Plead.

MCCALL and SHEDDEN against THOMAS WILLIAMSON. Dismissed.
JOHN MARNIX against JOSEPH MITCHELL. In Chancery. Dismissed at the Defendants costs.

GIDEON GOODRIGHT Plaintiff
Against Re: *In Ejectment for one MESSUAGE with the appurtenances situate and lying within the Borough aforesaid at the Demise of JAMES DAWSON*
TIMOTHY TURNOUT Defendant
This day came the Plaintiff by ANDREW RONALD Gentleman his Attorney and the Defendant TIMOTHY TURNOUT though solemnly called came not nor says anything in bar or preclusion of the action of the said JAMES DAWSON but made default whereby the said JAMES DAWSON remains thereof undefended against the said TIMOTHY TURNOUT. Therefore, it is considered that the Plaintiff recover against the

said Defendant his term yet to come of and in the premises together with his costs by him in this behalf expended. And the Said Defendants may be taken. And here upon the Plaintiff prays the writ of our Lord the King to the Sergeant of the Borough of Norfolk aforesaid to be directed to cause him to have his possession of this term yet to come and to him it is granted returnable here.

JOHN HUTCHINGS Gentleman thereof against JAMES ARCHDEACON Dismissed.

PAGE 218B
SAMUEL TUCKER against WILLIAM MCCORMICK, WILLIAM AITCHESON and JAMES PARKER and Company. ROBERT TAYLOR Gentleman this day came into Court and undertook for the Defendants that in case they shall be cast in this suit they the said Defendants will pay the condemnation of the Court or render their bodies to Prison in execution for the same or that the said TAYLOR will do it for them. Where upon the Defendants by their Attorney pleaded he did not assume issue joined and referred.

JOHN TATEM Sheriff against WILLIAM INGRAM and JOHN INGRAM. Dismissed.
CHARLES CONNOR against JOHN BROWN. Imparlance.

JACOB BISHOP against CHAPMAN MANSON. CHARLES COOPER B.L. this day came into Court and undertook for the Defendant that in case he shall be cast in this suit he the said Defendant will pay the condemnation of the Court or render his body to Prison in execution for the same or that the said COOPER will do it for him. Where upon the Defendants by their Attorney prays and has leave to IMPARLE here until the next Court and then to Plead.

ROE COWPER against CHARLES COOPER B.L., CHAPMAN MASON and JAMES BAKER this day came into Court and undertook for the Defendant that in case he shall be cast in this suit he the said Defendant will pay the condemnation of the Court or render his body to Prison in execution for the same or that they the said MASON and BAKER will do it for him. Where upon the Defendants by their Attorney prays and has leave to IMPARLE here until the next Court and then to Plead.

JOHN BARRET against JOSEPH CARY by attachment dismissed at Defendants costs.

Order is granted ANN JONES against WILLIAM NICHOLSON SR. for 25 pounds of tobacco for 1 day's attendance at this Court in his petition and summons against PAUL HERITER.

THOMAS SNALE and ELIZABETH, his wife against JOHN IVY admin of WILLIAM IVY deceased. The Defendant on his motion filed his answer to the bill of the Plaintiff and time is allowed them to consider.

JOHN BARRET against ROBERT FRY. Dismissed.

WILLIAM WAGER Plaintiff
Against Re: In Case
JOHN RANSBERG Defendant
This day came the parties by their Attorney's and the Defendant by his Attorney relinquishes his former plea, says that he cannot gainsay the Plaintiffs action nor but that he did assume in manner and form as the Plaintiff against him has declared. Therefore, it is considered that the Plaintiff recover against the said Defendant 7 pounds 17 shillings and 10 pence half penny and his costs by him about his suit in this behalf expended and the said Defendant in mercy.

WILLIAM MCCORMACK against SAMUEL TUCKER. On the motion of the Plaintiff by their Attorney A DEDIMUS is granted them to take the deposition of JAMES MOSELEY, WILLIAM WRIGHT, JAMES NEAL, and JAMES FORSTER giving defendant notice.

PAGE 219
JOHN IVY administrator of WILLIAM IVY Plaintiff
Against Re: In Case
THOMAS SNALE Defendants
This day came the parties by their Attorney's and there upon came also a Jury to wit: THOMAS ROBERTS, GEORGE GORDON, JOHN MEARNS, WILLIAM GOODCHILD, SAMUEL BACON, PAUL WATLINGTON, WILLIAM INGRAM, JAMES DISON, JAMES LEITCH, FREER ARMSTON, SAMUEL WHITE and WILLIAM JAQUES who being elected tried and sworn the truth to speak upon the issue joined upon their oath do say that the Defendant is guilty of the Conversion in manner and form as the Plaintiff against him has declared and do assess the damages of the Plaintiff by occasion thereof to 12 pounds besides his costs. Therefore, it is considered that the Plaintiff recover against the said Defendant his damages aforesaid in form aforesaid assessed and his costs by him about his suit in this behalf expended and the said Defendant in mercy.

MISTERS LOGAN GILMOUR and Company Plaintiffs
Against Re: In Case
ARCHIBALD BUCHANAN Defendant
This day came the parties by their Attorney's and there upon came also a Jury to wit: THOMAS ROBERTS, GEORGE GORDON, JOHN MEARNS, WILLIAM GOODCHILD, SAMUEL BACON, PAUL WATLINGTON, WILLIAM INGRAM, JAMES DISON, JAMES LEITCH, FREER ARMSTON, SAMUEL WHITE, and WILLIAM JAQUES who being elected tried and sworn the truth to speak upon the issue joined upon their oath do say that the Defendant did assume in manner and form as the Plaintiff against him has declared and do assess the damages of the Plaintiff by occasion of the non-performance of that assumption to 180 pounds 13 shillings and 7 pence 3 farthings besides their costs. Therefore, it is considered that the Plaintiff recover against the said Defendant his damages aforesaid in form aforesaid assessed and his costs by him about his suit in this behalf expended and the said Defendant in mercy.

SAMUEL HOSIER Plaintiff
Against Re: In Trespass Assault and Battery
JOHN HARDY Defendant
This day came the parties by their Attorney's and there upon came also a Jury to wit: JOHN CARMOUNT, JOSEPH CARY, ROBERT GILMOUR, WILLIAM HARGRAVES, JOHN WALKER, HARDRES WALLER, RICHARD BASSET, ROBERT FRY, BENNET BOUSH, ROBERT TUCKER, JOHN BROWN and ROBERT MACKIE who being elected tried and sworn the truth to speak upon the issue joined upon their oath do say that the Defendant is guilty of the Trespass, assault and Battery in the declaration mentioned in manner and form as the Plaintiff against him has declared. And do assess the Plaintiff damages by occasion thereof to 1 shillings and 1 penny half penny. Therefore, it is considered that the Plaintiff recover against the said Defendant his damages aforesaid in form aforesaid assessed and the Defendant may be taken.

Order is granted SAMUEL LANGLEY against JOHN IVY admin of WILLIAM IVY for 25 pounds of tobacco for 1 day's attendance in his suit against THOMAS SNALE.

Order is granted WILLIAM COLLEY against JOHN HARDY for 25 pounds of tobacco for 1 day's attendance at this Court in the Suit of SAMUEL HOSIER against him.

Order is granted WILLIAM BICKERDICK against JOHN HARDY for 25 pounds of tobacco for 1 day's attendance at this Court in the Suit of SAMUEL HOSIER against him.

PAGE 219B
WILLIAM FITCHBOURNE Plaintiff
Against Re: In Debt
THOMAS WALKER, ROBERT BARON and HENRY BRESSIE Defendants
This day came the parties by their Attorney's and thereupon came also a Jury to wit: THOMAS ROBERTS, GEORGE GORDON, JOHN MEARNS, WILLIAM GOODCHILD, SAMUEL BACON, PAUL WATLINGTON, WILLIAM INGRAM, JAMES DISON, JAMES LEITCH, FREER ARMSTRONG, SAMUEL WHITE, and WILLIAM JAQUES who being elected tried and sworn the truth to speak upon the issue joined upon their oath do say that the Defendants have not paid the debt as in pleading they have alleged. Therefore, it is considered that the plaintiff recover against the said Defendants his debt amounting to 380 pounds and his costs by him about his suit in this behalf expended and the said defendants in mercy. But this judgement is to be discharged by the payment of 190 pounds with interest thereon after the rate of 5% per annum to be computed from January 19, 1772, to the time of payment and the costs.

ROBERT GILMOUR admin of WILLIAM GRAY Plaintiff
Against Re: On a motion upon a replevy bond
THOMAS DICKERSON, AARON BARBER and JOSIAH HOFFMIRE Defendants.
This day came the Plaintiff by ANDREW RONALD Gentleman his Attorney and the Defendant BARBER and HOFFMIRE having had notice agreeable to the Act of Assembly as appeared by the Sergeant. Therefore, it is considered that the Plaintiff recover against the said Defendants 22 pounds 13 shillings and 9 pence and his costs by him in this behalf expended and the said Defendants in mercy. But this judgement is to be discharged by the payment of 11 pounds 6 shillings and 10 pence half penny with interest thereon after the rate of 5% per annum to be computed from September 13, 1773, to the time of payment and costs and discontinued against DICKERSON.

ROBERT SHEDDEN and Company Plaintiff
Against Re: In Case
ABRAM GIBSON Defendant
This day came the parties by their Attorney's and thereupon came also a Jury to wit: THOMAS ROBERTS, GEORGE GORDON, JOHN MEARNS, WILLIAM GOODCHILD, SAMUEL BACON, PAUL WATLINGTON, WILLIAM INGRAM, JAMES DISON, JAMES LEITCH, FREER ARMSTRONG, SAMUEL WHITE, and WILLIAM JAQUES who being elected tried and sworn the truth to speak upon the issue joined upon their oath do say that the Defendants did assume in manner and form as the Plaintiff against him have declared. And do assess the Plaintiff damages by occasion of the non-performance of that assumption to 34 pounds 8 shillings and 4 pence besides their costs. Therefore, it is considered that the Plaintiff recover against the said Defendant their damages aforesaid in form aforesaid assessed and their costs by them about their suit in this behalf expended and the said Defendant in mercy.

Order is granted JAMES THELABALL against FREDERICK BOUSH for 75 pounds of tobacco for 3 days attendance at this Court in the suit of CHRISTOPHER CALVERT against him

LOGAN GILMOUR and Company against EDWARD SPRUGG. The suit is dismissed.
AARON WHITEHURST against SAMUEL CALVERT. The suit is dismissed at the Defendants Costs.

PAGE 220
MISTERES M. REAND and BUCHANAN against ROBERT TUCKER. The Defendant by his Attorney pleaded that he did not assume issue joined and referred until next Court.

FREDERICK A. DOEBER against RICHARD TALBOT. The Defendant pleaded payment issue joined and referred until next Court.
THOMAS RASCOE against WRIGHT WESTCOAT. The Defendant pleaded that he did not assume issue joined and referred until next Court.

STEPHEN TANKARD against EDWARD BOOKER. Dismissed.
GEORGE CARLTON against THOMAS HUGHS. The Defendant payment issue joined and referred until next Court.

ISAAC THOMPSON Plaintiff
Against Re: In Debt on a note
MATTHEW PHRIPP and JOHN LAWRENCE executors of THOMAS THOMPSON Deceased Defendants
This day came as well the Plaintiff by THOMAS CLAIBORNE Gentleman his Attorney as the Defendant JOHN in his proper person and says that they cannot gainsay the Plaintiffs action nor but that their testator did assume in manner and form as the Plaintiff has declared. Therefore, it is considered that the Plaintiff recover against the said Defendant 15 pounds and his costs by him in this behalf expended. When assets after paying proceeding judgements of greater dignity and the Defendants own claims of equal dignity against the estate of the said testator to be levied of the goods and chattels which were of the said testator at the time of his death that shall hereafter come to the hands of the said Defendants to be administered and the said Defendants in mercy.

JOHN WYAT Plaintiff
Against Re: In Debt
TIMOTHY IVES Defendant
This day came the Plaintiff by THOMAS CLAIBORNE Gentleman his Attorney and the Defendant being solemnly called and not appearing. Ordered that the former order of this Court against the said Defendant and THOMAS HATTON his bail be confirmed. Therefore, it is considered that the Plaintiff recover against the said Defendant and FRANCIS HATTON his bail aforesaid his debt amounting to 20 pounds and his costs by him about his suit in this behalf expended and the said defendant in mercy. But this judgement is to be discharged by the payment of 10 pounds with interest thereon after the rate of 5% per annum to be computed from December 25, 1773, to the time of payment and the costs.

JOHN CRAMOND against WILLIAM ROBINSON. The Defendant pleaded that he did not assume issue joined and referred.
JOHN CRAMOND against WILLIAM ROBINSON. Dismissed at the Plaintiff's cost.

CELIA SOUTHERLAND admin of JOHN SOUTHERLAND deceased against SARAH CARNEY and JOHN TATEM executors of BARNABY CARNEY deceased. In Debt. Defendant pleaded payment issue joined and referred.

PAGE 220B
CELIA SOUTHERLAND admin of JOHN SOUTHERLAND deceased against SARAH CARNEY and JOHN TATEM executors of BARNABY CARNEY deceased. In Case. Defendant pleaded their testator did not assume and the Act of Limitations issue joined and referred until next Court.

Order is Granted JOHN GUY against JOHN IVY admin of WILLIAM IVY for 25 pounds of tobacco for 1 day's attendance at this Court in his suit against THOMAS SNALE.

This Court is adjourned to Court in Course, CHARLES THOMAS MAYOR, TESTE: JOHN BOUSH D.C.

NORFOLK BOROUGH
At a Hustings Court Held this 23RD day of May 1774
PRESENT: CHARLES THOMAS ESQUIRE MAYOR
GENTLEMAN ALDERMEN: GEORGE ABYVON, MAXIMILIAN CALVERT, PAUL LOYALL

COWPER and ADKINS against JOHN MORRIS. Order is granted the Plaintiff against Defendant and ROBERT SHEDDEN his bail.

MORTO BRIAN Plaintiff
Against Re: In Case
ROGER PEARCE Defendant
This day came the parties by their Attorney and by their mutual consent submitted all matters in difference between them to be determined of JOHN SHAW, JONATHAN EILBECK, BASSETT MOSELEY, and ALEXANDER MOSELEY Gentleman or any three of them and agreed that their award thereupon should be made the Judgement of this Court and they having returned their award in the premises in these words to wit: TALLOW MANUFACTORY DR. on account of ROGER PEARCE to amount of sundry debts L422.11.6

they having returned their award in the premises in these words to wit "Tallow Manufactory &c on acco.t

of Roger Pearce To amount of sundry det.s	£422.11.6.	By sundries by account rendered	£423.6.2½	
To a profit gained	5.14.8¾		428.6.2½	
	428.6.2½	By a profit gained £5.14.8¾		
To Morto Brian for wages	12.14.8	Balance	36.17.8¾ }	£42.2.5
Expences from Philadelphia	3.4.0			
Cash paid Singleton 16.3.9 d.o p.d E. Parke £ 10.10	26.13.9			
	42.2.5			
Morto Brian in account with		Roger Pearce	Cr	
To Balance of account rendered you	£16.8.4	By Balance from factory acc.t	£36.17.8¾	
Balance due by award	20.9.3¾		£36.17.8¾	

Norfolk Borough In pursuance of an Order of the Court of HUSTINGS to us directed to examine and settle all matters and differences between MORTO BRIAN and ROGER PEARCE. We the subscribers have duly examined the above accounts.

PAGE 221

And find the sum of 20 pounds 9 shillings and 3 pence 3 farthings Virginia Currency to be justly due to MORTO BRIAN. Therefore, we award the same with costs of suit to be paid unto the said MORTO BRIAN by ROGER PEARCE. In witness whereof we have set our hands this 11th day of April 1774. JOHN SHAW, JONATHAN EILBECK, BASSET MOSELEY. It is there upon considered that the Plaintiff recover against the Defendant the said 20 pounds 9 shillings and 3 pence 3 farthings and his costs by him in this behalf expended.

MORTO BRIAN Plaintiff
Against Re: In Covenant
ROGER PEARCE Defendant

This day came the parties by their Attorney's and by their mutual consent submitted all matters in difference between them for the determination of JOHN SHAW, JONATHAN EILBECK, BASSET MOSELEY and ALEXANDER MOSELEY Gentleman or any three of them and agreed that their award there upon should be made the Judgement of the Court and they having returned their award then premises in these words to wit: Norfolk Borough" In pursuance of an order of the Court of Hustings to us directed to examine and settle all matters and differences between MORTO BRIAN and ROGER PEARCE. We the subscribers have duly heard the parties and understood their differences in consequence of which we award the sum of 25 pounds Virginia Currency to be paid unto the Plaintiff MORTO BRIAN by the defendant ROGER PEARCE for forfeiture of agreement in witness whereof we have set our hands this 11th day of April 1774. JOHN SHAW, JONATHAN EILBECK, BASSET MOSELEY. It is there upon considered that the plaintiff recover against the Defendant the said 25 pounds and his costs by him about this suit in this behalf expended.

MISTERS ROBERT SHEDDEN and Company against ROBERT MATTHEWS. Dismissed.
DAVIS PURRELL against SAMUEL INGLES. Administrator of GEORGE SHEMELD. Imparlance.
LYDIA CAWSON against WILLIAM HUNTER. The suit is discontinued.

LYDIA CAWSON against WILLIAM CALVERT. In Case for slander. The Defendant by his Attorney pleaded justification of the words, issue joined and referred until the Next Court.

FRANCES ROBERTSON against JOHN SMITH and THOMAS TALBOT. Time is allowed to consider on a bill.

WILLIAM DONALDSON against ALEXANDER KEITH. In Case. ROBERT BAYNE this day came into Court and undertook for the Defendant that in case he shall be cast in this suit he the said Defendant will pay the condemnation of the Court or render his body to prison in execution for the same or that the said ROBERT BAYNE will do it for him. Whereupon the Defendant by his Attorney prays and has leave to IMPARLE here until next Court and then to plead.

MALACHI MAUND against SAMUEL CALVERT. In Case. The Defendant being called and not appearing. ON the motion of the Plaintiff by his Attorney an attachment is awarded him against the estate of the said Defendant for 30 pounds and costs returnable here the next Court.

HEPBURN and MITCHELL against DAVID DAVIS. The suit is dismissed.

PAGE 221B

WILLIAM NICHOLSON Senior against CHARLES RUDDER. In Debt. Order against the Defendant and GEORGE OLDNER his bail.

JOHN KELSICK against JAMES STEVENSON. The suit is dismissed.

EDWARD and ROE COWPER executors of PHILIP COWPER deceased against CHAPMAN MANSON. In Case. Order against the Defendant and WILLIAM WALKER his bail.

ROBERT GRAY and Company against WILLIAM AYLES, ALEXANDER LOVE, JOHN MITCHELL and ROBERT SHEDDEN and Company. In Case. Order against Defendants. AYLES and LOVE and Sergeant and discontinued against the other Defendants MITCHELL, SHEDDIN and Company.

ANN SYMONS an infant under the age of 21 years by ROBERT BANKS and SARAH his wife her next friend against ANDREW STEVENS. The suit abates by the intermarriage of the Plaintiff.

JOHN (INK BLOT) against JOHN MARLEY by warrant of the peace. Dismissed at Plaintiffs costs.

JOHN CHESHIRE against RICHARD BROWN. Order that the referrers proceed to settle and adjust the accounts between the said Plaintiff and Defendant on the 13th day of June Next.

CHRISTOPHER WRIGHT against WILLIAM WISHART. On the motion of the said Defendant by his Attorney A DEDIMUS is granted him to take the deposition of WALTER LYON giving the Plaintiff reasonable notice of the time and place.

THOMAS RASCOE against WRIGHT WESTCOAT. This suit abates by the death of the Plaintiff.

JAMES HALDANE was this day brought before the Court for misusing his servant ELIZABETH CASSARINE and the same being proved. It is ordered that the Sergeant sell the said CASSARINE for the time by her conviction unexpired and after deducting the expense of this prosecution that he pay the overplus to the said JAMES HALDANE.

WILL COWPER Plaintiff
Against Re: In Debt on a protested bill
WRIGHT WESTCOAT Defendant
This day came the parties by their Attorney's and there upon came also a Jury to wit: WILLIAM WILKINS, THOMAS HUDSON, ADAM BENNET, JOSEPH HARDING, DANIEL BARRAUD, WILLIAM SKINKER, SCARBROUGH TANKARD, MORTO BRIAN, PAUL WATLINGTON, ZACHERIAH HUTCHINGS, JOSEPH CARY and WILLIAM HARVEY who being elected tried and sworn the truth to speak upon the issue joined upon their oath do say that the Defendant has not paid the debt in the declaration mentioned. Therefore, it is considered that the Plaintiff recover against the said Defendant his debt amounting to 109 pounds 13 shillings and 8 pence sterling with interest thereon after the rate of 5% per annum to be computed from this day until the time of payment and the costs. And the Court says that the said sterling money may be discharged in current money at 30% for the difference of exchange.

JOSEPH CALVERT against THOMAS DICKERSON. The suit is dismissed at the Plaintiffs costs.

PAGE 222
WILLIAM TREBELL and ROBERT NICHOLSON executors of JOSEPH SCRIVENER deceased Plaintiff
Against: On a motion of replevy bond
JOHN WILLS and DANIEL HUTCHINGS Defendant
This day came the Plaintiffs by BENJAMIN CROOKER Gentleman their Attorney and the Defendants having had notice agreeable to the Act of Assembly. Therefore, it is considered that the Plaintiff recover against the said Defendants their debt amounting to 14 found 12 shillings and 5 pence with interest thereon after the rate of 5% per annum to be computed form September 28, 1773, to the time of payment together with costs.

WILLIAM MCCORNICK and Company Plaintiff
Against Re: In Case
SAMUEL TUCKER Defendant
This day came the parties by their Attorney's and thereupon came also a Jury to wit: GEORGE KELLY, JAMES MOORE, ALEXANDER WISEMAN, HENRY BRESSIE, HENRY BROWN, JAMES MARSDEN, THOMAS HEPBURN, WILLIAM HARVEY, ZACHERIAH HUTCHINGS, JOHN VALLENCIER, THOMAS WOODFORD and DANIEL HUTCHINGS who being elected tried and sworn the truth to speak upon the issue joined upon their oath do say that the Defendant did assume in manner and form as the Plaintiff against him has declared and do assess the Plaintiffs damages by occasion of the nonperformance of that assumption to 170 pounds besides their costs. Therefore, it is considered that the Plaintiff recover against the said Defendant their damages aforesaid in form aforesaid assessed and their costs by them in this behalf expended and the said Defendant in mercy. And the Defendant surrendered himself up in discharge of his Special Bail and Plaintiffs Attorney prays no committed.

AMELIA SOPHIA LEONERA FELTON against BARNABAS LORAIN. The suit abates by the death of the Plaintiff.
JOHN CRAMOND against HARDRESS WALLER. The suit is dismissed.

ALEXANDER KIDD and ANN WICKERSHAM admin of JOHN KIDD deceased against THOMAS WALKER, JOHN VALLENCIER and STEPHEN TANKARD. The Defendant VALLERICIER having sworn to this peal of duress is admitted to file it and continued

PHILIP CARBERY Plaintiff against JOHN WILLIAMS Defendant. In Case. The Defendant in Case. The Defendant by his Attorney pleaded that he did not assume issue joined and referred until next Court.

THOMAS HOWARD and WILLIAM WHITE executors of JOSEPH WRIGHT deceased Plaintiffs against JOHN TATEM SR. and JOHN TATEM JR. Defendants. In Debt. Defendants by their Attorney pleaded payment issue joined and referred until the next Court.

THOMAS HOWARD and WILLIAM WHITE executors of JOSEPH WRIGHT deceased Plaintiffs against JOHN TATEM SR. and FRANCIS WRIGHT Defendants. In Debt. Defendants by their Attorney pleaded payment issue joined and referred until the next Court.

WALTER LYON Gentleman Plaintiff against ROBERT BARRS Defendant. In Case. The Defendant by his Attorney pleaded that he did not assume issue joined and referred until next Court.

THOMAS APPLEWHAITE Plaintiff against THOMAS WILLIAMSON. Defendant. In Case. The Defendant by his Attorney pleaded that he did not assume issue joined and referred until next Court.

PAGE 222B

JOHN WILSON and Company Plaintiffs
Against Re: In Debt.
EPHRAIM BALL ANCE Defendant

This day came the Plaintiff by THOMAS CLAIBORNE Gentleman his Attorney and the Defendant being solemnly called and not appearing ordered that the former order of this Court against the said Defendant and SAMUEL BALLANCE his bail be confirmed. Therefore, it is considered that the Plaintiff recover against the said Defendant and SAMUEL BALLANCE his bail aforesaid. Their debt amounting to 19 pounds and their costs by them about their suit in this behalf expended and the said Defendant in mercy. But this judgement is to be discharged by the payment of 9 pounds 10 shillings with interest thereon after the rate of 5% per annum to be computed from January 1, 1766, to the time of payment and the costs.

MALACHI MAUND Plaintiff against ALEXANDER BELL Defendant. In Trespass. The Defendant by his Attorney pleaded that he is not guilty issue joined and referred until next Court.

MATTHEW PHRIPP and JOSEPH HUTCHINGS who as well and Plaintiff against MARY ROSS Defendant. In Debt. The Defendant by her Attorney pleaded not guilty issue joined and referred until next Court.

JAMES MARSDEN and JONATHAN EILBECK executors of ELDRED FISHER deceased Plaintiffs against WILLIAM SISSON Defendant. In Case. The Defendant by his Attorney pleaded he did not assume issue joined and referred until next Court.

JAMES MARSDEN and JONATHAN EILBECK executors of ELDRED FISHER deceased Plaintiffs against THOMAS WALKER Defendant. In Case. The Defendant by his Attorney pleaded he did not assume issue joined and referred until next Court.

MATTHEW PHRIPP and JOSEPH HUTCHINGS who as well and Plaintiff against JOHN BOGGES Defendant. In Debt. The Defendant by his Attorney pleaded not guilty issue joined and referred until next Court.

MATTHEW PHRIPP and JOSEPH HUTCHINGS who as well and Plaintiff against JOSEPH POPE Defendant. In Debt. The Defendant by his Attorney pleaded not guilty issue joined and referred until next Court.

MATTHEW PHRIPP and JOSEPH HUTCHINGS who as well and Plaintiff against JACOB WILLIAMS Defendant. In Debt. The Defendant by his Attorney pleaded not guilty issue joined and referred until next Court.

MATTHEW PHRIPP and JOSEPH HUTCHINGS who as well and Plaintiff against MATTHEW KELLY Defendant. In Debt. The suit abates by the death of the Defendant.

MATTHEW PHRIPP and JOSEPH HUTCHINGS who as well and Plaintiff against GEORGE JOSEPH FENWICK Defendant. In Debt. The Defendant by his Attorney pleaded not guilty issue joined and referred until next Court.

MATTHEW PHRIPP and JOSEPH HUTCHINGS who as well and Plaintiff against PETER KATZ Defendant. In Debt. The Defendant by his Attorney pleaded not guilty issue joined and referred until next Court.

PAGE 223

MATTHEW PHRIPP and JOSEPH HUTCHINGS who as well and Plaintiff against GEORGE ATKINSON Defendant. In Debt. The Defendant by his Attorney pleaded not guilty issue joined and referred until next Court.

MATTHEW PHRIPP and JOSEPH HUTCHINGS who as well and Plaintiff against JOHN BISER Defendant. In Debt. The Defendant by his Attorney pleaded not guilty issue joined and referred until next Court.

MATTHEW PHRIPP and JOSEPH HUTCHINGS who as well and Plaintiff against JUDITH DUNFORD Defendant. In Debt. The Defendant by her Attorney pleaded not guilty issue joined and referred until next Court.

JOHN MACLEAN, THOMAS TALBOT and HENRY LAMOUNT against JOHN WILSON and JOHN MEARNS. The suit is dismissed.
DAVID CROSS against JAMES MARSDEN and JONATHAN EILBECK executors of ELDRED FISHER deceased. The suit abates by the Plaintiffs death.

WARNER LEWIS Plaintiff against ALEXANDER LOVE. Defendant. In Case. The Defendant being called and not appearing. Ordered that the judgement be entered for the Plaintiff against the said Defendant and JOSEPH CALVERT Sergeant his bail for what damages that he has sustained to be ascertained at the Next Court upon a Writ of inquiry.

PHILIP HAYNES Plaintiff against JOHN WILLIAMS Defendant. In Case. The Defendant being called and to appearing ordered that the Judgement be entered for the Plaintiff against the said Defendant and JOHN GREENWOOD his bail for what damages the Plaintiff has sustained to be ascertained at the Next Court upon a Writ of Inquiry.

JOHN CRAMOND Plaintiff against THOMAS TAYLOR. Defendant. In Case. The Defendant being called and not appearing ordered that the judgement be entered for the Plaintiff against the said Defendant for what damages the Plaintiff has sustained to be ascertained at the Next Court upon a Writ of Inquiry.

RICHARD BARRON Plaintiff against FRANCIS BRIGHT. In Case. The Defendant being called and to appearing ordered that the Judgement be entered for the Plaintiff against the said Defendant and LEONARD TARRANT his bail for what damages the Plaintiff has sustained to be ascertained at the Next Court upon a Writ of Inquiry.

HENRY YOUNG against WILLIAM POOLE. The Suit is Dismissed at the Plaintiffs Costs.

WARNER LEWIS Plaintiff against SAMUEL ALLYNE. Defendant. In Case. The Defendant being called and to appearing ordered that the Judgement be entered for the Plaintiff against the said Defendant and WRIGHT WESTCOAT his bail for what damages the Plaintiff has sustained to be ascertained at the Next Court upon a Writ of Inquiry.

EILBECK ROSS and Company Plaintiffs against JOHN WHIDDEN. Defendant. In Case. The Defendant being called and to appearing ordered that the Judgement be entered for the Plaintiff against the said Defendant and JOHN WILSON his bail for what damages the Plaintiff has sustained to be ascertained at the Next Court upon a Writ of Inquiry.

MAXIMILIAN CALVERT against ANDREW STEVENSON. The suit is dismissed.

PAGE 223B
HUGH MORIARTY against PATRICK ROBINSON. The suit is Dismissed.
ALEXANDER SKINNER against JEREMIAH MATTHEWS. The suit is dismissed.

Order is granted ROBERT BARR against SARAH CARNEY and JOHN TATEM JR. executors of BARNABY CARNEY deceased for 25 pounds of tobacco for 1 day's attendance at this Court in the suit of CELIA SOUTHERLAND admin of JOHN SOUTHERLAND against them.

Order is granted CHARLES RANDOLPH against SARAH CARNEY and JOHN TATEM JR. executors of BARNABY CARNEY deceased for 25 pounds of tobacco for 1 day's attendance at this Court in the suit of CELIA SOUTHERLAND admin of JOHN SOUTHERLAND against them.

Order is granted HENRY GREEN against SARAH CARNEY and JOHN TATEM JR. executors of BARNABY CARNEY deceased for 25 pounds of tobacco for 1 day's attendance at this Court in the suit of CELIA SOUTHERLAND admin of JOHN SOUTHERLAND against them.

Ordinary Licenses are granted to ANDREW STEVENSON and SCARBROUGH TANKARD on their complying with the law.

The Court this day rated flour 16/8 per centum weight.

On the Petition of HERCULES DAVIS setting forth that although justly entitled to all the privileges which by the laws of this Colony a free Negro is a authorized to enjoy, is never the less detained in slavery by a certain REBECCA ELIZA TUCKER widow of JOHN TUCKER late of the said Borough deceased and being while in such state, incapable of acquiring or possessing any property so as to enable him to prosecute for his freedom and prays leave to be permitted to sue for the same in a form a paupers according to the course of this worshipful Court. On consideration it is ordered that ANDREW RONALD Gentleman inquire into the truth thereof and report his opinion to the Next Court.

This Court is adjourned to Court in Course. CHARLES THOMAS MAYOR. TESTE: JOHN BOUSH D.C.

PAGE 224
NORFOLK BOROUGH
At a Hustings Court Held this 21ST day of November 1774
PRESENT: GEORGE ABYVON ESQUIRE MAYOR
GENTLEMAN ALDERMEN: ARCHIBALD CAMPBELL, JAMES TAYLOR, CHARLES THOMAS

The King against DANIEL KELLY by warrant Dismissed.

THOMAS MCCARTY was this day brought before the Court by warrant for being a person of lewd life and conversation and a common disturber of the peace and the same being proved. It is ordered that the Sergeant take and keep him in custody until he gives bond and security himself in 50 pounds and 2 securities in 25 pounds each for his keeping the peace 12 months and pay the costs of this prosecution.

The King against ALEXANDER MUCKELBOY by warrant. Dismissed.
The King by NICHOLAS POWELL against WILLIAM ALLEN by warrant dismissed at the Defendants Costs.
The King against MARY WADE and JOHN YOUNG by warrant dismissed.
The King against WILLOUGHBY MORGAN against WARICK by warrant dismissed at his master's cost.
The King against ALEXANDER YOUNG by warrant Dismissed at the Defendants costs.
The King by WILLIAM MINETREE against WILLIAM BICKERDICK by warrant dismissed at the Defendants costs.

The King against JOHN HARDY by warrant dismissed at the Defendants costs.

SAMUEL PORTLOCK was this day appointed deputy Sergeant of this Borough in the Room of WILLIAM CALVERT and his having taken the oaths to the government and subscribed the test also the oath of a Deputy Sergeant of the said Borough enters upon the execution of this office.

Ordered that the Sergeant summon WILLIAM MINETREE to appear at the next Court to be held for this Borough to answer the complaint of his apprentice JOHN RODMAN.

Ordered that the rate of Flour be at 15 shillings per hundred weight

The King by LOUISA INMAN against JAMES MARSHALL Dismissed at the Plaintiffs cost.

Ordered that the Court be adjourned to Court in Course, CHARLES THOMAS MAYOR, TESTE: JOHN BOUSH D.C.

PAGE 224B
NORFOLK BOROUGH
At a Hustings Court Held this 20 day of February 1775
PRESENT: GEORGE ABYVON ESQUIRE MAYOR
GENTLEMAN ALDERMEN: PAUL LOYALL, JAMES TAYLOR, MAXIMILIAN CALVERT

The King by JOHN BOHANAN against PATRICK ROBINSON by warrant. Dismissed at Plaintiffs costs.
The King by ALEXANDER WISEMAN against WILLIAM PREISTMAN by warrant dismissed at Plaintiffs cost.
Ordinary License is granted to JOSEPH CARY on his complying with the law.
The King against ABRAM CLARKE by warrant dismissed at the Defendants costs.

WILLIAM LOVE and ALEXANDER MILLER were this day brought before the Court by warrant for being persons of lewd lives and conversation and common disturbers of the peace and the same being proved. It is ordered that the Sergeant take and keep them in Custody until they give bond and security themselves in 10 pounds each and two securities in 5 pounds each for their keeping the peace one month and pay the cost of this prosecution.

JAMES CUNNINGHAM, JOHN LOUNDS, and GEORGE ATKINSON were this day appointed Constables of this Borough and they having taken the oaths to the government and subscribed the test also the oath of a constable of the said Borough enters upon the execution of their office.

Ordered that the rate of rate of flour be at 15 shillings per hundred weight
CHARLES THOMAS MAYOR, TESTE: JOHN BOUSH D.C.

PAGE 225
COMPLETELY BLANK

PAGE 225B
NORFOLK BOROUGH
At a Hustings Court Held this 24th day of August 1778
PRESENT: CORNELIUS CALVERT Esquire Mayor
GENTLEMAN ALDERMEN: GEORGE ABYVON, PAUL LOYALL, JAMES TAYLOR,

SAMUEL PORTLOCK is appointed Sergeant of this Borough in the room of JOSEPH CALVERT removed and having taken the oath enters on the execution of the office.

ALEXANDER MOSELEY is appointed Clerk of this Borough in the room of JOHN BOUSH removed and having taken the oaths extension the execution of his office.

Ordered that the Sergeant summon WILLIAM SMITH and WILLIAM GOODCHILD to attend at the Next Court held for this Borough to qualify as constables of this Borough until the next election for mayor.

Ordinary License is granted WILLIAM SMITH on his complying with the law.

CORNELIUS CALVERT MAYOR, TESTE: ALEXANDER MOSELEY CLERK

PAGE 226
NORFOLK BOROUGH
At a Hustings Court Held this 24th day of January 1780
PRESENT: GEORGE ABYVON ESQUIRE MAYOR
GENTLEMAN ALDERMEN: THOMAS NEWTON JR., JAMES TAYLOR, CORNELIUS CALVERT

Ordered that JOSHUA PEED be summoned to attend at the next Court to be held for the Borough to qualify as constable for 1 year.
Ordered that the clerk give notice that this Court will proceed to business and enter on the docket the next Court.
Ordered that the Clerk and Sergeant apply to MR. WORMINGTON for the records of the records of this Borough.
Ordered that the Sergeant give public notice to all retailors of liquors and ordinary keepers that they must apply for license agreeable to the late act of assembly.

GEORGE ABYVON MAYOR, TESTE: ALEXANDER MOSELEY CLERK

PAGE 226B
NORFOLK BOROUGH
At a Hustings Court Held this 21st day of February 1780

PRESENT: GEORGE ABYVON ESQUIRE MAYOR
GENTLEMAN ALDERMEN: THOMAS NEWTON JR., JAMES TAYLOR, CORNELIUS CALVERT

Ordered that the Court Adjourn until tomorrow 10 o'clock, GEORGE ABYVON MAYOR, TESTE: ALEXANDER MOSELEY CLERK

NORFOLK BOROUGH
At a Hustings Court Held this 22nd day of February 1780
PRESENT: GEORGE ABYVON ESQUIRE MAYOR
GENTLEMAN ALDERMEN: THOMAS NEWTON JR., JAMES TAYLOR, CORNELIUS CALVERT

JOHN BOGGESS this day qualified as Deputy Sergeant of this Borough and enters on the execution of his office.
JOSHUA PRIDE was this day appointed and sworn constable of this Borough and enters on the execution of his office.
WILLIAM GOODCHILD appeared agreeable to the summons and refused to serve as constable of this Borough.
Ordered that the law be put in force against WILLIAM GOODCHILD

PAGE 227
Ordered that CHARLES COOPER be summoned to attend the next Court to qualify as constable of this Borough for 1 year.

Ordered that the Sergeant advertise a meeting of the inhabitants of this Borough on the 2nd Tuesday in March next to elect three commissioners of the tax for one year.

GEORGE ABYVON MAYOR, TESTE: ALEXANDER MOSELEY CLERK

NORFOLK BOROUGH
At a Hustings Court Held this 20th day of March 1780
PRESENT: GEORGE ABYVON ESQUIRE MAYOR
GENTLEMAN ALDERMEN: PAUL LOYALL, CORNELIUS CALVERT, JAMES TAYLOR, THOMAS NEWTON JR.

WILLIAM ROBINSON Gentleman this day qualified as an Attorney at law in this Court.
THOMAS MATTHEWS Gentleman. This day qualified as an Attorney at law in this Court.
WILLIAM GOODCHILD against JAMES DISON. Time to consider on bill.

WILLIAM GOODCHILD against WILLIAM SALMON. The suit abates. The Defendant being no inhabitant.
JAMES MOORE against WILLIAM HARVEY. The suit is continued.
HENRY TALBOT infant by MARY TALBOT his guardian against JOHN HUNT. The suit abates by the Defendant being no inhabitant.
EDWARD HACK MOSELEY against LEWIS HANSFORD. Dismissed.

PAGE 227B
THOMAS NEWTON SR., THOMAS NEWTON JR. and PAUL LOYALL Gentleman and THOMAS ROBERTS Distiller and JOHN TUCKER Gentleman against ROBERT TUCKER Gentleman eldest son and heir at law of ROBERT TUCKER Gentleman deceased. This suit abates by the Defendants death.

GEORGE WEBB and JOSEPH LANGLEY against JOHN BAYNES and NANCY ASHLEY. In Chancery. The suit is continued.
ALEXANDER GORDON against WRIGHT WESTCOTT. In Chancery. The suit is dismissed.

THOMAS SNALE and ELIZABETH, his wife against JOHN IVY admin of WILLIAM IVY deceased. This suit abates by the death of the Plaintiff.

THOMAS OLD by Justices against SPROWL and HUNTER abates by the death of the Defendant.
THOMAS LANGLEY against JOHN and JOSEPH HUTCHINGS. The suit is continued.
JAMES DAVIDSON against JAMES YOUNG and Company. This suit is dismissed.
THOMAS LANGLEY against JAMES PASTEUR. The suit is continued.

SARAH LANGLEY and JOSEPH LANGLEY executors of LEMUEL LANGLEY Plaintiff
Against Re: In Chancery
ARCHIBALD CAMPBELL administrator of JOHN DALGLEISH Defendant
The suit is dismissed.

NEWCOM DODD against SUSANNA LAMOUNTS. The suit is dismissed.
NEAL BROWN against JAMES ALLISON. The suit is dismissed.

ALEXANDER GORDON against PURDIE and DIXON. The Plaintiff be called and failing to appear. The Suit is dismissed.
WILLIAM and THOMAS FARRERS against GEORGE ALLISON Attorney Dismissed.

PAGE 228
JOHN WILSON against SAMUEL PORTLOCK. This suit abates by the death of the Plaintiff.

JAMES HALDANE against JAMES MARSDEN and JONATHAN EILBECK executors of ELDRED FISHER. This suit is dismissed.

JAMES CAMPBELL and Company against JAMES MARSDEN and JONATHAN EILBECK executors of ELDRED FISHER deceased. This suit is dismissed.

JAMES CAMPBELL and Company against JAMES MARSDEN and JONATHAN EILBECK executors of ELDRED FISHER deceased. This suit is dismissed.

JOHN RICHARDSON against WILLIAM HERBERT. Abates by the Plaintiffs death.
CHRISTOPHER WRIGHT against WILLIAM WISHART. Dismissed. Agreed.
JOHN EDWARDS against JOHN KNIGHT Abates by the Plaintiffs death.

ALEXANDER KEITH against WILLIAM LIDDLE. Abates by the Defendants death.
SAMUEL MCCASTLETON against WILLIAM SIMPSON. Dismissed.

WILLIAM and JOHN BROWN against WILLIAM SIMPSON. Dismissed.
THOMAS FLEMINGS against ANTHONY FLEMINGS. Abates by the Defendants death.
RICHARD SPENCER against JOHN FIELD. Abates by the Plaintiffs death.
JAMES ARCHDEACON against MARTIN MURPHY. Abates by the Plaintiffs death.

LOGAN GILMOUR & Co. against ALICE IVY. Dismissed.
GEORGE DIXON against JOSEPH YOWART*. Dismissed. (Listed 2x)
ANN BRAITHWAIT against JOSEPH COOPER. Dismissed.
DOUGALL GILCHRIST against JOHN SCOTT. Dismissed.

PAGE 228B
JAMES CAMPBELL and CO. against ELDRED FISHERS executors. The suit is dismissed.

ANDREW MARTIN against JOHN MEARNS. Abates by the Defendants death.
PHILIP CARBERY against JOHN SCOTT. Abates by the Defendants death.
JOHN SHEDDEN against ELDRED FISHERS executors. Abates by the Plaintiffs death.
MISTERS MCKEAND & CO. against ROBERT TUCKER. Abates by the Defendants death.*

JOHN BOWNESS & CO. against ELDRED FISHERS executors. Abates by the Plaintiffs death.
FREDERICK A. DOEBER against RICHARD TALBOT. Abates by the Plaintiffs death.
JAMES CAMPBELL & CO. against JAMES PATTERSON Admin. Dismissed.
THOMAS STEWART against JAMES PATTERSON Admin. Dismissed.
WILLIAM DONALDSON against JAMES PATTERSON Admin. Dismissed.

JOHN BOWNESS & Co. against THOMAS THOMPSON executors. In Debt. Dismissed (listed 2x)

JOHN CRAMOND against WILLIAM ROBINSON. Dismissed.
TULLY ROBINSON EXE. Against JOHN CRAMMOND dismissed suit by consent of Plaintiff
THOMAS BRYANT against SAMUEL GWIN. T.A.B. abates by the death of the parties.

THOMAS HOWARD and WILLIAM WHITE executors of JOSEPH WRIGHT against JOHN TATEM SR. and JOHN TATEM JR. abates by the death of the parties.

WALTER LYON Gentleman against ROBERT BARRS. In Case. Abates by the Plaintiffs death.
RICHARD TAYLOR against ROGER PEIRCE. Attachment. Abates by the Defendants death.

PAGE 228 # 2(CLERK LISTED TWO PAGES AS 228)
JAMES GILCHRIST against ROGER PIERCE. Abates by the Plaintiffs death.

THOMAS APPLEWHAITE against THOMAS WILLIAMSON. The suit is dismissed.

WILLIAM ROBINSON against JOSHUA WRIGHT. The suit abates by the Defendants death.
BARTHOLMEW TAYLOR against YOUNG &* POOK. The suit abates by the Plaintiffs death.
WILLIAM MCKEAND & CO. against EDWARD GOOD. This suit abates by the death of the Defendant.
RACHEL RICHARDSON against ANN BRAITHWAITE on this suit is dismissed.

Ordinary License is granted WILLIAM SMITH on complying with the law.

JAMES CARMICHAEL against RICHARD DAVIS. In Case. Abates by the Defendants death.
JOHN DUNN against GEORGE WINKLE. In Debt. Abates by the Defendants death.

ANDREW STEVENSON against JOHN MEARNS. In Case. The suit is dismissed.
JOHN MEARNS against ANDREW STEVENSON. This suit is dismissed.
GEORGE GORDON against JOHN WILSON. Admin. In Debt. The suit is dismissed.

ROBERT TUCKER against THOMAS THOMPSON exe. This suit abates by the Plaintiffs death.
SIMON BROWN and Co. against JOHN CRAMOND. The suit is dismissed.
JOHN CRAMOND against THOMAS TAYLOR. This suit is dismissed.

ELDRED FISHER exe. Against RODGER PEIRCE. Abates by the Defendants death.
JAMES CAMPBELL & CO. JOSHUA WRIGHT. The suit is dismissed.

JAMES WILSON against RICHARD BASSETT. In Case. The suit is dismissed.

ZACHERIAH HUTCHINGS against JOHN BARRET. In Case. The suit is dismissed.

PAGE 228B # 2(CLERK LISTED TWO PAGES AS 228B)

HARDESS WALLER against PAUL LOYALL & LATTIMER HALSTEAD admins of JONATHAN DISON abates by the Plaintiffs death.

CELIA SOUTHERLAND admin JOHN SOUTHERLAND against SARAH CARNEY and JOHN TATEM executors of BARNABAS CARNEY. Abates by the death of the parties (listed 2x)

SAMUEL FARMER against WRIGHT WESTCOTT. Dismissed.

EILBECK ROSS & co. against JOHN WHIDDON. Dismissed.

JEREMIAH FOREMAN against BARBER & HOFFMIRE and NATHANIEL POYNER Dismissed by the death of the Defendants

RICHARD BASSETT against PHILIP CARBERY abates by the Plaintiffs death.

MASON MILLER against CHRISTOPHER WILSON abates by the Plaintiffs death.

HUGH WYLIE against ARCHIBALD CAMPBELL admin of JOHN DALGLEISH. Dismissed.

ELBECK ROSS and Company against WILLIAM SAVAGE Dismissed.

THOMAS STEWART against JOHN LELLO abates by the Defendants death.

ANDREW STEVENSON & WIFE against JOHN HARDY Dismissed.

JOHN WILSON against ANDREW STEVENSON. Dismissed.

BALFOUR & BARRAUD against AARON BARBER. abates by the Defendants death.

JOHN SHAW against ROSANNA RITTER. Discontinued.

ANDREW STEVENSON against JOHN WILSON. Discontinued.

NEIL JAMIESON & co. against SARAH CARNEY and JOHN TATEM executors of BARNABAS CARNEY. Discontinued.

THOMAS CLAIBORNE against ROGER PEARCE. abates by the Plaintiffs death.

PAGE 229

JOHN BOWNESS against THOMAS TALBOT. Discontinued.

PREESON BOWDOIN against PHILIP CARBERY. Dismissed agreed.

JOHN EDWARDS against WILLIAM GREEN abates by the Plaintiffs death.

FRANCIS ROBERTON against JOHN SMITH. Dismissed agreed.

BENJAMIN CROOKER against GEORGE WRAY. abates by the Plaintiffs death.

JAMES NICHOLSON against JOHN CRAMOND. abates by the Plaintiffs death

GREIVE LOUDON & ROBB. Against JAMES AGNEW. Admin of ANDREW MCCAA. Dismissed. (2x)

JAMES & ROBERT DONALD and Company against RICHARD TEMPLEMAN. Dismissed. (2x)

THOMAS NEWTON SR. against CHARLES COOPER, CHAPMAN MASON, and JAMES BAKER. Dismissed.

DAVID PURCELL against SAMUEL INGLES admin of GEORGE SHEMELD abates by the Defendants death.

JOHN CALVERT against T.M. WILLIAMS abates by the Defendants death.

LYDIA CAWSON against WILLIAM CALVERT. Abates.*

FRANCES ROBERTSON against SMITH and TALBOT. Dismissed.

WILLIAM DONALDSON against ALEXANDER KEITH. Dismissed.

ROBERT GRAY & Company against WILLIAM AYLES & Company. Dismissed.

JAMES MOORE against JAMES NICHOLSON. abates by the Defendants death.

CHARLES SMITH against JOHN HOLLOWELL. Dismissed.

JAMES CARMICHAEL against JOHN FIELD and wife. Dismissed.

PAGE 229B

SAMUEL CALVERT against GEORGE CARLETON. abates by the Defendants death.

EDWARD MATHEWS against ANDREW STEVENSON and wife. Dismissed.

ANN MALLET against ALEXANDER CURRY. Dismissed.

DREW HALSTEAD against SAMUEL BRESSIE. abates by the Defendants death.

JOHN RODMAN against WILLIAM MINETREE. abates by the Plaintiffs death.

WILLIAM DONALDSON against JAMES MALCOM. Dismissed.

WILLIAM SWILVANT against WILLIAM JAQUES abates by the Plaintiffs death.

JAMES TANERS against CORNELIUS EMSON. Dismissed.

ARCHIBALD CAMPBELL against WILLIAM DEANE. Dismissed

JOHN CRAMOND against ARCHDEACON & INGRAM. Dismissed.

ELIZABETH STROUD against JOHN BAYNES. abates by the Plaintiffs death.

NEIL JAMIESON and Company against WILLIAM DEAN. Dismissed.
EDWARD MURFIELD against SAMUEL SONG. In Debt. Dismissed.
JOHN HARDY & WIFE against JOHN LOGAN and wife Dismissed.
JOHN WIGLY against WILLIAM BRYAN. Dismissed.
ALLAN FRAISER against ROBERT FERGUSON. Dismissed.

Ordered that attachment issue against WILLIAM GOODCHILD for refusing to serve as constable of this Borough.
Ordered that CHARLES COOPER be appointed Constable of this Borough for one year and that he be summoned to the next Court to qualify.

PAGE 230
The Court is adjourned to Court in Course, GEORGE ABYVON MAYOR, TESTE: ALEXANDER MOSELEY CLERK

NORFOLK BOROUGH
At a Hustings Court Held this 24TH day of April 1780
PRESENT: GEORGE ABYVON ESQUIRE MAYOR
GENTLEMAN ALDERMEN: PAUL LOYAL, CORNELIUS CALVERT, JAMES TAYLOR

JAMES NIMMO Gentleman this day qualified as an Attorney at Law in this Court.

MARY TRUSS executrix of JOSIAH TRUSS deceased Plaintiff
Against Re: In Case
RICHARD NESTER Defendant
This day came the parties by their Attorney's and by mutual consent submit all matters in difference between them to the determination of THOMAS BROWN and GEORGE KELLY who if necessary is to call in WILLIAM SKINNER as umpire and make their report to the Next Court.

WILLIAM GOODCHILD against JAMES DISON. In Chancery. The suit is continued
WILLIAM GOODCHILD against WILLIAM SALMOND* [SALMON]. In Case. Abates the Defendant is no inhabitant.
JAMES MOORE against WILLIAM HARDY. The suit is dismissed.

PAGE 230B
HENRY TALBOT by MARY TALBOT his guardian against JOHN HURT. The suit abates the Defendant no inhabitant.
RAMSAY, LOYALL and TANKARD against WILLIAM BASSET. The suit is dismissed.
JAMES BOUSHELL against WILLIS LANGLEY. This suit is dismissed. Agreed.

THOMAS NEWTON SR. against THOMAS NEWTON JR. and PREESON BOWDOIN executors of ROBERT TUCKER, deceased. In Case. The suit is continued.

CHARLES COOPER this day appeared agreeable to summon and refused to serve as constable of this Borough whereupon the Court ordered an attachment to issue against him for contempt.

Ordinary license is this day granted JAMES BOUSHELL on complying with the law. Paid in Full.

GEORGE WEBB and JOSEPH LANGLEY against JOHN BAYNES and NANCY ASHLEY. In Chancery. This suit is continued.

Ordered that the Clerk advertise that the Court of Hustings of the Borough of Norfolk will proceed to go through the docket the next Court being the 22nd day of May and dismiss such suits where the persons concerned fail to appear.

MAXIMILIAN CALVERT, THOMAS PRICE and ALEXANDER MOSELEY was this day returned commissioners of the tax for one year in this Borough.

Ordered that GOLDSBERRY HACKET be summoned to attend the next Court to qualify as Constable of this Borough for one year.

The Court is adjourned to Court in Course, GEORGE ABYVON MAYOR, TESTE: ALEXANDER MOSELEY CLERK

PAGE 231
NORFOLK BOROUGH
At a Hustings Court Held this 19TH day of June 1780
PRESENT: GEORGE ABYVON ESQUIRE MAYOR
GENTLEMAN ALDERMEN: PAUL LOYAL, CORNELIUS CALVERT, JAMES TAYLOR, THOMAS NEWTON JR.

HENRY TALBOT by MARY TALBOT his guardian against JOHN HURT. AN Imparlance.

CHARLES SAYER against PREESON BOWDOIN. This day came the Plaintiff by WILLIAM ROBINSON Gentleman his Attorney and the Defendant being solemnly called and not appearing. A conditional order is granted the Plaintiff against the said Defendant and GEORGE KELLY his bail.

SAMUEL CALVERT Plaintiff
Against Re: In Case
CORNELIUS CALVERT Defendant

This day came the parties by their Attorneys and by mutual consent submit all matters of difference between them to the determination of THOMAS RITSON and ALEXANDER MOSELEY who are to make their report to the next Court and their award to be the judgement of the Court and the same is ordered accordingly.

HENRY BRESSIE against GEORGE KERR. This day came the Plaintiff by WILLIAM ROBINSON Gentleman his Attorney and the Defendant being solemnly called and not appearing a conditional order is granted the Plaintiff against the Defendant and JOHN BOGGESS Deputy Sergeant

SARAH HUTCHINGS against JOHN JAMES. In Case. Imparlance.

JAMES WARREN against SAMUEL ROBERTS. The Defendant by his Attorney pleaded he did not assume issue joined and referred.

PAGE 231B
JOHN BATCH against TIMOTHY IVES. Abates by the Defendants death.
JOHN WARREN against JOHN POOL. Abates by the Defendant no inhabitant.
AMOS WEEKS against ZACH ROWLAND. Dismissed at Plaintiff's cost.

Ordered that attachment be issued against GOLDSBERY HACKET for contempt for refusing to serve as Constable of this Borough.

GEORGE WEBB & JOSEPH LANGLEY against JOHN BOYNES & NANCY ASHLEY. In Chancery. Continued.
THOMAS LANGLEY against JOHN & JOSEPH HUTCHINGS. Continued.
THOMAS LANGLEY against JAMES PASTEUR. Continued.
JOHN WILSON & Company against MARY ROTHERY executors of MATT ROTHERY. Continued.

JOHN CHESHIRE against RICHARD BROWN. Dismissed.
PETER BEVERLY WHITING against EDWARD DAWES Dismissed.
THOMAS NEWTON SR. assignee against WILLIAM SMITH Continued.

JOSEPH HUTCHINGS against RICHARD BROWN. Abates by the Plaintiffs death.

BARNABAS LORAIN against NATHANIEL WILSON. In Case. The Defendant being called and not appearing. Ordered that Judgement be made for the Plaintiff against the said Defendant and (blank space) his bail for what damages the Plaintiff have sustained to be as curtained at the next Court upon a writ of Inquiry.

JOHN WILLIAMSON against ROBERT SHEDDEN. The suit is dismissed.
PHILIP CARBERY against STEWART HOLT. The suit is dismissed.

PAGE 232
GEORGE WILSON and ARCHIBALD CAMPBELL admin of JOHN WILSON deceased against JAMES MARSDEN and JONATHAN ELBECK executors of ELDRED FISHER deceased dismissed.

ALEXANDER KIDD and AMOS WICKERSHAM admins of JOHN KIDD against THOMAS JOHN WALKER, JOHN VALLENCIER and STEPHEN TANKARD. In Debt. Dismissed.

ROBERT CARTWRIGHT against JAMES MARSDEN and JONATHAN ELBECK executors ELDRED FISHER deceased. The suit is continued.

JOHN SHEPHERD against JAMES MARSDEN and JONATHAN ELBECK executors of ELDRED FISHER deceased. The suit is continued.

JOHN PLUMER against JAMES MARSDEN & JONATHAN ELBECK executors of ELDRED FISHER deceased. The suit is dismissed.

FREDERICK BOUSH against JAMES MOORE. Dismissed. Agreed
THOMAS NEWTON SR. against THOMAS NEWTON JR. and PREESON BOWDOIN Defendants by their Attorney's pleaded did not assume issue joined.

PHILLIP* CARBERY against JOHN WILLIAMS. In Case. The Plaintiff not further prosecuting his suit the same is discontinued.

RAMSAY and TAYLOR against JAMES MARSDEN and JAMES MAXWELL admins of JAMES PATTERSON Deceased. In Debt. The suit is continued.

WILLIAM MILES against JAMES PATTERSON Admin as above continued.

THOMAS HOWARD and WILLIAM WHITE executors of JOSEPH WRIGHT against JOHN TATEM SR. and FRANCIS WRIGHT. In Debt. The suit abates by the death of the Defendants.

SAMUEL GRIFFINS executors against TIMOTHY IVES. In Debt. The suit is dismissed. Agreed.

PAGE 232B
JAMES MARSHALL against LOUISA INMAN. In Chancery. The Plaintiff further prosecuting his suit. The same is continued.

MALACHI MAUND against ALEXANDER BELL. In Trespass. The Plaintiff is not further prosecuting his suit. The same is continued.

MATTHEW PHRIPP and JOSEPH HUTCHINGS against MARY ROSS. Abates by the Defendants death.
MATTHEW PHRIPP and JOSEPH HUTCHINGS against MORTO BRYAN. Abates by the Defendants death.
MATTHEW PHRIPP and JOSEPH HUTCHINGS against JOHN BOGGUS. Abates by the Defendants death.

MATTHEW PHRIPP and JOSEPH HUTCHINGS against JOSEPH POPE, JACOB WILLIAMS, GEORGE J. FENWICK, PETER KATZ, GEORGE ATKINSON, JOHN BEISER and JUDITH DUNFORD, severally. These suits abate by the Plaintiff's death.

JAMES MARSDEN and JONATHAN ELBECK executors of ELDRED FISHER deceased. Against WILLIAM SISSON. In Debt. The suit abates by the Defendants death.

JAMES MARSDEN and JONATHAN ELBECK executors of ELDRED FISHER deceased. Against THOMAS WALKER. The suit continues.

THOMAS MORGAN against THOMAS EDWARDS JR. In Case. The Plaintiff not further prosecuting his suit the same is discontinued.

ARETAS AKERS & CO. against JAMES MARSDEN and JAMES MAXWELL admins of JAMES PATTERSON Deceased. The Plaintiff not further prosecuting his suit the same is discontinued.

WARNER LEWIS against ALEXANDER LOVE. In Case. The Plaintiff not further prosecuting his suit the same is discontinued.

PAGE 233
THOMAS GREEN against JOHN WILLIAMSON. In Case. The Plaintiff not further prosecuting his suit the same is discontinued.

PHILLIP HYNES against JOHN WILLIAMSON. In Case. The Plaintiff not further prosecuting his suit the same is discontinued.

SAMUEL PORTLOCK against ARCHIBALD CAMPBELL. Case Continued.

RICHARD BARRON against FRANCIS BRIGHT. In Case. The Plaintiff not further prosecuting his suit the same is discontinued.

JOHN LAWRENCE and Company against GEORGE WILSON & ARCHIBALD CAMPBELL admin of JOHN WILSON deceased. The Plaintiff not further prosecuting his suit the same is discontinued.

EDWARD ARCHER executor of EDWARD ARCHER deceased against PAUL LOYALL and LATTIMER HALSTEAD admin of JONATHAN DISON deceased. In Chancery. Continued.

JACOB SIKES against JOSIAH SIKES, JESSE SIKES, executors of JESSE SIKES. In Case. The Plaintiff not further prosecuting his suit the same is discontinued.

Ordinary License is granted to LEWIS MCLEAN on his complying with the law. Paid tax L40 & fee L6.
Ordinary License is granted to PRITCHARD JARVIS on his complying with the law. Paid tax L40 & fee L6.

WILLIAM GOODCHILD and CHARLES COOPER. This day qualified as Constables of the Borough for one year.

The Court is adjourned to Court in Course, GEORGE ABYVON MAYOR, TESTE: ALEXANDER MOSELEY CLERK

PAGE 233B
NORFOLK BOROUGH
At a Hustings Court Held this 24TH day of July 1780
PRESENT:
GENTLEMAN ALDERMEN: GEORGE ABYVON, PAUL LOYAL, JAMES TAYLOR, CORNELIUS CALVERT

JAMES WARREN against JOHN POOL. An Imparlance.
THOMAS LANGLEY against JOHN & JOSEPH HUTCHINGS. In Debt. The suit is dismissed at the Plaintiff's costs.
THOMAS LANGLEY against JAMES PASTEUR. In Debt. The suit is dismissed at the Plaintiff's costs.
THOMAS LANGLEY against JAMES WEBB. In Debt. The suit is dismissed at the Plaintiff's costs.

JOHN WILSON & CO. against MARY ROTHERY executor of MATTHEW ROTHERY deceased. In Case. The Suit is continued.
BARNABAS LORAIN against NATHANIEL WILSON. In Case. The Suit is continued.

ROBERT CARTWRIGHT against JAMES MARSDEN and JONATHAN ELBECK executors of ELDRED FISHER deceased. The suit is dismissed.
JOHN SHEPHERD against JAMES MARSDEN and JONATHAN ELBECK executors of ELDRED FISHER deceased. The suit is dismissed.
WILLIAM MILES against JAMES MARSDEN and JAMES MAXWELL admin of JAMES PATTERSON deceased. The suit is dismissed.
WILLIAM BELL against WILLIAM SIMPSON. In Debt. The Plaintiff not further prosecuting his suit the same is discontinued.
WILLIAM BELL against WILLIAM SIMPSON admin of FRANCES CLARK Deceased. The Plaintiff not further prosecuting his suit the same is discontinued.

PAGE 234
WILLIAM CARTWRIGHT against JAMES MARSDEN and JONATHAN ELBECK executors of ELDRED FISHER deceased. The Plaintiff not further prosecuting his suit the same is discontinued.

WILLIAM BELL against WILLIAM SIMPSON admin of FRANCES CLARK Deceased. The Plaintiff not further prosecuting his suit the same is discontinued.

JAMES WARREN Plaintiff
Against Re: In Case.
SAMUEL ROBERTS Defendant
This day came the parties by their Attorney's and thereupon came a Jury to wit: JOHN BAINES, JOHN VALLENTINE, JESSE EWELL, JOHN JAMES, CHARLES COOPER, WILLIAM SMITH, THOMAS PRICE, JOEL MOHUN, JOHN BRAMBLE, GEORGE WILSON, WILLIAM INGRAM, and

ARTHUR COOPER who being elected tried and sworn the truth to speak upon the issue joined withdrew and not returning any verdict on the premises, the cause is postponed until the next Court.

GEORGE WEBB and JOSEPH LANGLEY Plaintiff
Against Re: In Case
JOHN BAINES and NANCY ASHLEY Defendant
This cause was this day heard on the bill and the demurer thereto and the arguments of the Council on both sides in consideration where of it is ordered and decreed that the demurer of the Defendant be overruled and that they put in an answer the next Court so far as relates to the property of Negro NAN mentioned in the Plaintiff bill and it is further ordered that the cost be dived between the parties.

HENRY BRESSIE against GEORGE KERR. JOHN BOGGESS came into Court and undertook for the Defendant that in case he shall be cast in this suit he the said Defendant will pay the condemnation of the Court or render his body to prison in execution for the same or that the said BOGGESS will do it for him. A former order of this Court confirmed for the damages the Plaintiff has sustained to be ascertained the next Court in a WRIGHT* of inquiry.

PAGE 234B
SARAH HUTCHINGS against JOHN JAMES. In Case. The Defendant by his Attorney pleaded not guilty. Issue joined and referred until next Court.

HENRY TALBOT an infant by MARY TALBOT his guardian against JOHN HURT. In Case. The suit is continued.

JAMES MARSDEN and JONATHAN ELBECK executors of ELDRED FISHER deceased. Against THOMAS WALKER. In Case. The Plaintiff not further prosecuting his suit the same is discontinued.

SAMUEL PORTLOCK against ARCHIBALD CAMPBELL. Case is dismissed.

EDWARD ARCHER executors of JAMES ARCHER deceased against PAUL LOYALL and LATTIMER HALSTEAD admin of JONATHAN DISON deceased. In Case. The suit is dismissed.

JOSEPH MITCHELL against JOHN HARDY. In Case. The suit is dismissed.
HENRY GREEN against CELIA SOUTHERLAND admin of JOHN SUTHERLAND. In Case. The suit is dismissed.

SUSANNA MEAD executors of RICHARD RANDOLPH, GEORGE WALKER, and JOHN DIVER executors of DAVID MEADE deceased against THOMAS TALBOT. In Case. The suit is discontinued.

CHARLES COOPER against ANN BRAITHWAIT. In Case. The suit is discontinued.
JAMES MARSDEN and JONATHAN ELBECK executors of ELDRED FISHER deceased. Against JOHN SMITH and others. In Case. The suit is dismissed

RICHARD WEIS against JAMES MARSDEN. In Case. The suit is discontinued.
FREDERICK BOUSH against JAMES MOORE. In Case. The suit is discontinued.

MALACHI MAUND against ALEXANDER BELL. In Debt. Dismissed.
JAMES GRAYHAM against JOHN CRAMOND. In Case. The suit is discontinued. (2x)

PAGE 235
NATHANIEL BURGESS against WILLIAMSON & SNODGRASS. In Debt. Dismissed.
JAMES MURDOUGH against LOGAN GILMOUR & COMPANY. In Case. Discontinued.
JAMES LEITCH against THOMAS BURKE. In Case. The suit is discontinued.

MARY ROSS against WILLIAM PENN. In Debt. Dismissed.
RICHARD COLLINS & wife against JAMES CARMICHAEL. Dismissed.
ALEXANDER HODGE and wife against JAMES CARMICHAEL. Dismissed.

The Court is adjourned to Court in Course, GEORGE ABYVON SR. ALDERMAN, TESTE: ALEXANDER MOSELEY CLERK

NORFOLK BOROUGH
At a Hustings Court Held this 21st^H day of August 1780
PRESENT: THOMAS NEWTON JR. ESQUIRE MAYOR
GENTLEMAN ALDERMEN: GEORGE ABYVON, JAMES TAYLOR, CORNELIUS CALVERT

PAUL CLIPPER against JESSE EWELL. The suit is dismissed agreed.
AGATHY GRIMES against BENJAMIN HICKS. The suit abates by the Defendants being no inhabitants.

JOHN WILSON and Company against MARY ROTHERY Executrix of MATTHEW ROTHERY Deceased. The suit is discontinued.
THOMAS NEWTON & COMPANY against WILLIAM SMITH. In Debt. The suit is continued.
BARNABAS LORAIN against NATHANIEL WILSON. In Case. Continued.

PAGE 235B
WILLIAM SKINKER against LOYALL, NEWTON and others. The suit is continued.
CHRISTOPHER CALVERT against PAUL LOYALL. In Debt. Continued.

RAMSAY and TAYLOR against JAMES MARSDEN and JAMES MAXWELL admin of JAMES PATTERSON deceased. In Case. The suit is continued.

RICHARD COLLINS against JAMES CARMICHAEL. The suit is dismissed.
CORNELIUS CALVERT and wife against JOHN SMITH. In Debt. The suit is dismissed (listed 3x)

CHRISTOPHER WILSON against THOMAS TAYLOR abates by the Defendants death.
ALEXANDER LOVE and others against BARBER and HOFFMIRE. In Case. Discontinued.

SARAH HUTCHINGS Plaintiff
Against Re: In Case.
JOHN JAMES Defendant
This day came the parties by their Attorney's and thereupon came also a Jury to wit: WILLIAM INGRAM, JAMES LEITCH, JOSEPH LANGLEY, LEMUEL ROBERTS, GOLDSBERY HACKET, GEORGE WILSON, MAXIMILIAN MARLEY, JOEL MOHUN, THOMAS CALVERT, JOHN BRAMBLE, JOHN BOUSHELL and JOHN WOODSIDE who being elected tried and sworn the truth to speak upon the issue joined upon their oath do say that the Defendant did assume in manner and form as the Plaintiff against him has declared and do assess the Plaintiff damages by occasion of the non-performance of that assumption to 1500 pounds and the costs. Therefore, it is considered that the Plaintiff recover against the said Defendant her damages aforesaid in form aforesaid assessed and her costs by her about her suit in this behalf expended and the said Defendant in mercy.

Ordinary License is granted JOSHUA PEEDS on his complying with the law. Paid tax L49 & Fee L6

Page 236
WILLIAM GOODCHILD against JAMES DISON. In Chancery. Time to consider bill
CHARLES SAYER against PREESON BOWDOIN. In Case. The suit is continued.
HENRY BRESSIE against GEORGE KERR. The suit is continued.
HENRY TALBOT infant by MARY TALBOT his guardian against JOHN HURT. In Case. The suit is discontinued.

JOHN WARREN against JOHN POOL. In Trespass. The Defendant by his Attorney pleaded not guilty. Issue joined and referred.

JOHN SMITH against THOMAS TALBOT. In Chancery. Time to consider bill.
THOMAS BRESSIE admin of JAMES IVY against WILLIAM SMITH. In Case. Discontinued.
PHILLIP CARBERY against STAFFORD LIGHBURNE. In Case. Discontinued

WARNER LEWIS against SAMUEL ALLYNE. In Case. The suit is Discontinued.
WILLIAM SMITH against JAMES HALDANE. In Debt. The suit is Discontinued.
NICHOLAS POOLE against JAMES HALDANE. In Debt. The suit is Discontinued.

JAMES SOUTHERLAND against BAILEY WARREN. In Case. Discontinued.
HENRY BRESSIE against BRISTOL BROWN. In Case. Discontinued
JOSEPH MITCHELL against WILLIAM NICHOLSON SR. In Case. Discontinued

STAFFORD LYBURN against PHILIP CARBERY. In Trespass. Discontinued.
CHARLES CONNER against EDWARD ARCHER. In Case. Discontinued
YOUNG SMITH & Company against WILLIAM IVY. In Case. Discontinued
HENRY WHITEHURST against MAXIMILIAN CALVERT. In Case. Discontinued

PAGE 236B
This day came the Plaintiff by WILLIAM ROBINSON Gentleman his Attorney and the Defendant being solemnly called and not appearing. Judgement is awarded against said Defendant and CHARLES COOPER B.C. his bail. Therefore, it is considered that the Plaintiff recover against the said Defendant and CHARLES COOPER B.C. his bail aforesaid his debt amounting to 30 pounds with interest thereon after the rate of 5% per annum to be computed from the 20 day of February 1773 to the time of payment and the costs.

HERCULES ROSS against RICHARD TALBOT. In Debt. The suit is Discontinued.
ROE COWPER against CHARLES COOPER. The suit is Discontinued.

JAMES WARREN Plaintiff against LEMUEL ROBERTS Defendant. The Jury being called and failing to appear. Ordered they be discharged, and that the Sergeant summon another jury.

JAMES WARREN Plaintiff
Against Re: In Case
LEMUEL ROBERTS Defendant
This day came the parties by their Attorney's and thereupon came a Jury to wit: JOHN BAINES, JOHN VALLENTINE, JESSE EWELL, JOHN JAMES, CHARLES COOPER, WILLIAM SMITH, THOMAS PRICE, JOEL MOHUN, JOHN BRAMBLE, GEORGE WILSON, WILLIAM INGRAM, and ARTHUR COOPER who being elected tried and sworn the truth to speak upon the issue joined upon their oath do say that the Defendant did assume in manner and form as the Plaintiff against him has declared and do assess the Plaintiff damages by the occasion of the non-performance of that assumption to 150 pounds besides his costs.
PAGE 237
Therefore, it is considered that the Plaintiff recover against the said Defendant his damages aforesaid in form aforesaid assessed and his costs by him in this behalf expended and the said Defendant in mercy.

ALEXANDER BELL against MALACHI MAUND. In Case. The suit is discontinued.

MALACHI MAUND against SAMUEL CALVERT. The suit is discontinued.

JAMES YOUNG against ANDREW MCCAA'S Admin. The suit is discontinued.

THOMAS GILCHRIST & Company against BARNABAS CARNEYS executors. In Case. The suit is discontinued.

JAMES HALDANE against JACKSON & JUGER IVY. The suit is discontinued.

GEORGE TANKARD against WILLIAM AYLES. In Debt. Abates by the Defendants death.

WILLIAM BLACK against WILLIAM MEREDITH. In Case. Discontinued.

EDWARD MOSELEY, BETTY MOSELEY and LEMUEL THOROWGOOD executors of WILLIAM MOSELEY

Against Re: On a SCIRE FACIAS

ALEXANDER BELL Defendant

This day came the Plaintiffs by their Attorney WILLIAM ROBINSON Gentleman and the Defendant being solemnly called and not appearing. The Former Judgement of this Court is confirmed with costs.

MATTHEW PHRIPP and JOSEPH HUTCHINGS, Church warden of E.R. Parish against ABRAHAM WORMINGTON. In Debt. Abates by the death of the Plaintiff.

JAMES LEITCH against JAMES HALDANE. In Case. Discontinued

SAMUEL TUCKER against WILLIAM MCCORMICK and others. In Case. Discontinued

CHARLES CONNER against JOHN BROWN Writ of inquiry is awarded

COOPER and ADKINS against JOHN MORRIS. In Case. Discontinued

PAGE 237B

Order is granted MAXIMILIAN MARLEY against LEMUEL ROBERTS for 50 pounds of tobacco for 2 days attendance at this Court in the suit of JAMES WARREN against him.

Order is granted ANTHONY CONNER against LEMUEL ROBERTS for 50 pounds of tobacco for 2 days attendance at this Court in the suit of JAMES WARREN against him.

Order is granted THOMAS CARTER against LEMUEL ROBERTS for 50 pounds of tobacco for 2 days attendance at this Court in the suit of JAMES WARREN against him.

The Court is adjourned to Court in Course, THOMAS NEWTON JR. ESQUIRE MAYOR

NORFOLK BOROUGH

At a Hustings Court Held this 25th day of September 1780

PRESENT: THOMAS NEWTON JR. ESQUIRE MAYOR

GENTLEMAN ALDERMEN: GEORGE ABYVON, CORNELIUS CALVERT, JAMES TAYLOR, BASSETT MOSELEY

THOMAS NEWTON and Co. against WILLIAM SMITH G.B. The suit is continued.

WILLIAM SKINKER against LOYALL, NEWTON and others. In Case. The suit is continued.

RAMSAY and TAYLOR Plaintiff

Against Re: In case

JAMES MARSDEN and JAMES MAXWELL admin of JAMES PATTERSON deceased Defendant

This day came as well the Plaintiffs by his Attorney as the Defendants in their proper person and the said Defendants say that they cannot gainsay the Plaintiffs action nor but that their testator did assume in manner and form as the Plaintiff against them have declared.

PAGE 238

Therefore, it is considered that the Plaintiffs recover against the said Defendants 5 pounds 6 shillings and 11 pence and their costs by them about their suit in this behalf expended. When assets after paying debts of greater dignity and the Defendants own claims of equal dignity against the estate of the said testator to be levied of the goods and chattels which were of the said JAMES at the time of his death that shall hereafter come to the hands of the said JAMES and JAMES to be administered and the said Defendants in mercy.

WILLIAM STROUD against PHILLIP CARBERY. The suit is discontinued.

MALACHI MAUND against SAMUEL CALVERT. Dismissed.

WILLIAM NICHOLSON against CHARLES RUDDER. In Debt. Discontinued.

EDWARD and ROE COOPERS executors of PHILLIP COOPER deceased against CHAPMAN MASON In Case. The suit is Discontinued.

GEORGE PARKER against CHAPMAN MASON & others. In Debt. Discontinued.

THOMAS KING against MICHAEL SIMMONS. Discontinued.

ISAAC LUKE against BRYANT CROSBIE. In Case. The suit is discontinued.

JAMES MARSDEN and Company against JAMES THOMPSON. In case. Continued.

JOHN MCLACHLAN executors against JOSEPH MITCHELL. In Case. Discontinued.

CONSTANTINE RIDDICK against ANDREW STEVENSON. The suit is Discontinued.

CHRISTOPHER CALVERT against SAMUEL FARMER. Abates by the Defendants death.

AMOS TAYLOR against EDWARD CONNELLY. In Case. The suit is Discontinued.
JOHN MCDOUGALL against JAMES HALDANE. Discontinued.
WILLIAM SIMPSON against WILLS COWPER. The suit is discontinued.
HAMBLITON* and BLAINE against WILLIAM MAJOR. Trover*. The suit is discontinued
GEORGE HOBBS against JOHN MARTIN. Trespass Continued.

PAGE 238B
JOHN PARK and Company against HECTOR MCCALLISTER and Co. The suit is Dismissed.

MARY RUSSELL against JOHN MILLER & Co. The suit is Discontinued.
SAMUEL CALVERT against GEORGE CARLTON exe. In Case. Discontinued.
RICHARD CRATCH against WILLIAM NORTH In Case. Discontinued

ROBERT TUCKER exe. against WILLIAM TUCKERS exe. In Case. The suit is Discontinued
BARNABAS LORAINE against NATHANIEL WILSON. In Case. The suit is Discontinued
CHARLES CONNER against EDWARD ARCHER. In Case. The suit is Continued

WILLIAM GOODCHILD against JAMES DYSON. In Chancery. The demurer this day filed and until for arguing the Next Court.

CHARLES SAYER against PREESON BOWDOIN. The suit is dismissed. Agreed.
HENRY BRESSIE against GEORGE KERR. The suit is continued.
SAMUEL CALVERT against CORNELIUS CALVERT. In Case.

ABSENT MR. MAYOR & PRESENT: PAUL LOYALL Gentleman

THOMAS NEWTON SR. Plaintiff
Against Re: In Case
THOMAS NEWTON JR. and PREESON BOWDOIN executors of ROBERT TUCKER deceased Defendant
This day came the parties by their Attorney's and there upon came also a Jury to wit: DANIEL HUTCHINGS, JAMES MARSDEN, SAMUEL CALVERT, JOHN WARREN, THOMAS CALVERT, THOMAS PRICE, PAUL WADLINGTON, JOHN COOKE, ROBERT BARRON, JOHN HOLLOWELL, JAMES DYSON, and JAMES HUNTER who being elected tried and sworn the truth to speak upon the issue joined upon their oath do say that the Defendant's testator did assume in manner and form as the Plaintiff against them has declared

PAGE 239
And do assess the Plaintiff damages by occasion of the non-performance of that assumption to 1260 pounds 10 shillings. Therefore, it is considered that the Plaintiff recover against the said Defendant his damages aforesaid in form aforesaid assessed with interest here on after the rate of 5% per annum to be computed from this day to the time of payment and his costs by him about his suit in this behalf expended. To be levied of the Goods and Chattels of the said testator ROBERT TUCKER if so, much the said THOMAS NEWTON JR. and PREESON BOWDOIN have in their hands to be administered and if they have it not then the costs are to be levied of their proper goods and chattels and the said Defendant in mercy.

CHRISTOPHER CALVERT against PAUL LOYALL. In Debt. Discontinued.
PAUL LOYALL against HOG and ROWLAND. In Debt. The suit is continued.
PAUL LOYALL against NATHANIEL YOUNG. In Debt. Abates by the Defendants death.
JOHN SMITH against THOMAS TALBOT exe. The suit is continued.
JOHN WARREN against WILLIAM GOODCHILD. In Case. Discontinued.
MALBONE SHELTON against WILLIAM MARLEY. The suit is continued.
MAXIMILIAN CALVERT against SAMUEL ROBERTS. Abates by the Defendants death
SAMUEL CALVERT against JOHN HOLLOWELL. In Case. An Imparlance.
JOHN WARREN against JOHN POOL. In Case. The suit is discontinued.

PRESENT: MR. MAYOR

SAMUEL CALVERT against JOHN HOLLOWELL. In Case. Imparlance.
SAMUEL CALVERT against JOHN WAINWRIGHT. In Case. Imparlance.
JOHN BAYNE against HENRY GREEN. An Imparlance.

LEMUEL CORNICK against PAUL WADLINGTON*. Trespass. The Defendant by his Attorney pleaded not guilty issue joined and referred.

GEORGE WEBB and JOSEPH LANGLEY Plaintiff
Against Re: In Chancery
JOHN BAYNES and NANCY ASHLEY Defendants
Ordered that WILLIAM GREY, JOHN BOGGESS and JOHN WARREN do sell
PAGE 239B
Negro NAN mentioned in the complaint bill and whom by former order of this Court. The Defendants were to make answer so far as related to her and that JOHN BAYNES the Defendant who is now in possession of said Negro NAN do deliver him up to the said Commissioners to make sale of and that they make report to the Next Court in order for a final decree.

The Court is adjourned to Court in Course. THOMAS NEWTON JR. ESQUIRE MAYOR

NORFOLK BOROUGH
At a Hustings Court Held this 25th day of February 1782*
PRESENT: PAUL LOYALL ESQUIRE MAYOR
GENTLEMAN ALDERMEN: JAMES TAYLOR, CORNELIUS CALVERT, THOMAS NEWTON JR.

WILLIS WILSON against ROBERT BURLEY admin of JAMES HALSTEAD deceased Defendant.
The Defendant by his Attorney pleaded he did not assume issue joined and referred.

THOMAS NASH against ROBERT BURLEY admin of JAMES HALSTEAD deceased. Imparlance.
JAMES GRYMES against ROBERT BURLEY admin of JAMES HALSTEAD deceased. Imparlance.

ANN MCLEAN against JAMES GURTON. In Case. Dismissed. Agreed.

WILLIAM ROBINSON executor of WALTER LYON deceased against GEORGE OLDNER. In Case. Conditional order against Defendant.

JAMES BRADLEY against ROBERT BURLEY admin of JAMES HALSTEAD deceased. An Imparlance.
WILLIAM BYRD against WILLIAM MOSELEY abates. The Defendant is no inhabitant.
JOHN WOOLF* against PHILLIP RITTER. In Case. Dismissed Agreed.

PAGE 240
THOMAS HERBERT against PAUL WADLINGTON TROVER. Imparlance.

THOMAS NASH JR. against REUBEN HERBERT. In Case. ANDREW MARTIN this day came into Court and undertook for the Defendant that in case he shall be cast in this suit he the said Defendant will pay the condemnation of the Court or render his body to prison in execution for the same or that the said MARTIN will pay the said condemnation or render the body of the Defendant as aforesaid. Whereupon the Defendant by his Attorney pray and has leave to IMPARLE here until the next Court.

LEMUEL CORNICK against PAUL WADLINGTON. Trespass. Continued.
GEORGE WEBB and JOSEPH LANGLEY against JOHN BAYNES and NANCY ASHLEY. In Chancery.
The Commissioners appointed by a declaration order of this Court made their report in these words. In obedience to the written order, we have this day sold the with in mentioned NAN to MR. JOHN BAINES for the sum of 550 pounds. Witness our hands this 19th day of October 1780. WILLIAM GREY, JOHN BOGGESS, As ordered that the money arising from the sale of Negro NAN above mentioned be equally distributed between the Complainants and Defendants in the said bill mentioned by the Sergeant of this Borough.

Ordinary License is granted WILLIAM GOODCHILD and WILLIAM SMITH on their complying with the law.

CHARLES CONNER against EDWARD ARCHER. Case Continued.
JAMES MARSDEN & Co. against JAMES THOMPSON. In Case. Abates by the death of the Defendant.
GEORGE KELLY against JOHN MARTIN. Trespass Dismissed.
WILLIAM GOODCHILD against JAMES DYSON. Chancery Dismissed.
HENRY BRESSIE against GEORGE KERR. In Case. The suit abates by the Plaintiff's death

PAGE 240B
JOHN SMITH against THOMAS TALBOT exe. In Chancery. Further time to consider
MALBONE SHELTON against WILLIAM MARLEY. In Case. The suit is Continued.

SAMUEL CALVERT against JOHN HOLLOWELL. In Case. The Defendant by his Attorney pleaded, he did not assume issue joined and referred.

SAMUEL CALVERT against JOHN HOLLOWELL. The suit is discontinued.

SAMUEL CALVERT against GEORGE WAINWRIGHT. The Defendant by his Attorney pleaded he did not assume issue joined and referred.

JOHN BAINES against HENRY GREEN. In Case. The Defendant by his Attorney pleaded he did not assume issue joined and referred.

GEORGE ABYVON against JAMES TATE. In Case. Abates by the Plaintiffs death.

JOHN WARREN against WILLIAM GOODCHILD. Trespass. The Defendant by his Attorney pleaded not guilty issue joined and referred.

JOHN WARREN against JOHN POOLE. Trespass. Dismissed Agreed.
JOHN WILLIAMSON against REUBEN HERBERT. The suit abates by the Plaintiff's death. (2X)
WILLIAM GREY against RICHARD TALBOT. In Case. An Imparlance.
THOMAS HOLT against DAVID PEEPLES. In Case. The suit is dismissed.
MAXIMILIAN CALVERT against LEMUEL ROBERTS. In Case. Abates by the Plaintiffs death.
HUGH GIBSON against HENRY REEVES. In Case. Discontinued.
CHRISTOPHER WRIGHT against THOMAS TIMSON* In Case. Dismissed at the Defendants Costs.

PAGE 241
SUSANNA BOGGESS against WILLIAM BYRD. In Case. The suit is dismissed. Agreed.

MARY FERBIE against MATTHEW MAUND. The suit is dismissed. Agreed.

The Court is adjourned until tomorrow 9 o'clock, PAUL LOYALL MAYOR

NORFOLK BOROUGH
At a Hustings Court Held this 26th day of February 1782*
PRESENT: PAUL LOYALL ESQUIRE MAYOR
GENTLEMAN ALDERMEN: JAMES TAYLOR, THOMAS NEWTON JR. CORNELIUS CALVERT, BASSET MOSELEY

RALPH PICKET against ALEXANDER BELL. In Case. ANDREW MARTIN this day came into Court and undertook for the Defendant that in case he shall be cast in this suit he the said Defendant will pay the condemnation of the Court or render his body to prison in execution for the same or that the said ANDREW MARTIN will pay the said condemnation or render the body of the Defendant as aforesaid. Whereupon the Defendant by his Attorney pray and has leave to IMPARLE here until the next Court.

THOMAS NEWTON JR. Gentleman This day produced a Commission from his Excellency the Governor of this State, appoint him COLONEL of the militia of this Borough and having taken the oath of fidelity to the State and the oath of COLONEL of this Borough enters on the execution of his office.

PAGE 241B
GEORGE KELLY Gentleman is this day appointed Captain of the Militia of this Borough
JONATHAN CALVERT Gentleman is this day appointed first lieutenant of the militia of this Borough.
GEORGE LOYALL Gentleman is this day appointed second lieutenant of the militia of this Borough.
CARY HANSFORD Gentleman is this day appointed ENSIGN of the militia of this Borough.

The Court is adjourned to Court in Course, PAUL LOYALL MAYOR, TESTE: ALEXANDER MOSELEY CLERK

NORFOLK BOROUGH
At a Hustings Court Held this 25th day of March 1782*
PRESENT: PAUL LOYALL ESQUIRE MAYOR
GENTLEMAN ALDERMEN: CORNELIUS CALVERT, GEORGE KELLY, THOMAS NEWTON JR.

Ordinary License is granted ANN MCLEAN on her complying with the law.
Ordinary License is granted MARY BLEWS on her complying with the law.

THOMAS NASH JR. against ROBERT BURLEY administrator of JAMES HALSTEAD deceased. In Case. The Defendant being called and not appearing a Conditional order is granted the Plaintiff against the said Defendant.

PAGE 242
WILLIS WILSON against ALEXANDER BELL. A Conditional order is granted the Plaintiff against the said Defendant and THOMAS (BLANK) his bail.
WILLIAM BYRD against WILLIAM MOSELEY Detinue an Imparlance
Ordinary License is granted RICHARD JARVIS on his complying with the law.

MARY TRUSS executor of JOSIAH TRUSS deceased against GEORGE THOMAS HALL Imparlance.

MARY TRUSS executor of JOSIAH TRUSS deceased against WILLIAM SKINNER. In Case. Conditional order is granted the Plaintiff against the said Defendant and GEORGE THOMAS HALL his bail

MAXIMILIAN CALVERT exe against LEMUEL ROBERTS In Case. Imparlance.
JOHN SMITH against THOMAS TALBOTS exe. Chancery Continued

MALBONE SHELTON against WILLIAM MARLEY Dismissed.
THOMAS HOLT against DAVID PEOPLES. Case. Dismissed.
CHRISTOPHER WRIGHT against THOMAS TIMSON. Dismissed.
JAMES NIMMO against JAMES WARREN. Dismissed.

WILLIAM ROBERTON EXE of WALTER LYON Deceased against GEORGE OLDNER. The Defendant by his Attorney pleaded he did not assume issue joined and referred.

JOSIAH WILSON against ROBERT BURLEY administrator of JAMES HALSTEAD deceased. The Defendant by his Attorney pleaded not guilty issue joined and referred.

THOMAS NASH against ROBERT BURLEY administrator of JAMES HALSTEAD deceased. The Defendant by his Attorney pleaded not guilty issue joined and referred.

CHARLES GRYMES against ROBERT BURLEY administrator of JAMES HALSTEAD deceased. The Defendant by his Attorney pleaded not guilty issue joined and referred.

PAGE 242B
JAMES BRADLEY against ROBERT BURLEY admin of JAMES HALSTEAD deceased. The Defendant by his Attorney pleaded not guilty. Issue joined and referred.

THOMAS HERBERT JR. against PAUL WADLINGTON. The Defendant by his Attorney pleaded not guilty issue joined and referred.

RALPH PICKET against ALEXANDER BELL. The Defendant by his Attorney pleaded not guilty issue joined and referred.

WILLIS WILSON against ROBERT BURLEY admin of JAMES HALSTEAD. The suit is continued.

JOHN WARREN against WILLIAM GOODCHILD. The Defendant by his Attorney pleaded not guilty issue joined and referred.

For every quart of punch made with half pint of spirit and half sugar	3/
For every quart of grog	2/
For every quart of toddy	2/6
For every quart of wine	6/
Diet for each mean	1/6
Lodging per night	1
Oats and Corn per the gallon and hay & fodder for the pound	3

The Court is adjourned to Court in Course, PAUL LOYALL MAYOR, TESTE: ALEXANDER MOSELEY CLERK

PAGE 243
NORFOLK BOROUGH
At a Hustings Court Held this 22ND day of April 1782
PRESENT: PAUL LOYALL ESQUIRE MAYOR
GENTLEMAN ALDERMEN: CHARLES THOMAS, THOMAS NEWTON JR. JAMES TAYLOR, GEORGE KELLY, CORNELIUS CALVERT

SAMUEL CALVERT against GEORGE WAINWRIGHT. Dismissed. Agreed.
CHARLES CONNER against EDWARD ARCHER. The Defendant by his Attorney pleaded he did not assume, Issue joined and referred.
JAMES MARSDEN & CO. against JAMES THOMPSON. In Case. Discontinued.

LEMUEL CORNICK Plaintiff
Against Re: In Trespass
PAUL WADLINGTON Defendant
This day came the parties by their Attorney's and thereupon came also a Jury to wit: THOMAS MORRIS, JOHN COLLEY, GOLDSBERY HACKET, CHARLES BOUSHNELL, WILLIAM LECATT, THOMAS DRURY, ARTHUR COOPER, JOHN JAMES, WILLIAM BYRD, GEORGE WAINWRIGHT, HENRY GREEN and JOHN WOODSIDES who being elected tried and sworn the truth to speak upon the issue joined upon their oaths do say that the Defendant is guilty of Trespass in the declaration mentioned in manner and form as the Plaintiff have declared and do assess the Plaintiffs damages by reason thereof to 6 shillings besides 6 shillings for his costs. Therefore, it is considered that the Plaintiff recover against the said Defendant his damages aforesaid in form aforesaid assessed and 6 shillings for his costs by him about his suit in this behalf expended and the said Defendant in mercy.

SAMUEL CALVERT against JOHN HOLLOWELL. In Case. The suit is continued.
SAMUEL CALVERT against CORNELIUS CALVERT. In Case. Special Imparlance.

PAGE 243B
JOHN BAYNE against HENRY GREEN. In Case. Continued.
WILLIAM GRAY against RICHARD TALBOT. An Imparlance.

WILLIS WILSON Plaintiff
Against Re: In Case
ROBERT BURLEY admin of JAMES HALSTEAD Deceased Defendant
This day came the parties by their Attorney's and there upon came also a Jury to wit: JOEL MOHUN, JOHN BAINES, WILLIAM GOODCHILD, JOHN CALVERT, JAMES JOLLY, SAMUEL BACON, JOHN SINGLETON, JAMES MELLOW, WILLIAM COOPER, PAUL WADLINGTON, RALPH PICKET and PAUL PROBY who being elected tried and sworn the truth to speak upon the issue joined upon their oaths do say that the Defendants intestate did assume in manner and form as the Plaintiff against him has declared and do assess the Plaintiffs damages by the occasion of the non-performance of that assumption to 200 pounds. Therefore, it is considered that the Plaintiff recover against the said Defendant his damages aforesaid in form aforesaid assessed and his costs by him about his suit in this behalf expended and the said Defendant in mercy.

JOSIAH WILSON Plaintiff
Against Re: In Case
ROBERT BURLEY admin of JAMES HALSTEAD deceased Defendant
This day came the parties by their Attorney's and there upon came also a Jury to wit: JOHN COLLEY, GOLDSBERY HACKET, CHARLES BOUSHNEL, WILLIAM LECATT, THOMAS DUNN, ARTHUR COOPER, JOHN JAMES, WILLIAM BYRD, GEORGE WAINWRIGHT, HENRY GREEN and JOHN WOODSIDE who being elected tried and sworn the truth to speak upon the issue joined upon their oaths do say that the Defendants intestate did assume in manner and form as the Plaintiff against him has declared and do assess the Plaintiffs damages by the occasion of the non-performance of that assumption to 110 pounds. Therefore, it is considered that the Plaintiff recover against the said Defendant his damages aforesaid in form aforesaid assessed and his costs by him about his suit in this behalf expended and the said Defendant in mercy.

PAGE 244

CHARLES CONNER Plaintiff
Against Re: In Case
JOHN BROWN Defendant
This day came the parties by their Attorney's and thereupon came also a Jury to wit: THOMAS MORRIS, JOHN COLLEY, GOLDSBERY HACKET, CHARLES BOUSHNELL, WILLIAM LECATT, THOMAS DRURY, ARTHUR COOPER, JOHN JAMES, WILLIAM BYRD, GEORGE WAINWRIGHT, HENRY GREEN and JOHN WOODSIDES who being elected tried and sworn the truth to speak upon the issue joined upon their oaths do say that the Defendant did assume in manner and form as the Plaintiff against him has declared and do assess the Plaintiffs damages by the occasion of the non-performance of that assumption to 21 pounds 15 shillings. Therefore, it is considered that the Plaintiff recover against the said Defendant his damages aforesaid in form aforesaid assessed and his costs by him about his suit in this behalf expended and the said Defendant in mercy.

JOHN WARREN Plaintiff
Against Re: In Case
WILLIAM GOODCHILD Defendant
This day came the parties by their Attorney's and thereupon came also a Jury to wit: THOMAS MORRIS, JOHN COLLEY, GOLDSBERY HACKET, CHARLES BOUSHNELL, WILLIAM LECATT, THOMAS DRURY, ARTHUR COOPER, JOHN JAMES, WILLIAM BYRD, GEORGE WAINWRIGHT, HENRY GREEN and JOHN WOODSIDES who being elected tried and sworn the truth to speak upon the issue joined upon their oaths do say that the Defendant did not assume as I pleading, they have alleged. Therefore, it is considered that the Plaintiff take nothing by his bill but for his false claims be in mercy. And the Defendant go hence without day and recover against the Plaintiff his costs by him about his Defense in this behalf expended.

JOSIAH TRUSS executrix against WILLIAM SKINNER. Issue joined and referred to next Court.
WILLIAM RUSSELL against WILLIAM POWEL. Dismissed. Agreed.

THOMAS NASH Plaintiff
Against Re: In Case
ROBERT BURLEY admin of JAMES HALSTEAD Deceased Defendant
This day came the parties by their Attorney's and thereupon came also a Jury to wit: THOMAS MORRIS, JOHN COLLEY, GOLDSBERY HACKET, CHARLES BOUSHNELL, WILLIAM LECATT, THOMAS DRURY, ARTHUR COOPER, JOHN JAMES, WILLIAM BYRD, GEORGE WAINWRIGHT, HENRY GREEN and JOHN WOODSIDES who being elected tried and sworn the truth to speak upon the issue joined upon their oaths do say that the Defendants intestate did assume in manner and form as the Plaintiff

PAGE 244B

against him has declared and do assess the Plaintiffs damages by the occasion of the non-performance of that assumption to 147 pounds 18 shillings and 8 pence.
Therefore, it is considered that the Plaintiff recover against the said Defendant his damages aforesaid in form aforesaid assessed and his costs by him about his suit in this behalf expended. To be levied of the Goods and Chattels of the said intestate if so, much the said Defendant has in his hands to be administered and if he has it not then the costs are to be levied of his proper goods and chattels and the said Defendant in mercy.

CHARLES GRIMES Plaintiff
Against Re: In Case.
ROBERT BURLEY admin of JAMES HALSTEAD Deceased Defendant
This day came the parties by their Attorney's and there upon came also a Jury to wit: JOEL MOHUN, JOHN BAINES, WILLIAM GOODCHILD, JOHN CALVERT, JAMES JOLLY, SAMUEL BACON, LABON GOFFIGON, JOHN SINGLETON, WILLIAM COOPER, PAUL WADLINGTON, PAUL PROBY, RALPH PICKET and POWELL REINS who being elected tried and sworn the truth to speak upon the issue joined upon their oaths do say that the Defendants intestate did assume in manner and form as the Plaintiff against him has declared and do assess the Plaintiffs damages by the occasion of the non-performance of that assumption to 150 pounds. Therefore, it is considered that the Plaintiff recover against the said Defendant his damages aforesaid in form aforesaid assessed and his costs by him about his suit in this behalf expended. To be levied of the Goods and Chattels of the said intestate if so, much the said Defendant has in his hands to be administered and if he has it not then the costs are to be levied of his proper goods and chattels and the said Defendant in mercy.

WALTER LYON executors against GEORGE OLDNER. Issue joined and referred.
THOMAS HERBERT JR. against PAUL WADLINGTON. Dismissed. Agreed.

Order is granted ALEXANDER BELL, LEMUEL WILSON, MARY MILLER, and SMITH HALSTEAD against ROBERT BURLEY admin of JAMES HALSTEAD deceased for one days Attendance each as witnesses in the suit of WILSON against him.

PAGE 245

Order is granted ENOCH ETHEREDGE and THOMAS MCCOY against ROBERT BURLEY admin of JAMES HALSTEAD deceased for 3 days attendance each in the suit of NASH against him.

The Court is adjourned to Court in Course, PAUL LOYALL MAYOR, TESTE: ALEXANDER MOSELEY CLERK

NORFOLK BOROUGH

At a Hustings Court Held this 22ND day of July 1782
PRESENT: JAMES TAYLOR ESQUIRE MAYOR
GENTLEMAN ALDERMEN: CORNELIUS CALVERT, GEORGE KELLY, CARY H. HANSFORD

JOHN NASH against CHARLES RUDDER. An Imparlance
MARY THRUSTON against NICHOLAS GAUTIER. An Imparlance
LEWIS GUION against THOMAS HERBERT JR. An Imparlance
SAMUEL CALVERT against JAMES MARSDEN heir at law. In Chancery Continued

ANDREW STEWART against THOMAS HERBERT JR. An Imparlance
WILLIAM BYRD against JAMES DENBY continued

CHRISTOPHER WHITEHURST against JOHN BRUCE An Imparlance
JOICE BOUSH guardian of JAMES BOUSH against LEMUEL ROBERTS. NON DETINUE. An Imparlance
SAMUEL CALVERT against PETER SPARROW & REUBEN HERBERT . An Imparlance
SAMUEL CALVERT against GEORGE OLDNER. An Imparlance
SETH POINTER against ALEXANDER GUTHREY Dismissed Agreed.

PAGE 245B
JOHN CALVERT against JAMES MARSDENS ADMIN. An Imparlance
TULLY ROBINSON Executors against JOHN WILSON executors An Imparlance
CALEB WILSON against JOHN WILSON executors An Imparlance
CHARLES CONNER against EDWARD ARCHER Continued
PAUL LOYALL against HOGG & ROWLAND Continued

JOHN SMITH Plaintiff
Against Re: In Chancery
SOLOMON BUTT TALBOT executor of THOMAS TALBOT deceased Defendant
By consent of parties. It is ordered that PAUL LOYALL, JOHN KING and THOMAS RITSON or any two of them do arbitrate and settle all claims and demands between the parties and make their report to the next Court.

JOHN BAYNE Plaintiff
Against Re: In Case
HENRY GREEN Defendant
This day came the parties by their Attorney's and thereupon came also a Jury to wit: WILLIAM INGRAM, RALPH PICKET, JOHN SMITH, JESSE EWELL, JAMES MATTHEWS, POWELL RAINS, JOHN TALBOT, GEORGE THOMAS HALL, JOHN NASH, ALEXANDER BELL, THOMAS CALVERT, and WILLIS WILSON who being elected tried and sworn the truth to speak upon the issue joined upon their oath do say that the Defendant did not assume as in pleading they* have alleged. Therefore, it is considered that the Plaintiff take nothing by his bill but for his false claims be in mercy and the Defendant go hence without day and recover against the Plaintiff his costs by him about his defense in that behalf expended.

SAMUEL CALVERT against JOHN HOLLOWELL. Dismissed at the Plaintiff's costs.

PAGE 246
SAMUEL CALVERT Plaintiff
Against Re: In Case
JOHN HOLLOWELL Defendant
This day came the Plaintiff as well as the Defendant by their Attorney's and there upon came also a Jury to wit: BENJAMIN D. GREY, WILLIAM DEANS, EDWARD MOORE, THOMAS SHIPWASH, JOHN SHIPWASH, SHEARWOOD LEE, THOMAS DEANS, HENRY GREEN, JOHN BULLEY, SPIVEY WYATT, JOHN BAINES, and CHARLES WILLIAMS who being elected tried and sworn the truth to speak upon the issue joined upon their oath do say that the Defendant did not assume as in pleading they* have alleged. Therefore, it is considered that the Plaintiff take nothing by his bill but for his false claims be in mercy and the Defendant go hence without day and recover against the Plaintiff his costs by him about his defense in that behalf expended.

THOMAS NASH against REUBEN HERBERT. Continued

RALPH PICKET Plaintiff
Against Re: In Case
ALEXANDER BELL Defendant
This day came the Plaintiff as well as the Defendant by their Attorney's and there upon came also a Jury to wit: BENJAMIN D. GREY, WILLIAM DEANS, EDWARD MOORE, THOMAS SHIPWASH, JOHN SHIPWASH, SHEARWOOD LEE, THOMAS DEANS, HENRY GREEN, JOHN BULLEY, SPIVEY WYATT, JOHN BAINES, and CHARLES WILLIAMS who being elected tried and sworn the truth to speak upon the issue joined withdrew and returned and the Plaintiff being called came not but made default. Therefore, on the prayer of the Defendant it is considered that he recover of the Plaintiff 5 shillings current money and his costs by him about his defense in this behalf expended according to the form of the act of assembly and the Plaintiff for his false claims be in mercy.

THOMAS NASH JR. Plaintiff

Against Re: In Case
ROBERT BURLEY admin of JAMES HALSTEAD Deceased Defendant
This day came the parties by their Attorney's and thereupon came also a Jury to wit: RALPH PICKET, JOHN SMITH, JOHN MATHIAS, SHERWOOD LEE, POWELL REINS, JOHN BAYNE, GEORGE HALL, WILLIS WILSON, JOHN TALBOT, JOHN WOODSIDE, THOMAS CALVERT, and ALEXANDER BELL who being elected tried and sworn the truth to speak upon the issue joined upon their oath do say that the Defendants intestate did assume in manner and form as the Plaintiff against him has declared and do

PAGE 246B

assess the Plaintiffs damages by the occasion of the non-performance of that assumption to 64 pounds. Therefore, it is considered that the Plaintiff recover against the said Defendant his damages aforesaid in form aforesaid assessed and his costs by him about his suit in this behalf expended. To be levied of the Goods and Chattels of the said intestate if so, much the said Defendant has in his hands to be administered and if he has it not then the costs are to be levied of his proper goods and chattels and the said defendant in mercy.

Order is granted THOMAS SHIPWASH against RALPH PICKET for 125 pounds of tobacco for 5 days attendance as a witness in this Court in his suit against ALEXANDER BELL.

Order is granted JOHN SHIPWASH against RALPH PICKET for 125 pounds of tobacco for 5 days attendance as a witness in this Court in his suit against ALEXANDER BELL.

Order is granted AMBROSE SHIPWASH against RALPH PICKET for 125 pounds of tobacco for 5 days attendance as a witness in this Court in his suit against ALEXANDER BELL.

Order is granted RICHARD CAIN against RALPH PICKET for 125 pounds of tobacco for 5 days attendance as a witness in this Court in his suit against ALEXANDER BELL.

Order is granted ENOCH ETHERIDGE against THOMAS NASH for 100 pounds of tobacco for 4 days attendance as a witness in this Court in his suit against HALSTEAD admin.

THOMAS NEWTON against WILLIAM SMITH (G.B.) Continued
WALTER LYON executor against GEORGE OLDNER. Continued
JAMES BRADLEY against JAMES HALSTEAD admin continued.

PAGE 247

WILLIAM BYRD against WILLIAM MOSELEY abates by the Defendant's death
MARY TRUSS executrix of JOSIAH TRUSS against GEORGE THOMAS HALL issue joined and referred
MARY TRUSS executrix of JOSIAH TRUSS against WILLIAM SKINNER Continued.
MAXIMILIAN CALVERTS executors against LEMUEL ROBERTS issue joined and referred

FREDERICK BOUSH against WILLIS WILSON surviving partner of JOHN and WILSON WILSON*. Issue joined and referred to the next Court.

The Court allows WILLIAM SMITH 9 pounds per annum for the use of his house for holding of Courts.
The Court is adjourned to Court in Course, JAMES TAYLOR MAYOR, TESTE: ALEXANDER MOSELEY CLERK

NORFOLK BOROUGH

At a Hustings Court Held this 19TH day of August 1782
PRESENT: JAMES TAYLOR ESQUIRE MAYOR
RECORDER: HENRY TAZEWELL
GENTLEMAN ALDERMEN: CHARLES THOMAS , THOMAS NEWTON JR., CORNELIUS CALVERT, CARY H. HANSFORD

THOMAS NEWTON against WILLIAM SMITH. The suit is continued.
CHARLES CONNER against EDWARD ARCHER. The suit is continued.

PAGE 247B

Ordinary license is granted JOSHUA PEED on his complying with the law.
PAUL LOYALL Gentleman against HOG & ROWLAND Continued
ROBERT TUCKERS administrators against WILLIAM TUCKERS executors continued
SAMUEL CALVERT against CORNELIUS CALVERT. The Defendant pleaded did not assume, issue joined and referred.

THOMAS NEWTON JR. against JAMES TATE. The suit is dismissed.
WILLIAM GREY against RICHARD TALBOT. The suit is dismissed.
WILLIAM ROBERTSON executors of WALTER LYON deceased against GEORGE OLDNER Continued
JAMES BRADLEY against ROBERT BURLEY admin of JAMES HALSTEAD deceased Continued
CHARLES BOUSHNELL against SAMUEL CALVERT. An Imparlance

THOMAS NASH JR. Plaintiff
Against Re: In Case
REUBEN HERBERT Defendant
This day came the parties by their Attorney's and thereupon came also a Jury to wit: POWEL REINS, GEORGE T. HALL, JAMES LEITCH, GOLDSBERY HACKET, WILLIAM WILLOUGHBY, THOMAS BAKER, LEMUEL ROBERTS, LEWIS HATTON, JOHN WOODSIDE, JOSHUA PEED, ISAAC BARTIE and WILLIAM WISTERHOUSE who being elected tried and sworn the truth to speak upon the issue joined upon their oaths do say

that the Defendant did assume in manner and form as the Plaintiff against him has declared and do assess the Plaintiffs damages by the occasion of the non-performance of that assumption to 23 pounds. It is Therefore, considered that the Plaintiff recover against the said Defendant his damages aforesaid in form aforesaid assessed and his costs by him about his suit in this behalf expended and the said Defendant in mercy.

WILLIS WILSON against ALEXANDER BELL. The suit is dismissed at the Defendants Costs.

PAGE 248
FREDERICK BOUSH Plaintiff
Against Re: In Case
WILLIS WILSON surviving partner of JOHN and WILLIS WILSON
This day came the parties by their Attorney's and thereupon came also a Jury to wit: THOMAS NASH JR. JAMES BOYCE, JOEL MOHUN, JAMES WARREN, JAMES DISON, JOHN GUY, JOHN BAINES, ALEXANDER HARVEY, WILLIAM WALLACE, CHARLES WILLIAMS, TRIMAGEN BRETT and JOHN HUNTER who being elected tried and sworn the truth to speak upon the issue joined upon their oaths do say that the Defendant did assume in manner and form as the Plaintiff against him has declared and do assess the Plaintiffs damages by the occasion of the non-performance of that assumption to 147 pounds 6 shillings and 4 pence. Therefore, it is considered that the Plaintiff recover against the said Defendant his damages aforesaid in form aforesaid assessed and his costs by him about his suit in this behalf expended and the said Defendant in mercy.

JOHN NASH against CHARLES RUDDER. An Imparlance
MARY THRUSTON against NICHOLAS GAUTIER. An Imparlance

CHRISTOPHER WHITEHURST against CORNELIUS CALVERT by petition and summons. Judgement is granted the Plaintiff for 48 shillings. It is ordered the Defendant pay the same unto the Plaintiff with costs and fees.

Order is granted CHARLES WILLIAMS against THOMAS NASH JR. for 100 pounds of tobacco for 4 days attendance at this Court as a witness in his suit against HERBERT.

JOICE BOUSH guardian of JAMES BOUSH against LEMUEL ROBERTS. Continued.
MARY TRUSS executrix of JOSIAH TRUSS deceased against GEORGE T. HALL Continued

LEWIS GUION against THOMAS HERBERT JR. The Defendant by his Attorney pleaded not guilty issue joined and referred until next Court.

SAMUEL CALVERT against JAMES MARSDEN heir at law. Continued
WILLIAM BYRD against JAMES DENBY Continued

PAGE 248B
CHRISTOPHER WHITEHURST against JOHN BRUCE. The Defendant by his Attorney pleaded he did not assume issue joined and referred until next Court.
CHARLES CONNER against CORNELIUS CALVERT. An Imparlance.

SAMUEL CALVERT against PETER SPARROW and REUBEN HERBERT. The Defendants by their Attorney pleaded payment issue joined and referred until next Court.

SAMUEL CALVERT against GEORGE OLDNER. Continued

JOHN CALVERT against MARY MARSDEN administratrix of JAMES MARSDEN deceased. The Defendant by her Attorney pleaded payment and issue joined and referred until next Court.

MARY ROBINSON executrix of TULLY ROBINSON deceased against WILLIAM HAPPER Executor of JOHN WILSON deceased. The Defendant by his Attorney pleaded payment issue joined and referred until next Court.

CALEB WILSON against WILLIAM HAPPER executor of JOHN WILSON deceased. Continued
WILLIAM MARLEY against GEORGE JAMESON. The Defendant by his Attorney pleaded he did not assume issue joined and referred until next Court.

JAMES LEITCH against CHARLES COOPER. An Imparlance
NICHOLAS GAUTIER and wife against CORNELIUS CALVERT. Time to consider bill.
AFFIAH BOWSER against WILLIAM RUSSELL. An Imparlance.

ANDREW STEWART against ISAAC BARTIE. The Defendant by his Attorney pleaded tender and refusal of 25 pounds 10 shillings, issue joined and referred until next Court.

MARY TRUSS executrix of JOSIAH TRUSS deceased against WILLIS COWPER and Company. An Imparlance.

PAGE 249
The Court is adjourned to Court in Course, JAMES TAYLOR MAYOR, TESTE: ALEXANDER MOSELEY CLERK

NORFOLK BOROUGH
At a Hustings Court Held this 23RD day of September 1782
PRESENT: JAMES TAYLOR ESQUIRE MAYOR

GENTLEMAN ALDERMEN: CHARLES THOMAS , THOMAS NEWTON JR., CORNELIUS CALVERT, GEORGE KELLY

THOMAS NEWTON against JOHN POOL. Dismissed. Agreed
JOSHUA VENTRESS against GEORGE KERR. Abates. The Defendant no inhabitant

SAMUEL CALVERT against HENRY BANKS. Continued
JOHN CORPREW against ALEXANDER BELL. Continued.

JOHN CORPREW executor of MATTHEW SHIELDS against GEORGE OLDNER. JOHN BRUCE came into Court and undertook for the Defendant that in case he shall be cast in this suit he the said Defendant will pay the condemnation of the Court or render his body to prison in execution for the same or that the said JOHN BRUCE will do it for him. Whereupon the Defendant by his Attorney pray and has leave to IMPARLE here until the next Court.

HENRY WHITING against ROBINSON MATHIAS. The Defendant by his Attorney pleaded he did not assume issue joined and referred until next Court.

WILLIAM MORRIS against THOMAS DEBURK. Trover. The Defendant is ordered to give Special Bail or*

PAGE 249B
WILLIAM MORRIS against THOMAS DEBURK. An Imparlance.
JAMES BARTIE against ROBERT KEELE. An Imparlance.
WILLIS WILSON against GEORGE IVES. Continued.

CHARLES CONNER against ARTHUR DENBY. The Defendant by his Attorney pleaded not guilty issue joined and referred until next Court.

TULLY ROBINSON against LEMUEL LANGLEY. An Imparlance.
THOMAS NEWTON assignee of JOHN SMITH against WILLIAM SMITH. Continued.
CHARLES CONNER against EDWARD ARCHER. Continued.
PAUL LOYALL against HOG and ROWLAND. Continued
WILLIAM ROBINSON executor of WALTER LYON deceased against GEORGE OLDNER continued at the Plaintiffs costs.

JOHN CALVERT Plaintiff
Against Re: In Debt
MARY MARSDEN administratrix of JAMES MARSDEN deceased Defendant
This day came the parties by their Attorney's and thereupon came also a Jury to wit: ALEXANDER LOVE, LATTIMER HALSTEAD, JAMES BOYCE, JACOB WILLIAMS , THOMAS LOWREY, ARTHUR DENBY, ROBINSON MATTHIAS, GEORGE T. HALL, LEMUEL LANGLEY, ROBERT WILLIAMS, WILLIAM INGRAM, and JAMES LEITCH who being elected tried and sworn the truth to speak upon the issue joined upon their oath do say that the Defendants intestate has not paid the debt as in pleading set forth. Therefore, it is considered that the Plaintiff recover against the said Defendant his debt amounting to 311 pounds 3 shillings with interest from this day until paid at the rate of 5% per annum and the cost to be levied of the proper goods and chattels of the said JAMES MARSDEN if so, much thereof she has in her hands to be administered but if she has it not then the costs are to be levied of the said MARY*

JOHN NASH against CHARLES RUDDER. The Defendant by his Attorney pleaded not guilty issue joined and referred until next Court.

PAGE 250
MARY TROUSTON against NICHOLAS GAUTIER. The Defendant by his Attorney pleaded he did not assume issue joined and referred until next Court.

LEWIS GUION against THOMAS HERBERT JR. The suit is continued.
SAMUEL CALVERT against JAMES MARSDENS heir at law. The Suit is continued.

ANDREW STEWART against THOMAS HERBERT JR. The Defendant by his Attorney pleaded not guilty issue joined and referred until next Court.
WILLIAM BYRD against JAMES DENBY. The suit abates by the Defendant no inhabitant

MARY ROBINSON executrix of TULLY ROBINSON deceased against WILLIAM HAPPER executor of JOHN WILSON deceased Defendant. The suit is continued.

CALEB WILSON against WILLIAM HAPPER executor of JOHN WILSON deceased. An Imparlance

CHARLES BOUSHNELL against SAMUEL CALVERT. The Defendant by his Attorney pleaded payment issue joined and referred until next Court.
JAMES LEITCH against CHARLES COOPER. The Defendant by his Attorney pleaded not guilty issue joined and referred until next Court.
NICHOLAS GAUITER and wife against CORNELIUS CALVERT. Continued.

MARY TRUSS executrix of JOSIAH TRUSS deceased against CORNELIUS COWPER and Company. The Defendant by their Attorney they did not assume issue joined and referred until next Court.

WILLIAM MILLISON and THOMAS BAKER is appointed Constables in the replacement of JOSHUA PEED and WILLIAM GOODCHILD and ordered that they be summoned to the Next Court to qualify.

PAGE 250B

The Court is adjourned until tomorrow 9 o'clock, JAMES TAYLOR MAYOR, TESTE: ALEXANDER MOSELEY CLERK

<u>NORFOLK BOROUGH</u>
At a Hustings Court Held this 24th day of September 1782
PRESENT: JAMES TAYLOR ESQUIRE MAYOR
GENTLEMAN ALDERMEN: CHARLES THOMAS , GEORGE KELLY,THOMAS NEWTON JR., CARY H. HANSFORD

JOICE BOUSH guardian and next friend of JAMES BOUSH Plaintiff
Against Re: In Detinue
LEMUEL ROBERTS Defendant
This day came the parties by their Attorney's and there upon came also a Jury to wit: JAMES BOYCE, GEORGE T. HALL, JOHN CALVERT, THOMAS LOWREY, ARTHUR COOPER, JAMES BOUSHELL, WILLIAM MILLERSON*, WILLIAM LECAT, JOSHUA PEED, ISAAC BAILEY, JONATHAN CALVERT and JAMES MATTHEWS who being elected tried and sworn the truth to speak upon the issue joined returned a Special Verdict in these words to wit:
We of the Jury find that the Plaintiff JAMES is the son of SAMUEL BOUSH JR. deceased who was brother and heir at law of MAXIMILLIAN BOUSH deceased. We find that the said MAXIMILLIAN departed this life having made his last will and testament that by a clause in the said will he made the following devise:
Know all men that I MAXAMILLIAN BOUSH of my own free will and accord do leave to my father SAMUEL BOUSH the Negro wench named ROSE and the Negro girl named ISABELL to be disposed at his pleasure
PAGE 251
And for the benefit of my sister ELIZABETH BOUSH and for her only. To which (in fold) we refer. We find that ROSE and ISABELL have increased since the testator's death, VIOLET daughter of ROSE, JIM, and SAVANAH children of ISABELLA. We further find that ELIZABETH the devisee intermarried with LEMUEL ROBERTS the Defendant and that he has had possession of ISABELL and ROSE about 18 years and that ELIZABETH is dead leaving several children. We find that SAMUEL BOUSH the trustee is dead, and that the devisee ELIZABETH died about 3 years ago. We find that before the death of SAMUEL BOUSH the trustee, the Defendant LEMUEL ROBERTS had possession of the Negros. If upon the whole matter, the law before the Plaintiff find for the negroes mentioned in the Declaration to wit: ROSE, ISABELL, VIOLET, JIM, and SAVANAH but if they are not to be had then we further value to wit:
ROSE the value of 40 pounds.
ISABELL of the value of 75 pounds.
VIOLET the value of 75 pounds.
JIM of the value of 30 pounds.
SAVANAH of the value of 30 pounds. But should the law be for the Defendant then we find for the Defendant and the cause is continued until the next Court for the matter of law arising thereon to be argued.

JONATHAN CALVERT executor of MAXIMILIAN CALVERT deceased against LEMUEL ROBERTS. The suit is continued at the Defendants costs.

MARY TRUSS Executrix of JOSIAH TRUSS deceased against GEORGE T. HALL. The suit is dismissed at the Plaintiffs costs.
MARY TRUSS Executrix of JOSIAH TRUSS deceased against WILLIAM SKINNER. The suit is continued.

ANDREW STEWART against ISAAC BARTIE. Continued at the Plaintiffs costs.
WILLIAM MARLEY against GEORGE JAMESON. Continued.

PAGE 251B
APHIA BOWSER against WILLIAM RUSSELL. The Defendant by his Attorney he did not assume issue joined and referred until next Court.
SAMUEL CALVERT against CORNELIUS CALVERT. Continued.

SAMUEL CALVERT Plaintiff
Against Re: In Debt.
PETER SPARROW and REUBEN HERBERT Defendants
This day came the parties by their Attorney's and thereupon came also a Jury to wit: LEMUEL GODFREY, JAMES LEITCH, LEMUEL ROBERTS, JOHN GUY, ISAAC BARTIE, JESSE EWELL, ROBERT WILLIAMS , ALEXANDER HARVEY, JAMES DAVIS, WILLIAM WARREN, WILLIAM INGRAM, and WILLIAM SMITH who being elected tried and sworn the truth to speak upon the issue joined upon their oath do say that the Defendants intestate has not paid the debt as in pleading set forth. Therefore, it is considered that the Plaintiff recover against the said Defendant his debt amounting to 1280 pounds paper money and his costs by him about his suit in this behalf expended and the said Defendants in mercy. But his judgement is to be discharged by the payment of 5 pounds 4 shillings and 10 pence with interest thereon after the rate of 5% per annum to be computed from this day to the time of payment and the costs.

THOMAS BAKER this day took the oaths to the Commonwealth and the Oath of a Constable of this Borough and enters on the execution of his office.

THOMAS NEWTON assignee of JOHN SMITH against WILLIAM SMITH. On the motion of the Plaintiff by his Attorney a DEDIMUS is granted him to take the deposition of ROBERT FRY giving the defendant legal notice.

JAMES BRADLEY against ROBERT BURLEY admin of JAMES HALSTEAD CONTINUED.
CHRISTOPHER WHITEHURST against JOHN BRUCE Continued.

PAGE 252

WILLIAM MILLISON this day took the oaths to the Commonwealth and the Oath of a Constable of this Borough and enters upon the execution of his office.

Order is granted ALEXANDER HARVEY against LEMUEL ROBERTS for 75 pounds of tobacco for 3 days attendance at this Court in the suit of JOICE BOUSH against him.

Order is granted JOHN GUY against LEMUEL ROBERTS for 75 pounds of tobacco for 3 days attendance at this Court in the suit of JOICE BOUSH against him.

Order is granted LEMUEL GODFREY for 75 pounds of tobacco against LEMUEL ROBERTS for 3 days attendance at this Court in the suit of JOICE BOUSH against him.

Order is granted MARY BOGGESS wife of JOHN against LEMUEL ROBERTS for 75 pounds of tobacco for 3 days attendance at this Court in the suit of JOICE BOUSH against him.

The Court is adjourned until Court in Course, JAMES TAYLOR MAYOR, TESTE: ALEXANDER MOSELEY CLERK

NORFOLK BOROUGH
At a Hustings Court Held this 21ˢᵗ day of October 1782
PRESENT: JAMES TAYLOR ESQUIRE MAYOR
GENTLEMAN ALDERMEN: PAUL LOYALL, CHARLES THOMAS ,THOMAS NEWTON JR.,

THOMAS DEBURK against WILLIAM MORRIS. The suit is dismissed for want of security for costs.

PAGE 252B
ANN WALLER executrix of HARDRESS WALLER deceased against SAMUEL BURK. An Imparlance
WILLIS WILSON against ADAM LOVETT. Abates no inhabitant
THOMAS PRICE against JOHN JAMES. The suit is dismissed agreed.
MALACHI WILSON against WILLIAM HAPPER executor of JOHN WILSON deceased. An Imparlance. (2X)
JOSEPH MITCHELL against CHARLES COOPER. An Imparlance.
CHARLES CONNER against EDWARD ARCHER. The suit is Continued.
SAMUEL CALVERT against CORNELIUS CALVERT. The suit abates by the Plaintiff's death.
JOHN SMITH against THOMAS TALBOTS executors. The suit is continued.
WILLIAM ROBINSON Executor of WALTER LYON deceased against GEORGE OLDNER continued.

JAMES BRADLEY against ROBERT BURLEY admin of JAMES HALSTEAD deceased. The suit abates the Defendant being no inhabitant.

PRESENT: CARY H. HANSFORD, GEORGE KELLY, and CORNELIUS CALVERT Gentleman Alderman

JOICE BOUSH guardian and Next Friend to JAMES BOUSH orphan Plaintiff
Against Re: In Detinue on Special Verdict
LEMUEL ROBERTS Defendant
This cause was this day heard by the Council on both sides and the matter of law arising there upon fully argued in consideration thereof. It is the opinion of the Court that the law is for the Defendant. Therefore, it is considered that the Plaintiff take nothing by his bill but for his false claims be in mercy. And the Defendant go hence without day and recover of the Plaintiff his costs by him about his suit in this defense expended.

PAGE 253
Thereupon the Plaintiff by her Attorney prayed an Appeal to the Honorable the General Court which is granted her on her complying with the law in that case made and provided.

MARY TRUSS Executrix of JOSIAH TRUSS deceased against WILLIAM SKINNER. The suit is continued.

THOMAS NEWTON assignee of JOHN SMITH Plaintiff
Against Re: In Debt
WILLIAM SMITH Defendant
This day came the parties by their Attorney's and thereupon came also a Jury to wit:
WILLIAM WILLOUGHBY, JAMES BOUSHELL, THOMAS DRURY, GOLDSBERY HACKET, ARTHUR DENBY, ROBERT WILLIAMS WILLIAM MILLER, JOHN BURGESS, THOMAS LOWREY, JAMES DENBY, GEORGE BEATS and GEORGE COLLINS who being elected tried and sworn the truth to speak upon the issue joined upon their oath do say that the Defendant has not paid the debt in the declaration mentioned. Therefore, it is considered that the Plaintiff recover against the said Defendant his debt amounting to 82 pounds 12 shillings and 9 pence and his costs by him in this behalf expended and the said Defendant in mercy.

On the Attachment obtained by ROBERT KEEL against NATHANIEL BOUSH who has privately removed himself or so absconds that the ordinary process cannot be served on him and the Sergeant now making return that by virtue thereof he has levied the same on 21 pounds 14 shillings which he has in his hands. Therefore, it is considered that the Plaintiff recover the same against the said Defendant together with his costs by him in this behalf expended and ordered that the Sergeant pay the same.

PAGE 253B

On the Attachment obtained by WILLIAM GOODCHILD against NATHAN BOUSH who has privately removed himself or so absconds that the ordinary process of law cannot be served on him. The Sergeant now making return that he has levied the same on the balance if any after satisfying ROBERT KEEL attachment whereupon the Plaintiff proved his demand for 6 pounds to be just. Therefore, it is considered that the Plaintiff recover the same against the Defendant together with his costs by him in this behalf expended. And it is ordered that the Sergeant pay the Plaintiff whatever balance maybe in his hands after the paying the proceeding judgement of ROBERT KEELS and the costs.

JOHN NASH Plaintiff
Against Re: In Case
CHARLES RUDDER Defendant
This day came the parties by their Attorney's and thereupon came also a Jury to wit: JAMES BARTIE, RICHARD LANGLEY, GEORGE BISCOE, WILLIAM WARREN, JAMES BOYCE, WILLIAM MARLEY, JOHN HUTSON, MALBONE SHELTON, JAMES LANGLEY, RALPH PICKETT, WILLIAM INGRAM and JOHN WOODSIDE who being elected tried and sworn the truth to speak upon the issue joined upon their oath do say that the Defendant did assume in manner and form as in pleading set forth and do assess the Plaintiff damages by occasion of the non-performance of that assumption to 50 pounds. Therefore, it is considered that the Plaintiff recover of the said Defendant his damages aforesaid in form aforesaid assessed and his costs by him in his suit in this behalf expended and the Defendant in mercy.

LEWIS GUION against THOMAS HERBERT JR. The suit is continued.
SAMUEL CALVERT against JAMES MARSDENS heir at law. The suit abates by the Plaintiffs death.

ABSENT MR. MAYOR

PAGE 254
ANDREW STEWART against THOMAS HERBERT JR. The Suit is continued at the Plaintiffs costs.

The Court is adjourned until Court in Course, PAUL LOYALL, TESTE: ALEXANDER MOSELEY CLERK

BARROT, Jonathan 113B 114 114B

BARR, Robert 173 222 223B 228B

BARTIE, Isaac 247B 248B 251 251B James 253B

BARTLETT, Alexander 67B

BASSET, Richard 3B 4 8B 16 16B 36 78 78B 79 87B 92B 109B 124B 125 125B 126B 128 128B 188 188B 191 200 201B 202B 203B 219 228-2 228-B2 William 230B

BATCH, John 231B

BATES, Henry 96 CONFIRMED

BATTS, Henry 12B 14 CONFIRMED

BAYNE, Robert 221

BAYNES, Brudence* 135 James 118B 122B 188B 208 John 29B 36 76 151B 198 202B 203B 208B 209B 227B 229B 230B 239 239B 239B 240 243B 245B 246 Prudence 83B 148

BEAN, Zacheriah 3B 157B

BEATS, George 253

BEGG, John 202B 203 204B 205 205B 210B

BELL, Alexander 5 7 7B 11B 14 15 16B 21B 22 38 46 58B 59B 77B 81 81B 85 89 89B 91 91B 92 93 93B 94 98 99 105 108 108B 112 112B 113 113B 116B 117B 118B 122B 131 132B 136 141B 142B 143 144 147 149 152B 153 153B 166B 167B 174B 179B 182B 185 186 188 188B Alexander 200B 201 205B 209B 212B 213 218 222B 232B 234B 237 241 242 242B 245B 246 246B 247B 249 George 197B James 168B John 2B William 19B 40 40B 55B 78 172 232B 233B 234

BELT, Josmith 137

BENNET, Adam 177 197 221B

BERRY, James 159B 207B 211B

BESSIE, Irby 105B

BEVAN, William 124 211 212

BICKERDICK, Richard 3 3B 4 4B 5B 7 8 20 27 31B 32 34 39 40 40B 42B 43B 44 44B 62 64B 72 73 78B 81 89B 115B 120B 121 132 133 138B 139 140 143B 173 178 202B William 3 7 7B 37B 103B 105 106 108 138 140B 141 141B 142 142B 143 144 144B 145 147B 148 148B 149 149B 150B 151B 152 154 154B 173 219 224

BIRCH, John 21 Thomas 15 17B

BIRCKELL, John 74

BIRKBICK*, Charles 8

BISCOE, George 253B

BISER/BEISER, John 98 130B 151B 177 178 223 232B Peter 7B 23B 37B 50B 88B 104B 105 130 130B 152 154 178 SAME GUY SAME LAWSUIT

BISHOP, Jacob 129B 161 162 164 218B

BLACK, William 217B 237

BLAINE, Mr. 238

BLAIR, Mr. 146B 198B 204B SR. John 41B

BLEWS, Mary 241B Samuel 129 130 138B 139 140 161B 162B 189 192B 196 197B

BLINN, George 2 3B 4 7 7B 33 85B 92 92B 100 123B

BOGGESS, John 79 177 182B 192B 193B 194 222B 226B 231 234 239 240 252 Mary 252 Susanna 241

BOGUS, John 184B 186 194B 211 211B 232B

BOHANAN, John 224B

BOLDEN, Mr. 172 William 6B 54 60 62B 63B 119

BOLITHO, Zacheriah 183B

BOLSON, Betty 74

BOOKER, Edward 170 220 Richard 75B 121B William 114 162B 170

BOUCHER, Ann 24 37B 48 50B 79B 101B Richard 112 188 198

BOUSH, Arthur 60 Bennett 57B 219 Elizabeth 251 Frederick 42 46 79B 80 83B 92 102B 121B 122B 140 159B 169 187B 196 202B 207B 210 215B 219B 232 234B 247 248 Goodrich 59B 64 66 75B 90B 97 143B James 245 248 250B 252B John 3B 5B 7B 11 13B 18 20B 23B 27B 32B 35 39 41 42B 45 46B 49B 53 56B 58 60B 61B 65B 69B 71 75 79 81B 85 89 89B 92B 93 97 99 John 100B 105B 108B 111 115 117 122B 128 130B 133B 136B 140B 145B 146 151 156 160B 164 168B 169 175B 178B 184 186 190B 193 195 197B 201 202B 205B 208B 210B 212 215B 217B 220B 223B 224 224B 225B Joice 245 248 250B 252 252B Maximillian 250B Misters 98B Nathaniel 4B 5B 8B 19 38 39 42 46 80 88 89 102B 108 109B 121B 122B 128 130 140 144 150B 158 160 177 188B 199 203B 207B 211 212 253 253B Nicholas 130 Samuel 6B 54 62B 75B 85B 97 106 107 117 119 119B 122 123B 128B 131 132B 146 158 171 188B 190B 193 250B 251

BOUSHELL, James 230B 250B 253 John 235B

BOUSHNELL, Charles 5B 176B 177 178 178B 243 243B 244 247B 250

BOWDOIN, John 52 52B 82B Preeson 211B 212 212B 214B 229 230B 231 232 236 238B 239

BOWEN, William 93B

BOWERS, Robert 14

BOWNESS, George 109 109B 110 169B John 3B 4 6B 16 16B 54 62B 63B 119 169B 172B 210 210B 228B 229

BOWREY*, Robert 61B

BOWSER, Affiah* 248B Aphia* 251B

BOYCE, James 248 249B 250B 253B

BOYD, Bathsheba 2B John 201B Robert 97 Teresa 19

BOYER, Elias 146B 198B 204B

BOYNES, John 231B

BRACEGIRDLE*, Frederick 85B

BRADDIN*, William 202B

BRADLEY, James 239B 246B 247B 251B 252B

BRAG, Henry 136B 145

BRAITHWAIT/E, Ann 107 160B 165 183B 191B 193B 196 202 228 228-2 234B

BRAMBLE, John 234 235B 236B Willis 143

BRAY, Henry 98

37B 77 107B 161B 169 177 184B 197 213B 219B 221 229B 231 235B 237 238 238B 239 240B 243 245 245B 246 247B 248 248B 249 250 251B 252B 253B William 19 23 25 25B 26 114 128 196 197 213B 221 224 229

CALVILL, John 12B

CAMPBELL, Alexander 79 Anna 191 214B 215 215B Archibald 5B 6B 8 11B 16 21 21B 28 29 33 35B 39B 45B 46B 49B 54 58 61 62B 63 71 75 79 85 89 90 93 93B 95B 99 100 100B 105B 106 107 107B 109 111 111B 112 112B 115B 118 119 119B 122B 128 131 133 133B 135 137 137B 140B 144B 146 148 151B 154 155 156 158B 161B 164B 169 173 175B 179 184 184B 186B 187 188 190 190B 191 193B 195 195 198 202 209 210 216 217 217B 224 227B 228-B2 229B 232 233 234B Charles 151 191 214B 215 215B Donald 58B 110B Duncan 6B 54 62B 63B 78 119 130 James 64 71B 75 75B 78 94 107B 121B 122 122B 132 133 133B 135 136B 138B 144B 146 155 167B 168 170B 191 216 228 228B 228-2 John 100B 107B 120

CANN, John 18B 39 74B 77B 78 177B 178 Sarah 39 74B 77B 78 177B 178 180B 181 181B 190

CANNON, Edward 74 81 81B John 24

CAPLE, Hanbury 12B 13

CARBERY, Philip 3 4B 5 7 10 23 25 25B 26 48 49 59 60B 76 76B 77 78 83B 89 93B 106 107 114 114B 115B 116 116B 127B 138 139 147B 148 148B 149 149B 150B 160B 167B169B 170 184B 186 192 201B 202B 203 204B 205 205B 206B 207B 209 210 210B 212B 213 214B 215B 216B 222 228B 228-B2 229 231B 232 236 238

CARLSON, George 53B 132 133B CONFIRMED

CARLTON, George 14 42 79 120B 127 177B 220 229B 238B CONFIRMED

CARMICHAEL, James 58B 141 141B 142B 147B 148 148B 157 157B 158 158B 161 162B 164 165 167B 177 180B 181 183B 190B 194 194B 196 197B 199 199B 200 200B 202B 203 204B 205 205B 206 208B 209 211 211B 214B 216 228-2 229 235 235B John 199B

CARMICKHAIL*, James 93 131B 132 133

CARMOUNT, John 138 140B 141 141B 142 142B 143 144B 145 174 184B 185 185B 186 200B 202B 214B 215 217 219

CARNEY, Barnaby/Barnabas 61 107B 110B 113 117B 128 144B 153B 155 B165 169 177 177B 185 185B 196 209B 213B 220 220B 223B 228-B2 237 James 149 149B 150B Richard 128 Sarah 196B 209B 213B 220 220B 223B 228-B2

CARR, Alexander 9 42 94B Alice 94B 144B Ralph 9 10

CARRIE/CORRIS, John 6B 54 62B 63B 119 [SAME PERSON]

CARTER, Charles 52 52B 82B John 124 163 Thomas 237B

CARTWRIGHT, Robert 168 216 232 232B 233B Susannah 172B Thomas 172B William 234

CARY, Archibald 52B 82B 208 Joseph 218B 219 221B 224B

CASON, Hilary 81B

CASON/CASSON, Charles 81 83 170

CASSARINE, Elizabeth 221B

CASTLE, William 209B

CASTLETON, Samuel 124

CAWSON, Lydia 221 229

CHALMERS, John 10B 13 William 24B 57B 58

CHAMBERLAIN, Philip 93B

CHAMBERLAYNE, Parnell 210

CHAMBERS, David 91

CHAMPION, James 79B 92B

CHAPMAN, Ann 67 68 Elizabeth 66B 67 68 John 2 35B 43 59B 64B 65 65B 66 66B 67 67B 68 71 78B 83 John Jr 68 William 66B 67

CHERRY, John 201 Matthew 94 136B 149B Thomas 94 136B 149B Thomas Jr 215

CHESHIRE, John 24B 31 32B 33 34B 35 38 39 48 49 56B 57 57B 123 129 139 173B 174 188B 189 192B 199 203 204B 205 205B 215 215B 221B 231B Richard 36B

CHEVIS, David 6B 54 62B 64 119

CHISHOLM, William 6B 18 22 23 25 25B 26 28B 38B 53B 54 60 60B 62B 76 119 122 125B 130 131B 132 132B 192B

CHRISTIAN, Matthias 78 78B Michael 53B 94 101 105 116 136 142B 143 144 186

CLAIBORNE, Thomas 146 158 169B 173B 184 191 191B 195 201 201B 209B 212 214 220 222B 228-B2

CLARK, Frances 232B 233B 234 Francis 109B 156B 172 Thomas 89 Willilam 49

CLARKE, Abram 224B Francis 83 99B 199 208 James 98B

CLAYTON, Jasper 213B Sarah 33B

CLEMONS, Luan 101

CLIPPER, Paul 235

COAKLEY, William 4B 8B

COBURN, Charles 190B

COCKIN, William 165

COCKRAN, David 46 50B Matthew 97

COKE, Robey 80

COLEMAN, John 6 40 57 59

COLES, John 80B 122 131B 184 199B

COLLEY, James 137 John 243 243B 244 William 64B 80B 81 219

COLLINS, Elizabeth 206 George 57 111B 152 167 185 253 Henry 57 Richard 162B 163 183 191 203 206 235 235B

COLLINS/COLINS, John 74 165B 173

COLVILLE, John 19 40 43 49 49B 61B 74B 77 123 160B 165

DELACOUDRE, Lewis 5 7 7B
DEMOUNT, Peter 99
DENBY, Arthur 204 249B 253 James 245 248 250 253
    Samuel 7 7B 10 22 73 74 85B
DENNY, Catherine 193B
DIACK, Alexander 86 104B 132B
DIBBS, Robert 70B
DICKERSON, Elira 104 Judah 104 Thomas 88B 103B
    104 104B 106 107 166B 167B 216B 219B 221B
    Thomas 49B
DINGLEY, Benjamin 136
DISON, Francis 154B
DISON/DYSON, James 57B 76 76B 77 78 89 100 101B
    102 102B 103 103B 154B 219 219B 227 230 236
    238B 240 248 John 3 9 12B 21B 72 73 Jonathan 1
    6B 10 16 16B 17 35 38 39 48 49 54 55 57B 58 60B
    62 62B 63 64B 75B 81 81B 90B 91 92B 98 106B
    107 119 193B 196B 228-B2 233 234B Sarah 1 35
    60B 75B 92B 193B
DIVER, John 234B
DIXON, Daniel 137B George 195B 228 John 159B Mr.
    227B Thomas 107
DIXON*, James 3B 32
DOBSON, Margaret 146
DODD, John 215 Newcom 227B CONFIRMED
    Newcomb 157B 199 201B 207 CONFIRMED
DOE, John 65
DOEBER, Frederick Augustus 111B 118B 131B 132B
    133 169B 220 228B
DOEGOOD Obediah 1
DONALD George 12 15B
DONALD James 213B 229
DONALD Robert 51B 52B 82B 99 213B 229
DONALDSON William 146 171B 198 204B 221 228B
    229 229B
DOWN Wentworth PAGE 172B
DREWREY/ DEWRY/DRUREY Thomas 43 65 65B 91
    112 135B 141 152B 162B 163 243 244 253
DRIVER, John 191B
DRUREY/DRURY, John 70B
DUGAN, David 5B
DUNBAR, Richard 5B 14 54B 74B 77
DUNFORD, Judith 156B 182B 199 205 223 232B Judy
    99 Willis 49B 103 88B
DUNLAP/DUNLOP, James 4B 10B 16 17B 28B 87B 96
    113B 114 137B 146B 188 197
DUNN, James 8 19 28 39B 43 48 74B 75 90 94 100 109
    109B 115B 116 116B 130 133B 134 134B 135
    149B 153 154B 155 155B 192 192B 193B 194
    194B 207 John 1 39B 43 72 73 73B 183B 228-2
    Thomas 243B
DURELL, John 18B William 18B

EASTHER, Thomas 215

EASTWOOD, Enoch 149B Enos 162B Judith 162B
    Richard 177B Willis 177B
ECHORD, Baultis/Baltis 6B 163
EDGE, Thomas 173B
EDINBURGH, Slave 12
EDMONDS, Isaac 191
EDMUNDSON, James 112 153 185B 193
EDWARD, Peter 103B 104B
EDWARDS, John 83B 88B 113B 114 114B 123 127B
    128B 133B 134 134B 135 165B 166 166B 174
    188B 194 194B 199B 200B 212B 214B 215 216
    217 228 229 Joshua 23B 38B 39 49B 103B 104
    [note: Joshua is listed as Mary's husband all times
    except 1] Mary 49B 88B 103B 104 Thomas Jr 183
    185 232B
EDY, Solomon 165 188
EILBECK, John 4 24B 57B 58 84B 185B 187B Jonathan
    16 16B 17B 31B 32 84B 164B 165 167B 168 168B
    169 169B 171 171B 172 172B 173 174 174B 175B
    176 176B 180 181B 182 183 187 187B 188 193B
    194B 195 196B 197B 206B 207 211 211B 216
    216B 220B 221 222B 223 228 232 232B 233B 234
    234B
ELIZA TUCKER, Rebecca 223B
ELLEGOOD, Jacob 6 29 29B 30 45B 50 62 206B
ELLERY, Elias 23B 31B
ELLIOT, Ralph 157B 160 174 174B 190 196B 197
    Robert 42 47
ELLIS, Mr. 10B Thomas Jr 74
EMSON*, Cornelius 229B
ERRICK, Robert 201B CONFIRMED
ESDALE, John 51 52B 82B
ESTAVE, Andrew 5B 117
ESTHER, James 42B 48B 58 62 72 73 78 78B Susannah
    112 133 158B
ETHEREDGE, Enoch 245 246B
ETHERIDGE, Amos 2B 9B 40B 54B 56B 113B David
    98B 143B 150
EVANS, John 163B
EVE, John 4 13
EWELL, James 123B 137B Jesse 234 235 236B 245B
    251B

FAIREY, Andrew 183B
FARMER, Samuel 51 52B 82B 104B 196B 228-B2 238
FARRER, George 7 24 38B 40 43B 44 44B 98B 104
    206B 208B Thomas 3B 4 5B 10 13B 15 16 16B 17
    17B 33B 34B 62 81 81B 84B 89B 95B 96B 100
    115B 116 116B 129B 146B 164B 176 190 194B
    197 227B William 5B 17 30 38 39 84B 104B 106
    108 108B 110 146B 159 164B 176 183B 189 190
    197 203B 210B 227B
FEARSON, William 159
FELTHAM/FELTON, Amelia Sophia Leonora 183B 222
    CLEARLY SPELLED BOTH WAYS.

GOODRIGHT, Gideon 218
GOODWIN, Elizabeth 35B 59B
GORDON, Alexander 80B 159B 173 177B 188 198 216
　　227B George 6B 54 60 60B 62B 72 73 75B 89
　　113B 115 115B 119 161 162 164 174 184B 185
　　185B 186 187 192 199B 200 200B 210B 211 211B
　　219 219B 228-2 Robert 28 87B 96
GORHAM, Prince 4B 16
GOUGH, James 199 207 Joshua 146B 147B 148 148B
　　149 149B 150B 156B 198B 199 205 207
GOVAN, Archibald 169B 184 CONFIRMED
GRAHAM, Alexander 159 187 James 201 Mr. 204
　　William 99 151B 189B
GRANBERRY, Josiah 51B 52B 82B
GRANBERY, Gibson 160B Mr. 167B William 96
GRANFIELD, John 19
GRANT, John 25B Thomas 24B 33B
GRAY, Benjamin 93B 141B Edward 67B Elizabeth 177
　　James 1 37 Lodwick 93B 136 141B Robert 194
　　194B 221B 229 William 3 7 8 9 10 13 14 30 31 32B
　　55 58B 60 75B 79B 85B 92B 93 123B 124 128B
　　161 166 177 188B 200 201 216B 219B 234B
GRAYHAM, James 234B CONFIRMED
GREAR, Alice 32B Else 24 Joseph 3B 5B 19 24 32B
　　48B 55 62 72 73
GREEN, Henry 61 110B 128 177 177B 185B 191 223B
　　234B 239 240B 243 243B 244 245B 246 Thomas
　　187 233 William 212B 229
GREENHOW, John 10B 17 22B
GREENSON, Gilbert 203 203B 204
GREENWOOD, John 14 15 30B 36 38B 41 42 47 48
　　50B 54B 55B 60 60B 64 75B 83 85 88 88B 90
　　100B 108 109B 111 111B 112B 115 127B 133B
　　134B 140 152 162 165B 167B 170B 175 187B 191
　　198 209 214 214B 223
GREIVE, Mr. 213 213B 229
GREY, Benjamin D. 246 William 239 240 240B 247B
GRIFFIN, John 21 153 154B 155 155B Mary 179B
　　Samuel 18 23 25 25B 179B 232
GRIMES, Agathy 235 Charles 244B Mary 79B 122 126
　　Maximilian 2B 173B
GRISTOCK, Henry 70B
GRYMES, Charles 242 James 239B
GUION, Lewis 245 248 250 253B
GURTON, James 239B
GUTHREY, Alexander 245
GUTTERY, Dinah 50B 72B
GUY, Elizabeth 79 James 78B 79 John 14B 18B 74B 78
　　78B 79 220B 248 251B 252
GWIN, David 212 Samuel 163B 172B 179 203 210B
　　228B

HACKET, Goldsbery 230B 231B 235B 243 243B 244
　　247B 253
HADDON, Nancy 70B Thomas 50B

HALDANE, James 115B 161 162 164 165 165B 167
　　170B 180B 181B 183 184B 185 185B 186 186B
　　190 193B 195B 196 202B 203 203B 204 204B
　　209B 210B 211 213B 214B 215 216 217 218 221B
　　228 236 237 238
HALL, Amy 213 George 242 246 247B 249B 250B 251
　　George Thomas 245B 247 248 Mr. 172B Philip Jr
　　88B
HALSTEAD, Drew 229B Henry 91B James 81 81B 91B
　　239B 241B 242 242B 243B 244 244B 245 246
　　246B 247B 251B 252B Lattimer 22 28B 76 98
　　106B 107 122 125B 129B 189B 193B 196B 228-B2
　　233 234B 249B Smith 244B
HAMBLITON*, Mr. 238
HAMILTON, Gustavus 157 John 1367B 167 212B
HAMOT, George 133B
HANBURY, Caleb 113 188 200B 201 Capel 1 40B 41B
　　Osgood 1 12B 13 40B 41B Solomon 22B
HANCOCK, Simon 70 William 42B 88 109
HANNON, John 202 209 212B
HANSFORD, Cary 241B 245 247 250B 252B Edward 4
　　5B 10B 18 20B 46B 48B 49 72 73B 90B 91B 117B
　　135 141 146B Lewis 1 3B 5B 6B 8 10B 11 11B 13
　　13B 14 16 18B 21 23B 28 29 29B 33 35B 38 39B
　　46B 49B 53 54 56B 58 61 62B 63 64 64B 71B 74
　　75 79 85 87 89 90 92B 93B 97 99 100B 105B 111
　　115B 117 119 122B 128 131 133B 137 146 151B
　　156 160B 164B 169 175B 179 184 187 190B 193B
　　201 203 207 217 217B 227
HAPPER, Samuel 90B 143B William 248B 250 252B
HARDIE, John 1 3 7 7B 8 10B 18 19 25B 44B 144
HARDING, Joseph 58B 83 86 86B 95B 96B 103B 104B
　　107 128B 208 221B
HARDY, Elizabeth 22 42 85 127B 156 John 6 9 27B 28
　　39B 42 54B 74 75 80B 81 85 98 105 106 127B 146
　　156 165B 179 191 206 209B 216 219 224 228-B2
　　229B 234B William 123 128B 188B 200B 230
HARGRAVES, Mr. 209B William 208B 219
HARMANSON, John 101 144 157B 186
HARPER, David 54B 158 199 214B 215
HARRIS, John 106 107 113B 114 114B 144B 152 154
　　161 161B 162 164 174 174B 178B 191 212B
　　William 46B
HARRISON, James 123 Thomas 123 188B 200
HART, Stephen 201B 202
HARVEY, Alexander 215B 248 251B 252 William 192B
　　193B 194 194B 221B 222 227
HARWOOD, John 128 166 188B 203B William 192
HASTIE, Mr. 128B 148B
HATTON, Francis 25 25B 27B 158 179 199 211B 212
　　214B 215 220 Lewis 247B Robert 19B 31 32B 86
　　86B 87 89B 165 188 199B 200 200B Thomas 220
HAWKS, John 133B
HAY, Alexander 53B 55B
HAYES, Michael 50

JACKSON, George 13 86 86B 98 171B 174 176B 177 178 178B 179 209 211B 212 214 214B John 196 214B Jonathan 99B 144 155 Mathew 209 214

JACOB, William 6B 54 62B 63B 119

JACOBS, Isaac 127

JAMES, John 231 234 234B 235B 236B 243 243B 244 252B William 81

JAMIESON, David 86 114 George 210 248B 251 Mr. 210 214 Neil 6 29 29B 30 33B 45B 50 50B 52B 62 82 82B 83 90B 127B 135B 139 141B 184 199B 209B 228-B2 229B

JAQUES, Jaques 229B William 131 131B 132B 133B 134 134B 135 138 203 204B 205 205B 209 214 214B 215 217 219 219B

JARVIS, David 83B James 196 196B Pritchard 233 Richard 183B 190B 242

JENKINS, Charles 19 21B 30B 58B 75 76 77B 87B 89B 91B 92 93 96B

JENKINSON, William 55B 127

JOHNSON, Benjamin 42B 88 93 Elizabeth 42B 88 93 George 210 211 215B John 28 87 97B 101B 183 213 Priscilla 113 198B Richard Jr 14 74B 77B 86B 87 William 79B

JOHNSTON, Labon 94 136 143 Mr. 166B

JOLLIF, James Sr 14 74

JOLLIFF, James 40B 191 201

JOLLY, James 243B 244B

JONES, Ann 218B Edward 170B 208 211 James 93B 136 142 Jesse 79 John 43 76 76B 77 78 85B 86 91 92B 111 113 131 131B 149B 157B 206 207B 210 211 215 215B 216B 217 Joseph 85B 93 93B 136 142 Margaret 202 Philip 110B Philistria 86

JUNIOR, George 153

JUNKERSON, William 108

JUQIEZ*, Martin 196 214B

KATE, Slave 19B

KATZ, Peter 94 136B 146 146B 182B 198B 204B 206B 222B 232B

KAYS, William 104 178B

KEATING, William 198 204 207 208

KEATON, William 120B 137B 143B

KEEL, Robert 253 253B

KEELING, Thorowgood 178

KEEN, John 68B 70B

KEETON, William 3 14 22B 40B 80 81B 84 101B

KEETON/KEATON, Edmond 13B 19B 20 23 25 25B 26 27B 31 32B 33B 34B 50B 57 58 80B 86 123 125B 126 126B 192B

KEITH, Alexander 166B 216B 221 228 229

KELLY, Ann 22B 24 30 31B 32 33B 80B 84 87B 99 102 127 144 Daniel 224 George 5 10 29 40 40B 72B 80B 86 95 100 107 137 144B 155.174 174B 175 175B 179B 180 183 183B 192 203 203B 204 209 211B 212 213 215 217 222 230 231 240 241B 243

245 249 250B 252B Hugh 48B 72B Mathew 3B 4B 5 7 7B 12B 21 22B 24 30 31B 32 32B 33B 40 41B 42B 49 50B 58 62 72 73 80B 84 87B 93B 99 102 107 112 122B 127 144 150B 151 155B 156 182B 222

KELSICK, John 221B Richard 7 7B 40 40B 85B 89B 92B 128B 188B 203B

KELSO, John 15 47

KEMPE, James 6 60B 74 77B 109 114

KENNEDY, John 147 Joseph 50B

KENNY, Hugh 81

KERR, George 231 234 236 238B 240 249

KID, William 53B 208

KIDD, Alexander 55B 94B 95 95B 113B 165B 222 232 John 94B 95 95B 113B 165B 222 232

KING, Ann 32B Henry 216B John 245B Thomas 238

KIPPIN, George 51B 52B 82B

KIRBY, Bennet 59B 65B 66 66B

KNIGHT, Henry 155B James 165B John 166 216 228

LAMBERT, Solomon 79

LAMOUNT, Hardress 2B 44 Henry 183B 223 Susannah 157B 199 227B

LANCASTER, Hyndman 186B

LANDS, Samuel 204B 205 205B

LANGELY, Thomas 184

LANGLEY, Elizabeth 116B Frances 204 Ivy 215 James 138B 139 140 253B Joseph 61 76 91B 129B 137B 138B 139 140 148 151B 189 194 194B 197 198 199B 200B 203 203B 204 227B 230B 231B 234 235B 239 240 Lemuel 98 100 116 122B 137B 193B 194 227B 249B Mary 116 Moses 33B 74B 76 89 115 175B 192 Richard 109B 253B Samuel 41B 76 80 88 148 Sarah 137B 148 203B 227B Thomas 116 118B 154B 174 174B 194 227B 231B 232B 233B Thomas Sr 97 97B 115B 116B 136B 184 192B 193B Willis 3 5 7B 46 88B 100 230B

LANGSTON, Thomas 205B

LATCHWELL, Matthew 160

LATHBURY, George 28 87B 96

LAWRENCE, John 4 6B 38B 54 54B 59B 60 60B 62B 63B 79 98 100 101 106 111 111B 112B 117B 118B 119 120 122B 123 147B 152 168 171 172B 176 176B 180 187 191 191B 192B 198 207 209 214B 220 233 Jonathan 124 214 Martha 117B 207 Mr. 172

LAWSON, Anthony 5B 8 14 16 21 23B 28 29B 43 49B 53 56B 82 93 93B 135B 141

LEAH, Thomas 201B

LECAT, William 243 243B 244 250B

LEDIMORE*, George 129 199 215

LEE, John 1 24B 33B 34B 43B 44 44B 45 60 60B 72 73B 79B 109 109B 110 113B 122 126 176B 177 178 178B 199B 200B 202B Jonathan 214B Sherwood 246

OSHEAL, David 139
OVE, William 209 CONFIRMED
OWEN, Archibald 74B

PACHICO, Francisco 5 7
PACKER, Mr. 185
PAGAN, George 23B 31
PALMER, Henry 163 163B
PANE, Anthony 163B
PARK, John PAGE 238B
PARKE, Edward 11B 19B 33B 74B 76 76B 77 89 98B
    115 125B 126 126B 133 143B 150 161B 162B
    175B 192 192B 193B 194 194B 214B 215
PARKER, Charles 98B George 238 James 75 111 135
    218B Mr. 112 152B
PARNAL, Elizabeth 46B
PARROT, Mary 196B
PARSONS, John 98B 104 162B 163B Jonathan 104
    Thomas 53 88B
PASSONS, John 143B CONFIRMED
PASTEUR, James 59B 97B 115B 116 116B 208 214B
    215 217 227B 231B 232B 233B John 72 73 81 81B
PATEON, Abraham 100 118 138 154 161 161B
PATRICK, James 118B
PATTERSON, James 170B 171 171B 172 183B 197B
    228B 232 232B 233B 235B 237B
PAYNE, Anthony 163 Richard 174B 193 193B
PEAD, John 133B Joseph 141 141B Joshua 135B 142B
    143 Mary 78B
PEARCE, Robert 79B Roger 43 81B 187 188 189B 190
    196B 197 197B 206B 209B 210 211 220B 221 228-
    B2
PEARCE/PEARSE Teresa 179 183B 207
PEARSE, Roger 85B 89B 178 179 179B 180B 186B
    192B
PIERCE, Roger 25 25B 27B 55 97B 99 99B 100 107B
    120 129B 144 151B 153 154B 157B 158B 160B
    161 207 209 228 228-2
PEARSON, John 57B 156B 199B 215 Thomas 31B 32
    33B 34B 36B 48B 57 125B 126 126B 152B 174
    185 187B 191 194B 195B 203 205
PEART, Francis 6B 54 62B 63 115B 119 Griffin 6B 54
    62B 63 87 100 113B 115 116 116B 119 124B 125
    125B 126B 130 133B 134 134B 135 154B 189B
    197 199B 200 200B
PEATON, Abraham 174 186B
PEBWORTH, Thomas 133B
PECK, Daniel 86 86B 87 106 128B 137 144 146B 158
    159B 166 192
PEED, Joshua 91 143B 226 235B 247B 250 250B
PEEPLES, David 240B
PENN, William 205B 235
PEOPLES, David 242
PETER, Walter 58 116B 183B
PETERS, Robert 197B

PEYTON, Abram 189B
PHIDALL, Joseph 138
PHRIPP, John 104B 147B 186 John Jr 86 104B Mathew
    2 6 29 29B 30 36 45B 50 53B 54B 60 62 75B 86
    90B 98 100 101 104B 120 122B 124 131 132B
    143B 147B 157 158 168 171 172B 176 176B 180
    181B 182 182B 187 188 191B 196B 198 199 202
    207 209 211 214 214B 218 220 222B 223 232 237
PICKET, Ralph 241 242B 243B 244B 245B 246 246B
    253B
PIGOT, William 157B
PLUMBER/PLUMMER, John 137B 158B 169 232
PLUME, William 3 7 8 9 183 209
POINDEXTER, Richard 21
POINER, Nathaniel 105 158
POINTER, Seth 8 10 16 16B 113 211B 212 245
POLLOCK, John 100 128 131B 132 133 144 151B 157B
    160 188B 200 Thomas 136B 144B
POMEROY, Robert 107B 113B 114 114B 130 197B
POOK, Mr. 182B 209B 212B 228-2 Richard 4B 5 10
POOL, Mary 165B 168 204B 209B 211B
POOLE, Howard 6 39B 48B 60 60B 64B 72 72B 73
    187B John 98B 209 231B 232B 233B 236 239
    240B 249 Nicholas 8 13 15 37B 43 56B 57B 60
    60B 61 72 73 89B 98B 105B 117 143B 150 165B
    168 204B 209B 211B 236 Thomas 108 200B
    William 170B 171 177B 185B 195 223
POPE, Joseph 75B 83B 122 131 138B 139 140 179 182B
    222B 232B
PORTER, David 90B 143B
PORTLOCK, Annis* 106 John 90B 143B Lemuel 191
    Samuel 21B 42 46 49B 50B 53 61B 80 88B 89 94
    102B 109B 111 111B 114 115B 121 124B 132B
    133B 156B 158 160B 173B 179 179B 188 214B
    224 225B 228 233 234B Simon 53B 72 73 92B
POWELL, John 167B Nicholas 224 Seymour 6 40 57
    William 244
POWERS, Samuel 70B
POYNER, Nathaniel 61 109 201B 228-B2
PREESON, Thomas 112
PRESTON, John 200B
PRICE, Adam 130B Thomas 74 230B 234 236B 238B
    252B William 80 84
PRIDE, Halcot 1 24B 34 Joshua 226B
PRIESTMAN, William 85B 106 127B 127B 134B 144
    154 154B 224B
PRIOR, Dickerson 30B 45 50B 98 101B 102 102B 103
    103B 115B 131B 132 133 143B 151 177 182 204
    211B 212 Frances 30B 50B 103B
PROBY, Bartram 216B Paul 100 101B 102 102B 103
    103B 108 130 138 177 192B 193B 194 194B 204B
    205 205B 208B 243B 244B
PRYOR, Dickerson 88B 100 Frances 88B
PULLETT, Mary 28 79B 122 126
PURCELL, David 229

SAVAGE, Nathaniel Littleton 52 52B 82B William 202 228-B2

SAWYER, Charles 80B 127 138

SAYBOURN, Stafford 206B

SAYER, Charles 231 236 238B

SCOTT, Ann 9 50B 88B 104B 105 James 141 John 50B 88B 90B 104B 105 128 133 167 170 196B 209B 216B 228 228B Mary 55 Walter 191

SCRIVENER, Joseph 146 198B 204 222

SEABROOK, Nicholas brown 99B 144 152 190B 196B

SELDEN, Cary 218 John 3B 4 31B 32 38B 86 86B 87 192

SEVILLS, Taylor 23

SHAKELFORD, John 91

SHARP, Duncan 24 34B 35 Reuben 45 103B 104B 156B 168B

SHAW, John 60 60B 81 81B 108 118B 122B 123B 128 132 188B 197 206B 208 211 211B 220B 221 228-B2 Mary 118B 122B 188B 208

SHEDDEN, John 86 94B 103B 104B 108 110 115 115B 132 141 141B 168B 169 173B 203 204B 205 205B 216 228B Jonathan 109B Mr. 218 Robert 1 2B 9B 12 13B 24B 35 40B 56 83 100B 113B 124 127B 135 144 150 159 167 188B 192 216B 219B 220B 221 221B 231B

SHELTON, Christopher 98B Malbone 78B 107B 144B 154B 239 240B 242 253B

SHEMELD, George 221 229

SHEPHERD, John 112B 164B 174B 190 191 216B 232 232B 233B Robert 6 Solomon Jr 118B 188B William 173 181B

SHERLOCK, John 23B 38B 39.55

SHEWSBERY, Peter 201B 209 212B

SHIELDS, Matthew 249 William 79B

SHIPWASH, Ambrose 200B 246B John 94 97 246 246B Thomas 200B 246 246B William 37B 46 88B 102B 115B

SHORE, John 33B 34B 38B 40 40B

SHURLEY, Margaret 22B

SIKES, Jacob 191 233 Jesse 191 233 Josiah 191 233 Walter 92

SIMMONS, Amy 78B Michael 238 Samuel 18 25B 80B 83 109B 127B 138

SIMPSON, Abram 118B Jonathan 6B 54 54B 62B 63 119 William 2 6B 18B 19 28 29 36B 37B 46B 49 50 54 55 58B 62B 63 74B 76B 77 83 85B 86 88B 99B 101 106B 109B 110B 114 119 120B 156B 167 172 187B 188 191B 196 198 199 207 208 228 232B 234 233B 238

SINGLETON, Henry 99B 104B John 243B 244B Peter 157B 158B 192B

SISSON, William 181B 199B 200 208 222B 232B

SKINKER, William 4 5B 17B 35B 53 57 74 126B 132 133 141 141B 142B 145 159B 173 180 192 192B

193B 194 194B 207B 208 214B 215 217 221B 235B 237B

SKINNER, Alexander 170B 197B 209 213 223B William 230 242 247 251 253 244

SLACK, Thomas 12B

SLAVE, Aberdeen 9B Edinburgh 9B Frank 9B

SMALLWOOD, Charles 5 7 Mary 30B

SMITH, Charles 229 Jo 70B John 2 3B 4 4B 10B 15 18 19 20B 23B 31B 33 34 34B 35B 36 36B 38B 42 43B 46 49B 50 52B 53B 56B 57B 60 60B 62 74B 75 76 76B 82 82B 88B 100 105 109B 113 114 1166 118 118B 121B 122 125 125B 126B 127 131 131B 132B 140B 141 141B 142 142B 143 144B 145 153 153B 154B 155 155B 157B 159 161 184B 185 185B 186 186B 189 196 199 206 207B 209B 210B 213 215 221 229 234B 235B 236 239 240B 242 245B 246 251B 252B 253 Jonathan 214B 215 217 Josiah 69 Mathias 54B Mr. 99B 100B 138 180 210 214 Robert 66 66B Samuel 68 69B 70B 191 201B Samuel Jr 69B 70 Sarah 130B Thomas 5 58 William 10B 12B 13 24B 33 43B 44 44B 53 88 88B 91 102 104 112 113B 114 114B 118B 130B 131 132B 152B 159 162 163 163B 206B 207 209B 215B 225B 228-2 231B 234 235 236 236B 237B 240 246B 247 251B 253 Young 212B 236

SNALE, Elizabeth 46 83B 198 207B 218B 227B Thomas 46 47 57B 78B 79 81 81B 83B 89B 90B 94 130 131B 132 133 135B 198 207B 213 218B 219 220B 227B Thomas Capt 47B

SNODGRASS, Mr 116B 235 Neil 201B

SOMMERVILLE, John 211B 212B

SONG, Samuel 229B

SOUTHERLAND, Celia 191 196B 220 220B 228-B2 223B 234B James 209B 236 John 61 82B 105 105B 191 196B 220 220B 223B 228-B2 John Jr 23 John Sr 23

SPARLING, George 5B 15 19B 25 25B 27B 112

SPARROW, Peter 245 248B 251B

SPENCER, Richard 195 228

SPRIGG, Edward 209

SPROWLE, Andrew 22 37B 90B 111B 138 143B 147 152 159B 185 198 198B 205 205B John 90B 111B 152 185 Mr. 135B 227B

SPRUGG, Edward 219B

STABLER, Edward 168B

STANHOPE, John 4 7 7B 9B 10 13B 78 78B 99 107 120B 144 150 161B 162B 173 177 197 202B 203 203B 204

STANLEY, Nathaniel 50

STANTON, Giles 201B

STAUNTON, Eleanor 151 Mary 30 99 144 155B 156

STEAD, Andrew 209B Robert 24B 31 34B 38 39 204B

STEAL, Robert 4B JURY

STEED, Robert 32B 40B 42 42B 56B 88 110 165B 168

STEELE, Elizabeth 160B 179 179B Sarah 18B

THOMPSON, Ann 65B 66 66B Bartholomew 5 7 8B 9
    13B 15 166 17 17B 25 25B 27B 33 34B 40 40B
    48B 62 76 76B 77 78 81 81B 95B 96B 104B 115
    115B 129B 141 141B 142B 145 161 161B 162
    Christopher 2B Elizabeth 69B Isaac 171 176B 220
    James 185 238 240 243 John 87 Talbot 10B 16B
    123 129 188B 199B Thomas 6 8 20 26B 39B 48B
    54 54B 57 60 60B 62B 63B 64B 72 72B 73 98 100
    101 119 122B 124 147B 168 171 172B 176 176B
    180 187 191B 198 220 228-2 228B Victor 191B
THOROWGOOD, Adam 37 87B 96B Lemuel 218 237
THRUSTON, Mary 245 248 250*
THURMER, Molly 57B Samuel 21B
TILKINS, Henry 206
TILLIDGE, Thomas 113 153B 185B 186
TIMSON*, Thomas 240B 242
TINNIE, John 139
TODD, John 174 184B 185 185B 186 194 194B Joseph
    99B 144 153 154B
TOMLINSON, Samuel 33B 34B 103B 104B 109B 145
    176B 177 178 178B
TRACEY, Mary 183
TRAVIS, Edward 158B
TREBELL, William 146 198 204 222
TRISTRAM, James 196 197 201B
TROUSTON*, Mary 250
TRUSS, Josiah 78 194B 230 242 244 247 248 248B 250
    251 253 Mary 230 242 247 248 248B 250 251 253
TRYTITLE, Timothy 64B 65 69 70B
TUCKER, Eldred 41 147B Gavin Corbin 50 50B 51 51B
    52 52B Henry 42 50B 88 88B 90B 135B 137 141B
    184 199B John 5 11 13B 39B 77B 80B 122 131B
    158B 185B 194 210 223B 227B Robert 2 2B 3B 5
    5B 6B 8 14 15 16 20 22B 24 26B 27 31 33 33B 36
    39B 50 50B 51 51B 52 52B 54 54B 60B 62B 68B
    70B 73 74 74B 75 77 77B 82 82B 89 91 92B 102
    108 109 119 158 169B 174 174B 180 187 194 199
    209 210 213 214B 215 217 219 220 227B 228B
    228-2 230B 238B 239 247B Samuel 218 218B 222
    237 Travis 184 199B William 238B 247B
TULLY, Robinson 245B
TUMBLINSON, Samuel 13 15 55B
TURBIT, Peter 173B
TURNER, James 86
TURNOUT, Timothy 218
TYLER, John 171B
TYSON, Joseph 139

VALLAROS, Joseph 75
VALLENCIER, John 85B 94 117 136 143 156B 157 158
    165B 180 222 232
VALLENTINE, John 148B 234 236B
VEALE, Dempsey 107 144B 149B George 74 90B 143B
    185 George Jr 2B 39B 44 113 173 Thomas 2B 40B
    56 90B 113B 143B 158 199 214B 215

VENTRESS, Joshua 249
VERLING, William 9
VICKERS, James 188 196B 207 Mr. 202
VOSS, Edward 2 2B 4 8 11 39B 44 55B

WADE, Mary 224
WADLINGTON, Paul 238B 239 240 242B 243 243B
    244B
WAGER, William 166 216B 218B
WAINWRIGHT, George 240B 243 243B 244 John 239
WALDROND, Frances 2
WALKE, Anne 114 129B John 3B Thomas 194 194B
WALKER, George 191B 243B Hardress 124B Henry
    213 James 33B 34B 49 72 73 74 86 86B 87 100 108
    115 123B 131 170 176B 177 178 178B 192 193B
    194B 195 John 23 25 48B 60 60B 93 103B 104B
    109 109B 110 130 131B 132 153 154B 155 155B
    167 193B 205B 219 Mr 170 Robert 110B Thomas
    61B 81 94 111 136 143 148B 157 165B 173 182
    189 190B 197 199B 200 200B 209 216B 219B
    222B 232 232B 234B William 4B 5B 17 37B 79B
    120B 121 140B 141 141B 142 142B 143 144 144B
    145 152 154 158B 164 166B 173 186B 189B 207B
    212 221B
WALKINSHAW, Captain 47 John 100B 137B
WALLACE, Ann 8 19 37B 105B 117 James 45B William
    18 23 109B 248
WALLER, Ann 252B Hardress 4 6 6B 7 7B 9 10 13B 31
    32B 43 48 54 59B 62 62B 63 74 76 111B 118 119
    123 124 125B 126 126B 140B 141 141B 142 142B
    143 144B 145 157B 1677B 170 182 195B 196B 199
    201 208 208B 219 222 228-B2 252B Robert 132
    132B 195 Thomas 129
WALMSLEY, Thomas 81
WANNAL, Henry 209B
WARD, Robert 81B Thomas 166 177B
WARDEN, Hugh 13 15 25B
WARING, Francis 51B 52B 82B
WARNER, Samuel 24 74 81 81B
WARREN, Bailey 28B 36 38B 47 47B 55B 104 123
    123B 183 188B 200 209B 236 Charles 75 93B 101
    James 231 232B 234 233B 234 236B 237B 242 248
    John 231B 236 238B 239 240B 242B 244 Peter 75B
    121B William 251B 253B
WARWICK, Anthony 96 113B 188 197 Cumming 1066
    129B 144 149 192
WATERS, Robert 5 9 36B
WATLINGTON, Paul 1 20 27 87 174 192 193B 211
    211B 213B 214B 219 219B 221B
WATSON, Andrew 209B Ann 80B 112 135 143B 151
    188 198 George 80B 98B 112 135 143B 151 188
    198 Peter 37B
WEBB, Aphia 3 5 7B 46 49B 88B 100 George 61 76 129
    151B 198 199B 200B 202B 203 203B 204 227B
    230B 231B 234 239 240 James 3 3B 4 4B 5 7B 8B

www.ingramcontent.com/pod-product-compliance
Lightning Source LLC
Chambersburg PA
CBHW080417270326
41929CB00018B/3061